D1610171

POULENC

poulenc a biography

roger nichols

YALE UNIVERSITY PRESS
NEW HAVEN AND LONDON

For information about this and other Yale University Press publications, please contact:
U.S. Office: sales.press@yale.edu   yalebooks.com
Europe Office: sales@yaleup.co.uk   yalebooks.co.uk

Set in Fournier MT by IDSUK (DataConnection) Ltd
Printed in Great Britain by TJ International Ltd, Padstow, Cornwall

Library of Congress Control Number: 2020931416

ISBN 978-0-300-22650-8

A catalogue record for this book is available from the British Library.

10 9 8 7 6 5 4 3 2 1

To Sarah and Sidney,
this volume's twin *anges gardiennes*

TABLE OF CONTENTS

	List of Plates	viii
	Acknowledgements	x
	Preface	xii
I	Overture and Beginners: 1899–1918	1
II	'Now We Are Six': 1919–1924	29
III	Dreaming of Maturity: 1924–1928	62
IV	Depression and Recovery: 1929–1934	85
V	Surrealism and Faith: 1934–1939	112
VI	The Years of Darkness: 1939–1944	142
VII	'Liberty, I Write Your Name': 1944–1952	172
VIII	Mad about Nuns: 1952–1956	215
IX	Joy, Suffering and Farewell: 1957–1963	249
	Appendix	292
	Envoi	294
	Endnotes	295
	Chronology	322
	Catalogue of Works	347
	Select Bibliography	353
	Index	359

PLATES

1. Francis sets out.
2. Francis joking, his nanny unimpressed.
3. Francis's father, Émile.
4. Francis's mother, Jenny, with Raymonde Linossier.
5. Francis with his elder sister Jeanne.
6. Poulenc's grandparents' house in Nogent.
7. Poulenc in 1924, photo by Man Ray.
8. Ricardo Viñes, staying with the Latarjets.
9. Guillaume Apollinaire.
10. Paul Éluard.
11. Le Grand Coteau.
12. Wanda Landowska and Poulenc duetting.
13. At the Noailles' Paris residence, after the premiere of *Le Bal masqué* in 1932.
14. Yvonne Gouverné and Poulenc descending the steps of the Rocamadour shrine in August 1936.
15. Les Six with Jean Cocteau in 1931.
16. 'In praise of intelligence': Poulenc and Pierre Bernac.
17. 'Self-satisfaction': Poulenc and Pierre Bernac.
18. The Princesse de Polignac playing her Cavaillé-Coll organ.
19. Les Six with Jean Cocteau, probably in the early 1950s.
20. Poulenc with his niece Brigitte Manceaux.
21. Poulenc with his lover Raymond Destouches in the late 1940s.
22. Poulenc's lover Lucien Roubert.
23. Poulenc teaching Mickey table manners.
24. Pierre Bernac, Simone Girard and Poulenc in England in the mid-1950s.
25. Fiorenza Cossotto during the world premiere of *Dialogues des Carmélites* at La Scala in January 1957.

26. Joan Sutherland in the British premiere of *Dialogues des Carmélites* at Covent Garden in January 1958.
27. Poulenc's commentary on *Le Travail du peintre*.
28. Poulenc at Oxford on 25 June 1958.
29. Poulenc the flower lover.
30. Poulenc and Cocteau looking through the score of *La Voix humaine*.
31. Poulenc and Denise Duval.
32. Poulenc in a bar in Cannes.
33. The last photograph of Poulenc, Holland, January 1963.

ACKNOWLEDGEMENTS

One of the pleasures of writing this book has come from the enthusiasm that has greeted all my enquiries: for this, as well as for the information supplied, I am grateful to the following: Michelle Biget-Mainfroy, Beatrice Brooke, Sidney Buckland, Sir Humphrey Burton, Fiorenza Cossotto, Evelyne Crochet, Alan Crumpler, Sister Philippa Edwards, Dom Michael Evans OSB, Barrie Gavin, Yvonne Gouverné, Henri Hell, Eva Hornstein, Daniel Jaffé, Hervé Lacombe, Richard Langham Smith, Marie-Ange Lebedeff, Dame Felicity Lott, Andrew McCrae, Graham Melville-Mason, Otfrid Nies, Robert Orledge, Roger Pines, Yves Pouliquen, Manuel Rosenthal, Rohan de Saram, Benoît Seringe, Rosine Seringe, Nigel Simeone, Nicolas Southon, Charles Timbrell, Jon Tolansky, Sir John Tooley, Bishop Erik Varden, Marina Vecci and Virginia Zeani. I am equally grateful to the personnel of the following libraries for their assistance: Bibliothèque nationale de France (Département de la Musique), Bodleian Library, Hereford Public Library, Médiathèque musicale Mahler, Morgan Library and Museum, Harry Ransom Humanities Research Center of University of Texas at Austin, Music Faculty Library of Oxford University, Beinecke Rare Book and Manuscript Library of Yale University.

I am happy to acknowledge generous financial help from the Association des Amis de Francis Poulenc, the British Academy/Leverhulme Small Research Grants and The Society of Authors' Authors' Foundation.

Picture credits: Collection Francis Poulenc 1–8, 11, 12, 14, 19, 23, 28–33; Collection Lucien Berton 9, 10, 13; Collection Winifred Radford © S. Buckland 16, 17, 24; Estate of Felix Aprahamian by kind permission of The Arabesque Trust 27; Fiorenza Cossotto 25; Fondation Singer-Polignac 18; Lipnitzki/Roger Viollet/ Getty Images 15; Pierre Miscevic, *Francis Poulenc, Lettres inédites à Brigitte Manceaux*, by kind permission of Éd. Orizons, Paris, 2019 21, 22; Roger Wood: Royal Opera House/Arena Pal: www.arenapal.com 26

Note: A brief comment on the thorny question of comparative prices. In March 1935 the French franc was valued at 71 to the pound sterling; £1 in 1935 was worth roughly £68 in 2018. By these computations, the 25,000 francs from the Princesse de Polignac for Poulenc's Concerto for two pianos and the same sum from the Noailles for *Le Bal masqué* are each equivalent today to about £24,000. These sums are made less secure by France's abandonment of the Gold Standard in 1936, but nonetheless give some idea of their generosity and that of Edward James at the end of the decade.

All translations are mine.

Roger Nichols
Kington
Herefordshire
April 2019

PREFACE

In retrospect, the first years of the twentieth century in Paris must have seemed golden to those who subsequently survived two world wars and the financial and political turbulence of the intervening years – *l'entre-deux-guerres*. For this short period, tradition and innovation seemed to be held in some kind of balance. If, in the last of the five international exhibitions in 1900, one of the most visited exhibits was one 'displaying le Vieux Paris in all its picturesque glory',[1] by contrast Picasso's Blue period would lead to his Pink one on the way to Cubism. Throughout the period the horse was gradually giving way to the bicycle, and then the bicycle to the motor car, no doubt with some confusion. But the opening of the first *métro* line in July 1900 meant that instead of taking 90 minutes to cross from the Porte Maillot to Vincennes, you could now do it in 25 minutes. Life was further accelerated by general electrification, by the telephone and by the *pneumatiques* which sped messages through the city by tubes of compressed air. Then on 25 July 1909, a cause of huge national pride, Louis Blériot made his first airplane flight over La Manche (otherwise known as the English Channel).

While the Dreyfus Case had dragged on until 1906, much of public opinion seems to have felt the injustice of it and accepted the truth of the matter sometime before that, even if not all the friendships it had shattered would be restored. Whether as a result of this case or not, anti-military novels began to appear around this time, and Romain Rolland's ten-volume saga *Jean-Christophe*, published between 1906 and 1912, contained pleas for Franco-German understanding. Elsewhere on the French diplomatic front in the early years of the century, relations with Russia and Italy were now good, followed in April 1904 by the Entente Cordiale with Britain, promoted to some extent by King Edward VII's popular visit to France the previous year. Internal politics too were now more stable, no politician being assassinated between President Sadi Carnot in 1894 and Jean Jaurès in 1914.

Meanwhile the café-concert continued to flourish, as did the theatre with Sarah Bernhardt its uncrowned queen. In the musical theatre two cultural icons were paramount. In 1908 the impresario Sergei Diaghilev brought Musorgsky's *Boris Godunov* to Paris with Chaliapin in the title role, and followed this up with Stravinsky's three great ballets in 1910 (*The Firebird*), 1911 (*Petrushka*) and 1913 (*The Rite of Spring*). But before that, in 1902, Debussy had not been quite as revolutionary with his opera *Pelléas et Mélisande* which, though not wholly free of Wagner's influence, passed it through a prism of nuance and understatement. These two cultures together were crucial in the musical development of the young Francis Poulenc.

Alistair Horne sums up: 'Whether on stage or screen or in the cabarets, the message of that first decade and a half of the new century before the deluge was one of relentless optimism.'[2] Did Poulenc share this optimism? In his youth, probably. But as we shall see, in the longer term it was crucially undermined by his internal contradictions: between religious faith and doubt, between hetero- and homosexuality, between popularity and profundity, between tonality and modernity, between the axioms of the *haute bourgeoisie* and a *nostalgie de la boue*, this latter expressed in his affection for 'rough trade' or something similar. He himself described the struggle as involving 'Poulenc, who despises the all-too-vulnerable Francis'.[3] There were of course saving graces. One of these was a wholehearted embrace of his French heritage. We begin, then, with him following Debussy's line in his thoughts on the musical tradition of France's north-eastern neighbour.

I
OVERTURE AND BEGINNERS
❖ 1899–1918 ❖

On 6 September 1919 the twenty-year-old Francis Poulenc wrote to Otto Marius Kling, the director of the London publishers J. & W. Chester, 'I detest Wagner because I don't like fake music, cardboard dragons and flighty goddesses';[1] then, in an interview in 1954[2] with Claude Rostand, he admitted 'seriously hoping never again as long as I live to hear *Die Meistersinger*'; and finally, at the end of his life, he complained that 'composers who, like Vincent d'Indy, absorbed the example of the *Ring* unthinkingly, ended up inescapably swamped in a pathos that was contrary to the French temperament'.[3]

If it's true that we are defined as much by our antipathies as by our enthusiasms, it may be worth asking what, in Poulenc's opinion, was this 'French temperament' which, by implication, accorded with his own; whether indeed it existed (given that, for Pierre Boulez, there was no such thing as a valid 'French musical tradition');[4] and, if so, to what extent did he remain true to it. Again, we may proceed by a process of negation: in place of counterpoint and motivic development, Poulenc preferred accompanied tunes and juxtapositions; in place of pathos ('music to be listened to head in hands', as Cocteau described it),[5] charm and delight; in place of textures that swamp the listener, primary colours with plenty of space around them.

Of course these general characteristics admit of exceptions. But the main thrust of Wagner, as of Brahms and Bruckner, was towards a seriousness that demanded respect and unyielding concentration. If there are jokes (and one can't be sure that Siegfried's 'Das ist kein Mann', on finding Brünnhilde on her mountain top, qualifies as such), they are mostly peripheral to the main argument. Born as he was (at 2 rue Cambacères, now place des Saussaies, in the 8th arrondissement) on 7 January 1899, Poulenc the composer avoided the full flood of French *wagnéromanie*, but still from 1917 onward he had to combat the widespread, unspoken devaluation of comedy as against tragedy in music. The mixture of the two elements in *Carmen* was allowed to have produced a masterpiece, while *Falstaff* was acceptable from someone with Verdi's long record in operatic tragedy. Even so, there remained a long legacy dating back to Berlioz, who had insisted that moving the ladies in the audience to tears was the true test of success.[6]

Berlioz, though, for all his incontestable genius, was never a typically French composer, and suffered profoundly because of this. Despite Boulez's misgivings, it is surely possible to compile a family tree of French composers from Gounod through Massenet, Saint-Saëns, Bizet, Fauré and Poulenc's beloved Chabrier to Debussy, Ravel and Satie, for all of whom grace, elegance, humour, lightness of touch and sense of proportion are key ingedients, but all of whom also have the power to move us, and often beyond our expectations. These qualities surely go to make up the 'French temperament' that Poulenc refers to; it did, and does, exist; and with two or three brief exceptions he was true to it throughout his life. As to establishing where his gifts came from, this is, as always with creative artists, a matter of surmise, but one can do worse than begin from his own prescription: that his was essentially a dual nature, and not so much conflicted as compounded.

On his mother's side, he came from a Parisian family of tapestry workers, bronze workers and cabinet makers. Jenny Zoé Royer was born on 20 June 1864, a couple of years after her brother Marcel who, like her, was to play a large part in Poulenc's musical life. An accomplished pianist, she preferred 'mainly Chopin . . . And then Mozart, Schubert, Scarlatti'.[7] After the two-year-old Francis had been given a little toy piano in white lacquer with cherries painted on it, the keys activating slips of glass, it was she who in 1904 gave him his first lessons on a proper instrument and who appears first in the list of dedicatees for his opera *Dialogues des Carmélites*: 'to the memory of my Mother, who revealed music to me'. Her brother Marcel, a confirmed bachelor with a penchant for valets and hotel waiters[8] and always known to Poulenc as 'Papoum', was his godfather and from an early age encouraged Francis's interest in painting and in the theatre. Papoum also had friends in the operatic world and Poulenc later remembered, 'I was brought up on the knees of the tenor Edmond Clément and, by the time I was ten, *Carmen*, *La Bohème* and *Manon* held no secrets for me.'[9]

Happily, Clément is well represented on CD and we can treasure his impeccable diction and, in the famous 'Vainement ma bien aimée' from Lalo's *Le Roi d'Ys*, recorded in 1911 during Poulenc's impressionable youth, his effortless top As; the voice, perhaps somewhat grainy for modern tastes, could well have predisposed him to appreciating Pierre Bernac's a quarter of a century later. At all events, Clément's elegant phrasing belongs unmistakably to the 'French temperament', eschewing what the French call 'emphase', a term which goes some way beyond the English 'emphasis' to embrace 'bombast' and 'grandiloquence', and which Poulenc specifically condemned as a German disease. In this, as in many other respects, Poulenc was following Debussy, who in 1902 had demanded of his cast in *Pelléas et Mélisande* to 'forget you are singers' – that is, to speak their lines rather than declaiming them.[10]

His father Émile's family came from Espalion, some 30 kilometres from Rodez in the Aveyron, and in 1900 Émile, born on 5 July 1855, and his two brothers Gaston and Camille took over the family chemical firm under the name 'Poulenc Frères', based at 7 rue Neuve-Saint-Merri in Paris, with further outlets throughout the city's suburbs. The firm flourished throughout Poulenc's youth and beyond, bringing in a comfortable income for the family, and eventually morphed into the current enterprise Rhône-Poulenc.

Whereas Camille, the youngest brother, was the researcher of the family, Émile was more interested in photography: he had had his own studio since 1887 and in 1903 Poulenc Frères opened a photographic studio at 19 rue du Quatre-Septembre, 'dedicated to photographic products and materials with a projection room in the basement with room for 100 people'.[11] It is tempting to set off this forward-looking establishment against the long-standing, traditional *métier* of Poulenc's maternal forebears, finding expression in his own compositional blend of old and new, but Poulenc himself seems not to have done so. On the musical front, according to his son, Émile favoured 'Berlioz, César Franck, Massenet . . . And then Beethoven! Oh yes . . . Beethoven, Beethoven!'[12] But the library in Poulenc's own country house at Noizay contains a number of vocal scores, embossed E.P. on the back cover, of operas also by Gounod, Bizet, Delibes and Lalo, with lighter ones by Grétry, Offenbach and Messager, and more challenging ones by Wagner (*Lohengrin*, *Tannhäuser*, *Tristan*) and Debussy (*Pelléas et Mélisande*), suggesting that Émile was musically more open-minded than his son remembered.

The contrast Poulenc did make between his parents, and many times over, was between his mother's free-thinking, agnostic family and the committed Roman Catholic one of his father's. There has been much discussion during the last decade or so over the question of Poulenc's religious faith. It has for years been the case that, in families where one Roman Catholic parent has married a non-Catholic, the non-Catholic must accept that any offspring will be baptized in the faith and instructed in it until their first confession and communion, which can be as early as eight – hence the claim that St Francis Xavier borrowed from Aristotle: 'Give me a child until he is seven, and I will show you the man.' We know that Francis celebrated his first communion in 1910, aged eleven, and his friend Jacques Soulé remembered going with him around then 'several times to Sunday mass in the church at Nogent [the home of his maternal grandparents], but we never discussed religion. His faith was not unduly displayed at the time, but you could feel its presence during the ceremony.'[13] The general view is that during the heady days of Les Six and the 1920s he was (to quote from the libretto of Britten's *The Turn of the Screw*) 'so deep in the busy world' that he paid religion scant attention. Even so there can be no doubt that Francis had been well schooled in Catholic doctrine. One question that does remain unanswered is how Émile was able to accept Papoum, by Catholic standards a loose-living individual, as Francis's godfather: perhaps it just came down to the man's charm and Jenny's advocacy.

Francis's parents had been married on 16 March 1885 and their daughter Jeanne Élise Marguerite was born on 24 May of the following year. It is not unknown for Francis to be wrongly described in the press as an only child – the reason being the gap of nearly thirteen years between the two. Although biographers seem not to have commented on this, it was only through Hervé Lacombe's diligent researches that we have learnt the truth: that between these two children lay the birth of Louis Étienne on 8 July 1888, and his death on 17 May 1891; and then the stillbirth of a child of unrecorded gender on 23 June 1892. No biographer's gloss is needed to imagine the parents' suffering, or indeed Jeanne's. But we can also imagine the emotions surrounding the birth of Francis Jean Marcel on 7 January 1899 and his early childhood, making of him what the French call an 'enfant choyé', a 'coddled child' – if not exactly spoilt, then one whose health and well-being might have been monitored on a daily if not an hourly basis. Writing to Marie-Blanche de Polignac in August 1929 to tell her of the serious illness of his nanny Nounou (Françoise Lauxière), Poulenc revealed that she had stayed with the family until he was fifteen.[14] Was this careful upbringing perhaps a source of the adult Poulenc's hypochondria and of his being, in the words of Jeanne's daughter Rosine, all his life 'un inquiet'?[15] Certainly this 'inquiétude' makes things difficult for the biographer, not least in the domains of money and sexuality. The following pages will testify to Poulenc's variable statements, both of his wealth, or penury, and of his amorous dispositions. Can this *haut bourgeois*, joint heir to a flourishing business, really be on one occasion, according to his own account, reduced to a balance of 83 francs? As for the details of his love life, especially during the 1920s, these remain obscure and are likely to remain so: in particular, we know practically nothing about when he became aware of his homosexuality until his first declaration of it in letters at the end of the decade. Thereafter, he would be regularly 'inquiet' about the state of his relationships, with jealousy playing a major role.

But, outwardly at least, Francis's early childhood was settled, with all the material comforts that an affluent bourgeois family could command, including the pleasures of the table: 'I grew up in a family for whom gastronomy was a rite; I've inherited a taste for good food and a wide range of recipes. It's my culinary ancestry.'[16]

In 1907 his mother passed him over for piano lessons to Mlle Melon, an assistant to César Franck's niece, Mlle Boutet de Monvel, and Poulenc later remembered, 'Every evening, after school, I'd spend an hour of serious work under her tuition, and whenever I had five free minutes during the day, I'd rush off to the piano and do some sightreading.'[17] The same year, he first heard the music of Debussy when a harpist friend of the family played the *Danses sacrée et profane* with a string orchestra and Francis exclaimed, 'It's so pretty! It's a bit out of tune!', going on to try out on the piano the dangerous chords of the 9th in the second dance. He also surreptitiously bought copies of 'La Soirée dans Grenade' and 'Jardins sous la pluie', although for the moment they were beyond his manual capabilities. The composer was, of course, still very much in the public eye, as Poulenc remembered:

> I'd often seen Debussy at the Concerts Colonne rehearsals, on Saturday mornings at the Châtelet, which he came to with his daughter Chouchou. My dream was to meet him. Well, one day I saw Debussy and his wife going into a shop that sold mourning clothes (such shops existed before 1914). While Mme Debussy and my mother were trying things on in adjoining rooms, I took advantage of a moment when Debussy was telephoning to touch the lining of his hat, which he'd left on a chair. If I'd dared, I'd have kissed it. Debussy returned a moment later, I was blushing with pleasure, shame and timidity. I think he saw this, because he gave me a little smile when he saw me gazing at him with such admiration.[18]

Debussy would probably have been equally amused by another event that took place around this time. One of his mother's female friends was a firm advocate of d'Indy's rigorous teaching methods, based on Beethoven and Franck, as practised at the Schola Cantorum. Calling on the Poulencs, she spotted:

> . . . the Grieg Concerto on my piano – I still like the first movement. I was 14 at the time. The poor lady, brandishing her lorgnette, exclaimed: 'Oh, Jenny! You let your son play this!' Then, glancing at the rest of my music which included the Schönberg *Six little pieces*, *The Rite of Spring* and *The Nightingale*, she cried out, literally horrified: 'My dear, it really is time to make him work seriously.' 'Not with your boring old f . . . s at any rate,' said I, slamming the door noisily.[19]

He was composing too, and from somewhere around this time dates the earliest known of his compositions, a piano piece of fifty-seven bars entitled *En Barque*. It demonstrates no signs of precocity, nor of Debussyan influence, but the opening phrase of eleven bars may be the first sign of Poulenc's penchant for avoiding too much rhythmic regularity.[20]

In January 1910, after weeks of rainfall, the Seine overflowed its banks and much of central Paris was flooded. The Poulenc family moved out to Fontainebleau and it was here, in a music shop, that Poulenc discovered Schubert's *Die Winterreise*. It was one of the defining moments of his life. In the words of Hervé Lacombe:

> By turning his piano round, he can, at about 4pm, see the sun moving through the forest trees covered with frost. The song he is then singing harmonizes with the countryside. This fusion of the visual, the musical and the poetic is the open sesame of his future aesthetic, in the same way that the expressive restraint and the accuracy of declamation, the balance and interplay between piano and voice are a lesson for his future as a song composer.[21]

From the summer of 1910 dates the only surviving letter from Jenny Poulenc to her son. She and her husband were taking the waters at Vichy, and she mentions seeing quite a lot of the family of one of the doctors who used to practise there in the summer, Dr Linossier, whose eldest daughter, Suzanne, was at school with Francis's sister Jeanne. She also says she will pass a drawing by Francis on to the youngest daughter, Raymonde – the first evidence we have of a relationship that was to be crucial to Poulenc's intellectual and emotional life.[22]

The following year, according to his friend Hélène Jourdan-Morhange, he discovered Musorgsky's *Nursery Songs* and in February 1914 the music of Chabrier.

'He put two sous into a nickelodeon,' she wrote in 1955, 'to play a disc in a new shop and heard Chabrier's "Idylle" played by Risler. He told me just the other day, with an excitement that went right back to that youthful experience, that he'd played the disc more than ten times.'[23] But at the same time he remained true to his love of opera. In August 1911 the family went down to Bagnères-de-Luchon on the Spanish border and Poulenc kept a holiday diary:

> We went off to gargle with the thermal waters. It's a real laugh! The women make noises like badly oiled machines. The men spit and sniff [. . .] We came back for lunch, then off to the open-air theatre with Campagnola singing the role of Cavaradossi in *Tosca*. Jean Laure was Scarpia and Arlette Bergès Tosca [. . .] Campagnola very much in the Italian style, which was marvellous. Also he has a splendid voice. As for Bergès, she has a very pretty voice and excellent diction. She was particularly good in the last two acts because her voice is a bit screechy at the top; in the first act she had a horrid costume, orange and canary yellow. Campagnola's wasn't really appropriate, it was the one for Werther. Jean Laure's was very sinister, especially in Act I where he wears his cloak. I really like the first act because everything was good – the role of the sacristan especially is very funny.[24]

Not bad for a twelve-year-old . . . And already the musical is mixed with the visual.

Holidays such as this and the one the following year at Biarritz were the exception rather than the rule. By far the most common place for relaxation was the estate belonging to Poulenc's maternal grandparents at Nogent-sur-Marne on the edge of the Bois de Vincennes. 'For me it was paradise, with its open-air dance halls, its sellers of French fries and its *bals musettes* . . . It was there I got to know the tunes by Christiné and Scotto which, for me, became my folklore. The "vulgar, naughty boy" side of my music, you see, isn't artificial, as people sometimes think, because it goes back to very tender childhood memories.'[25] At Nogent he also saw more of the Linossier family, especially Raymonde, as well as a young pianist Simone Tilliard; and Édouard Souberbielle, who was both a pianist and a budding composer, and to whom Poulenc would become very close in the years around 1919. Both grandparents lived into their eighties, outliving Poulenc's parents by some years, and Nogent was a haven for him until his grandmother's death in 1924. A photograph of the young Poulenc survives, on the back of which he later wrote, 'Poupoule, in the days when he was well behaved!!!!! Nogent 1906'.[26]

Some of the most detailed, and spirited, recollections of Francis before the Great War come from his friend Jacques Soulé, his exact contemporary, who used to come to the Royer property to play tennis:

I used to beat him easily. He was heavy on his feet, lacked vivacity and, while he defended himself resolutely, showed no passion for winning. Often, after tea, we'd go up to his bedroom. Here he had an upright piano to which he'd immediately gravitate. I was amazed then to see his great hands with their rounded fingers running nimbly over the keyboard; and when I listened to him playing with that velvet touch that was already his, I wondered whether it was really the same Francis I'd just seen messing up so many easy shots.

Two further extracts show that the fun-loving composer was already in the bud:

One day he played me on the piano a wild tune of his own composing which ended with one of those furious passages he favoured and which he accompanied with some characteristic miming. When I asked him what this tune claimed to represent, he said, 'Hold on, I'll show you.' He disappeared into his bathroom and came out with just a towel tied round his waist and began a savage dance, singing the tune he'd just played. Then he went off to get dressed, and we talked about something else.

A few years later, two other members of the tennis party provided inspiration:

Maybe as a result of remarks made in confidence, or because he'd overheard a meaningful exchange, he was sure that a boy and girl we knew, older than us, were considerably interested in each other. He gave this hypothetical affair a frame in the form of a certain Parisian haberdashers which was, so he said, well known as a covert meeting place. He imagined that the boy and girl in question had decided on seeing each other in this haberdashers, and on the piano improvised a scene on the spot which portrayed the girl agreeing the rendezvous, the boy waiting anxiously in the shop, the girl arriving all flushed. Finally, after a moving love duet, the curtain fell. Francis sang both roles in his curious voice and I was dumb with admiration.[27]

In retrospect we can see that a difficult balance had to be struck between this theatricality, fed by contact with Edmond Clément and by a fervent admiration for Sarah Bernhardt, and a distaste for 'emphase'. In later life he could not remember a time when he had not been thinking of writing an opera, while at the same time harbouring plans to become a singer (abandoned when his voice broke, leaving him with what he called 'a composer's typical sorry squawk'),[28] or else a tragic actor.[29] If his theatrical leanings led him to temper the lonely life of a composer with one as a performing pianist, at the same time both his own operas and his performing style refused to bear down on an audience in a grandiloquent manner: which is not to say that he scorned virtuosity – probably his admiration for Horowitz's playing stemmed to some extent from that pianist's genius for producing marvels of dexterity to the maximum delight of audiences, but with minimum apparent effort. Poulenc's finest compositions are models of 'the art that conceals art', in fruitful combination with his supreme lyrical gifts.

Until the autumn of 1912 Francis had been educated first of all at home with the same governess who had taught his mother and sister, and then at the Petit Condorcet, a feeder for the lycée of the same name, where he loathed science, mathematics and geography, but enjoyed French and history. Now, though, a serious decision had to be made about his future. As he later recalled:

> My mother, who had immediately sensed that music was my sole vocation, would have been happy for me to enter the Conservatoire; since artists had always ruled the roost in her family, to her that seemed entirely natural. But my father, despite his love of music, couldn't accept that the son of an industrialist shouldn't pass the two parts of his baccalaureat. 'He can do what he likes afterwards', my father used to insist.[30]

Francis's years at the Lycée Condorcet were not distinguished by any great intellectual success, and indeed his second year produced worse results than the first ('Must make more effort in Greek and *especially in Latin*. Little progress').[31] Nor did he complete this second year, being removed from the school list on 31 March 1914 with the note 'ill', and not returning until the autumn of 1916. This may have been an early onset of the depressions that would plague him in later life. Even so, he would look back on his days at the lycée rather fondly, and had made a good friend in Jean-Marie Legrand, the son of Franc-Nohain, whose play *L'Heure espagnole* had just been set to music by Ravel. Jean-Marie, under the pseudonyms

Jean Nohain or Jaboune, would later provide the words for Poulenc's *Quatre Chansons pour enfants* of 1934 and for two of the replacements for the *Sept Chansons* of 1937 – in a sense continuations of the school exercises he had allowed Poulenc to copy from him in order to keep his head just a little above water.[32] Poulenc's 'maladie' might possibly have been a realistic acceptance that scholarly enterprise, at least of a kind in keeping with the tenets of the Lycée Condorcet, was not his forte. Perhaps he promised his father to return there in due course. But we need to remember that this was a boy who had learnt Mallarmé's poem 'Apparition' by heart at the age of ten, so he was no literary dunce,[33] and although he claimed to hate mathematics, he was hooked on bridge from the age of about twelve,[34] so must have had some aptitude for figures. For the time being, it seems, he was put under the care of a private tutor, José Vincent.

In any case, his mother's intuition was proving accurate and already in 1913 he had composed a piano piece and a song. *Mélopée d'automne* was completed on 14 March,[35] while the song, *Viens! une flûte invisible*, set to a poem by Victor Hugo, dated 2 June, was almost certainly a wedding present for his sister, who was married that day to André Manceaux.[36] Again, there are no signs in either piece of undue promise. But nearly a year later Poulenc had one of the most exciting experiences of his life – one that might almost be interpreted as sanctioning his departure from the lycée and the time he was now left to concentrate on his music. On 5 April 1914 Pierre Monteux, who had conducted the stage premiere of *Le Sacre du printemps* the previous May, gave a concert performance of the work at the Casino de Paris. After the concert, Poulenc recalled:

> I came home so shocked and thunderstruck that, during the evening, I couldn't conceal from my parents how I'd spent the day. 'It's not a concert for someone of your age,' said my father, as if the memorable scandal had been caused by some indecency or other. My mother smiled, approving internally, and said nothing. 'You really have got some weird tastes, my poor boy!' my father finally grumbled. 'Ah well!!!' His 'Ah wells' were a sign of resignation, and the incident was closed.[37]

Thunderstruck Poulenc might well have been, but despite all his admiration for Stravinsky (and before this incident he had already heard *Fireworks*, *The Firebird* and *Petrushka*), it was not mainly *Le Sacre* among the latter's compositions that would influence his own: the work's wildness and savagery were, like Wagner's grandiloquence, essentially foreign to his French temperament. Far more to his taste, if briefly, was *Le Rossignol*, premiered at the Opéra on 26 May 1914, which he later claimed 'visibly inspired' his early piano piece *Processional pour la crémation d'un mandarin*. In this, he was clearly following the French attraction towards the Middle and Far Eastern exotic, triggered by Félicien David's 1844 ode-symphonie *Le Désert*. But once this extravaganza was out of his system, he would only once return to orientalism, in his 1932 Concerto for two pianos.

We know of no further compositions by him for the next couple of years. Certainly, his father would have seen to it that he treated M. Vincent's ministrations seriously, and no doubt Papoum continued to take him to the opera and the theatre, but it seems likely that the boy was pondering the crucial question of whether composition was to be a *métier* or merely a *divertissement*; and if a *métier*, what path should he follow? In a 1952 interview he said that two ways forward had suggested themselves: Schoenberg and Stravinsky; and that 'My Latin taste in harmony led me to choose Stravinsky, and not Schoenberg who grew out of Wagnerian counterpoint.'[38] But as explained above, Stravinsky was not in fact a determining influence at this stage.

Materials for a truer answer to this question came at some point in 1914 or 1915. Through a friend of his mother, Geneviève Sienkiewicz, herself an accomplished pianist, Poulenc was introduced to the celebrated virtuoso Ricardo Viñes, who had given first performances of many of Debussy and Ravel's piano pieces. From his (sadly small) recorded legacy we can hear the sparkling, colourful tone and elegant phrasing that made Viñes such a successful pianist, and Poulenc never ceased to be grateful for the keyboard skills he passed on, especially with regard to use of the pedal, recalling his 'button boots with which he used to rap my shins when I didn't change the pedal enough. Viñes was paramount in the way he handled pedalling, that essential factor in modern music. He succeeded in playing crisply even through a wash of pedal! And what cunning he showed in distinguishing between staccato and full legato!'[39] His influence did not end there. It was through him that Poulenc met Satie and Auric, which was perhaps partly what he had in mind when, after Viñes's death in 1943, he wrote to the pianist's sister Elvira about 'my dear Viñes whom I adored and to whom I owe everything about my musical career, both as a pianist and as a composer'.[40] In addition, his studies with Viñes inspired him to write piano music. 'At the time of my first lessons, I composed some Preludes of unbelievable complexity, which would amaze you today. They were sub-Debussy, written on three or four staves . . . Then I dedicated to Viñes three Pastorales in 1918.'[41] These formed the basis of the *Trois pièces* of 1928.

France's entry into the war on 1 August 1914 has left no visible trace in the Poulenc literature, and we may reasonably accept Edith Wharton's evidence that the Parisian populace 'scorned all show of war, and fed the patriotism of her children on the mere sight of Paris's beauty . . . It seemed as though it had been unanimously, instinctively decided that the Paris of 1914 should in no way resemble the Paris of 1870, and as though this resolution had passed into the blood of millions born since that fatal date, ignorant of its bitter lesson.'[42] It is perhaps debatable whether this insouciance persisted through the later bombing of the city and the blaze and blast of searchlights and anti-aircraft guns.

But in any case the Poulenc family suffered a loss of its own, in the death of Poulenc's mother on 7 June 1915 at the age of only fifty. Again, there is no reference to this in Poulenc's correspondence of that time or later, but references to the great debt he owed her do appear in the dedication, already noted, to *Dialogues des Carmélites*, and in a number of his recorded conversations. Most telling of these is the memory of how once, when he was in a melancholy mood as a child, she had cheered him up by playing Rubinstein's *Romance in F*, an example of what Poulenc later dubbed 'délicieuse mauvaise musique'. 'I found it so entrancing that I said "Again!" [. . .] It's perhaps through this simple romance that I imbibed, unconsciously, a whole spectrum of uncomplicated melody in Tchaikovsky's music, at a time when Stravinsky had not yet provided him with a passport of respectability.'[43] His deep devotion to his mother is not in doubt. But although the trauma of her death was something he preferred to internalize, it certainly prompted him as an adult to seek out and value highly the support of kind, clever, musical women, often of a certain age, who seem to have acted as maternal substitutes. The names of Marthe Bosredon, Nadia Boulanger, Colette, Simone Girard, Wanda Landowska, Marie Laurencin, Princesse Edmond de Polignac, Geneviève Sienkiewicz and Virginie (Tante) Liénard will be found regularly in the following pages.

Some months after his mother's death, Poulenc engaged in an exercise which, puzzling as it is, admits of a variety of explanations. He wrote to nine French composers and Stravinsky, asking them 'what they thought of Franck' and of his place in the development of music. Some inkling of his reasons for doing this may be gained from his letter to Stravinsky, the earliest from his pen so far discovered, in which he includes himself among those who 'are floundering in uncertainty', not a condition the answers he received can have helped him very much to cure. Debussy underlines the need to hold on to old traditions, while describing Franck as 'one of the greatest Flemish composers'; Saint-Saëns says effectively 'time will tell'; Ropartz, as a Franck pupil, is predictably enthusiastic; and Satie points out that Franck's music is 'amazingly franckish, in the best sense of the word'.[44] But if Poulenc's enquiry was intended seriously, and not, as he later suggested, just for the composers' autographs, it could have stemmed from the division in contemporary music between the d'Indystes, who followed Franck and looked askance at flashy objects like concertos, and the younger composers such as Debussy and Ravel, bringing with them the charismatic figure of Fauré, who favoured music that didn't necessarily take itself so seriously – not that their technique could possibly be called into question.

To some extent, this division was mirrored on the social and political fronts of the time. In the dark days of 1870–1, poor Offenbach had been widely blamed for sapping the French patriotic spirit with uproarious works such as *La Grande-Duchesse de Géroldstein*, in which the French military were not treated with the respect some felt they deserved. Now Wharton's mention of 'the mere sight of Paris's beauty' being peddled as some kind of moral support was picked up by writers such as Maurice Barrès, complaining that the French 'came to be regarded as jaded triflers, far too affluent and light-hearted, with pleasure as our only concern; the French people were supposed to allow impulse and passion to determine the course of their lives . . .'[45] For the young Poulenc, what kind of shadow did such condemnation cast over the concept of 'the French temperament'?

This problem was not one that had to be solved immediately: for one thing, there was no question at the moment of any public performance of Poulenc's music. Even if he, or his father, had thought any of it worthy of such attention, the war, which saw public dancing banned in Paris, also silenced such institutions as the Société nationale de musique (from May 1914 to November 1917) and the Société musicale indépendante (from January 1915 to April 1917). In any case, even when these institutions returned to life, they showed no great enthusiasm for the young composer: before 1939 the SMI featured his music just once (the Sonata for two clarinets on 4 December 1919), the SNM likewise (the Suite in C, played by Viñes, on 10 April 1920). For the moment, then, Poulenc was free to listen to as much music as possible, to enjoy the company of his new friend Georges Auric, introduced to him by Viñes, and, perhaps with less excitement, to concentrate on his renewed studies for the *baccalauréat*. He passed the first part of the exam early in 1916 as an independent candidate despite, as he later recalled, marks of the order of 5/20 in geography, 6/20 in physics, but 36/40 for an essay on Diderot. Came the oral exam, and the examiner told him he was either a cheat or else a very extraordinary student. The authorities, he went on, were minded to pass him: what would he like to talk about? The eighteenth-century writer Montesquieu: result, 18/20 and a pass, for which his father duly delivered the promised present of a camera.[46] But after his return to the Lycée Condorcet on 3 October 1916 his bad habits took over again and, although he stayed there for the whole three terms of that academic year, he never passed the second exam.

The first public performance of music by Poulenc, which eventually took place on 11 December 1917, was clearly designed to distinguish him as somebody different. 'From 19 November to 5 December 1916 the opening exhibition took place at the venue on the rue Huyghens – a famous moment in the history of art, since beside works by Picasso, Matisse, Ortiz, Kisling and Modigliani there were 25 sculptures and masks from Africa and New Caledonia, lent by the gallery-owner and collector Paul Guillaume. It was one of the very first exhibitions of black art in Paris.'[47] There is no incontrovertible evidence that Poulenc attended, but the likelihood at the very least is suggested by his engagement during the spring of 1917 on a *Rapsodie nègre* for singer, flute, clarinet, string quartet and piano. But as he was putting the finishing touches to this, another crucial event intervened: the premiere on 18 May 1917 of Satie's ballet *Parade*.

Poulenc went to it with Jacques Soulé and 'was conquered. With all the injustice of youth, and although I idolized Debussy, I agreed to disown him a little because I was so eager for the new inspiration Satie and Picasso were bringing us. That was the time Ricardo Viñes introduced me to Satie [. . .] Satie was suspicious of the young Poulenc because he came from middle-class stock, but my admiration for *Parade* seemed so genuine to him that he adopted me completely.'[48] As Nancy Perloff has pointed out, 'Many of the ballet's elements of varied repetition, musical quotation, brevity and spoof were familiar from Satie's piano pieces of the 1910s. Yet *Parade* was Satie's first concert work to explore a popular language and his first to become known to a large French public.'[49] Knowledge, though, did not imply approval and, accompanied by Picasso's cubist set and elements such as a pantomime horse, the work offended those who thought the talents of Diaghilev's Ballets Russes might have been better employed. The work was even described as 'boche', and its reception was probably not helped by Cocteau proclaiming it as 'the greatest battle of the war' at a time when hundreds of French frontline troops were in mutiny.[50]

But in the longer term there was no gainsaying the 'new spirit', the 'esprit nouveau' identified by Guillaume Apollinaire, who wrote an introduction to the work in the ballet programme. Whether *Parade* had any effect on the composition of *Rapsodie nègre* is arguable. Poulenc's work could simply be heard as an example of the 'exotic', but it shares with *Parade* a refusal to employ the brilliantly sensuous orchestration that French ears had come to expect from their musical exotica: hence Ravel's complaint about *Parade* to Cocteau, that 'It is not bathed in any sonorous fluid' – to which Cocteau's reply was that 'It was precisely the novelty of Satie not to bathe anything in sonorous fluid, not to use any magic philtre, but to take the public by the hand, by the cravat, by the back of the coat, maybe by the nose!'[51] If this was the message Poulenc took from the ballet, it can only have been reinforced by attending a performance of Apollinaire's play *Les Mamelles de Tirésias* on 24 June (a letter to the director Pierre Albert-Birot asks for four tickets on 10 June, so the premiere must have been delayed by a fortnight).[52] Satie had refused to write the incidental music for it (Poulenc later sensed that 'Satie was incapable of adapting to a sense of humour different from his own'), so the score ('unspeakable, dumbfounding') was composed by Albert-Birot's wife. But this was made up for by the quality of the audience: in alphabetical order, Aragon, Auric, Braque, Breton, Cocteau, Derain, Diaghilev, Dufy, Éluard, Léger, Massine, Matisse, Modigliani, Picasso, Satie – for an eighteen-year-old, just to be in the same theatre with all these artists must have felt like being touched by genius.[53]

But whatever élan the young Poulenc felt, it was dashed exactly three weeks later when his father died at the age of sixty-two. Once again, no immediate response is to be found in Poulenc's surviving correspondence, though Satie wrote to offer his condolences the following day, addressing the young man as 'Mon pauvre Ami'.[54] The orphaned Francis went to live with his sister, her husband André Manceaux and their three-year-old daughter Brigitte at 76 rue de Monceau, where they stayed until the summer of 1919, when they moved to no. 83 in the same street. This was a very comfortable *haut bourgeois* residence containing Louis XVI furniture. Here Poulenc lived in a probably less splendid bachelor flat on the other side of the courtyard, above the ancient stables. Brigitte was joined by siblings Rosine in 1918 and Denis in 1921.

It would be natural to hope that Émile Poulenc went to his grave with at least some inkling of what his son would become. But on two counts this has to be doubtful. Firstly, Francis's vain struggles with the second part of his *baccalauréat* must have been a concern, even if he would not have been left in immediate financial need. Secondly, Francis being a composer who was also proficient on the piano, Émile must have heard the strains of the *Rapsodie nègre* and surely, as a Beethoven lover, must have wondered where on earth his son was heading. We do not know whether he expressed any concern, but if he did, certainly he was not the last to do so.

The French have never bought into the ancient British cult of the talented amateur. Art, like business, is a serious matter and, as evidenced by both sides of Poulenc's family, one needs to be properly trained. Viñes's teaching had obviously been vital, and Poulenc had also benefited from lessons given from time to time by other helpful musical friends, but this did not constitute a teaching programme comparable with that of the Conservatoire or the Schola Cantorum. Satie's immediate judgement of Poulenc as a dilettante 'fils à papa' (Daddy's boy) was one that other trained musicians were only too likely to make. So, on Viñes's advice, Poulenc asked Paul Dukas whether he would take him as a pupil. Dukas claimed he was no longer taking pupils, and suggested Paul Vidal, winner of the Prix de Rome in 1883 when Debussy was runner-up, now a professor at the Conservatoire and musical director of the Opéra-Comique. Poulenc duly presented himself at Vidal's door on 26 September, and later that day wrote to Viñes with his news:

> . . . he asked if I'd brought him a manuscript. I handed him the manuscript of my *Rapsodie nègre*. He read it closely, wrinkled his brow and, on seeing the dedication to Erik Satie, rolled his eyes in a rage, got up and yelled these precise words:
> 'your work's disgusting, inept, a load of tasteless garbage. You're trying to make a fool of me with these consecutive fifths everywhere. And what the hell is this Honoloulou? Ah! I see you're a member of the gang of Stravinsky, Satie & Co. Well good-day to you!'
> And he more or less threw me out. So here I am, high and dry, not knowing what to do, who I should go and consult, and so on . . .[55]

This is the only reference we have, and an oblique one at that, to his newly orphaned status. Viñes duly tried again by arranging a meeting with Ravel. Again, things didn't quite turn out as hoped. Ravel explained that:

> Schumann . . . pooh! pooh! pooh! . . . was a nonentity . . . that Mendelssohn . . . was wonderful . . . that Mendelssohn's *Songs without Words* were a thousand times better than Schumann's *Carnaval*, that all the later works by Debussy . . . which I worshipped – which, in fact, I was one of the very few to worship – that is *Jeux* and the *Études pour piano* . . . were none of them 'good' Debussy. That

Debussy's musical old age wasn't up to much; that Saint-Saëns was a musician of genius . . . that Chabrier wasn't equal to orchestrating his own music, and so on. All this bowled me over. I came out as though I'd been K.O'd . . .[56]

It was to be four years before Poulenc did finally find a teacher. In the meantime, Satie provided consolation, saying 'What did you think would happen?', and at least some influence in the form of his own music: over the next two years the *Sonatine bureaucratique*, *Socrate* and the five *Nocturnes* for piano. But one of the most startling aspects of the *Rapsodie nègre* is its independence of any obvious model and the unmistakable sound of an individual voice.

It hardly seems likely that Vidal was, in 1917, objecting to consecutive fifths *per se* – Debussy had been using them for years, not to mention Puccini at the start of the second act of *La Bohème* in 1896. Probably far more disturbing was the fact that for much of this work they form the harmonic bedrock, sometimes gaunt and spare, every now and then richly chromatic. As an ostinato pattern they are the substance of both the vocal intermezzo 'Honoloulou' and the following 'Pastorale', while in the 'Prélude', which they open and close in a style marked 'assez uniforme' (possibly a nod here to Satie, who thought boredom had its uses),[57] they enclose four bars redolent of the lyrical Ravel – in other words, this wretched young man *could* write respectable music if he chose. In the 'Ronde' Vidal might have sensed, and censured, a dark energy to match that of black sculpture and masks, and if he had persevered as far as the 'Final', would have found little here to his taste either, in the relentless iteration of a single chord[58] and the brash instrumentation. Altogether Vidal's fury might have been stoked not merely by the consecutive fifths but by these pitiless repetitions of tiny phrases, turning their backs on the whole traditional idea of 'development', in the search for a 'primitive' musical discourse.

In this we can find some backing for the statement in *The Chesterian*, the house magazine of the publishers Chester & Co who brought out the score of the work in 1919, that *Rapsodie nègre* was written 'under the influence of Stravinsky', a claim that they 'were fortunate enough to obtain from the composer'.[59] But we should also bear in mind that it was Stravinsky who now persuaded Chesters to take Poulenc on, so the statement may have contained an element of gratitude. It has also been suggested that the instrumental grouping may have been influenced by that of *Pierrot lunaire*, but this could only have been through a perusal of the score, published by Universal in 1914, since, despite interest from Ravel, the work was not heard in Paris until January 1922.

17

The eighteen-year-old Poulenc was probably unaware that in espousing this new simplicity he was anticipating the artistic mindset of the following decade. These final war years were a time of flux in which conservative and radical ideas fought it out with considerable vigour. The Nabi painter Maurice Denis let fly from the far right a damning volley, raging that 'Revolutionary prejudices, the excesses of individualism, the penchant for paradox, the craze for the unfinished, for the original, all the defects of our art are also the defects of French society.'[60] Against this, a more measured analysis came from André Derain, prophesying that 'Everything is going to change, and we will have simpler ideas.'[61]

But even the most equanimous of commentators could feel some sympathy with Vidal's outburst, 'And what the hell is this Honoloulou?', faced as he was not only with this word as the title of the third movement, but with a text whose first verse reads 'Honoloulou, poti lama!/Honoloulou, Honoloulou,/Kati moko, mosi bolou/Ratakou sira, polama!' This poem is part of a collection *Les Poésies de Makoko Kangourou* supposedly 'publiés par Marcel Prouille et Charles Moulié' in 1910, though they were in fact its authors. While this nonsense verse undoubtedly appealed to Poulenc's naughty side, already touched on and regularly in evidence hereafter, nothing in his setting reveals its ludicrous nature: and, as would be the case in all such Poulenc enterprises, performers need to keep an absolutely impassive demeanour, free of nods or winks. For Poulenc a further incentive to setting it might have been the statement in the authors' spoof biography of one M. Kangourou that 'he was educated at the petit lycée Condorcet: his teachers say that he was never an outstanding student, though well-behaved.'[62]

In the six months between his father's death and the first performance of *Rapsodie nègre* in December 1917, Poulenc seems to have strengthened and established his ties with the Parisian intellectual community – as to whether he felt liberated as well as disturbed by his orphan condition, we can only guess. But certainly in these final years of his teens he found support in at least four institutions, two of them musical, two literary.

In 1913 the actor/manager Jacques Copeau had founded the Théâtre du Vieux Colombier in the street of that name, but in 1917 he felt moved to take his troupe to New York. When the soprano Jane Bathori turned down the opportunity to come with him, he suggested to her that she might take over the theatre in his absence. She seized the chance and, thanks to her stellar reputation (she had given first performances of Ravel's *Histoires naturelles* and Debussy's *Promenoir des deux amants*, among many other works), had no trouble finding artists to perform at her concerts. *Rapsodie nègre*, performed on 11 December 1917, was one of her earliest discoveries and was repeated regularly over the next couple of years. But by 1920 Copeau had to accept that the hoped-for success in New York had eluded him, and he returned to his Paris theatre.

In 1914 the Swiss painter Émile Lejeune had introduced a series of concerts in his large studio on the rue Huyghens, measuring some 17 by 7 metres and with a gallery, for the benefit of unemployed musicians and artists. The enterprise was then taken over by the cellist Félix Delgrange, with help from Blaise Cendrars and the actor Pierre Bertin, and their concerts were given initially under the name 'Lyre et Palette', then as 'Peinture et Musique'.[63] A recital of Debussy's music was held in early April 1916 and a Satie/Ravel concert on 18 April, at which the writer and composer Roland-Manuel delivered a lecture on Satie. Between then and the ending of the concerts in 1920 the studio became a favourite venue for the young composers promoted by Satie, the Nouveaux Jeunes, and their subsequent incarnation as the Groupe des Six, while among the painters exhibited were Picasso, Matisse, Braque, Gris and Modigliani. Milhaud later recalled that 'the seats without backs were uncomfortable, and the atmosphere unbreathable because of the smoke from the stove, but the whole of Paris high society, together with artists as well as supporters of new music, did a certain amount of elbowing to be part of it'.[64]

Poulenc's two literary supports were both bookshops:

From November 1915 Adrienne Monnier ran a bookshop at 7 rue de l'Odéon, 'La Maison des Amis de Livres', which was also a lending library. She would stay there till 1951. Her visitors soon included Paul Fort, Jules Romains, Léon-Paul Fargue, Breton, Aragon, Apollinaire, Cendrars, Reverdy, Gide, Valéry . . . Satie came by regularly. The spirit of fantasy that animated the Amis de Livres led Fargue to invent a group of 'Potassons', bringing together those friends who had the privilege of finding their way into the room behind the shop, especially on Wednesday afternoons when the shop was closed. Valéry Larbaud, Raymonde Linossier and Francis were among them.[65]

'Potassons', according to Monnier, were a 'variety of the human species that is distinguished by its kindness and its sense of life. For the *potassons*, pleasure is a positive; they are immediately in the know, they have good-heartedness and pluck. When the *potassons* meet, everything goes well, everything can be put to rights, they enjoy themselves without effort . . .' 'Potassons' were an outgrowth of a tiny novella, one page long, entitled *Bibi-la-Bibiste* by Linossier, fifty copies of which were published on 7 February 1918 on imitation Japanese vellum. It was dedicated to Poulenc. Monnier described 'Bibisme', inspired by the book, as 'a sort of Dada before its time. It displayed a taste for the baroque and the primitive. It cherished primitive arts and those forms of popular arts that expressed themselves in animal skins, boxes made of shells, surprise postcards, pictures made of postage stamps, constructions out of cork, etc . . .'[66] As Sophie Robert remarks, 'Bibists and Potassons had many things in common, above all the playful nature of their meetings, and their essential interest in eating good things.'[67] Poulenc was no ascetic when it came to eating good things, nor was he an enemy of playfulness – one of the things that allied him with Stravinsky, whose ludic nature remains, as in Poulenc's case, one of the joys of his *oeuvre*. Beyond that, we can trace a line of playfulness that stretches from Ravel's 'Apaches' in the years after 1900, on to the group 'Gloxinia' that embraced *résistants* during and after the Second World War (of whom Poulenc would be very much a member).

Poulenc's second literary support came in the form of the bookshop Shakespeare & Co., founded by the American Sylvia Beach in 1919. As such, it will figure in the next chapter; suffice to say here that the two shops soon ran as one, with Beach and Monnier living together.

Amid all this supporting activity, and in the wake of his father's death, Poulenc composed little in the last six months of 1917. In August he took a holiday at Paramé, now part of the commune of St Malo, which was, as he complained to Viñes, somewhat short on pleasure, 'because the scenery is ugly and the weather so-so, but I've had a rest and that's really all I wanted after the sad times I've just been through. I haven't played any music at all because the hotel piano is abominable. As for composing, for the same reason I'm still where I was when I arrived, that's to say I've got a scherzo for two pianos on the go. It's called *Zèbre*, inspired by a Cocteau poem. I think you'll like it because rhythmically it's quite fun.'[68] Six bars on the autograph of *Rapsodie nègre* may be the remains of this piece, which otherwise has vanished,[69] but we do learn that Poulenc's habit of composing at the piano was already established – any qualms he might have had about this were eased by remembering Rimsky-Korsakov's advice to Stravinsky: 'Some composers compose away from the piano, some at the piano: you compose at the piano.'[70]

In August 1917 Poulenc continued his African productions with three *Poèmes sénégalais* for voice and string quartet, but these have not survived and we do not even know who wrote the texts. Then in the autumn he wrote the *Trois Pastorales* for piano and dedicated them to Viñes. As on many other occasions, Poulenc's recollections of these and their subsequent history were faulty. The facts have been clearly set out by Carl Schmidt,[71] namely that the 1917 originals were revised twice, in 1928 and again in 1953, both under the new title *Trois pièces*. The 1928 revision was drastic, including an entirely new 'Hymne'; but the 1953 revision merely extends the final 'Toccata' by a couple of bars.

The first performance of the *Rapsodie nègre* does not seem to have provoked any reviews – perhaps luckily, since things did not go quite as planned: 'At the last minute the singer threw in the sponge, saying it was too silly and that he didn't want to look a fool. Quite unexpectedly, masked by a big music stand, I had to sing that interlude myself. Since I was already in uniform, you can just imagine the unusual effect produced by a soldier bawling out songs in pseudo-Malagasy!'[72] Despite this, Poulenc, happy that Jane Bathori as impresario had accepted it in the first place, was no doubt equally encouraged by her decision to repeat it and by seeing Stravinsky and Diaghilev in the audience. She also now accepted the *Pastorales* for performance at the Vieux-Colombier, as Alfredo Casella did the *Rapsodie nègre* for a concert in Rome, being, according to Poulenc, 'très emballé' (very excited) by the piece.[73] In the meantime Poulenc enjoyed what was to be a brief love affair with jazz in the persons of Harry Pilcer and Gaby Deslys at the Casino de Paris.

Poulenc was in uniform because, having turned nineteen on 7 January 1918, he now had to perform his military service. He just had time to attend a concert at the Vieux-Colombier by members of the group Nouveaux Jeunes that included works by Tailleferre, Honegger, Auric, Roland-Manuel, Durey and himself (*Rapsodie nègre*) on 15 January, before reporting for duty two days later. This month saw the beginning of the bombardment of Paris by the German howitzer *La Grosse Berthe*, leading to the closure of the Vieux-Colombier in March. But Poulenc, even if enlisted for the duration of the war in artillery regiments in Vincennes, Arnouville-lès-Gonesse and Châlons-sur-Marne and then, with the end of the war, in air defence batteries at Villenauxe-la-Grande and Pont-sur-Seine, had probably been in no greater danger than most of the civilian population. It's abundantly clear from his letters that his main enemy was boredom, which he alleviated from time to time by overstaying his leave, duly punished by days in solitary. Although friends did come to see him occasionally, as he mentioned in a letter to his sister,[74] to fellow potasson Léon-Paul Fargue he complained 'if only I had someone to talk to, but here I have nothing but imbeciles as companions',[75] while in Arnouville 'military life leaves me precious little leisure for practising my art'.[76] While there in August 1918, he had the idea of enlisting as a driver for the Red Cross unit set up by the Comte de Beaumont, but nothing came of this.[77] Finally in the summer of 1919, he took up a secretarial post in the War Ministry in Paris before being demobilized on 17 January 1921.

Shortly after the outbreak of the Second World War, Poulenc wrote to Nadia Boulanger, 'It's sad to think that the other war impeded my musical education considerably.'[78] On the face of it this was certainly true, but we may agree with Hervé Lacombe that to have escaped the formal teaching of, say, the Paris Conservatoire might not have been all loss for a talent such as his, leaving him free to enjoy 'la délicieuse mauvaise musique' without incurring the frowns of M. Vidal and Co.[79] In any case, he was able to come back to Paris on leave (of the four places mentioned above only Châlons is more than 120 kilometres from Paris), and pleasures are often sweeter for being tasted in spite of encumbrances – as the conductor Manuel Rosenthal later remembered, the fact that opportunities to hear a particular work in Paris were fewer in the 1920s than in the 1980s meant that you treasured them all the more as being 'plus rares'.[80]

The catalogue of Poulenc's musical activities in the three years from December 1917 proves that he was anything but out of the swim. The group Nouveaux Jeunes was set up by Satie, who introduced Auric and Durey to Honegger, with Poulenc and Tailleferre then joining them; Milhaud, who had gone to Brazil early in 1917 as Claudel's secretary in the French Embassy, was added on his return to Paris in February 1919, while Roland-Manuel remained a peripheral member of the group. Their first concert on 1 December contained works by Auric, Durey, Honegger and Tailleferre.

By now Poulenc had met Jean Cocteau who, with his sensitive ear for the ʒeitgeist, realized that Parade had started a musical movement to which he could attach himself with profit. Although his pamphlet Le Coq et l'Arlequin, written in the spring of 1918 and published the following year, has often been taken as a precursor of the music composed from 1920 by Les Six, the new group which had formed from the Nouveaux Jeunes after Satie's break with them in November

22

1918, in fact it may be more accurately seen as a description of what had been already happening in the spring of 1918 – which is not to deny its influence, aided by Cocteau's magical way with words. 'Build me music I can live in like a house', 'the café-concert is often pure; the theatre always corrupt', 'a composer always has too many notes on his keyboard', 'a young man should not invest in gilt-edged stock', 'to be daring with tact is to know how far we may go too far' – these snappy sayings lodge in the brain, though the book found detractors as well as enthusiasts: not least Satie who, in Frederick Brown's words, 'was appalled by Cocteau's tentacular intimacy. It seemed to him that the writer had been riding his coat tails, and *Le Coq et l'Arlequin* confirmed his dark suspicions.'[81]

In those three years from December 1917 Poulenc wrote some fifteen works; not all of them have survived (one is intrigued by the single mention of a *Fanfare* for four pianos),[82] but those that do contain some of his best-loved pieces. From the spring of 1918 dates the Sonata for two clarinets, written or completed in Boulogne. What suggested this instrumentation is unknown. It was not composed with any particular performers in mind, and the only examples of the genre by well-known composers before Poulenc are some Duos by C. P. E. Bach and Crusell and a couple of tiny pieces by Rimsky-Korsakov, this last using both B flat and A clarinets as Poulenc does. Ostinatos abound, as in the *Rapsodie nègre*, as well as short phrases within a small compass that evoke the Russian folk songs which were engaging Stravinsky at this same time. Here and there we find echoes of *Petrushka* and *Le Sacre*, but maybe the strongest Stravinskyan influence is that of the *Three Japanese Lyrics* (especially the second song): Poulenc must surely have heard these at the concert of the Société musicale indépendante on 14 January 1914, together with the premiere of Ravel's *Trois poèmes de Stéphane Mallarmé*, both works being sung by Jane Bathori. Poulenc enjoys himself exhibiting the flexibility and wide range of the clarinet, as Boulez was to do much later, but virtuosity never gets out of hand. Already Poulenc had an instinctive feeling of when to put an end to one idea and start on another, and he was rightly proud in a letter to the work's dedicatee Édouard Souberbielle of how, with such simple means, he had composed a finale which, 'when you hear it, you can't say how it's written'.[83] The initial joyful whoops of the B flat clarinet are so delightful, the critical spirit retires abashed. Of these sonatas and the two for woodwind and brass that followed it, Poulenc later said that they 'retain a certain freshness that's not unlike the early paintings of Dufy',[84] but at the same time we note in this sonata the markings 'incolore' and 'sans nuances' which link it 'undeniably to the period of Satie and Les Six'.[85]

The spring of 1918 also saw three events that were, for Poulenc, of varying importance. On 19 March the *Poèmes sénégalais* were premiered at the Vieux-Colombier by the Quatuor Merkel and an unspecified singer. No review has survived and we have no record of Poulenc ever mentioning them again, though there must be a good chance that the singer was Jane Bathori, and her participation so obvious as not to need mentioning. Nor is there mention of the death of Debussy six days later, while Paris was cowering under the bombardments of *La Grosse Berthe*; the mourners at his funeral were few, and it is doubtful whether Poulenc was among them. But the third event, the private performance at the home of the Princesse de Polignac of extracts from Satie's *Socrate*, again sung by Jane Bathori, left Poulenc dumbfounded. In 1926 he remembered that 'the language of the work, so pure and luminous, surprised and moved us at a time when a whole host of debussyan and ravelian techniques were still casting a cloud over music,'[86] and at the end of his life he said that 'the music of *Socrate* is static by virtue of its purity, balance and reserve. The work is very difficult to sing because you risk confusing unity with monotony. I cannot myself hear the last section of the triptych, "La Mort de Socrate", without a lump in the throat.'[87] It may be worth noting that, by the time of this avowal, he himself had already faced the unity/monotony problem in writing *Dialogues des Carmélites*.

The lessons of *Socrate* in the form of 'purity, balance and reserve' manifest themselves first of all in parts of his Sonata for piano duet, finished in Boulogne in June 1918. It's fair to say that the work as a whole owes almost nothing to the essentially lyrical piano duets of Bizet, Debussy or Ravel. Instead, 'purity' is at work in the central 'Rustique' in its twenty-two bars of C major with no accidentals, 'reserve' in its ostinatos and short-winded phrases. The outer movements, though, are a good deal less pure. The 'Prélude' testifies to the young Poulenc's enthusiasm for Bartók's *Allegro barbaro* and Prokofiev's *Sarcasmes* and 'Suggestion diabolique',[88] even if it never approaches the mobile chromaticisms of the latter. Novelty also makes a claim at the very start in the layout of the four hands, with the left hand of the *prima* player playing below both those of the *seconda*, making performance an even more intimate exercise than usual. Repetitive, folksy little snippets do duty for melodies, as they had in *Rapsodie nègre*, and the only Debussyan feature, a passage of major ninths (like those that had so fascinated the young Francis in the 'Danse profane'), has its seductiveness brutally nullified by additional chromatics marked 'féroce' and 'strident'.

The 'Final' begins in purity, but this is soon sullied by locomotive-like hoots in the *prima* part and the rest of the movement is driven by interplay between good and bad harmonic behaviour. The last two bars introduce a feature that will mark many of Poulenc's pieces from now on: a kind of ambiguous 'sign-off' that seems to cast doubt retrospectively on the nature of what we've been hearing – has it been serious, comic, anxious, joyful, sarcastic, tender? Or a mixture of some or all of these? The extraordinary exactness of Poulenc's intuition is displayed by the fact that these sign-offs, while often appearing on the page to be unrelated to what's gone before, nonetheless do make a forceful impact, even if we can't put into words what precisely that impact is. In the present instance the simultaneous markings 'Presto' and 'subito *ppp*' add to the ambiguity.

Poulenc's late summer and autumn of 1918 were largely taken up by a collaboration with Jean Cocteau (a sonata for piano and orchestra joins the *Fanfare* and a, possibly spoof, sonata for cimbalom and wind quartet in meriting only a single mention).[89] For any Parisian artist of the time, Cocteau was a hard man to avoid. As Milhaud's widow Madeleine later put it, 'He liked to be in charge of everything, and generally was at that time: if he wasn't doing everything, he didn't think he was doing anything.'[90] But where music was concerned, Cocteau suffered, as he didn't in his literary and visual enterprises, simply from a lack of training. Enthusiasm – he could deliver that in spades. But musicians learnt to be wary of his forays on the musical front, as witness Cocteau's lunchtime bout with Satie, recalled by Auric:

> . . . at a particular moment [Cocteau] ventured to speak at rather too great a length about music. Satie suddenly went white with anger, got up and went over to Cocteau's chair. We were terrified, seeing him, pince-nez and serviette in hand, looming over Cocteau who had stopped talking or even moving, ready to receive a serviette and a plate on top of his head. Satie lifted his arms as though about to brain him, then delivered a single word: 'Imbecile!'[91]

The young Poulenc was, of course, in no position to behave likewise, and in any case for the moment he saw Cocteau as a useful vehicle for capitalizing on the limited success of the *Rapsodie nègre*. He was therefore quite ready to accept Cocteau's invitation late that summer to join other members of the Nouveaux Jeunes in a 'Séance Music-Hall', which Jane Bathori had asked Cocteau to put together for a fortnight at the Vieux-Colombier. The theatre would, wrote Poulenc, 'be turned for the time being into a Music Hall. There will be performances four times a week. Real acrobats, jugglers, wrestlers and boxers will do their stuff onstage and will perform to the sound of music by Messrs Satie, Auric, Durey and Poulenc . . . No scenery . . . In the intervals furniture music by all of us.'[92] 'Furniture music' was the phrase invented by Satie for what we would nowadays call 'wallpaper music'. According to the programme, Honegger and Tailleferre were also due to contribute;[93] Milhaud was still in America. Poulenc later explained that he and Milhaud, who had first met on a tennis court in 1915, had become friends at once, but with Honegger this took a little longer, thanks to a meeting in the spring of 1917. Jane Bathori got a few musicians together, including Honegger, Koechlin, Viñes and Poulenc, to go through Ravel's *Trois Chansons* for unaccompanied choir. But Poulenc 'made mistakes once or twice. Arthur Honegger turned round and said to me: "Ear training . . . young man?" . . . I was very intimidated, and perhaps it was because of that first contact that Honegger scared me for a very long time.'[94]

Sadly, nothing of the music survives from any of these composers except a single song, *Le Toréador*, by Poulenc. His main contribution, entitled *Le Jongleur*, was for a twenty-piece orchestra of fairly conventional make-up, and the music was to be 'very simple, it will be noble and majestic, a sort of uniform background to the movements of the actors'. But the instruments for the *Prélude percussion* before it are worth detailing: '2 Chinese trumpets with a unique sound, marvellous instruments that one of my friends stole from a temple in China, timpani in G, D ♯ and F, castanets, tambourine, bass drum with cymbals, cymbals, triangle, glockenspiel and xylophone'.[95] Two points of interest here are, firstly, the 'exotic' Chinese trumpets, showing a side of Poulenc which, as already mentioned, would be heard again only once, in the early 1930s; and secondly, the tuning of the timpani, which suggests that he might possibly have been planning something in the whole-tone scale. He later described *Le Toréador* as 'une fausse chanson de caf' conc' and admitted that when writing it he had in mind the voice and style of Maurice Chevalier. The 1933 published score bears the subtitle 'chanson hispano-italienne', a knowing hit at the rather casual geography of the chansons of 1918 'in which a Japanese girl would go to the bad in Peking and Sappho would fire questions at the sphinx'.[96] There are a few Spanish ornamental triplets, but otherwise the song gives a first glimpse of Poulenc's lyrical gifts and his easy command of modulation, and it remains arguable whether he in fact fulfilled the second half of Cocteau's ambivalent request that 'the song should not be as good as Chabrier – you must make it *good* but *lousy* [il faut la faire *bien* mais *moche*]'.[97] But maybe by 'moche' he merely meant 'populist'. If so, Poulenc obeyed, and the commission 'prompted [his] first experiments with an approach to songwriting that he employed throughout his career [which included] the imitation of written features of French music-hall songs (syllabic setting, alteration of stress patterns)',[98] the first of which occurs in the very opening line: 'Pépita reiné de Venise'.

For reasons which are now obscure, plans for *Le Jongleur* dragged on and on and, although Poulenc says his own contribution was completed before 20 November 1918,[99] the piece was not finally performed until June 1921. The set and dancer's costume were by Valentine Hugo, to whom Poulenc explained that he hadn't asked Picasso because he didn't want anything that would remind people of *Parade*.[100] In the meantime he turned his attention to other works, initially a Violin Sonata and a Sonata for piano trio. The Violin Sonata set a pattern for Poulenc of destroying works for this combination, despite what any of the violinists concerned might say in their favour. This sonata, unlike some of its successors, did actually receive a performance, in the Salle Huyghens on 21 December, played by Hélène Jourdan-Morhange and Marcelle Meyer, together with the first performance of the Sonata for piano duet played by Meyer and the composer.[101] According to Jourdan-Morhange, Poulenc hadn't finished the piano part and they played only the first two of its three movements, but she remembered them as being 'fort jolis'. Her general impression was that 'all this young group was in a hurry to fulfil its destiny of escaping the vampires of the previous generation'[102] and, if Poulenc had felt the sonata fell short of this destiny, it could well have been a reason for him destroying it. Another possible reason could be found in a letter he wrote to Cocteau on 14 November, saying 'I've just finished the sonata for violin and piano. This one in rag-time': otherwise jazz in any shape or form is notably absent from his music and he doubted the value of its influence on the music of his colleagues, notably on that of Ravel.[103] We know still less of the Sonata for piano trio, which was never performed and may not even have been completed, nor is Poulenc known ever to have considered writing for this chamber combination again.

Bad and good news reached him in November 1918, in the form of Satie's defection from the Nouveaux Jeunes on the 1st, Apollinaire's death on the 9th, and the armistice two days later. Satie's burst of hostility against the group he himself had founded was in keeping with his explosive character, not improved by drink. Poulenc's error was to try and heal the rift by arranging a ceremony of reconciliation, a move that sparked off a further response:

Poulenc's comico-idiotic manoeuvres – which everyone wants me to 'swallow' and which utterly disgust me – compel me to ask you to withdraw the 'homages' prepared for me by the good 'N.J.' gentlemen. I won't accept them at any price.[104]

None of these three events is mentioned in Poulenc's letters, maybe because December found him in low spirits, stationed in 'a terribly grim little country town', Villeneuve-la-Grande, in which 'all work seems to me impossible'.[105] To Adrienne Monnier on the 28th he sent New Year wishes in the form of a 'petite complainte', complete with music and instructions for performance by the potassons, thinking of whom he confessed to 'blubbing like a little boy'.[106] But this bout of depression makes for curious reading in light of the little work he had written earlier that month, which was to be the first of his great successes: the *Trois Mouvements perpétuels* for piano.

II
'NOW WE ARE SIX'
✦ 1919–1924 ✦

On 4 January 1916 Albert Roussel, like Ravel serving in the army as a lorry driver, wrote home to his wife, 'This war will have created a new world in which many things from the old one will have disappeared.'[1] How prescient he was is easy to see on many musical fronts, most notably in the field of language and in the abandonment of Romantic features such as the 'clouds, waves, aquariums, water nymphs and perfumes of the night' so roundly condemned by Cocteau in *Le Coq et l'Arlequin*.[2] By 1919 Poulenc had, for the moment, exorcized the influence of Debussy's piano music through his multi-stave preludes and can have found little on which to model solo piano music of his own in that of Stravinsky, though the eight little piano duets of 1914–17 might well have been of more interest in their imaginative use of ostinato. In this respect Satie too had much to offer, most notably in his *Avant-dernières pensées* of 1916, rather naughtily dedicated to three eminently respectable figures in Debussy, Dukas and Roussel.

In calling his three pieces *Mouvements perpétuels*, Poulenc neatly headed off criticism of what might seem a limited technical procedure. In fact, as Stravinsky and Satie would no doubt have agreed, to compose anything valuable, let alone individual, under such a constraint is far from easy. The great pianist Alfred Cortot, writing in 1930, had the measure of Poulenc's achievement in these three pieces:

> . . . acclaimed by virtuosos as well as by amateurs with a welcome that was as justified as it was immediate, and which resolve the delicate problem of instantly adapting the ironically subversive aspects of Satie's technique to the easily outraged taste of middle-of-the-road salons. There is nothing, in fact, in these three amiable pieces, clearly inspired by the manner of the composer of the *Gymnopédies*, which does not lend itself to delightful listening, and equally to a calm and contented spirit. There is no dissonance, however fleeting, that does not find itself clothed in the attractiveness of an engaging melodic idea; no

daring passage, even if it is concealed, which does not recover through a charming display of goodheartedness.[3]

Cortot's testimony that the pieces were 'acclaimed by virtuosos as well as by amateurs' reflects another sense in which 'the war had created a new world', in that it no longer seemed necessary for a composer to pass through a period of apprenticeship before he/she joined the ranks of the successful; nowadays they 'arrived' at what many older heads felt was an unseasonably early age. As a result, their 'arrival' was accepted in some quarters, but not in others; and Poulenc was no exception.

As for Cortot's 'charming display of goodheartedness' ('charmant accent de bonne compagnie'), this is perhaps not as innocent as it might superficially appear; certainly if we observe the instructions included on the autograph, but not in any of the three editions Poulenc put through the press in 1919, 1939 and 1962: 'The second piece should be played three times consecutively: the first time in a casual manner; the second with plenty of rubato; the third with fury, accentuating every note.' A second set of instructions demands that 'These three pieces must only be played as a group, and one smartly after the other. They should all flow in a uniform way that is without colour. Pianists must forget they are virtuosos.'

It may be that Poulenc intended these instructions just for the dedicatee, his friend Valentine Gross, rather than for public consumption. But in any case Hervé Lacombe has some reason to be brought up short by 'this opposition between "rage" and "lack of colour", between rubato (elsewhere forbidden) and uniformity'.[4] No less surprising is the very idea of giving three consecutive performances of a piece in quite differing styles – one that smacks rather of Mallarmé or Boulez than of a nineteen-year-old devotee of Satie. But it does fit quite well with what was to be Poulenc's lifelong determination not to be written off as just a purveyor of 'easy listening'. As he wrote to his friend, the distinguished Belgian critic and entrepreneur Paul Collaer, 'The Belgian critics find me "agreeable, charming". They should be aware that no one realizes the chemical combinations of acrid odours that go to make up the scent of the rose.'[5]

If there are acrid odours in these three pieces, they are certainly well disguised. Most of the performing instructions on the score, as opposed to the 'rage' advertised on the manuscript, promote a cool rendering: 'sans nuances', 'doucement timbré', 'incolore', 'indifférent', 'uniforme', 'avec charme', 'gris'; and on the final pair of scales that separate off towards the two ends of the keyboard (with a wonderful sense of liberation after the close textures so far) players are asked to 'ralentir en s'effaçant' (slow down in a self-effacing manner). One of the most remarkable aspects of these extraordinary pieces is indeed the self-effacement of the composer, mirrored in his warning 'Pianists must forget they are virtuosos' – not a million miles from Debussy's already quoted adjuration to those taking the solo roles in *Pelléas et Mélisande* to 'forget you are singers'.[6] Self-effacement can also be seen as taking two other forms. First of these is the borrowing from another composer in the opening of the first piece, where the descending right-hand phrase seems to have been copied from 'Es kehret der Maien', the fifth song of Beethoven's cycle *An die ferne Geliebte*.[7] This may have been unconscious, and certainly there is no question of his taking a leaf out of Satie's book in the *Sonatine bureaucratique*, which is plainly a deliberate retake of a well-known Clementi sonatina. The second act of possible self-effacement comes in those little 'sign-offs' at the end of each piece, and especially of the second, which Vladimir Jankélévitch describes as seeming 'to say to us airily: You know, I don't attach any more importance to it than this. Don't take my romance too seriously!'[8] Quite apart from their purely musical value (the sceptical reader is encouraged to try and find equally persuasive alternatives), these sign-offs neatly cut the ground from under the feet of those who would accuse Poulenc of *arrivisme* or self-importance.

Viñes gave the first performance of these pieces at a Lyre et Palette concert on 9 February 1919 and they were the first of Poulenc's works to spread worldwide. Viñes played them again on 5 April at another Lyre et Palette concert in the Salle Huyghens, which also included the first performance of the Sonata for two clarinets as well as first performances of works by Auric, Durey, Milhaud (now back in Paris) and Tailleferre. In 1930 Poulenc described his pieces as 'still no more than three simple little touches of colour, on a ground of white paper'[9] and by the last decade of his life he claimed merely to 'tolerate' them.[10] But even so, for him they also carried the memory of his beloved Viñes and 'the first time I returned to Barcelona after the Second World War, I was asked to play the *Mouvements perpétuels* as an encore in his memory. As I announced them, I burst into tears.'[11]

If we are looking to take something positive from the horrors of the First World War, we may consider the fact that the small amount of free time left to Poulenc by his military activities meant that it was easier to write short works rather than long ones, extended and uninterrupted periods of time being the crucial need of composers for major works, and one lamented by many of them in the busy twentieth century and beyond. Undoubtedly short works fitted with Poulenc's undeveloped compositional technique, but at the same time they demanded an accuracy of perception that could not be taken for granted. Roland-Manuel put his finger on the problem when, with regard to the simplicity that tended to accompany such brevity, he warned that 'our music must . . . take care . . . not to confuse "stripped-down" art with the "left-overs of the arts"' ('notre musique . . . doit se garder . . . de confondre "l'art dépouillé" avec les "dépouilles des arts"').[12] In other words one had to be careful not to flush out the baby with its bathwater.

But not the least of Poulenc's abilities was that of knowing when to stop. 'Longueurs' in his music are very few and far between, so that the unhurried discourse of *Dialogues des Carmélites* was to represent a serious challenge for him, and one he was proud of having overcome to his own satisfaction. In the early months of 1919, though, it was Adrienne Monnier who, with her *potassonesque* instincts, enabled Poulenc to build on the experience of the *Mouvements perpétuels*. In January of that year she sent him the new edition of Apollinaire's collection of short poems *Le Bestiaire* with woodcuts by Dufy. By mid-May he had completed twelve settings of Apollinaire's thirty poems (twenty-six about animals together with four entitled 'Orphée') and, after one private performance, he accompanied the soprano Jeanne Borel in the first public performance of all twelve on 8 June. Auric had attended the rehearsals, so Poulenc was disposed to take his advice seriously when he recommended publishing only six of the songs. This too was the advice of Raymonde Linossier, though Poulenc later chose to efface her part in this decision, for reasons that have never been satisfactorily explained.

Although the cycle is now generally performed with piano accompaniment, the original one was for flute, clarinet, bassoon and string quartet, adding just a bassoon to the ensemble used for the *Rapsodie nègre*. It is instructive from time to time to hear this instrumental original: to savour the bassoon tone in the descending semiquaver figure of 'Le dromadaire', the clarinet's acciaccaturas in the fourth bar of 'La chèvre de Thibet', and its seductive doubling of the vocal line on the final 'Poissons de la mélancolie' – a phrase that unmistakably proclaims Poulenc's genius as a songwriter. Where the two versions would seem to differ profoundly is in the overall texture: clean in the instrumental version, and clouded with pedal in the piano one, as heard in Poulenc's 1928 recording with Claire Croiza. This difference does pose the question of whether Poulenc's pedalled textures are to be taken as definitive, speaking as he regularly did throughout his life of wanting pianists to use the pedal 'like a good sauce'.[13]

The style of the word setting clearly shows the influence of Satie, in a conversational tone with predominantly small intervals, so that the final upward octave leap on 'mélancolie' strikes home with all the greater effect. Three of the performing instructions echo those on the *Mouvements perpétuels*: 'uniforme', 'sans nuances', très égal', and the whole set is redolent of 'the French temperament'. The only reference Poulenc ever made to German music in relation to this cycle was to the bass Doda Conrad, saying 'The first time one heard Marya Freund [Conrad's mother] sing *Le Bestiaire* as though it were Schubert, one understood that it was serious!'[14] It might also seem that the brevity of these songs separated them from the German tradition, but Benjamin Ivry could be right in suggesting that Poulenc's choice of such short poems might have been encouraged by the fact that 'since childhood he had had on his music stand the example of Schoenberg's *Six Little Piano Pieces* op. 19 as a precedent for concentrated emotional statements'.[15] As to reactions from his listeners, no more touching words could he have received than those from Apollinaire's mistress Marie Laurencin in September 1921 when, as discussed below, he was in need of intellectual support: 'Since I've been back I've been humming your *Bestiaire* as best I can and you can't have any idea, Francis Poulenc, how well you've managed to convey both the nostalgia and the musical quality of these admirable quatrains. And what almost overwhelms me is that you'd think it was the voice of Guillaume Apollinaire himself reciting these very lines.'[16] Auric's memories of Apollinaire are also to the point: whereas the poet left a performance of *Parsifal* in some mental disarray, 'a tender, straightforward tune would captivate him, provoking – and very successfully – a straightforward, tender vein which too often he felt obliged to dissimulate.'[17] Finally it's notable that Poulenc 'carefully avoids the most aggressive poems' in Apollinaire's collection, and that 'the cycle of songs clearly presents a progression towards silence and immobility'.[18]

As happens in Satie's music, at least one passage in 'L'écrevisse' is for the delight of the pianist alone, where the last word in the phrase 'As crayfish move, Backwards' finds the right hand plunging way below the left. Finally, ' "The Carp" found its visual counterpart in a melancholy pond where, in melancholy fashion, my melancholy captain used to fish.'[19] Whatever the doubts expressed by Poulenc and his comrades about Debussy and the lure of Impressionism, in this song he dares to succumb, with magical results. Three of the omitted songs, 'Le serpent', 'La colombe' and 'La puce', have since been recovered, but it's hard to quarrel with Auric's and Linossier's judgement, though the energetic, populist 'Le serpent' looks forward to the songs that followed.

These next populist settings were not long in coming. Around the time of the first performances of *Mouvements perpétuels* by Viñes on 9 February and before that of the Sonata for two clarinets on 5 April, Poulenc wrote to Cocteau:

Let's find something – no question, we must organize something in May / June. What? It's up to us to find it. Where? That's up to us too. We'll be all the more successful because at that time the public will have got fed up with Caplet – Léon Moreau – Louis Aubert who are going to give one concert after another at the Indépendante, the Colombier, the Nationale etc. . . . I have to say that at this moment there's not *a minute to lose*, as the other groups are being very active.[20]

Who 'the other groups' were is not entirely clear. But there's no mistaking Poulenc's determination to distance himself from the mediocre mainstream represented by Moreau and Aubert, even if Caplet operated on an altogether higher level. As for the venues, we have already noted the single performance at the Société musicale indépendante of the Sonata for two clarinets on 4 December 1919 and that by the Société nationale, the most prestigious of the Parisian concert-giving bodies, of the Suite in C for piano, played by Viñes on 10 April 1920. But his plans notwithstanding, Poulenc did not succeed in getting Cocteau to organize anything for that summer. Instead he used the three months of April to June in setting three of Cocteau's poems entitled *Cocardes (Petites Pièces plaisantes)*.

Although the settings were published in 1920 as 'Chansons populaires', Poulenc's later performing partner Pierre Bernac took issue with the title, stating that 'neither the poems nor the music suggest popular songs. The texts (I hardly dare call them poems) are kind of word puzzles in which the last syllable or syllables of one word are repeated to begin the next one, as for example in the titles: "Miel de Narbonne, Bonne d'enfant, Enfant de troupe".'[21] The pattern is repeated in the texts themselves: 'Les clowns fleurissent du crotin d'or / Dormir' . . . 'Mandoline / Linoléum'. The popular, or populist, element lies rather in the instrumentation for a band of violin, cornet, trombone, bass drum, triangle and cymbals. Poulenc claimed that this combination reflected the influence of Stravinsky, 'even if it's less visible here than elsewhere', but it's not clear what Stravinsky work or works he was referring to. The most likely candidate would be *Rag-time*, completed by the end of 1918 and published in Paris during 1919, though Stravinsky might have shown Poulenc a score of this and / or of *Histoire du soldat* during a private visit; we do know that Poulenc did not hear *Piano-Rag Music* before Stravinsky played it at the home of Jean and Valentine Hugo early in September 1919.[22] In any case, it would seem that the sounds of Parisian street and circus bands had some influence on the instrumentation. As with *Le Bestiaire*, 'this cycle must be sung without irony. The crucial thing is to believe in the words which fly like a bird, from one branch to another . . . I class *Cocardes* among my "Nogent" works with an atmosphere of chips, accordions and Piver perfume.'[23]

This essentially Parisian work is not designed to touch the heartstrings of non-Parisians, and still less those of non-French listeners for whom the names 'Carnot', 'Joffre', 'Mayol' and 'Touring Club' lack any particular resonance. Even for an expatriate Frenchman like Varèse it spoke, according to his wife, of 'that particularly frivolous period of the *Boeuf-sur-le-toit*, which Varèse disliked and called pure "Parisianism", one of the worst adjectives in his vocabulary'.[24] But the music itself cannot ever have caused real alarm except in the stuffiest of circles. It never strays far from a basic key (D major in the first song, C major in the last two) despite seasoning from an array of wrong notes, while the phrases, mostly of two or four bars, suggest a popular provenance, even if, as Bernac suggests, they never blossom into a popular song as such. The last song, 'Enfant de troupe', centres around the note G, sounding about 100 times in the 46 bars – a wilful distortion of accepted practice, as evidenced in André Gedalge's caustic enquiry of the young Milhaud over his First Violin Sonata: 'Why have you put the note D sharp 17 times on the first page?'[25] Although Poulenc complained to Cocteau during the summer that 'militarism makes itself felt all round me at a moment when I would particularly have need of liberty',[26] it would be easy to assume that these three songs could not have taken up much of his time. However, the fact that they nonetheless sound unmistakably like Poulenc may well be attributed to some hard thinking on his part – despite the charge of 'facility' that was to dog him throughout his career, and almost always in error.

In June 1919, the same month in which he finished *Cocardes*, steps were being taken to publicize the music of the 'tout jeunes' of the French school. On the 28th Roussel wrote to Georges Jean-Aubry, the editor of *The Chesterian*, the house magazine of the publisher Chester, 'As for your review, I have the vague intention of offering you a little article on the "tout jeunes" of the French school, Darius Milhaud, Auric, Durey, Poulenc etc. . . . who are truly interesting.'[27] Not that Roussel has anything very startling to say about Poulenc, but it was surely enough that he recognized his 'charming musicality', noting that 'The influences which reveal themselves in these works do not by any means conceal a personal temperament which will free itself entirely in the composer's next works';[28] and when in September Poulenc sent him a copy of the Sonata for two clarinets, Roussel admired its 'freshness and spontaneity'.[29] It would also seem to have been at some point in 1919 that Stravinsky recommended Poulenc to Chester Editions as a composer worth promoting. Many years later Poulenc remembered Stravinsky's helping hand:

> It was Stravinsky who got me published in London – by Chester, my first publishers, the publishers of *Mouvements perpétuels*, my Sonata for two clarinets, my Sonata for four hands. All those beginner's pieces, stammering little pieces, were published thanks to Stravinsky's kindness. He was really a father to me.[30]

This, while true, was not quite the whole story, given Poulenc's letter of 28 April 1919 to Diaghilev, thanking him 'from the bottom of my heart for what you've done for me. Everything is sorted out between Mr Kling [the director of Chester] and myself. What's more, he's written me a charming letter, and I can sense that the promptness of his reply is due to your warm recommendations. That's why I insist on expressing to you my deepest gratitude.'[31] What else beyond *Rapsodie nègre* Diaghilev knew at this time of Poulenc's music is unclear, but Chester's publication of his works over the coming years meant that Diaghilev (who, despite one or two doubting comments expressed over the years, was musically literate) could keep track of Poulenc's progress without having to attend performances, with results we shall be considering shortly.

In August Poulenc could announce to Cocteau that the voice and piano version of *Cocardes* was done, his exclamation 'Ouff!' indicating that, as suggested above, this was far from being the work of a moment. He noted that Chester were bringing out the Sonata for four hands in a week's time and told Cocteau that, if he was agreeable, they would also be sent *Cocardes*. It is probable that they were, but refused, given the songs' narrowly Parisian nature. Finally he mentioned the rather curious title 'Disques' for an 'album collectif' – possibly the first evidence of the coming mutation of the Nouveaux Jeunes into Les Six.[32]

The word 'possibly' is very much required here since the early history of Les Six remains unclear in many respects. While Satie's letter to Durey of 1 November 1918 (p. 27) may have put an end to the Nouveaux Jeunes for official purposes, that was no reason for this group of friends to disband; in any case, Satie did not entirely cease to collaborate with them, despite his misgivings. The clearest exposé of their combined efforts during 1919 comes from Robert Orledge:[33]

During 1919 Les Six crystallized as a group, giving joint concerts both with and without Satie, in which the added presence of Milhaud as an organizing and as a conciliatory force should not be underestimated. The 'Samedistes', as they called themselves in 1919, began and ended their informal Saturday evening gatherings at Milhaud's apartment in Pigalle, enjoying a meal at a nearby bistro, or visits to the music hall, the Cirque Médrano, or the Montmartre fair in between [. . .] Between March and August 1919, Cocteau's 'Carte Blanche' column in *Paris-Midi* aimed to create a new public for what he saw as his group, and the dedication of a copy of *Le Coq et l'arlequin* to the musicologist Henri Collet in January 1919 strongly suggests that Collet's seminal article 'Les Cinq Russes, Les Six Français et Erik Satie' in *Comoedia* on 16 January 1920 was the result of a carefully organized plan masterminded by Cocteau.[34]

Certainly Collet was being kept abreast of the group's activities, as attested by a letter to him from Poulenc of 24 October 1919 mentioning works by Auric, Durey and Tailleferre, and indicating that Chester would be sending Collet one of his own (unidentified, but quite probably the Sonata for two clarinets).[35] But for all the outward appearances of cohesion, Milhaud for one was not entirely happy with the publicity and what it portended:

Auric and Poulenc embraced the ideas of Cocteau, Honegger German romanticism, and I myself Mediterranean lyricism. I disapproved fundamentally of communal aesthetic theories and considered them as a limitation, an unreasonable brake on the imagination of the artist who must, for each new work, find different and often opposing means of expression; but resistance was useless! Collet's article made such an international splash that the 'Groupe des Six' was founded and I was part of it, whether I liked it or not.[36]

In July 1919 Poulenc wrote a 'Valse' for the 'album collectif' mentioned above, which on publication in 1920 by the Parisian firm Demets carried the title 'Album des Six'. Of the six pieces, Poulenc's and Auric's (written in December) are by some way the simplest, to some extent presaging future developments of the composers in question, as certainly do those of Milhaud and Honegger. In the 'Valse', indications such as 'très chanté', 'souple' and 'avec charme' show Poulenc's intention to honour the traditional mood of the waltz, as does the almost uninterrupted sounding of C major; but oversweetness is avoided through a couple of contrary markings ('très articulé' and 'sans pédale') together with an unusual instruction to 'cinglez les appogiatures' – literally 'lash' or 'bite' the appoggiaturas, bringing out a sudden ferocity in the B flat and D flat against an innocent C major chord. It may be worth mentioning that in July 1919 Ravel had still to begin work on *La Valse*.

During the late summer and autumn Poulenc seems to have needed a rest from composing, to judge by a remark to Jean-Aubry that 'For me, I've written *Cocardes* and that's enough to make me cheerful.' The only other pieces Poulenc mentions there, before the end of 1919, are a *Quadrille* for piano duet, now lost, and the Suite in C for piano solo which he would complete in March. But whereas he described writing the *Quadrille* as 'simple recreation', the Suite was said to be the recipient of 'une discipline énorme'.[37] What this meant is hard to figure out from the finished work, or rather from its 1926 revision. In 1954 he described it as 'si franchement Satie' ('so obviously Satie')[38] and perhaps in this case the influence was not to his benefit, even though he would later include the piece among the limited number of piano works of his that he 'tolerated'.[39] Keith Daniel refers to its 'bareness and mundane melodies',[40] and a review of its first performance, given by Viñes, on 10 April 1920, while praising the player, criticized the superficiality of the first of the three pieces and felt the central Andante 'shows this slender work's intrinsic emptiness, and a very academic one to boot'. But then, no doubt mindful of the *éclat* of the recently published *Le Coq et l'Arlequin*, the critic goes back to sit on the fence, declaring that 'M. Poulenc is part of the little group that appropriates the avant-garde of our most recent music: those who were expecting to meet someone engaged on reconnoitring appeared disappointed to find merely someone on sentry duty; but then, as you know, that's the necessary apprenticeship of the best and bravest soldiers.'[41]

Poulenc, now a secretary at a war office in Paris, had no need of physical bravery nor, for the moment, of the mental kind. Collet's 16 January *Comoedia* article and its follow-up a week later provided a launching pad for 'the new music', confirming Roussel's judgement on French music that 'if its silence has been almost complete for four years, its awakening after the armistice has proved all the more lively.'[42] As a result, for the next few months at least, Poulenc's easy musical style fitted the Parisian bill perfectly. Perhaps attending the Ballets Russes premiere of Stravinsky's *Le Chant du rossignol* on 2 February led him to muse on how his own exotic tendencies were now in abeyance, and he must have been pleased by the overall tone of the Spectacle-Concert organized by Cocteau three weeks later which included, together with an orchestration by Milhaud of the finale of his Piano Duet Sonata called *Ouverture* and the first public performance of *Cocardes*, a fox-trot by Auric, Satie's *Trois petites pièces montées* and Milhaud's *Le Boeuf sur le toit*.

There were, however, limits to what Poulenc was prepared to accept in the way of new music. On 8 March Satie organized a 'spectacle-concert' of his own, made up of piano duet music, performed by Milhaud and himself, pieces played by other unspecified performers on clarinets and trombone, a three-act play by Max Jacob and an exhibition of children's drawings. The sticking point for both Poulenc and Auric was the introduction of Satie's *musique d'ameublement*, or 'furniture music'. The first page of Satie's autograph explains that this 'replaces "waltzes" and "operatic fantasias" etc. Don't be confused! *It's something else!!!* No more "false music" . . . Furniture music completes one's property; . . . it's new; it doesn't upset customs; it isn't tiring; it's French; it won't wear out; *it isn't boring*.'[43] Turning his back on the whole notion of a work of art, sneeringly designated an 'oeuvre', Satie wanted the music to be ignored, like furniture and, when the audience obviously started to pay attention, was driven to shouting 'Go on talking! Walk about! Don't listen!' . . . to no avail.[44] Had he foreseen the 'muzak' of the future, maybe he might have embraced Poulenc's and Auric's scepticism.

During March, Poulenc was finishing the Suite in C for its first performance the following month, and also probably saw his music used for one of the first ballets put on by the Ballets Suédois at the Comédie des Champs-Élysées on the 25th, a solo item entitled *Sculpture nègre* for their *premier danseur* Jean Börlin. In it, 'dressed in a costume imitating a wooden African statuette (later echoed in *La Création du monde*), he danced this piece in a deliberately ponderous fashion.'[45] It has been reasonably assumed that the music used was all or part of *Rapsodie nègre*.

Although Diaghilev was given to appropriating artists and turning tetchy if they took their talents elsewhere, he had not as yet commissioned anything from Poulenc and could not really regard any such collaboration with the Ballets Suédois as treason. So it was that the young Poulenc was honoured by being allowed to sit in on one of the defining events of the 1920s: Ravel's presentation of his ballet *La Valse* in two-piano form to Diaghilev. To a select band of listeners (Diaghilev, Massine, Poulenc, Stravinsky) Ravel and Marcelle Meyer duly performed the work: 'Now at the time,' recalled Poulenc at the end of his life:

I knew Diaghilev very well . . . and I saw the false teeth begin to move, then the monocle. I saw he was embarrassed, I saw he didn't like it and was going to say

39

'No'. When Ravel had got to the end, Diaghilev said something which I think is very true. He said, 'Ravel, it's a masterpiece . . . but it's not a ballet . . . It's the portrait of a ballet . . . It's the painting of a ballet.' Ravel proceeded to give me a lesson in modesty which has lasted me all my life: he picked up his music quite quietly and, without worrying about what we all thought of it, calmly left the room.[46]

This was a defining event in several ways. Firstly, despite Diaghilev's immediate reaction, over the next few years he came round to a process of dethroning narrative in his ballets, telling the American composer John Alden Carpenter in 1924 to write a ballet about the modern city without regard to story or action;[47] secondly, this volte-face obviously had repercussions for *Les Biches* in 1924, where the ballet's subtexts are certainly far more important than the tenuous storyline; and thirdly, Ravel's attitude – 'without worrying about what we all thought of it' – allowed him to break all the structural rules in *Boléro*, on whose long crescendo all kinds of narrative can be imposed. Modesty, one suspects, was not the only lesson Poulenc learned on this occasion.

No firm date has ever been arrived at for this encounter, but early May seems a likely time, with rehearsals beginning for the premiere of Stravinsky's *Pulcinella* on the 15th. This too can be called a defining event, notably for the progress of neo-classicism, Stravinsky carrying on where Satie left off in the *Sonatine bureaucratique* of 1917. Poulenc, even if he never went down the route of basing his music so narrowly on someone else's, could remember twenty years later 'playing the overture to *Mavra* and the finale of *Pulcinella* 20 times'.[48] As a lesson in the art of managing diatonicism plus 'wrong' notes, it would be a hard work to beat.

At this time two roles that Poulenc was to fulfil in the future remained as yet relatively or completely unexplored: those as concert pianist and as critic. He had accompanied Suzanne Peignot in *Le Bestiaire*, but with Viñes and Marcelle Meyer on hand there was for the moment no incentive for him to tackle more difficult piano works such as the Suite in C. Even when he did accept Jean-Aubry's request to play this piece in London on 22 November 1920, he did so 'since you want me to', admitting 'je ne suis pas grand pianiste'.[49] There are grounds indeed for thinking that he did not appear as a solo pianist in Paris until the Auric/Poulenc concert of 10 June 1928 in the Salle Pleyel, when he gave first performances of the *Deux Novellettes* and of one ('Hymne'), and possibly all, of the *Trois pièces*. Perhaps he felt that the critics in London were less demanding. However, Poulenc does seem to have played his six *Impromptus* at Salzburg in the summer of 1925, when the critic of *The Chesterian* noted that he 'shone no less as a pianist than as a composer'.[50]

As for himself becoming a critic, this too was not an automatic choice. Although in later years Poulenc was happy to remember that the Lycée Condorcet had at least not spoilt his love of literature, his early letters are not notable for their orthography (in the letter just quoted, he misspells two of his colleagues in Les Six as Honneger and Taillefer, and throughout his life his letters regularly eschewed accents). But what are editors for?

François Bernouard, who launched the magazine *Le Coq* at a dinner on 6 March 1920, intended it as a mouthpiece for Les Six and supporters such as Satie, Max Jacob, Raymond Radiguet, Blaise Cendrars and Marie Laurencin. Poulenc contributed articles to three of the four numbers that appeared during the year. In the May number he took issue with the critic Jean Marnold, who had presumably complained about the shortness of the new works on show – to which Poulenc replied, in Satiesque mode, 'We shall never give you any "oeuvres".' He also, with less than total regard for the truth, claimed that 'As for Henri Collet, we barely know him. His articles were a surprise and we thank him for his clairvoyance.' In the June number, with his ears still full of *Pulcinella*, he defended Auric's Fox-Trot for piano, *Adieu, New York* as 'an example to all those composers who are happy to deform a modern dance'. Finally, his complete contribution to the final November number reads: 'A vulgar tune is good if it works. I love *Roméo*, *Faust*, *Manon* and even the songs of Mayol. Refinement nearly always makes modern French composers lose their popular accent. When refinement and this accent combine in a country (as they do with the Russians) then that country finally possesses its own music'[51] – a remarkably prescient description of the line his own music was to take.

The friendly support of Roussel and his receipt of several Poulenc scores led the latter to visit him in July at his home in Varengeville-sur-mer, from where letters were sent to friends back in Paris. To Milhaud, several of whose scores Poulenc gave to Roussel, Poulenc wrote, 'He's really a charming man and exceptionally lucid. I spend all my time with him because he's giving me advice on various points.' To Cocteau came the same report of Roussel's charm as well as of his clairvoyance 'so different from Maurice R.' (that old interview still rankling). To Cocteau's 'adopted son' Raymond Radiguet, Poulenc perhaps hints at a little too much seriousness in the Roussel household and 'would love to have all my friendly Samedistes here to get up to all kinds of nonsense'. On these lines he is 'thinking of writing a cycle of 5 or 6 songs in the "Ile d'amour" style – I'll talk to you again about them. When I get back, I'm going to spend a lot of time in Nogent sur Marne.'[52] These were the *Quatre Poèmes de Max Jacob*, not performed until 1922.

While Poulenc was staying at a hotel in Varengeville, Roussel was at work on his Second Symphony, which on its first performance in April 1922 was the subject of some unsympathetic reviews, notably that of Émile Vuillermoz, who complained that 'the orchestration is dull, gloomy and uniformly grey with attempts at idiosyncrasy that break out here and there, but don't work. This style gives evidence of research . . . but it never gets as far as discovery. The mixtures of timbres are without interest and add nothing to the repertory of modern orchestration.'[53] Other critics found the language itself dissonant and difficult. We don't know whether Roussel played Poulenc parts of it on the piano, but something happened over that summer with the result that the piano pieces Poulenc began, when back in Paris in September, suggest that the emollient style of *Mouvements perpétuels* and the Suite in C may have begun to pall and that the composer felt it needed spicing up from time to time with more acerbic elements. Carl Schmidt rightly notes that this new style shows 'struggles with greater complexity of texture, flirtation with increasing dissonance juxtaposed with more familiar popular elements, experimentation with changing metres, and a general lack of formal counterpoint'.[54]

As well as the Jacob songs, in the second half of 1920 Poulenc was working on three other projects: three pieces entitled *Napoli*, which underwent long revision and were not finally performed until 1926; six *Impromptus* written between September 1920 and March 1921; and incidental music to *Le Gendarme incompris* written in October and November 1920.

Nothing can be said about the original version of *Napoli*, since the revision of it was probably as radical as it was prolonged. The six *Impromptus* were published in early 1922, then in revised versions in 1924 and 1939: in 1924 the second piece was dropped (Poulenc cautiously demanding that the blocks of this be destroyed), no. 3 became no. 2, a new no. 3 was inserted, nos. 4 and 5 remained and no. 6 was also dropped. The aurally most demanding pieces, nos. 1 and 4, are highly chromatic, no. 2 the most Satiesque and no. 5 mostly modal. No. 3 was chosen as a supplement for *The Chesterian* and, with no. 5, was given the honour of separate publication. Undoubtedly the most attractive of the five, it was taken, with a few changes, from the 'Madrigal' in Poulenc's incidental music for *Le Gendarme incompris* (see below): a left-hand ostinato is much in evidence and what chromaticism and bitonality there is never stretches the ears unduly. Despite the serious challenges to both player and listener of nos. 1 and 4, we have no reason to doubt the puff in *The Chesterian* that 'Four of these delightful pieces were written in 1920–1, and so great was their success that a new edition has already become necessary . . .'[55] Sales figures do not lie, and it may well be that, despite the grittiness of nos. 1 and 4, Poulenc's name was already becoming the guarantee of a certain quality.

'A comic play in one act mixed with songs', *Le Gendarme incompris* was put together by Cocteau and Radiguet, the highlight of the piece being the role of the village policeman, improbably named La Pénultième, whose part is quoted entirely from Mallarmé's prose poem 'L'Ecclésiastique'. It is hard to believe that, as claimed subsequently, nobody in the first night audience on 24 May 1921 recognized the quotations, and certainly many of them must have known the text of the judge's 'Madrigal', which is none other than 'Placet futile', a poem set by both Debussy and Ravel in 1913. In spirit this is an utterly 'potasson' work, even if neither Cocteau nor Radiguet was ever a member. The policeman has spotted a 'priest' in the shrubbery behaving in a suspicious manner and brings 'him' before the judge. Then it transpires that 'he' is in fact the Marquise, who owns the land on which she was trying to reach some inaccessible flowers. The judge, a shameless social climber, finally dismisses the policeman and wangles an invitation to supper at the Marquise's château. The fun of quoting Mallarmé is compounded by the policeman's traditionally uncouth accent, as though Hamlet's 'To be, or not to be' soliloquy were interrupted by a beadle sharply enquiring 'Allo, allo, allo, wot's goin' on 'ere then?' The music freely mixes dissonance with popular elements, while never losing itself in incomprehensible complications, and the little orchestra (violin, cello, double bass, clarinet, trumpet, trombone and percussion) is clearly a relation of that in *Cocardes*. For some reason, although the complete work and a suite derived from it both had a few performances in the 1920s, a score was never published until the one by Salabert in 1988. Quality was surely not an issue in this work, described by Milhaud on the day of the first performance as 'a wonderful thing in its instrumental form, so clear in expression and you can feel so much music everywhere. The charm and abundance of tunes make it an extremely successful piece'[56] – a claim certainly substantiated by performances at the Northcott Theatre, Exeter in 1987.

A similar fate met the *Quatre Poèmes de Max Jacob*, originally entitled *Poésies pastorales*. Poulenc had been asking Jacob for some poems to set and these four, described by Jacob as 'rimes fragiles',[57] were still unpublished when the songs were written. The popular savour of Nogent that Poulenc had envisaged in mentioning

'Ile d'amour', a nearby island in the Marne, is certainly present in nos. 2 and 4 but, as a contemporary critic wrote, is 'deformed by the "modern" language (often close to polytonal Milhaud), and hardly rises to the "madly jolly" ["follement gai"] that Poulenc wants to convey there. Like the substance of no 1, the atonal instrumental fugato of no 3 sounds wrong, not because it is dissonant but because the dissonances are forced, against Poulenc's nature . . .'[58] In February 1921 Poulenc described the group, honestly enough, to its dedicatee and first conductor Milhaud as 'not without surprises and of course with mistakes as large as you are',[59] but two years later he looked back with undisguised contempt on this work 'adrift in polytonality and other "1920-style" garbage',[60] and tried to destroy the work. And yet the first performance had been encored! From his more mature vantage point in 1923, Poulenc was wise enough to recognize that the audience's enthusiasm had been excited less by quality than by fashion and by the Parisians' habitual passion, like that of the Athenians described by St Paul, for 'neon ti' – something new. It's possible to argue that Jacob's surrealist wordplay made an 'outlying' musical style imperative, and that the rediscovery of a score by Milhaud's widow Madeleine in 1993 was a blow for freedom. Or should Poulenc's wish have been honoured? In asking this, we have to take account of the fact that in 1993 his letter condemning the work as '1920-style garbage' was not yet in the public domain.

He was still working on these four projects at the time of his demobilization on 17 January 1921. To these another was added shortly afterwards, and one that took Poulenc back to his more amenable style. During the previous winter Jean Cocteau had put together another of his 'spectacles', originally entitled *La Noce massacrée* (The destroyed wedding), until Stravinsky explained that his ballet *Les Noces* was due to be performed by the Ballets Russes, and could he please change the title – which he did to *Les Mariés de la Tour Eiffel* (The wedding couple on the Eiffel Tower).[61] One of the points about Cocteau's 'spectacles' was that they should not adhere to any previously known format, so we should not be surprised by his summary of the work: 'Ballet? No. Play? No. Revue? No. Tragedy? No. Rather a kind of secret marriage between antique tragedy and the end-of-year revue with chorus and music-hall numbers.'[62]

Whatever the truth of this, the storyline is as bizarre as that of *Le Gendarme incompris*, with the addition of various surrealist items: an ostrich crosses the stage followed by a hunter who fires at it, upon which a large blue telegram flutters down from the flies; it's a dead telegram; the general makes a speech (polka by Poulenc); a photographer clicks his shutter and a Trouville bathing beauty emerges (cue dance, music again by Poulenc); a lion emerges from the camera, eats the general, goes back in the camera. In the final pages, the camera, feeling queasy, wants to bring up the general – 'Je voudrais rendre le général' – to which comes the reply 'Il saura bien se rendre lui-même' – 'He's quite capable of bringing up/surrendering himself.' Seventy years later Milhaud's widow remembered, all round the Théâtre des Champs-Élysées, the sharp intakes of breath.[63]

It is a truth universally acknowledged that the divided self is a prime creator of misery and self-doubt. The gulf between the jollity of the general's polka on one hand and on the other the gritty dissonances of the *Quatre Poèmes de Max Jacob*, and also of the ten *Promenades* for piano, written for Arthur Rubinstein during the summer of 1921 (and barely spoken of again by Poulenc), might have caused even the most experienced composer to halt and take stock, even if the purposes of the two styles were acknowledged as being widely disparate. By July 1921 Poulenc had on his desk or in his mind *Trois Études de pianola*, a *Première Suite d'orchestre*, a String Quartet and a Trio for piano, clarinet and cello, all of which were duly abandoned or destroyed or lost, or possibly never even begun. As a further incitement to cultural disarray, he had to take on board one or both of the two preliminary performances, with piano, of Honegger's *Le Roi David* in early June, about which he exploded to Paul Collaer: 'For me the whole thing is a bad cantata for Rome, falsely grandiose, idiotic. I make no distinction between *Le Roi David* and [Saint-Saëns's] *Le Déluge* . . . As for the musical technique, it's 30 years old, hellishly Wagnerian, utterly German-Swiss, as ridiculous as polytonality . . . What can you like in "The Dance before the Ark" and "The March of the Philistines" (with its arbitrary wrong notes) etc . . .'[64] But what of his own 'wrong notes' in the Max Jacob songs and *Promenades*? As for 'falsely grandiose', we may note the, not wholly unreasonable, lament of the *Daily Mail* critic, responding to:

> . . . bouquets from Mlle Germaine Tailleferre and MM. Poulenc and Milhaud, three of the much-talked of 'Six' who interpret the new spirit of the age. It is an irreverent age. Was music once a holy art? Did the masters once contrive sublime syntheses of Love, Life and Death? We are much too knowing nowadays for any such hollow romance. Nothing today sounds more absurd than a grand symphonic apotheosis.[65]

Not surprisingly, similar sentiments were expressed by various of the older generations of French composers. In December 1921 Vincent d'Indy, as a visiting professor, complained that 'the pupils at the University of Montreal are in too much of a hurry and want to learn about *the whole of music* in 3 months and don't produce anything except what follows the gospel of Poulenc and Darius Milhaud. This tendency needs to be checked and they should be taught the real meaning of *Art*.'[66] While a London audience was also vigorously hissing a three-movement suite from *Le Gendarme incompris* (a response which, the composer vainly hoped, might actually encourage Chester to publish it!), in the same letter Poulenc claims, perhaps not wholly tongue-in-cheek, that 'I'm working so as to become one day a great composer.'[67] Despite Roussel finding the suite 'bien amusante',[68] the question remained: what sort of 'working'? Clearly Poulenc was now in need of some wise advice.

Encouraged by Milhaud, and possibly also by Germaine Tailleferre, that September he wrote to Charles Koechlin asking for lessons. Admitting that until now he had been following instinct rather than intelligence, he stated that 'I should like, thanks to you, to become a *musician*'.[69] (Here one must query this translation of the word 'musicien', which can mean either 'musician' or 'composer'; but since any desire 'to become a composer' hardly made sense, given that he had been known as one for some four years, 'musician' seems a more likely candidate, on the lines of the question posed to the young Milhaud by André Gedalge: 'What do you want to do, learn your *métier* or win a prize?'[70] Like Milhaud, Poulenc wanted to be a true musician, to learn his *métier*.)

His lessons with Koechlin, fifty-eight in all, lasted from November 1921 to March 1925.[71] At the end of his life, Poulenc expressed his gratitude for Koechlin's openness to his pupils' character: 'Having felt, as a result, that like most Latins I was more of a harmonist than a contrapuntist, he made me write four-part realizations of Bach chorale themes as well as the usual counterpoint exercises . . . It was thanks to this I acquired a feeling for choral music.'[72] Koechlin also acted discreetly in turning Poulenc away from his initial harsh, and one might say uncontrolled, dissonances like those in *Promenades*, and towards more clearly tonal harmonies that nonetheless included dissonances that would not have been tolerated by such as Paul Vidal or any of his Conservatoire colleagues. We can see this by comparing Poulenc's offering in December with one the following March.[73] We can also see that Koechlin was sharpening Poulenc's ear not just for harmony, but also for rhythm – a lesson he took into his later choral writing, and indeed into his chordal writing generally.

It seems to have been around this time that he began to make sketches for a ballet commissioned by Diaghilev, who had liked his contributions to *Les Mariés*. In a letter to Poulenc from London of 15 November, Diaghilev acknowledged receipt of details of a ballet entitled *Les Demoiselles*, which he thought were 'très amusants', though he was confused about when Poulenc thought he might deliver a score.[74] He agreed to keep the idea between themselves of what was to be *Les Biches*, and expressed his delight at having secured as 'maître de ballet' Nijinsky's sister Bronislava, who was to choreograph not just *Les Biches*, but Stravinsky's *Renard* and *Les Noces*, Auric's *Les Fâcheux* and Milhaud's *Le Train bleu*.

Meanwhile, in the midst of his chorale exercises, Poulenc sent copies of his music to Bartók, who was very interested in the Piano Duet Sonata and the Sonata for two clarinets, wrote to Kodály and received congratulations from Roussel on the suite from *Le Gendarme incompris*.[75] The 15 December concert had also included the first French performance of the first part of *Pierrot lunaire* – the whole work would be given on 12 January. The promoter of this 'concert-salade' was the pianist Jean Wiéner, who not only formed a two-piano group with his partner Clément Doucet that excelled in jazzed-up versions of the classics, but was a staunch supporter of the new music. Milhaud was happy to conduct *Pierrot*, but the soprano Marya Freund needed some persuasion to be the female reciter, as 'everyone will think I've lost my voice'.[76] However, the concert was instantly recognized as an event of considerable importance, and Wiéner followed up with 'Feuillage du coeur' from Schoenberg's *Herzgewächse*, in which Poulenc played the celesta.[77]

Poulenc's growing reputation in the musical world also came in the form of a request for two reviews for the British magazine *Fanfare*, and he wrote to Jean-Aubry asking for the score of Malipiero's *Rispetti e strambotti* which he was reviewing together with Bartók's Second String Quartet and Stravinsky's Concertino.[78] The magazine, of which Philip Heseltine (Peter Warlock) was joint editor, lasted as an independent production for just seven numbers between October 1921 and January 1922, its other contributors including Cocteau, Satie and Egon Wellesz. Satie also wrote for it his *Sonnerie pour réveiller le bon gros Roi des Singes*, Manuel de Falla a rather less extravagantly entitled *Fanfare pour une fête*, and Poulenc himself contributed an *Esquisse d'une fanfare*, written as an overture to Cocteau's version of Shakespeare's *Romeo and Juliet*, though this would not be performed until 1924 (see p. 63). Poulenc's first review was of a concert by the Flonzaley Quartet, an American group founded in 1902, including the first performance of Stravinsky's Concertino, specially written for them. Although Alfredo Casella claimed that 'its performance by the Flonzaley Quartet showed an almost complete lack of understanding and resulted in a clamorous failure',[79] Poulenc appreciated the work's unity:

> It's like a perfectly-rounded object, a billiard-ball, a ball of crystal or of wood. It exists because it is a whole, because it pre-supposes, because it necessitates, an irreproachable construction, almost mathematical. A modification, a cut, would destroy it as surely as a notch destroys a croquet ball. It is uniform and smooth; everywhere of the same diameter, the ground is always firm and we have a certitude of security. This is because no foreign element enters. Literature is banished. It is music pure, the ultimate of Mozart.[80]

Here surely the young Poulenc is dreaming of what, perhaps, he himself might some day achieve on the same lines. Stephen Walsh writes of 'the sheer variety of device' the work employs, and that 'the mixture is held in a kind of tension, brilliantly sustained'.[81] In truth, nothing Poulenc had composed so far exhibited such tension to any perceptible degree, and he must have been hoping that Koechlin's tuition would point the way to such a prize. He was less impressed by Malipiero's *Rispetti e strambotti*, in which he felt 'the melodic invention seems to have been found at fault', but was deeply impressed by Bartók's Second String Quartet, ending his review with the plea 'Do not break this beautiful toy to find out how it works. We are in the presence of a masterpiece. Let us make obeisance'[82] – the first of many adjurations he was to make in his lifetime not to kill beauty by an excess of thinking. The fact that this was the composer who also worried because so far he'd been relying too much on instinct rather than on intelligence merely goes to show that Koechlin had more than a purely technical task on his hands.

Poulenc's second article is less interesting, saying nothing much about his friend Roussel's *Pour une fête de printemps* apart from its 'mastery of instrumentation' and the 'serene beauty' of its conclusion, and continuing to find Rimsky-Korsakov's *Antar* 'insipid and crude'. He ends by noticing a separate performance of Milhaud's *Le Boeuf sur le toit* – in his view 'an epitome of the sadness of towns, of their places of amusement, and of the night-birds who inhale, instead of fresh air, the feeble whiffs of electric ventilators'.[83] Perhaps Paris, its arcades and its Cirque Médrano were allowed to be exceptions? We do indeed have testimony from others that Paris life for Poulenc was continuing to be enjoyable. Virgil Thomson, remembering 'the first time I saw Paris', recalled meeting:

... at tea Darius Milhaud, Francis Poulenc, Georges Auric and Arthur Honegger, all near my age and all well disposed to accept me as a colleague. There came also my revered Erik Satie, and Marcelle Meyer, pianist, married to the actor Pierre Bertin. And there were musical evenings at the Bertin flat, boulevard de Montparnasse, where Marcelle, athletic like the women on the banknotes, and Poulenc, holding his elbows in and his wrists up like a dancing pig on a postcard, played music by Satie and by Satie's young friends.[84]

On 7 January 1922 a group of wind players headed by flautist Louis Fleury accompanied the singer M. Jobin in the first, and for many years the last, performance of the *Quatre Poèmes de Max Jacob*. The flag of modernity was then hoisted again by the complete performance of *Pierrot lunaire* on the 12th. As already mentioned, Poulenc certainly knew the *Six Little Pieces* for piano and possibly also the *Three Pieces* op. 11, but otherwise knowledge of Schoenberg's music among French composers before the war had been limited to a tiny group: to Ravel, Debussy, Koechlin and perhaps Milhaud. After the war, the return of Schoenberg's music occurred most dramatically in the form of the *Five Orchestral Pieces*, played by the Pasdeloup Orchestra under André Caplet on 22 April 1921: the performance caused a riot in which animal noises were freely voiced, Florent Schmitt was physically attacked, ending up with a swollen face, and one woman in the audience was heard shouting, 'It's a disgrace to subject war widows to stuff like this.'

In his autobiography, Milhaud simply writes that 'As Francis Poulenc and I wanted to renew contact with the Austrian composers from whom we had been separated by the war, we undertook a journey to central Europe', without any mention of *Pierrot*, though the fact that they were accompanied by Marya Freund, and that in Vienna Milhaud conducted a performance of the work including her, strongly suggests that *Pierrot* was the motive force. Alma Mahler who, as with Ravel's visit in 1920, was the presiding genius over this 1922 enterprise, suggested a second performance, conducted by Schoenberg, with Erika Wagner, Schoenberg's favoured interpreter, and Milhaud noted the differences between her rendering – in a harsh voice, with considerable freedom in treating the text – and Freund's – possibly too respectful of it, he thought.[85] Perhaps this may have caused Poulenc to consider the ancient question regarding the 'French temperament'. At all events, on a visit to Schoenberg in Mödling he played his *Promenades* and joined Milhaud in a piano duet version of *Le Boeuf sur le toit*; and on 7 February he accompanied Freund in *Le Bestiaire* in a public concert, leaving the *Trois Mouvements perpétuels* to Milhaud. On a less aesthetic level, Poulence later recorded an event at lunchtime in Mödling: 'just at the moment when Arnold Schönberg, the sorcerer, was about to serve the soup, I can confirm that a football, violently expelled from his son's bedroom, landed in the tureen and turned into an edible melon'.[86]

While in Vienna Milhaud and Poulenc were introduced to the leading musicians of the city – Berg, Webern and Egon Wellesz – and the only serious problem was a throat abscess that Poulenc suddenly developed, necessitating an operation on 13 February; Milhaud was deeply impressed by Wellesz's expression of sympathy, a pot of jam – at the time 'for a Viennese a real sacrifice, especially as he had children'[87] – and they experienced further evidence of post-war poverty going on to Warsaw and Kalisz, where Freund had been born.

Poulenc's home life, however, continued to be comfortable. The twenty-year-old Jean-Pierre Poupard, newly arrived from Bordeaux on 15 January and newly named as Henri Sauguet, had been encouraged to come to Paris by Milhaud, who put him up in his flat at 5 rue Gaillard. Together they went off to see *Les Mariés de la Tour Eiffel*, where Sauguet was introduced to Cocteau. On 10 March Sauguet was invited to supper by Poulenc's sister and was impressed to find himself in a circular dining room not only full of Louis XVI furniture but also with Corots on the walls. The party then went off to the Salle Gaveau to hear the second complete performance of *Pierrot lunaire*. From these profound experiences Sauguet 'felt most powerfully that it was truly in Paris that tone and progress are decided, and that it only remains for us poor provincials to fall in line and follow the flow, while avoiding wrong notes and wrong directions'.[88] Not that provincials were alone in this trajectory. At least he, like Poulenc, realized that he needed advice, and likewise turned for it to Koechlin.

In April Poulenc extended his foreign contacts by four meetings with Bartók. The first was at a presentation at the Sorbonne on the 4th entitled 'Le mouvement musical contemporain en Europe' at which Bartók and Jelly d'Aranyi played his First Violin Sonata, Poulenc turning the pages for Jelly ('Ravel and Poulenc like the 2nd and 3rd movements,' the composer reported to his wife);[89] on the 8th, Poulenc organized a lunch *chez lui* at which Bartók and Satie met for the first and last time, followed by an entirely Bartókian concert that evening organized by *La Revue musicale*, including the composer playing his Suite op. 14 and a repeat of the Violin Sonata; and on the 9th he heard Bartók and d'Aranyi yet again, with her taking the opportunity to ask him for 'a sonata, a concerto . . . of which I shall never write a note'.[90] Poulenc's message to Bartók of 14 April thanks him for bringing 'pleasure to all the young French composers', not presuming to speak for the older ones. This message was sent in the form of a dedication on a copy of *Le Bestiaire*, Poulenc further promising him a copy of the *Impromptus*. At some point in April he at least planned to perform himself in a concert at Le Havre and to include the *Mouvements perpétuels* and a selection of the *Impromptus*. But he was still not confident of his keyboard skills, adding 'The *Suite* [*in C*] is too difficult for me because of the precision needed for the phrases, which is why I've substituted the *Impromptus*.'[91]

Hard on the heels of his visit to the members of the Second Viennese School, then that of Bartók to Paris, the 1922 season of the Ballets Russes brought to the Opéra two works by another major composer of the time. The premiere of Stravinsky's *Renard* on 18 May did not please everybody. But while puzzlement might have been engendered by its status as 'the most radically anti-Italian, most hermetically Russian work of his that Parisians had yet heard', there were more appreciative comments from such as Louis Laloy, delighting that 'From the first notes, that flourish on the brass marking the entrance of the characters, one is gripped as if by the throat, or even bodily, with an urge to join in the dance and never let up.'[92] Although Poulenc seems never to have said or written much about *Renard*, we cannot assume that it left him unmoved; more likely, its joyful spirit chimed so easily with the wind sonatas he wrote around this time that he simply accepted it with gratitude as sanctioning his own path.

The second Stravinsky work, however, was 'une autre paire de manches'. Premiered privately at the Hôtel Continental on 29 May and publicly at the Opéra on 3 June, *Mavra* set an aggressively sharp-clawed cat among the pigeons. Milhaud would later explain that 'The simplicity of *Mavra* appeared scandalous to a public who had taken ten years to "digest" *Le Sacre*! . . . The press's incomprehension was disgraceful; it exclaimed that Stravinsky was no longer writing Stravinsky, that he had become incapable of expressing himself, that his music was dull and savourless, that his tunes were "old hat".'[93] Poulenc's reaction at the time was similarly vigorous:

The whole musical clan of the *S[ociété] M[usicale] I[ndépendante]* and the *Revue musicale* has taken against this 'Domino noir' (Ravel's description). Result, agitation of our friend Igor, off hooks with Delage, our Maurice [Ravel], Schmitt etc. . . . Only Auric and I are absolutely and sincerely passionate for *Mavra* . . . But I should say to the glory of our Beethoven [Honegger] that he's excellent and on *Mavra*'s side. Both in the press and among the composers it's the post-*Parade* spirit that reigns, minus the scandal. My current opinion is that we are looking at a *very important* work; together with *Pulcinella*, it's a wonderful landmark for Stravinsky, the equivalent of 'Picasso's nudes', but the dreadful thing now is that people want musical cubism. We're too traditional for them.[94]

This certainly was Ravel's reason for citing *Le Domino noir*, the 1837 opera by Auber. In Poulenc's article on *Mavra*, the first sustained piece of his music criticism to be printed, he defends it on several points, but perhaps most persuasively on the harmonic one:

Ultimately, it is the harmony of *Mavra* that is under attack for its lack of *originality*. It is amusing on this front to observe that the composers of the post-Debussy generation, drunk on 'rare harmonies', have got into the habit of finding perfect cadences banal. [. . .] In *Mavra*, Stravinsky has addressed all his efforts to the system of modulation. It is through the horizontal juxtaposition of distant keys that he has obtained a kind of music that is precise, springy and decidedly tonal (a rare quality these days). No critic has remarked on that. You can see, the ear drums are hardening.[95]

This espousal by Poulenc of perfect cadences and 'the horizontal juxtaposition of distant keys' shows unmistakably the way his mind was now tending. At the same time, he never followed *Mavra*'s habit of dissociating melody from harmony and rhythm – not the least striking, even disturbing aspect of the score is the unexpected placing of 'oom-cha' chords: often the tonic accent in the voice will occur on the 'cha' rather than the 'oom'. Perhaps the most curious thing in responses to the work was the widespread refusal to recognize that it is a *comic* opera, with all the latitude that genre has always been allowed in respect of musical detail.

During the summer Poulenc worked on a set of *Marches militaires* for piano and orchestra that never saw the light of day, sorted out the general drift of *Les Biches* ('there won't be a story but just dances and songs'),[96] attended the Salzburg Festival in August (fellow composers included Bliss, Ethel Smyth, Webern – 'garçon exquis et plein de talent' – Bartók and Hindemith), where pieces by Milhaud and himself were generally judged too raw.[97] He also began to compose two sonatas, for clarinet and bassoon, and for horn, trumpet and trombone, as well as a lost *Caprice espagnol*, and a *Chanson à boire* for the Harvard Glee Club which sadly fell foul of prohibition in the United States, though it was published in France in 1923. The anonymous seventeenth-century words are adorned, à la *Pulcinella*, with a variety of laughs and glissandos.

The two wind sonatas were intended to form a group with that for two clarinets, as is clear from the binding round the autographs[98] and supported by the fact that Poulenc's piano transcriptions of all three were published together in 1925.[99] Even before starting the last two, Poulenc could write to Collaer, '*Mavra* has proved to me that the common chord is fine. Once again Satie is right. Believe me, polytonality is an *impasse* whose uselessness will be acknowledged 5 years from now, unless it's a means of expression for a kind of genius like Darius. I'm not talking about atonality, that's shit.'[100] Actual work on the sonatas only confirmed his opinion, as later letters show.

Of all the words written about these three sonatas, perhaps the most illuminating came from Milhaud, claiming that Poulenc 'in his chamber music copied the form of short sonatas, in the way used by Scarlatti in which the elements are reduced to a minimum. His Sonata for clarinet and bassoon is a marvel of precision, of gaiety, of charm and grace, and his Sonata for horn, trumpet and trombone is a true masterpiece. It's a work whose classical form is balanced with wonderful exactness and whose novelty resides in the ease with which he juggles his simple elements of sound.'[101] The name of Scarlatti is especially well chosen, given the fondness of both composers for decisive themes, often based on scales and arpeggios. In the first bars of the Sonata for clarinet and bassoon, the clarinet's descending scale, recalling the one that opens the first *Mouvement perpétuel*, finds its D major lightly contradicted by an E flat, C natural and B flat from the bassoon, but leaving us in no doubt about the overall key of D; and when this opening scale, now in F major, recurs to begin the slow movement, B naturals similarly lend a discreet touch of exotic colour.

It's worth noting that for all his diatribes against atonality and polytonality, Poulenc never inveighed against bitonality – clearly, two conflicting keys should be enough for anybody (except Milhaud). But Poulenc's bitonality is often exercised against a background which is not just tonal, but goes back to the simple tunes of his nursery and childhood.[102] For the listener (and for anglophones perhaps the best-known example is 'Frère Jacques'), this immediately creates a feeling of security, of being in safe hands, so that 'wrong' notes here and there cause no great alarm. Finally, Poulenc's past also caught up with him in the final bar of the Sonata for clarinet and bassoon, where the concluding 'sign-off' borrows from that of the second of the Debussy *Danses* for harp and strings, which had made such an impression on him as a boy – and at the same pitch.

Milhaud's testimony is a compendium of terms that belong to the traditional understanding of the 'French temperament' espoused by Poulenc (see p. 1): 'précision', 'gaieté', 'charme', 'grâce', 'équilibrée', 'justesse', 'aisance', 'simples'. But to these one needs to add the colouring Poulenc wanted for these pieces: 'only homophonic instruments tempt me at the moment'.[103] In this he was following the prescription not only of Cocteau in *Le Coq et l'Arlequin* ('a poet always has too many words in his vocabulary, a painter too many colours on his palette, a composer too many notes on his keyboard'),[104] but also of Picasso ('Work with three colours, too many colours makes Impressionism'),[105] from whom Cocteau borrowed the idea. At the same time Poulenc was critical of Prokofiev's ballet *Chout*, now revived by the Ballets Russes, as being 'slightly monotonous in its colourful glow',[106] but delighted to report to Koechlin that the latter's Sonata for two flutes had greatly impressed the composers at the Salzburg Festival, who were 'surprised at so much music in such a short space of time and with such limited means'.[107] Calibrating the correct colour dosage required all of one's 'précision' and 'justesse'. Almost certainly Auric would have shown Poulenc the letter he had from Stravinsky praising the two sonatas for their freshness and individuality, and for being 'very, very French'.[108]

Through the autumn Poulenc worked on the previous two sonatas, on his ballet now named *Les Biches*, and on the piano suite *Napoli*, which would not be completed until 1925. These last months of the year were quiet, animated only by 'considerable correspondence' with Stravinsky, who was encountering serious money problems in Biarritz, the belated discovery that Milhaud, like Poulenc, was an avid bridge player,[109] and the French premiere of Webern's *Five movements for string quartet*, of which the composer had already sent Poulenc an inscribed copy.[110]

The year 1923 began with a Wiéner concert on 4 January that included *Socrate* and also the first performances of the previous two wind sonatas. But whereas Satie was granted four recalls, the sonatas were met with 'some whistling, some ironical calls for encores, but overall bewilderment. The end of the one for brass provoked a huge gust of laughter followed by "hou! hou! hou!" in a parody of the trombone.'[111]

But a couple of months later in Brussels the Sonata for clarinet and bassoon was described as being 'youthful, clear spontaneous, witty and sincere'.[112] Writing to Stravinsky, Poulenc expressed enormous enthusiasm ('je *suis* fou') on attending rehearsals of *Histoire du soldat*, adding 'you can't imagine the perfection of the performance they're giving here', with surely a subtext of 'unlike Paris'.[113] Other problems aside, Poulenc was outraged that during *Socrate* Honegger was fooling around. He also noted sourly that Honegger was giving his companion and wife-to-be Andrée Vaurabourg a hard time and was moved to pour scorn on his *Cantique de Pâques* as 'right royal rubbish'.[114] A few months later, the critic Émile Vuillermoz pointed out that the works of Les Six 'have always been sympathetically received, according to their merits, which have been very unequal and very different from each other. But these young people have, deservedly, been refused the right to bear a standard and represent an aesthetic position.[115] [. . .] They are independents, of very disparate character, who are not following in the slightest the programme announced on the cover of their manifesto.'[116] We need then to be aware that not everything among Les Six, whether in music or in personal relations, was unending sweetness and light.

A further commission from Diaghilev was for a joint enterprise. As part of his 1924 season in Monte-Carlo, Diaghilev was planning to put on four *opéra-comiques* and replacing their spoken dialogue with recitative, with this as far as possible conforming to the style of each composer. The three Gounod operas (*Le Médecin malgré lui*, *La Colombe* and *Philémon et Baucis*) were entrusted to Satie, Poulenc and Auric respectively, and Chabrier's *Une Éducation manquée* to Milhaud, although Gounod's heirs refused Auric's efforts. Diaghilev, with the wisdom of experience, would seem to have given his composers plenty of time, so that already in January 1923 Poulenc was studying the scores of Gounod's operas in the Opéra library.[117] However, as late as 3 September he was explaining his long silence to Koechlin because 'a most perilous piece of work has come my way – commissioned by Diaghilev. I have had to do the recitatives, often very long and eight in number, for a comic opera by Gounod, *La Colombe*, which will be performed this winter in Monte-Carlo. Fortunately I am very familiar with the stage works of good old Charles, and so I have been able to draw on everything I know about the style – by the way admirable – of this too often disparaged composer.'[118] (While Poulenc's letters are a priceless source for the biographer, this one shows that he was not above myth-making when it suited: neither 'has come my way' nor 'I am very familiar with the stage works' is strictly concordant with the facts.) However that may be, when Satie saw the recitatives he wrote to Collaer that 'Poulenc has done a *Colombe* that is astonishing in its verve and extremely accomplished'.[119]

Apart from the throat abscess he suffered in Vienna, Poulenc's health seems in general to have been fairly sound, despite his entrenched hypochondria. But during the first fortnight of April he was laid low with jaundice, living on milk and forbidden by his doctor to walk about. His doctor also insisted that he go to Vichy for a cure at the end of May, which meant missing the Comte de Beaumont's Louis XIV ball on the 30th.[120] More annoyingly still, he remained too ill to play one of the pianos for the premiere of *Les Noces* on 13 June, though he allowed himself a twenty-four-hour dash to Paris to attend it. Over the following years he reckoned he played in *Les Noces* over forty times, and that under Ernest Ansermet's baton it became easier to do,[121] but he never enthused over the work in the way he did over *Mavra* – not that he questioned its stature as a masterpiece, more likely because its essentially Russian nature had nothing important to say to him as a composer.

Jaundice was not allowed to prevail over two other premieres. On 1 June the Opéra finally mounted Roussel's opera-ballet *Padmâvatî*, which Poulenc found 'moving, powerful and *admirably* orchestrated'.[122] Although three-quarters of the work had already been written by August 1914, Roussel managed to retain the same spirit in the remainder, despite his prophecy of 1916.[123] More important for Poulenc's future was the premiere on 25 June of Falla's *El retablo de maese Pedro*, commissioned by the Princesse de Polignac. Like Roussel, Falla had become a good friend of Poulenc, and a couple of months earlier had sent him an inscribed score of the work. For the French premiere, Ricardo Viñes and his nephew Hernando worked the marionettes and, as for the earlier Spanish premiere, the harpsichord was played by Wanda Landowska. Other composers apart, 'After Viñes and Bathori, the important encounters that had a profound influence on him were with Wanda Landowska, Pierre Bernac and Paul Éluard'.[124]

In July Poulenc had letters from both Cocteau and Radiguet who, with Auric, were on holiday on the bay of Arcachon, Cocteau writing *Le pauvre Matelot*, Radiguet revising his novel *Le Bal du comte d'Orgel*, and Auric, naked in the hot sun, typing out Radiguet's finished text. Radiguet had also been writing poems:

> . . . some of them very long. It would be a great pleasure for me if you would set some of them to music as, even if the habit of setting poems in threes is now quite out of fashion, songs even so are not to be sneered at, would you agree?

And since people these days only compose short ones, it might perhaps be rather good to write one as long as *Le Promenoir des deux amants*.[125]

Since Debussy's three settings of stanzas from this poem by Tristan l'Hermite are each only of three four-line verses, the reference must surely be to l'Hermite's poem which is of no fewer than twenty-eight verses! This suggests such a total misunderstanding of Poulenc's oeuvre as to defy belief. As Jacqueline Bellas rightly remarks, 'Poulenc had a predilection for poems that could be contained on a postage stamp. In this way he could profit from an essential virtue of music, that of expanding the texts which engage with it.'[126] In fact Poulenc had set at least one Radiguet poem some three years earlier. In an undated letter to Milhaud, now attributable to 5 April 1920, he wrote, 'I'm continuing with my Radiguet poems. "Côte d'azur" (no 1) is on the way, and after that "Paul et Virginie" and finally, I think, "Victoire".'[127] Of the 'Paul et Virginie' he did set, in 1946 he wrote to Bernac, 'In 1920 I wrote a song on this ravishing little poem by my poor Radiguet, but at that time I didn't know how to manage in a song where I had no place to modulate [. . .] I think the idea of a silence and the final unprepared modulation is a happy one.'[128]

With the coming of autumn and winter, Satie was struggling with his recitatives for *Le Médecin malgré lui*, Falla was having fun singing the *Chanson à boire* in the Alhambra, Ravel was complaining that no one had sent him scores of *Le Boeuf sur le toit* or Poulenc's *Promenades*,[129] and Stravinsky, congratulating Poulenc on finishing *Les Biches*, added, 'If you need me for any advice, don't hesitate to come here [to Biarritz] – you know the sympathy I've always had for what you're doing, and especially for *Les Biches*; the rest of the score, which I don't know, still interests me enormously.'[130] On 1 October Poulenc had played the completed piano score of *Les Biches* to Diaghilev and Auric, and on the 27th (after attending the premiere on the 25th of Milhaud's ballet *La Création du monde*, about which his only comment at the time was 'nice orchestration')[131] he was heading for Monte-Carlo where he would finish his own orchestration of *Les Biches* and, at Diaghilev's command, cast an eye over the choreography. In any case, with his long-standing love of pictures he would have been keen to see that this was to his liking. Happily it was: 'The choreography of *Les Biches* is, surprisingly, *ravishing*,' he enthused to Milhaud. 'This time Nijinska has really understood my music. It's very Marie Laurencin, very *Sylvia*.'[132] What he meant by 'this time' ('cette fois') is unclear, since Nijinska had never choreographed any of his music before; perhaps it was merely to distinguish this treatment from the regulated, angular, brutal kind she had recently meted out to the dancers in *Les Noces*. Thirty years later, Poulenc remembered that:

> Diaghilev had said to me, 'Don't worry, she'll suss it out without understanding it.' Precisely that. As the ballet didn't have a storyline, we worked together on a choreographic structure: here, an ensemble; here, a *pas de deux*; here, a *pas de trois* and so on. Imperceptibly, the dance of the two ladies in grey, a simple feminine *pas de deux*, became a dance that was very secretly Proustian (Albertine and a female friend at Balbec). It was Nijinska's instinctive genius that made such audacity possible.[133]

If we are to assume that this use of the word 'Proustian' reflected Poulenc's view back in 1923, then it could possibly have been an indication of his doubts about his own sexuality. But this is quite a large assumption, and it has to be repeated that evidence from the early 1920s as to his homosexuality is little more than nil. In any case, the claim that Poulenc's variations on accepted musical structures are a subversive, 'camp' activity cannot be verified when any admission of this aim by the composer is absent: or as one reviewer on a quite different subject has somewhat waspishly put it, to do so shows 'this amazing ability to infer someone's inner thoughts from their actions, and state the former as fact'.[134] This is not to say that the subversively 'camp' attribution is wrong – merely that by its nature it cannot be proved. In any case, playing around with musical structures has always been the province of *homo ludens*. It would be a brave critic who classed as 'camp' the regular reversal in the recapitulation of the two sonata-form subjects in the music of Honegger, who in the 1920s married Andrée Vaurabourg within days of Claire Croiza giving birth to his son.

What is beyond doubt is the pleasure Poulenc took in the risqué elements of Nijinska's choreography: the very title of the ballet is suggestive, 'biches' meaning both 'darlings' and 'does', with its implication that love never goes beyond an animal instinct. While Poulenc's correspondence from mid-December is filled with the terrible fallout after the death of Cocteau's beloved Raymond Radiguet from typhoid fever on the 12th, work on the ballet continued unabated and we are indebted to Diaghilev's two-day absence at some point in the month for Poulenc's letter to him, describing the progress of the choreography in some detail:

Nijinska is truly a *genius*. I explain: realizing that the sofa is a 'star' on the same level as herself, she makes it dance during the whole Jeu movement!!! So Grigoriev asked the Casino for a magnificent sofa and work began (decently, of course). I can't begin to describe what happened then. In a Presto passage the female dancers sit down, jump up into the air, fall back on the seat and roll around on their backs, while the two men straddle the sofa back, and then the poor sofa, which must be particularly solid, is thrown around in every direction. When the music calms down in the middle of the scene, the Star [Nijinska] and Wilzak cuddle each other. The 'Biches' then use the sofa (which has its back to the audience) as a lookout post, poking their heads above the back, then dropping them down again – and when the game restarts, *please believe this*, the two men suddenly swing the sofa round and we see two women lying down in a position which, with Barbette in mind, I would describe as head to tail . . .[135]

Barbette was a female impersonator, much admired by Cocteau among others.

Further elements can be found in Lynn Garafola's superb analysis of the choreography,[136] from which one small detail must here suffice: 'To some extent, all ballets are about performing and looking. In *Biches*, however, Nijinska takes both to their logical extreme, giving us a critique of the narcissism and voyeurism that make up the business of sex. Again and again she uses arms to draw attention to the body's erogenous zones. Her mannequins parade with a hand to one shoulder; her Garçonne with a hand cupped to the face or, when posed in arabesque, with a hand on each thigh – emphasizing the crotch between.[137]

The presence of the Garçonne, a girl dressed as a boy, is itself provocative, not merely because it anticipates the transgendering issues prevalent a century later, but because of the 1922 book *La Garçonne* by Victor Margueritte in which the hero(ine), angry at her husband's infidelity, embarks on multiple affairs, adopting an Eton crop, flat chest, no corset, and ideas about liberating herself from her traditional secondary role in French society. Margueritte, for his pains, was stripped of his Légion d'honneur rosette. As to the ballet's meaning (one hesitates to use the word 'thrust'), the last words go to Poulenc himself, in two sources. First, an article originally published in English in 1946:

In this ballet, as in certain of Watteau's pictures, there is an atmosphere of wantonness which you sense if you are corrupted but which an innocent-minded girl would not be conscious of. One such simple creature said to me:

'*Les Biches* is the modern *Les Sylphides*', to which I replied, 'I am so glad that is how it strikes you.' [. . .] This is a ballet in which you may see nothing at all or into which you may read the worst [. . .] Diaghilev wanted a ballet in the spirit of the Fêtes Galantes, and that is why he chose Marie Laurencin to do the décor; for her pictures have the same ambiguous blend of innocence and corruption.[138]

In a talk given in 1962 Poulenc expanded on this description, recalling that Diaghilev specifically wanted the ballet to be 'erotic' and that, as mentioned above, they agreed it should copy *Les Sylphides* in having no storyline.[139] This decision was in keeping both with Nijinska's general approach at that time, and with Diaghilev's.[140]

Les Biches, with a premiere on 6 January 1924 that provoked eight curtain calls for the composer, was the undoubted hit of Diaghilev's French festival, his seventeenth season of productions; only his habitual money worries seem to have prevented it being played for more than six nights. Stravinsky sent his congratulations, as did Satie, who was in Monte-Carlo for his version of *Le Médecin malgré lui*, but sadly this was where Poulenc's friendship with him ended. Satie had chosen Louis Laloy, a critic and the secretary of the Paris Opéra, to be another on his fairly long list of *bêtes noires*, and now warned Poulenc against this individual. Satie believed that Laloy had intentionally omitted his name from the festival programme and no doubt Laloy's enthusiastic review of *Les Biches* ('from the first numbers, applause burst forth from every corner of the theatre') didn't help matters,[141] any more than the present that Poulenc and Auric then sent Satie of a doll with an old man's head stuck on it that was the image of Satie himself.[142]

If one had to choose one single, overriding reason for such applause, it might well be the tunes: surely not since Tchaikovsky's ballets had they poured forth in such abundance, instantly delightful, persistently memorable. But even so, all eight movements of this ballet, like so much of Poulenc's music, speak of a dichotomy between joy and melancholy. As the influential critic Boris de Schloezer wrote, 'The great difficulty and danger for Poulenc is that his music is essentially aristocratic; it is in general a courtly art which, by force of circumstances, finds itself obliged to approach the masses.'[143] This courtliness finds its apogee in the 'Adagietto', a solo for Vera Nemtchinova, and here the dichotomy can be read in the phrasing: the twenty-seven bars of the opening paragraph comprise phrases of ten, ten and seven bars, and yet the whole sounds beautifully balanced. But at the same time the tension between the music's smooth, smiling surface and its disordered structure deliver both the joy and the melancholy. Milhaud goes still further, writing of the work's 'graceful and enchanting allure [which] ends up achieving true grandeur that becomes melancholy and even tragic in the Rag Mazurka'.[144]

Away from the theatre, Poulenc was earning other garlands, not least from the Ukrainian-born Vladimir Dukelsky, now reinvented as the American composer Vernon Duke, who participated in the great transatlantic invasion of musical Paris. 'Auric and Poulenc were wonderful company,' he wrote thirty years later; 'Poulenc much more of a *mondain* than his friend. Auric was a big, unwieldy creature, a *mégot* [fag-end] always dangling from his lips, the smile childishly good-hearted, the small Balzacian eyes malevolent and crafty. Francis, on the contrary, although fairly portly too, spoke and moved with the easy assurance of a salon habitué; his voice lazy and nasal, his clothes unobtrusively right, his light hair cut *en brosse*, somewhat in the Prussian military manner, Poulenc was at his best when playing the piano, which he did with an impish nonchalance immediately attractive to the listener.'[145]

Les Biches marked Poulenc's first major and almost unanimous success. Over the next four years it was danced in thirteen major European cities to similar acclaim, so perhaps the most surprising thing is that, as far as we know, in the five years left to him Diaghilev never spoke about commissioning a sequel. Instead he chose to ask Auric, who duly composed *Les Matelots* (1925) and *La Pastorale* (1926) as successors to *Les Fâcheux* of 1924. Cocteau certainly was on Poulenc's side, complaining that *Les Fâcheux* was 'peppered with broken bottles and stinging nettles'.[146] One reason for Diaghilev's disinclination may have been that Poulenc was not happy with the conducting in Monte-Carlo of the relatively unknown Édouard Flament,[147] and his strictures may have found their way to Diaghilev's ever-open ears. On the other hand, in May Poulenc was certainly thinking of writing a sequel, if only he could find a subject.[148] However, not only has *Les Biches* outlasted Auric's ballets by many a mile (especially in the form of the orchestral suite, without the three choral numbers in which, as in *Les Noces*, singers performed in the pit), but in August 1924 Poulenc received a letter from Cocteau, still distraught at Raymond Radiguet's death the previous December: '*Les Biches* are helping me to stay alive. That's no small tribute. Georges plays them to me and their charm works upon my poor shattered nerves.'[149]

III
DREAMING OF MATURITY
✦ 1924–1928 ✦

Obviously Poulenc could not have foreseen the triumph of *Les Biches*, and indications are that he took some time to fully absorb it and what it meant for him as a composer. Triumphs are all very fine, but they do pose the problem of acting as markers against which anything you write thereafter will be judged. In the whole of 1924 Poulenc, as well as pursuing the *Marches militaires*, now sometimes given the title of a piano concerto, began only two new works: in May the Trio for oboe, bassoon and piano, which would take him two years to finish; and in December the *Poèmes de Ronsard*, which took him at the most two months. He also worked on the third movement of *Napoli* and, as already mentioned, revised the *Impromptus*, but the Violin Sonata for Jelly d'Aranyi ultimately met the familiar fate of most of his works for strings.

Meanwhile the year 1924 witnessed over half a dozen major works by Poulenc's colleagues and (in Satie's case, his ex-colleague), all of which he attended and of which he voiced criticisms in sharply varying tones. The first of these, on 14 March, was the third version of *Le Roi David*, for which the Salle Gaveau was sold out so that a repeat performance was required for the 19th. Waspishly, Poulenc explained to Collaer that in calling it Honegger's masterpiece he was not calling it a masterpiece *tout court*. 'It's actually a sterile work, of no significance, conventional, melodically weak, in a word a success in the d'Indy mould.'[1] Relations between the members of Les Six were not, as already noted, always smooth, and Milhaud lumped Poulenc and Auric together as 'adolescents, hypnotized by the idea of instant success. I'm coming to the end of my patience with it.'[2] While Poulenc could not help admiring in *Le Roi David* an orchestration which saved certain passages that on the piano sounded 'detestable',[3] he never really came round to liking the piece because of its heaviness and maybe (though he never admitted the fact) because of its essentially Protestant seriousness. Certainly it doesn't contain much of the 'fraîcheur' and 'jeunesse' he admired in Sauguet's comic opera *Le Plumet du colonel*,[4] premiered on

24 April as part of the *Soirées de Paris* organized by the Comte de Beaumont in competition with the Ballets Russes, and perhaps with an eye to the crowds assembling for the Olympic Games. We don't know whether Poulenc attended a later performance so that he could hear the first Paris performance that night of Stravinsky's *Histoire du soldat* – perhaps not, as he had already enjoyed the Brussels rehearsals of that piece.

Next, on 17 May, came the premiere of Milhaud's 'ballet chanté' *Salade*, also for Beaumont, which Poulenc variously described as 'excellent', 'a masterpiece' and 'one of his best things', though by 1933 this had declined somewhat to being merely 'agréable'.[5] The Paris premiere of *Les Biches* on 26 May continued its successful career, though Poulenc's tireless adversary Émile Vuillermoz took the opportunity to fulminate against Les Six in general for their 'platitudes, trivialities, clichés'.[6] Then on 2 June Cocteau's *Roméo et Juliette* finally reached the stage, including Poulenc's 'Fanfare'. But the premiere of Satie's ballet *Mercure* on the 15th, also as part of a *Soirée de Paris*, provoked Auric to a sour review, Satie to a retaliation, this to the disobliging present for Satie already mentioned (a doll with an old man's head, depicting Satie himself), and that to the ending of two friendships. It was an eventful evening for other reasons, 'greeted by boos from a group of people who, at the instigation of the surrealists Aragon and Breton, had a great time shouting: "Long live Picasso: down with Satie!"'[7] But a few days later Francis Picabia wrote 'I've just had a letter telling me that at La Cigale the other evening Satie had a triumph with the musicians who went to *Mercure* . . .' Of the demonstration he said 'Aragon and Breton have often admitted to me that they didn't understand a thing about music; so what's the point of this blackmail and this wild admiration for Picasso?'[8] Not that everyone was pro-Picasso: Marie Laurencin asked a friend 'if I've been to the Cigale to see Picasso's ballet, of which she said she understood nothing, that it was too highbrow, that she can't make out why he turns solids into steel wire, that he takes himself too seriously because he is Spanish'.[9] For Poulenc, *Mercure* belonged in the same boat as Satie's final ballet, *Relâche*, given by the Ballets Suédois on 4 December: 'An evening wasted at *Relâche*. Music of an old dotard, better orchestrated than *Mercure*, thank God, but even more empty of content. I came away feeling really sad. I hate seeing people I admire grow old.'[10]

The other ballet premiere of 1924 no doubt gave him more pleasure, though he is not known to have committed himself to any comments. Milhaud's *Le Train bleu*, on a scenario by Cocteau, was the only commission Diaghilev gave this composer. Milhaud's progress report of 16 February (the ballet seems to have taken him all of three weeks) gives the flavour of the piece: 'Music in the tradition of Offenbach, Maurice Yvain, and a real Verdi finale with nice bland harmonies and not a single syncopation. It's typically Parisian – naughty, sly and sentimental, spiced with a little polka, galop, waltz etc. ... The whole thing is a little appalling, but fascinating.'[11] Cocteau's notes on the work proclaim that '*Le Train bleu* is more than a frivolous work. It is a monument to frivolity!'[12] If nothing else, elements of Maurice Yvain would have endeared it to Poulenc, for whom that light music maestro was a lifelong model.

With *Le Train bleu* at one end of the aesthetic spectrum and *Le Roi David* at the other, Poulenc could be forgiven for becoming a little confused. However, early signs of the Trio for oboe, bassoon and piano were that 'it's much more important than my other chamber works. It lasts about as long as a Haydn or Mozart trio, but not at all in that style. More "objective" music, as that idiot Prunières would put it.' 'Important' here refers to character rather than to size: when it was reported as being nearly done in October, he boasted that the Andante lasted six minutes;[13] but his 1959 recording is shorter at 4 minutes 25 seconds, and his 1928 one shorter still at just 4 minutes. Be that as it may, revision continued for some months and it was not performed until 2 May 1926. An undated letter to Stravinsky, presumably from April of that year, says 'How kind of you to have given me all of that good advice. I've modified the first tempo in the trio. It's completely different.'[14] Here we see a conjunction of minds with the Russian composer who once said 'My music can stand anything except being played at the wrong speed.'

In the first movement, the 'importance' is manifest from the opening nine notes on the piano – a call to attention involving harsh dissonance, as opposed to the impertinent 'wrong-note' kind. Here, combined with the succeeding dotted rhythms and trills, it unmistakably refers to the ceremonious French overture and the Versailles of Louis XIV. But with Poulenc, at least at this stage of his life, seriousness cannot be expected to last for long and the minor mode is soon obliterated by the major one in a scampering Presto. In due course the lyrical Poulenc does proclaim himself but the form follows the pattern that was to become the norm, that is 'episodic, with the themes or sections following one another in sequence. The trio, for example, contains nine distinct tunes or motives, with no development or evolutionary order, between rehearsal number 2 and four bars after number 13 in the first movement.' As one reason for this additive style, Keith Daniel reasonably suggests that at least four of his admired composers – Chabrier, Debussy, Satie and Stravinsky – were likewise unattracted to traditional kinds of development.[15]

Unusually, Poulenc later confided to Claude Rostand what he claimed were the formal bases of the Trio: 'For those who think I don't care about form, I've no objection to unveiling my secrets here: the first movement follows the plan of a Haydn Allegro, and the final Rondo the shape of the scherzo in Saint-Saëns's Second Piano Concerto. Ravel always recommended this method to me, which he often followed himself.'[16] Daniel throws both light and doubt on the question[17] and it seems Poulenc was to some extent myth-making once again. This, however, is far from being the most striking feature of the Trio, which undoubtedly is its 'importance' and even more its depth of feeling, especially in the central Andante where, in his favourite B flat major and over a continuously pulsing quaver movement, he gives full rein to his lyrical gifts. Here too, as in the Adagietto of *Les Biches*, though without suggesting the unease of that movement, the four-bar phrases are occasionally elided, avoiding any tedious predictability. If Mozart lies behind this movement, it also looks forward: in one chromatic downward sequence of piano chords, to the harmonic palette of Messiaen in the form of one of his 'modes of limited transposition'; and in one repeated woodwind phrase to the setting of the words 'Pater omnipotens' in the 'Domine Deus' movement of Poulenc's own *Gloria* of 1959–60. He had reason to say, 'I'm rather fond of my Trio because it sounds well and its sections balance each other.'[18]

The year 1924 marked the 400th anniversary of the birth of the poet Pierre de Ronsard. During the previous autumn, the editor of the *Revue musicale*, Henry Prunières, approached nine composers (Fauré, Dukas, Roussel, Aubert, Caplet, Honegger, Delage, Roland-Manuel and Ravel) for settings of his poetry to appear in a special number on 1 May 1924, Ravel's *Ronsard à son âme* being the best known of the results. It's always possible that the inclusion of Honegger spurred Poulenc on to show Prunières what he had missed, but the immediate cause was the critic André Schaeffner, who had sent Poulenc some of Ronsard's poems. 'I haven't finished my Trio,' he wrote to Schaeffner, possibly around January 1925. 'Instead I've produced five Poems by Ronsard. That's the splendid result. If my songs are good, as I hope, because I've put them together with great care, then you're pardoned, but if not, how am I going to punish you?'[19] The dates of the original piano version are December 1924 to January 1925, and Poulenc made a version with full orchestra in September and October 1934.[20]

They may have been 'put together with great care', but Poulenc soon fell out of love with them. His most observant comment came in 1958: 'I'm not suited to poetry on classical lines. Each time I've tried it, for example in the *Cinq Poèmes de Ronsard*, it hasn't been a success.'[21] This was also the advice from his friend Auric, who urged him to 'stay with Apollinaire, set Max Jacob, Éluard and Reverdy', and Poulenc spoke of Picasso's cover as being, without question, the best thing about the work. On the technical front, he admitted that 'at that time I was studying counterpoint with Koechlin and I was trying to fill out my style. What happened to me was the same (with due regard to the difference in our abilities, naturally) as what happened to Debussy when he composed his songs to poems by Baudelaire after the *Ariettes oubliées*.'[22] Overall, they give the impression not only of trying too hard, but of wilful examples of harmony and texture that do not seem to correspond with anything in the text. Certainly it's true that 'he does not lose his inspiration in the dusty corridors of learning. No more does he try and find the 16th century through Debussy.'[23] But why paint Ronsard's elegant tributes to the immortals Ceres, Chloris, Phoebus, Minerva and others with a jaunty staccato bass line? Altogether the set is much easier to appreciate in the 1934 orchestral version than in the piano one, the rich variety of colours illuminating the syntax.

For the first performance on 10 March 1925 Poulenc accompanied one of his favourite singers, the mezzo-soprano Suzanne Peignot, and the set was very well received, Poulenc commenting with the slightest edge of bitterness that 'For the first time in a review of my music I read the words "magnifique, très émouvant" ["magnificent, very moving"] for the fourth song ("Je n'ai plus que les os") – I'm slightly surprised to find these adjectives replacing "charmant, délicieux" ["charming, delightful"]. I didn't think I'd made such a major breakthrough.'[24] Here Poulenc is questioning, whether deliberately or not, an aesthetic position taken up in a review of *Les Biches* by the widely respected critic Boris de Schloezer over a year earlier: ' "Délicieux! Charmants!" These over-employed adjectives have these days taken on an almost pejorative meaning and in declaring a work to be "charmante" or "jolie" one has the impression of wanting to belittle a work; but I should like, in Poulenc's honour, to revive the value and true significance of these adjectives, because an art that charms us is worth every bit as much as one that troubles or bowls us over.'[25] Poulenc's use of the same two words does suggest that his denial was deliberate, and that he truly wanted his music to go beyond charm and delightfulness, however popular these attributes might prove to be. That he had some way to go before winning ubiquitous approval is shown by a passing reference to him in a 1925 compendium – that is, a year after *Les Biches*: 'M. Francis Poulenc, still quite young and inexperienced, but not without talent.'[26]

Poulenc mentions only *en passant*, and over twenty years later, that he was in Monte-Carlo for some of the rehearsals and the premiere of Ravel's opera *L'Enfant et les sortilèges* on 21 March. One assumes that he was there on his own initiative, since relations with Ravel were not such as to lead to an invitation. However, when he got there, he learnt that:

> . . . the orchestral material had been so hastily copied that at odd moments the harp and first bassoon parts were to be found in alternation on the same sheets. The orchestra had to be stopped all the time and Ravel, wearing a tightly fitted grey flannel jacket, was threatening to block the premiere. But at the dress rehearsal everything went like magic and we understood, various friends and I who had been sharply attacking Ravel around 1920 that, now he had at last emerged from the purgatory in which his imitators had immersed him, Ravel was, in his lifetime, making his entrance into eternity.[27]

Whether Poulenc was drafted in to help correct the parts, he doesn't say, but ten years later he added: 'In 1925, at the premiere of *L'Enfant et les sortilèges*, Georges Auric and I made our peace with Ravel. In fact he then thanked us warmly for not having been among his followers.'[28]

That same month Poulenc went to Koechlin for the last seven of his fifty-eight composition lessons. There is no record of what was studied on these final occasions, and Poulenc's memory of 'studying counterpoint' seems to contradict what he said elsewhere; but maybe by this last session Koechlin felt Poulenc was ready to move on from purely harmonic issues. The remainder of the year was fairly uneventful. He still had not abandoned the *Marches militaires*, and also continued working on the Trio and *Napoli*. The only two new projects were a piano version of Mozart's *Ein musikalischer Spass*, made for reasons unknown, and the eight *Chansons gaillardes* on more or less scurrilous seventeenth-century poems.

These are dated 'Nazelles-Clavary 1925–1926', reminding us of Poulenc's perpetual journeying, which often combined work and pleasure. Writing to Auric on 15 March, he announced his holiday plans: 7 May, a return to Monte-Carlo for the revival of *Les Biches* (Osbert Lancaster not wholly impressed: 'The revival of *Les Biches*, I think, worked visually pretty well, but I thought musically not at all. It didn't seem to me that the orchestra or conductor really understood what Poulenc was getting at. All the snap had gone out of that side of it');[29] around the 18th to Cannes and his elderly friend Virginie Liénard, always known as 'Tante Liénard'; then to Aix-en-Provence for Milhaud's wedding on 4 May to his cousin Madeleine (when this letter was published in 1994, his note to Auric, 'Darius is madly in love.

I approve but would have chosen another wife', was read with great amusement by the lady in question who, looking back on her forty-nine years of happy marriage, commented 'Je crois avoir fait mes preuves' – 'I think I passed the test').[30] Then came a fortnight with the wealthy American Russel Greeley and his companion Comte François de Gouy d'Arcy at Clavary, near Grasse, during which Poulenc clearly spent at least some time on his latest group of songs.[31]

However, he seems not to have travelled to London for the first British performance at the Coliseum of *Les Biches* on 25 May under the title *The House Party*, which the critic Cyril W. Beaumont recorded as having had 'a most enthusiastic reception' and having 'become a popular item in the repertory'. Beaumont himself had reservations about the piece, if expressed with supreme tact: 'This artificial hothouse atmosphere provoked the strangest emotions, although they were masked by an affected and nervous air of gaiety . . . It was not a pleasant theme, and it was presented with an insight that could only be derived from an intimate knowledge of such occasions, but it was a genuine cross-section of a phase of contemporary life, a presentation rendered the more piquant by the very delicacy of its considerable imputations.'[32] Nothing naive about Mr. Beaumont . . .

After his attack of jaundice, and perhaps even earlier, Poulenc had followed the family habit of going to Vichy every summer to take the waters, and he was there when Raymonde Linossier's telegram reached him announcing Satie's death on 1 July. Thanks to the generosity of the Comte de Beaumont, Satie was in a private room at the St Joseph Hospital and, although the newly married Milhauds were welcome, he had refused to see Poulenc or Auric, saying 'One must be intransigent up to the end'.[33] Linossier followed up her telegram with a letter written very late on the evening of the funeral on 6 July – sadly the only letter between them that we know, but one that fully explains the attraction Poulenc felt for this remarkable woman. In 1925 she was not only a probationary barrister at the Paris lawcourts, but was just joining the staff of the Musée Guimet, the national museum of Asiatic arts.[34] Therefore, since both she and Poulenc lived in Paris, we can assume these two *potassons* saw each other quite regularly and correspondence was required only for an occasion such as Satie's death. Her letter mixes sadness and humour in a very Satiean manner:

For some days he had been living on nothing but champagne and paregoric. Now that he's dead, I'll tell you about that horrifying visit that so upset me. Without any warning, I found myself in the presence of a man whose mind had gone and who rambled on deliriously for two hours. This disintegration of what had once been our *bon maître* was terrible to behold. [. . .] The burial in Arcueil was fine. No doubt many people were unable to attend, and only the smart, leisured, homosexual set was well represented. But the setting was pleasant and the good people of Arcueil – his café companions and others – followed the funeral procession. [. . .] Cocteau sobbed rather noisily. Valentine [Hugo] was made up to the nines. Forgive me, but I couldn't help looking at the ceremony through Satie's eyes. [. . .] And it's hard to give up running everyone down over a drink, with the inevitable umbrella between us.[35]

This letter not only makes clear that Linossier was, in American terminology, 'one smart cookie', but also perhaps tells us something about Poulenc: if in 1925 she had known that Poulenc was homosexual, would someone of her literary and emotional intelligence have used the phrase 'l'élément chic, inoccupé et pédéraste'? – although 'pederast' literally means a lover of boys, in French it is still also used, either in full or abbreviated to 'pédé', to mean more generally 'homosexual'. It can at least be argued that at the age of twenty-six Poulenc was either able to conceal his orientation from such a close and sharp-witted friend, or was himself still unsure of what this was. It is a question which an event in 1927 would render irrelevant.

In August Poulenc arranged Mozart's musical joke (*Ein musikalischer Spass*) for piano and at Nazelles in September put the finishing touches to his piano suite *Napoli*. For this group of three short pieces to have taken five years merely shows how problematic Poulenc found the whole business of writing for piano, as it was to remain all his life. In the work's earliest mention, in a letter to Jean-Aubry of 22 June 1920, the three movements are already settled: 'a Nocturne, a Barcarolle, finishing with a grand caprice "Vesuviana"'.[36] Then on 17 March 1924 Marcelle Meyer had played the first two movements, so it would seem that the final Caprice was the sticking point. Both the first two unashamedly celebrate the tonality restored in *Mavra* and therafter in *Les Biches*. The 'Nocturne' never leaves the key of D major, with occasional alien notes acting as no more than spice to the mixture, while in the 'Barcarolle', although the central section of the ABA form is chromatic, the outer ones are entirely in D flat major until the final bar. Here, as in the 'Nocturne', Poulenc again indulges his love of the quirky sign-off. The final 'Caprice italien', which lasts as long as the previous two together and on the page is twice as long as that, is more complex, mixing tonality with moments of scatty dissonance. The last two pages, in which the tonic E major fights successfully against attempts to dislodge it, may well have taken Poulenc time to get right, as may his juggling throughout the piece to combine memories of Scarlatti, Chopin, Chabrier and Prokofiev, not forgetting the Finale of *Les Biches*. Both volcanic and tuneful, it makes a sparkling end to a recital.

The most serious event in the last months of 1925 was the accident on a train arriving in Amboise station, which braked very suddenly. Poulenc's left hand went through a window, severing two tendons in his thumb. Mercifully, after an operation, ten days in the clinic, fifteen changes of bandage and two months' rest, by 11 January the thumb had recovered to being no more than a trifle stiff.[37] By this time he had completed his eight *Chansons gaillardes* and they were going off to the engraver. Like *Napoli* and the never-to-be completed *Marches militaires*, these enjoyed a long gestation, being mentioned first in a letter of August 1922.[38] 'Gaillard' has a number of meanings: vigorous, merry, sharp, sly, free, ribald, all of which (especially the last) apply at various points to these songs on anonymous seventeenth-century texts. Where the sexual references in *Les Biches* are largely coded and subterranean, here their blatancy in the texts is obfuscated by the sheer beauty of Poulenc's music. For once this composer who was ever doubtful of his gifts knew what he had done, and wrote to Paul Collaer: 'I hope you'll like these songs. I set perhaps more store by them than by anything else I've composed. It seems to me they're very uniquely "Poulenc" and that no one else could have succeeded with semi-erotic, semi-elegiac songs of this kind.'[39] He also had a set purpose in writing them, namely 'to show that obscenity can sit comfortably with music'.[40]

This it certainly does in the faster songs, which leave little time for moralizing. The modal flavour of 'La Maîtresse volage' and Poulenc's favourite switches between major and minor, as in 'La belle jeunesse', give off a flavour of the untutored countryside, where bawdy is more to be expected. By contrast the slow, heavy chords in 'Chanson à boire', indebted to Musorgsky,[41] tell us a universal truth, that the final destruction of the body cannot be cheated, as the gods of Egypt and Syria believed, by embalming it: embalming the living body in drink is presented as almost a holy exercise (and this is the only song of the eight not to boast even a slightly 'gaillard' text). But in 'Invocation aux Parques', a similarly grave atmosphere is used to distract from the verbal double entendre: the whole text reads 'I swear, as long as I live, to love you, Sylvie: Fates, who hold in your hands the thread of our life, lengthen mine as much as you can, I beg you.' 'Fil' can mean 'thread', but also 'current' of a stream or a 'wire' or, by analogy, something more sexual. False innocence is at the heart of the concluding 'Sérénade', a sicilienne with all the unassuming quality of the genre. Only the discreetly grinding semitonal clashes warn that wiping the tears of Cupid is not the innocent pastime it might superficially appear.

One of the 'must-hear' occasions of 1926 Paris, after the city's premiere of Ravel's *L'Enfant et les sortilèges* on 1 February, was the Auric/Poulenc concert in the Salle des Agriculteurs on 2 May, containing six works by Auric, including two first performances, and four by Poulenc: a repeat of *Poèmes de Ronsard* and first performances of the Trio for oboe, bassoon and piano, *Napoli* played by Marcelle Meyer, and the *Chansons gaillardes* sung by a baritone introduced to Poulenc after he had been searching a long time. Years later Poulenc remembered the singer as 'a young man who came, like me, from the bourgeoisie. His father was a stockbroker. To tell the truth, and especially for a group of songs like these, I wasn't entirely happy with him, just as Satie had previously been unhappy with "Poulenc the little daddy's boy" [. . .] I rehearsed him in the *Chansons gaillardes*, which he sang superbly and with great success. Then I completely lost sight of him.'[42] Eight years later, he was to catch up again with Pierre Bernac.

According to Poulenc, they had to turn away more than 200 people and the aged André Messager had a job reaching his reserved seat. The critics' reaction was generally good, though René Chalupt, while registering the audience's delight, cautioned that 'one soon grows tired of too easy pleasures and it may be presumed that the present reaction in which they have taken the lead will in its turn, and probably before long, provoke a counter-reaction.'[43] André George was surprised to hear these texts sung in front of 500 people,[44] but Boris de Schloezer, whose review did not appear until February 1927, thought only one of the texts 'borders on obscenity'. He also felt, understandably, that the musical style looked back to Poulenc's earliest pieces but also, curiously, that Poulenc 'seems deliberately to have turned his back on any kind of sensual seduction.'[45] Perhaps Schloezer could be seduced only by rich romantic textures.

After going to a Satie memorial concert on 17 May and playing at two more on the 19th and 26th, on 2 June Poulenc was joined by Sauguet on a visit to London, where Poulenc was to play one of the pianos in the Ballets Russes production of *Les Noces* on 14 June. On the 29th London again saw *Les Biches*, and Poulenc '*finally heard*' it,[46] suggesting that he agreed with Lancaster's view of the Monte-Carlo revival. An unidentified cutting in the dancer Anton Dolin's album records that, compared with previous London performances, the orchestra under Eugene Goossens was certainly better than ever.[47] Poulenc returned to France on 7 July and spent the summer in Nazelles, from where he wrote to Milhaud that he was 'very seriously at work' on the violin sonata begun in 1924, now with a view to performing it in Copenhagen as early as 23 October. He could already describe it in detail ('instrumental style: 18th-century violin school – Vivaldi, Leclair, Loeillet. Four movements: Largo, Allegro, Sérénade, Gigue')[48] and, although the work missed the Copenhagen concert, which he gave with Auric, on 17 November he was still in the middle of it: 'I think that it's quite unusual as a violin and piano duo, albeit very 18th-century. The opening largo is done; the third movement romance likewise; I'm struggling with the second movement presto; the fourth movement gigue is in limbo.' Then comes the killer sentence: 'Que c'est difficile la musique.'[49] As with its predecessor, limbo was to be the destination of the whole work.

The many false starts and indeed false continuations in Poulenc's creative life give the lie as much as anything can to the notion that, because his music was not 'difficult' in the sense of being full of chromatic counterpoint and because it favoured tunes and plainly logical discourse, therefore it must have been easy to write. Instead it was hard writing that made for easy listening – and not in the pejorative sense of that phrase. The calendar tells us that in the year between the concert with Auric on 2 May 1926 and Poulenc's start on his *Airs chantés* in May 1927, he completed no more than a *Récitatif pour précéder Orphée* for cornet and piano in that month for Cocteau's play, a tiny *Vocalise* in February 1927, and the 'Pastourelle' for the combined endeavour *L'Éventail de Jeanne* in April. But that is to ignore this Violin Sonata and the *Marches militaires*, both of which were ultimately abandoned, the latter not until 1932! Then of course there were the hours spent (as any composer reading the following paragraph will testify) agonizing over details. Manuel Rosenthal recalled the case of Ravel:

> He finished the work [*L'Enfant et les sortilèges*] in Monte-Carlo, just days before the opening. When it was finally completed he said to me, 'You know, at night when I was walking along the shore, wondering whether something should be in B flat or B major or how to choose a chord or manage a melodic line, I said to myself, 'Oh, I'm tired of this! I'd like to be finished with it, just sitting at last in a café, enjoying an apéritif, looking at the sea.' And when I was finally through and could sit in a café having my apéritif, the taste of it was bitter! I was longing for the time I'd spent walking at night, thinking 'should it be B flat or B major?'[50]

Poulenc's lack of production in the last half of 1926 should not, therefore, be attributed to idleness. One further object of his musical thoughts seems to have been the Harpsichord Concerto requested by Wanda Landowska back in 1923 after the performance of Falla's *El Retablo*, since she wrote to Poulenc from New York on 19 January 1927 that 'I have spoken to Koussevitzky about your *Concert champêtre*'. The fact that she gives the work its final appellation makes it certain that Poulenc had already vouchsafed this to her and almost as certain that he had at least the general spirit of the work in mind. Koussevitzky was enthusiastic in advance and wanted to play it the following winter in both Boston and New York. But if that was to happen, she needed to have the work 'in my hands, of rather under my fingers by the end of May or the beginning of June'.[51] Certainly Poulenc had begun the presto Finale by March, as noted on the manuscript, but he did not put the finishing touches to the work until August 1928. If Landowska refused to be hurried (in this letter she complained bitterly about having had to work up Falla's Harpsichord Concerto in less than two months), then Poulenc was similarly determined to take his time, especially as the harpsichord was to him a fairly unknown quantity.

The *Vocalise* he composed in February (sometimes known as *Air sans paroles*) was first sung by Jane Bathori, possibly on 7 May 1927, or else certainly on 3 March 1928. It was published in 1929 as one of the pieces in A-L. Hettich's long-running series *Répertoire moderne de vocalise-études*, to which most French composers of the time contributed, and conforms to the usual requirements of agility, breath control and accurate intonation. Altogether more interesting, for us listeners anyway, is his 'Pastourelle' for a multi-authored one-act ballet for children *L'Éventail de Jeanne*, also including music by Ravel, Pierre-Octave Ferroud, Ibert, Marcel Delannoy, Roussel, Milhaud, Auric and Florent Schmitt. The Jeanne of the title was Jeanne Dubost, who was married to a stockbroker and whose father, Adrien Bénard, was most noteworthy for having persuaded Hector Guimard to design the entrances to the Paris métro. She was known as an anti-conformist, given to wearing strange hats, but the visitors to her salon were beyond reproach, including, in addition to the composers above named, Satie, Casella, Szymanowski and Bartók. As was often the case with salons, her husband, though footing the bill, had no interest whatever in the results and so missed the occasion when, as Madeleine Milhaud remembered, the guests were entertained 'by a Red Indian chief who sang at the top of his voice and jumped all over the place'.[52] Sadly, on this occasion Mme Dubost's good nature was imposed upon, as the 'chief' had been born in the United Kingdom.

Mme Dubost was only one of several hostesses who were included in Poulenc's salon circuit. Another *salonnière*, Mme de Saint-Marceaux, invited him to come and play his own music on three occasions and was rewarded with a dedicated copy of the *Airs chantés*. But this did not prevent her from seconding the concerns voiced to her by André Messager, that these young composers 'are content with banalities which they spice up with dissonances in the hope that this will give the impression of being something' – and that after he had conducted *Les Biches*! On 18 March Poulenc came to dinner together with Marguerite Long, Messager, Ravel and the pianist Jacques Février, and their hostess recorded that in the course of the evening he 'sang his *Chansons gaillardes* and played his *Napoli*. He plays the piano well. His compositions don't lack talent but he's not a genius, and I'm afraid he thinks he is. It's the great failing of all this young group.'⁵³

The ballet *L'Éventail de Jeanne* was a present to Mme Dubost from its composers, to thank her for her support and for the ballet class she ran for the 'petits rats', the up-and-coming child dancers at the Opéra. The first performance, conducted by Désormière, was given in her drawing room on 16 June 1927 with a cast of twenty-six girl dancers and two boys. The light-hearted tone was set by Ravel's opening 'Fanfare' (in fact a multiplicity of bitonally clashing fanfares, marked to be played 'wagneramente') and continued by the quotation in Ibert's 'Valse' from Ravel's longer work of the same name. Poulenc's two-minute 'Pastourelle' in his favourite B flat major continues his love affair with the pentatonic scale and with its third degree, disturbed only by a sudden switch at the end to the minor. Are we in for a bout of melancholy brooding? The abrupt sign-off reassures. Among the audience was Jacques Rouché, the Opéra director, who was so delighted that he programmed the ballet for his larger stage two years later, while Paul Morand passed on to Poulenc Ravel's remark that 'what you gave the other evening at Madame D. was excellent'.⁵⁴ Carl Schmidt notes that, with the help of Horowitz's 1932 recording, by 1952 the 'Pastourelle' had sold more than 31,000 copies.⁵⁵

While writing this piece took Poulenc only a few weeks, the *Concert champêtre* remained on his table until August 1928, and even the four *Airs chantés*, lasting altogether no more than some eight minutes, took him a full year from May 1927 to May 1928 . . . and in the latter's case deliberation turned out to be no guarantee of satisfaction. Later on he would give two differing versions of his attitude to Jean Moréas's texts. In his 1954 interviews with Claude Rostand, Poulenc said that he only set them as a joke, to please his publisher François Hepp who liked the sonnets, that he himself didn't, but that he confined his displeasure to a single distortion of the prosody by setting 'sous-la-mou-sou-la-mousse-à moitié', in imitation of a *café concert* habit. His account in the posthumously published *Journal de mes mélodies* is more damning: 'I detest Moréas and I chose these poems precisely because I found them ripe for mutilation [. . .] This set put me off writing songs for a long time. In a word, a bad mistake.'[56] But does any composer really decide, even to please a friend, to set words by a poet he 'detests'?

Jean Moréas, who lived from 1856 to 1910 and whose real name was Yannis Papadiamantopoulos, had left Athens for Paris in 1879 and in 1886 gave the Symbolist school of writers that name. Although the poems Poulenc set came from his later *Stances*, which represented something of a turning back to the classical world, Moréas is nevertheless the only 'romantic' poet he ever set, following Ravel's example of concentrating on poets of classical and modern times. As for being 'put off writing songs for a long time', after the first complete performance of these songs on 10 June 1928, it's true he wrote none in 1929 and only a single one, *Épitaphe*, in 1930, but then twelve more in 1931.

We are entitled to ask: are the *Airs chantés* really as bad as all that? Technicians may frown at his reliance on the diminished seventh, that old warhorse of heightened emotion, but there are felicities too. The piano introduction of 'Air champêtre' marries beautifully an eighteenth-century mood with the playfulness of a five-and-a-half-bar phrase, and playfulness appears too at the end of the song in a blatant borrowing from Chopin's G flat Étude op. 25 no. 9. If we are looking for word painting and lyricism, then it can surely be found in the 'Air grave' on 'Sentiers de mousse pleins, vaporeuses fontaines' where the deliberate inversion of accents on '*vaporeuses*' gives a wonderful sense of floating spray. This is the first but far from the last instance of Poulenc taking a violent and highly disputable dislike to one of his own creations.

The summer of 1927 provided a trio of offerings from the Ballets Russes, but only one that contained anything to teach Poulenc. Sauguet's ballet *La Chatte*, premiered on 27 May, pleased him with its suave charm, and he was delighted that his young friend should have had a success. But he had little to say about Prokofiev's ballet *Le Pas d'acier*, premiered on 7 June, other than that it was a triumph,[57] a verdict not necessarily endorsed by Diaghilev who had expected the first night of this deliberately Soviet ballet to be disrupted by a White Russian demonstration, 'and when *Le Pas d'acier* was greeted with applause, relieved by only a few cat-calls, he was rather disappointed and thought the public "spineless"'.[58] It's understandable that Prokofiev's music, deliberately provocative in its almost relentless percussive pounding which nullified the composer's hopefully emollient remark that most of it was on the white notes, was not really to the taste of a Poulenc who had got this sort of thing out of his system with the *Rapsodie nègre*.

Between these two premieres, however, was another that was to have a far deeper and more lasting influence on him: on 30 May Stravinsky conducted *Oedipus Rex*. That morning, after attending the dress rehearsal the previous evening, Poulenc wrote to the composer:

> Dear Stravinsky, I couldn't find anything to say to you yesterday evening that precisely expresses my enthusiasm. I feel that this evening it will be the same thing. Even so I do want you to know into what a state of *superior* emotion you plunged me yesterday. Your art has risen to such a height that it would need the language of Sophocles himself to speak of it. My God, it's so beautiful! Permit me to embrace you. It is a rare honour for me. Your faithful Poulenc.[59]

Given Poulenc's reverence for Stravinsky in general, this response is not exactly surprising. But two contextual details deserve our attention. Firstly, Stravinsky's take at the dress rehearsal, given just with him accompanying the singers on the piano in the Princesse de Polignac's spacious salon: 'from the reactions of the guests I foresaw that *Oedipus* was not likely to succeed with the Parisian ballet audience'. As for the premiere, 'my austere vocal concert, following a very colourful ballet [*Firebird*], was an even greater failure than I had anticipated. The audience was hardly more than polite [. . .] Performances were rare in the next two decades [. . .]'[60] So Poulenc's enthusiasm was going very much against the general trend. Secondly, in asking what it was he found that eluded others, we are to some extent helped by his underlining of the word 'supérieure' and the possibility it offers that the work tapped into some kind of religious feeling. But Stravinsky pointedly asked, 'In what sense is the music religious? I do not know how to answer because the word does not correspond in my mind to a state of feeling or sentiment, but to dogmatic beliefs' – a position closely connected to the fact that 'the music was composed during my strictest and most earnest period of Christian Orthodoxy'.[61] We may nonetheless agree with Stephen Walsh in admiring the work's 'extraordinary spiritual grandeur'[62] and even tie this up, tendentiously, with Stravinsky's admission that 'I do, of course, believe in a system beyond Nature'. But whether or not some residue of religious feeling remained with Poulenc during the 1920s and early 1930s, there can be little doubt that *Oedipus* also taught him lessons in musical technique. A further quotation from Stravinsky about the work is relevant: 'My audience is not indifferent to the fate of the person, but I think it far more concerned with the person of the fate, and the delineation of it which can be achieved uniquely in music … Crossroads are not personal but geometrical, and the geometry of tragedy, the inevitable intersecting of lines, is what concerned me.'[63]

As if this aesthetic excitement was not enough for the summer of 1927, Poulenc also surprised everyone by (suddenly, as it seemed to his friends) buying a large country house. They might have surmised that he was following the example of his sister and brother-in-law who had recently bought a château called Le Tremblay in Normandy, or that of Roussel, whose newly bought house in Varengeville-sur-mer he had visited in 1920. One of the main reasons – perhaps *the* main reason – would not be vouchsafed by him, as we shall see, for another twelve months. In the meantime Poulenc could only visit a house that had to undergo considerable restoration. But at least now he would have a workplace away from the distractions of the capital and one that, being at Noizay in the Touraine, was close to Nazelles and his dear Tante Liénard. Her house, La Lézardière, had for some years been the repository of various of Poulenc's belongings and would, together with the auberge Le Lion d'Or, continue to welcome him. He could also now continue to enjoy the peace of 'ma chère Touraine', where had had composed *Les Biches* and much of the *Chansons gaillardes*.

No sooner had the house been bought than rumours began to do the rounds that Poulenc was engaged to be married, the instigator of these being the painter and part-time gossip Jacques-Émile Blanche, who even named the fiancée as a daughter of the director of the Royal Academy in London. Writing to Milhaud, Poulenc scotched the rumours and gave yet another explanation of his purchase, namely that the family were now letting out the house in Nogent (in the end it was sold). He therefore had to find somewhere to put all the belongings of his that had accumulated there since his childhood, a task that involved 'weeks of dust and dirt' and no doubt considerable nostalgia.[64] However, his good humour was not seriously dented, as we can see from his card of September to the said Blanche, showing a photo of Le Grand Coteau:

> Here's the house I've bought in Touraine, but for the moment I have *no* desire to get married. Even so it's very kind of you to have thought of me. However charming your delightful miss may be, I'm afraid I prefer a French lady to her. Perhaps my lack of matrimonial internationalism will strike you as bourgeois. I'm not making a general rule. I speak only for myself.[65]

November found Poulenc less sanguine about the ongoing work at Le Grand Coteau, with the various workmen all blaming each other for delays. Otherwise a letter to his sister mentions three *Novellettes*, of which he would have only two to play the following June, as well as the original plans for performing the *Concert champêtre*.[66] But his known correspondence says nothing about an enticing collection of performances over the ensuing four months: Schoenberg's visit to Paris and the premiere at the Opéra-Comique of Milhaud's *Le Pauvre Matelot* in December, Berg's Chamber Concerto and Prokofiev's Classical Symphony in February, and in March the Opéra-Comique's production of all three of Falla's operas, followed by the French premiere at the Opéra of Puccini's *Turandot*.

But we need to be aware that failure to mention such events in his immediate correspondence has little or no bearing on the importance to Poulenc of the works performed, merely of his occupation elsewhere, in this case with his new home. This reservation is borne out by his epistolary silence in 1928 over Stravinsky's ballet *Apollon musagète* as against his subsequent opinion of the work. In 1962 Poulenc contributed an article on the Ballets Russes to a history of music, published in 1963, after his death. In it he writes that 'In 1928, Stravinsky returns to classical ballet with *Apollon musagète*, which is a homage to the music of Tchaikovsky and one of his finest scores.'[67] In 1954 Poulenc had already explained to Claude Rostand that 'it's from *Pulcinella*, *Mavra*, *Apollon* and *Le Baiser de la fée* that I've gathered my honey [. . .] there's the rhythmic echo of *Les Noces* which you can find, very Frenchified, it's true, in the sung dances of *Les Biches*. But it's obvious that there's much more of *Le Baiser de la fée* and *Apollon* in *Aubade*, for instance and of *Pulcinella* in *Les Biches* and the *Concert champêtre*.'[68]

We know of no letter from Poulenc to Stravinsky on the lines of the one he wrote under the impact of *Oedipus Rex*, and it's easy to understand that the influence of *Apollon musagète* would be more gradual, less of a knock-out blow. Certainly the pairing of this work with *Aubade* fits the chronology, since both the French premiere of the former and the commissioning of the latter date from the summer of 1928. Boris de Schloezer reckoned that Stravinsky's ballet revealed his 'thirst for renunciation, his need of purity and serenity [. . .] What this peace and clarity have cost him can be witnessed only by the long series of precedent works whose exasperated dynamism would almost seem, by comparison with the *Apollo*, to be a vain agitation.'[69] The rival claims of serenity and agitation also occupied Poulenc throughout his life, with serenity undoubtedly the harder of the two to achieve.

He almost certainly attended the French premiere of *Apollon musagète* on 12 June since he had been in Paris only two days earlier to take part in another Auric/Poulenc concert, at which he had given first performances of the *Deux Novellettes* and the *Trois pièces*, and accompanied Suzanne Peignot in the first complete performance of the *Airs chantés*. The *Novellettes* are examples of serenity and agitation in that order. The note E in its role as the major third in C major exercised a particular charm on Poulenc, and having started with it in the first piece he finds it hard to escape from: in the forty-one bars of the first of the three sections, no fewer than nineteen begin with the E at the top of the treble stave, so that it seems to ring out like a bell. More generally, his use of the major third as the bringer of serenity does of course follow nineteenth-century practice. What is typically Poulencquian is the chromatic stress it occasionally undergoes, and conquers. Composed in October 1927, the piece is dedicated to Tante Liénard, no doubt in gratitude for housing the belongings from Nogent. The second piece from 1928, marked 'très rapide et rythmé', is one of Poulenc's scampering exercises of the sort that left audiences amazed at the dexterity of his large, ungainly looking hands. The instruction 'rythmé' is confirmed in the middle section in the major, where a relaxed serenity might be thought appropriate, with a firm 'absolument sans ralentir', followed up by another 'sans ralentir' over the final bars. Not for the first or last time with Poulenc do we feel a Baroque undertow, and only on the final page do a couple of 3/2 bars momentarily interrupt the almost mechanical series of two- and four-bar phrases. The composer's declared hatred of rubato is nowhere better exemplified.

The *Trois pièces* were reworkings of the three *Pastorales* Poulenc had written for Viñes in 1917. According to Poulenc in 1954, 'They remained unpublished for some time, but in 1928 Casella wrote to me: "What happened to your pastorales? I liked them a lot", so I had the idea of going back to them [. . .] The first of them is almost identical with the original version; I kept the opening four bars and the conclusion of the second and turned it into a "Toccata", well known now thanks to Horowitz; finally I replaced the last one with a "Hymne", in the style of my *Concert champêtre*.'[70] The earlier provenance of the first piece is hinted at by the instruction 'Calme et mystérieux', mystery being in rather short supply in the Poulenc of the 1920s. This is emphasized by chromatic harmony that sounds more like Florent Schmitt than Poulenc, until the sun suddenly comes out on the second page and we are in an atmosphere which, in its dotted rhythms, anticipates that not only of *Aubade* (figs. 26–29) but, more curiously, of the final 'Apothéose' of *Apollon musagète*. The imposing opening bars of 'Hymne' would later return to begin the

Gloria, while the scampering of the 'Toccata' would find a charismatic interpreter in Horowitz. If his increase in tempo from the marked crotchet = 160 to 184 is quite breathtaking enough, his sudden pianissimo on the final page is no less so, and we can absolutely understand why Poulenc adored his playing.

Wanda Landowska's command of the harpsichord was no less supreme and in writing the *Concert champêtre* Poulenc took full advantage of her technical know-how:

> We went through it bar by bar, note by note. Even so, we didn't change a single bar or melodic line – our most intense work was on the piano writing [sic] and the choice of orchestral instruments. For the most part we clarified the writing, either by simplifying chords or by taking out notes [. . .] Most of all, I wanted to use the harpsichord in a manner that was both French and modern, and did not sound like a pastiche. I wanted to prove that the harpsichord was not an obsolete, inefficient instrument of merely historical interest, but on the contrary that it was and remains an instrument that had reached its point of perfection, with its specific characteristics, its own properties, timbres and accents that no other instrument can replace. I also wanted, while using a modern language, to take inspiration from the pure French style of the seventeenth century, imbued with majesty and ceremony and absolutely distinct – and I insist on this – from the 'pastorals' of the subsequent era.[71]

This combination of clarity with majesty is perhaps one of the most striking features of the work, and Landowska can take credit for explaining to Poulenc that on the harpsichord too much doubling of notes is counterproductive: by its essentially percussive nature the instrument thrives on plenty of vertical space. Although, as already noted, Landowska expressed herself determined not to suffer again the chronological trials imposed on her by Falla over his concerto, Poulenc found he too needed time for composing such an adventurous piece, so what with his delays and Landowska's appendicitis, the first performance did not take place until May 1929.

Poulenc had undoubtedly attended the two Paris performances on 14 May 1927 of Falla's Harpsichord Concerto, played by the composer in the same concert, first on a piano, then on a harpsichord and, although Poulenc's orchestra far exceeds Falla's five instruments, some comparison might seem desirable between these two works which together restored the harpsichord to the mainstream. But in fact they could hardly be more different. Falla's lighter scoring is negated by a far more complex harmonic palette involving much bitonality and by a parallel complexity in the syntax, to the point that the listener has to work quite hard at times to make sense of the discourse. Poulenc on the other hand uses his large orchestra to expound clearly tonal or modal material in the shape of his usual wealth of memorable tunes, scales and arpeggios abounding. The rural nature of the work is expressed in much writing for horns, and the composer's explanation of the bugle calls in the last movement tells us that 'For me, the eternal city dweller, the trumpets of the fort of Vincennes, heard from the neighbouring wood, are as poetic as the hunting horns in a vast forest were for Weber.'[72] While Fred Goldbeck could later complain that the work displayed 'the most savage mixture of styles any composer has ever dared to offer',[73] there are signs too of more self-confidence, not least in the slow movement, a Sicilienne, which, as Keith Daniel points out, is, 'except for immediate repetitions of each theme [. . .] nearly through-composed, a rarity for Poulenc.'[74] Perhaps boldest of all is the very end, where simplicity wins out over majesty, nostalgia over joy.

The change in 1925 from acoustic to electric recording persuaded many doubters that the gramophone was here to stay and its superior trustworthiness over the player-piano could now come fully into its own. In 1928 Poulenc engaged with the new system on two fronts, as both pianist and critic. The considerable speed of the faster numbers (the 'Rondeau' from *Les Biches* and the third *Mouvement perpétuel*) leads to some untidy playing, but overall there is an unmistakable authority and character, and thanks to the speed of the latter the slow final bars acquire a magic glow. Poulenc had to record the two excerpts from *Les Biches* several times, not liking the sound he made on playback. Finally the recording engineer said that 'as I preferred "the American taste", he'd move my Pleyel further away. You can see that in gramophone language "American taste" means something entirely different from what it does to champagne merchants.'[75] In the other work, the Trio, the special timbres of the French oboe and bassoon and the superb phrasing of Messieurs Lamorlette and Dhérin still enchant ninety years later.

As critic Poulenc contributed to the new gramophone magazine *Arts phoniques*. It is no surprise to find that he's as sharp a listener to the sonorities of discs as to the value of the works themselves or the quality of the interpretations. In the June 1928

POULENC

number, after castigating the famous flautist Marcel Moyse for his dull sound in the middle and higher registers, and for choosing a work by Georges Hüe 'd'une parfaite nullité' and a 'pâle étude' by Paul Taffanel, he recommends that listeners can increase the volume by putting the gramophone on the lid of a grand piano. 'You may laugh,' he adds, 'but it works.' In the January 1929 number, he thinks the Andante of the Debussy Quartet may have been recorded further away than the previous two movements ('if so, someone should have marked the position of the chairs with chalk'), and in comparing piano discs by Francis Planté (1839–1934) and Alexandre Brailowsky (1896–1976) he notes that 'a gulf separates these two conceptions of piano playing. The instrument makers have not been deaf to this evolution. You can't play an old Erard and a modern Steinway in the same manner.'

Having dared to say in an earlier number that Fauré was 'a master, but a minor master', Poulenc not surprisingly was rewarded with a number of indignant letters. His reply, in a P.S. to his January article, sets out his current attitude towards that composer:

I recognize that Fauré's output contains passages that are moving, poetical, always technically perfect and worthy of a master (the Quartets, the first act of *Pénélope*, *La bonne chanson* and some other songs), but I do not accord them the same importance as most of the works of Debussy or Ravel. *Pénélope* is not *Pelléas* and in all Fauré's piano music there is not an *Isle joyeuse* or a *Gaspard de la nuit*.

For the November-December number, Poulenc was asked to review his own solo recording of the *Mouvements perpétuels* mentioned above! He neatly evaded any difficulty by describing instead the problems he faced and, for all the occasional untidiness of the result, it's worth quoting him at some length as testimony to his professionalism and his devotion to the quality of sound:

People who have heard me play these three pieces live will be surprised by certain differences of interpretation I have brought to the recorded version. For the two sides of the disc I made more than six attempts, and the mistakes in the first ones led me to introduce various changes. To begin with, I played the pieces as usual, that's to say in a slightly colourless fashion with quite a bit of pedal; result: like a piano inside a bottle. The second time, I played the same pieces very cleanly; you would have said it was a conscientious pupil entirely

82

devoid of talent. After this I tried to play differently each time, being careful to release the pedal at every change of harmony and to soften my attacks. In this way I hope I have achieved a result that is more satisfactory from the point of view of clarity, without being dry.

He finished by noting what every recorded pianist knows only too well: 'The gramophone is a terrible mirror that shows us the slightest blemish. We must learn from its unyielding lessons.'

In the August of 1928 Poulenc had finally finished the *Concert champêtre*. We could well think that, buoyed by this, by the success of another Auric / Poulenc concert on 19 June including the complete *Airs chantés*, and by a commission from the Vicomte and Vicomtesse de Noailles for a danced work of his own devising (which would be the *Aubade*) and forces of his own choosing as well as with a generous fee of 25,000 francs,[76] and if we also judge his mood by the spirit and indeed the wisdom of his record reviews, then altogether he was psychologically in a good place. Not so.

On 21 July he had written what was certainly one of the most extraordinary documents he ever penned. From Nazelles he sends to Raymonde's elder sister Alice a letter 'which will surprise you, I think . . .' The gist of it is that for two years he has been thinking of proposing marriage to Raymonde. For the last six months he has been miserable and now he begs her to intercede for him with Raymonde – after all, 'did you think I had bought a large house just for me?' He does not have the courage to speak to Raymonde directly, but 'I have reached the point where the idea of losing her is intolerable to me, and it is because of the terrible fear of being refused that, until now, I have remained silent – and cowardly, I admit. The truth is that I suffer because I have the impression that her attitude to me has changed a lot for some time now and I don't know why. [. . .] I'm so afraid I'm speaking too late. Japan is a formidable rival.'[77]

By 'Japan' he seems to have meant her studies at the Musée Guimet but, whether he knew it or not, we ourselves can now read the word in a different sense, being aware of the rumour that Raymonde was already in some kind of relationship with a Japanese man. It has to be admitted that much in this whole matter is unclear, and seems likely to remain so. Poulenc explains to Alice that he would leave Raymonde entirely free to pursue her own career with any travelling this might entail, positing a similar liberty for himself. The general opinion within the Poulenc family is that he had in mind a *mariage blanc*. But on the most basic level, we do not even know whether Alice in fact approached her sister on Poulenc's behalf, nor, if she did, what the answer was, though a plain 'no' seems by far the most likely; and the picture would become even more uncertain over the coming months.

We may be certain that during the autumn he attended three first performances of works by his friends. Of Honegger's *Rugby*, given on 19 October, he would say that it was 'an authentic masterpiece',[78] even though its gritty textures were far from his own; he never pronounced in detail about Ravel's *Boléro* other than regarding it as 'a success';[79] but Stravinsky's *Le Baiser de la fée* was an altogether different matter:

> So this *Baiser de la fée*, what a marvel! I'm talking about the music. The décor doesn't matter [. . .] But this music that overwhelms you, or better, that wins you over simply by its sweetness and by this lucid intelligence which is no different from love. It's more than prodigious: it's a prodigy. I'm in no way reluctant to talk about it, indeed I've asked to write about it. I loathe writing about music, but people are bound to write nonsense about this work. Why should we expect our professional critics to appreciate a miracle? The tiger has assumed the voice of a nightingale.[80]

Poulenc's admiration for the work even led him to write quite sharply to his friend Paul Collaer: 'Your opinion of *Le Baiser de la fée* has got me worried because I'm afraid we no longer understand one another. I've played this score again and again and I'm *certain* that it's a *marvel*.'[81] Clearly, of the three works mentioned above, Stravinsky's is by some measure the nearest in tone to what *Aubade* would become, especially in numbers such as the 'Pas de deux' and the 'Adagio' from the third scene.

Music aside, Poulenc was still working through the autumn to make Le Grand Coteau habitable ('My life is more like that of a builder's foreman than a composer's,' he wrote to Sauguet, excusing himself from the premiere of the latter's ballet *David* on 4 December).[82] Otherwise he was trying to keep Maurice Lecanu, the artistic director of Columbia Records in France, up to the mark over his recordings, and succeeding in getting out his two movements from *Les Biches* in December, because 'January is such a terrible month'. And so it proved.

IV
DEPRESSION AND RECOVERY
✦ 1929–1934 ✦

What it was that made that January, and indeed both the first two months of 1929, terrible is not easy to decipher. Quite possibly the arrival of his thirtieth birthday on 7 January had something to do with it. Then of course there was the ongoing question of Raymonde and how she might fit into his future – or not. At all events there is no doubt about the depression itself, documented in Poulenc's letter of around February to Charles de Noailles. In other circumstances, the composer might have kept his low mood to himself but, as it was, the Vicomte, having commissioned a work specifically for his 'Bal des matières' on 19 June, needed to be told the situation:

> I came back to Paris yesterday evening in a state that was pitiful to behold. My liver problems have *such a serious, such a serious* cause that Vichy water doesn't touch them. [. . .] As for my poor *Aubade*, which was begun in happiness, I can't find a way to finish it in tears. I've done and tried everything, but I'm giving up because I don't even know what a ♯ is any more. Whatever you do, don't hold it against me. I'm suffering so much and my sadness is made five times worse because of how it affects you. I'm leaving tomorrow to go and hide away in a distant corner of the Jura, which will *hold no memories* for me, where no one will know who I am and where I'll be able to indulge my tears.[1]

The underlining in the last sentence ('dans un coin du Jura, qui ne me *rappellera rien*') does suggest that he was determined to avoid areas that recalled past times with Raymonde, but again nothing is certain. Whether with the Jura's assistance or not, by March Poulenc's gloom had lifted, though sadly it was very far from being the last depressive episode of his life. In the first letter that is known with the heading 'Le Grand Coteau', he thanks Koechlin for offering to pay back a loan of 2,000 francs, and congratulates him on the publication of the first two volumes of his *Traité de l'harmonie*, assuring his teacher that 'you've planted within me a seed that I am working hard to raise as well as possible.'[2] This sounds more like the Poulenc his friends knew and loved, even if his assurance to Charles de Noailles, 'Don't imagine that I'm forgetting you, quite the opposite',[3] gives reason to suppose that his recovery was fairly recent. What the Vicomte was not told was that Poulenc had not yet started on his commission: indeed the first bars of *Aubade* were not composed until May 1929, at best seven weeks before the Noailles' ball! It could be that his earlier reference to the *Aubade* being 'commencée dans la joie' referred merely to some kind of general outline of the work.

In the meantime, in February Poulenc had happened to see in the street a young man he knew slightly called Richard Chanlaire, a talented painter and amateur violinist. They got talking and Poulenc felt Chanlaire was sympathetic enough to listen to his woes. Shortly afterwards he sent him several phonograph records by way of thanks for his friendship, offered 'at the bottom of his abyss', and invited him to come and listen to Ansermet conducting *Les Noces* on 24 February. Suddenly, and it seems quite unexpectedly, Poulenc found himself in love. Lacombe describes his situation acutely, namely

> the double attachment to Linossier and Chanlaire and the opposition between two outcomes, one heterosexual, the other homosexual. The move from the 'amitié amoureuse' for Raymonde to the 'désir amoureux' for Richard, the terrifying descent into his inner being, the experience of the vanity of things, such as the loss of the person he had been and which he believed he was, these are accompanied by the discovery of another self.[4]

This loss of identity was to have immediate repercussions on the musical front. But at the same time, meeting Chanlaire did at least offer hope, and gave Poulenc a sympathetic ear outside the people most nearly concerned in his relations with Raymonde.

One other event that no doubt helped his mood was the production at the Opéra on 4 March of *L'Éventail de Jeanne*. Poulenc's 'Pastourelle' was much admired, prompting the usual responses: 'fraîcheur', 'délicieuse', 'adorables', 'mignonnes', 'piquant', 'exquis', 'grâce, 'charme', etc.[5] More 'piquant' than 'exquis' was the *Pièce brève* he wrote that month on the letters of the name Albert Roussel as one of eight contributions for an *Hommage* to the composer for his sixtieth birthday, published as a supplement to the *Revue musicale*. Roussel thanked him warmly for this little piece, and promised to play it for himself, if rather more slowly than the 'Très animé' indicated.[6]

The first performance of this piece by Lucie Caffaret on 18 April coincided with the private premiere of the *Concert champêtre* at Saint-Leu, before the public premiere on 3 May. Amid no doubt desperate work on *Aubade*, Poulenc found time to write to Chanlaire enclosing a manuscript of the *Concert champêtre*, telling him 'I offer it to you today because you are the person in the world I cherish the most. You have changed my life, you are the sun of my 30 years, a reason to live and work.'[7] This gift matched that of the manuscript of the same work sent to Raymonde the previous August. But whereas she was, for Poulenc, always 'vous', Richard was already 'tu'.

The impact of his love for Richard can be gauged both through his behaviour and through the music he now had to write for the Noailles commission. Whereas his love for Raymonde had been kept secret even from its object, over Richard he 'came out' unreservedly in letters to friends such as Valentine Hugo and Wanda Landowska. On the musical front, the *Aubade* in a sense takes up emotionally where the *Concert* left off. In the above letter to Richard of 10 May, Poulenc goes on to say 'During long months of loneliness I called to you without knowing you. Thank you for coming at last.' Now that the desired person had arrived, the generalized anguish that had nourished the *Concert* could become particular. If, as seems likely, Poulenc's initial move in this direction was in writing the ballet's scenario, this can only support the notion that until meeting Richard in February, Poulenc had done very little work on *Aubade* of any substance.

As the vehicle for this particularization Poulenc chose the person of Jupiter's daughter Diana. His treatment of her, however, varies considerably from her showing in classical legend, rendered in greatest detail by Callimachus in the third century BC in his *Hymn to Artemis*.[8] In his version, Diana chooses chastity at the age of three! Sitting on Jupiter's knee, she makes this choice together with a host of others, including a bow and arrows like those of her brother Apollo. There is no indication anywhere that, having chosen chastity, she ever even considered renouncing it. We can therefore (one almost says 'must') read Poulenc's scenario as being dictated by his own situation, as described by Lacombe: for the time being at least, one of chronic indecision and the anxiety 'the divided mind' always brings with it.

The scenario, while it has a slightly more definite storyline than *Les Biches*, is nonetheless static rather than dynamic, since it deals entirely with Diana's unhappiness, portrayed in various attitudes. We learn that she is 'on fire with a love that attacks her purity'. She twice leaves her female companions in the glade while she runs off into the wood and then returns, before doing so a third time, accompanying her flight with 'a final gesture of farewell'. As with *Les Biches*, this simple scenario allowed Poulenc the composer free rein. The opening fanfare warns us that this is to be, in the composer's words, 'une oeuvre de poids' – a weighty piece.[9] The fanfare's basic key of A minor is poisoned by dangerous D sharps that will return, most powerfully in the final pages. As well as being weighty, this opening portrays dawn, the time when, as for most depressives, 'my anguish reached its height, for it meant that one had to live through another horrible day'.[10] Then a fiendish piano solo, 'passionate and violent', portrays Diana's torment on another level. From here on wildness alternates with sensuous calm, dissonance with Poulenc's familiar tonal seductions, the whole shot through with quotations from Stravinsky and from himself. The apogee of the moments of calm comes with 'Diana's variations', whose first ten notes on solo clarinet are taken from the 'Larghetto' of the fourth of Mozart's five Divertimentos for two clarinets and bassoon K.439b. But this is soon invaded by unease leading to the 'Allegro feroce' of 'Diana's despair' and ultimately to her final farewell and departure for the wood. A tainted A minor returns, reminiscent of the magical apotheosis of *Apollon musagète* but, for some listeners at least, with none of Stravinsky's calm acceptance. Here Poulenc carries indecision into his own reading of the ending; it signifies either resignation and calm, as he wrote at the time;[11] or, as he said a decade and a half later, continuing anguish through the tension from fig. 54 between the flutes, whose arabesques are in triple time, and the duple metre of the rest of the instruments below them.[12] As Diana flees finally into the forest, we are left wondering why, and what lies in store for her, mirroring the situation of Poulenc himself. Whatever the 'correct' reading of both choreography and score, did Poulenc perhaps have in mind that Diana and Apollo were twins, with her A minor a 'relative' variant of his (that is, Stravinsky's) C major?

Although *Aubade* was generally judged a success, there were one or two dissentient or lukewarm voices. Désormière wrote to Collaer that 'Poulenc's *Aubade* is at least as bad as the *Concerto* [*Concert champêtre*]',[13] while a few years later, still the best Collaer could write to Poulenc was 'I agree it's very prettily orchestrated.'[14] Poulenc himself described the audience at the premiere of the costumed ball as 'a gossiping, frivolous crowd', no doubt encouraged to be so by wearing costumes made of cardboard, paper, cellophane and other unusual 'matières' – all, he added, dreadfully bad for the acoustics.[15] At least Nijinska as choreographer had stuck to his scenario, unlike Balanchine who presented the public premiere of the ballet version on 21 January 1930 as the story of Diana being spied bathing naked by Actaeon. Poulenc accepted this version at the time, but soon came to hate it, since '*Aubade* is a female ballet, about female loneliness. So I absolutely disapprove of any storyline other than my own.'[16]

In July he enjoyed a stay at Fontainebleau with Charles de Noailles's mother, the Princesse de Poix, but then was, like so many in the musical world, shocked to hear of the sudden death of Diaghilev on 19 August. Not that everyone was an admirer: only five days before the impresario's death, Sauguet had complained to Poulenc of how 'that wretched man has been able to sow discord and hatred around him his whole life'.[17] While Poulenc suffered less than some, he had certainly been warned early in 1924 that if he contributed anything to the Comte de Beaumont's *Les Soirées de Paris*, *Les Biches* would not be performed that May in Paris.[18] But in the wake of his demise he could only write to Marie-Laure de Noailles, 'as you may imagine, Diaghilev's death has bowled me over. What a break with the past. Suddenly one feels 80 years old.'[19]

For a full year after the premiere of *Aubade*, he produced no completed work, if we except the single bar (to be repeated *ad lib*) of a whole-tone *Fanfare* for twenty clarinets, ten trumpets and ten trombones to thank Marie-Laure for the silver service she had sent him in gratitude for *Aubade*. He worked on a third Violin Sonata, to no avail, and the fragmentary sketch of a piano waltz is of interest only for the dedication: 'For Raymonde, her score, amid tears because she's going away, and in memory of her *first* stay at Noizay. Tenderly, Francis, 3 November 1929.'[20] This must indicate that whatever cooling there had been in their relationship was now over and, similarly, that if Raymonde had indeed received his plea through Alice, it had occasioned no rancour or reserve. Furthermore, Poulenc's underlining of 'premier' meant that he still had some hopes of her staying many more times, even if not as a wife or permanent companion. A busy December included him as pianist in the first concert performance of *Aubade*, conducted by Ansermet, on the 1st, and two concerts celebrating the tenth anniversary of Les Six on the 11th and 18th, with other concerts on the 10th, the 14th and the 21st.

Then, on 30 January ('the terrible month'), came the news that Raymonde had died of peritonitis.

Writing the next day to her sister Alice, Poulenc explains that he had not come to see her body, wanting to keep 'intact the memory of her eyes and her voice [. . .] I should like her, to whom I always gave the least bad of myself, to take a little of me away with her. Rather than burning the manuscript of *Les Biches* which is hers, I beg you to place it in her hands, since it is the whole of my youth that departs with her, the whole of that period of my life which *belongs to her alone*. I sob, thinking of Monte-Carlo. I am now twenty years older.'[21] Whether or not Poulenc kept a copy of the original score we do not know, since neither that score nor the parts from it were ever published, but only the vocal score: so it seems more than likely that he had only this to work from when he re-orchestrated the ballet in 1939–40.

Shocked and desolate, for the whole of February Poulenc went to ground. His only information about Raymonde's death was, as stated above, that she died of peritonitis, and he never lived to hear the rumour within her family that she in fact died of a botched abortion, the baby's father presumably being the Japanese man whom she was seeing. Her family's long silence on the subject might have reflected not only the disgrace of her pregnancy outside marriage, but also the fact that in 1930 abortion in France was illegal. Whatever the truth of this, for Poulenc her death remained 'the irremediable departure of a face I have never replaced and of a beautiful, wakeful intelligence that I shall miss for ever.'[22]

The next sign of life is a letter from Poulenc to Falla announcing his forthcoming visit to Spain and asking him to recommend an oboist and a bassoonist for his Trio, as well as a pianist to play the orchestral part in the *Concert champêtre*. Starting in Madrid and going on to Barcelona, Bilbao and Málaga, he was to give a series of 'conference-concerts', employing for the first time his skill as a raconteur.[23] However, this accompanied another plan, to stay in Granada (that is, near Falla), for five weeks from 12 April in order to compose – only after Easter, on 20 April, was he to be joined by Richard Chanlaire (two bedrooms required for renting). He planned to return to Paris only on 20 May.[24] If he did any composing, there seems to be nothing to show for it, and we may surmise that, like his earlier quest for a distant corner of the Jura, the conference-concerts gave him an excuse to leave Paris, where memories of Raymonde would bring too much pain. He and two colleagues wrote a postcard to Ravel saying 'Madrid talks of nothing but your Bolero, which everyone admires!!',[25] otherwise he was happy to do some networking, his letters to Marie-Laure mentioning at least one comtesse, one duchesse and an ambassadeur. He was staying in an English *pension*, though there is no mention of Richard. It did have a piano and he says, on 1 May, 'je *vais* travailler' (author's italics). Among the possible subjects may have been sketches for the piano suite *Les Soirées de Nazelles*, which certainly date from some point in 1930, but to which he would devote serious attention only six years later.

After a couple of concerts back in Paris, he went on further travels to stay with the Noailles and Polignacs, then with his sister in Normandy. He also made an emotional visit to Burgundy: 'My old nanny is dying,' he had written a year earlier to Marie-Blanche de Polignac. 'It is absolutely a duty for me to go there because she stayed with me for 15 years until I was a big boy. Alas, where is that time long ago when she used to stuff me with sweets . . .'[26] Regrets for past years also continued to dog him through memories of Raymonde: 'I try to work in memory of her, but I'm physically very much beaten down and can't produce anything that's any good,' he wrote to Alice during the summer.[27]

However, in July mourning did inspire a single song, the first he had written for two years. Of *Épitaphe*, on a poem by François de Malherbe, Poulenc later wrote, 'While I was composing it, I thought of Louis XIII architecture. It's to be sung "without grandiloquence" [sans emphase], because grandiloquence was the ultimate bugbear of Raymonde Linossier in whose memory I composed these two pages.'[28] The song was meant to be included in a small volume honouring Raymonde, but this was never published. Marked 'calmement', the song is pitched low in the baritone range and includes some of the murkiest textures to be found in Poulenc's vocal output, with little in the way of incidental colouring. But it is enough that in the final one of the last two lines, 'But at least you see in the cinders/ That I still love the fire', he abandons quaver movement for seven even crotchets to suggest acceptance; it is for the piano then to add two bars that turn this acceptance into doubt.

Meanwhile Poulenc was still labouring on the *Marches militaires*, as well as beginning two pianistic projects that would finally reach completion later in the decade: the set of eight *Nocturnes* and the suite *Soirées de Nazelles* (to be considered in due course). Work on Le Grand Coteau continued ('the surveyor is coming tomorrow to raise the level of the terrace'),[29] but a further concern was that the aftershocks of the Wall Street Crash of 1929 were beginning to tell on French banks. As yet these were not serious enough to cause Poulenc grave concern, but money was continuing to flow out on renovations to Le Grand Coteau ('beautifying Noizay is ruining my finances, worse than if I were supporting Josephine Baker')[30] and he had to give them some thought. Years later, his friend Stéphane Audel gave an idea of the house's ambience: 'The organization of the interior revealed the proprietor's infallible taste. There was not a piece of furniture, a painting or a decorative object that had not been chosen with care and placed in such a way that you immediately had an impression of perfection. The library, full of books of art in rare editions, was matched by his record collection, whose variety demonstrated Poulenc's eclecticism. The large studio, in which an upright and a grand piano stood side by side and loaded with photographs of his friends, boasted a large fireplace. In the evenings, logs flared and crackled there joyfully.'[31]

Later in the decade he would boost his bank balance by writing light pieces for piano, but in 1931 he opted for twelve songs, supposedly by three authors: Louise Lalanne, Guillaume Apollinaire and Max Jacob. These last two might be seen as participating in the 'nostalgia syndrome' provoked by the deaths of Diaghilev and Raymonde, taking Poulenc back to the time when he had shared these authors with her in Adrienne Monnier's bookshop.

In fact all three authors shared this privilege, since Louise Lalanne did not exist, being an amalgam of Apollinaire and his mistress Marie Laurencin – part of a prank of 1909 into which Apollinaire had entered wholeheartedly. In the review *Les Marges* 'under the name of Louise Lalanne he supplied coy articles on lady poets, wrote "feminine" poems of his own, and threw in a few by Marie Laurencin. To halt the hoax a year later, the review announced that Mlle Lalanne had been abducted by an army officer, and finally revealed her true identity.'[32] Of the *Trois Poèmes de Louise Lalanne*, Apollinaire was the author of the middle one, 'Chanson', she supposedly of the outer two, 'Le présent' and 'Hier'.[33] According to Pierre Bernac, the Apollinaire poem, the first by him that Poulenc had set since *Le Bestiaire* over a decade earlier, is pure nonsense and no attempt should be made to instil any sort of meaning into it.[34] 'Le présent' clearly echoes Verlaine's 'Voici les fruits', set by Debussy and Fauré, in which the most valuable present is the poet's heart. But Poulenc's setting turns rather, by his own admission, to the implacable octave writing in the finale of Chopin's B flat minor sonata.[35] The tempo markings of the two songs are respectively 'Follement vite' and 'Presto possible', and they mark the beginning of a series of whirlwind songs in which necessarily the listener can appreciate an overall mood rather than intricate detail. By the time we reach the slower third song we are more than ready to be seduced by its beauty, mingling, as so often with Poulenc, sound with sight: the melodic clarity of the popular singer Yvonne Printemps with an interior as painted by Vuillard.[36]

Having made contact again with the poet, Poulenc was reluctant to let him go, and in that same February began the set of *Quatre Poèmes de Guillaume Apollinaire* which he completed the following month. Bernac tells us that Poulenc was always particularly fond of these songs[37] and it's not hard to hear why. Poulenc himself admitted a predilection for 'L'anguille', with its 'atmosphere of a seedy hotel, punctuated by the little patter of felt slippers'.[38] Bernac goes on to warn that, for all the popular, suburban tone of both poem and song, at all costs the singer must avoid vulgarity: 'no one managed better than Poulenc to convey the dark poetry of a certain kind of sordid Parisian atmosphere. It is this poetry that one has to try and recreate.' For those singers not born in Paris this is undoubtedly easier said than done: Bernac's concrete suggestions are that on certain words the accent may be placed unusually on the first syllable: 'gentille', 'chichi', 'Dimanche', and that slides are useful at certain points. Among Poulenc's own indications, pride of place must go to the demand, made six times during the set in varied phraseology, to maintain a steady pulse – only over the last two bars of 'Carte-postale' is a slight rallentando permitted. Elsewhere the indications 'sans nuances' and, for the piano at the start of 'L'anguille', 'sans pédale, très sec et ponctué', are emblems of that distaste for the 'emphase' that Raymonde hated so much (pianists should note Poulenc's fingering on the first two bars, testimony to his complete professionalism, allowing a dry accompaniment under 'le chant lié').

Such details aside, the most extraordinary feature of these songs is the way they catch 'la voix de Guillaume', as far as one can judge just from the poetry. To take one example, in 'Avant le cinéma' the word painting of the 'vieux professeurs de province' through a dry delivery against legato phrasing in the right hand catches both the crotchety nature of these gentlemen and the extent to which they are out of touch with the sweep of the modern world. Throughout, the music is energized, not least by jumps between one key and another, until the sharp emotional sting of the final, heart-rending, untranslatable line – 'Que ne t'avais-je entre mes bras' – where the 'amoroso' injunction to the singer has to fight against the piano harmonies. Calm resignation or continuing anguish? As in *Aubade*, no easy answer comes to mind.

After a Poulenc festival in Strasbourg on 9 February, on the 24th Poulenc was in Paris for the first French performance of Stravinsky's *Symphony of Psalms*, conducted by the composer (as Poulenc no longer had his own flat in the city, he used to stay with his friend Georges Salles at 24 rue du Chevalier de La Barre in the 18th arrondissement). Since an article by him on the symphony appeared in the February number of the new journal *Le Mois*, he must have had prior knowledge of it, either through reading the vocal score or through attending the world premiere in Brussels on 13 December, or indeed both. He places it 'very high on the long list of masterpieces stretching from *The Firebird* to *Capriccio*'[39] and once more follows Raymonde's lead in praising the absence of grandiloquence. On 2 April he sent a copy of his article to Stravinsky as 'a small testimony of my admiration and affection'[40] and had a reply a few days later thanking him and making the friendly and surely insightful remark, 'You are truly good and that is what I always find again and again in your music.'[41] Although Poulenc would admire the orchestration of *Jeu de cartes* and defended Stravinsky stoutly when he was attacked by André Jolivet and others just after the war, it seems no other Stravinsky work after the *Symphony of Psalms* fed into his own music in the way of *Mavra* or *Apollon musagète*, among others. Maybe this signalled maturity, or maybe he simply felt this influence had become dangerous? His article states the undeniable truth that 'there is no example of a Stravinsky work not spawning an infinite number of copies while *he* is already a long way along another path'. Certainly Poulenc had no intention of belonging to any herd.

Depression struck again during the spring of 1931, this time provoked by losing a considerable sum of money in a bank failure, in which of course he was far from being alone. As a result he even had to consider the possibility of selling Le Grand Coteau, after all the effort he had put into restoring it. But through the gloom he joined many millions of other visitors to the Exposition coloniale that opened on 6 May in the Bois de Vincennes, a visit that would have repercussions the following year. He also continued planning an all-Poulenc concert for 1 June, later postponed to the 19th, which included first performances of the seven Apollinaire songs mentioned above and a first version of the Sextet for piano and wind instruments, which does not survive. A project for a film with the music-hall singer Damia came to nothing, and in July Poulenc was still in low spirits.

But he went on working. That same July saw the beginning of the *Cinq Poèmes de Max Jacob* and the first mention in Poulenc's correspondence of the name Éluard, even though this would not inspire any music until 1935. Then, in August, a means of deliverance from his financial anxieties appeared in the form of a commission from the Princesse de Polignac for 'a piano work, on the lines of the Landowska Concerto, if possible arranged for 3 pianos: a solo one and two as accompaniment'.[42] It seems probable that this did not come entirely out of the blue, since an earlier letter from Poulenc to her niece, the Comtesse Charles de Polignac, makes clear that he had been laying out to the Comtesse his desperate financial situation and expresses his gratitude for the commission. At the same time he pleads with her, 'Please be good enough not to keep me waiting too long for a reply, whatever it may be, so that I can know how to proceed.'[43]

Whatever the exact sequence of events, Poulenc had already decided by mid-September that it would become the Concerto for two pianos, and by the following month had decided the key of D minor and the make-up of the orchestra,[44] although in the event the size of this grew considerably. Nor did the aristocratic network end its favours there: in November the Noailles commissioned a work (in the event *Le Bal masqué*) for the 'spectacle-concert' to be given on 20 April 1932 at the theatre (newly restored for the occasion) in Hyères, just east of Toulon, where they had a country house.

After the débâcle of the *Quatre Poèmes de Max Jacob* in 1921, it could well be that Poulenc, ever faithful to his friends, felt he owed Jacob another attempt. It could also be that tackling surrealist poetry was a way of distancing himself from Stravinsky, for whom the movement had never been a major interest. So on the compositional front the second half of 1931 was largely devoted to another group of songs that became the *Cinq Poèmes*. They were taken from Jacob's collection *Chants bretons signés Morven le Gaëlique*, which recalled the poet's birth and childhood in Quimper. Whether or not deliberately in a parallel revisiting of his own childhood and adolescence, Poulenc wrote some of the cycle during two months spent in his grandparents' house in Nogent, even though it was now stripped of most of its furniture, and was able to indulge in his ancient delights of fortune-tellers, fried potatoes and Pernod. The poems don't entirely conform to the judgement of Henri Fabureau that in Jacob 'His enthusiasm is defeated by irony. With sombre delight he tortures his poetic soul with parody and burlesque caprice. So that in the end poetry becomes for him an actual laboratory experience.'[45] Irony there is, but no defeat of the poet's *joie de vivre*. Poulenc's own torturing never strays outside what is easily comprehensible, though as Bernac says, 'vocal difficulties are not lacking: in tessitura, leaps and rhythms which must be victoriously overcome'.[46]

In 'Chanson bretonne' the young girl has lost her hen and her cat, and her urgency to find them is 'described' by the incessant quaver movement. Poulenc's term 'descriptive' in relation to the whole cycle[47] needs to be taken with a slight pinch of salt, since much of the poem defies any such thing – though in this first song high trills certainly 'describe' the birds' twittering. At the same time their arrival produces a sudden change in atmosphere, becoming 'poetic and unreal' with the singer adopting a 'very white voice', as the girl moves from reality to memory. 'Cimetière' follows a similar pattern, with memory taking over on the final page, the voice 'très doux' and its running triplets momentarily solidifying nostalgically into duplets on 'quand nous jouions sur le quai'.

The final quiescence in 'La petite servante' serves a different purpose. Until then, the servant girl's fears have been reasonable, while the piano is wild and frantic in Poulenc's familiar manner and, at the mention of scabs and pimples, harmonically at total variance with the voice. But when she asks, in Jacob's ironical manner, for a husband who doesn't get drunk or beat her too often, Poulenc responds with his own brand of irony, turning on his most lush, seductive harmonies. In 'Berceuse' his choice of a waltz could be 'descriptive', since the grumpy babysitter tells us that the baby's mother is 'au cabaret', which could be either a tavern or a night club, but the mismatch between title and content persists. Again the song ends with the singer dreaming, 'mélancolique, subito dolce', of how, if the baby died, she could be on the beach catching crabs – and the last dissonant chord (Poulenc's favourite dominant 13th) says 'if only' . . . In the final 'Souric et Mouric', the change of tone comes earlier, with the injunction to the tree-frogs to sing, at which Poulenc turns finally to his most easy-going, tuneful style, all but four of the last twenty-six bars being firmly in F major. In the first four songs, the persistent four-bar phrases speak of childhood ditties, while in the last one the return to four-bar phrases coincides with (helps produce?) the change in tone.

The death of Vincent d'Indy on 2 December left no discernible trace on Poulenc's life. The only points of interest in that month were the first concert of a new concert society, *La Sérénade*, on the 1st and a very informative letter from him to Marie-Laure on the 12th. The foundation of the society is described by Henri Sauguet:

> The marquise de Casa Fuerte, Yvonne Giraud, who had been a fellow pupil of Milhaud at the Conservatoire where she studied the violin (she won a first prize, she was a virtuoso performer), came to live with us in the hôtel Nollet. She had the splendid idea of forming a concert society which would play our music and that of contemporary composers of all tendencies, given that she thought their compositions to be of value.[48]

The committee comprised the marquise, Auric, Désormière, Igor Markévitch, Milhaud, Nicolas Nabokov, Poulenc, Rieti and Sauguet – and for the twenty-two concerts the society put on between December 1931 and June 1939 these composers provided a number of the works performed: Milhaud 11, Poulenc 9, Sauguet 7, Rieti 5 and Markévitch 3. The historian Michel Duchesneau comments that 'the Society's concerts constituted a kind of general, public "salon" that ensured visibility on a grand scale for a certain group of the Parisian aristocracy, while satisfying aspirations that were in clear contradiction with social currents in France at the time'.[49] It was of course the case that in 1931 France was only five years away from the rise to power of the left-wing Front National. But it was also the case that the French aristocracy, like aristocracies through the ages, held much of their wealth in the form of land and so were less seriously affected by the Wall Street Crash than those who relied on the money markets. Given that the French government would not normally commission new music until the Exposition of 1937 (Berlioz's *Requiem* and *Grande symphonie funèbre et triomphale* a century earlier had been almost the exceptions that proved the rule), it could be argued that the aristocracy were taking on a social duty that no other group either would or could fulfil, least of all in 1931 which marked the peak of the financial crisis in France. As for the repertoire, music by members of the committee was well seasoned by interesting works from other hands: in 1932 alone, Satie's *Le Piège de Méduse*, Stravinsky's Octet, and on 11 December Weill's *Mahagonny* and *Der Jasager* as well as Falla's Harpsichord Concerto. Marie-Laure funded the two Weill works, for which the original German performers were invited, including Lotte Lenya and the conductor Maurice Abravanel.[50]

The letter of 12 December to Marie-Laure shows that the final plan of *Le Bal masqué* was already decided and that Poulenc was about to start composing 'Madame la dauphine'; also that the work was 'an invaluable diversion from a black mood that I chase off as best I can using flats and sharps', the mood being dictated by his continuing fear of having to sell Le Grand Coteau, despite commissions – 'not a word to anyone,' he warns. At the same time he was working on the Concerto for the Princesse de Polignac (alias Tante W – Aunt Winnie), the first movement of which is 'very Balinese' (which the ending indeed is),[51] and we may note that it was surrealism rather than Far Eastern exoticism that was effective against the 'black dog'. When 'too much reality' impinges, perhaps surrealism offers relief? Further relief may well have been had by playing the solo part in the first known private performance, also at Tante W's, of Lucien Garban's two-piano arrangement of Ravel's G major Concerto with Février playing the orchestral part.[52]

The New Year of 1932 brought two wonderfully gossipy Poulenc letters that tell us, in case we needed telling, what a marvellous companion he could be once the black dog had departed. To Auric's wife Nora: Milhaud's opera *Maximilien* at the Opéra a total dud with 'unvaried declamation and prosody out of the textbook'; then supper at the Café de Paris talking about everything except the music; then at 2 a.m. Sauguet 'dances a fantastic ballet on the Opéra steps, scarves flying, leaving a dozen onlookers banjaxed'. The following Thursday he's in Paris again for the premiere of Ravel's G major Concerto – 'stuffed with music and with the verve of a composer of 30 [. . .] Filthy weather here but the tulips are out which is a good sign.'[53] To Marie-Laure: in Satie's *Le Piège de Méduse*, 'Baron Méduse will be wearing the waistcoat my grandfather had for my sister's wedding'; 'the pious ladies who make their confessions at 5 a.m. in the church of St Augustin come out of the church in disarray thanks to the organist practising Milhaud's Organ Sonata'; '*Le Bal masqué* progresses [. . .] Georges Salles's servants turn up in the morning singing the bit of the Finale I'm sending you.'[54]

At a Sérénade concert on 22 February 1932 Poulenc accompanied Suzanne Peignot and Roger Bourdin in the *Trois Poèmes de Louise Lalanne* and the *Quatre Poèmes de Guillaume Apollinaire* respectively, and letters to Falla and Collaer both point to 'Souric et Mouric' as one of Poulenc's favourites among his songs.[55] The autograph of *Le Bal masqué* sports the information 'Noizay Février 1932 Cannes le 10 avril 1932', but, as already mentioned, sketches date back at least to December 1931. The terminal date, though, of just ten days before the premiere, seems to indicate that here, as with *Aubade*, Poulenc was daring to let necessity be the mother of invention.

For that premiere Poulenc, of course, played the taxing piano part, Désormière conducted, the costumes were by Christian Bérard, the producer was Diaghilev's ex-secretary Boris Kochno and the solo baritone was Gilbert Moryn, described by Poulenc as 'singing wonderfully and being amazingly reasonable' (no doubt over his fee – a quality close to the composer's heart in his financial travails).[56] Remembering the occasion over thirty years later in his interviews with Claude Rostand, Poulenc described Moryn as singing with 'marvellous earthiness' and gave a vivid description of the work's atmosphere:

For me, *Le Bal masqué* is a sort of Nogentais carnival with the portraits of various odd characters I saw during my childhood on the banks of the Marne. Max Jacob's 'Blind Lady', for example, who gets drunk with her young brother-in-law, I knew her. In 1910, her double used to live in a little Swiss chalet, in the style of [the cartoonist and illustrator Albert] Dubout on the Ile de Beauté in Nogent. In a spangled silk dress, she spent her days in her garden playing *belote* [a popular card game] with her so-called husband who, beneath his Panama hat, looked like [the serial murderer] Landru.

Poulenc was also quite clear as to his intentions. 'I'd already written *Aubade* for these patrons. The first time, I'd tried to move them; this time, I fully intended to entertain them'.[57] Not the least ingredient in this entertainment came from the mismatch between the posh and intellectual clientele, including aristos, musicians, surrealists and communists, and the low life so vividly resurrected in the music and in the words, from Jacob's collection *Le Laboratoire central* of 1921. Poulenc was proud of what he had achieved in this respect:

> It's the only one of my works in which I think I found a way of heightening a suburban atmosphere which I cherish. This is thanks to Max's words, full of unexpected links, and to the instrumental ensemble I've used. Here *colour* underlines the bombastic [emphatique], the ridiculous, the piteous, the terrifying. It's the atmosphere of the colour prints in the *Petit Parisien* of the Sundays of my childhood. 'Ow 'orrible!' my grandmother's cook used to exclaim in those days, '*anuvver* bloke wot's done in 'is sister-in-law.'[58]

The entertainment, then, has a sinister undertow and to help bring this out Poulenc makes two further points: 'The rhythms, slow or brisk, are *implacable*. At the end of *Le Bal masqué*, which lasts 20 minutes, the public should be stupefied and exhilarated like people who get off a merry-go-round at the Foire du Trône [a Paris funfair]'; and in a further endorsement of Moryn, 'He would not have sung Scarpia with more conviction and more seriousness.'[59] The 'double' nature of the work resides also in the dichotomy between the folky tunes, as so often using parts of scales (initially at fig. 1: up and down the first three notes of G major), and harmonizations which are deliberately crude and dissonant. But, thanks to the rhythmic brio and fast tempi with which these are delivered, they register as no more than local colour, causing no puzzlement even to the most naive ear. Colour is also the predominant feature of Poulenc's orchestration as he juggles adroitly with his eight players, including a percussionist in charge of twelve instruments. No single combination is allowed to dominate for long and the changes of tone are, in best surrealist fashion, abrupt (see *implacable* rhythms above). At the furthest point from the work's often manic energy is the outburst at fig. 37, *très expressif* in the traditionally warm key of D flat major, on the words 'Malvina oh Fantôme, que Dieu te garde!', in the manner of a prayer from nineteenth-century French opera. But again, after six bars we're back to manic energy. As Lacombe says, '*Le Bal masqué* achieves an astonishing equilibrium between the trivial and the poetic.'[60]

After the premiere on 20 April, the work was given again in the Noailles's Paris house on 9 June and then, in the first public performance, as part of La Sérénade's fourth concert in the Salle Chopin Pleyel four days later, where it was accompanied by the other commissions for Hyères by Sauguet, Auric, Markévitch and Nabokov. Poulenc was able to report to André Latarjet that it 'made a fairly lively impact in Paris during the spring',[61] and it was always a work he particularly treasured, claiming 'I'm sure no one who belittles it can truly like my music. It's a hundred per cent Poulenc'.[62]

By now the *Marches militaires* had joined various violin sonatas in an eternal limbo, the last known mention of the *Marches* being in a letter to Marie-Laure of 27 October 1930, while the first version of the *Sextuor* for piano and wind was already undergoing changes, Poulenc telling Sauguet in September 1932 'in ten days I'm going to finish the Sextet'.[63] The final revisions were made in August 1939.

In mid-May, with Le Grand Coteau apparently reprieved, it was the venue for a Whitsun weekend party including Rieti and Sauguet, and Prokofiev and Auric and their wives. Bridge seems to have played a role. This would also seem to have been the weekend Poulenc remembered with some sadness thirty years later (with slightly later dates) as the last in a long series of Parisian bridge evenings with Prokofiev through 1931 and 1932. This time the meeting extended almost to a whole week, in which the two of them also rehearsed together (on two pianos?) in the Salle Gaveau. Poulenc then saw Prokofiev on to his bus, said 'Write!' . . . and never saw or heard from the Russian again.[64]

But throughout the summer Poulenc kept his head down over the manuscript paper: the Two-Piano Concerto commissioned by Winnie was to be premiered in Venice on 5 September at the International Music Festival and delivery could on no account be delayed. In the event the work was completed in just two and a half months, with help from Poulenc's niece Brigitte Manceaux, 'rehearsing certain passages a thousand times'.[65] As already mentioned, there seems to have been no correlation for Poulenc between time spent composing and the value of the result. As already seen, both *Aubade* and *Le Bal masqué* were similarly written quite quickly, though not as fast as this Concerto; but one cannot say that works which took much longer to write – *Dialogues des Carmélites* is the obvious example, and the song 'Montparnasse' another – necessarily suffered from the fact. More to the point was the strength of the impulse to compose. Poulenc frequently claimed that whatever virtues his songs might have, they derived from his love for the poems rather than from any kind of ratiocination. So with this Concerto, the commission for which 'enchanted' him.[66] Another inducement was that he was to perform the work with his close friend Jacques Février. As a pupil of Marguerite Long, whose mantra was 'Les doigts! Les doigts!', he might seem a curious partner for Poulenc's own kind of expansive, extensively pedalled pianism, but Février had, with Viñes's help, gone some way beyond her influence and the two men were now a perfect match, honed by years of playing duets together. The conductor Manuel Rosenthal said that from the point of view of sonority he had three favourite French pianists, Jean Wiéner, Poulenc and Février, because their tone was 'moelleux': not just mellow and velvety, but with a warm centre inside the brilliant surfaces – marrow in the bone.[67]

Février came to Noizay for play-throughs, then the two left on 30 August for Venice, stopping off at Milan to rehearse with the La Scala orchestra that would be playing with them in Venice, and including a visit to Lake Como. In Venice they stayed at the Palazzo Polignac on the Grand Canal, where Fauré had been inspired to write his *Cinq Mélodies de Venise* some forty years earlier, and where they now found Falla and Arthur Rubinstein. But, if anything, the grandeur of their apartment was overshadowed by the quality of the rehearsals and of the performance itself. 'Venice has been,' he wrote to Nora Auric, 'I must confess immodestly, a triumph. [. . .] I'm very happy with the new Concerto which sounds stunning. It's true that Toscanini's orchestra performed it in a way to render all other performances feeble. [. . .] The violins are heavenly in the upper register, the clarinets seductive, the oboes gentle and gay. It's marvellous!!! Jacques played with me perfectly and apparently we performed very well. Anyway we're heavily booked for the winter.' By 'winter' he meant 'from January onwards', when performances were already in hand in 'London, Berlin, Prague, Marseilles, then Italy again, and probably Madrid and Barcelona'.[68]

In choosing to write for two pianos and orchestra Poulenc was fully aware that in the past examples had been confined to those by Mozart and Mendelssohn. Intriguingly, in his 1954 interviews with Claude Rostand he said, 'Now, there are plenty',[69] but without specifying any that might have influenced him twenty years earlier (a brief search suggests Villa-Lobos's *Chôros 8*, published in 1928, as the only possibility, but there is no evidence of Poulenc engaging with this composer in any way). Two possible models that he did admire at the time were the two Ravel solo piano concertos, both premiered in Paris in January 1932: the G major 'Marvellously entertaining', the D major 'without question one of the high points of his art'.[70] Renaud Machart proffers an interesting comparison between the concertos of the two composers:

In the various areas of vocal composition Poulenc displays an innate sense of dramatic construction. In the concertos it is perhaps the very opposite of this that makes them interesting; in them he develops what could be called an 'aesthetic of discontinuity'. Against the Brahmsian post-romantic concerto in which the overall arch is dominant, the opposite is the 'fantaisie' (in the strictly musical sense of the term), a genre employed by Ravel in his two piano concertos [. . .] Poulenc, who is so fond of 'verbal kaleidoscopes' in the texts that he sets, employs in his Two-Piano Concerto a kaleidoscope of musical ideas.

Although Machart categorizes the first movement as tripartite, he admits there are a number of divergences from this generalized form, not least in the appearance of a new theme where the recapitulation usually was (fig. 18).[71] Overall, perhaps Poulenc's most impressive technical feat was to impose unity of tone onto the myriad disparate elements, beginning with the pseudo-Bach enlivened and interrupted by extravagant leaps and wildly dissonant scrunches. At the other extreme are the contemplative gamelan sounds at the end of this first movement, recalling the Balinese music Poulenc had heard at the Exposition coloniale – the only truly exotic music to be found throughout his whole oeuvre, and a passage he counted as 'one of my most complete successes'.[72] Even here, though, the exoticism is mixed with a quotation from the beginning of the slow movement of Ravel's G major Concerto, itself borrowed from the Marguerite movement of Liszt's *Faust Symphony*!

The slow movement might have been entitled 'Souvenirs de Mozart', since there are at least two direct quotations from his piano concertos: the opening theme from the slow movement of K.537, the Coronation Concerto, and the passage at fig. 33 from the slow movement of K.467.[73] Around these, Poulenc appears wearing a powdered wig, and often awry. Neo-classicism here does duty for a nice piece of social flattery, since the Princesse de Polignac's money came from a decidedly post-eighteenth-century source, she being the heiress of the Singer sewing-machine family. The hectic finale recalls the high jinks of *Le Bal masqué*, complete with almost a superfluity of tunes that would not disgrace a café-concert, a brief, decidedly uncontemplative return to Bali, and a final couple of bars which deliberately flirt with the 'artificial pathetic' that Poulenc so passionately loathed.

The Concerto remains one of Poulenc's best-loved and most often played works. In a letter to Paul Collaer he wondered whether his desire for perfection had perhaps drawn him away from his true musical nature, but in general his judgement, spiced with a dig at the critic Henry Prunières who had never been one of his greatest fans, and ending with a naughty touch of 'emphase', is surely just:

> I must confess to you immodestly that it really knocked the festival audience sideways. Even poor Pruneton in this week's *Les Nouvelles littéraires* has been obliged to agree it had 'a triumphant reception'. You will see that it's an enormous advance over my earlier works, and that I am truly entering my great period.[74]

Concert champêtre, *Aubade*, *Le Bal masqué*, Two-Piano Concerto: altogether something under one and a half hour's music in just over five years. For some of Poulenc's contemporaries, such as Koechlin or Milhaud, this might amount almost to idleness. But two factors need to be taken into account. Firstly, all the works were commissioned, the last three having to be delivered for a fixed occasion. And secondly, and more importantly, all four broke absolutely new ground in one way or another. We might wish to add a third point, namely that all four are still in the mainstream repertory nearly ninety years later.

The orchestral polish and hummable tunes that feature in so much of Poulenc's music led several critics of the time to assume that for him composing was a feet-up, Vouvray-in-hand activity – an unthinking echo of the *fils à papa* syndrome first mooted by Satie a decade earlier. When he told Marie-Laure in August 1932 that he was '*fou* de travail' after a month of 'labeur formidable', he was barely exaggerating.[75] We may speculate that a Conservatoire training in his teens might have given him a technique that could have speeded up the composing process; but equally such a concentrated exposure to tradition might also have blunted his individuality. After the serious intellectual labour of writing, composers often need time to wind down by writing less demanding pieces,[76] and history shows that in general such spin-offs may to some extent bear the imprint of their weightier predecessors.

Poulenc would receive no more major commissions until the one for the cantata *Sécheresses* in 1937. Until then, writing for himself, he kept to short piano pieces and vocal music and the occasional piece of incidental music for the theatre. The *Valse-improvisation sur le nom de Bach*, commissioned by the *Revue musicale* and dashed off at Le Grand Coteau on 8 October 1932 and lasting just over a minute, is dedicated to Horowitz and perfectly designed for his brand of fireworks. Poulenc is not tied too closely to B-A-C-H and Jean Roy writes of the piece causing something of a scandal; certainly it sounds odd against its companion pieces by Roussel, Casella, Malipiero and Honegger, and Roy is surely near the mark when he says that 'asking [Poulenc] to write a homage to J.S. Bach was a fairly preposterous idea'.[77]

Whether or not the idea of a set of improvisations followed on from the above, what would eventually be the collection of fifteen *Improvisations* was among the few of his piano works for which Poulenc always retained considerable affection, recording four of them (nos. 2, 5, 9 and 10) for Columbia in 1934. He wrote the first six at Noizay during 1932 before, mysteriously, giving the first performance of *seven* Improvisations at the sixth La Sérénade concert on 4 February 1933 – but the seventh one in the set was not written until October or November of that year. Although nos. 1, 3 and 4 are marked 'Presto' and no. 6 'A toute vitesse', the melodist in Poulenc wins out. There are indeed some echoes of things past: in no. 1 the alternation of the two hands, *très sec*, recalls the opening of the Two-Piano Concerto which Poulenc attributed to the example of Alfredo Casella[78] and, in no. 2, bar 14 onwards looks back to the bareness of Stravinsky's *Symphonies of Wind Instruments*. But the modulatory sleight of hand is Poulenc's own, as is his determination not to outstay his welcome by a single bar: nearly all the fifteen pieces except the last lie between 1 ½ and 2 ½ minutes. No better idea can be given of La Sérénade's catholic taste than the conjunction on 4 February of these six (or seven?) pieces with Schubert's C major Quintet and, ending the concert immediately after the Poulenc, Berg's *Lyric Suite*.

In November 1932 Poulenc wrote to Marie-Blanche to apologize for not finishing his revisions to the Sextet, which he judged would not manage to find a publisher. His financial state was not improved by an unlooked-for difficulty: 'Would you believe that at the moment nobody wants this summer's Concerto, despite the press and the success! I know perfectly well that one should work for the love of art, but even so there are times when one also has think of coal and cutlets. So as I stand on the brink of a winter without commissions, I'll have to "write for the piano" what these "gentlemen-publishers" want.'[79] Given that the immediate result was the first set of *Improvisations*, it's hard to cast too many stones in that direction. But it brings home the reason for Poulenc's five-year gap in commissions: through the mid-1930s money in France was tight, and when Poulenc's dearth was finally ended in 1937, it would be thanks to an English millionaire.

The first two months of 1933 found Poulenc in concert: 12 January in Strasbourg playing in his Trio; then back in Paris for the 16th and *Le Bal masqué*, then on the 23rd a private performance for the Princesse de Polignac of the Concerto with Février, given again in London on 1 February with Thomas Beecham conducting; in February playing seven *Improvisations* at La Sérénade on the 4th (as mentioned above) and on the 12th in Lyon for another performance of the Concerto, this time with Ennemond Trillat, a piano professor at the Lyon Conservatoire.

In the meantime the occasional opportunity came his way to write incidental music for the theatre, first of all for a play called *Intermezzo* by Jean Giraudoux. Because the author wanted unusual instruments used, Poulenc thought of the harpsichord, to which he then added oboe, clarinet, trumpet and trombone to give the impression of a wind band from the Limousin region. These four wind instruments would be heard only in the third and final act, Poulenc improvising on the harpsichord during the first two.[80] The play, directed by Louis Jouvet, was premiered on 1 March 1933 to general acclaim, but only three pages of musical sketches survive. We have to guess at what Tony Aubin meant in suggesting that Poulenc 'could be introducing a new and curious kind of incidental music'.[81] We know that when the play was revived in New York on 18 January 1950, Poulenc fell in with the director's request and 'improvised with a bad grace' some ten minutes of music.[82] In the following months of 1933 he contributed music to two other plays, Jules Romains's *Monsieur le Trouhadec saisi par la débauche* and Marcel Achard's *Pétrus*, both scores now being lost. He also spent more time on the latest, ill-fated Violin Sonata and on the Sextet, performed on 16 December. The only other music that survives complete from this year is the tiny song *Pierrot*, his only setting of Banville and, written on Christmas Eve, the second of his piano *Nocturnes*, 'Bal de jeunes filles'.

But elements of the music for *Intermezzo* do survive, according to Keith Daniel, in the little piano pieces *Villageoises*, written in Montmartre in February 1933 and dedicated to Giraudoux and Jouvet. The autograph of these six pieces bears the additional titles 'Niaiseries Villageoises, Petites niaiseries, Petites pièces faciles'. But, even when deliberately writing 'nonsense', Poulenc retained his enviable talent for writing catchy tunes. This facility did not preclude echoing music by others – in this case Satie, whose 'Tyrolienne turque' and second piece of *Trois Morceaux en forme de poire* lie behind Poulenc's 'Valse tyrolienne' and 'Rustique'.[83] One tribute to these charming pieces is the number of Russian arrangements made of them in the 1970s and 1980s, for accordion, guitar and balalaika. As for the piano pieces written in 1933 and 1934 to please his publisher Lerolle (three *Feuillets d'album*, *Presto in B flat*, two *Interme*ʒʒ*i*, *Humoresque*, *Badinage*), only the second Intermezzo in A flat retained Poulenc's favour; otherwise he would have agreed entirely with Alfred Cortot, who in 1941 felt bound to confess that:

> . . . it is only because I regard Poulenc as one of the most gifted composers of his generation that I feel I have the right – and perhaps even the friendly duty – to reproach him for his indulgence towards himself, and for not having tried more often to go beyond those boundaries of waggish facility within which a dangerously complaisant popularity has kept him captive.[84]

Poulenc spent the New Year of 1934 performing (two outings for the Concerto with Février) and composing *Huit Chansons polonaises* for the Polish singer Maria Modrakowska, which occupied him until the end of April. She was said to be able to sing in ten languages and on 30 June 1933 had taken part 'in the first major Hôtel Singer-Polignac gala concert conducted by [Nadia] Boulanger'.[85] In his 1954 conversations with Claude Rostand, Poulenc unintentionally muddied the chronological waters by claiming his Polish songs came after a tour of North Africa with Modrakowska, whereas in fact this tour did not take place until 1935.[86] Modrakowska chose the folksongs, which all spring from the 1830 revolution, leaving Poulenc to harmonize them. According to him, 'I didn't look either for local colour or originality. I simply imagined, in French fashion, a Polish atmosphere, just as others have evoked Spain without knowing it.'[87] This 'imagining' also involved writing preludes and postludes which, as we should expect, are never predictable: in the first song, in G major, the melodically independent prelude is in G minor, providing the link to a central verse in B flat before a final one back in G; the other prelude, to the last song, is a pre-echo of the vocal line, but with a curiously twisted ending. Meanwhile we are left guessing to find out whether there will be a postlude and, if so, how relevant it will be to what has gone before, the postlude to the sixth song, 'Le drapeau blanc', being the only one that conforms to the 'sign-off' pattern of *Le Bestiaire*. The accompaniments themselves are often spiced with chromatic inflections (in the third song, on the words 'the Pole always hopes for justice', with the marking 'très sec'), though in the fourth song and the last composed, 'Le dernier mazour', the soldier's desperate pleas for a last mazurka are all the more telling for the plainness of the harmony. Poulenc dedicated the songs to the Polish ladies in his life, including Ida Godebska, Misia Sert, Marya

Freund, Madame Arthur Rubinstein and, of course, Wanda Landowska. The last song, 'Le lac', dedicated to Modrakowska herself, stands out from the rest in its stark dissonances, reminiscent of Poulenc's harmonic adventures of a decade earlier. The girl's wreath of rosemary is withering, its flowers falling one by one – like the Polish warriors in their failed 1830 uprising?

Quite by accident, setting these revolutionary songs coincided with the nearest that France came during the 1930s to a *coup d'état*. Only two years earlier the President, Paul Doumer, had been assassinated by a mad Russian, and in January 1934 the cover of a popular magazine warned that '1934 opens anxious, panicked eyes on a future heavy with hatred, tragedies and catastrophes'.[88] Nor was farce absent from the scene: when the director of the Comédie-Française was dismissed for putting on Shakespeare's *Coriolanus*, with its clear incitement to anti-democratic demonstrations, he was replaced by a chief of police. On 6 February, when that evening's major social charity event, the Bal des Petits Lits Blancs, was cancelled, right-wing patience was finally exhausted and in the fighting fifteen people died and 1,500 were injured. Although Poulenc was never a close reader of political runes, there is a coded reference in a letter to his publisher in which he writes, 'I'm working hard, trying to forget the uglinesses and sadnesses of life at present, both public and personal.' Inevitably, the latter overrode the former, in the shape of continuing financial worries, although these cannot have been helped by fears of what the political situation might become. 'You will do me a great service,' he went on, 'in making out to me a crossed cheque for 2,240 francs and sending the rest to me as a money order. My current fortune amounts to 83 francs, which is to say that I wait on you with anxiety.'[89]

Some balm was poured on his woes by going to the premiere of Stravinsky's danced melodrama *Perséphone*, put on at the Opéra by Ida Rubinstein on 30 April with the composer conducting. As Stephen Walsh notes, partly because André Barsacq had been chosen as designer without his knowledge, Stravinsky 'never had a good word to say about Barsacq's designs, and his name is not mentioned in the autobiography or conversations'.[90] And there was criticism elsewhere. Boris de Schloezer said of Rubinstein that 'the fact she was not a dancer, nor an actress' was 'so evident that it would be bad taste to insist on it, and in any case futile', while Schloezer's colleague Julie Sazonova found the danced solos 'nothing but conventional leaping and prancing'.[91] These were presumably some of the deficiencies Poulenc had in mind when he wrote to Stravinsky on 11 May, explaining that he had not come round to embrace him after the performance a few nights earlier because 'I was so furious with all your collaborators that I didn't want to show you my bad temper, magnified a hundred times by my admiration for your music. [. . .] The orchestration is so noble that everything by comparison sounds like instrumental botchery.'[92]

The epithet 'noble' may seem a rather strange one to use about *Perséphone*'s sound world if we judge by the jauntiness of the early chorus 'Ivresse matinale', but as the work proceeds nobility grows upon it. In any case the term needs to be glossed by Poulenc's description of the work eighteen months later, in his article 'Éloge de la banalité', as 'entirely white, entirely pure perfection, that of Racine'.[93] The strident or explosive Stravinsky is banished – perhaps a factor in Pierre Boulez's dismissal of the ballet as 'a very weak work'.[94] But for Poulenc, it was further confirmation from his Russian friend that there was still mileage in such a readily understandable language, full of absolutely tonal ideas (if not traditional harmonies) sometimes held for long stretches, and clothed in such clear, economical colours. Rhythmically, too, Stravinsky's favourite irregular bar lengths chimed with Poulenc's own habits, even if in his own settings Poulenc would never have dreamt of inflicting such damage on French prosody.

Between Christmas Eve 1933 and the following May he added five more *Nocturnes* to the single one of 1929/30. 'Bal de jeunes filles' proceeds almost entirely on the lines of tune plus accompaniment, animated by Poulenc's elegant switches of key, until the slow coda, when the young girls' excitement is quenched by a 'très expressif' sign-off, ending enigmatically with a major/minor triad. Poulenc in general enjoyed the sound of bells, but the third Nocturne, 'Les cloches de Malines', suggests a sleep fatally disturbed by their incessant clanging; the piece was, however, a favourite with Alfred Cortot.[95] The fifth, 'Phalènes', describes the 'presto misterioso' fluttering of moths ('phalaena' being an early classification by Linnaeus), and may be regarded as Poulenc's response to 'Noctuelles' in Ravel's *Miroirs*. While the sixth piece is enigmatic in a different way from the ending of the second, seeming to lose its way but then recovering just in time, the most successful of the five is undoubtedly the elegantly expressive fourth, entitled 'Bal fantôme'. Clearly inspired by Chopin and, unusually for Poulenc, entirely in four-bar phrases, it bears an epigraph from Julien Green's novel *Le Visionnaire*, published only a few weeks earlier: 'Not a note of the waltzes or schottisches was lost through the whole house, so that the ailing man could take part in the festivities and could dream on his sickbed of the happy days of his youth.' Over half a century later, Poulenc's friend Sir Lennox Berkeley, suffering from dementia in the last few years of his life, would play the piece over and over again.[96]

During the summer Poulenc continued his keyboard activity with three of the short piano pieces already mentioned (two *Intermezzi*, *Presto in B flat*), a little *Villanelle* for pipe and piano, and the delicious *Quatre Chansons pour enfants*, but apparently nothing more. In July he spent a week in a hotel in Vichy, then a week in early August with Jean and Marie-Blanche de Polignac in their castle at Kerbastic in Brittany. During autumn he orchestrated the *Poèmes de Ronsard*. So what had happened to his 'grande période'? The two years since finishing the Two-Piano Concerto had produced nothing remotely 'great'. Maybe his financial worries deprived him of the impetus to write anything on the grand scale? Maybe his love life was in trouble (lack of evidence for this period precludes any certainty)? In a letter from Vichy to Marie-Blanche he says he will stay with her for just a week from 4 August, needing to be in Salzburg by the 13th: 'I'm paying for my imprudence of the spring when I asked for an engagement at any price.'[97] In fact he was facing two engagements, one for two review-articles for *Le Figaro* on events in the Festival, another for a concert with Suzanne Peignot and instrumentalists. For each of the articles, which were to be of three typed pages or more, he was to be paid a no doubt welcome 500 francs. In fact he wrote three articles, which appeared in *Le Figaro* on 1, 4 and 29 September, as well as a more general article on the Festival for an unidentified journal.

The Salzburg Festival, founded in 1920 by Max Reinhardt and Hugo von Hofmannsthal, with support from Richard Strauss, billed the 1934 series as containing a 'Richard Strauss cycle', including *Der Rosenkavalier*, *Die ägyptische Helena* and *Elektra*. Poulenc either chose or was deputed to review the last of these, with a few passing swipes at *Der Rosenkavalier*.

To set the tone, he begins his review with a pun, his identification of *Elektra* as 'l'éloge de la fureur' being a riff on Hitler's newly minted titles of 'Führer und Reichskanzler'. Then the put-down direct: 'Certainly a single phrase of Mozart is enough to dissipate this terrifying rapture, but we should cultivate a taste for these poisons, if only to appreciate more fully, with a sense of coming home, the divine purity of Mozart or the human sensibility of Debussy.' Nor is there much left that is truly Greek: 'All the action could as well take place in the entrance hall of a Prussian railway station.' As for the music, 'it proceeds by leaps, ever developing, as slippery as mercury, corrosive and yellow as acid'. After which *Der Rosenkavalier* is despatched by a damning comparison: 'While I was listening to those waltzes launching out ineffectually and crashing every time on rocks in the orchestra, I found myself regretting that Strauss the waltz king (the one of *Die Fledermaus*) was not on the programme.'[98]

Weber's *Oberon* receives a rather different reception:

My passion for *Oberon* dates from my earliest childhood. [. . .] On a Moorish
pedestal table, brought back from Granada, sat a musical box carved out of oak
in a shape that was half edelweiss, half fir cone, precious souvenirs of a summer
in the Black Forest. One turn of the handle and the finale of *Oberon* took wing
in a light tinkle, filling me with joy and taking me off to a fairyland in which I
saw appearing, as in a kaleidoscope, a succession of ever-changing images. One
day, with a clumsy gesture, I broke the spring and I have had to wait 30 years
– some punishment! – to recapture, one evening in Salzburg, that innocent joy
I had felt so long ago. [. . .] No race expresses the woods and waters of fairyland
better than the Germans. The French are too cerebral, and always introduce an
architectural plan into the most immaterial scenes of nature, so that the Siren
immediately becomes Susanna in her bath. In Weber's music we swim, we fly,
without the burden of human knowledge, without fear of ridicule, in a
Christmas pantomime atmosphere that delights all ages.[99]

Poulenc's third article, probably cleared with the editor of *Le Figaro* from Salzburg,
was a plea, after hearing *Fidelio* conducted by Clemens Krauss with Lotte Lehmann
as Leonore, for the work to figure in the repertory of the Paris Opéra. Although it
had been given there by foreign opera companies in 1925 and 1928, it's possible that
Poulenc's encouragement may have helped towards the Opéra's own production in
1937, when Germaine Lubin sang Leonore. His article contains some telling detail,
among which we may treasure the description of the work's palette, by this deeply
visual composer, as 'rich in browns and oranges'.[100]

If his article on *Fidelio* possibly had an impact, one of his appearances in Salzburg
as pianist had repercussions that were to be a dominant part of his life for the next
twenty-five years. This was not the concert, organized by Pierre-Octave Ferroud,
containing Debussy songs with Suzanne Peignot, his Violin Sonata with Robert
Soëtens and Poulenc's own Trio with members of the Vienna Philharmonic
Orchestra, but a last-minute affair with the baritone Pierre Bernac. After their
performance of the *Chansons gaillardes* in 1926 the two had lost touch, but in June
1934 Poulenc went to a concert organized by Edmond Rostand's sister at which
Bernac was singing songs by Debussy. Poulenc intimated to Bernac that he would
like to work with him on these songs as well as his own, and Bernac agreed, but put
him off until the autumn because of a Salzburg engagement. We must presume that

his accompanist had to cancel at the last moment, when Bernac wrote to Poulenc: 'I'm being asked to sing some Debussy in three days' time. Would you agree to accompany me? Nice fee. Let me know quickly.'[101] Their recital ended a long evening financed by a rich American lady, Mrs Moulton, consisting also of an orchestral concert conducted by Herbert von Karajan and Serge Lifar dancing *L'Après-midi d'un faune*; after which:

> . . . one could choose between a song recital in the open air and a performance of the [Debussy] *Preludes* in a well-heated library. Shivering beneath a willow-tree bathed in moonlight, with the piano going more out of tune every second, we came out of it fairly well and it was a marked success with the professional musicians. The next day I said to Bernac: 'If you like, we can do this again this winter in Paris, in a room that's nice and warm.' 'Agreed,' he replied. So began our collaboration.[102]

V
SURREALISM AND FAITH
✦ 1934–1939 ✦

In September 1934 Poulenc gave a sign that he was ready once more to embark on a 'great' work, for organ. On the 16th the Princesse de Polignac replied to a letter from him which had not only suggested this project but done it 'so frankly that I have to tell you quite candidly that, thanks to Mr Roosevelt, my musical budget is considerably reduced. I can only offer you half of what you kindly accepted for the [Two-Piano] Concerto – that's to say 12,500 francs.'[1] Since Poulenc himself was the instigator of this project, it can in only a limited sense be termed a commission. It figures sporadically in his correspondence before its final elaboration and completion in 1938.

After Poulenc's North African tour with Maria Modrakowska in February 1935, the first Bernac/Poulenc recital took place on 3 April at the École normale de musique.

In his talk 'Mes mélodies et leurs poètes' in 1947, Poulenc remembered that 'Bernac's vocal style naturally encouraged me to try and find a lyrical poet. I thought at once of Paul Éluard [. . .]'[2] This is not strictly true, since he had thought of setting five poems by Éluard in July 1931,[3] but undoubtedly his return to the poet in March 1935 was prompted by his new collaboration with Bernac. Twenty years later he told Claude Rostand:

> I'd admired Éluard from the day I met him in 1917, in Adrienne Monnier's bookshop on the rue de l'Odéon. [. . .] I have to say, I was immediately attracted to Éluard. First of all, because he was the only Surrealist who could tolerate music. And also because all his poetry is musical vibration. [. . .] These five poems [. . .] opened the door for me to the whole of Éluard's poetry. At last I had found a lyric poet, a poet of love, whether of human love or that of liberty.[4]

On the other hand, this was poetry he 'regarded with apprehension, full as it is of pitfalls. I took the plunge and in less than a month I set five of his poems to music.

[. . .] I owe to him the fact that I finally found the lyrical style I'd been dreaming of for years.'[5] The words 'pitfalls' and 'plunge' show that Poulenc regarded these poems as a risk, a view confirmed by his entry in *Journal de mes mélodies*: 'A tentative work. Key turned in the lock. An attempt at giving the piano the *maximum* with the *minimum* of means.'[6] His model was a collection of Matisse drawings reduced from multiple hatchings to a single line, giving him the same 'less is more' advice as Landowska had over the *Concert champêtre*. It cannot be said that the advice was taken entirely – the piano writing in 'Amoureuses' reaches a climax that could be by Rachmaninov, and Hervé Lacombe may be right in claiming that here 'Poulenc has not yet got the measure of exaltation and of pathos, which from time to time takes on the character of melodrama.'[7] Poulenc himself thought the best songs were 'Plume d'eau claire' and 'Rodeuse au front de verre', both of which belong to his more familiar style, with an almost classical arrangement of harmonies spiced up with a few unimpeachable chromaticisms. In the other three songs Poulenc's attempts to follow Éluard's abrupt changes of perspective are not totally convincing, even prompting one to think (most unusually in a Poulenc song) 'why this rather than that?' The fact that they were heard together with songs by Chabrier, Debussy and Ravel, as well as Poulenc's *Épitaphe*, *Le Bestiaire* and *Quatre Poèmes de Guillaume Apollinaire*, may either have sweetened the pill or made it stand out all the more. The reviews at least were favourable.

The last song was written at Cannes, and Carl Schmidt is probably right in suggesting that he was visiting Tante Liénard who was seriously ill.[8] On 11 May she died at the age of eighty-nine. Writing to his sister the day before, Poulenc says he had explained his arrival to the old lady as wanting to make sure she was not alone when making the journey from Cannes back to Noizay. He also emphasized that notices of her death should follow strictly the wording that he was sending her, which was 'exactly what she had always asked me to use'. Both demonstrate a tact and a punctiliousness not always allowed to a man sometimes regarded as rather too observant of his own creature comforts. Without any doubt, he felt her loss deeply: 'Need I tell you that I am going through very difficult moments, but such an example of a life so noble to the end is a lesson.'[9]

His compositions during the remainder of 1935 turned their back temporarily on surrealism in favour of less demanding fare, including two pieces of incidental music. Although Poulenc had no intention of following Auric's and Honegger's example and devoting himself seriously to film music, he was not against the occasional collaboration, writing five scores between 1935 and 1951. In the summer of 1935 he composed a score for a six-minute animated film *La Belle au bois dormant* produced by Alexandre Alexeieff to advertise Vins Nicolas. Billed for many years as lost, the film has now been brought out as a DVD by Cinédoc as part of a collection of films by Alexeieff.[10] Poulenc himself plays the harpsichord in the small, wind-dominated ensemble, and the instrument's loud, crunchy chords well illustrate Prince Charming banging on the castle doors, while elsewhere the composer exercises his familiar binding together of tuneful snippets. Not only was the wedding ceremony of Sleeping Beauty and the Prince loudly applauded by the journalists at the first showing, they actually insisted on an encore. Still further, Émile Vuillermoz, by no means a general admirer of Poulenc's music, confided that 'we are here in the presence of a complete and perfectly balanced composition, which underlines the tiniest details of the action and is close to being the ideal formula for accompanying an animated film'.[11] A first small step maybe towards *Les Mamelles de Tirésias*?

The other piece of incidental music, composed while Poulenc was staying with Jean and Marie-Blanche de Polignac at Kerbastic in August, was for a play called *Margot* by Edouard Bourdet, premiered at the Théâtre Marigny on 26 November with a cast including Yvonne Printemps as Margot, Stéphane Audel (later to become a close friend of the composer and provide an illuminating preface to *Moi et mes amis*) as King Charles IX, and an eleven-year-old Charles Aznavour as one of the cast's twenty children. The Margot of the title was Margaret of Valois, sister of Charles IX and in due course bride of Henri of Navarre, later Henri IV. Although highly intelligent, after her marriage she was unwise enough to conceive a passion for her own brother Henri III, while on the political front the war of religion had been stoked by the St Bartholomew's Day massacre in 1572, in which Catholics murdered Huguenots throughout France, up to 4,000 dying in Paris alone. Auric wrote the music for Act I, Poulenc for Act II. He was less concerned with details of the plot than with the general sixteenth-century setting. Nadia Boulanger suggested he arrange dances from Claude Gervaise's *Livre de danceries*, which coincidentally Maurice Emmanuel was doing at precisely the same time (Anglo-Saxon music lovers may remember that Peter Warlock had done something similar in 1928 with settings of Arbeau's *Orchésographie* in his *Capriol Suite*). Poulenc's original score is lost, but he reused material from it in the song *À sa guitare* (sung in the play by Printemps) and in the seven movements of the *Suite française d'après Claude Gervaise* which he produced in three versions: for keyboard alone (piano or harpsichord), for small orchestra, and for cello and piano.

In the play Margot sings her song at her window, accompanied by a guitar, in the separate published version replaced by either a harp or a piano. The words, by Ronsard, were presumably those sung in the play and accepted by Bourdet. After a decidedly modern, pseudo-improvisatory introduction, the song proper begins with four bars that might pass for sixteenth-century originals; but chromaticism increasingly invades, until a repeat of the four bars briefly restores historical accuracy – then a memory of the introduction rounds off the song. The same juxtaposition of old and new informs the *Suite*. If the balance of harmonies is tipped more in the direction of old than in *Pulcinella*, Poulenc's recompositions would seem to derive unmistakably from that source, while the generally garish orchestration (wind, percussion and harpsichord) sports echoes of the *Symphonies of Wind Instruments*. The general impression is that a good time is being had by all. The year ended with the premiere on 11 December of this orchestral version, conducted by Charles Münch, at a concert of the Triton society. A rival of La Sérénade, this was founded by Pierre-Octave Ferroud and would put on just three works by Poulenc between March 1935 and the society's last concert in May 1939.

Two of Poulenc's most interesting literary contributions appeared during October 1935. 'Mes maîtres et mes amis', published that month in *Conferencia*, had been given as a talk on 15 March with music performed by Maria Modrakowska and five wind players, and offers a good idea of his tastes and preoccupations: a spring away from Paris (the 16th arrondissement aside) was a spring wasted; his favourite composers were Mozart, Schubert, Chopin, Debussy, Ravel and Stravinsky; those who had 'never touched my heart' included Wagner, Brahms and Fauré; painting is, together with music, the art to which he's most responsive; as for jazz, he listens to it in the bath, 'but for me it's frankly odious in a concert hall'; and 'I need a certain musical vulgarity as a plant desires compost.'[12]

He followed up this last admission with an article provocatively entitled 'Éloge de la banalité'. Writing to prepare audiences for performances in Lausanne and Geneva of *Le Bal masqué*, he explained first of all that he was not a composer who created his own syntax, but one who 'arranged known materials in a new order'. He warned that 'In our day, when we must have the new at any price, the taste for a system has found its way into painting as well as music, with a rigour that threatens to become instantly old hat.' A saying of Picasso, echoing both Cocteau and Ravel, won his admiration: 'The truly original artist is the one who never manages to copy exactly'; and on the subject of banality so did two quotations from Max Jacob's *Art poétique*: 'Authors who make themselves obscure in order to win esteem get what they want and nothing more' and 'There is a purity of the guts which is rare and excellent.'[13]

The article understandably provoked a lively response, including a long one from Ernst Krenek in the same review setting out a contrary position:

> The most advanced feature of musical language we find currently is the dissolution of tonality, brought about chiefly by Wagner and later by Debussy. Schönberg has merely identified the final consequences of this evolution in penetrating the non-tonal region. The composer who, while fully aware of the results obtained in this development, wants to take the situation back to a previous stage, could only repeat the journey made by his predecessors and end up in the same positions. I have personal experience of this fact.

Further, Krenek had no time for banality, when the true composer should be bent on elaborating a new language. To which we can only reply that he was not Poulenc . . .[14] The basic idea behind Poulenc's article was better realized by Florent Schmitt, who wrote that the praise was, as near as might be, of humanity in its entirety, referencing the well-known claim by the Roman playwright Terence: 'Homo sum, humani nihil a me alienum puto' [I am a human and think nothing that is human is foreign to me]. Scriptural authority comes from the Acts of the Apostles (X:15), 'What God hath cleansed, that call not thou common', and from Romans (XIV:14), 'I know, and am persuaded by the Lord Jesus that there is nothing unclean of itself.' For Poulenc the art lover, support for his thesis came from paintings such as Rembrandt's *Flayed Ox* and any number by Chardin, such as the skate slit open and hanging from a hook, in which we are forced to readjust our senses of what is beautiful, so often based on habit and on opinion received from an élite. Nearer to Poulenc's own time are musical works such as *Le Sacre* and *Parade*, as well as physical objects such as Duchamp's readymades which deny élite authority, no doubt encouraged by a perception of the First World War as one fought by lions led by donkeys. The *Dictionnaire abrégé du Surréalisme* of 1938 defined a readymade as 'an ordinary object elevated to the dignity of a work of art by the mere choice of the artist'. The dictionary was edited by André Breton and Paul Éluard.

On 30 December Poulenc sent a letter to his publisher Jacques Lerolle prefaced with a tiny quotation identified as 'Intermède de la Sonate pour piano et violon', promising it for 1936. But yet again a Violin Sonata project fell on stony ground, as did a 'Chanson espagnole' that Éluard sent him which 'I was never able to set',[15] though the two men were already corresponding over the poems Poulenc might use for an, as yet untitled, song cycle.[16] Instead the spring of 1936 saw him at work on his first major work for unaccompanied chorus. André Latarjet, the husband of Raymonde Linossier's sister Suzanne, was the co-founder and president of the Chœurs de Lyon, and he now commissioned Poulenc to compose something for them. Poulenc's acceptance had something to do with the fact that Lyon had not responded favourably to either *Aubade* or the Two-Piano Concerto, in the latter of which a local paper had lamented 'the vulgarity of the materials employed'. The *Sept Chansons* were intended to be a means of righting this evident wrong, but for whatever reason they seem never to have been performed in that city in these pre-war years.[17] Writing to the Latarjets in March, Poulenc is clearly surprised by his own response: 'Genius (well, let's call it genius) descended on me in answer to your request and one of the little choruses for the Lyon singers is already done. Regardless of the music, the poem is exquisite – it's by Apollinaire. Not wanting on any account to write old French, but rather young Francis, I've decided to use contemporary texts. I've chosen 2 Apollinaires, 3 Éluards and 2 Max Jacobs.'[18] Composition continued apace and the set was completed on 22 April.

The dangers of writing 'old' music, if not specifically French, could have been increased by one particular influence: 'In March 1936, in the house of the Princess Edmond de Polignac, I listened to several performances of Monteverdi motets given by Nadia Boulanger's vocal ensemble. I possessed the complete edition of Monteverdi's works and so, when I got back home, I read through these marvels of polyphony again with enthusiasm.'[19] As to what 'young Francis' might consist of, he would probably have been heartened by a letter from Koechlin emphasizing that 'with old means one can produce new things', a viewpoint further expressed in a typically forthright article in *Le Ménestrel*, stating that 'The old tonal region is sterile only to the inexperienced amateur and to the clumsy idler who no longer knows how or wants to cultivate it, or indeed to the young composer seduced by the magic of atonality.'[20]

Poulenc soon decided the Max Jacob poems did not fit the cycle and instead chose five poems by Éluard, four from *La Vie immédiate* of 1932 and one from *Répétitions* of 1922. Since Éluard was still alive and more than willing to have his poems set by Poulenc, there were no copyright problems, but these then arose over the two Apollinaire poems 'Marie' and 'La blanche Neige' which appear together in the collection *Alcools* of 1920. Whatever the real situation might have been, Poulenc blamed the 'malveillance' of the publishers Gallimard[21] for refusing permission to publish songs on these two texts, even though these were already composed. Even the intervention of Apollinaire's widow Jacqueline had no effect.[22] As a result, the first edition of 1936 included just the five Éluard settings, premiered by the Chœurs de Lyon at a La Sérénade concert in the Salle Gaveau on 21 May 1937. That year Poulenc then produced a second edition with the music for the two Apollinaire poems now fitted to new words, 'La Reine de Saba' on 'La blanche Neige', 'Marie' on Apollinaire's poem of the same title. The task of writing these new words fell to Poulenc's schoolfriend from Le Petit Condorcet, variously known as Jean Nohain, Jaboune and, in this case, Jean Legrand. Finally, in 1943 Gaston Gallimard relented and the cycle was printed and performed as Poulenc had originally envisaged.

In his 1954 interviews with Claude Rostand, Poulenc remembered that 'As the Éluard poems are rather static, I added two by Apollinaire that are more lively and rhythmical; "La blanche Neige" and "Marie".'[23] It might seem strange therefore that he placed 'La blanche Neige' first. But calling this poem 'lively and rhythmical' was in no sense to deny its lyrical power, and it could well be that he wanted this power to declare itself early and to cast its spell over the whole cycle. Like the rest of the songs, it displays what one might call the virtues of its failings. In the words of Hervé Lacombe, 'Poulenc, who regularly composed at the piano and who did not have a polished contrapuntal technique, does not always give the accompanying voices the contrapuntal lines one expects [. . .] [Having] also through his studies of chorales with Koechlin learnt to follow a medium way between vertical and horizontal thinking, [he] thereby discovers a logic that is different from that of counterpoint in the traditional sense.'[24] These lines are often highly chromatic – and, as a result, harder to sing in tune than would appear from the page. At the same time, in this first song eleven of the first thirteen phrases all end on a consonance. Only the fourteenth and final phrase, the heart-rending '[et que n'ai-je] Ma bien aimée entre mes bras', concludes with a seductive, widespread dissonance on 'bras' – in fact one of Poulenc's favourite chords, here rendered even more tender by the diminuendo from *mf* to *pp*.[25]

The second song, 'À peine défigurée', begins with another Poulenc fingerprint, the alternation of minor and major (more often in that order). Is this, as has been suggested, a mirror of Poulenc's own basic unease? Or is it simply that he is wary of exact repetitions that could become wearisome, whereas this minor/major practice marries gentle variation with a lack of necessary harmonic progress? The music moves, yet stays in the same place. Opposites are also blended in the song's textures. The traditional four-part harmony, beginning and ending in F major, is broken up by brief passages for solo sopranos, solo basses, three-part women's voices, three-part mixed voices and two-part sopranos, all within a song lasting a mere 1½ minutes or so. But within this fragmentation there are harmonic links: the final chord of A flat on the phrase 'Par un sourire' (marked 'clair') is the same chord, but now in F major, that ends the last phrase, 'beau visage': both of these happy phrases balance the more tortured lines of poetry elsewhere.

To judge by the markings in the third song it contains, successively, violence, mystery, precision and sweetness, all at a hectic 'Presto, véhement'. The dissonances are now extreme and a challenge for any choir, especially at this pace, finally dissolving at fig. 8 into a 'magic' chord borrowed, not for the last time and with little in the way of disguise, from *Symphonies of Wind Instruments* (fig. 1). 'Tous les droits' begins with the savage octaves that Poulenc liked to produce from time to time, and here they alternate with more serene music, one of the passages Hélène Jourdan-Morhange might have had in mind when she spoke of the voices being 'treated like an ancient concerto in which the instrumental groups challenge and answer each other'.[26] 'Belle et ressemblante' is the most sheerly beautiful of the songs, not least because it is the most tonal, barely moving out of F minor/major (see Koechlin above!) and legato throughout, contrasting with the scattered texture of 'Tous les droits'.

After which 'Marie', the second Apollinaire setting, shows how 'young Francis' can, whatever he may have said, do 'old French' with the best of them – its repeated 'la la la's and clean-cut tunes hark back to Jannequin, and even if some of the harmonies are those of 'young Francis', E minor/major inhabits some thirty of its forty-nine bars (the familiar minor/major colouring the final 'Marie'). Finally 'Luire' emphasizes this embrace of tonality, but in quite different colours. Taking its cue from the opening words, 'Terre irréprochablement cultivée', the song is almost brutally declarative, with no cause for reproach on grounds of sentimentality, and only in the last two bars is this brutality explained as evoking the white heat of the 'clair soleil d'été'. After the key that turned in the lock in the *Cinq Poèmes de Paul Éluard*, here the door is opening.

On 30 April Poulenc wrote to Marie-Blanche that the Organ Concerto 'is nearing the end [. . .] It's not the genial Poulenc of the Two-Piano Concerto but rather

Poulenc on his way to the cloister, very 15th century if you like.'[27] Not for the first or last time he was being unduly hopeful, and there were radical changes to be made before the work's true completion in August 1938. Less speculative, indeed fairly definitive, was his move that April to a flat in the same block as Oncle Papoum at 5 rue de Médicis: he changed flats within the block after Papoum's death, but lived at that same address until his own. The first of the two flats was not ready for occupation until September, when he also pronounced Georges Salles, who had put him up for years in the rue du Chevalier de La Barre, to be 'toujours adorable', for whatever reason. Probably Poulenc felt that at thirty-seven he was not too young to have a Paris flat of his own, and the fact that he could now maintain two homes suggests that, despite his later mention of 'a host of annoyances on the financial front',[28] such pressures had nonetheless eased – gloomy prognostications of having to sell Le Grand Coteau no longer figure in his correspondence.

Now that Poulenc and Bernac had decided to form a partnership, they set up a pattern of leaving the bright lights in August and rehearsing their programmes intensely for the coming year. In 1936, as in the previous year and the following three, they were joined in the Hôtel du Commerce in Uzerche by Yvonne Gouverné, the chorus mistress of the French Radio Choir from 1935 to 1960. As a pupil of André Caplet, she had got to know Bernac in the 1920s, and after Caplet's death in 1925 had continued to advise him. Both he and Poulenc knew she could be relied upon for help both in setting up their career and in the choice and performance of their repertoire. But this year, no sooner had they reached the hotel than news reached them that the thirty-six-year-old composer Pierre-Octave Ferroud had been decapitated on the 17th, hit by a car while walking along a road near Debrecen in Hungary. Although the three of them had seen Ferroud at Salzburg for the last few years, he was not, as has often been stated, one of Poulenc's friends: three days after the accident, Poulenc admitted to Sauguet that he had listened to Ferroud on the radio from Salzburg, talking about Mozart, and that Ferroud's voice (or what he said?) put him in a rage, about which he now felt guilty.[29] The effect of this news on Poulenc has been much discussed, and with good reason.

There is no denying that it showed up an egocentric side in him. In a letter to Auric eight days after the accident he wrote frankly, 'Ferroud's death has knocked me back from all points of view. Think of the emptiness of an output like his, once the composer is no more. Of course my music's going well and it would be monstrous of me to complain, especially as I have invitations this winter for Belgrade, Prague etc. . . . but I wonder, if I conked out today, whether . . .'[30] At least this is honest. For any composer with a modicum of ambition the fate of his music cannot possibly be a matter of unconcern. Ferroud was, almost to the day, a year younger than Poulenc, who had already been deeply distressed by the false news, as broadcast on Seville Radio, that Falla had been killed in the Spanish Civil War (he lived until 1946). Also Poulenc admitted that 'a host of annoyances on the financial and editorial fronts has left me terribly nervous and melancholic' before going to Uzerche.[31]

As a result, Poulenc was forced to take a good look at himself and what he had achieved. Was banality something he should eschew? Why did he find writing piano music so difficult? And at the age of thirty-seven why was he so far from having written a song cycle to be mentioned in remotely the same breath as *Die Winterreise* or *Dichterliebe*? In short, for all its memorable tunes, delightful surfaces and stylistic variety, his music could be accused of lacking depth. But, as Graham Johnson writes, 'It is at this point that the Poulenc enthusiast begins to talk about certain pieces of his music being profound. This is a matter of non-comprehension as far as many more casual listeners are concerned. Profound Poulenc?'[32] At this crucial juncture in his life, Poulenc turned to religion: specifically to the shrine of the Black Virgin of Rocamadour, one of the many Black Virgins of southern France famous for their healing properties. Poulenc's father had often talked about the Rocamadour shrine and, on 22 August, Poulenc visited it with Bernac and Gouverné (Plate 14).

Reaching some kind of truth about Poulenc's religious life is far from easy: the evidence is scattered and sometimes contradictory, his attitude depends to no small extent on his mood, and clearly he finds it a hard thing to describe in words – which is certainly not to say that his religious feelings were faked. One thing we can say with certainty is that visiting the Black Virgin and taking back with him the little pamphlet which a few days later would inspire the *Litanies à la Vierge noire* offered not only immediate comfort but also the glimpse of a way forward. As Yvonne Gouverné wrote many years later, 'Nothing seemed to happen and yet everything changed within Poulenc's spiritual life.'[33] But even she found it hard entirely to grasp the nature of the event. Shortly before her death she was asked about Poulenc's 'return to the faith'. At this, her charm turning abruptly to severity, she proclaimed 'On ne fait pas de retour à la foi.'[34] In saying this she was following the precept of

St Francis Xavier, already quoted in Chapter 1: 'Give me a child until he is seven, and I will show you the man.' If this is true, then Poulenc had, from baptism and confirmation, remained a Catholic at his core whatever the impact of superficial events. It was therefore not a return, but an epiphany, the reappearance of something long hidden beneath worldly cares. As a final piece of evidence one may look at the photograph mentioned above, taken by Bernac as Poulenc and Gouverné descended the steps of the shrine, in which, while she seems absorbed in her own thoughts, and despite Poulenc's passing protestations of nervous melancholy, his face appears to shine out with happiness and confidence, ready to face the world once more.

Back at Noizay in September, while putting the finishing touches to *Les Soirées de Nazelles* and trying to find a replacement for 'the ⅛th of the [Organ] Concerto messed up last spring', he wrote to Nadia Boulanger that the *Litanies* was 'one of the two or three works I'd take with me on my mythical desert island [. . .] It's very special, humble and, I think, rather striking. Suddenly a whole half of my Aveyronnais blood triumphs roughly over my Nogentais half. And I'm cleaving fiercely to this richer, more austere blood "which should" grant me a good old age.'[35] Humility, ferocity, austerity: these three are combined throughout the work which, for all its simple materials of three high voices and organ, is leagues away from the milk-and-water sentimentality such forces might suggest. Humility and austerity reside in the generally conjunct movement of voices, and often of organ as well, with their reminiscences of plainsong; austerity too in the frequent harmonization with seconds and sevenths, avoiding the lushness of thirds and sixths. Against these the moments of ferocity are, in a good performance, terrifying, especially the rising three invocations to the Queen of Heaven, not only 'éclatant' but 'assez libre' in contrast with the regularly pulsing quavers around them. Each of these ends with 'priez pour nous' on piercingly dissonant chords in which Verdi's agonized diminished sevenths play their part. The peaceful coda, 'of a suffocating, almost supernatural beauty',[36] confirms the work's gradual progress from an initial D minor to a final G minor, the key of the contemporary Organ Concerto, and to a last, gently decorated G minor chord which, Poulenc put it years later, 'opens (for me) on to . . . the infinity of Heaven as MESSIAEN would say'.[37]

Exactly where this miraculous work is placed with regard to Poulenc's religious epiphany is open to debate. Is it at one with the happy, confident face we see on the steps of the shrine? Or does it rather reveal a desperate wish to believe? Some credence is lent to the latter claim by Poulenc's admission to Auric, in the middle of the very week it took him to write the *Litanies*: 'I wish I could think as you do and have your faith, because then we should be in exactly the same situation, but what can one do when one does not believe. If I had even a contrary faith, that would be something, but I absolutely do not.'[38] It is not clear what he means by 'une foi même contraire': would a settled atheism be preferable to this troubling doubt? In 1954 he recalled that 'In this work I tried to get across the atmosphere of "peasant devotion" that had struck me so forcibly in that lofty chapel.'[39] But for a man of Poulenc's intellectual stature peasant devotion was not easily achieved. A similar problem, in reverse, arose with the lovers he took from the milieu we may unkindly dub 'rough trade' who, not surprisingly, tended to be left cold by his music's sophistication. They would also surely have been perplexed, shocked even, by the organ's terrifyingly dissonant chords that follow seven of the pleas for divine intervention. Of course we have no way of knowing, of his desire to believe, whether it remained unfulfilled or, if so, whether in the short or longer term. It may not be irrelevant to think of Proust's 'les intermittences du cœur', a title he at one time considered giving to his great novel; and if Poulenc suffered 'les intermittences de la foi', he would certainly not have been alone among professing Catholics. One thing at least was sure: the undated, anonymous text would not be subject to royalties.[40]

Buoyed by his success in the *Litanies*, that September he also composed a secular spin-off in the shape of *Petites voix*, five settings of prose poems by Madeleine Ley, again for three high voices. As he intended them to be sung in schools, the harmonies are straightforwardly tonal spiced with a few chromaticisms, though the agility required in nos. 3 and 5 would call for careful rehearsal. On 1 October, at long last, he completed the piano suite *Les Soirées de Nazelles*, first sketched in 1930, but now dedicated 'à la mémoire de ma tante LIÉNARD, en souvenir de Nazelles'. As a preface to the score, Poulenc explained that 'The variations which form the centre of this work were improvised at Nazelles during long evenings in the country when the composer was playing the game of "portraits" with friends gathered round the piano. We hope that now, enclosed by a "Préambule" and a "Final", they will be able to evoke this game in the setting of a salon in the Touraine, with a window open to the night.'

Poulenc never revealed the identity of the 'friends gathered round the piano', though we may imagine that 'L'alerte vieillesse' is a portrait of Mme Liénard herself, especially as it rounds off the collection. At the time of writing it, Poulenc described the work with some affection, explaining that it 'is inspired by the banks of the Marne, where I was so happy as a child: Joinville with its pleasure gardens, its fried potatoes, its trumpet-shaped phonographs, its boats full of lovers',[41] and he performed it first on the BBC on 1 December and then at La Sérénade on 19 January. But over time he became disenchanted with its loose structure, pronouncing that it was, with *Napoli*, one of the piano works 'I condemn beyond redemption', and that in it 'I'm unhappy with myself [. . .] for letting myself get lost along paths that weren't mine'.[42] Critics have found fault with its extreme contrasts and over-reliance on Chopin and Schumann, but the fact remains that pianists like to play it. While it certainly contributes nothing to any 'grande période', it lies well under the fingers (Poulenc would probably interject 'too well!') and his melodic invention is as fertile as ever. Scholarly honesty compels one to note that Poulenc later insisted that the performer omit movements four to six (as on recordings by Jacques Février, and by Gabriel Tacchino; Poulenc made the latter promise he would always do this).[43] At least the run-on between the end of the third movement and the beginning of the seventh is musically tidy.

On the practical front, the last months of 1936 were spent seeing the *Sept Chansons* and the *Litanies* through the press and helping organize their first performances. On the compositional front, they also witnessed one total failure and, stemming directly from it, one outstanding success. Bernac later recalled that at Christmas he was at Le Grand Coteau working with Poulenc on the repertoire for their forthcoming tours, which included songs Poulenc had written on six of the thirty-three poems from Cocteau's 1923 collection *Plain-chant*. He now intended to try out four of these. Bernac tried to hide his lack of enthusiasm, but in vain. 'Suddenly, to my alarm, to my horror, Poulenc took his manuscript and threw it on the big fire that was burning in the grate. He began to laugh and said, "Don't worry, you'll have something much better for 3 February!"'[44] So it was that Poulenc published none of Cocteau's words between *Le Toréador* of 1918 and *La Voix humaine* of 1958; and that instead he composed, at considerable speed, one of his indubitable masterpieces.

There must have been something in the air of France during those later months of 1936 and the January of 1937. That summer, Olivier Messiaen, looking out at the peaks of the Dauphiné mountains from his newly acquired little house near Grenoble, composed *Poèmes pour Mi* on his own love lyrics to his wife Claire Delbos; six months later Poulenc composed *Tel jour telle nuit* on love lyrics by Éluard. Together they form a summit of the *mélodie* that over the last eighty years or so has, in many people's estimation, never been surpassed, or even equalled.

If the *Cinq Poèmes de Paul Éluard* had been the key turning in the lock, *Tel jour telle nuit* may be said to represent the discovery of the treasure within. In fact work on the cycle had, in some subterranean part of Poulenc's psyche, already begun before the destruction of the Cocteau poems, provoked, not unusually, by a visual stimulus. 'One Sunday in November 1936 I was feeling perfectly happy. I was ambling down the avenue Daumesnil, looking at a train in a tree. It was so pretty and so close to my childhood journeys when I used to return to Nogent by the Bastille railway. Since the trains left from the second storey of the station, I didn't need surrealism to place a locomotive in a plane tree. Moved by this childhood memory, I began to recite the poem "Bonne journée" from *Les Yeux fertiles*. That evening, the music arrived of its own accord.'[45]

'Bonne journée' was to be the first song of the new cycle, all of which set poems from Éluard's collection *Les Yeux fertiles*, published in October 1936. The nature of the treasure is well described by Keith Daniel: 'a clear sense of Éluard's prosody, a musical portrayal of the inherent lyricism of the verse, a musical clarification of the difficult verbal imagery, a limpid purity of diatonic harmony in certain songs, and the influence, for the first time in a non-religious work, of Poulenc's rapidly developing sacred style.'[46] Of these five attributes, perhaps the third and the last belong most particularly to this cycle. Evidence of Poulenc's care for prosody, lyrical invention and pure diatonic harmony can be found in both earlier and later settings of other poets. But Poulenc's ability to clarify 'difficult verbal imagery' here reaches new heights, justifying Éluard's claim, made to the composer nearly a decade later: 'Francis I was not listening to myself / Francis I owe it to you that I am hearing myself' – while a translation of this second line ('Francis je te dois m'entendre') could well be a more powerful 'I am understanding myself'.[47] As for Poulenc's newly found 'sacred style', this was to be a major item in the composer's gallery of musical costumes, often together with a repetitive, litany-like structure towards which Éluard's poetry also tended.

In the course of a fascinating article on the cycle, Sidney Buckland notes that in it 'Images of darkness and light, strength and frailty, obstacle and ease abound, interact, unite. All move towards the ecstatic "harmonisation of opposites" of the final poem', and she ends her article by quoting from Éluard himself: 'Everything is comparable to everything. Everything finds its echo, its reason, its likeness, its contrast, its perpetual becoming, everywhere. And that becoming is infinite.'[48] The relevance to Poulenc of such inclusiveness is not hard to find – as Buckland says, he 'lived in a constant state of reconciliation of opposites':[49] the juxtaposition of his new-found religious feeling with both his populist propensities and his homosexuality, of simple with complex harmonies in his musical language, and of outward ebullience with inner 'inquiétude'.

Of the four titles Éluard suggested for the cycle,[50] Poulenc's choice of *Tel jour telle nuit* (As is the day so is the night) makes clear his embrace of opposites and their possible reconciliation. Part of this reconciliation, and one that Poulenc himself would never have wished to claim, is simply that every bar of the work sounds like Poulenc. Added to this, in each of the nine songs, with just a single exception, the piano maintains the texture and articulation of its opening. This exception, the eighth song 'Figure de force', is, like the fifth 'À toutes brides', what Poulenc calls 'une mélodie tremplin' – 'a springboard song', whose value is to introduce by its violence and speed (respectively 'presto' and 'prestissimo') the lyrical songs that immediately follow it. Overall, he was always attentive to what artists call the 'hanging' of a picture, in his view 'as crucial in music as in painting',[51] a fact that can easily be tested in this song cycle by changing the order of songs – always to their detriment and that of the whole. The most obvious structural feature of the cycle is the correspondence between the first song and the last: both move in steady quavers at almost exactly the same tempo (crotchet = 63 and 60), both are in the key of C, thus reconciling the opposition between 'Bonne journée' and 'Nous avons fait la nuit'.

Within that basic tonality, Poulenc's harmonic control is unfailing: we may note how the opening pedal on a low C, initiating the threefold invocation of 'Bonne journée', diminishes from six bars to three and finally to two, driving the music on to the singer's climactic high A flat. At the same time Poulenc demanded that the singer perform 'with a *very calm* joy', adding 'A *bonne journée* is so rare and wonderful. *Belles journées* are so much more banal.'[52] In its context this distinction, making clear that the title had nothing to do with the weather, ties up with the song's dedication to Picasso who, early in 1936, had agreed to a combined project with Éluard before suddenly disappearing from his life for eight weeks; the poem 'Bonne journée' celebrated his equally sudden reappearance. It seems more than likely that Poulenc was aware of the story . . . The final 'Nous avons fait la nuit' (We have turned out the light) is dedicated to Yvonne Gouverné, like Picasso someone whom Poulenc deeply respected, perhaps to the point of awe, a sentiment reflected in the song's profound and powerful beauty. Éluard's poem, a hymn of love to his wife Nusch, had first appeared in his collection *Facile* in 1935, where all the poems were accompanied by naked photos of her taken by Man Ray, so that a visual impact was here added to the verbal.

The key of C now comes in the minor mode, yet the feeling is not of sadness but of great tenderness, emphasized by the markings 'doux et clair', 'doucement chanté', 'très lié', 'doucement lié', and by the effortless flow of the harmonies, memorably expanding at one point into the nineteenth century's favourite 'romantic' key of D flat major, coloured by Poulenc's beloved Lydian G naturals. The end crowns the work. The three flats of the key signature were removed earlier for seven bars, but that was to usher in A minor. C major is reserved for the piano coda designed 'as in Schumann's *Dichterliebe*, to prolong the audience's emotion'.[53] Here Poulenc was remembering from nearly twenty years later and, while Schumann was almost certainly his model, the coda in question might rather have been the one to *Frauenliebe und Leben* with its long notes in the middle of the bar.

Happily Poulenc's insistence that the cycle would be ready for the recital in the Salle Gaveau on 3 February was justified, and it concluded a programme that also contained songs by Weber and Liszt, Debussy's *Trois Ballades de François Villon* and Ravel's *Histoires naturelles*. Ravel attended the concert and Poulenc recalled that 'he had been touching in his kindness both to the accompanist of his music and to the composer, but I remember that at the time he was already unable to find the words he wanted'.[54] Éluard, though far from well, was also in the audience and reported 'Great success.'[55] Two days later *Litanies à la Vierge noire* were given their first Paris performance by Nadia Boulanger's group of singers, including Hugues Cuénod and Doda Conrad, following the world premiere by the same forces in a BBC broadcast on 17 November.

During that spring Poulenc, though hampered by a serious bout of flu, continued his long-drawn-out work on the Organ Concerto and was then commissioned to write four short pieces for (to give it its full title) the *Exposition Internationale des Arts et des Techniques appliqués à la Vie Moderne*, all of which were premiered on 24 June 1937 (exactly a month after the opening, delayed from 1 May by a combination of wet weather and Communist-inspired strikes among the workforce). Poulenc's 'Bourrée, au Pavillon d'Auvergne' was one of eight piano pieces by French composers making up the *Exposition* and including contributions by Auric, Milhaud and Tailleferre. It is perhaps indicative of Honegger's standing at this time that his contribution to the fair, 'Scenic Railway', was for a piano suite, *Parc d'attractions, Hommage à Marguerite Long*, in which his eight collaborators all joined him in hailing from outside France. However, 'internationale' though the *À l'Exposition* was, patriotism also had its part to play, Poulenc's taking the form of a pseudo-bagpipe texture with a drone beginning and ending on C.

His *Deux Marches et un intermède* for chamber orchestra were performed at a dinner given in honour of the writer and diplomat Harold Nicolson and other British intellectuals, 'Marche 1889' with the 'Ananas aux îles', 'Intermède champêtre' with the cheese, 'Marche 1937' at the end of the meal. Poulenc clearly took his task seriously, and the final march, with its simultaneous major/minor chords, would have needed strong coffee to wash it down: echoes of it were to reappear two decades later to introduce the final tragic scene of *Dialogues des Carmélites*. If Poulenc felt neglected at not being asked to contribute, as Milhaud, Honegger and Messiaen were, to the spectacular 'Fêtes de la lumière' illuminating the Palais Chaillot, the Trocadéro gardens and the Eiffel Tower, there is no mention of this in his correspondence. In any case, a longer view assures us that the twin 'clous' of the occasion were not musical, but two pictures: Dufy's *La Fée electricité* and Picasso's *Guernica*.

At some point before this year the critic and historian Paul Landormy had asked Poulenc whether he was thinking of writing an opera. 'He sincerely amazed me by saying he had no interest in this form of art. The theatre leaves him cold and he's interested only in chamber or orchestral music. At the end of the day it could be that the theatre is always inclined towards emphasis, a touch rudimentary and heavy, the sort of thing that doesn't suit his delicate nature.'[56] Poulenc's 'delicate nature' aside, the broadcast of an opera by Milhaud on 3 April 1937 was to change his mind utterly: the tragi-comic opera *Esther de Carpentras*, on a libretto by Milhaud's friend Armand Lunel, conducted by Manuel Rosenthal. Within days Poulenc was writing to Lunel, asking for a libretto. 'I don't want an opera buffa. I'd like a good love story with maybe a slightly erotic atmosphere and some drama (nothing except that!!!). Do you know Verdi's *Otello*?'[57] From here on various works by Stendhal and Balzac were considered and rejected as well as *La Jeunesse de Gargantua*, based on Rabelais. Of this, Denis Waleckx writes, 'Poulenc's reasons for abandoning a project that already seemed so well advanced remain a mystery. Nevertheless, it is possible to put forward a hypothesis. It was about this time [more precisely August 1938] that Poulenc rediscovered Apollinaire's text *Les Mamelles de Tirésias*. And Poulenc frequently described his opéra bouffe as a "Rabelaisian" work.'[58]

As well as a possible opera, and of course the Organ Concerto, Poulenc now engaged on two other projects: a Mass for mixed chorus unaccompanied and a work for mixed chorus and orchestra, both intended for the Chœurs de Lyon. For some weeks in August, Poulenc and Bernac shared a little country cottage at Anost in the Morvan, his nanny's birthplace, planning their recitals for the coming year and leaving Poulenc time to compose. For the time being at least, the days of depression and anxiety seemed to have been banished. Thanking Auric in a letter to his wife for sending him copies of various masses (sadly not specified), he tells her that 'Mine is making serious progress. I've copied out the Kyrie, Benedictus and Agnus Dei and the rest is sketched. I can't manage to understand why choral music is easy for me. I ought to have lived in the XVIth century.'[59] Still more euphoric is the letter two days later to his sister: 'This is truly primitive living, but wonderfully profitable. My Mass is going splendidly. I've only got the Gloria to write. I think it's really good from the point of view of both choral writing and music. The themes have real character and nothing smells of the lamp. What's more, I feel in perfect shape in every way and thrilled to see long months of work stretching ahead of me.'[60] The only sadness was in learning of the death on 23 August of Albert Roussel 'whom all musicians venerate and admire'.[61]

Poulenc's father Émile had died on 15 July 1917, and it would seem likely that the composer's decision to write a mass in his memory was moved by the twentieth anniversary of the loss of the man from whom he had inherited his Roman Catholic faith, although other, less personal motives may also have been at work (see p. 131 below). He gave a succinct account of his musical intentions in one of his interviews with Claude Rostand:

> As my ancestors are from the Aveyron, that's to say they were mountain and in a sense Mediterranean people, the Romanesque style has naturally been my favourite. So I tried to compose this act of faith which is the essence of the mass, in this rough, direct style. The roughness is particularly striking in the opening 'Kyrie', but don't forget that in the early Church those who had not been baptized were allowed to sing this hymn with the priests. This explains the almost savage side of my *Mass*.[62]

The roughness of the 'Kyrie' consists largely in two features: in the first two bars in the spread of the four voices over three octaves with no harmonic softening; and thereafter in the occasional harsh false relation (figs. 6.1, 6.2, 9.3, 9.4). These no doubt were among the details that caused one choirmaster of the time to write the Mass off as 'unsingable'.[63] While evidently within the capabilities of today's choirs, these 'scrunches' (to use a technical term), especially as they are all sung fortissimo, point up the supplicatory tone of the text. For listeners accustomed to a more flowing style, as in the surviving movements of Mozart's Requiem, Poulenc's chopped-up delivery can be disconcerting, not least because, as in his songs, the phrases are presented in bars of variable length, but also owing to accentuations that depart from the accepted norm. The first ten bars of the 'Gloria' offer 'b<u>onae</u> volúntatís', 'b<u>e</u>nedicímus té', 'gra<u>ti</u>as agimus' (underlining for longer note lengths, acute accents for downbeat positions). Pedants will point out that classical Latin requires 'benedícimus'; others may rejoice in the pleasure of sheer shock – though this was to be surpassed in the *Gloria* of 1961 with its perky 'bénedicimús te'. Then there is the splitting of key words by rests: 'lau – damus', 'Do – minus', 'De – us'. So even the most devoted Poulencquians might question his claim that 'in all my religious works I have always tried, in line with Victoria's example, to follow the sacred text as closely as if it were a poem by Éluard or Apollinaire'.[64] Whether he actually needed to make this claim remains arguable.

The 'Sanctus', marked 'moving along and gently rejoicing', is one of Poulenc's litanies, with the opening almost-pentatonic phrase repeated nearly twenty times with variations in texture, the mesmeric spell at last broken by the rich, widespread, eight-part chords of 'Hosanna in excelsis'. The final cadence recurs not only in the 'Benedictus' but also, with the addition of a soprano E in alt, will crown *Figure humaine*. Until the 'Hosanna', the 'Benedictus' is harmonically cumulative, passing from simple consonances to more anguished dissonances, then returning to the opening before a wrenching modulation leads into 'Hosanna' at its original pitch. Finally, an ethereal soprano (ideally for Poulenc a boy) introduces the 'Agnus Dei', followed by a reminiscence of the rough octaves that began the 'Kyrie'. The work ends with the soprano again, pleading 'Dona nobis pacem' in a cadence that would later conclude the opera *Dialogues des Carmélites*.

'Dona nobis pacem' . . . For a Frenchman in the 1930s this phrase held more than ritual meaning. The rise of Nazism up against the north-eastern border could not leave anyone in France free of anxiety, despite the hopeful messages of politicians about the impenetrability of the Maginot Line. Even if Poulenc declared a number of times that he was entirely apolitical, he cannot have missed the fact that, in promoting the 1937 Exposition, the Popular Front 'had intended this Exhibition to unite the nation behind its belief that war was not possible'.[65] If contrary proof were needed, one had only to look at Picasso's tragic masterpiece, reminding the world that 'on 26 April 1937 German planes, acting on orders from General Franco, bombed the small Basque town of Guernica, killing 1,564 women, children and old people'.[66] So it is possible to read Poulenc's *Mass*, together with the later *Quatre Motets pour un temps de pénitence* and the song *Priez pour paix*, as a trio of religious works written under the looming shadow of war and towards the end of a decade characterized as 'les années creuses', the hollow years.

More immediately, though, his thoughts turned to an entirely secular project. Intended for the Chœurs de Lyon, it was a work for chorus and orchestra commissioned by the English millionaire Edward James, a godson of Edward VII, James also providing the texts. Initially called *Quatre Sécheresses*, then *Sécheresse*, then *Les Pays de la Sécheresse*, and finally *Sécheresses*, this four-movement work has enjoyed a mixed press. On the face of it, it was a strange project for Poulenc to have undertaken. For one thing he believed he couldn't set any poetry that he didn't love, and nowhere in his correspondence or elsewhere concerning *Sécheresses* is there the slightest hint of any such sentiment. For another, how could he not feel about James and the French language the way he later did about Ned Rorem, on being shown his setting of Ronsard: 'Stick to American and leave French to us'?[67] Poulenc's biographer Henri Hell notes severely that the work 'is far from having the perfection of the *Sept Chansons*' and lays the blame on James's poem, 'a feeble copy of Éluard'.[68] Poulenc's response to the doom-laden text ('anxious and bitter, fear like a cicada rules over the pale Acropolis' gives the general flavour) takes him much of the time not only outside his harmonic comfort zone with sounds that are 'jagged … harsh … gaunt'[69] but, as Wilfrid Mellers remarks, imposes an unconvincing sectionalism on the discourse.[70]

Poulenc completed the score in December and in the meantime, as well as the Rabelais collaboration with Lunel, began to consider writing 'a ballet for Massine on the fables of La Fontaine. I think it suits me very well.'[71] This fits with Poulenc's later remark to Claude Rostand that Jacques Rouché, the director of the Paris Opéra, had been asking him for a ballet for some years;[72] the La Fontaine project, begun in 1940, would reach the Opéra in 1942 under the title *Les Animaux modèles*.

The other project completed in December was *Trois Poèmes de Louise de Vilmorin*. Poulenc found Vilmorin very attractive both personally and as a writer of novels, and it was he who persuaded her to make the move to poetry. He had come across her poem *Chevaliers de la Garde blanche*, written in the summer of 1937, and now asked her for two more to form a short cycle. Just as the *Cinq Poèmes de Paul Éluard* had signified 'the key turning in the lock', his *Trois Poèmes de Louise de Vilmorin* were to bear more tasty fruit in the months ahead in the form of a second Vilmorin cycle, *Fiançailles pour rire*, and also more generally in a generous outpouring of *mélodies* – no fewer than eighteen between that December of 1937 and October 1939. On one level, now that he had formed the settled partnership with Bernac, Poulenc wanted to write also for the female voice, and for this Vilmorin suited him perfectly: 'I found in Vilmorin's poetry a sort of sensitive impertinence, a licentiousness, a gluttony which recaptured, in the songs, what I had expressed when I was very young in *Les Biches*, with Marie Laurencin.'[73]

As in the *Trois Poèmes de Louise Lalanne*, Poulenc places the slow 'Officiers de la Garde Blanche' after the two fast songs rather than between them, fulfilling its role as an emotional climax. In 'Le garçon de Liège', marked 'vertigineusement vite', the diatonicism anchors the mostly remorseless semiquavers. It also gives Poulenc a chance, as he sums up the girls' boredom 'dans ma chemise, à mourir', to show the ineffably personal touch he can give to textbook harmonies, as again a year later at the end of *La Grenouillère*. In the central 'Au-delà', the diatonic style allows the major/minor alternations to paint the girl's anxiety over who she should choose as her lover (and even, if we choose to read the text this way, what sexual practice she favours . . .). At the start of the final song, the repeated semiquavers within heavy pedal, an effect Poulenc was proud of discovering, 'evoke the guitar Louise used to take with her when she went to have dinner with friends.'[74] At the same time these twenty bars of A minor entirely free of accidentals conjure up the required 'mélancoliquement irréel' of the guardian angels, until more dangerous harmonies enter with 'les tourments en tourmente/De l'aimer un peu plus d'aujourd'hui'. The cycle as a whole emphasizes how, in Poulenc's hands, less can be more.

The final event of that December was a particularly sad one. After years of struggling with a brain disorder (still not analysed to everyone's satisfaction over eighty years later), in the early morning of 28 December Ravel died after an operation. Poulenc attended the civil funeral two days later in the cemetery of the north-western Paris district of Levallois-Perret, together with Jacques Rouché, Reynaldo Hahn, Ricardo Viñes, Milhaud and Stravinsky among others. Although never a member of Ravel's intimate circle – the twenty-four years' distance in age perhaps worked against this – Poulenc had remained an admirer since the Monte-Carlo premiere of *L'Enfant et les sortilèges* in March 1925 and always treasured Ravel's remark that 'Poulenc invents his own folklore'. If further testimony is needed of Poulenc's affection, it can be found in the article he wrote in 1941, 'Le coeur de Maurice Ravel'. Finding himself in January 1940 with a day to spare in Ravel's home town St-Jean-de-Luz:

> I went into the church where the baby Maurice was baptized. In this Basque church, fitted with wooden balconies and where the word 'nave' truly recaptures its maritime meaning, it was already quite dark. A few candles were burning on the altar of the Virgin. Then Ravel, I prayed for you; do not smile, dear sceptic, because if I am sure you had a heart, I am even more certain that you had a soul.[75]

The early months of 1938 were full of concerts with Bernac. After recitals in Orléans and at the Concertgebouw on 19 and 25 January, they gave their major Paris concert at the Salle Gaveau on 7 February and another there on the 13th, pairing *Tel jour telle nuit* with Ravel's *Histoires naturelles*. Then followed a fortnight's stay in London from 19 February during which they performed Debussy's songs for the BBC, with the final broadcast on 4 March. From there they travelled to Avignon on 12 March and thence to Milan, Turin, Lugano and Florence. But at some point in March Poulenc found the time to compose *Le Portrait* on a poem by Colette. Not that he was particularly happy with the result: 'I must confess that my music expresses my admiration for Colette very inadequately. It's a very ordinary song.'[76] Certainly in its headlong and rather complicated course it says nothing new or memorable.

On 3 April the Lyon choir gave the first performance of the *Mass* in the Dominican Chapel in the Faubourg-Saint-Honoré, rewarded by a warm review in *Le Figaro*. But the following month at the Concerts Colonne the reception of the first performance of *Sécheresses* was altogether different. Overcoming the disadvantages mentioned above demanded at the very least a superior rendering, but this was not to be. In a retrospective defence of the work, Poulenc slightly exaggerated the practical difficulties, claiming the Lyon choir had sung his *Mass* in the morning of *Sécheresses*'s first performance on 2 May 1938,[77] whereas the two were in fact separated by some thirty-six hours. But certainly the conductor Paul Paray was delayed in Sweden by problems with the aircraft, and then proceeded to change the chorus layout, carefully prepared by the Lyon choirmaster, so that at the performance the singers could no longer hear the cues they were used to.[78] The result, Poulenc was forced to admit, was 'un four', a disaster. Despite two revisions, the work has never appealed to choirs or promoters, and it's tempting to conclude that the composer's initial response, to destroy the work, may have been the right one, though countermanded by Auric, Gouverné and Désormière. The fact that Durand did not publish the score until 1952 also suggests a certain lack of enthusiasm on their part. Finally, and sadly, one must confront the fact that James was paying the sum of 20,000 francs (less than Winnie's 25,000 francs for the Two-Piano Concerto, but still, in 2020 money, something of the order of £19,000) and that Poulenc regretted adding some orchestral bars in the last movement – 'what I would never have conceded to Éluard or Apollinaire – oh! irony – I conceded to James . . . because he had . . . paid me . . . for the work. I wanted him to be happy. You saw the result.'[79] On the financial front, the initial terror of the early 1930s that he might have to sell Le Grand Coteau might be over, but could one be sure, in 'the dreadful drift into darkness that defined European politics during the Thirties',[80] that it would not recur?

Some more successful performances followed, but the blow of the first one left a permanent scar. For years, every work of his had been well received by almost everyone, even rapturously so. The failure of *Sécheresses* mirrored that of the Paris premiere in 1931 of Honegger's cantata *Cris du monde* in which the composer issued 'a prophetic warning about matters that then had no name, but now have their own government departments: quality of life, the environment, pollution, enlistment, mass culture, pressure of noise, of the media, of collectivism'.[81] Like Poulenc, Honegger had been until then the golden boy of French music and he reacted to the blow by publishing an article 'Pour prendre congé' (Leaving the Ranks) in which he lamented that 'what is discouraging for a composer is the certainty that his work will not be heard or understood in the way he conceived it and tried to express it'.[82]

Poulenc, probably wisely, issued no such tract, but over the following years we can trace his continuing attempts to find homes for this difficult child and his profound gratitude when they succeeded. Nor were detractors of his music in general totally absent or silent. The setback of *Sécheresses* came on the heels of an especially virulent attack which ended by proclaiming that 'his music is for precocious, nasty children who read the classics listlessly, rip the pages and scribble on them cartoons of the teacher or the girlfriend they fondle in dark corners. Let's leave these amusements to one side. Enough of these farandoles and quadrilles. Let's be careful not to dramatize these empty pleasures, and let's not pursue these games in which the heart finds itself so ill at ease. Ravel, that conjuror of genius, is no more. All that's left on the scene now are a few garishly decorated clowns tumbling about in his shadow.'[83]

A response to this bitter tirade was already in hand in the shape of the Organ Concerto, now in its fourth year of gestation. As usual, the spring and summer found Poulenc moving around France with some rapidity: April at Noizay, May in Paris, July at Kerbastic, then with his sister at Le Tremblay, and the whole of August with Bernac at Anost. He worked at the Concerto first in Paris and then finished it at Anost.

Critical responses over the years, while generally positive in tone, have tended to imply puzzlement as to what the Concerto is saying. References to its sectional structure, like that of *Aubade*, and to a possible inheritance from Buxtehude steer clear of any real musical engagement. The earliest clues from the composer himself came in two letters of 1936 in which he claimed 'It's not the genial Poulenc of the Concerto for two pianos but rather a Poulenc on his way to the cloister, very 15th-century, if you like', also describing it as 'grave and austere'.[84] We have no way of knowing exactly what changes he made between 1936 and 1938 (though we know he did make some), but the denial of anything 'amusing' hardly fits with the Concerto we have. Perhaps his view was coloured by the problems he had composing it. The Princesse de Polignac had commissioned the work at Jean Françaix's suggestion after he had turned down her offer, and throughout its long gestation Poulenc remained aware, and indeed guilty, about its non-appearance. He explained to her that 'since I've been writing music I've never had such trouble finding my means of expression, but I hope, even so, that it now flows without sounding too effortful. At any rate it is a noble piece.'[85] Around the same time he wrote to his sister, 'I don't know what to think of it as it's so different from what I've done, and I've written it with a technique so new for me (almost from my desk) that I don't know what I feel about it.'[86] In the light of such apparent disarray, perhaps critical puzzlement might be a reasonable response. But the fact that the Concerto 'works' and has become one of his most popular pieces suggests that, as so often, his unconscious was really in control.

The mention of writing it 'from my desk' seems to indicate that Poulenc was aware of the necessary difference in composing for organ and for piano. Maurice Duruflé, who was the soloist in the first three performances and who made a notable recording of the work in 1961 with Georges Prêtre, remembered that Poulenc 'loved the organ, speaking to me about Louis Vierne, Charles Tournemire, Marcel Dupré, André Marchal and Joseph Bonnet. He often used to go and listen to them.' Since he'd joined Papoum's apartment block in the rue de Médicis in 1936, it was only natural that of these five he would hear more of Marcel Dupré at Saint-Sulpice, a mere 400 metres away. But the Concerto contains no terrifying demands on virtuosity. Contrast comes from the continous changes of texture and colour. When Duruflé and Poulenc were discussing the organ registration in Saint-Étienne-du-Mont, where Duruflé was organist, 'I realized he was very aware of the timbres he wanted, but that he couldn't define them, not being familiar with organ stops. [. . .] At a certain place in the organ part he said to me: "Now, here I'd like a neutral timbre, you know, that boring organ noise." ' Duruflé, as any organist would, offered him 8′ diapasons. '"That's it, that's exactly it," he said delightedly.'[87]

Regarding the work's structure, Renaud Machart helpfully points out that it adheres to a kind of symmetrical form, ABCA'C'BA, even if the repetitions are as much of general feeling as of precise material. As to its gravity, this certainly obtains in the opening organ flourish, recalling that of Bach's G minor Fantasia, one of Winnie's favourites, but elsewhere, at the opposite extreme, we find both long, lyrical melodies and, more strangely, the noises of a fairground steam organ. Of this curious conjunction, Wilfrid Mellers suggests that 'Stravinsky is again the catalyst between the "old" styles and the quick, balletic music in somewhat frenzied dance rhythms.'[88] Memories of what Stravinsky memorably referred to as the 'mortuary tarantella' at the end of *Oedipus Rex* are reinforced at the start of the Concerto by the timpani's minor thirds, recalling 'Adest pestis, Oedipus'.

After a private performance in Winnie's apartments on 16 December, conducted by Nadia Boulanger, the first public performance took place in the Salle Gaveau on 21 June 1939, conducted by Désormière. Poulenc much preferred Nadia's efforts, telling her 'Désormière was perfectly accurate but you, you also had the heart and the lyricism, and God knows, my music needs that'[89] – as far as I'm aware, the only negative response to Désormière's conducting known to mankind.

Apart from a little *Hymne à la Touraine* for four-part male chorus, preparations during August at Anost for the winter recitals with Bernac included five new songs from Poulenc which would include 'Le portrait'. Two of them, 'Dans le jardin d'Anna' and 'Allons plus vite', were settings of Apollinaire, and two, 'Tu vois le feu du soir' and 'Je nommerai ton front', of Éluard. For Poulenc the order of individual songs was every bit as important as those in a cycle, and in his *Journal de mes mélodies* he places them in the order of their intended performance.

He had thought of composing 'Dans le jardin d'Anna' in 1931 and 'the lyrical conclusion and the few Spanish bars came to me at once. The rest would not come.' Although he insisted that 'a tempo that is continuous and strict is essential', he does mark three deviations, most notably the wonderfully 'calm, expressive' conclusion; and, working against the steady tempo, in the song's seventy-one bars there are no fewer than twenty-seven changes of metre. This tension underlies the irony of the poet, sitting with Anna on a bench dated 1760 and wondering what they would have said to each other in those days – if he'd unfortunately been German, and talked to her about Pythagoras, and put on his Spanish coat to meet his grandmother . . . who refuses to speak German. The occasional bursts of lyricism finally flower in the final bars in Poulenc's favourite lyrical key of D flat major.

'Allons plus vite' was also a later version of a 1935 sketch, 'subsequently burnt and, thank heaven, forgotten [. . .] The poem by Apollinaire opens like Baudelaire: "Et le soir vient et les lys meurent" then, abruptly, after taking flight with a few noble lines, comes back to earth on a Paris pavement. [. . .] If you don't understand the poem's sexual melancholy, it's pointless to sing this song.'[90] The sexual undertow is presented in an extended form of the title, 'Allons plus vit' nom de Dieu allons plus vite', urged on the prostitute by her impatient client. Poulenc's own take on the proceedings was to admit 'I've so often spent the night loitering in Paris that I think I recognize better than any other composer the rhythm of a felt slipper sliding along the pavement on a May evening.'[91]

'Le portrait' was envisaged as the third song in the group, useful only as a 'mélodie tremplin' to lead into the fourth one, 'Tu vois le feu du soir', of which Poulenc wrote 'I wonder, if I was to play that silly game of "Desert Island Discs", whether this might not be the song of mine I'd choose to take with me.'[92] It belongs to an archetype that would include many of his most successful songs: the 'calm, magical' flow of quavers, often in pairs, is unceasing, untroubled by any change of tempo, so that the voice seems to float on a cushion of sound. The shape of the whole is dictated by the movements of the bass – long pedals at the beginning and end, and in the middle, on 'Tu vois un bel enfant quand il joue', the fifth of the six litanies starting with 'Tu vois', quicker movement and basic harmonies that underline the image's innocence. The great mystery is not that Poulenc should have written something so deeply moving, but that he should have paired it with the final song of the group, 'Je nommerai ton front'. In his *Journal* he admitted frankly that it is a 'mélodie ratée' (a dud song). Although work on it was interrupted by news of Bernac's father being seriously ill, this can really be no excuse for a brutal song that seems to lack any redeeming qualities. Whereas the duo recorded 'Tu vois' three times, its successor was left out in the cold, and on tour they regularly replaced it with 'La belle jeunesse', the seventh of the *Chansons gaillardes*.[93] Bernac's own opinion says it all: 'Éluard and Poulenc were both better suited for singing of love than of hate.'[94]

The puzzle is all the greater because in September and October Poulenc did compose two songs in a similarly contemplative vein to 'Tu vois le feu du soir' and was content to leave them without partners. After performing with Bernac at the Venice Biennale from 5 to 8 September, he had returned to Noizay and on the 29th wrote *Priez pour paix*, setting a poem he had found the day before in *Le Figaro* in a section entitled 'Les prières pour la paix'. This was a crucial moment in the lead-up to the war. On the very day Poulenc wrote the song, Hitler, Mussolini, Daladier and Chamberlain met in Munich and signed an agreement on the sovereignty of Czechoslovakia, from which Chamberlain returned waving his famous 'piece of paper', promising 'Peace for our time'. The poem, by the fifteenth-century poet Charles d'Orléans who had been captured at Agincourt and imprisoned in England for twenty-five years, took Poulenc back to the *Litanies à la Vierge noire* in its simplicity and devotional atmosphere, while its diatonic/modal harmonies are interrupted only for a couple of bars at the mention of Christ's people 'whom he wanted to redeem with his blood'. Published in two versions, the original low one in C minor and the one for medium voice in F minor, it is one of the few songs for which Poulenc sanctioned such transposition.

The second contemplative song on the other hand, written a few weeks later, is determinedly secular, and perhaps more so than is generally realized. Poulenc says *La Grenouillère* was one of the Apollinaire poems he had been intending to set for a long time and which had been 'waiting its turn'.[95] The pairs of piano chords, 'very much blurred by pedal', evoke a dreamworld of couples out in punts on the Marne near the island called La Grenouillère; Poulenc explained that it was inspired by Renoir's paintings, one of which the dedicatee, Marie-Blanche de Polignac, had just been given as a Christmas present by her mother. (Sending Marie-Blanche an autograph copy, Poulenc added 'obviously a Renoir would be much better. Even so, accept this little present from your old Francis.')[96] What Poulenc does not explain is that the island, as recorded by Maupassant in his 1881 story 'La Femme de Paul', 'reeked of vice and corruption, and the dregs of Parisian society in all its rottenness gathered there: cheats, conmen and cheap hacks rubbed shoulders with under-age dandies, old roués and rogues [. . .] Cheap sex, both male and female, was on offer in this tawdry meat-market [. . .]'[97] Perhaps, by the time Poulenc got to know it, the island had become respectable. Certainly his recorded view was that the song 'evokes a beautiful, lost past, Sundays of ease and contentment.'[98] On the other hand, as we learn from 'Allons plus vite', the seamier side of life was not unknown to him.

The last three months of 1938 saw Poulenc and Bernac giving concerts in Holland and eastern France, followed by the premieres of *Trois Poèmes de Louise de Vilmorin* – Poulenc accompanying Marie-Blanche on 28 November – and, as already mentioned, the Organ Concerto *chez* Winnie. Finally, to complete a very full year, Poulenc not only continued work on *Quatre Motets pour un temps de pénitence*, begun in the summer, but also found time in December to write an eighth Nocturne to form a coda to its predecessors, published separately between 1929 and 1935. Twenty years later he admitted to being very fond of certain of these, but without specifying which.[99] Sadly, he recorded only three of them (nos. 1, 2 and 4) in 1934 and never returned to the cycle.

The political situation did not prevent Poulenc and Bernac from touring England and Ireland between January and early March 1939, including five sessions for the BBC and a serious bout of flu caught in Ireland. Meanwhile the unlucky songs 'Je nommerai ton front' and 'Le portrait' received their first performances on 7 January and 16 February respectively. Altogether more successful was the first performance of the *Quatre Motets pour un temps de pénitence*, given on 7 April, Good Friday, by the Petits Chanteurs à la Croix de bois in the church of Saint-Nicolas-des-Champs. A year earlier, Poulenc had been very impressed by their performance of Milhaud's cantata *Les Deux Cités* on words by Paul Claudel and, after composing 'Vinea mea electa' in July, completed the cycle over the following months.

Although he always chose Victoria as his favourite among Renaissance choral composers, only one of the four texts, 'Tenebrae factae sunt', appears in that composer's oeuvre and there seems to be no link between the two settings. It was undoubtedly from Lassus that Poulenc borrowed the piecemeal text of 'Timor et tremor' (although it was also set by Giovanni Gabrieli) and both composers responded to the disruption latent in the final 'non confundar', Lassus by a top line syncopated against the rest, Poulenc by a succession of four triads that mix the bland and the colourful (B ma, D ma, A ma, C mi) – and, so that we take this on board, he repeats the succession louder and with a more active tenor part. In 'Vinea mea electa' the comfortable, diatonic opening, expressing Christ's hopes embodied for the vine he planted, soon veers off into dissonant bitterness, especially on the key word 'crucifigeres', so that the final return to the tonic major chord comes over as harshly ironic. The writing for a solo soprano in the final 'Tristis est anima mea' looks forward to similar moments in the *Stabat Mater* and *Gloria* where the emotion culminates in an outpouring of angelic beauty. Equally moving are the last ten bars of the motet, a *locus classicus* of Poulenc's genius in combining heterogeneous elements of a tonal scale to express emotional depth: 'and I go to be sacrificed for you', marked 'Très calme, doucement en dehors'. As to a performing style for these pieces, in a 1962 talk Poulenc praised a recording by the choir of the Académie Philharmonique Romaine for their warm tone, mentioning the name of the famous operatic soprano Renata Tebaldi – one of the many instances where he was happy to mix sacred with secular.[100]

The next five months were a time of planning, sketching and tidying up. If the idea of Poulenc writing incidental music to either *The Tempest* or *Pericles* seems curious,[101] he was certainly on the right track in making early sketches for *Les Mamelles de Tirésias*. Meanwhile he returned to two earlier works, beginning a re-orchestration of *Les Biches* (the only version known to us) in May, and in August making a definitive version of the Sextet, which had been a 'work in progress' since 1931 and never published. He told Nadia Boulanger that he had 'redone it entirely. It contained good ideas but the whole thing was badly put together. Now I'm happy with it.'[102] At the end of his life he added one detail that went beyond the ideas to the actual sound. He had been very struck by Ravel saying to him that young composers missed a trick by treating the double bass only as a foundation instrument, Ravel himself being a great one for harmonics on the instrument (see the beginning of *L'Enfant et les sortilèges*). Poulenc took this comment further, remarking that young composers tended to write too low for the strings, producing a dull texture, and specifically mentioned that he had borne this in mind while re-orchestrating *Les Biches*.[103]

The manic energy of the opening of the Sextet, recalling *Le Bal masqué*, demands considerable virtuosity from all concerned, before a plaintive phrase on solo bassoon introduces a lyrical section over regular quavers on the piano – here it's the melancholy of *Aubade* that's remembered. The manic energy is then briefly reactivated. In the central 'Divertissement' the structure is reversed to slow-fast-slow, from bel canto to perkiness and back, with the initial ideas now redistributed between the wind instruments. The finale revisits the crazy logic of the first movement through which lyricism is heard from time to time, but all seems set for a noisy ending – until another plaintive recitative on bassoon pours shame on all such vulgarity. Henri Hell might question the work's 'lack of a dorsal spine', but he was surely right in claiming that 'from the sole point of view of technique, the Sextet is a success of the rarest quality',[104] as is Benjamin Ivry in suggesting that the work needs to be played by individualists and not in too 'ensemble' a manner.[105]

On a more general front Poulenc wrote that 'since 2 September I admit courage fails me for attempting anything major since I don't know whether I shall be here the next day'.[106] This of course refers to France's declaration of war on 3 September, which led to Le Grand Coteau being full of refugees for the rest of that month.[107] Nevertheless Poulenc was more sanguine than, for example, Stravinsky who, caught up in Paris by the outbreak of hostilities, 'could neither eat nor sleep, he could not work; an occasional bomb blast made him jumpy; he got angry, nervous and irritable.'[108] Poulenc's letters to friends offer sympathy where required and explain that he's waiting to be called up, though as a soldier of the First World War he probably won't be needed instantly. Meanwhile he had returned to Vilmorin's poetry. By 26 September he had sketched six songs and is searching for a seventh, which he regarded as 'crucial', but which would in fact never materialize. 'I'm adopting the title *Fiançailles pour rire*,' he wrote to Boulanger, 'with all that that contains of nervousness, sensuality, disillusionment and melancholy.' Sensuality apart, an unsurprising response to events. But Poulenc's critical antennae were far from being neutralized. 'Of course,' he goes on:

I think all the time about music, about my music, about all the music I like and even what I don't like. As I'm not putting on any heroic posture, can I do otherwise? Absolutely not. Have you thought about what music will be like after the war? We shouldn't be trying to imagine a new fashion, as fashion is something that passes, but rather a new way of feeling, of communicating with our spiritual brothers. The other day two discs by a composer I won't name sent shivers down my spine. It was *terribly* 'pre-war'.[109]

VI

THE YEARS OF DARKNESS
✦ 1939–1944 ✦

The darkness did not descend immediately. Until the Germans occupied Paris on 14 June 1940, the French were subjected to what was called *le drôle de guerre*, 'the phoney war'. As for Poulenc, he would serve his country in uniform for little more than six weeks, and during those phoney months, his creativity, perhaps in sympathy, became muted, and would remain so for at least three years. To Stravinsky's anguished 'How can one work amid disorder?'[1] he seems to have answered 'Slowly'.

The emotional motivation behind *Fiançailles pour rire* was Vilmorin's departure with her husband for his castle in Hungary. When, if ever, would Poulenc see her again? The undertow of anxiety and melancholy in these songs is impossible to miss, even if Poulenc paints them with a light hand, and they do tend to raise questions of style and even of content. To begin with, how to translate the title? 'Light-hearted betrothal'? 'Whimsical betrothal?' If we take the line that Poulenc did not want the songs to be taken entirely seriously, then Bernac's view, that they do not really constitute a cycle and that the poems 'lack the same richness, the same density as the admirable poems of Éluard'[2] is tenable (though an uncharitable critic might point out that, as they were definitely intended to be sung by a woman, his opinion might not have been entirely unbiased). Other critics have noted Poulenc's later description of the songs as 'more fabricated' than his *Cinq Poèmes de Max Jacob*,[3] but perhaps not too much should be made of this, since Poulenc, as we have seen and like many other composers, was given to sporadic bouts of unhappiness with his own works.

On the positive side, the songs are now regularly sung round the world and work charm of an unusually refined and delicate kind. Partly this stems from their contrasting elements of strictness and abandon. In 'La dame d'André' the regular four-bar phrases are offset by a more 'romantic' piano part, including grinding semitones on the phrases 'A-t-elle eu peur, la nuit venue', while in 'Dans l'herbe' the singer's lament over a dead lover proceeds in the piano's steady crotchets but also in a succession of swiftly changing tonalities; these are then halted momentarily by one of Poulenc's favourite cycles of fifths to help register the '*p* subito' on the words 'Mais comme j'étais loin de lui', giving the reason for his lonely death. 'Il vole' is another of the 'mélodies tremplin', marked 'presto implacable', to act as an introduction to the calm of the fourth song, and pianists may find a wry justification for its strenuous demands in the two final bars, borrowed from Chopin's G flat Étude op. 25 no. 9.

The last three songs are linked by tempo: the crotchet markings being respectively at 60, 63 and 56, the area regularly inhabited by Poulenc's lyrical *mélodies*. 'Mon cadavre est doux', like 'Dans l'herbe', belongs to the numerous family of songs that take as their basis the regular pulsations found in those of Schubert, Schumann and Brahms. 'Violon', though, is specifically a portrait of the Hungarian gipsy fiddlers Vilmorin's husband, Count Palffy, had brought to a Hungarian restaurant on the Champs-Élysées. From the A minor of this song to the D flat major of 'Fleurs' was a deliberate leap 'from afar' and, if ever a singer wanted to preface 'Fleurs' with a different song, Poulenc insisted it should also be in a distant key. 'I believe,' wrote Poulenc, that in 'Fleurs' 'there is such unassuageable melancholy that from the opening bars the listener will assign to the song its role as a coda. It must be sung with *humility*, the lyricism coming from *within*.'[4] Writing to Marie-Blanche he said it 'produces tears, or ought to produce them.'[5] Graham Johnson, who has played this song more often and to a higher standard than most critics, is firm in its defence: 'It breathes at the tempo of a heartbeat and moves forward as a living, feeling thing, the plaint of a real person with real needs. This is simply a sign that Poulenc is in touch with the expressive needs of singers, and as a result they love him like few other twentieth-century composers.'[6]

Poulenc's first musical recognition of war, rather than of separation, dates from that same October in the song *Bleuet*, to a poem by Apollinaire that records the imagined thoughts of a squaddy who is to 'go over the top' at 5 p.m. By an extraordinary coincidence (or was it divine intervention?), as Poulenc was working on the song he received the news, false as it later turned out, of the death at the front of a young man he had known from childhood. This song too 'breathes at the tempo of a heartbeat' and, since it also eschews the pomp of bugle calls and flags, he considered marking it to be sung 'intimement', though in the end he settled for 'très lié, très simplement'.[7] As, in the final two lines ('O douceur d'autrefois/ Lenteur immémoriale'), Apollinaire indulges in nostalgia for the lazy days of peace, the music moves from C♯ minor to the major on the last word. Is this comfort

realistic? Just when we are thinking it might be, the piano ends with a high
D♯ – a questioning compression of those Poulenc sign-offs that have so often had
the last word.

❦

After the departure from Le Grand Coteau of the evacuees at the end of September,
Poulenc began his wait to be called up and committed his thoughts and fears to his
letters in some detail. He reads Bossuet and Valéry, commenting 'If we did not
constantly take care of our souls, life these days would truly be one of slavery'.[8] He
worries about Bernac who had never been in the army (he was declared unfit at the
end of the first war because of tuberculosis), but has now been called up, and is
sorry for 'those who, in these dark days do not have the faith that embraces all
faiths'[9] and explains 'I have confidence in my guardian angel. That's a great deal.
In exchange I've promised him some religious pieces.'[10] Then, in December, he is
thrilled to learn that, thanks to his networking, including appeals to Alfred Cortot
who on 21 November had instituted 'L'action artistique aux armées',[11] Bernac has
been given three months' leave so that the two of them can tour Portugal from 2 to
10 January, promoting French song. And so, 'a few days after leaving behind the
uniform, the truck, the snow, and the cold of a terrible winter, I found myself in
tails, giving a recital with Francis on the stage of the opera house in Lisbon!'[12]

But throughout the eight months between October and the following June, in
unwitting accord with Stravinsky, Poulenc wrote a mere one and a half minutes of
new music. Instead, like Apollinaire in *Bleuet*, his thoughts turned to the past.
Initially they were guided in that direction by an aesthetic disaster. On 3 November
he wrote:

What a frightful day!!! On the radio a lady has just been caterwauling, for a
whole quarter of an hour, some songs which could possibly have been by me!
Ah! female singers who follow only their own instinct. I ought to say 'instincts',
since I presume this lady is gifted in quite other areas than music. People often
massacre my piano pieces, but never as much as my songs and, God knows, I
place a higher value on the songs than the piano pieces. I'm undertaking this
diary in the hope it may serve as a guide to those interpreters who entertain
some feeling for my poor music. I say 'poor', but I ought to write 'miserable',
for that's how it felt to me, sung like this.[13]

144

Poor Poulenc! But those who love his songs and appreciate his *Journal de mes mélodies* have good reason to be grateful to the caterwauler: what would we not give to have a *Tagebuch meiner Lieder* by Schubert? In the short term, though, the experience seems to have been traumatic since he would begin no more solo songs until the *Chansons villageoises* in October 1942. In other genres too he kept an almost total silence, the one and a half minutes mentioned above consisting of a *Française d'après Claude Gervaise* for piano on the lines of the previous *Suite*. He concluded 1939 by orchestrating three Satie piano pieces (two posthumous preludes and the *Gnossienne* no. 3). We know neither the motive behind this work nor the details of any first performance.

Poulenc marked the beginning of a new decade by finishing his re-orchestration of *Les Biches*. Hervé Lacombe says that the Opéra was to mount it,[14] but for whatever reason this never happened. He and Bernac then made their tour of Portugal, followed by trips to Italy and Holland during February and Switzerland in March. In April Cortot arranged a recital for them in Casablanca and in due course thanked them profusely for the 'magnifique résultat' and the evidence it provided for their 'légitime popularité'.[15] Then in May they broadcast on French Radio, drawing thanks from Casella's wife Hélène for 'a moment of perfect beauty, and an interpretation worthy of the music, giving that rare impression that it could not be otherwise.'[16]

Finally, on 2 June 1940, Poulenc's call-up papers arrived, sending him to Bordeaux to join the 72nd battery of the Anti-Aircaft division. But it seems he was still in Paris around 10 June when the astonishing exodus from the Paris region took place of some two million people, graphically described by Irène Némirovsky in her book *Suite française*. As related by Marcel Schneider many years later, Poulenc's ex-lover Raymond Destouches, being a professional chauffeur, was prevailed upon to load up his enormous Panhard-Levassor limousine with the gold rings, silver and precious documents belonging to Poulenc's sister and her husband and to head south. 'But great embarrassment when it came to lunch. It was not thought proper to eat with the chauffeur, but neither could you let him eat on his own at a nearby table. "I found the solution," Francis told me. We had a picnic on the edge of a wood. The open air and fresh grass did the trick . . ." '[17]

On 14 June the Germans entered Paris and the government moved to Bordeaux, and on 29 June from there to Vichy where, on 10 July, the National Assembly voted full powers to Marshal Pétain. On that day, as Poulenc's brief mobilization was coming to an end, he gave Marie-Blanche an account of his life under arms. He's now in Cahors and doesn't:

. . . regret for a second the time I've spent in uniform. I'm with tough peasants from the Périgord, Limousin and Dordogne. Their intelligence is far superior to that of the Parisians who 'think they know it all'. [. . .] The under-officer who's in charge of 'supplies' is a figure of fun for the men. He's a pork butcher by trade and yesterday decided to buy a pig. They killed it this morning. To general hilarity it became clear that the butcher had always had his pigs slaughtered by an underling. The poor beast screamed for all of 15 minutes. [. . .] Shortly afterwards, the village bell rang for mass. Cool as you like, my companion in the straw (I'm sleeping in a barn, all very 'La Fontaine') announced, 'Ah, that's Cazot (the butcher) sounding the knell for his pig.'[18]

On the same day he wrote to Bernac in similar good spirits: ' "I have my hands," that's what I keep saying to myself all day long with a wild gratitude. Paris is intact. I would happily sacrifice Noizay for it. It's rather strange in fact how little I care about things.'[19] Poulenc was not alone in being immune to the bitterness of defeat. As Jean Dutourd recounted in his chronicle of 1940, while some of the several thousand French prisoners at Auray 'had anxious looks on their faces, the majority had the good humour of people who have been disencumbered of a great weight. As nobody felt responsible, they took unreserved pleasure in the defeat.'[20] But as the Occupation continued it became clear, as Poulenc wrote to Milhaud, now safely with his wife and son in America, that there were 'spiritual values to be defended'. But how? If in Paris a German soldier asked you the way to the Opéra, did you tell him? Did you tell him wrong? Or did you walk past, ignoring him? And if such a person was billeted on you, did you have the courage and determination of the family described by Vercors and refuse to speak to him?[21] Most acute of all could be the problem of how to make a living, especially for musicians who depended on performance for their existence.

Poulenc, like all his compatriots, would face these problems in due course. For the moment, after being demobilized on 18 July he had to wait while the bureaucracy sorted out his travel from the 'free zone' to the 'occupied zone' that included Le Grand Coteau. Four days later he reached Brive where he stayed with cousins and where he was visited by Papoum, his sister and his niece Rosine. Here he began to work on the tunes and sketches he had made during his time in the straw: a piano piece: *Mélancolie*, a Cello Sonata, not completed until 1948, and *L'Histoire de Babar*, a setting of Jean de Brunhoff's children's story. He also sketched out all the movements of a ballet, *Les Animaux modèles*, fulfilling the long-expressed wish of the Opéra director Jacques Rouché and which, as he wrote to Auric, he was largely happy with 'because they're all conceived *orchestrally* [pensés *orchestre*].'[22]

Mélancolie is, by any computation, one of Poulenc's most touching piano pieces, so it is surprising that commentators have tended to bypass it. One obvious question is, why the title? Wilfrid Mellers offers the observation that 'Rather than melancholy as it is usually understood, the mood is rather of resignation, of a happiness that recognizes its fragility, immanent in the continual modulations.'[23] Poulenc might almost be saying, 'France is at peace for the moment. But for how long?' And what about those spiritual values that had to be defended?

L'Histoire de Babar also turns out to be different, and indeed more, than just a children's story. The tale of its genesis gives us a glimpse of Poulenc's incarnation as 'l'oncle Francis'. One day he was playing some of his music on the piano, when 'the granddaughter of one of his cousins came up to him and said: "Oh, Uncle Francis, what you're playing is so boring! Why don't you play this?" And she put on the piano Jean de Brunhoff's *L'Histoire de Babar, le petit éléphant*. So Poulenc started to improvise for her, responding to the ideas the little girl suggested to him.'[24] As often, Poulenc then put these musical ideas aside and let them germinate. But what he finally produced would, as we shall see, be far from childish in the sense of incompetent or emotionally naive.

At last, on 9 September, Poulenc was cleared for travel to Paris, in a cattle truck: 'Be duly grateful for your American sleeping cars!' he wrote to Milhaud.[25] He stayed in Paris for some of October, since it was from there and in that month that he dated a new project, incidental music to Jean Anouilh's play *Léocadia* at the Théâtre Michodière, which Yvonne Printemps and Pierre Fresnay had just taken over. The score, written for soprano, violin, double bass, clarinet and bassoon, is most notable for the warmhearted song *Les Chemins de l'amour*, made famous in Printemps's recording. Otherwise it follows two of Poulenc's prescriptions: either cod eighteenth-century with wrong notes or, as in the song Printemps sang in Act III, leisurely waltzes that look back to his early years in Nogent. To the first group, but without the wrong notes, belongs the overture to Act II which would appear, in developed format, as *Improvisation 11*, in all probability the sightreading piece for the Conservatoire piano *concours* requested by the director, Claude Delvincourt, to be 'a single page, not too tough, but even so with one or two traps';[26] both are dated

June 1941. If Poulenc was happy to borrow from Mozart, Stravinsky and others, what reason could there be not to borrow also from himself? The play opened on 3 November and ran for 173 performances until the following April, surpassing Poulenc's expectations and momentarily healing 'the anxieties I didn't imagine being able to avoid this winter'.[27]

He finally returned to Noizay in October,[28] and during November and December continued to move between there and Paris. On 24 November he attended a Mozart/Ravel concert conducted by Charles Münch in the old concert hall of the Conservatoire, where Berlioz's *Symphonie fantastique* was first performed in 1830. The little hall was packed, so Poulenc heard the concert in a corner of the stage sitting on a harp case. But, true to form, he turned this into a profitable exercise:

> When it comes to music by Ravel, it's absolutely fascinating to hear an orchestration the wrong way up, that's to say with more wind instruments than strings, more percussion than bows. Few orchestrations pass this formidable test. You won't be surprised if I tell you that Ravel's balancing of sounds comes through this cross-examination with flying colours.[29]

Ravel did indeed believe in making the different departments of the orchestra as far as possible self-sufficient, and Poulenc may well have tried to take this lesson into his score of *Les Animaux modèles*.

But this was still some months in the future. Poulenc's immediate interest lay in five further settings of Apollinaire and, thanks to a happy mixture of inspiration and hard work, they were ready for his recital with Bernac in the Salle Gaveau on 14 December, five days after the first performance of the revised Sextet. Poulenc took the title *Banalités* for the group of five songs from its appearance over two *vers de mirlitons*, pieces of doggerel, he discovered when sorting out his library on his return to Noizay. But there was almost certainly a further reference to his 1935 article 'Éloge de la banalité', in which he had stated, 'I detest in equal measure synthetic cuisine, synthetic perfume and synthetic art – I want garlic with my mutton, real rose perfume and music that says clearly what it wants to say, even if it has to use vulgar words. I praise banality, "yes, why not", if it is intentional, felt, earthy and not born of weakness.' He also explained, 'I made the decision a long time ago to put the unusual harmony and the common-or-garden cadence into the same pot.'[30] The result, as Bernac says, is a heterogeneous group, rather than a true cycle such as *Tel jour telle nuit*.

The two doggerel songs, 'Hôtel' and 'Voyage à Paris' (nos. 2 and 4), belong to the Nogent fraternity, the latter recalling for Bernac the style of Maurice Chevalier, though he differs from Poulenc in claiming that 'this great music-hall singer was, for half a century, the incarnation of a certain type of sentimentality and Parisian waggish humour, which never descended into vulgarity . . .' – an interesting remark, implying that the Poulenc/Bernac duo contained tensions that needed some working through during their summer rehearsals. As for 'Hôtel', few would quarrel with Bernac's description as 'undoubtedly the "laziest" song ever written!'[31] The laziness resides in several aspects: the hypnotically regular four-bar phrases in the piano part; the lush, sensual harmonies, underpinned by a long cycle of fifths in the bass (lasting for half of the song, from the G♯ in bar 6 to the B flat in bar 18); and the relaxed, conversational tone of the vocal line. But formless the song is not. How cunningly Poulenc places F♯s – as his favourite major third in the song's D major – once in bar 3, then not again until the singer's very last note in bar 21, on completing the crucial word 'fumer'! But perhaps the greatest miracle comes in the last two bars of the piano's coda: four simple chords that in an inexplicable way sum up the tone of the whole song. Readers may like to try finding any other group of chords that succeeds so effortlessly . . .

'Voyage à Paris', the other doggerel song, swings along with splendid abandon: the duo often performed it as the last item of a foreign tour before returning to the capital. The opening 'Chanson d'Orkenise' also eschews sentimentality, being marked 'briskly, in the style of a popular song', as does the stark 'Fagnes de Wallonie', which Bernac identifies as 'a high plateau in the Belgian Ardennes where Apollinaire spent a holiday at Stavelot in 1899. It's a place of moors and peat bogs, of knotty trees twisted by the wind.'[32] The group ends with 'Sanglots', on a poem which, like 'Fagnes de Wallonie', Poulenc had long wanted to set. Here, as Henri Hell, says, 'the tone changes. No more games or waggish humour or laziness. The poem, one of Apollinaire's most poignant and discreetly heart-rending, evokes the common humanity that each of us carries within us since the beginning of time.'[33] 'Heart-rending' is indeed the effect of Poulenc's music, culminating in thirteen bars that circle desperately round F♯ minor before finding it, as the singer declaims 'Et rien ne sera libre jusqu'à la fin du temps' . . . and this, at that first performance, in Occupied Paris.

Looking back over the year in December, Poulenc admitted to his sister that he was relishing his solitude at Le Grand Coteau, allowing him to compose in peace. He was happy with the progress of *Les Animaux modèles*, in addition to which he had written a tiny piece for solo flute, two Latin motets for the wedding of his previous landlord Georges Salles with Hélène de Wendel (though this ceremony never took place), a setting of a poem by Paul Valéry as *Colloque*, and an article on Chabrier for his upcoming centenary.

The piece for flute, vaguely recalling Debussy's *Syrinx*, was written for an album published in 1940 by Marie-Thérèse Mabille under the title *Ruines de Tours 1940* and stays close to its tonic C minor throughout.[34] In *Exultate Deo*, a 'motet for ceremonious occasions', the early promise of imitative entries is soon quashed in favour of joyful triads floating freely through various keys. The mood changes only for the last line, 'insigni die solemnitatis vestrae', where the word 'solemnitatis' provokes a standard Poulenc texture of descending sequences over a low pedal. In contrast, the four-part *Salve Regina* is couched almost entirely in minor triads, taking its cue from the phrase 'gementes et flentes' ('groaning and weeping') and perhaps warning the couple (unnecessarily, as it turned out) that marriage is not all lutes and trumpets. Of *Colloque*, a duo for soprano, then baritone, Poulenc explained at the end of his life that 'I admire Valéry as much as Verlaine, Rimbaud or Mallarmé, but, as far as those poets are concerned, I couldn't find a note of music to set their lines. The result was that my [*Colloque*] sinks into the worst sort of dullness.'[35] The problem was that Valéry had sent the poem to him with the request that he set it. The result proves the rule that politeness has little or nothing to do with art.

Happily, in writing about Chabrier, politeness was not called for: Poulenc's article, written for *La nouvelle Revue française* and celebrating, among much else, the 1941 Paris performances of *L'Étoile* and *Gwendoline*, was effectively a dry run for his biography of twenty years later. Completing his production for 1940 was another article, entitled simply 'Igor Strawinsky', complaining that for the whole of the autumn season the Parisian Sunday concerts had been a Stravinsky-free zone. Probably he was moved to write because Stravinsky was now in Manhattan and so unable to promote himself; in a roundabout way, it can also be read as publicity for the upcoming performance of *Les Noces* on 2 March in which Poulenc was one of the pianists. But he was also, as if by some instinct, ahead of his time, in that the Nazis didn't quite know what to do with Stravinsky's music: it could hardly be termed 'degenerate', and yet its vast distance from the German tradition was unsettling. Just not playing it might be the safest course.

Away from the concert hall, we know little about Poulenc's love life. Raymond Destouches was now married with a son Jean, to whom Poulenc had dedicated one of the *Petites voix* in 1936. To Raymond, Poulenc had dedicated *Mélancolie* (with what intention we can only guess) and the two men remained close until the end of Poulenc's life. The same was true of Richard Chanlaire, in both cases the intimate relationship turning into one of friendship. The fact that the Poulenc *Correspondance* contains no mention of Chanlaire between 1930 and 1954 cannot be taken as signifying any kind of break – merely that, from the passionate letters of the early 1930s until those of the 1950s, either Poulenc became more guarded in mentioning his amorous liaisons, or that the recipients of passionate letters have preferred to keep them private. The result has been that, quite simply, Poulenc's later love life is a closed book until his liaisons with Lucien Roubert from 1950 to 1955, and with Louis Gautier from 1957 until his death.

Whether from Paris or Noizay, he also wrote that January of 1941 to Sauguet, enthusing that 'I can't get over how much progress I've made with my ballet. I feel, thanks be to God, in that same state of creative richness as in the days of *Les Biches*. I hope technique will be the only thing to show signs of the 20 intervening years.'[36] But the visit to Le Grand Coteau was undoubtedly short, because between 25 January and 25 March he was involved in no fewer than nine concerts in Paris, including first performances of *Ce doux petit visage* and *Colloque* on 4 February;[37] then there followed that of *Mélancolie* by Marcelle Meyer on 23 May. The February occasion was a 'concert causerie' with the theme 'Chabrier-Debussy-Poulenc' in a series entitled 'La musique contemporaine française et ses affinités'. To his composing and piano playing, Poulenc now added his skills as raconteur, and so successfully that these 'causeries' would become a staple of his performances. Another one took place on 15 March with the title 'Baudelaire, Verlaine, Apollinaire et cinq de leurs musiciens, Henri Duparc, Gabriel Fauré, Debussy, Honegger, Poulenc'. Poulenc explained that 'I would talk first of all about these gentlemen, and afterwards why not about their relationships with the composers? And one could alternate words and music.'[38]

Quite unusually, work on *Les Animaux modèles* seems to have taken absolute preference over almost everything else. Apart from a score of the film *La Duchesse de Langeais*, on a script by Jean Giraudoux based on Balzac and not to be shown until March 1942, so probably not engaging Poulenc until the end of 1941, the next new pieces are not heard of until September, when an announcement appeared in *L'Information musicale* of a still unfinished String Trio, destined for 'the marvellous

Pasquiers'.³⁹ News of the work persists in Poulenc's correspondence for a while, but no score has survived, neither does an article on the use of the pedal, promised to the editor of *L'Information musicale*. This, Poulenc reckoned, would upset the mothers of some young pianists he had examined, and he sounded off about their pedalling, no doubt on the usual lines of 'pas assez'. The other work mentioned is the song 'Montparnasse'. This, not finally completed until January 1945, was to be held up by Poulenc as proof against the persistent assumption that his largely unchallenging musical vocabulary derived from easy writing.

Recitals continued through the summer – a 'Séance Francis Poulenc' on 10 June, a concert with Bernac in Biarritz on 25 July – but in a letter to Milhaud he admits that in general 'work is the best comfort at the moment. Indeed I'm living at a distance from everything. [. . .] The musical life is intense and everyone plunges into it as a way of forgetting present sorrows. [. . .] Alas, Henri Mat[isse] is rather ill. Pablo is full of genius. I see him regularly.'⁴⁰ There is conflicting evidence as to when exactly Poulenc completed the piano score of his ballet and moved on to the orchestration, but his overall mood of high seriousness is unmistakable. To Marie-Blanche he writes that 'I shall be living amid anxiety, so no holidays or idle wanderings or delicious Breton cooking. One has to resign oneself and be well-behaved if one wants to become a great composer. At the moment I'm really haunted by this craving for greatness. So I must accept the consequences.'⁴¹ According to a letter of 13 September to Jacques Rouché, the director of the Paris Opéra, Poulenc was then planning to deliver six of the eight numbers to the engraver and could play Rouché the remaining two from memory.⁴²

At some point in September or October he wrote incidental music to a play called *La Fille du jardinier*, premiered on 22 November, but the score is lost, and the only completed piece that remains from these last months of 1941 is the twelfth *Improvisation* in November, dedicated to the actress Edwige Feuillère who was playing the title role in *La Duchesse de Langeais*. But even this is a slightly developed version of the 'Valse brillante' that forms the second number of the film score. Subtitled 'Hommage à Schubert', it asks the pianist to play 'smartly' (pimpant) and to emphasize the first beats of each bar. In the simple structure AABAcoda, the B section introduces an element of questioning, even of melancholy, and varies the predominantly four-bar phrases with five- and three-bar ones, while on the fade-out ending we find the typical instructions 'sans ralentir' and, twice, 'toujours sans ralentir'. It may count as 'Romantic' music, but there's no call to over-egg the pudding. The rest of the score is neatly summarized by

Lacombe as consisting of 'waltzes, a mazurka, a minuet, ländler and pages of delicate melancholy'.[43]

Meanwhile on the larger stage December 1941 saw a number of crucial events: on the 7th the Japanese attacked Pearl Harbor, and the United States entered the war; on the 12th, 750 French Jews were arrested in Paris; and on the 20th the German assault on Moscow failed. In the French capital, the Nazis were anxious not to stir up more animosity than was strictly necessary and in general allowed the French a certain autonomy in their musical activities. For some French musicians there were organizations they themselves shunned, notably Radio-Paris which had become a blatant arm of Nazi propaganda. Of course Jewish composers were banned, but there could be ways round this: rumour has it that the teenage Yvonne Loriod would, without censure, include in her repertoire piano pieces by a certain 'Bartholdy', otherwise known to the world as Mendelssohn. Indeed, the Nazi authorities were not always as vigilant as one might suppose. Honegger's daughter Pascale remembered, fifty years later, the *frisson* that ran through the French in the audience for her father's oratorio *Judith*, at the words 'Israël revivra!'[44]

More damaging on many fronts were the banning of Jewish performers, which decimated the musical life of the capital, and the export of young men to work in factories in Germany, the hated STO (Service de travail obligatoire). Around 600,000 workers were extradited between June 1942 and July 1944. In a move to stem the loss of young musicians, Claude Delvincourt, the director of the Conservatoire, started up the Orchestre des Cadets du Conservatoire, and it is testimony to a certain ambivalence among Nazi administrators that he succeeded. Indeed one of the clichés of French novels during the war was the figure of 'the musical German', a source of ambivalence among the French, to add to their early, surprised appreciation of the enemy's correctness and good manners. Despite these difficulties and others such as lack of heating and bomb alerts, 'concerts were now more frequent and audience numbers much greater. [. . .] During the four seasons of war, the four Paris associations organized more than 650 [Sunday] concerts.' But for orchestral players there were difficult choices to be made. 'In exchange for attractive salaries, the authorities of Radio-Paris demanded exclusivity. They insisted on a regular presence which forced musicians playing for Radio-Paris to arrange replacements in other orchestras. So it became difficult to manage both functions, with the result that numerous replacements took over the duties of official members: it was a frequent occurrence for a conductor to hold a rehearsal with players who were then absent for the concert.'[45]

❧

Poulenc escapes the attentions of a biographer for much of the first half of 1942, undoubtedly because he spent much of it closeted with the orchestration of *Les Animaux modèles*, 'a great labour because I orchestrate very slowly'.[46] There were two premieres during this time – the screening of *La Duchesse de Langeais* on 27 March and the performance of *Fiançailles pour rire* with Gérard Souzay's sister Geneviève Touraine on 21 May – but the first known letter concerning the ballet, to the director of the Opéra Jacques Rouché, dates from 4 June. The news is good. A third of the work is already rehearsed, he is delighted with the choreography by Serge Lifar (who, rather unusually, is praised for his 'docility'), the score and orchestral parts are complete – but now to a question of money: 'It seems to me, since I have written this ballet specially for the Opéra after reading you the scenario for it, that *Les Animaux* comes within the scope of commissions allocated through the budget of the Beaux-Arts, and that consequently it would be fair to allot to me (as I am both librettist and composer) the sum of 10,000 francs, mandated for a work of one act. I hope, dear Director, that this will also be your own point of view.'[47] Whether it was or not, we don't know.

The whole question of what the ballet is 'about' has exercised many minds. Perhaps the first point to make clear is that the idea of it went back at least as far as 1937, when Poulenc wrote to Collaer, 'I'm starting a ballet on the fables of La Fontaine. I think it suits me very well.'[48] It thus has no initial grounding in the war, and its supposedly Pétainist leaning towards a glorification of the French countryside is entirely accidental. More to the point is the resumé offered by Wilfrid Mellers:

> . . . it makes sense in the evolution of Poulenc's theatrical art, since in being based on the fables of La Fontaine it fuses Poulenc's preoccupation with childhood with his love of France's *grand siècle*. [. . .] *Les Animaux modèles* is, as Francis put it, 'très Louis XIV' [. . .] La Fontaine's wit, tenderness and intermittent gravity have precisely the ambivalence between a mature classicism and an elegiac romanticism – looking back to the Golden Age of Louis XIII – that so entranced Poulenc in the music of Couperin.[49]

The composer's own thoughts about the ballet are perhaps best appreciated in the responses he made to criticisms of it by two friends whom he held in high regard. Charles Koechlin had written to him the previous December asking, unavailingly, whether he might, through his connections with Rhône-Poulenc, have access to saccharine, which Koechlin could no longer obtain. Instead, Poulenc invited him to the ballet's premiere on 8 August (the Nazi Occupation had turned upside down the usual calendar, under which August had always been a 'dead' month for music). Koechlin thanked him for this, but not until the 19th, which Robert Orledge remarks as being 'an unusually long gap for him, perhaps because he had been putting off expressing his opinion, which was less than enthusiastic'.[50] The crucial passage reads:

> It seemed to me that in the matter of orchestration you are more your own master than in *Les Biches*. Even so, for now I really think that I prefer *Les Biches*. There are some very amusing and characteristic passages in *Les Animaux modèles*, for example the bear and also the charming children's dance before that. Elsewhere some of the dances seemed to me a bit long, I mean 'musically' (for instance, the final ensemble) and not to have as much character as some other compositions of yours, for example the set of songs you sent me and which were very much to my taste.[51]

This letter, headed 'Cher Ami', provoked a response headed 'Cher Koechlin' in which Poulenc regrets his teacher's preference for *Les Biches* and admits being equally distressed that in *Les Animaux* 'you seem to have been chiefly struck by its burlesque aspects. You are one of the few who have not been touched by the death, the dawn and the midday meal. Coming from you, these reservations grieve me greatly.'[52] These three movements, nos. 6, 1 and 8, do indeed display Poulenc at his most heartfelt, and his distress is understandable, quite apart from Koechlin's comments touching again the old sensitive spot of Poulenc being essentially a clown, repeated in English-speaking countries in the form of the tiresome pun 'le leg-Poulenc'. It is in these three movements that we hear the truth of Poulenc's admission in his 1954 conversations with Claude Rostand, 'As far as harmony goes, I also owe a lot to Ravel, especially in *Les Animaux modèles*.'[53] On the overall tone of the ballet, he was already insisting less than a week later, and before receiving Koechlin's letter, that 'I must repeat, my ballet is a serious one, and so it was vital that the impersonations should not at any point engender a "Casino de Paris" atmosphere.'[54]

The other friend who offended was Colette, in an article published in *Comoedia* on 22 August, in which she waxed lyrical about a side of Poulenc not hitherto widely explored: 'Beneath a rocky hillside, Poulenc, surrounded by vines, lives in a large, airy house where he makes and drinks his wine. Through his spangled orchestration listen to the sound and gaze at the gold and bubbles issuing from a rich patch of earth! Look at Poulenc: are those the features of a water drinker? He has a strong, sensitive nose, an eye quick to change expression. He is confiding and wary, at ease in friendship, and as poetical as a peasant.'[55] The assumption that, because he lived in the Touraine, Poulenc was a native Tourangeau, was one he combated all his life; on this occasion he explained to Colette that such agricultural influence as manifested itself in the ballet came rather from the Morvan, the Dordogne and the Périgord. But by far her worst sin was to take issue with the production, not realizing that Poulenc, visually aware as ever, had exerted a determining influence on its tiniest details.[56]

The six movements representing the La Fontaine fables are topped and tailed by movements evoking the peasants going off into the fields at dawn, and then returning at midday for lunch. These movements are allied in their material, including a quotation from *Litanies à la Vierge noire* that serves finally as a pre-prandial 'Benedicite', and in their key of D major which summons up memories of the song 'Hôtel'. The title *Les Animaux modèles*, found for Poulenc by Éluard despite his distaste for La Fontaine's poetry, indicates that animal sentiments inform the behaviour of the dancers, but they put a human spin on these and so wear entirely human dress apart from the chorus of hens, who are permitted white feathers on their tutus and three red ostrich feathers on their heads – 'but this hair decoration is more to indicate their femininity'.[57]

The characters and events in the six movements take their origins from La Fontaine without following him in every detail. 'L'ours et les deux compagnons' targets greed. Two hard-up friends sell a bearskin to a merchant before actually killing the bear. The animal's appearance sends one up a tree, while the other plays dead. Poulenc interposes a little dance for the bear in the course of which 'he blows kisses at the audience, clearly being an educated bear who's escaped from a zoo'. Having sniffed at the 'corpse', the bear shambles off and the two friends escape in terror. In 'La cigale et la fourmi', the first and one of the best known of the fables, the cricket (or dancer), having sung (or danced) all summer instead of hoarding food against winter, dances a fast waltz in ever greater desperation. She calls on the miserly ant to ask for money, but is rebuffed. In Poulenc's version, the ant then throws a violin and a bow at the cricket – his rendering of the poet's 'Eh bien! dansez maintenant.'

The human version of 'Le lion amoureux' is a long-haired, ne'er-do-well hippy who captures the eye of a shepherdess. In the poet's version, her father insists that the lion has his teeth and claws filed; in Poulenc's, more visible to a stage audience, he demands that, after dancing a 'java' with his girl, the hippy disarm himself of both pistol and dagger. The lion is duly (La Fontaine) killed by dogs or (Poulenc, less upsettingly) chased away by the father's servants. In either case, La Fontaine's motto is applicable: 'Love, Love, when you've got hold of us, we can truly say "Farewell Prudence!"', but Poulenc ends with a gentle waltz for the girl as she returns to her house in tears. At various times in his life hereafter, the composer proudly recounted how in this ballet he had surreptitiously inserted the refrain to a patriotic song from the Franco-Prussian war, 'Non, vous n'aurez pas l'Alsace et la Lorraine', and how delighted he was to see the German officers in the audience totally oblivious of the quotation. Curiously, he always wrongly referred to this as occurring in the seventh movement, 'Les coqs', whereas it appears in fact, repeated six times in a row, at the start of 'Le lion amoureux'. This mistake persevered in the Poulenc literature until Yannick Simon sensibly looked at the music. But even so, the quotation is so thoroughly 'Poulencquified' that even those who knew the original well could be forgiven for missing it. In any case, the sentiment was out of date since both provinces were now firmly under Nazi control: speaking Alsatian, Lorraine Franconian or French there was now illegal, and speaking German obligatory, while 200,000 of the inhabitants, being deemed unassimilable, were expelled.[58]

In 'L'homme entre deux âges et ses deux maîtresses' Poulenc follows La Fontaine precisely in charting the experience of the middle-aged man and his two mistresses, one old, one young, the old one pulling out his dark hairs, the young one pulling out his grey ones. The motto: 'Either one I chose would want me to live according to her lights, not mine.' Did this perhaps resonate with Poulenc who never, after Raymonde Linossier (to whom the ballet is dedicated), seems even to have considered close, continuous cohabitation? As for 'La mort et le bûcheron', the story of the woodcutter who, exhausted by labour and poverty, calls on Death to visit him and who, when finally faced with the reality, backs away (or, in La Fontaine's more ironical version, asks Death to give him a hand with some logs), must surely have resonated with the audience at large as representing an all too familiar reality. In 1942, depression at being powerless was widespread among the French populace[59] – but, when it came to the point, was death a better fate? Not everyone got to choose. Poulenc's chilling take on Death is to make her an elegant lady who 'is nothing but charm and seduction', and whose music, mostly in his favourite lyrical key of D flat major, comes straight out of his *mélodies*. Only at the very end do we hear the timpani tapping out the 'fateful' minor thirds from *Oedipus Rex*. After this, 'Les deux coqs' mixes fowl noises with light dancing and, for the cock fight, thick textures that suggest Honegger, and still thicker ones when the winner is carried off by a vulture. La Fontaine's motto: 'Beware of Fate, and take care after winning a battle.' A message to the Nazis, perhaps?

The premiere was a resounding success, ending with six curtain calls accompanied by ovations. The critics too were enthusiastic, none more so than Honegger in his article for *Comoedia* that included the sentence, 'The influences of Chabrier, Stravinsky and Satie, which he showed at the beginning of his career, have been assimilated, as does always happen when there is real youthful vitality, and they are now so well combined with his own talents that it is impossible to spot them, while at every moment the curve of a melody or a chain of harmonies makes us say: ' "That's very Poulenc." '⁶⁰ It may be germane to note that the ballet's run at the Opéra coincided with that of the German composer Pfitzner's opera *Palestrina*, given thirteen performances between 30 March and 13 December. No doubt the grey/green uniforms in the best seats thought *Palestrina* was wonderful. If the French members were less impressed, that was certainly the case of a young *chef de chant* called Henri Dutilleux, who remembered rehearsals many years later as being 'some of the worst moments of my life'.⁶¹

Poulenc spent the next few months in Noizay, continuing work on the Violin Sonata he had sketched out in 1940 and which, this time, would lead to a more or less finished work in 1943, though he was never happy with the result. He spent a lot of his time playing through music from between the wars. 'What rubbish,' he wrote to Schaeffner, 'and how the names that count are so clearly those that we had always predicted. Only the kind of mediocrity that prevails today could so easily brush aside Stravinsky, Prokofiev, Satie, Hindemith, Falla etc. . . . Apart from Françaix and Messiaen, all the young composers are quite happy with what was done before 1914.'

Anxious as he habitually was about his own standing in the musical world, Poulenc nevertheless listened more closely to his own instincts and desires, and the success of *Les Animaux modèles* encouraged him to spend a little more time in the countryside, in the form of six songs for voice and orchestra on popular texts by Maurice Fombeure. 'Imagine a kind of *Pribaoutki* from the Morvan,' he told Schaeffner, thinking of Stravinsky's 'song games' from 1914.[62] His relationship with the countryside and its peasants was a complex one. As we have seen, when marooned in Cahors at the end of his military service he wrote of the peasants round about that 'their intelligence is far superior to that of the Parisians who "think they know it all" '.[63] Towards the end of his life the Noizay locals wanted to repay such an attitude by making him mayor, but there was a limit to his involvement in the town's life and he refused. For him Noizay spelt peace and quiet in which he could compose, and perhaps the essential distance between him and even his less rustic neighbours is best caught by Ned Rorem in his obituary tribute:

> I remember a pair of elderly female instructors from the Tours lycée, each sporting a shirt and tie, who came for tea at his country home. While his big, liver-spotted hands popped tiny raspberry tarts into his mouth – washed down with *tilleul* (he seldom touched liquor) – he held forth on private Paris gossip, then talked for an hour about orchestration, all this to his uncomprehending listeners, including the chauffeur, who was also of the party.[64]

In the *Journal de mes mélodies* Poulenc wrote, 'Composed in September 1942, just after the run of *Les Animaux modèles*, the *Chansons villageoises* stem directly from that work in their orchestration and even in their harmonic style ('C'est le joli printemps' and the end of 'Le mendiant' from 'Petit jour' and 'Les deux coqs' respectively).'[65] Pierre Bernac's comments suggest an amicable disagreement between him and Poulenc over the nature of these songs, noting that, 'being written in the style of "chansons", they are really "mélodies", and very difficult'.[66] This judgement subscribes to the entirely tenable view that 'chansons' are basically simple and unsophisticated. What Poulenc has done is take the 'chanson' and its earthy language (even breaking up the syntax in 'Les gars qui vont à la fête' with a final shout of 'chapeau'), but then pass it through his sophisticated prism. While there are only three changes of metre in the group,[67] against this, some of the harmonies are, in short bursts, highly dissonant and it's only the rhythmic regularity that holds them together (for example, at the end of 'Les gars' on the phrase 'mis la fleur au chapeau'). It's fair to say, then, that these are a new brand of 'chanson/mélodie', and this combination extends to the texture too: whereas the ensemble of eight woodwind, three brass, timpani, percussion and harp deliberately overwhelm the string quartet to produce a shrill, Nogentais roughness, the singer has to be a powerful, classical Verdi baritone capable of singing Iago.[68]

In the fast patter songs the presiding genius is Maurice Chevalier, set off, on the one hand, against the dreamlike invocation of spring in 'C'est le joli printemps' – Poulenc at his loveliest – and on the other against the thick, brutal, Musorgsky-inspired chords of 'Le mendiant' – Poulenc at his most terrifying and not to be heard again until *Dialogues des Carmélites*. In its vitriolic condemnation of the abbot and the well-fed shopkeepers who have turned away the tramp Jean Martin, now found dead upon the ice, it's the nearest to a political statement in all Poulenc's music. As with *Les Animaux modèles*, its stand, embodied in the repeated 'Long live the passer-by', an ironic statement of the hospitality that should ideally be a keystone of our civilization, can only have gathered further resonance during the Occupation.

During the final months of 1942 Poulenc was not only making plans for another composing project, but also travelling to the south of France with Bernac for recitals. The first mention in his published correspondence of *Les Mamelles de Tirésias* comes in a letter to Marie-Blanche in 1938, followed by news of early sketches for it to Sauguet in 1939 and a further mention in his reply to Koechlin of August 1942 – a sop to his one-time teacher in his role as a fan of 'le Poulenc burlesque'.[69] This news flies in the face of the reminiscence already quoted from the critic Paul Landormy that 'The theatre leaves [Poulenc] cold'. We should be aware that Landormy's friendship with Poulenc went back some way, and that this is a useful reminder of how radically Poulenc could change his mind, something to bear in mind when assessing his opinions.

That autumn the pace began to pick up, Poulenc telling Rouché that 'yesterday I asked *Apollinaire*'s widow to reserve for me the right to set *Les Mamelles de Tirésias* to music. It'll make one act in two scenes (same set) lasting about 35 minutes. I warn you straight away that it'll be a *folie* and I beg you not to read the play until I've arranged it to my liking and for the eyes of the public. If my bet comes off, I think it'll make people laugh for 5 minutes.'[70]

In November he and Bernac gave a series of recitals in what had been the Unoccupied Zone, in Cannes, Marseille and Lyon among other towns. His mention that the zone was still 'libre' must reflect the fact that although, in response to the Allied landings in North Africa on 8 November (Operation Torch), the Nazis had taken over that zone only three days later, the administration had not yet caught up with the realities. For Poulenc one benefit of this was that he could write direct to Ansermet in Switzerland instead of routing his letter through the Swiss consulate in Paris. Apart from giving Ansermet news of musical life in the capital, he asks him to contact Chesters and see if they will take over the edition of the *Mouvements perpétuels*, copies of which are proving hard to find for pianists,[71] not that the publisher Rouart Lerolle was necessarily to blame, since the allocation of paper during the Occupation was something the Nazis controlled with particular care, and publication of these so un-German pieces might well have been low on their list of priorities.

Poulenc signed that letter 'Votre mélancolique Francis'. He had no especial reason for melancholy, so far as we know, but for the Allies the year 1942 marked the lowest point in the war, and his antennae may simply have responded to a general malaise. But with the British victories at El Alamein between July and November, the arrival of Allied forces in North Africa, and the surrender of the German army outside Stalingrad on 2 February 1943, the war would now take a decisive turn: the French communists brought their well-organized cells to the Resistance, and fear and despair were, slowly but increasingly, replaced by hope. It was a piecemeal business. In the Southern Zone the opposing forces crystallized into two groups. 'Entering the popular vocabulary at more or less the same time, the words *maquis* and *milice* together defined the new realities: the one a little-known word for the back country of Corsica, which became a synonym for militant resistance; the other a familiar word meaning simply "militia", which became a synonym for militant repression.'[72] Worse than that, the members of the *milice* were all French, and as traitors an immediate target of revenge. The first *milicien* was assassinated by the *maquis* on 24 April, and by October nine more would follow.

For Poulenc, of course, whether in Paris or Noizay, such activities in the Southern Zone were of no immediate consequence. Even so, the notion that resistance now had a real purpose would soon impinge on his composing life. In the meantime, amid multiple recitals, in March he wrote a third and last *Intermezzo* – in Fauréan fashion, a lyrical tune generates considerable passion before returning, in a piece Poulenc variously categorized as one of his lesser works, while admitting he was very fond of it.[73] Affording less comfort was his completion in April, at last, of a Violin Sonata, incorporating we know not what elements of earlier attempts, and due to undergo further modifications of the finale in 1949. Poulenc gave the first performance, with Ginette Neveu, on 21 June at the first public concert of the newly formed Concerts de la Pléiade, inaugurated by Gaston Gallimard under the auspices of the *nouvelle Revue française*. Also performed were his *Sept Chansons* (repeated from the opening concert on 8 February), both Poulenc pieces being surrounded by vocal works of Debussy and Ravel – programming that testified to Poulenc's emergence, at least in some minds, from the confines of *petit maître*. A week later, at the same venue, Roger Bourdin sang in the first performance, with orchestra, of the *Chansons villageoises*.

The sonata is dedicated to the Spanish poet and playwright Federico García Lorca, whom some recent researches claim was assassinated on the order of the Nationalist Civil Governor during the first days of the Spanish Civil War in 1936. Rumours, though, have also circulated that his homosexuality was an aggravating, if not primary factor in his death, which might have given further impetus to the dedication beyond what Poulenc admitted. Noting that it contains three movements, he explained that 'at the head of the intermezzo I inscribed this line by Lorca, so beautiful in Spanish with its resonance of a plucked string, and which, despite the translation, retains in French its evocative power: "The guitar makes the dreams weep." '[74] A dozen or so years later Poulenc had fallen out of love with the work, pronouncing it to be 'frankly no good [. . .] because of its tone of artificial pathos. To be honest, I don't like the violin, as a solo instrument. In the plural, quite the contrary, but how could I resist a suggestion from Ginette Neveu!'[75]

'Frankly no good' (oeuvre ratée) seems harsh, and no doubt reflects disappointment at not being able to surmount his natural antipathy to the solo violin. But if not 'ratée', the work is certainly 'problématique'. Surreal contrasts of material only work when that material has a strong character of its own. In this sonata this is sadly not the case, either with the unusually dissonant, even aggressive passages, or with those that subscribe to the lyricism of *mélodies* such as 'Tu vois le feu du soir', but without its persuasive shaping. A further problem is that in the whole sonata the piano has only a single bar's rest, and that near the end of the finale. Altogether the whole piece emits a surprising whiff of 'emphase', all the more extraordinary in that Poulenc composed it hard on the heels of orchestrating *Les Animaux modèles*, dedicated to 'emphase's arch-enemy, Raymonde Linossier. On 29 April, a few days after he finished the Sonata, another link with his past was broken with the death in Barcelona of Ricardo Viñes. As there is no mention of this in Poulenc's correspondence, it is possible that, given the difficulties of wartime communication, he learned of it only sometime later. At all events he must have been deeply saddened to hear not only that Viñes had died but that, having gambled away all his considerable earnings, he did so in penury.

A letter from Poulenc to Marie-Blanche indicates that two critics at least, Tony Aubin and Gustave Samazeuilh, had had harsh things to say about the Sonata, but that he has settled down for the time being in a boarding house at Beaulieu in the Corrèze. Raymond was with him and, as Poulenc jokingly mentions, was surprised when the composer admired the muscles of a Parisian teacher of 'culture physique';[76] but relations with the married Raymond may now have been platonic. Poulenc was thinking of two new works, neither of which seem to have progressed beyond outline planning, if that: a Violin Concerto for Neveu (surely piling Pelion upon Ossa) and, again, a String Quartet. As he says in the same letter, 'I have a piano but inspiration is lacking.' Whether or not it was the fault of the piano, whose mediocrity he still remembered a decade later, the solution to the impasse appears in another letter to Marie-Blanche later that month:

> I'm working patiently. A few bars are beginning to come here and there. I'm writing a cantata for unaccompanied double choir (a commission from Belgium) on admirable poems by Éluard (currently censored). As I imagine it, it will be a kind of *Tel jour* for chorus. I've come up with one or two snippets that aren't bad. A very pure style with no bits of clever writing, variety coming just from the musical expression. It's very difficult.[77]

'It's very difficult' – the most negative comment that has come down to us from Poulenc about *Figure humaine*, written in just six weeks at Beaulieu: no revisions, no anguished wondering as to its value, of the kind that followed so many of his compositions. Three years later he could still write to Collaer that 'I place my *Cantata* above everything that I've done.'[78] The only thing wrong with it is, indeed, that it is extremely difficult to perform, both because it needs two six-part choirs and because of the music's complexity. Nor was he prepared to accept chamber choirs, suggesting initially a choir of around 200:[79] when, for the premiere in London, it was suggested that sixty singers might be enough, Poulenc retorted that eighty-four would be nearer the mark, with seven singers to each part.[80] For the Carnegie Hall premiere in 1950 he accepted eighty singers (with sixty rehearsals!).[81] No doubt he was thrilled to have a performance in Belgium with 250.[82]

He gave two different accounts of what prompted the work which cannot, even with a little goodwill, be made to harmonize completely. The first, from 1944, assures us that

. . . it was following a Pléiade concert, including my *Sept Chansons* [so on either 8 February or 21 June 1943] [. . .] that M. Screpel, the director of the Compagnie des Discophiles, asked me to set to music Paul Éluard's poem 'Liberté' which opens *Poésie et vérité 42*, with a view to recording it:

Sur mes cahiers d'écolier	On my school notepads
Sur mon pupitre et les arbres,	On my desk and the trees
Sur le sable et sur la neige	On the sand and on the snow,
J'écris ton nom . . .	I write your name . . .

[. . .] At the time I was terrified by the difficulty of the task. But then I went off to give a concert in Lyon where, in a bookshop, I found the little Swiss edition of these poems. I read them again. The different layout of the work showed it to me in a new light, and impressed it on me once again. Instantly, I had the idea of setting not only 'Liberté', but of writing a cantata for which 'Liberté' would merely provide the finale.[83]

The second account, from ten years later, tells us that 'During the Occupation, certain privileged people, including myself, had the consolation of receiving by the morning post some marvellous typed-out poems, at the bottom of which, under assumed names, we guessed that of Paul Éluard. That was how I received most of the poems of *Poésie et vérité 42*. [. . .] The idea of a secret work, a work one could write and publish clandestinely and produce on the long-awaited day of the Liberation, came to me after a votive pilgrimage to Rocamadour, quite near Beaulieu.'[84] A possible means of reconciling these two versions to some extent lies in the admission, in the earlier one, that 'I read them again', possibly after receiving the typed version through the post. But more importantly, in both versions the emotional source of the work lay in the prospect of Liberation; to which we may add the, typically Poulencquian, visual point that in the Swiss edition 'the different layout of the work showed it to me in a new light'.

One of the main things that strikes the listener at a first hearing is, as Lacombe says, that 'Poulenc hardly employs any moderate expressive zone'.[85] The work is one of extremes, both in tempi and in styles of singing. Of the eight movements, nos. 2 (partly), 5 and 7 (wholly) are very fast, while the rest of the music is very slow – the tempi of the first seven movements all beginning with the adverb 'très' – and on the dynamic front the range is from *pppp* to the final *ffff*. This 'extreme' style is obviously inspired by the text and combines with Poulenc's decision not to include instruments, which would have made performance so much easier: but the sound he wanted was that of a people both oppressed and rebellious. The riches of *Figure humaine* really deserve a book to themselves. Here some half-dozen observations must suffice regarding detail and structure.

The first line of the first poem encapsulates the dichotomy to which the whole piece resounds, between order and disorder, and here particularly between peace and war: 'De tous les printemps du monde/Celui-ci est le plus laid'. Poulenc picks up on this distinction, setting the first ten words as a pseudo-folksong and then hitting us amidships with an 'ugly' dissonance on 'laid'; and this ambivalence will be echoed throughout, pitting false serenity (if you like, the comfortably set-up Poulenc) against actual evil (friends subject to deportation and worse). The extreme of terror comes in the seventh, penultimate movement, 'La menace sous le ciel rouge' where, initially, liberation still remains an unvoiced hope. Here Poulenc deliberately moved outside his comfort zone and wrote, uniquely in his output, the opening 'exposition' of a fugue. We can only guess at the relevance of this to the text: 'The menace beneath the red sky came from under the jaws the scales the links of a slippery heavy chain' – in any case, after four entries orthodoxy is abandoned for mere echoes of the subject. Easier to explain is the fact that this subject pays partial homage to twelve-note technique, shortly to be labelled 'dodécaca' by Poulenc despite his admiration for the music of Webern – partial because the twelve-note set is not complete until note fourteen, with two notes (A natural, E natural) 'incorrectly' repeated. Certainly the angular subject, incorporating the swoop of a diminished seventh following that of Bach's *Musical Offering*, sets this movement in stark relief with what has preceded and will follow it. A final detail illustrates the (genetically inherited?) careful craftsmanship apparent in every bar. It is only at the end of this seventh movement that, for the first time, we find hope of better things in the phrase 'And base conduct gave way/To men who were brothers/No longer fighting against life/To men who were indestructible [hommes indestructibles].' Normally that last phrase would contain a liaison between the two words. But Poulenc specifically forbids this, determined that 'indestructibles' should stand alone in all its glory.

The structure of the work is both strong and individual. The two choirs mingle in myriad ways, though with the soprano line mostly dominant, and Poulenc gives each choir one movement to itself (nos. 4 and 6) both for colouristic variety and as a practical move to ease the considerable burden of concentration. But as always he is on the qui-vive against the obvious. In the last movement, he gives the repeated refrain 'J'écris ton nom' twice to Choir 2 as a response to Choir 1 but then breaks the pattern, saying effectively, 'I'm sure you've got the message.' Finally, to give shape to this very long poem, he uses tempo markings, first to accelerate, then to slow down to the final bars which return to the speed of the opening. The result is to give these last eleven bars extraordinary weight in every aspect: in tempo, in register, in fullness of texture, and in reliance on the ever-present cycles of fifths in the bass. With basses singing a low E and two sopranos singing E in alt, the E major chord on the final syllable of 'Liberté' covers four octaves in sixteen parts, its brilliance largely due to ten of those sixteen singing the tonic E.

It goes without saying that a cantata with such a revolutionary text could not be performed in public during the Occupation, and even copies from the clandestine printing of it in May 1944, all set to be sent out by lorry, were then delayed by the Allied invasion of Normandy (D Day) on 6 June.[86] During the autumn of 1943 Poulenc continued to indulge his love of vocal music in two sets of songs, and these too reflected the Occupation in their different ways. *Métamorphoses* contains settings of three poems by Louise de Vilmorin, written especially for Pierre Bernac who was a great admirer of her poetry; but he wanted masculine poems instead of feminine ones such as *Fiançailles pour rire*, which for him were unsingable.[87]

By 1943 Vilmorin had left her Hungarian husband Count Palffy and was back in the family château at Verrières-le-Buisson, a south-western suburb of Paris. Poulenc had worried about her being so far away in Hungary in wartime, but even now he seemingly felt she needed support. So it was at Verrières in August 1943 that he performed for her the first two songs of the cycle, the third not being finished until October. The two outer songs are springboard ones, fast and rather superficial. But the central one, 'C'est ainsi que tu es', belongs to that family of slow, heartfelt, bittersweet songs that show the composer at his best.

The other set of songs, *Deux Poèmes de Louis Aragon*, are more directly linked to the Occupation. Poulenc remembered that 'at the end of the summer of 1943, a friend brought back for me from Switzerland *Les Yeux d'Elsa*. Two of the poems resonated so precisely with my state of mind that in a single week I wrote "C" and "Fêtes galantes".'[88] This Swiss edition of September 1941 had by then been smuggled into the Southern Zone but was unobtainable in the Northern one. The two poems record in powerful detail the misery and disruption of life under the Nazis and the only questionable point about Poulenc's settings is that he should have placed 'Fêtes galantes', by his own admission a 'mélodie tremplin', after and not before 'C'. Marked 'incroyablement vite', it paints the total abolition of peacetime hierarchies, beginning with the sight of marquises on bicycles and going on to that of dead bodies floating under the bridges. Poulenc's setting of the poem as something from the café-concert underlines the casual ordinariness that such sights have now assumed.

'C', on the other hand, marked 'très calme', is a lament and without doubt one of Poulenc's greatest songs. The poem begins 'J'ai traversé les ponts de Cé', and at once the French listener of the day would have been taken back to the year 1620, when the army of the teenage Louis XIII easily defeated that of his mother, Marie de Médicis, in the commune of Les Ponts-de-Cé, a suburb of Angers some 80 kilometres west of Tours. This not only avoided a civil war but, in the view of at least one historian, initiated the 'absolutism' that was to last until the Revolution more than a century and a half later.[89] Known in France as the 'Drôlerie des Ponts-de-Cé' (The Ponts-de-Cé Joke), the battle is probably as familiar to French schoolchildren as the Battle of Hastings to the British. The poem builds on this historical background to muse on distant memories, of a wounded horseman and of a crazy duke with swans in his castle moat. The river Loire bears these memories away, together with the overturned vehicles, the decommissioned weapons . . . and the ineffectually stifled tears. In any other composer these deep emotions could so easily have provoked *emphase*. Instead, the regularly pulsing quavers and the continuous four-bar phrases, each ending in an appreciable cadence, produce the effect of a hymn, the sense of unity increased by the fact that all eighteen lines end with the sounds 'é' or 'ée', in various spellings. This regularity is brought to a sudden standstill only on the penultimate line 'O ma France, ô ma délaissée', by a surprising harmony, *p* subito, and in the voice a held high A flat dying away on a molto portando descent, all of which mark these two bars off as the song's emotional climax – a cry of inconsolable anguish.

These two songs, together with *Métamorphoses*, were premiered by Bernac and Poulenc on 8 December. Before that, Poulenc played 'C' privately to Désormière, and the soprano Irène Joachim recalled Déso's reaction and that of the public later: 'I saw him arrive, absolutely overcome; he was on his way back from Poulenc's flat where the composer had just played him a new song, sung by Bernac. [. . .] The poetry and the music are as magnificent as each other: it's on a poem by Aragon, an overwhelming song. In fact the audience, who were surprised, became so wildly enthusiastic, the artists had to perform it again.'[90] Well might they have been surprised, since this blatantly incendiary text was being performed in the Salle

Gaveau, at 45 rue La Boétie, from where the *Propaganda Staffel*, which had to sanction all cultural activity in Paris, was a mere five minutes' walk away at 52 avenue des Champs-Élysées.

❦

The autumn had been a quiet time for Poulenc, who left Beaulieu first for Brive, then Paris, then Nogent, before again settling down to work in Noizay. But his mood was not entirely sunny. Congratulating Paul Collaer on his activities in Brussels, he felt Collaer:

> . . . ought to pass on some of your enthusiasm to the music lovers of Paris whom I find increasingly odious. They're happy with any old thing and, in ever greater numbers certainly, seem to treat music as a run-of-the-mill commodity whose sole attraction is that you can consume it without consulting a menu. Only the Pléiade concerts have tried to do something new, but in fact they've fallen back into the mode of La Sérénade in 1936 with an audience of snobs, taking no notice of the absence of Da [Darius] and other composers.[91]

Back at Noizay in October, he developed this theme to André Jolivet:

> I'm now thinking of writing my Concerto for piano and orchestra for my American tour after the war. It's by thinking of the future, which I regard boldly and optimistically, that I find the impulse to compose, because you have to admit the present mediocrity of audiences is far from inspiring. Without being a Jew-lover, one has to confess that the Jewish yeast is indispensable for getting the concert flan to rise, and what's more I prefer my *Mouvements perpétuels* played by Horowitz rather than by Lucienne Delforge.[92]

Others noted by Poulenc's critical pen included Stravinsky ('*Mavra* is more old-fashioned than *L'Heure espagnole*') and Honegger ('I see you've persuaded Arthur to give up writing articles – rather disordered ones, it has to be said in passing. Bravo. When one is Monsieur Arth. Hon. it's enough to write music, if you don't have the literary gifts of M. Croche.')[93] It's hard to avoid the feeling that Poulenc was in a lowish, even grumpy mood between finishing the Aragon songs in October and rehearsing for the Paris concert on 8 December. The sense that composing

Figure humaine had taken its toll is compounded by the tally of the next five months, during which he wrote no more than a brief film score, before embarking on *Les Mamelles de Tirésias* the following May.

In his illuminating book *The Shameful Peace*, Frederic Spotts makes the basic point that 'it was the arts – literature, theatre, film, art exhibitions, concerts, recitals and opera – more than anything else that helped the French to retain some sense of dignity and to get through the daily miseries of the Occupation. [. . .] in the arts the French had a weapon – their only weapon – to continue the war. [. . .] For the French during the Occupation [films] promised, more than any of the other arts, a brief escape from prison or at least a glimpse outside the prison window. In the vast majority of towns and villages, with dancing forbidden, it was the only form of entertainment available. Not surprisingly, cinema receipts in those years doubled and in Paris trebled.'[94] With coal and wood in short supply, cinemas and theatres were also havens of warmth.

Le Voyageur sans bagage, written as a play by Jean Anouilh, was premiered in that form on 1 April 1944, and as a film the previous 23 February. The missing 'bagage' is Gaston's memory, lost as a result of trauma in the First World War: when it returns, after he has rediscovered his family, he learns that the original Gaston was ruthless and violent. The story is one concerned with memory, loss and identity and, though written in 1937, clearly resonated with a French audience of 1944. Of the nine movements Poulenc composed, for a long time believed to be lost, no. 6 would appear again in *Les Mamelles*, and no. 2, either taken from or contributing to *Babar le petit éléphant*, has now been published in Poulenc's own version for cello and piano under the title *Souvenirs*.[95]

Apart from performances and showings of *Le Voyageur sans bagage*, for Poulenc the first months of 1944 were of little interest, except for the arrest of Raymond for black market activities (though luckily he escaped deportation),[96] and less happily that by the Gestapo of Max Jacob, who died in Drancy transit camp on 4 March. But a couple of letters no doubt cheered him. On 6 April Reynaldo Hahn wrote to deny that he didn't like Poulenc, as seemed to be the rumour believed by the latter: probably this was a misunderstanding born of the fact that the two composers 'didn't have the same conceptions about writing music and that we were of different grammatical upbringings'.[97] Even more heartening was a letter written four days later by the writer Claude Roy, a reader for the publishers Gallimard, assuring Poulenc that 'You play in the darkness that surrounds us, as someone sings in order not to be afraid. And we are no longer afraid. [. . .] We know that France still exists. There are not many of you who remind us of this: Aragon, Éluard, Lurçat, one or two others. How not to be forever grateful to you for it?'[98]

The summer brought considerable disarray both before and after the Normandy landings, not least owing to the Allied bombing raids: on 8 June a munitions train was blown up only a few kilometres away from Le Grand Coteau, electricity and water supplies were interrupted, and through it all the house was now once again home to various refugees: entirely welcome was the presence of Oncle Papoum and Raymond Destouches, who undertook a number of useful duties as courier; rather less so was that of three members of Raymond's family. Whether or not as a direct result of this invasion of his privacy, at the end of June Poulenc began to suffer from rheumatism, fluctuating temperature and throat trouble. 'I'd always thought,' he wrote to Bernac on 24 June, 'that I'd write *Les Mamelles* during a happy summer. It has, alas, been nothing of the kind.'[99]

But write he did, and gave Bernac a detailed account of progress, beginning with the prologue: 'It's a tough job because there isn't a phrase whose prosody and tone are not chosen with care. Sometimes this even gives me a bar less in which to modulate. Even so I don't think it'll be disjointed because, in the prologue for example, there's a firm tonal plan.'[100] Here, and in all his comments on the opera, Poulenc is at pains to show that comedy does not entail any slackening of technique – in line with what any comic actor will say, for whom timing is of the essence. 'I'm reserving my worst follies for the second act in order to keep the interest on the increase. [. . .] What with my words, my tessituras, my instrumentation, you see what tortures I'm subjecting myself to. Uncle Royer, a typical member of the Opéra-Comique's traditional audience, is unaware of my sufferings and declares himself content. This is already a great deal.'[101] It could also be the case that this careful, solid foundation affects the opera's tone where, in the words of Jacques de Menasce, 'A sincere human quality prevails throughout, lending grace to peculiar situations and dignity to the individual figures, their drollery notwithstanding.'[102]

The large number of letters from Poulenc, a dozen or so mostly to Bernac, that survive from this summer show the composer necessarily confined to Le Grand Coteau by the military situation, and this enforced residence gave him the leisure to consider various matters other than the work in hand. He has heard on the grapevine that Messiaen has completed a work Poulenc calls the *Liturgies* – the

Trois petites Liturgies de la Présence divine – and asks Bernac for news of these, which in fact would not be performed until 21 April 1945. Poulenc has been playing a number of Messiaen's works to himself and comments 'when he sticks to the form of his *Visions* [*de l'Amen*] it's truly remarkable; in other more contrived passages the influence of Dukas is irritating. It's the worst possible, I think, and that goes for everybody. Saint-Saëns's form could, for instance, guide Ravel. Dukas's is a form based on other forms.'[103] A fortnight later Bernac sent him a copy of Messiaen's *Technique de mon langage musical*, with the rider that 'its stupidity goes beyond anything you can imagine!'[104] Later in the decade, the *Turangalîla Symphony* was to exercise Poulenc's sense of taste still further.

On the practical front, the possibility now seemed to emerge of Bernac being appointed to a teaching post at the Conservatoire. Unlike Poulenc, Bernac had no store of family money behind him and the war's effect on performances was for him a serious matter. Poulenc made great efforts over the following years to obtain this post for him, and now assured him 'of course, you must make sure that you'll still be free to go on long tours. Mind you, with air travel these days, everything's so easy.'[105] He wrote to Sauguet in Paris to congratulate him on the success of his opera *La Gageure imprévue*, premiered at the Opéra-Comique on 4 July, and was delighted to have a long letter back full of news of the capital.[106] Of course, like everyone he knew, he was anxious about the liberation of Paris on 25 August and its human cost: 'We were told that 100,000 had been killed in Paris alone. The improbability of this extraordinary figure was enough in itself to reassure me. [. . .] Is it true they shot Chevalier? That would be too stupid. On the other hand we must be implacable regarding all those bastards, while never forgetting that punishments must be *appropriate*.'[107] But overall, despite problems of health and propinquity, he was relieved. 'When I think that Noizay is so totally untouched I feel almost ashamed. I hope that *Figure humaine* and *Les Mamelles* will prove a sufficient tribute from a Frenchman.'[108]

VII

'LIBERTY, I WRITE YOUR NAME'

✦ 1944–1952 ✦

With communications gradually becoming easier now that France had been liberated, word had reached the BBC of the existence of *Figure humaine*, and the accepted wisdom has been that at some point in the late autumn they sent a producer, Vera Lindsay, over to France to meet Poulenc and discuss plans for a performance. However, researches by Richard Langham Smith cast doubt on this journey, unattested anywhere in the BBC archives.[1] What is certain is that the efforts of Edward Lockspeiser, a BBC producer and the author of a seminal biography of Debussy, were crucial in setting up the project. Poulenc's willingness for the premiere to take place in Britain may seem surprising, but he was under no illusions about the work's difficulty, nor generally about the capabilities of French choirs. In 1898, after Fauré had conducted the Leeds Festival Choir in his *Naissance de Vénus*, and then heard them in the B minor Mass and Beethoven's Ninth, he praised the 'utter perfection and absolute splendour' of the result, commenting 'Alas, when will we decide to do the same! We don't lack the means.'[2] Over *Figure humaine*, Sauguet said quite bluntly that French choirs weren't up to it.[3] Although Poulenc had written the work for the Sainte Cécile Choral Society of Antwerp, the Allied landings and continued military activity in northern France and Belgium made performance there impossible.

Poulenc finished orchestrating *Les Mamelles* in October and so was free to give full consideration to the first known approach from the BBC in the shape of a letter dated 6 November from the Director of Music, Victor Hely-Hutchinson, expressing gratitude for the chance to peruse the score and agreeing enthusiastically to record and perform it.[4] Poulenc replied happily, agreed that time was needed for singers to absorb the music and said he would be in London in January, when they could confer further.[5]

During December and January he completed three other works: incidental music for *La Nuit de la Saint-Jean*, a French version of J. M. Barrie's well-known play *Dear Brutus*, the score of which has not survived; a choral setting of four short poems by Éluard under the title *Un Soir de neige*; and two more songs by Apollinaire.

Individual phrases in the Éluard poems are sufficient indicators of mood: 'pieds glacés', 'ciel noir', 'branches mortes', 'proie atroce', 'bois mort'. The cycle, written in six parts, continues where *Figure humaine* left off in its use of ever-varying textures; Renaud Machart regards it, despite its brevity, as an outright masterpiece, while Jean Roy observes its 'intimate character: it evokes night, cold, solitude, and sings of the years of misery, the months without heat, the days without hope.'[6] Two details give some sense of the whole. Stephan Etcherry notes the opening of the fourth piece, where a tune is given 'to the 2nd sopranos as well as to the 1st baritones. So the listener hears just one tune but with an entirely individual timbre – inorganic, glacial. The absence of intermediate voices (altos and tenors) creates a "hollow", a kind of void, of emptiness that suggests "la nuit le froid la solitude" of the prison described by Éluard.'[7]

The second observation, by Daniel Albright, takes us into the familiar world of Poulenc the magpie. Various commentators have mentioned that the opening of the third piece paints the words 'Bois meurtri bois perdu' with two leaps of a tritone, the mediaeval 'devil in music', but it has been left to Albright to identify these four bars as a transposed borrowing from The Tree's melancholy complaint 'Ma blessure . . . Ma blessure . . .' in *L'Enfant et les sortilèges*.[8] As has been noted above (see p. 67), Poulenc had felt that with this opera Ravel was 'making his entrance into eternity' and, following Stravinsky's advice, here borrowed only from one of the best sources in evoking a ravaged wood.

The two Apollinaire songs, 'Montparnasse' and 'Hyde Park', conform to the pattern of the two Aragon songs: a lyrical one followed by a 'mélodie tremplin'. Poulenc has nothing of interest to say about the latter, a brisk sort of Maurice-Chevalier-with-wrong-notes. But 'Montparnasse' repays attention both for what it is and for how it came to be. For Graham Johnson 'there has never been a greater song written about Paris than "Montparnasse",'[9] and many would agree. For Poulenc it is a dreamworld, initially still, then moving, as so often, in regularly pulsing quavers, coloured by his beloved sevenths, with sequences in echo, cycles of fifths in the bass – all the elements of the Poulenc vocabulary brought into a single, ecstatic vision. And yet this is far from how it came to be, which was in fragments, beginning with the line 'Un poète lyrique d'Allemagne' that occurred to him in 1941. Others arrived over the next three years (his account of the chronology is not entirely clear) and he then put all the pieces together in February 1945, a task which posed particular problems:

> As I *never* transpose music I've imagined for a certain line, or even for several words, into another key to make life easier for myself, it follows that the linking up is often problematic, and I need to stand back so as to find the exact place where I sometimes need to modulate.[10]

Without Poulenc's sketches, we cannot identify the problematic moments for certain, but we can at least guess that two of them (after 'prospectus', and then 'réalité' which leads into 'Un poète lyrique') were solved by using diminished sevenths, chords which Herbert Howells used to call 'Clapham Junctions' because they can switch in all directions. But equally, and in some sense despite his explanation, Poulenc would often simply go directly from one harmony to a distant one, relying on the strength of his melodic line, as here between 'Paris' and 'Vous connaissez'.

After writing *Un Soir de neige* between 24 and 26 December, Poulenc celebrated the New Year of 1945 by visiting London from 2 to 15 January. As well as giving recitals with Bernac at the Wigmore Hall, the National Gallery and recording for the BBC, on 6 January he was joined by Benjamin Britten in a performance of the Two-Piano Concerto with the London Philharmonic Orchestra under Basil Cameron. Probably to some extent owing to their friendship with Lennox Berkeley, the two men had been aware of each other's work for some time, Britten admiring the songs 'Le tombeau' and 'Attributs' when sung for the BBC by Marya Freund in 1937 and regularly performing *Tel jour telle nuit* with Peter Pears during the war. But this was the first time they had met, and an exchange of scores sealed their friendship. We don't know whether Britten showed Poulenc that of *Peter Grimes*, to be premiered on 7 June, but over the Concerto Philip Reed is undoubtedly right in surmising that, since Britten 'by this stage had more or less given up making solo piano appearances [. . .] it says a great deal for the esteem in which Poulenc was held by Britten that the latter was prepared to undertake this rôle.'[11] The performance was well received and a decade later Poulenc said to Claude Rostand, 'You can imagine how happy I was, after four years of the Occupation, to see England again, a country which, thanks to Stravinsky, provided me with my first publishers, Chester, and with my most faithful public up to 1940.'[12]

After returning to give concerts and make private recordings in Paris in February, Poulenc and Bernac spent much of March back in London. Again there were recordings, and concerts in which Poulenc also accompanied Ginette Neveu, and Maggie Teyte with Bernac in the final scene of *Pelléas* in a memorial concert for the music critic Edwin Evans.[13] But the main reason was the premiere of *Figure humaine*, now definitely fixed to be given by the BBC Chorus conducted by Leslie Woodgate on Sunday the 25th. As the choir was not thought capable of mastering the original French as well as the demanding music, Éluard allowed the English translation by his friend Roland Penrose to be used as a basis, which Poulenc's friend Rollo Myers then adapted to fit the music. Scheduling the broadcast for a Sunday also meant that a number of singers were unavailable owing to church commitments, and 'the assistance of members of the Variety Chorus – hardly used to this kind of music – therefore became indispensable'.[14] Before the broadcast concert Poulenc delivered a talk translated by Lockspeiser, introducing the work, the concert itself being attended by a broad swathe of the great and good, including Éluard, Britten, Peter Pears, Edward Dent, Maggie Teyte, Lady Violet Bonham Carter, Roger Désormière, Ginette Neveu, Kenneth Clark and Sir Adrian Boult. Although the broadcast was received in Britain, unexplained technical problems prevented it being heard in France. Even so, Lockspeiser's retrospective comment that '*Liberty*, the first poem in the book and the last in the cantata, assumed a significance comparable to the *Marseillaise* during the French Revolution' was surely no exaggeration, building as it did on the impact of copies of the poem previously dropped over France by the RAF.[15]

Two days later Poulenc sent Milhaud one of his regular accounts of musical life in Paris, mentioning that 'The Messiaenists are very much "against Stravinsky's last period" [in English]. For them, Igor's music stops at the *Sacre*. They whistled at the *Danses concertantes* which I adore.'[16] Poulenc went public with his views in an article on 7 April, including the *Four Norwegian Moods* in the works targeted and absolving Messiaen himself from any blame.[17] In fact Messiaen had gone backstage afterwards and apologized for his pupils, including a certain Pierre Boulez, to the conductor Manuel Rosenthal who shrugged off the incident, saying effectively 'boys will be boys'.[18] Then, on 21 April, Poulenc and Messiaen found themselves celebrating premieres in the same concert, Poulenc of *Un Soir de neige*, Messiaen of *Trois petites Liturgies de la Présence divine*, hailed by Poulenc as 'a triumph'.[19]

Nine days later, Adolf Hitler shot himself. The outcome of the war was thus effectively decided, but too late for the poet Robert Desnos who died of typhoid on 8 June after the liberation of Terezin concentration camp, to which he had been committed for his Resistance activities. But on a happier note, Poulenc could now start to think of Milhaud's return to France and the welcoming present he would offer him: *Les Mamelles de Tirésias*. This would not be possible for some time, not least because the 'épuration', the 'political cleansing' of suspected collaborators, made any casting of roles uncertain. Meanwhile, though, he got on with the orchestration and, in the same light-hearted spirit, filled out the sketches for *L'Histoire de Babar* which he had made in 1940. He also, more seriously but less successfully, meditated on the elusive String Quartet . . .

It's easy to regard *Babar* as just a light-hearted *jeu d'esprit* – and indeed it is partly that. The composer, ever alert to the dangers of complacency, told Sauguet that he had thought of the subtitle '18 glimpses of the tail of a young elephant', a not entirely respectful gloss on Messiaen's *Vingt Regards sur l'Enfant-Jésus*.[20] But the quality of the music suggests that deeper forces were also at work. Machart points out that 'When "Babar weeps, thinking about his mother", there is a reminiscence of "C'est ainsi que tu es" from the *Métamorphoses* of 1943, with exactly the same type of texture, of tune, and with the same appoggiaturas of quick notes.'[21] Lacombe reasonably posits a relationship with Poulenc's own history: 'the premature death of his mother, nostalgia for his original environment (for Babar, the forest), the child's gratitude and success (King Babar), naive enjoyment and love of parties, a taste for funny situations, the ideal life of the idealised couple (papa-maman or Francis-Raymonde) and dreamy thoughts of the stars (coda)'.[22] Finally, evidence that it was more than just a joke comes from another letter to Bernac, saying 'It's much better than I thought and the text, with portions of unequal length, read between pieces also of unequal length, goes very well. The ending is a happy inspiration in the poetic style: chaste night of love for the use of children.'[23] We have seen already that another danger to which Poulenc was ever alert was the boredom attendant on excessive regularity, hence his pleasure over these unequal lengths. What he does not say – compounded by his careful refusal to acknowledge that the ending is in any way profound – is that the preceding irregularity helps this regular coda achieve its extraordinary emotive power. After the piano's final low staccato E flat, there is always a silence, then maybe a collective sigh. And not infrequently tears.

With the ending of the war, Poulenc was keen to renew his previous recital schedule as far as possible. A letter to Bernac of 10 September shows this determination and his ideas for as far as two years ahead, and will do duty for much of his concertizing from here on:

1. If you'd prefer Rheims before Brussels, fine. 2. I'm writing to Collaer about *Figure*, also to the Radio. 3. I'm dealing with Dublin. 4. Agreed for Besançon and Mulhouse. Isn't Strasbourg going ahead? If not, phone Paul Rouart who's taken over Wolf's business and he'll fix that. Then we'll go on to Switzerland. 5. Find someone to go with you to Egypt. 6. Good idea for Algeria with Simone [Tilliard].

[. . .] From 46–47 I want to return to my pre-war schedule, especially as by this time I hope to have coal again at Noizay. So: October, Noizay; November, concerts; December, Noizay; January–May, concerts; June, concerts (London, I suppose); July, August, holidays; September, Noizay. That's five months of concerts, five working at Noizay, two for holidays.[24]

But despite this show of organization, the first year of peace found Poulenc ill at ease. A few weeks after writing the above letter, he complained that 'all I like is composing and my terrible winter of concerts does not fill me with joy',[25] and even composing had its limits, since 'I don't know why, but I have no desire to write songs. Let's hope it'll return one day.'[26] Writing to Milhaud at the end of the year, he was sorry to see that 'There is in the musical world at the moment a kind of hesitation, of confusion and floundering, utterly different from our clear refusals in 1918.'[27] What he did not yet know was that a young pupil of Messiaen named Pierre Boulez, quite apart from whistling at the lesser Stravinsky, was committed to refusals just as clear as those of 1918: turning the pages for the vibraphone player at the premiere of Messiaen's *Trois petites Liturgies*, he found all that A major hard going, and was far more interested in the quasi-oriental sonorities – what he called 'the side order' – which he would develop in works such as *Le Marteau sans maître*.[28]

Poulenc's only contact with twelve-note music at this time was through the advocacy of René Leibowitz, a considerably less talented musican than Boulez. Responding to a 1945 article by Leibowitz, who wrote 'of the twelve-tone system as the only lifeboat for contemporary music', Poulenc claimed that Berg's Violin Concerto had 'solved instantly, through the power of genius, all the problems posed by Schoenberg, and to such an extent that the music of the latter has, over the last 25 years, become no more than a desert, a broth of pebbles, ersatz music, poetry reduced to atoms.'[29] Although Poulenc came to have great respect for Boulez, he never really deviated from his view of twelve-note music as 'dodécaca'. In any case, Boulez later condemned Leibowitz's conducting and analysis of it as doing more harm than good to the cause: 'He was serviceable at the beginning, but I began to resent him when I saw how narrow and stupid he was. His analyses of Schoenberg are an arithmetical countdown.'[30]

Confusion was further sown by the lowering of Honegger's prestige (nothing to do with politics, says Poulenc) and by Auric's embrace of film music and the money it brought him. Music publishing also was having a difficult time, and through all this Poulenc felt 'it's my duty as a Frenchman to be a commercial traveller in music',[31] advising, encouraging, making contacts, as he did in recommending to Lockspeiser the Jewish pianist Lazare Lévy as a soloist for the BBC, 'a pianist of the good old school of [Emil von] Sauer, [Francis] Planté etc. . . . and by far the best French teacher since the departure of [Isidore] Philipp'.[32] On a larger front, some of the confusion and dislocation he detected stemmed from the political scene. The *épuration sauvage* (unoffical purge) affected anyone who had had dealings with the Germans, whether willingly or not (Isaiah Berlin's definition of acceptable conduct, 'that to survive, you might have needed to do business with the Germans, whether as a waiter, a shoemaker, a writer or an actor, but "you did not have to be cosy with them"', clearly left room for individual interpretations). The fact that the great pianist Alfred Cortot, deemed altogether too close to the occupiers, should have spent three days and nights on a bench in a police station meant that no one could feel exempt.[33] There was also great fear, especially after Charles de Gaulle's resignation in January 1946, that the Communists, bolstered by their Resistance record, might take over the government.

Poulenc's composing too was going through a difficult patch: he wrote songs, since lost, for a play *Le Soldat et la sorcière*, premiered on 5 December, and began work on a group of eight French *chansons* to popular texts which had been commissioned by Henri Screpel, the director of the Compagnie des Discophiles, and which he didn't finish until the following April. Meanwhile, amid the confusion, news of performances of *Figure humaine* and *Les Mamelles* remained wholly absent. Happily, Raymond had come through the war unscathed, though Oncle Papoum died on 24 November of heart trouble, even if quickly and without pain. Poulenc's sister Jeanne took over his flat, while Poulenc moved up to a flat on the seventh floor.

On 18 January Poulenc's contributions to French culture were finally recognized by his appointment as chevalier de la Légion d'honneur. For the delivery of the insignia, he needed a 'godfather' and approached the writer François Mauriac, himself a grand officier of the order, to take on the task. The (untranslatable) terms of his request show his habitual resistance to pomposity. The French for 'to stand as godfather to a child' is 'tenir un enfant sur les fonts baptismaux' – literally 'to hold a child over the baptismal fonts'; Poulenc hoped that Mauriac would hold him over the republican ones 'despite his age and weight . . .' The writer did so on 17 June.[34]

Much of Poulenc's time during the first three months of 1946 was spent giving concerts with Bernac in France, Belgium, Switzerland and Holland, and in June and July they were in England for three weeks, during which time Poulenc played *Babar* on the BBC, following its French Radio premiere on 14 June. On the compositional front, Poulenc was labouring at his last attempt towards a string quartet: 'I'm working simply to get well clear of my fiftieth year with the benefits of my age, since I shall have its defects, alas!'[35] The strain would ultimately tell, and we may imagine he was happier writing the last two of the *Chansons françaises*.

Almost simultaneously with their despatch, his friend Lennox Berkeley was writing to Nadia Boulanger, 'I think that certain natures easily confuse beauty with pleasure and have to make a continual effort to keep them apart – I think that Poulenc for instance is apt to do this, but though it is dangerous to people like him and me, it is perhaps a good thing that the element of pleasure should return to music after all the grim and false austerity of the 1920s. Stravinsky has the true austerity, and at the same time pleasure is by no means absent from his music.'[36] We might venture to say that the 'true austerity' does also find a place in works such as *Figure humaine*, which maybe gives Poulenc leave to indulge in pure pleasure from time to time. It is certainly hard to think of any music more utterly delightful than these eight songs for three, four and five mixed voices, using popular tunes, in which the tradition of the *chanson* is both respected and developed. Tonality, modality and chromaticism coexist in the happiest of ways, with plenty of 'forbidden' consecutive fifths, the balance between repetition and variety changing all the time. But underpinning everything is Poulenc's melodic gift: nowhere more clearly do we hear the truth of Ravel's oft-cited comment, 'what I like is his ability to invent popular tunes'.[37]

Despite Poulenc's earlier fear that songwriting had abandoned him, in July Apollinaire once more came to the rescue, but again it was a question of building on ideas that had occurred to him earlier. In *Le Pont*, music for the line 'Qui vient de loin qui va si loin' arrived at Noizay in 1944, and for 'Et passe sous le pont léger de vos paroles' in 1945 when he was working on the *Chansons françaises* at Larches, while the initial impulse to set this difficult poem had sprung from finding a satisfactory setting of the treacherous phrase 'c'est pour toi seule que le sang coule'. The dedication of the song to the memory of Raymond Radiguet stems from the song's roots in Nogent, almost certainly provoked by working on the eight popular songs, and the need to perform it without artifice or sentimentality is expressed in the composer's habitual command to play *Le Pont* 'very evenly, at a steady tempo, without rubato, and above all without slowing down the piano solo at the end.'[38] The mood of *Un Poème* is very different. For Poulenc the words suggested 'a great silence, a great void', and the bold, spare dissonances of the music take us away from Nogent into some spectral territory, barely made more comfortable by the final consonant chord.

Of the three other songs Poulenc began that summer, Radiguet figures once more as the poet of *Paul et Virginie*, provoked not only by *Le Pont* but by the news that Radiguet's *Le Diable au corps* was being turned into a film – for which Poulenc would have loved to write the music. 'One rainy day, a deep melancholy allowed me to find the mood that I think is right.'[39] The two other songs belonged to those subjected to lengthy perusal, both finally finished in the summer of 1947. *Le Disparu* is one of Poulenc's strangest songs, telling the story of André Platard abducted by the Nazis and never seen again, prayers to various saints proving unsuccessful. The strangeness lies in the song exhibiting, Poulenc tells us, the style of Edith Piaf, and only the gradual rallentando of the last page tells of hope lost. *Main dominée par le coeur*, on the other hand, belongs to the family of Éluard settings which flow smoothly on a bed of regular semiquavers, taking in their stride Poulenc's characteristic modulations. Two examples of word painting stand out: on the line 'Aucun secours tout m'échappe', C major clashes with C minor, and on the phrase 'Les yeux purs' we find the major 13th chord (C7 with added A naturals) that, for him, always speaks of deeper emotion – immediately after which, dead on cue, Poulenc pens the admonishment 'Ici, on ne mettra jamais assez de pédale'.

During the twelve months between July 1946 and that of 1947 Poulenc the performer and organizer largely took over from Poulenc the composer. No doubt some part in this was played by post-war freedom and easing of travel restrictions and the psychological relief these brought, on the lines of Pelléas's 'Ah! je respire enfin' as he emerges from the castle dungeons. But some part may well have been due to a need to take stock within the general atmosphere of unease. A third reason may also have been that traditionally Paris had responded to the public presence of composers: working away in monk-like seclusion was all very well but, as Cocteau's example demonstrated, the capital's fickle public needed constant prodding, and long periods of invisibility too easily led to oblivion.

The outstanding event of that autumn, though, involved Poulenc neither as pianist nor as organizer. On 13 September he became a father. A recently published letter (see Appendix) tells us a New Year party was the occasion responsible. He had known the baby girl's mother, Frédérique or Freddy, since the 1920s when she used to spend her holidays at the château de Perreux in the Touraine. She was a cousin of Richard Chanlaire's sister-in-law Suzette. Poulenc had dedicated two songs to her, 'Une ruine coquille vide' from *Tel jour telle nuit* and 'Dans l'herbe' from *Fiançailles pour rire*. However, the paternity of Marie-Ange was kept a close secret and even she herself believed that Poulenc ('Payen', as she called him) was her godfather, learning the truth only after the composer's death in 1963. The reasons behind this secrecy can only be guessed at. By 1946 Poulenc was generally known to be homosexual, so news of his paternity could possibly have given rise to ribald comment of some kind; and of course, in the social circles in which he moved, begetting a child out of wedlock might still cause disapproval. Beyond this, though, his treatment of his daughter could not be faulted for its kindness and loving attention, and he made sure that after his death she would be well provided for.

To set against this birth came two deaths in November. On the 14th Manuel de Falla passed away peacefully a few days before his seventieth birthday, in Argentina where he had gone at the outbreak of war. Poulenc had always admired his religious fervour, apparently untainted by the doubts that assailed himself. The second death, of Éluard's wife Nusch from a cerebral haemorrhage on 28 November, was more shocking since she was only just forty. A woman of stunning beauty, painted by Picasso and Magritte and photographed by Man Ray and Dora Maar, her death had a powerful impact on the whole surrealist world. The following October Poulenc dedicated his song . . . *mais mourir* to her memory.

On the musical front, the December of 1946 saw both a birth and a death-plus-rebirth. Negotiations with Brussels for a first performance of *Figure humaine* had been going on for some time, and far from smoothly. But at last on 2 December Paul Collaer conducted the work in a broadcast with the 140 members of the

Belgian Radio Choir, much to Poulenc's delight, more than eighteen months after the BBC broadcast. 'One doesn't find much of this quality in a lifetime!' he wrote to Collaer. 'Suddenly, for 20 minutes I could believe I was a great composer! A very nice feeling!'[40] Altogether less happy was a private playthrough of his just completed String Quartet by the Calvet Quartet. 'I've destroyed my Quartet,' he told Milhaud, 'and thrown it into a gutter in the place Péreire. I'd made a total mistake and it was bad, bad, bad despite a certain musicality. I intend to save several tunes and use them for an orchestral sinfonietta with double woodwind. It seems one can be wrong at any age.'[41] A decade later he added further details of his disappointment: 'Right from the opening bars I was saying to myself: "Whatever else, that'd be better on an oboe, that needs a horn, there it should be a clarinet." This surely served to condemn the work out of hand? I had only one desire: to run away.'[42] But at least some of the tunes did have a rebirth in the *Sinfonietta* he wrote over the next couple of years.

With the original French version of *Figure humaine* now successfully launched, and the Paris premiere settled for 22 May with the same forces, Poulenc could begin to direct all his attention towards the premiere of *Les Mamelles*. Rehearsals of the opera had been planned for the spring of 1945 ('if we're still here!', glossed Désormière),[43] then for May or June 1946, but these too were cancelled owing to changes in personnel: from 1944 the collaborationist Lucien Muratore had handed over to a committee of four, including Désormière, which was succeeded in turn by Albert Wolff and then, in 1946, by Henri Malherbe, while Jacques Rouché, the overarching director of both the opera houses, was dismissed from his post in February 1945. In his letter of 28 December to Milhaud, Poulenc could announce that rehearsals for the work had now begun, but these covered only the men's parts of the opera because the soprano for the central role had yet to be found. Poulenc knew the work was likely to offend the more straitlaced members of the Opéra-Comique audience, 'so I thought, reasonably enough, that I'd put up a better defence with a pretty girl who had a bit of zip and go about her. But by February 1947 I still hadn't found this rare bird.' Then the producer suggested he attend a rehearsal of *Tosca* – where he first saw and heard Denise Duval. 'Immediately I was struck by her luminous voice, her beauty, her chic, and above all that healthy laugh which is so wonderful in *Les Mamelles*. I made up my mind on the spot. Here was the singer we'd dreamt of.'[44]

The producer's suggestion was made as late as 19 March. A letter from Poulenc to Duval contains not only detailed instructions ('Try to find some other slippers.

Don't forget to undo your dress before launching on the phrase with the top C') but the final apostrophe 'Je vous embrasse tendrement mon trésor' – the beginning of a long, deep and fruitful friendship.[45] Poulenc, as would be the case with all his three operas, was assiduous in attending rehearsals and the months up to the premiere on 3 June were some of his happiest. Duval, as well as learning her part in three or four days, stunned everyone with her elegance, shown to good effect in the dresses Poulenc obtained for her from his friend Christian Dior. Although Christian Bérard turned out to be too busy to take on the role of designer, his replacement Erté was a marvellously apt choice given his experience at the Folies Bergère, where Duval had performed since 1944: James Harding refers to his decor and costumes as the work of 'the suave magician of high camp', the earliest use of that phrase in Poulenc criticism.[46] The composer was also delighted to have as conductor Albert Wolff, who had first exercised his skills at the Opéra-Comique as long ago as 1910, a man whose performances took place 'in an atmosphere of security, order and equilibrium' and whose quick reflexes had qualified him to be a pilot in the First World War.[47]

The first night was one of those splendidly scandalous occasions in which Paris has always specialized, Erté recording that seats were smashed amid animal noises and shouts of 'Hou-hou!' and 'Décadence!'[48] 'The Puccinistes in the gallery are indignant,' wrote Poulenc to Milhaud,[49] and they continued to be so for the revivals. Roger Shattuck, attending some of these, was surprised to find himself 'politely presented with a lantern-slide request from the management that violent expressions of opinion be withheld until after the performance. Nevertheless, reactions are strong among the habitués, and noisy demonstrators occasionally have to be expelled from the house.'[50]

The causes of the uproar, provoked by the action rather than by the music, are not hard to discern (though the premiere of *Figure humaine* less than a fortnight earlier may have given some of the audience the wrong idea of what to expect). The underlying message, as explained in the Prologue, is that the French should 'heed the lesson of the war and produce children, you who have almost given up doing so'. Given that the collapse of the French army in 1940 was partly attributed to lack of manpower, this was a hard enough pill to swallow, but it was made even more indigestible by the 'gender fluidity' of the plot which, while representing almost a norm in twenty-first-century culture, was far from being so in 1947. Then there was the threat by one of the babies born during the opera 'to denounce and blackmail his father for imaginary crimes' – all too close to the realities of the

Occupation.[51] Altogether it was not surprising that 'one mother, rendered purple by heat and indignation, left her box noisily, taking her daughters with her'.[52] But the music was not wholly exempted from blame. Over the years Poulenc would identify as partial sources for the score those of Chabrier's *L'Étoile* and Ravel's *L'Heure espagnole*, in the case of the latter admitting to 'reading the orchestral score with unusual care, the piano reduction in the other hand. What an astonishing masterpiece but what a dangerous example (like that of all masterpieces). When you don't have Ravel's magical precision which, sadly, is the case with me, you have to set the music on solid feet.'[53] But another Ravelian influence, not mentioned by him, is surely *L'Enfant et les sortilèges*, in the premiere of which, as we have seen, he was closely involved and which, like *Les Mamelles*, is built on an apparently disconnected variety of styles. For Henri Hell the work is one where 'we find ourselves in the middle of a series of more or less successful "gags" that only feebly illustrate the poet's basic premise: exhorting the French to have children' and so 'not really a piece of theatre but a *fantaisie poétique*'[54] – possibly a deliberate reference to *L'Enfant*'s nomenclature as a *fantaisie lyrique*.

The music aside, another possible influence on the opera was the project enthusiastically embraced in Poulenc's letter to Armand Lunel of 12 October 1937 for a work called *La Jeunesse de Gargantua* which, for no reason given, then faded from view.[55] Some light though may be thrown on this by Poulenc's remark in an interview of 1944: 'I have just this summer composed an *opéra bouffe* on *Les Mamelles de Tirésias* . . . a very Rabelaisian play in which the grotesque attains a kind of grandeur. It is quite the opposite of a light work. What is more, I prefer Rabelais' obscenities to the smutty little jokes of most 18th-century authors.' As Denis Waleckx says, 'It is therefore plausible that the *Jeunesse de Gargantua* project prepared the composer for the discovery of Apollinaire's text'.[56] The apparent dissonance between Poulenc's two descriptions of *Les Mamelles* as both an *opéra bouffe* and as being 'quite the opposite of a light work' is one that has understandably drawn critical attention. A brief look at the history of the play and an annotated synopsis of the opera may be the most convenient ways of joining in this debate.

Commenting on the play's premiere on 24 June 1917, which Poulenc attended, Apollinaire wrote to a friend, '*Les Mamelles de Tirésias* was played in an atmosphere most suitable to a work which I think resembles nothing known, but which, if we must have comparisons, could be said to have affinities with Plautus and Beaumarchais, as well as Goethe'.[57] Plautus and Beaumarchais seem plausible, but Goethe? Light is shed on a more serious subtext to the play by an article Apollinaire wrote for the *Mercure de France* shortly before the play's premiere, quoting 'the old French saying, "God blesses large families". Had there been more children in France, the war would not be dragging on so long. Great fortunes belonging to wealthy couples with only one child are almost always doomed to sterility; the heirs content themselves with what they have, and most often squander it [. . .] Many children are needed, for the happiness of the home and of the nation.'[58]

The prologue of the play continues in the same vein, in the lines already mentioned that come twice, sung by 'le directeur' wearing evening dress (possibly reminding Poulenc of *Oedipus Rex?*). He left no doubt over the seriousness of his music in this prologue, telling Bernac that it was 'an aria in the style of Iago for Beckmans or Etcheverry'[59] – José Beckmans having made his Opéra-Comique debut in 1925 as Escamillo, and Henri Etcheverry in 1937 as Golaud, repeating the role in the famous production conducted by Désormière. In his *Journal de mes mélodies*, in an entry of 6 October 1945 long before the premiere, Poulenc went further, insisting that 'cheerful music and lighthearted music are not necessarily humorous. So *Les Mamelles* must be *sung*, from one end to the other, like Verdi.'[60] In this sense, the serious and comic elements should be welded together by the Verdian style, made a touch less surprising by the fact that in the months before the premiere Duval had launched two dramatic Puccini roles at the Opéra-Comique: Madam Butterfly on 5 March and Tosca on 28 March. That the action takes place in somewhere called Zanzibar, though designed to look more like Monte-Carlo, should detract nothing from the heroic atmosphere.

As always with Poulenc's music, the performers must evince total belief in what they are doing, with no conspiratorial winks to the audience. Again, the prologue needs to be listened to, in which the audience is assured that 'You will find here actions that are added to the main drama and decorate it: changes of tone from the harrowing to the burlesque and the reasoned use of the unlikely' and that the poet's aim is 'to evoke life itself in all its truthfulness': '*Les Mamelles de Tirésias* is authentic,' glosses Daniel Albright, 'in that there is not one moment of our lives in which there isn't a funeral march playing somewhere in the back of our skulls – and yet these corpses always resurrect themselves, at least in our dreams. Poulenc's authenticity lies in his faithfulness to the coextension of tragedy and farce, dissonant yet inextricable, throughout human life.'[61] From this viewpoint, Hell's complaint about ' "gags" that only feebly illustrate the poet's basic premise' seems beside the point. Modern brain research has shown that humour acts on the brain as a stimulant to understanding things both burlesque and harrowing.[62]

The first act shows us Thérèse in feminist mode, depicted 'Presto très agité' with forceful rhythms, as she ignores her husband's requests for food (he is 'Le Mari', name unknown) and looks forward to a career as soldier, artist, politician or indeed President. Balloons doing duty for her breasts float up to the sky and she sings to them a luscious waltz, as she replaces them with a beard and moustache. The husband thinks she's an intruder, but she shrugs him off. Two drunken layabouts, one short and fat, one tall and thin, enter and argue about who cheated at cards, and dance a polka before finally shooting each other (though their deaths are greatly exaggerated), accompanied by lyrical fourths and fifths in the orchestra that recall the opening and closing bars of *L'Enfant*. In scene 5, Thérèse appears as a smart young man, the husband in a dress with his hands tied, while the chorus comment on the comics' duel. A gendarme (described as 'of the absolutely classic type' – for Poulenc undoubtedly recalling *Le Gendarme incompris*, even if not spouting Mallarmé) takes a fancy to the husband and unties him. Overall Poulenc makes some cuts in Apollinaire's text and allows himself repetitions, but it is at this point that he makes his only significant addition: after the husband exclaims 'Il me prend pour une damoiselle' Poulenc inserts the lines 'Ce gendarme est un vieux fou coucou' (before fig. 59), with 'coucou' in falsetto, undoubtedly echoing Don Inigo's falsetto 'coucou' at the end of scene 9 of *L'Heure espagnole*. The husband rebuffs the gendarme's overtures and explains that he will now fill the vacuum by producing children himself.

An entracte reminiscent of Stravinsky's *Symphonies of Wind Instruments* introduces a ceremonial gavotte danced by members of the chorus, some of whom, ensconced in the orchestra, then take the role of newborns singing 'Papa' in falsetto. The second act begins with the husband boasting of his fecundity in fathering 40,049 babies in a single day. A Parisian journalist shows up avid for details, and Papa explains to him that children, far from impoverishing you, make you rich: one baby called Joseph has just sold 600,000 copies of his latest novel. But after producing a journalist his Papa, finding himself (as mentioned above) facing threats of extortion from one of his children, decides the next one will be a tailor so he can attract the girls – but the gendarme arrives to complain that, with all these extra mouths to feed, Zanzibarians are dying of hunger. A fortune-teller enters, complete with complex roulades (no problem for Duval), reinforcing the message of fecundity and warning the childless gendarme that the outlook for him is bleak. They fight, she strangles him, Papa throws himself on her . . . and she reveals herself as Thérèse once again. From here all is peace and love, expanding *Babar*'s magical finale with a brief memory of Thérèse's ascendant breasts, and the opera ends with the command 'Dear audience, make children'. Despite (or because of) the scandal, the opera was performed twelve times in 1947, nine times in 1948 and seven times in 1949.

As well as regularly attending rehearsals of *Les Mamelles*, Poulenc also joined Bernac in concerts in England during February and March, mostly for the BBC but also on stage in Welwyn Garden City and Oldham. Another stage appearance on 20 March was made under the auspices of the Université des Annales in Paris to deliver his talk 'Mes mélodies et leurs poètes', a useful summary of his history and beliefs in this area. Refusing the invitation of his hostess to sing excerpts from *Les Mamelles*, then in rehearsal, out of a reluctance to inflict on the audience his 'nasty nasal braying', he engaged Bernac's help in performing, after Schubert's 'Die Nebensonnen', his favourites among his own songs, from *Le Bestiaire* to 'C'. Much of what he said is to be found elsewhere in his writings, but two points deserve repetition. Of Apollinaire he said, 'He was in truth the contemporary poet I needed because, I have to tell you, I don't feel musically at ease except with the poets I have known [. . .] A crucial fact: I heard the sound of his voice. I think that's an essential point for a composer who doesn't want to betray a poet. The timbre of Apollinaire's voice, like that of his work as a whole, was both melancholy and cheerful.' He then turned, with rather more urgency, to the topic of pedalling in his music: 'Now playing my music without pedal is the end of everything, and especially the end of my music. Just as I can't imagine cooking without butter, I demand that pianists must use the pedal madly, fantastically, to distraction. It's the only way to get the real sound of my music. That doesn't mean you shouldn't change it constantly. But it must always be present.'[63]

As if all this was not enough to occupy Poulenc, Edward Lockspeiser took advantage of Poulenc's stay in the Piccadilly Hotel to bring to the BBC's notice his willingness to write a sinfonietta to mark the first anniversary of the start of the Third Programme on 29 September 1946. Lockspeiser, though by now a friend of the composer, was nonetheless realistic: 'He has in mind something like Prokofiev's "Symphonie Classique". I think he might be able to do something good with this idea if he continues to remain in the right mood, and it would be a credit to us if he pulled it off successfully. I am aware that Poulenc is by no means an expert nor always a skilful orchestrator. I am aware too that commissioned works can so easily be a flop. Nevertheless I have the feeling that among all the ideas we [he and I] discussed it is here that he is most likely to succeed.'[64] Lockspeiser's caution over 'the right mood' proved prophetic, as the *Sinfonietta* would not finally be performed until 24 October 1948.

With *Les Mamelles* successfully launched, Poulenc seems to have taken time out, announcing in a letter of 17 July that 'After a more than excitable spring I've come to have a rest in the Corrèze and cure my soul at Rocamadour.'[65] Between then and September he did return to composition, putting the finishing touches to *Main dominée par le coeur* and writing the *Trois Chansons de F. Garcia Lorca*. For once, it is hard not to find a link between the subtlety of Lorca's poems and the problems Poulenc acknowledged this caused him,[66] together with the two less than enthusiastic remarks the songs engendered in his *Journal*, even if the second is slightly warmer than the first.[67] Enthusiasm is lacking in their general reception, the most that Graham Johnson can find to say being that Poulenc was not disgraced by them.[68] He did begin the Sinfonietta in August and in the autumn also composed two pieces of incidental music and . . . *mais mourir* in memory of Nusch. Rarely did Poulenc encapsulate so much emotion in the space of just twenty-four bars. The shaping of the vocal line is almost that of *art nouveau* in its elegant curves, perfectly set off by the regular quavers that so often grace the composer's most heartfelt songs.

On 23 August Poulenc wrote to Schaeffner that he had completed a score in the style of 1900 for Anouilh's play *L'Invitation au château*, using the playwright's recommended instruments of violin, clarinet and piano and that it was 'without importance', being mainly 'pretty waltzes'. He was also 'starting a score that is far more difficult and grave (in every sense of the word) for Molière's *Amphitryon* which [Jean-Louis] Barrault is putting on at the [Théâtre] Marigny with sets by B.B. [Bébé Bérard].'[69] The Anouilh score has not survived, but the Molière one was recently discovered in the Département des Arts du Spectacle of the Bibliothèque nationale de France. Jean-Louis Barrault wrote to Poulenc on 12 July, telling him he had August and September in which to write all the music, and that the enterprise involved 'an outpouring of joy, of passion, of Jovian virility, and we must provide this in sufficient quantity to ensure the straightforward fabrication of a baby Hercules!!'[70] This was a reference to the myth in which Jupiter disguises himself as Amphitryon in order to seduce Amphitryon's wife Alcmene, Hercules being the result of the encounter. Poulenc replied to Barrault that there could be no question of 'a Jupiter in all his pomp processing to the sound of five or six miserable players. I'll let you know the make-up of my orchestra (not absolutely fixed as yet) which I shall try and make as economical as possible (15 at the maximum). Don't forget that good incidental music can only work through colour, since we musicians don't have the time, or so little time, to express ourselves.'[71] To Bernac, Poulenc wrote that he was 'working on Amphytrion [sic]. It's *terrifyingly* difficult, but not exhausting as to length. Imagine this (indications by Barrault): "Act I, Sosie half opens the door of Alcmene's house. A warm breath of sensuality leads us to think that Jupiter and Alcmene are making love (10 seconds)." And so on.'[72] At the time of writing, this score has not been revived either in concert or on disc.

Composition went on hold between November and May, not least because of Poulenc's concerts in London in December with Bernac, the premieres of *L'Invitation au château* on 5 November and of *Amphitryon* exactly a month later, the tour with Bernac of fifteen concerts in Holland during January and February and his talks broadcast on French Radio between 27 December and 29 May.[73] At some point during the spring, at a party given by Tailleferre, Poulenc met the young American piano duo of (Arthur) Gold and (Robert) Fizdale, who remembered how, possibly with those 'coucous' still sounding in his head, 'he sang a nonsense-syllable imitation of Gertrude Stein's English in a hilarious falsetto, and was especially compelling in the role of America's pioneer suffragette Susan B. Anthony.'[74] He became very fond of 'les boys', as he called them, and would write three works for them over the next decade or so.

With those events out of the way, composition returned. Having toured Europe widely since the end of the war, Poulenc now had America in his sights, knowing that his music was becoming popular there. 'I shall present myself,' he wrote to Virgil Thomson, 'just for this year, with my *only* speciality – songs. As it's a field in which I have no serious competitor, for me it's a way of playing my trumps as a pianist.'[75] Clearly such an important tour required songs specially written and, as so often, he turned to Apollinaire, though in a quite different vein from *Les Mamelles*. In choosing poems from the collection *Calligrammes*, published in 1918 and the last poems Apollinaire read in proof, he wrote that 'For me it represents the culmination of a whole series of experiments in setting Apollinaire to music. The more I turn the pages of his writings, the more I feel that I no longer find anything to nourish me. Not that I love Apollinaire's poetry any the less (I've never loved it more), but I feel I've taken from it everything that suited me.'[76] It was to be his last Apollinaire cycle.

The 1918 collection bears the title *Calligrammes: poèmes de la paix et de la guerre*, and of the seven poems only two, 'Il pleut' and the final 'Voyage', are ones of peace. Of the warlike songs, Poulenc singled out two, sadly unnamed, which 'like soldiers' songs will stand out well from their surroundings'.[77] Determined that *Calligrammes* should be a true cycle and not just an arbitrary grouping, Poulenc explained first of all that it was built on a strict out-and-back plan of tonalities with the B major of 'Il pleut' at the centre:

	Poulenc's list	Reality
L'espionne	F♯ minor	F♯ minor
Mutation	E flat major	E flat minor
Vers le sud	E major	E minor/major
Il pleut	B major	B flat minor?
La grâce exilée	E major	E major
Aussi bien que les cigales	E flat major	E flat minor
Voyage	F minor	F♯ minor

Although he lists 'Voyage' as being in F minor, this is clearly a slip of the pen. More puzzling is the attribution of B major to 'Il pleut', which begins and ends nearer to B flat minor, and then the mention of E flat major which is in fact nearer to E flat minor.[78] But puzzlement gives way to blank incomprehension over his claim that he wanted to 'attempt a tonal exercise, namely that each song should be the prolongation of its predecessor, and for that I feel happy with a sort of tonal underpinning which compels me not to finish a song in its initial key ...'[79] In fact every song ends on its initial tonic. The only charitable explanation for this disjunction might be that he simply changed his mind. It is certainly the case that changes were made quite late in the whole process. On Bernac's autograph copy of *Calligrammes*,[80] in the performing instructions over 'Il pleut', 'brouillard' became 'buée' ('fog' becoming the less dense 'vapour'), in bar 16 Poulenc's '*p* subito' over the top G was crossed out in red by Bernac, so changed to 'forte', and in the final 'Tempo subito' one bar three from the end was removed, and the bar after it removed but then reinstated. Almost certainly this double act operated on every Poulenc song that 'the team' performed.

Despite these problems, the quality of *Calligrammes* has never been seriously questioned since its wildly successful American premiere. In stating that the cycle was 'still more carefully structured than *Tel jour telle nuit*',[81] Poulenc would seem to have wanted to do for Apollinaire what he had done a dozen years earlier for Éluard, telling Lockspeiser that for him they were 'of an importance equal to that of *Tel jour*'.[82] The obvious difference between the two cycles (though how crucial this might be remains a matter of conjecture) is that Apollinaire arranged the texts of some of his poems as ideograms, forming shapes like those of Lewis Carroll, hence the overall title. Of the seven poems chosen by Poulenc, three were in the ideogram form: 'Il pleut', 'Aussi bien que les cigales' and 'Voyage'. The composer's clearest echo of this comes over in 'Il pleut', where the rainlike parallel verticals of the poem inspire regular semiquavers in the accompaniment, 'sec et précis' and with the unusual instructions 'sans pédale . . . toujours sans pédale'.

But these details are really incidental to the uninstructed listener's appreciation of the music which, with its emphasis on love, takes over where *Les Mamelles* left off, for all the disparities of tone between the two works. Apollinaire wrote the poems while on military service and even in the trenches, thinking of his mistress Marie Laurencin, safely away in South America. Poulenc's two bouts of military service, even if they did not include any fighting, enabled him to sympathize with the poet's cry in the brutal waltz 'Mutation': 'Et tout a tant changé en moi', and, as the final song would show, also with the phrase that follows: 'Tout sauf mon amour.' These references to the 1914–18 Great War took Poulenc back too to his past and Nogent, his grandmother's house, the smells of flowers, the sound of crickets. In 'Aussi bien que les cigales', almost certainly the second military song with 'Mutation', the poet tells the peasants to take their cue from the crickets, even to pissing like them (for those of a delicate constitution Apollinaire's widow sanctioned the replacing of 'pisser' by 'siffler', though 'whistling' doesn't really work . . .). The song seems sure to end in a triumphant celebration of 'the adorable delight of sun-drenched peace' – but the two loud, final chords are of E flat minor. The G flat becomes F♯ and for the final song we are back in F♯ minor. In keeping with the nostalgic atmosphere, the seven songs are dedicated to childhood friends, the last and best of whom is, of course, Raymonde Linossier. Poulenc said that 'Voyage' was one of the two or three of his songs he liked best, passing as it did from emotion through melancholy and love to silence. 'The ending is, for me, the silence of a July night when, from the terrace of my childhood home in Nogent, I would listen to the distant trains which were "going on holiday" (as I used to say then). Today this is accompanied by the irremediable departure of a face I have never replaced and of a beautiful, wakeful intelligence that I shall miss for ever.'[83] Like *Tel jour telle nuit*,

Calligrammes has a piano epilogue: but loving contentment is here replaced by spare two-part writing in octaves, shorn of comforting harmonies.

Whether even Raymonde's 'beautiful, wakeful intelligence' would, over time, have eased Poulenc's difficult relationship with solo strings must be doubted. But after a Violin Sonata he didn't really like and a String Quartet by now somewhere out in the North Sea, he still didn't abandon the chase. Poulenc's own version is that he had first made sketches for a Cello Sonata at Brive in the summer of 1940 when, in his post-military euphoria, he also composed *L'Histoire de Babar* and *Mélancolie* and started on *Les Animaux modèles*. That of the cellist Pierre Fournier is rather different, claiming that Poulenc said he wanted to write a cello sonata around 1925–8, and then again in 1937–8, using their mutual friend Jacques Février as an intermediary. Fleeting references to progress on the Sonata appeared in Poulenc's correspondence during 1942 and 1943 and, when the score was finally completed in 1948, Fournier saw it was difficult, so gave advice on bowing and fingering, but without changing anything radically in the score itself, 'just little things to make performance easier'.[84] Rehearsals for the first performance on 18 May 1949 would go well, Poulenc even commenting 'I have the feeling of playing with Bernac, he's so on-the-ball (précis).'[85]

Poulenc had very little to say about the work, although suggesting it was better than the Violin Sonata, and his opinion can be fairly accurately judged from his homage to the cellist and conductor Jean Witkowski, which ends with the memory 'of that evening when, thanks to your enthusiasm, I felt I loved my Cello Sonata, since you imbued it with so much poetry'.[86] His reservations about it are clear too from a letter of 1957, saying 'how correct the Turin critic was to write, after the Cello Sonata: "It's amazing that the composer of *Les Biches* should borrow his form from d'Indy's Schola Cantorum." '[87] The general opinion has been that the slow 'Cavatine' is the best movement, beginning with a quotation from the end of the first movement of the Two-Piano Concerto. There's a feeling of great freedom about it, perhaps induced to some extent by the composer's 'off-handed, anti-architectonic treatment of tonality', since 'it begins and ends in F♯ major, but very little of the movement is in that key'.[88] The following 'Ballabile', this time borrowing from *Les Animaux modèles*, is full of delightful moments, but the outer movements are less convincing, even after Poulenc had cut bars from the finale in 1953. If there is anything of architecture in the work, it lies in the sporadic passages of D flat major, as often involving his equally beloved Lydian G natural.

Both at home in Noizay and staying with his sister at Le Tremblay, Poulenc found the summer of 1948 particularly productive. In addition to *Calligrammes* and the Cello Sonata, in August he composed *Quatre petites prières de Saint François d'Assise* (his first religious music since the *Exultate Deo* and *Salve Regina* of 1941) and put the finishing touches to the *Sinfonietta*. The prayers were commissioned in a letter of 15 August from his great-nephew Gérard, known as Frère Jérôme, a grandson of Poulenc's uncle Camille, who was in a seminary studying theology for the priesthood. The invitation reached Poulenc just as he had returned from a visit to Assisi that had greatly impressed him, and thirty years later Frère Jérôme recalled that 'when he came [to the seminary] in October, he explained to me that the texts I sent him had immediately interested him and he had set them to music at once'.[89]

In his 1953 broadcast conversations with Stéphane Audel, Poulenc explained that 'In architecture, Romanesque art and especially that of southern France has always been my religious ideal, whether it's Vezelay, Autun, Moissac, les Vierges du Puy or Conques. I like the religious spirit to express itself clearly in the sunshine with the same realism we see in Romanesque capitals.'[90] Written for a cappella men's choir, these *Prières* are among the simplest music Poulenc ever wrote, but within that simplicity – of harmony, melody and texture – the least deviation from the norm can assume extraordinary power. In the first prayer, the litanic procession is magically halted by the quiet seventh chords on 'qui par la grâce et l'illumination du Saint Esprit', and at the start of the second, after a succession of eighteenth-century harmonies, the force of 'bien' in the sense of 'goodness' is underlined in pairs of harmonies of increasing unexpectedness. In the third prayer the first mention of 'amour' brings with it a touch of Poulenc's more sensual harmony, leading to the final phrase 'de mon amour' set to the last cadence of *Figure humaine*, and in the same key (though of course without the E in alt). The last prayer, delivered by a figure of authority, presumably the abbot, to his 'dearest brethren', begins understandably with a tenor solo. From here it grows, through the harsh minor chord on 'la peine éternelle', to an expansion of Poulenc's 'love' harmonies on the best-known phrase in these texts: 'many are called, but few are chosen'. The final Amen ('Ainsi soit-il') is unique in being repeated, as Poulenc takes us down emotionally from exaltation to calm acceptance.

The other work Poulenc was engaged on this summer was the Finale of the *Sinfonietta*, whose first three movements had already been composed the previous August and two of them orchestrated. But, as he complained at the time to Lockspeiser, 'The *Sinfonietta* has turned into a symphony [. . .] Explain that, with all your sympathy, to the BBC. But there is no way I can be ready on time not, alas, being a Hindemith or a Milhaud, but rather a Falla or a Ravel, that's to say a slowcoach.'[91] It was not until 8 September 1948 that he could tell Lockspeiser, 'This morning I put down the last barline on the *Sinfonietta*. I can talk seriously to you about it. As some people have said that because of it you no longer *loved me*, others have added that you are *vexed*, and nasty rumours have insinuated that you were *furious*, all that leads me to revise my schedule, especially as the BBC is always like a mother for me.'[92] His disarray even prompted him, very unusually, to offer a financial sacrifice: 'As a mother always rewards her well-behaved children, could you obtain £50 (tax free) from the BBC for this premiere? We previously agreed £100 for 12 minutes and a dedication. I reckon that 25 minutes without dedication for £50 is very reasonable. Please manage this, as in February (when the money's due) I've a very heavy bill to pay with my tailor.'[93]

The sad truth is that, more than seventy years on from its first performance, the *Sinfonietta* has still not entered the general orchestral repertoire. It has had its admirers: Keith Daniel comments that it contains 'his first truly successful string writing' and admits 'it remains a mystery to me why the *Sinfonietta* is not heard more often, for it is rich in ingratiating tunes and intriguing orchestral colours'.[94] This is undoubtedly true, but the problem may reside less in the material than in the way it is organized. Daniel himself makes the point that there are passages in both the outer movements 'that hint at development, but in these cases we begin to tread a fine line between it and altered restatement with the aid of flexible modulations'.[95] Undeniably, Poulenc did not think naturally in the form of developments, but rather, in Wilfrid Mellers's phrase, 'kaleidoscopically'.[96] The result is that much of the score sounds like ballet music – which is true of Tchaikovsky, but then he also had the knack of making such material work symphonically. Deprived of text, stage action or contact with any individual performer, Poulenc, dependent as he was on words, images and friends, lost his guiding stars, and his sporadic use of four cyclic themes was not enough to compensate. As has been pointed out already, it doesn't do to believe uncritically everything he himself said about his music, but honesty demands quotation of his overall view on what he composed between 1944 and 1949: 'I didn't recognize my age and I wanted to write music that was too young, like the *Sinfonietta* with its characters of 48-year-old "biches" . . . I didn't recover my true self until the *Stabat Mater*.'[97]

With the *Sinfonietta* completed, Poulenc was free to concentrate on his forthcoming American tour, something he had first dreamt of twenty years before, and again in 1943.[98] He and Bernac left on 22 October 1948 and were back in Paris on 23 December. From New York, Washington and Boston they went to Chicago and then spent five days in Los Angeles, returning to New York via Salt Lake City with excursions to Pittsburgh and Philadelphia. They had been working intensively on *Calligrammes* and on 16 October had given a private performance in Paris chez Marie-Blanche de Polignac in preparation for the public premiere in the New York Town Hall on 24 November.

Although a New York agency was in overall charge of the tour, the bass Doda Conrad played a large part in smoothing their way, helped by the idiomatic English he'd picked up in the American army. In his memoirs, Conrad relates how Bernac warned him that Poulenc was suffering from a throat infection and that his doctor, fearing it was cancerous, was urging him to call off the tour. Conrad, recalling the experience of some of his wartime comrades, begged Poulenc to take a blood test in case he was suffering from a sexually transmitted disease. This turned out to be true, he was duly treated and the tour went ahead.[99]

Another old friend was the composer Virgil Thomson, also the music critic of the *New York Herald Tribune*. Poulenc's letter to him of 15 September alerts him to the arrival of *Calligrammes*, but asks 'What will the famous Virgil Thomson think? That's the problem. As you normally like my songs, I'm hopeful. Mind you tell everyone that Poupoule is a Parisian type who speaks English badly, sometimes rough, but full of goodwill.'[100] The goodwill won out over the roughness. As Lacombe reports, 'The first recital in the Town Hall on 7 November was a triumph; the second on 20 November caused delirium: the première of *Calligrammes* [on the 24th] had seven recalls and the concert was extended by five encores.'[101] Among the other friends he met were Lily Pons, Wanda Landowska, Horowitz and Christian Dior, and thus began a love affair with the United States that would last until his death. Among the benefits was 'also the pleasant possibility of having some commissions': to which he adds the curious rider, 'It would be very nice finally to earn a crust with some real music.' So what was the 'unreal' or 'fake' music he'd been condemned to write so far for a pittance? But maybe it was the just the effect of the expensive Hotel Saint-Moritz, where he pronounced himself 'divinely installed [. . .] with a piano sent by Baldwin and a divine view over the park'.[102]

His room was also so quiet that, to thank Conrad for all his organizing, he was able to compose a song for him, *Hymne*, the last music he would write until the following May. In a couple of ways this song is unique. It is his only setting of Racine; and it is the only song which, apart from one minim rest, engages the singer throughout, with no prelude, interludes or postlude. Racine's text is a translation from the Roman Breviary, banishing the shadows and demons of night and rejoicing in the brightness of day and in Christ, our one and only light. This movement from darkness into light may well refer to Conrad's medical intervention, since the copy sent to his mother Marya Freund bears the dedication 'For the mother of my guardian angel, and she will never know how true that is.'[103]

The opening music of darkness poses problems for the pianist in its low-lying dissonances, somehow to be reconciled with the familiar 'mettre beaucoup de pédale'. With the appearance of sunlight the piano texture naturally rises, but equivocation between minor and major indicates that mankind is still struggling against 'the dense veil that was covering nature'. The pianissimo apostrophe 'O Christ' brings with it more sensuous harmonies and from here the play continues between dark/sin and light/salvation. Although the song cannot be accused of demonstrating Poulenc's regrettable return to youthfulness, it did not find total acceptance in his eyes: 'There are passages in this *Hymne* that satisfy me completely, others that I would have liked to be more supple. It's impossible to set alexandrines to music when you don't feel the rhythm *in a living sense*. That's the case with me!'[104] Given the mostly thick piano textures, variety has to be sought out. As usual, Bernac is a wise counsellor:

The poem consists of five verses, made up of one octosyllabic line and three alexandrines. Curiously, Poulenc begins each verse of his song *pianissimo* (except the last which is only *piano*). It's vital to observe these nuances which allow for a large crescendo that should lead to a broad *forte*. In every case the start of each verse is marked by a change of lighting and of vocal colour which should not be missed [. . .] The indicated speed, crotchet = 60, seems good and natural.[105]

Bernac's mention of 'lighting' (éclairage) proves, if proof were needed, how well attuned he was to the visual component in Poulenc's inspiration.

Despite the triumphant success of the tour, not to mention his dinner in Salt Lake City with a Mormon gentleman whose father had eighteen legitimate wives ('This charming custom was abolished in 1895. So much the worse for me!'),[106] Poulenc's letters are full of his nostalgia for France, his return to which he celebrated in January with a group of radio talks under the title *À bâtons rompus* [Off the Cuff]. His first response, if we are to judge by the title 'Retour de l'Amérique', would seem to be to tell French listeners about his American tour. But in fact the article turns, after praising the clarinettist Woody Herman and his Woodchoppers, to tales of his own youth.

The first months of 1949 were largely taken up by touring with Bernac: in England during February, including the first British performance of *Calligrammes* for the BBC on the 14th, and in Spain for the first fortnight of April. This tied up with a request to write a preface for a book on Ricardo Viñes, prompting thoughts of Viñes's 'miraculous' recordings 'which must absolutely be reissued'.[107] Fournier joined him in the first public performance of the Cello Sonata on 18 May, and before that in a private one chez Marie-Blanche – to which, unusually, he wanted Raymond to be invited since 'he'd listened to me hammering away at it all last summer'. Poulenc insisted that Raymond would understand 'the exceptional nature of this invitation', the composer normally keeping a clear distinction between his social and intimate lives.[108]

Apart from a single song, the main focus of Poulenc's attention in 1949 was on his Concerto for piano and orchestra for Boston, presumably commissioned in the course of his first tour for his second one in 1950. The idea of a concerto for himself to play went back to October 1943, when he told André Jolivet 'I'm now thinking of writing my Concerto for piano and orchestra for my American tour after the war'[109] – a plan that incidentally shows how the defence of Stalingrad and its aftermath had come to make Allied victory seem inevitable. Two years later he wrote of 'a new piano concerto for the winter of 46–47',[110] but then no more is heard of the idea until July 1949 when he announced to Marie-Blanche, 'I've just finished the first movement of my concerto for Boston', followed by a note to Bernac that 'the best definition of the Concerto is that it is raked like my terrace. The orchestration is very spruce and varied, the piano writing brilliant and fitting my capabilities.'[111] The other two movements duly followed over the summer and autumn and the Concerto was complete by early October.

In June Poulenc made a short visit to England to play the Cello Sonata with Fournier, and in July wrote the song *Mazurka* at Le Tremblay as one of seven settings of Louise de Vilmorin's poetry: published as *Mouvements de cœur*, it is dedicated to Doda Conrad who had conceived the album as a tribute to his fellow Pole Frédéric Chopin on the 100th anniversary of his death. Conrad gave the first performance in New York on 6 November 1949, accompanied by David Garvey.

Poulenc's prompt dismissal of the song ('In the style of Poulenc by a Poulenc who was bored with this kind of thing')[112] is a little harsh. Its waltzing character refers back to the fourth Nocturne where a ball becomes a mysterious vision, steeped in nostalgia, and even if the texture is not particularly varied, a sensitive singer can make up for this. But at the end of the year Poulenc had to admit, 'I think Doda didn't like either the *Mazurka* or the advice in my letter.'[113]

As he was putting the finishing touches to the Concerto in September, two of the other matters he noted concerned Messiaen and Bernac. To Milhaud he wrote on 18 September, 'It seems to me that Messiaenism is not rampaging through America. You'll tell me all about that.'[114] Although Poulenc made no secret of his allergy both to Messiaen's verbose prefaces and to his Dukas-based orchestration, there was still a voice in his head warning him that Messiaen could not simply be written off; and his anxiety about Messiaen's standing in America touched painfully on worries about his own in a land where he was keen to be loved – hence his request for Milhaud's support. Whether coincidentally or not, this letter was written only a matter of weeks before the world premiere on 2 December under Leonard Bernstein of the *Turangalîla Symphony* in Boston, where Poulenc was due to play his Piano Concerto on 6 January – and Poulenc's engagement with Messiaen's *magnum opus* would not end there . . .

Poulenc's concern for Bernac was of a quite different order. On 12 September he wrote a letter showing that the kindness between them was reciprocal:

> Thank you for your card from Solesmes [a religious retreat run by Benedictines] – I'm certain that this short stay will have done you a world of good – I'd felt you were unhappy for some time, and for a nature like yours this kind of immersion in grace is perfect. Don't be so worried then about your autumn. I reckon you've still got five or six good years in front of you. After that will come true autumn happiness, that's to say when you'll live surrounded by pupils to whom you'll communicate your experience. I've been playing all our discs lately. Brigitte was very struck by how much stronger your voice is in the more recent ones.[115]

This was reinforced a week later by an assurance that '*No*, you are not in decline, thank God . . .'[116] Bernac's artistry and sensitivity to language had never been in question. But it has to be admitted that not everyone found the voice itself to their taste. Ned Rorem, who first met Poulenc on 6 July 1949, later wrote of Bernac:

Primarily he is an actor, a multi-masked *diseur*; much of [his] vocality is actually faked (especially high notes), smoothed over with poignant suavity and with the tastefully vulgar twang of Opéra-Comique. Bernac's chief quality was, and is, that he knows what he's singing about, and how to persuade you that his version is definitive. He does this through a flawless, if sometimes coy, diction . . .'[117]

Nearer to home was a 1957 article by Émile Vuillermoz who, after praising Bernac's many fine qualities, explained that exactly because of the those qualities he should be prepared to accept some direct advice:

Pierre Bernac seems to be evolving, for some time now, towards an ideal of singing that is rather too specialized. He thins out his voice dangerously, with a surfeit of unemphatic suavity. In this way he has succeeded in 'tenorizing' the whole upper register of his baritone voice so that it's losing its deep resonance and timbre, which used to be more incisive [. . .] What's more, the entirely praiseworthy aim of making intelligible all the words of his texts is leading him to put weight on every syllable, in a slightly irritating manner. He has a way of deliberately sinking his teeth into the flesh of a word and chewing up their consonants which is leading him into a certain affectation.[118]

It is fair to answer these critiques with the plain statement that in 1949 Bernac had, not five or six years in front of him, but ten, and that applause throughout this time was as loud as ever, both in France and abroad. They do, however, go some way to explaining the problems over an institutional post that would now increasingly occupy Poulenc as well as Bernac.

Not surprisingly, Bernard Gavoty failed to invite Poulenc to answer his September questionnaire in *Le Figaro* about the value and future of twelve-tone music. Perhaps worried that someone might have to decide whether the term 'dodécaca' could appear in a respectable newspaper, he turned instead to Honegger, Schmitt, Dutilleux and Ibert among others.[119] As it happened, Poulenc was 'turning serious' in another direction, reflecting on the sudden death of his dear friend Christian Bérard on 12 February. He told Milhaud, 'After the Concerto I'm going to write . . . a *Stabat Mater* in memory of Bérard, the first performance of which I shall give with Robert Shaw during the winter of 1950–51 in New York.'[120] As mentioned above, it was with this work that Poulenc felt he would emerge from his second composing adolescence.

Whereas for their first American tour in 1948 he and Bernac had travelled by boat, Poulenc now flew on his own to New York on 28 December, to be joined by Bernac around 12 January. On the flight he determined to write a diary of this second tour, and was clearly stimulated by new sights and new people. In Boston the day before the first performance of the Piano Concerto he met a professor who astounded him by his perfect French and encyclopedic knowledge of music. Talk turned to Debussy:

> It's astonishing, really, how a mere 30 years after Debussy's death the true meaning of his message has been lost. How many players betray Debussy for lack of *sensuality*. The word 'sensuality' amazes my companion. I realize it's not a term he's in the habit of using about music. 'Surely you mean eroticism?' 'Not necessarily, sensuality being sometimes a more accidental form of eroticism.' Then, going on to a more concrete example, I explain to him that if Toscanini revealed *La Mer* and Sabata *Jeux* to the general public, it's because, being true Italians who don't blush at Puccini (bravo!), they can't conceive how we might fight shy of the Massenet influence on many passages of Debussy. I add that conductor A putting *Jeux* in the ice house and conductor B in the sterilizer do more damage to this jewel than silence does.[121]

Poulenc's admiration for *Jeux* was at least one thing that linked him with the avant-garde: it was in Messiaen's supplementary class in 1944 that Boulez 'discovered Debussy's *Jeux*, then almost unknown and seldom studied',[122] and only in 1959 did the German scholar Herbert Eimert publish his detailed analysis, claiming the ballet as 'one of the most important works in the development of modern music'.[123]

On 6 January 1950 'the concerto went well. Five recalls, but more sympathy than outright enthusiasm. The "Rondeau à la française" caused shock, by its sauciness and its naughty boy side. From the keyboard I could feel the audience's interest fading. I was hoping that this view of Paris, obviously more of "its Bastille than its Passy side", would amuse the audience. Basically I think it was disappointed.

Too bad.'[124] It seems to have been the tiny, sparky Finale that caused the trouble, leading to the whole work being 'judged a little "disrespectful" by the very Sibelius-minded critics of certain cities' after he had taken it on tour.[125] He had hoped that quoting 'Way down upon the Swanee River' would appeal to American audiences, but not so. It's clear from his remarks about the work that he never intended it to be more than a divertimento, a work that 'wears its cap over one ear'[126] – maybe calling it a Concertino would have helped. Keith Daniel notes that there are only thirty bars of solo piano in the whole work and finds the change of mood in the Finale disconcerting.[127] Certainly there are moments of warmth and seriousness in the first two movements, the first beginning with a tune that insists on minor rather than major thirds, the slow movement with one that is among Poulenc's most lyrical and which leads to piano chords of Rachmaninovian grandeur. But although he might shrug his shoulders with a 'Tant pis!' and later almost disown the Concerto, at the time he was undoubtedly hurt, explaining to Henri Hell, 'I've done exactly what I wanted to and this French lucidity, this balance has been taken here (except by the young) for pettiness'. His pride damaged, he even went as far as adding 'It's so hard to explain to them that Watteaus are great pictures'[128] – an implied comparison he wisely kept to a private letter.

The charge of pettiness ('mesquinerie' also carries whiffs of 'shabbiness', even 'dishonesty') also led Poulenc to think again about his standing in the musical world, and especially in America. In 1945 the critic Claude Rostand had considered writing his biography, but the project fell into abeyance. Now Poulenc was pinning his hopes on Henri Hell, a critic and a good pianist, though he had never thought of himself as a biographer.[129] Poulenc recounted how his modest confession that he had never composed the *Kreutzer Sonata* or the *Coronation Concerto* led a journalist to write of Poulenc admitting that 'apart from his vocal and stage works, his music is only of minor interest'. Hell was duly enjoined to 'destroy my legend as a miniaturist in this land of Sibelius'.[130]

These annoyances aside, the tour was a great success, one of the pinnacles being the performance on 17 February of *Figure humaine* in Carnegie Hall: 'Splendid performance,' wrote Poulenc, 'with 80 singers and 60 rehearsals. That has been my real success of the year and I'm delighted with it. My American colleagues greatly astonished by its great effect without recourse to trumpets and drums.'[131] Bernac also played a large part in the tour's success, Poulenc being 'so happy for Pierre, for whom it's his only joy in life'.[132] On 25 and 27 March they recorded songs by Poulenc, *Chabrier* (Poulenc's italics), Satie and Debussy. On the

28th Poulenc shared a box with the Stravinskys for Virgil Thomson's Cello Concerto, and the next day he and Bernac flew back to Paris.

At some point that spring Poulenc met Lucien Roubert, a forty-one-year-old married commercial traveller living in Toulon and working in Marseille, though the marriage seems not to have lasted long after his meeting with Poulenc. In 1955 the composer attested that 'If Raymond remains the secret of *Mamelles* and *Figure humaine*, Lucien is certainly that of the *Stabat* and *Carmélites*,'[133] from which we may infer that his relationship with Raymond was by now platonic, and probably had been so for some time. Maybe it was in some sense only right and proper, given that these last two works dealt with suffering, that the relationship with Lucien would be one of Poulenc's most harrowing experiences.

But for the time being, after nearly six months away from composing, he came back to it almost immediately. Although he had already mentioned the *Stabat Mater*, he does not seem to have worked on this until August. Between April and July he wrote his penultimate Éluard cycle, *La Fraîcheur et le feu*, on a poem in seven sections entitled 'Vue donne vie' from the poet's 1940 collection *Le Livre ouvert I*; Éluard himself provided the title for the set of songs. Its source and character are well captured by Graham Johnson:

> Here a composer of great personal inner contrasts writes a cycle which uses the interplay of slow and fast tempi, and major and minor tonalities, to embody the extremes of the work's title: the contrasts between water and fire, coolness and heat, light and dark are encapsulated by the human polarity of man and woman, difficult and puzzling certainly, but essential for the miracle of life.[134]

A need to contain the stress of these opposites could well lie behind Poulenc's description of the songs as being without doubt 'mes mélodies les plus concertées', in which 'concertées' is surely to be taken in the sense of 'structured, planned out'. Part of this planning was the removal of anything superfluous, following the practice of Matisse (though pianists may wonder at some points what the original can have looked like!). In dedicating them to Stravinsky and claiming they were 'in some sense derived from him' he was no doubt referring to the inexact quotation in the third song from the last movement of Stravinsky's *Serenade in A* (though not from the final cadence, as recalled here, but, as printed on the copy, from the opening three bars).[135] If the challenge of structuring a single long poem was, as he wrote, one of his main motives, then another, referring to Stravinsky, may have been the one he naughtily confided in a letter to Milhaud: 'this is to tell you that I took the trouble to cook up one of the only dishes to which he does not possess the secret'.[136] Not a thought he would have entrusted to just anybody . . .

The climax of the cycle, built up through the usual juxtaposition of fast and slow songs, comes in the sixth one, 'Homme au sourire tendre' whose calmly majestic F♯ major is further marked out from the distant C minor/major of its predecessor by a 'très long silence'. But at the end the calm is shattered in a stroke of genius – a single, dangerous, low C natural, *ppp*, that leads immediately to the last song whose ending, 'très violent', brings us back to the cycle's Chopinesque opening bars and a final, abrupt confrontation between the minor and major modes that have stalked the work.

In early June Poulenc had a run-in with Bernard Gavoty, operating under his critical cognomen 'Clarendon', in which, in defence of Milhaud's *Bolivar*, Poulenc claimed it was 'impossible to state, honestly, the day after the first performance of an opera, whether it was a flop or a success' and quoted the examples, among others, of Enesco's *Oedipe*, Granados's *Goyescas*, Massenet's *Grisélidis* and Puccini's *Turandot* where initial scorn later turned to admiration. He ended his public letter with harsh words for 'la mesure française' too often confused with 'la médiocrité académique' – only for Gavoty to reply that Milhaud himself had claimed 'mesure', in the sense of a middle-of-the-road balance, as one of French music's defining characteristics.[137]

Poulenc may have had to leave the song cycle in its final stages in order to play in the first French performance of the Concerto at the Aix-en-Provence festival, again with Münch conducting, on 24 July. Remembering the occasion the following March, Poulenc complained that 'the hastily prepared performance was in any case execrable', a judgement we have no reason to doubt, despite his general admiration for Münch. In any case, the reception by some of the critics was even more damning than in Boston, though Claude Rostand took the opportunity of inventing a description of the composer that was to persist, and with Poulenc's blessing: 'there will always be inside me the "moine" and the "voyou".'[138] 'Moine' as 'monk' is straightforward enough, but 'voyou' has always caused slight problems, translated variously as 'guttersnipe', 'loafer', 'hooligan', 'blackguard', 'lout', 'ruffian', none of which really suit Poulenc. 'Cheeky street-arab' might be nearer (though probably now politically incorrect) and 'subversive' nearer still, though the word's political connotations are adrift; perhaps 'rascal' or 'ragamuffin' are nearest. But even if no exact English equivalent exists, the thrust of Rostand's nomenclature is clear: if you were looking for someone to blow raspberries at Sibelius or Bruckner, Poulenc was your man.

As it happened, the Aix-en-Provence festival in 1950 gave an opportunity for something of the same sort, namely the French premiere on 25 July, the day after that of Poulenc's Concerto, of Messiaen's *Turangalîla Symphony*. The head of music at Radio France, Henry Barraud, later condemned the work as offering 'baneful echoes of a certain *In a Persian Market* by Ketèlbey, now it seems largely forgotten, but at the time one of the most dreadful tunes in bars and music halls', and recalled the meeting, in a café after the performance, of Auric, Sauguet, Honegger, Poulenc, Roland-Manuel, Daniel-Lesur and probably Jolivet at which decorum was thrown to the winds, Auric and Honegger being in favour, Poulenc and Roland-Manuel against.[139] Poulenc gave his own account several weeks later:

> At the end of Messiaen's atrocious *Turangalîla-Symphonie*, in the place de l'Archevêché, in front of an astonished crowd, Roland [-Manuel] and Arthur [Honegger] set upon each other; as for Georges [Auric] and me, that was a real drama. Georges was green, still unwell from a mixture of flu and a frozen melon, and I was red as a beetroot. For seven minutes we said dreadful things, Georges defending Messiaen, while I was at the end of my tether about the dishonesty of the work, written to please both the crowd and the élite, the urinal and the Holy Water stoup, all in the awful tradition of Dukas and Marcel Dupré. People surrounded us as if they were at a cock-fight. After seven minutes we kissed and made up. But it's all over the radio and the papers . . .'[140]

That being so, Poulenc was quick to limit the damage, writing only a week later to Messiaen:

> I'm sure people have not failed to tell you, more than once, that I don't like your *Symphony*, which is true, but since I also think that no one, with the exception of Paul Rouart, has told you how *thrilled* I was by your [*Cinq*] *Rechants* this spring, I insist on doing so in order to assure you that my attitude in the present case is strictly limited and based entirely on a difference of aesthetics. I love *Les Corps glorieux*, *Les Visions de l'Amen* and many of your other works. I have said

so and say it again. So do not hold it against me if the conception of *Turangalîla* has shocked me profoundly.[141]

It is reasonable to suppose that this view of *Turangalîla*, together with the success of *Figure humaine* despite its lack of 'trumpets and drums', may have played a role in the genesis of the *Stabat Mater* to which Poulenc now turned his attention. 'I had thought initially,' he wrote, 'of a Requiem, but I felt that was too ceremonious. Then I had the idea of an intercessional prayer, and the overwhelming text of the *Stabat Mater* seemed to me the perfect vehicle for entrusting the soul of my dear Bérard to Our Lady of Rocamadour [. . .] it's true that the *Stabat Mater* is perhaps more *noble* than my other sacred works.'[142] A decade later, he would look back and distinguish it as being 'a large *a cappella* work enshrined within the orchestra', whereas the *Gloria* was more 'symphonic'.[143] At the time he explained that 'the *Stabat*, in its tone of a funeral oration, is closer to the Jesuit style of Saint-Eustache or Saint-Roch, churches in which Bossuet, for one thing, used to deliver his sermons'.[144]

Since Poulenc was a fervent reader of Jacques-Bénigne Bossuet's writing, it is as well to touch on those points that united them: Bossuet's description of faith ('It is, without evidence and in the midst of obscurity, wholehearted persuasiveness, total freedom from anxiety, absolute conviction, a perfect acquiescence in the truth') clearly spoke to the composer's 'inquiétude', as did his acceptance of fear ('I tremble, in truth, to the very marrow of my bones, when I consider the lack of solid grounding I find in myself'). Beyond that there was comfort in Bossuet's embrace of simplicity ('Only pray to that Spirit, that bloweth where it listeth, to scatter on my lips *those two ornaments of Christian eloquence: simplicity and truth*'). Finally, Bossuet was no friend to narrowness ('There has to be fullness to produce fecundity, and fecundity for variety, without which there is no delight').[145] For a composer who craved a solid faith, who lamented his lack of it, who distrusted complexity (embraced in *Turangalîla*, expunged in *La Fraîcheur et le feu*), but who relished a wide variety of musical styles, Bossuet was a mentor *sans pareil*.

Poulenc's determination to avoid portentousness suited the character of the work's dedicatee: Christian Bérard was, in Benjamin Ivry's description, 'an obese man who bathed rarely and spent days in bed with his dog, eating and joking with friends. Welcome in the upper reaches of high society, he had a taste for transvestism in seedy Paris dives.'[146] If such tastes made the idea of a Requiem seem overwhelming, it's easy to see how, in addition to Bérard's painterly skills, they might appeal to Poulenc, to the extent that he lamented to Denise Duval, 'It's a whole piece of my youth that has departed with him.'[147] Not the least of the work's many beauties are its moments of intimacy, where we feel we are there, with the Virgin as she weeps for her Son on the cross, and also with Poulenc as he laments his friend, dead so suddenly at only forty-six of a cerebral haemorrhage while Poulenc was away in London. Just as the composer was moved to think back to his youth, so he looked for inspiration in a more distant past, that of the eighteenth century, not only by following Pergolesi's twelve divisions of the text rather than Rossini's, Dvořák's or Verdi's, but at times in the music itself. A further borrowing from that century is the chorus in five parts, with tenors and basses separated by baritones (or 'basses-tailles'), as in the *grands motets* of Lully, Lalande and Charpentier, who may well have been in his mind when he used the word 'noble'. Simultaneously, though, he acknowledged Bérard's standing as a modern painter in his treatment of the Latin text, imitating Stravinsky in his wilful play with accentuation: 'dol*o*rosa' instead of 'dolor*o*sa', 'g*e*mentem' instead of 'gem*e*ntem', 'mo*e*rebat' instead of 'moer*e*bat' – leaving himself free to opt for standard accentuation when he felt like it.

As Keith Daniel points out, movements two, seven and eleven could be regarded as 'tremplins', as in Poulenc's song cycles, without any suggestion that their texts may be less meaningful than the surrounding ones,[148] but, as in those cycles, the emotional weight does reside in the more lyrical movements, here especially in the three that include the soprano soloist. Originally he had Suzanne Danco in mind for this role, which she was greatly looking forward to taking ('It is a joy and an honour to agree to sing for you and with you!').[149] Her apparently effortless tone would indeed have suited the part superbly, but for whatever reason she did not perform in the Strasbourg premiere. Poulenc's progress on the score during the summer of 1950 also seemed relatively effortless: 'I'm attacking the *Stabat* with patience and calm,' he told Bernac,[150] while to Hélène Jourdan-Morhange he announced proudly, 'You know anyway that I'm as sincere in my faith, without any messianic [Messiaenic?] shouting, as in my Parisian sexuality. My musical style is spontaneous and in any case, I think, quite characteristic.'[151]

The opening bars, consisting of some ten seconds of unalloyed A minor, speak of a composer sure of himself, untroubled by the publication that year of works such as Boulez's Second Piano Sonata. The steadily pulsing quavers, 'très calme', join those in so many of his finest songs, possibly echoing the opening 'Gute Nacht' of his beloved *Winterreise*? But the mood here is sombre, the unyielding minor thirds looking back not only to *Oedipus Rex* and what Wilfrid Mellers calls its 'grim purgatorial motives',[152] but to the supplicatory text of the first movement of *Symphony of Psalms*: 'Auribus percipe lacrimas meas', 'Hearken to my tears'. After the second movement 'tremplin', the chorus alone sings 'O quam tristis', joined sporadically and briefly by the orchestra which signs off with three quiet chords. How it is that the chorus's diminished sevenths do not sound hackneyed is one of those mysteries . . . Poulenc, fully aware that the presence of a soprano in front of the orchestra would alert the audience that at some point she would sing, in line with Chekhov's celebrated maxim that 'if in Act I you have a pistol on the wall, then it must fire in the last act', deliberately keeps them waiting until the sixth movement. A further action of Poulenc the dramaturge is initially to give the soprano just the phrase 'Vidit suum dulcem natum' (She saw her dear son) and allot 'morientem, desolatum' (dying, desolate) to the chorus, leaving the impression that the Virgin is too horrified by those two words to pronounce them. At last, she takes courage, but by changing the order of the two words Poulenc somehow manages to intensify her sorrow. Finally she sings 'Dum emisit . . .' (until he gave up . . .), but now her courage fails again, and it's left to the chorus to complete the sentence with 'spiritum'.

In the eighth movement, 'Fac ut ardeat', Poulenc makes obeisance to contrapuntal practice as found in religious music for centuries, but three bars of it is enough before the texture dissolves into his familiar chordal writing, part plainsong, part *mélodie*, with a sprinkling of 'forbidden' consecutive fifths. The romantic élan of the 'Sancta mater' is then channelled into the classicism of the second of the three movements with soprano, 'Fac ut portem', where the French overture double dotting of her previous solo is reinterpreted as part of a sarabande, marked as such, with the rising minor third in A minor again prominent as at the beginning of the work. (Incidentally, Poulenc sent the opening four bars to the organist André Marchal as the subject of an improvisation to end his recital on 7 November at St Peter's, Cranley Gardens in London.)[153] The soprano line, though, sails lyrically above the urgent orchestra, rising up to a top C flat, and culminating in the phrase 'Ob amorem filii' (For love of the Son) – after which the chorus are left to mutter 'Fac ut portem Christi mortem' (Make me bear the death of Christ). The eleventh movement, 'Inflammatus et accensus', is possibly too dramatic to be heard as a 'tremplin', and in any case it soon resolves into an Adagio. The last movement, 'Quando corpus', truly crowns the work, the soprano's ecstatic, threefold 'Paradisi gloria' being based on the piece's opening bars, and eventually summoning their pulsing quavers.

On the technical level, the *Stabat Mater* demonstrates Poulenc's increasing skill at any number of points. By reserving the soprano until the sixth movement, he not only increases anticipation, but by then bringing her back in movements ten and twelve produces a kind of accelerando of soprano sound. Harmonically too, he makes the links between movements harsh and uneasy, often by shifting the keys by a semitone; the pay-off comes between the last two movements where the link is more natural and relaxing, the last movement duly marked 'attaquer de suite' – the path to paradise beckons irresistibly. The final chords themselves are also carefully differentiated. Once again he engineers a kind of accelerando, this time of harmonic colour: the first seven movements all end on common chords; then movements eight, ten, eleven and twelve all end on discords, the final unresolved dominant seventh leading us decisively out of this material world into a blissful infinity.

Poulenc spent August and September of 1950 at Noizay, completing the vocal score of the *Stabat Mater* on 3 October. Not without reason, he was startled at having written thirty-five minutes of music in just two months,[154] though the orchestration would take him until the following April. But for whatever reasons, the next two years would see only minor pieces in various formats, while concert-giving continued in force. On 15 October he was back in Paris, the concert season beginning on the 28th both in Paris and in England. After he and Bernac had given the public premiere of *La Fraîcheur et le feu* in Birmingham on 1 November, on the 8th and 9th he played the Piano Concerto with the BBC Symphony Orchestra under Basil Cameron. At least two British critics, writing for *The Musical Times*, joined the ranks of the unimpressed. One wrote the work off as 'the usual harmless, amiable collection of oddments, the treatment of which, in an avowed Parisian "divertissement" way, makes me think how much better old Saint-Saëns would have brought it off'. The other felt that 'Poulenc has been overcome by the sentimentality that he has often parodied in the past, and is now inexpertly trying to express romantic ideas that he once scorned.'[155] The French premiere of the song cycle took place in the Salle Gaveau on the 22nd, where the programme, largely a repeat from the Wigmore Hall, also included songs by Duparc, Debussy and Ravel and, rather more surprisingly, by Verdi and Brahms. Éluard thanked Poulenc for all his 'intelligent, clear and intelligible music' and Bernac 'for the infinite purity of his singing'.[156] The year ended on a sad note with the death on 31 December, at his home on the Mediterranean, of Charles Koechlin to whose teaching Poulenc could still trace, at the end of his own life, his 'feeling for choral music'.[157]

One of his 'round-up' letters to Milhaud, of 6 March 1951 from Agadir, gives the flavour of his concert life: 'For various reasons (of no interest to you) I've agreed to make one last tour of Morocco and Algeria with Pierre. Before that I was in Italy, before that in Holland, in November in England. Thank God, on 20 March I become a composer again until 30 October.' While admitting the critical reception of the Piano Concerto, he could retort, 'As I was in great demand, I turned into a commercial traveller (Amsterdam with Klemperer, Rome with Clemens Krauss, Florence, Turin, Milan, Bologna etc. . . .) Finally I retired with military honours.'[158]

'Becoming a composer again' meant chiefly orchestrating the *Stabat Mater*, but he also found time to write two less important works. In February he had one of his sporadic financial crises: having received 'a horrible tax bill, I was thinking of selling my jewellery. Normally I say no to films, but non-material considerations [. . .] have decided me to say yes in principle.'[159] Directed by Henri Lavorelle, *Le Voyage en Amérique* was authoritatively stated by Yvonne Printemps, certainly one of the non-material considerations in question, to contain new songs for her by Poulenc, but the music has come down to us as forming most of the two-piano valse-musette *L'Embarquement pour Cythère*. Intended for the duo of Gold and Fizdale, 'Les boys', as an encore of the kind identified by the composer as 'delicious bad music', it is dedicated to Lavorelle as 'this evocation of the banks of the Marne dear to my childhood'. Altogether stranger, and frankly less successful, is the *Thème varié* for solo piano, begun in February and completed in late summer or early autumn for him to play on tour. Lasting some twelve minutes, it was his final attempt at a virtuoso piece and Poulenc told Sauguet it was 'a serious work, but I hope not boring. The coda of the variation finale is strictly the Theme in retrograde. You see, Monsieur, Leibowitz, we too can . . .'[160] But can he? The first sixteen bars of the theme do indeed reappear thus transformed, beginning in bar two of page fifteen, but to no clear aesthetic purpose. The best music comes in the less aggressive variations such as 'Pastorale', which could have come from the *Nocturnes* or *Improvisations*, and 'Mélancolique', whose D flat major with Lydian G naturals recalls *Mélancolie*. Like the *Impromptus* and *Promenades* from the 1920s, the piece is today barely heard outside performances of the complete piano music.

For Poulenc the undoubted *clou* of 1951 was the premiere in Strasbourg of the *Stabat Mater* on 13 June. In January he had taken the partially orchestrated score to Fritz Münch, Charles's brother, who was to conduct it, and wrote to Bernac, 'Fritz

Münch, very calm, very serious, found the *Stabat* superb. I have the feeling he's the first person to appreciate the novelty of the work's choral writing. I'm certain of a magnificent performance because we understood one another (thank God he doesn't have his brother's semi-religious, semi-spaced-out temperament). He knows precisely what he has to do. "The work is perfectly written and singing it will bring my chorus joy, but it's a demanding *work*." I think that's the perfect word.'[161] Here Poulenc was certainly referring to 'demanding' (exigeante), but his italicization of 'work' (oeuvre) also suggests that Münch admired the technical skill Poulenc had put into it. As for his brother's temperament, Poulenc may possibly have been referring to Charles's occasional habit of leaving pieces slightly under-rehearsed in order to give the performance a tang of danger. He was thought by some to rely in general on his personal magnetism rather than on perfection of detail.[162]

The second half of the year was relatively uneventful. During the first week of September he gave concerts in Edinburgh, London and Bournemouth, then wrote an article on Prokofiev's piano music, promised for 1 October[163] but not delivered until the following month. Fondly remembering how Viñes would seize on the new Prokofiev pieces that reached Paris around 1917, he singles out the later Sonatas nos. 6, 7 and 8 as the high point of Prokofiev's solo writing, with Sonata no. 7 as the absolute summit.[164] No doubt the obsessive minor thirds in the bass of the headlong finale spoke to him, but did he not recognize that Prokofiev's control of complex, dissonant harmonies far outshone his own? Also in November he started on his *Quatre Motets pour le temps de Noël* which he would finish the following May. But testimony to Poulenc's divided self appears in a letter to Simone Girard in case, with both these motets and the *Stabat Mater* in mind, she felt he was becoming overly holy: 'I am, alas, not as religious as I'd like to be. Half of me remains in opposition. If I'm not entirely impious, my piety is, alas, that of a horse.'[165]

No detailed record exists of rehearsals with Bernac for their third American tour, due to begin in January. But, even if Poulenc had written nothing specifically for it, in December he could write that 'My hand is working very well and I'm preparing for America with our friend Pierre who is *on excellent form* both temperamentally and vocally'.[166] Whereas the second tour had lasted for three months and taken in Canada and San Francisco, this tour lasted only seven weeks and centred on New York, with a week and four concerts in Caracas. Poulenc flew out on 4 January and was joined by Bernac on the 10th. They gave their first recital on the 21st at Dumbarton Oaks in Washington D.C., and on 10 February gave

1. Francis sets out.

2. Francis joking, his nanny (Nounou) unimpressed.

3. Francis's father, Émile, featuring the Poulenc nose.

4. Francis's mother, Jenny, with his first love Raymonde Linossier.

5. Francis with his elder sister Jeanne.

6. Poulenc's grandparents' imposing house in Nogent.

7. A thoughtful Poulenc in 1924.

8. A quizzical look from Ricardo Viñes, staying with the Latarjets.

9 and 10. Guillaume Apollinaire and Paul Éluard, Poulenc's two favourite poets.

11. Le Grand Coteau and environs.

12. Wanda Landowska and Poulenc happily duetting.

13. At the Noailles' Paris residence, after the premiere of Poulenc's *Le Bal masqué* in 1932. Left to right: Yvonne de Casa Fuerte, Vittorio Rieti, Charles Koechlin, Igor Markévitch, Francis Poulenc, Nora Auric, Henri Sauguet, Georges Auric, Roger Désormière and Nicolas Nabokov.

14. Yvonne Gouverné and a radiant Poulenc descending the steps of the Rocamadour shrine in August 1936, following his religious experience before the Black Virgin.

15. Les Six with Cocteau in 1931. Left to right: Francis Poulenc, Germaine Tailleferre, Louis Durey, Jean Cocteau, Darius Milhaud and Arthur Honegger. Georges Auric presides from the wall as drawn by Cocteau.

Eloge de l'intelligence —

16. Poulenc and Pierre Bernac. Poulenc's title, 'In praise of intelligence', possibly reflects the critics' praise for Bernac's 'intelligent' interpretation of song texts.

17. 'Self-satisfaction': Here Poulenc's jokey title may indicate his awareness that all the praise for their performances might lead to overconfidence.

La contentement de soi —

18. The Princesse de Polignac playing her Cavaillé-Coll organ.

19. Les Six with Cocteau, probably in the early 1950s. Left to right: Darius Milhaud, Jean Cocteau at the piano, Georges Auric, Arthur Honegger, Germaine Tailleferre, Francis Poulenc and Louis Durey. Cocteau was no pianist, but the photo does display his elegant hands.

20. Poulenc with his beloved niece Brigitte Manceaux.

21. Poulenc with his one-time lover, then devoted friend, Raymond Destouches in the Luxembourg Gardens at the end of the 1940s.

SOUVENEZ-VOUS DANS VOS PRIÈRES

DE

LUCIEN ROUBERT

rappelé à Dieu à Toulon

le 21 Octobre 1955

22. Poulenc's lover Lucien Roubert, whose illness and death shadowed the composition of *Dialogues des Carmélites*. Poulenc kept this photograph in his missal.

23. Teaching Mickey table manners.

24. In England in the mid-1950s. Bernac and Poulenc with Simone Girard, one of the many female friends who cheered and supported Poulenc in his depressive moods.

25. Fiorenza Cossotto (Sister Matilda) in her dressing room at La Scala during the premiere run of *Dialogues des Carmélites* in January 1957. Poulenc's moustache was a passing phenomenon.

26. Joan Sutherland (Madame Lidoine) in the British premiere of *Dialogues des Carmélites* at Covent Garden in January 1958.

Le travail du peintre,
cycle de 7 mélodies sur
les poèmes de Paul Éluard
appartient à la dernière manière
de Francis Poulenc.

Depuis le Stabat Mater (1950)
Poulenc s'est engagé de plus
en plus dans la voie d'un
lyrisme qui a trouvé son
apogée dans l'opéra
Dialogues des Carmélites
représenté cette année à
la Scala de Milan avec un
vif succès.
Composé durant l'été 56,

immédiatement après l'achèvement
des Dialogues, le travail du
peintre est un cycle de mélodies
à la gloire des maîtres:
Picasso. Chagall - Braque.
Gris - Klee - Miró - Villon.
On y retrouvera l'accent
d'un autre cycle d'Éluard.
Poulenc: Tel jour telle nuit
mais largement amplifié
et plus délibérément humain

27. Poulenc's commentary on his last song cycle *Le Travail du peintre*, explaining that since 1950 his music has become ever more lyrical.

28. Poulenc at Oxford wearing his D.Mus. robes on 25 June 1958. For his comment on the regalia, see p. 258.

29. 'One of my ancestors was a gardener under the First Empire.'

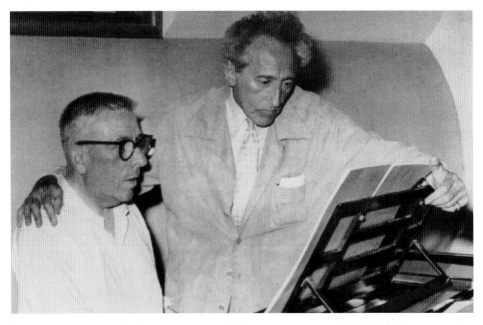

30. Poulenc and Cocteau looking through the score of their opera *La Voix humaine*. The composer was amazed at Cocteau's musical perceptiveness.

31. Poulenc and his adored soprano Denise Duval. What *can* he have said . . . ?

32. Poulenc sharing a joke in a bar in Cannes.

33. *Salut!* The last photograph of Poulenc, taken in Holland during a concert tour in January 1963, a few days before his death on the 30th of that month.

another in New York which included the song cycle *Mélodies passagères* by Samuel Barber, who became a close friend. Meanwhile Bernac was undergoing a transformation:

> If on his departure from the Invalides you saw an old, grumpy, down-in-the-dumps singer, you wouldn't recognize the sprightly man-about-town now strolling down 5th Avenue. He's like some adolescent, gazing at the packed schedule we have until we leave. We're on evening television on Wednesday the 19th, which here is the best it gets, and then, as you know, we're off to Venezuela. He's recording with Robert[167] and with me. What more could he ask for? [. . .] Things are going well for me too. Great success in Cincinnati with the Concerto. Shaw's splendid chorus are giving my *Stabat* on 27 April.[168]

Poulenc's disappointment at having to miss this occasion was later underlined when the New York Critics' Circle voted it the best choral work performed in the city during 1952. He was sorry too to miss Horowitz, on tour in Cuba, but spent a happy time with Wanda Landowska in Lakeville, from where he confessed to Doda Conrad that he had experienced 'faint temptations in the direction of the manager of my hotel, a handsome male of 45. Maybe I didn't displease him, as I'm paying only eight dollars for a bedroom, a sitting room and a kitchen. Don't tell your noble mother all these dreadful things. Persuade her I'm a Parsifal.' And he continued, 'What I like about Wanda is, she doesn't suffer from Nadia's musical bulimia. After four preludes and fugues she turned off the gramophone, saying that was enough and we wouldn't listen properly to any more.'[169] Not the least of his pleasures was hearing the 1949 radio recording of her playing the *Concert champêtre* with Stokowski and the New York Philharmonic.

He and Bernac returned to France on 5 March, after which his schedule ran 'a week in Paris – a week in the Midi of delightful love – a week in Munich – three weeks' solid work in Noizay – a month at the XXth-century Festival – another fortnight's work in Noizay – a fortnight's tour in England, and finally a little peace and quiet in Normandy with my sister.'[170] The week of 'delightful love' was spent in Marseille with Lucien, but the 'solid work' is harder to define. To balance this came the distressing news that Roger Désormière had suffered a paralytic stroke while on tour in Italy and was now not only paralysed down his right side but was affected in both speech and recall of events. His musical receptivity was also touched – Irène Joachim reported that 'he would whistle music, leaving out whole passages that were so many blanks in his memory'.[171] He would remain in this condition until his death in 1963, a tragic loss for French music of a man who had impressed Boulez most forcibly by his 'rhythmic exactness, the vital precision of his metrical impulse (a magnificent feature of his Stravinsky performances)', and no less by 'the moral rectitude of his attitude towards both works and composers'.[172] Désormière's appeal for Poulenc, enemy of rubato and amorphous caterwauling, can easily be understood.

The only music on Poulenc's desk at this time seems to have been the *Quatre Motets pour le temps de Noël*, but he gave these precise dates: in chronological order, no. 3/November 1951; no. 2/December; no. 1/April 1952; no. 4/18 May 1952 – from which it appears that only the last two would have been the subject of his labours between March and May, though he did revise no. 2 considerably when preparing the set for publication in July. He told Yvonne de Casa Fuerte that either no. 2 or no. 1 was 'assez exceptionnel', sadly without specifying which.[173]

Details of the first performance of these motets are unknown, but Carl Schmidt suggests that it was given sometime in 1952 in Madrid by the Netherlands Chamber Choir conducted by Félix de Nobel;[174] certainly they were heard on French Radio on 21 December.[175] Poulenc envisaged them as pendants to the *Motets de pénitence*, and likewise indebted to those of Victoria. He emphasized their simplicity, explaining that in the opening 'O magnum mysterium' 'the four parts practically never divide and, on the tonal front, in this motet I keep coming back to the original key of B flat minor'.[176] Keith Daniel notes that these motets contain more musical repetition than their companions:[177] indeed in 'Quem vidistis' all the material is heard twice, some of it three or four times, albeit with changes of texture. As for simplicity, it would be hard to write anything simpler harmonically than the opening of 'Videntes stellam' which uses merely the three basic chords of Western tonality (I, IV, V; A major, D major, E major – and back to A major) – which, by some magic of his own, Poulenc makes memorable. Here the threefold repeat of 'Videntes stellam', culminating in a full texture, wonderfully conjures up the Magi's growing exaltation. The set ends with the extraordinarily percussive articulation of 'Hodie Christus natus est', a bracing wake-up call to the joys of Christmas.

Poulenc, having had to miss the American premiere of the *Stabat Mater*, conducted by Robert Shaw in New York to great acclaim on 27 April, was present at the French one three days later, even if for him its singers paled beside 'the sublime chorus of my beloved Shaw'.[178] French provincial cities such as Avignon, Strasbourg, Aix-en-Provence and Besançon having introduced music festivals in the years immediately after the war, Paris was, as ever, determined not to be outdone, and in 1952 Denise Tual, with her Pléiade concerts reaching their conclusion, collaborated with Nicolas Nabokov in putting on a festival of music from the first half of the twentieth century. Nabokov may have reneged on the title 'festival' as 'already prostituted' in favour of 'L'Oeuvre du XXe siècle', but a festival it was nonetheless, and a highly ambitious one, including the French premiere of Virgil Thomson's *Four Saints in Three Acts*, Strauss's *Arabella*, Gian Carlo Menotti's *The Consul*, *Oedipus Rex* and Covent Garden's production of *Billy Budd* both conducted by their composers, and *Wozzeck* with the Vienna Opera conducted by Karl Böhm. Georges Balanchine also came with his American Ballet Theater and the Musée national d'art moderne hosted an exhibition of twentieth-century art.[179] Poulenc noted the 'astonishing flop' of *Billy Budd*, with 'a half-empty hall by the end'.[180] He himself was among those truanting, while Clarendon in *Le Figaro* called it 'long and boring',[181] and Sauguet was pleased he didn't have to pay for his ticket.[182] But for Poulenc *Wozzeck* was 'the high point of the festival: sublime, wildly enthusiastic reception'[183] and, for all his devotion to Shaw and his chorus, he cannot have been insensitive to the honour done him in opening such a prestigious enterprise – in Bossuet's Église Saint-Roch, what's more, and with Fritz Münch on the podium.

Poulenc spent the last few weeks of June with Bernac in England for two recitals and, according to the ledger of the musical agents Ibbs and Tillett, for an appearance at the Aldeburgh Festival on the 27th. But as no other evidence for an Aldeburgh visit is to hand, and it is not mentioned in Philip Reed's article 'Poulenc, Britten, Aldeburgh: A Chronicle',[184] it could be that this was merely an unfulfilled intention. Certainly Poulenc would have had a problem deflecting any enquiry from Britten as to his thoughts on *Billy Budd* . . . That June also saw two events of vastly different importance.

Firstly, Poulenc finished a tiny orchestral piece for a *Guirlande de Campra*, commissioned by the critic Marc Pincherle for the Aix-en-Provence festival as one of seven homages 'to an unjustly neglected composer'[185] and based on a theme from Campra's 1717 opera *Camille*. Poulenc's 'Matelote provençale' takes its name from the 'Matelotes provençales' in Couperin's *Troisième Ordre*, but the only link would seem to be that both pieces are in duple time, unlike Campra's original whose '3/4 in G major is too monotonous'.[186] Poulenc retains G major, but seasoned with various excursions and ending with one of his impolite sign-offs. Secondly, sometime that June, 'A most friendly visit from the most directorial Director of the publishers Ricordi brought me comfortably down to earth. With great ceremony (these Italians are a laugh) a visit was made to ask my hand for La Scala. Major ballet for winter 1953/4. I was delighted to accept. Think of it, with 10 orchestral rehearsals and Monsieur Sabata [. . .] I'm going to write a ballet on the life of a holy martyr.'[187] In the event there would be several martyrs, it would be an opera, not a ballet, and it would turn upside down not only his own life, but to no small extent the perception of what a contemporary opera might be.

VIII

MAD ABOUT NUNS
✦ 1952–1956 ✦

As Carl Schmidt observes, preparations for the opera *Dialogues des Carmélites* and its subsequent composition and performance occupy more space in Poulenc's letters and writings than any of his other works.[1] This is not surprising. The twelve-year-old who could write a meaningful review of *Tosca* (see p. 7) had gone on to be a regular visitor to opera houses wherever he might be and, although the Paris Opéra would not be the *Carmélites*' first home, and the glory days of Jacques Rouché were long over, the hope of being performed there still stirred the hearts of his generation of French composers. But it was vital that any serious opera should be a success, Poulenc no doubt remembering the 1932 premiere of Milhaud's *Maximilien* and his own comments that after it, even 'Milhaud's best friends put on their gloves to applaud' and that 'a little supper at the Café de Paris . . . was the best part as, with astonishing off-handedness, we talked about everything except the opera'[2] (see p. 97). So, as the project slowly came into focus, Poulenc would have been prepared for the long haul, if not for the problems it would bring.

One of these had already made itself felt. Although his love affair with Lucien would last until the latter's death in 1955, Lucien did not accept fidelity as part of the arrangement. The thought that his love was not enough caused Poulenc deep distress, which underlay much of the depression that haunted him in these years. At the end of 1951 he wrote to Simone Girard, 'Stopping with you was a delight, and a comfort. I was indeed profoundly miserable, and thanks to you I avoided a solitary lunch in Marseilles with my dark thoughts.'[3] A further problem was that the affair had to be kept secret from Raymond. Even though Raymond had just got married for the second time, his continuing attachment to Poulenc was attested by the fact that the first thing he did after the marital bed was installed was to put Poulenc's photo on his bedside table.[4]

Meanwhile Poulenc addressed himself to three very different works. In August a wrote an *Ave verum* for women's voices, commissioned by the Howard Heinz

Foundation to be performed at the Pittsburgh International Contemporary Music Festival, of course unaware that he would set the text again as part of *Carmélites*. This early version is indeed 'very simple, very pure and, I think, very successful'.[5] The other two works were both for two pianos, dedicated to friends, but of directly opposite characters. Why the *Capriccio d'après Le Bal masqué* should have been dedicated 'To Sam Barber' is unknown – perhaps it was the result of a private joke. Certainly the work gave rise to one of Poulenc's jokes. As the duo of Gold and Fizdale later recalled, the work:

> . . . had been commissioned by another American two-piano team who, when they received it, wrote to Poulenc that they were disappointed it was so short and would like to keep it 'on approval' for a while before they decided whether to pay for it and perform it – or return it to him. This infuriated Poulenc who told us he was not accustomed to such treatment. He sent it to us as a gift and urged us to play it as soon and as often as possible in 'order to drive the other team mad'.[6]

At all events it's a jolly five-minute romp, technically quite challenging, using some of the more striking elements of its source.

The Sonata for two pianos, dedicated to Gold and Fizdale, goes to the other extremes of language and emotion. Poulenc had had such a piece in mind for some years, but only began work on it in the autumn of 1952 in Marseille, according to him in the same hotel room occupied by Chopin on his return from Majorca.[7] If, as Poulenc felt, the Andante is the very centre of the work, inspired by his affection for Lucien,[8] it is for some listeners hard to reconcile this with the dissonances, at times extremely harsh, to be found in the movements around it, starting with the loud tintinnabulation at the very opening of the work, which returns at the very end. Admittedly the sonata has had, and still has, its admirers. Hélène Jourdan-Morhange regarded it as 'one of the piano works in which Poulenc is at his most authentic',[9] and Hervé Lacombe finds it 'magnificently written for two pianos'.[10] Less enthusiastic listeners may wonder whether it was one last (desperate?) fling in the direction of modernism, since such extreme dissonance does not recur in any of his subsequent music; they may also find a modicum of support in Poulenc's own admission that he was looking forward to time off in Aix-en-Provence 'to recover from an apocalyptic suite for two pianos (Ah! Messiaen, where are you?) which is exhausting me with its noise and tension'.[11] He also claimed, with reason, that 'I've always done my best, conscientiously. I don't want to survive through an acquired ability and worn-out dodges'.[12] 'Les boys' gave the first performance at the Wigmore Hall on 2 November 1953.

Poulenc stayed in France through the rest of 1952 and, apart from the Sonata for two pianos and early attempts at a Flute Sonata, his focus was on more material matters. In August he suffered serious eye problems and headaches that made work impossible for a fortnight. Then the question came up again of Bernac's possible post at the Conservatoire, Roland-Manuel assuring Poulenc that Bernac and Henri Etcheverry, the Golaud of Désormière's *Pelléas* production and recording, were certainties for 1953 or 1954. There were thoughts of a fourth American tour (which did not eventually come about until 1960), but Poulenc felt an Australian one was not advisable because of heavy taxes and expenses, with no long-term prospects at their ages.[13]

In September he was pleased to tell Bernac their duo was widely recognized as having paved the way for the successful appearance of Benjamin Britten and Peter Pears at Aix. Once again, he emphasized what important lessons Bernac had to teach the young, and admitted that he himself had not taken sufficient notice of them. A politician friend had told him that 'the young are afraid of me. I must do my best to counteract that. Milhaud's example is excellent in that respect. Arthur is too pontifical. As for Georges, he's like me. That's why the young don't come knocking on our doors.'[14] He spent October in Lyon and Avignon, making trips to Marseille, as ever unknown to Raymond. A visit from Sauguet left him momentarily depressed because he had come with Désormière. 'It's overwhelming to see this poor speechless man with his useless hand pointing, with his stick, at what he wants to talk about. For most of the time his spirit is extraordinarily present, at others you feel it fading.' The sudden deaths of Bérard and Max Jacob seemed to Poulenc infinitely preferable.[15] But he was deeply distressed by that of Éluard on 18 November and interrupted his stay in Marseille from 20 November to 20 December to attend the funeral at Père Lachaise on 22 November. The final musical event of the year was Février's first performance of the *Thème varié* in the Salle Gaveau on 15 December.

On 4 January 1953 Poulenc left France for Ouchy-Lausanne. Here until the 28th he wrote and recorded for Swiss Radio a series of six interviews with Stéphane Audel which would later form the first part of the volume *Moi et mes amis* published six months after his death; and simultaneously he began another series of eighteen interviews with Claude Rostand as interlocutor, which would be broadcast by French Radio between 13 October 1953 and 16 February 1954, and published later that year as *Entretiens avec Claude Rostand*. Whether either interviewer knew of the other's project is not clear. But whoever was paying for his room at the Hôtel Beau-Rivage knew their subject's partiality for comfort – in Poulenc's words he was 'paradisiaquement installé', quite apart from the presence of various royalty and Charlie Chaplin and family.[16] To Simone Girard he outlined the perfect timetable he was observing. Going to bed at 9.30, he wakes at 6, then:

> Reading in bed. Toilet at 7. Breakfast (tea and wonderful cakes) at 7.30. From 8 to 9.30 I work on my 20 conversations with Rostand. 9.30 walk round the garden. 10 till 1 music. I have a piano tucked away in a little private salon. 1 p.m. lunch. 2 to 3 walk round the lake. 3 to 6 music. 6 to 7.30 short trip into Lausanne. 8 a light dinner and 9.30 bed.[17]

To which, upon Audel's later arrival, work on the conversations with him would have been added. The only outside event impinging on this paradise was, suitably enough, the news, already mentioned, that the New York Critics' Circle had just voted the *Stabat Mater* best choral work of 1952.[18]

During February and early March Poulenc was in England and then the south of France, from where he began a tour of Italy with the cellist Pierre Fournier. For Poulenc, Fournier was the greatest living cellist, 'but he doesn't have that rich background [tous ses arrière-plans] of my dear old Pierre [Bernac] which makes him my irreplaceable double'.[19] After a cool reception in Turin, the tour was a success, Poulenc being moved to rewrite the finale of his Sonata for a second edition that appeared later that year.

But the most important event took place outside the concert hall. Since the previous summer, Poulenc had been mulling over the idea of a sacred ballet for La Scala, possibly on St Margaret of Cortona about whom his friend François Mauriac had published a novel in 1945. But although dancing nuns had figured famously in Meyerbeer's opera *Robert le diable*, they had never been the main subject of a French ballet. For whatever reason, Poulenc's initial enthusiasm had cooled by the time he took advantage of his presence with Fournier in Milan to go and see the director of the Ricordi publishing house, Guido Valcarenghi. How about an opera instead?:

'No problem there, I commission you on the spot,' replied my host. 'But the libretto?' 'Since you're looking for a mystical subject, why not make an opera out of Bernanos's *Les Dialogues des Carmélites*?' [. . .] Of course I knew Bernanos's play which I had read, reread and seen twice, but I had no idea of its *verbal rhythm*, which for me is crucial [. . .] Then, two days later, right in the middle of a bookseller's window in Rome, I saw *Les Dialogues* which seemed to be waiting for me [. . .] I bought the book and decided to read it again. So I sat down on the terrace of the café 'Tre scalini' on the Piazza Navone. It was 10 o'clock in the morning [. . .] At half past midday I was drunk with enthusiasm, but there remained the acid test: could I find the music for such a text?

He opened the book at random at the First Prioress's speech, later to begin Act I scene 2. 'Incredible as it may seem, I immediately found the melodic curve for this long speech! The die was cast. At 2 o'clock I telegraphed to M. Valcarenghi, true psychic that he was, that I would write the *Dialogues*.'[20] In fact, the psychic was not Valcarenghi but Margarita Wallmann[21] who, according to her, not only suggested the play but, in an extension of her psychic powers, would produce the opening run of Poulenc's opera. Of course Poulenc continued to play the piano and give talks, but Bernanos's nuns now became the centre of his attention for the next three years and more. Between this March and May 1956 his other work consisted merely of finishing the Sonata for two pianos in July 1953, making a transcription for cello and piano, never published, of the *Suite française*, and writing three short songs lasting altogether less than four minutes.

The true story goes back to June 1794 (Messidor year II in the Revolutionary calendar) when the Revolutionary Committee of Compiègne voiced its suspicion of the sixteen Carmelite nuns now, after the closure of their convent, living separately and in secular clothing in the town, namely that 'these women still live in a community; that they do so still in submission to the fanatical regime of their recent cloister; and that there may exist some criminal correspondence between these recent nuns and the fanatics of Paris'. They were duly arrested on 22 June, as it happened, 'their washing day. With their civilian clothes in the wash, they had been packed off to prison in religious robes that by law they were banned from wearing in public. They wore them throughout their trial – thus predisposing the jury to believe they were inveterate law-breakers – and indeed to the scaffold.'[22] They were sent to Paris in a cart on 13 July, and three days later the president of the Revolutionary Tribunal arraigned them as being 'simply a collection, a gathering of female rebels and plotters who nourish in their hearts the desire and hope of seeing the French people returned to the chains of its tyrants and in slavery to priests as bloodthirsty as their power is illegitimate, and who want to see its liberty drowned in the streams of blood that their wicked machinations have rendered visible to the sky above'.[23] The next day, 17 July, the sixteen nuns were guillotined, together with twenty-four other victims. Only ten days after that, Robespierre fell and the Terror came to an end.[24] The Sub-Prioress of the convent, Sister Marie of the Incarnation, having previously gone to Paris on business of her own which took longer than expected, escaped martyrdom and between 1832 and 1836 wrote the account of her sisters' deaths that underpins all future literature on the subject.

Shortly after the First World War, Gertrud von le Fort, a Catholic convert, began a novella based on this story, *Die Letzte am Schafott* (*The Last to the Scaffold*), finally published in Munich in 1931. It was she who introduced the fictional character of Blanche, this child in perpetual anguish, known familiarly as 'the little hare', this young woman who, for fear of the world, enters a convent and there tries, mystically, to meld her religious life to the Agony of Christ. Jacques Maritain read a French translation of the novella which he sent to a Dominican friend, Father Raymond Bruckberger who, in 1946, had the idea of turning it into a film. He and another friend, Philippe Agostini, put together a scenario and he asked Georges Bernanos to provide the dialogue. Bernanos, now terminally ill with cancer, completed the dialogue, but the film was never made, and after his death in 1948 his script was saved only through the efforts of his literary executor, Albert Béguin. It was published to great acclaim in 1949 and, duly retranslated into German, was turned into a play produced in Zurich in 1951, and then in French at the Théâtre Hébertot in Paris. None of this took into account that the American author Emmet Lavery had, in 1949, negotiated exclusive rights for theatrical adaptations of the piece.

Poulenc, sitting down in August 1953 to compose the first scenes of his opera, was blissfully unaware of any copyright problems and the music flowed out of him: scenes 1 to 4 were completed on 18 September, 3 October, October and December respectively, with the first three scenes of Act II following by March 1954. Enthusiasm radiates from the pages of his correspondence. 'I've caught the atmosphere of the great scene between the [First] Prioress and Blanche with an excellent form: calm at the start, fierce in the middle (rules of the order), calm again at the end':[25] 'I don't want to think about anything else because it's going (I venture to say) too well. I'm doing a scene a week. I hardly recognize myself. I'm besotted with my subject to the point of thinking I've known these women':[26] 'In a fortnight

I've sketched the first three scenes of the *Dialogues* which I shall write next week. I can't get over it. It flows, it flows and doesn't sound like anyone except me. It's madly vocal.'[27]

To add to his happiness, on 1 September he was promoted from chevalier to officier de la Légion d'honneur, as if to reward him for having begun on the *Dialogues*! The presentation was made by Colette, herself a grand officier, on 31 October. Meanwhile Poulenc received further encouragement on learning that Pathé-Marconi were going to record *Les Mamelles*, starting on 17 September, with singers from the Opéra-Comique including Denise Duval as Thérèse, conducted by André Cluytens (in fact the sessions took place between the 14th and the 25th). The composer was delighted with the result, admitting that it brought tears of joy to his eyes.[28] He had only two complaints about his life. The first was that, although the recent visit to Le Grand Coteau of Raymond and his wife had gone very well, Poulenc was the one who found it hard since, although he and Raymond saw a lot of each other, 'I missed sharing a bathroom after 20 years of doing so'[29] – a remark that has to find a place in the curious mix that was their relationship. Secondly, his initial enthusiasm about *Dialogues* followed the familiar pattern over the following weeks, as in a letter of 24 September to Yvonne Gouverné confessing 'Sainthood is difficult but sacred music like *Carmélites* is terrible. I alternate between satisfaction and discouragement, because if this opera's a flop, it'll be a terrible one.'[30]

The first of his conversations with Rostand was broadcast on French Radio on 13 October, and on 2 November Gold and Fizdale gave the first performance of 'their' Sonata at the Wigmore Hall, which Donald Mitchell noted 'from time to time extended itself beyond the intrinsic interest of its material', though he applauded the 'good tunes'.[31] But with December appeared the first copyright difficulties over *Dialogues*. For the moment Poulenc made light of them, claiming 'I'm certain to overcome them since Saint Antony of Padua and Saint Thérèse [of Avila] are looking after me',[32] a confidence which, bolstered by another comfortable stay in the Hôtel Beau-Rivage, carried him over into the New Year.

Undoubtedly the most important musical event in Paris in January 1954 was the first concert on the 13th of the Domaine musical, including Webern's Concerto op. 24, Stravinsky's *Renard* and works by Luigi Nono and Karlheinz Stockhausen. Founded by Pierre Boulez, the organization became the main Paris forum for new music, with Poulenc as one of its most loyal audience members. His reactions to that first concert were to condemn Hermann Scherchen's conducting of *Renard*, and to wonder 'am I an idiot to think that there was nothing there to equal Boulez's

Soleil des eaux?'[33] Despite his occasional cracks at 'dodécaca', he was honest in taking serial music as he found it, without any *parti pris*, and it would have been only human for him to wonder whether this was a path he himself should tread. It was a hard decision to make for several reasons.

There is a move in current scholarship to downplay the depth of the rift that had already been opening up between conservatives and serialists, probably in part owing to the elderly Boulez's reinvention as a cuddly international treasure. It was not always thus, either with him or his colleagues. In May 1952 Boulez and Messiaen gave the first performance of Boulez's *Structures Book I*. A female member of the audience was thought to have shown disrespect towards the work so, when the fifteen-minute piece was over, a posse of young serialists moved to attack her physically and the *garde municipale* had to intervene.[34] A major impulse behind the practice of serialism was to make a complete break with the past: Boulez later remembered 'people saying "Oh, you should have tasted the meat before the war!" I was not interested in "the meat before the war".'[35] Serialism being a German invention, the situation in Germany was, if anything, more radical still: in 1953 the thirty-seven-year-old Henri Dutilleux wrote from Cologne to explain to his father that 'one must either be a 12-toner or not be a composer'.[36] Later, Dutilleux would claim, maybe not entirely in jest, that it was only with his inclusion of serial elements in *Métaboles*, premiered in 1965, that Boulez took his music seriously; certainly, finding himself near Dutilleux after the premiere in 1951 of the latter's tonal/modal First Symphony, Boulez abruptly turned his back.[37]

A further problem for Poulenc was that by 1953 Stravinsky, for so long a vital composing model, was well and truly launched on his final, serial career: the Septet was finished in February 1953 and the *Three Shakespeare Songs* in the autumn. Poulenc's decision to stay with the tonal system ('I shall continue to write *do mi sol do* and do not approve of Stravinsky putting on hats that are too young for his age')[38] was therefore a brave one, though he has rarely been given credit for this (an exception being Honegger's testimony to Poulenc that he had 'remained himself with that rare courage that commands respect').[39] On the contrary, it has been interpreted as a form of cowardice, especially in the years immediately following the early 1950s, labelled by Dutilleux 'the serialist terror'. Writing from Cannes, where various events had been organized around Les Six and where Poulenc started on the opera's second act, he asked Sauguet, 'How's Paris? Is it twelve-toning itself at full speed? The Carmelites, poor things, can only sing in keys. One must forgive them.'[40]

In March Poulenc and Bernac toured Egypt (the third scene of Act II was finished in Alexandria) and then had a relaxing break in Greece and Italy. Back in Noizay in April, perhaps in order to leave his nuns in peace for a while, Poulenc composed the two songs making up *Parisiana* on poems by Max Jacob. In his *Journal* he wrote 'At the time of *Le Bal masqué* I had intended to include in the cantata the poem "Jouer du bugle", but I had to give up the idea because it was too similar to "La dame aveugle". It's joined by the extravagant "Vous n'écrivez plus", so typically Max Jacob, and in 1954 I gave them the overall title of *Parisiana* to fix the Parisian atmosphere of them both.'[41] Marked 'sans ironie, très poétique', the first song typically sets the crazy poem ('The three women who were playing the trumpet late in their bathroom . . .') to the most equable, unsurprising music that hovers round G minor, finally for the last fifteen bars settling on to a low G. As usual, the performers are commanded (three times) not to interrupt the steady tempo, and the singer simply has to find a new voice colour in order to sound 'très mélancolique' on the (for Poulenc, magic) phrase 'Au pont d'Iéna'. The second song is all over in some forty seconds, during which, Bernac warns, the singer has to lace the common, suburban accent with a certain tact.[42] Before returning to his nuns, in May Poulenc followed these two songs with a single one, 'Rosemonde', taken from Apollinaire's collection *Alcools*. This one is marked 'calmement' and the steady tread of the quavers is decorated only with a faster little piano figure to signal the poet blowing kisses from his fingers, echoed in the piano epilogue. In their measured tread, both 'Rosemonde' and 'Jouer du bugle' sound rather like offcuts from the opera.

At this point, however, the measured tread of Poulenc's life was brutally interrupted. With hindsight, it's tempting to see forewarnings as far back as his very first work on the opera, when he wrote to Bernac 'The *Carmélites* are begun, so I'm no longer sleeping (literally)'[43] and the same on the same day to Simone Girard.[44] Then on 13 December he wrote to Bernac, 'I've just spent a *terrible* week because of these ladies. The first two thirds of the fourth scene are done and the last one sketched out. The scene is *terrifying* in its austerity, fear, pity and sorrow. I've put my whole heart into it. [. . .] I knew perfectly well that this work would gut me, but not to this extent, because one is all the time on peaks of emotion.'[45]

Poulenc's morale was not helped by the fact that at the end of January 1954 he had learned of the response to Bernac's application for a post at the Paris Conservatoire. Claude Delvincourt wrote:

I am dictating these few words to tell you that I too was very disappointed by the result of the preliminary rounds for the nomination of a future professor. Personally, I did not fail Pierre Bernac either at the first or the second or the third round of voting. Impossible to find a way of getting him a majority. I have written to him to say that I had good hopes for next year. It's [Ketty] Lapeyrette's class that will come vacant and I know that in her he has a supporter. So it's a small campaign we now have to wage; the chance must not be lost yet again.[46]

Apart from these two worries were three others that contributed to darkening his mood. He was having gall bladder problems which at any moment might require surgery; by now Lucien had been diagnosed with cancer, suggesting to the ever-suggestible Poulenc that maybe he had cancer too; and still no accommodation had been reached with Emmet Lavery over the copyright of *Dialogues*, Lavery being on bad terms with Bernanos's heirs (to the point, according to Gianfranco Vinay, of bringing an action against them),[47] and unwilling to co-operate. As a result Poulenc now fell into a deep depression, the impact of which can be read in the opera's chronology: he completed the second interlude of Act II in April, but then, although he began orchestrating Act I in August, he would write no new music until the fourth scene of Act II in March 1955. He also had to tell Britten that he could not accept the invitation to come to Aldeburgh in June. In July he went with a doctor friend, Paul Delmas-Marsalet, to stay in the Pyrenees, which allowed him to visit both Lourdes and Rocamadour,[48] possibly in search of healing. But his old friend Sauguet had the measure of his distress: 'it's difficult to heal Francis from the outside; his egocentricity makes him impervious to influences. It's within himself that the trouble lies. It's himself one has to persuade that there's nothing wrong.'[49]

Meanwhile Poulenc had begun to correspond with an American acquaintance, John Howard Griffin. Of this exchange of letters, with one exception, only Poulenc's have survived. These are not only harrowing to read, but also throw up various problems that Poulenc was clearly not aware of. In a letter to his niece Brigitte Manceaux he refers to Griffin as 'le Père Griffin supérieur des Carmélites de Dallas E-Unis'. This was untrue. Griffin, born in Dallas in 1920, had gone to France to study at Poitiers University and had met Poulenc before the war in Tours, and once again after it. As Carl Schmidt records, this second meeting with Poulenc left Griffin 'with an oversweet taste and always an undercurrent of panic, of suspected tragedy under all this – of some man helplessly trapped behind a mask'.[50]

Accessing the name John Howard Griffin on the Internet reveals that during the war he had helped smuggle Jews out of France to England, then returned to America, then to the Solomon Islands where he married a local girl before being totally blinded in an explosion in 1946. Back in Dallas, he became a Roman Catholic in 1952, but his sight did not return until 1957. So not only was he not a monk, let alone a Superior, but at the time of the correspondence with Poulenc he was totally blind. So someone else (his wife? a monk in the Dallas Carmelite Seminary?) would have had to read Poulenc's letters to him and, presumably, write back to the composer, whether at Griffin's dictation or not.

The single letter from Griffin has survived through being quoted *in toto* by Poulenc, writing to his other niece Rosine Seringe. Griffin assures Poulenc that all the Carmelites of the United States are praying for him and that 'one of us [monks] who is blind has just learnt, two days ago, that from now on he will be paralysed in both legs. He has wondered to whose intention he could offer up this sacrifice and, behold, it has fallen into his lap!'[51] As to the truth of this, who can say? What is beyond dispute is that Poulenc was in serious need of emotional support. As late as October from Amsterdam, where he was giving three recitals with Bernac that included first performances of *Parisiana* and 'Rosemonde', he could still write to Griffin:

I am in a state of the deepest neurasthenia. I can no longer play, no longer work. I despise myself. [. . .] Solitude is so dreadful to me that I leave my hotel room in order to calm myself, in the main hall, through contact with people I don't know. I truly have the feeling that I'm the plaything of the devil. Redouble your prayers for me and may Heaven allow me to sleep again, to work again, to forget, to pray. At the moment I am a dual personage, and Poulenc despises with all his might the all-too-vulnerable Francis. I so much want to finish my *Carmélites* but how to recover calm, how to *sleep*? [. . .] Will God forgive me all my mistakes, all my folly? I so want to honour him again with music that is free of evils. [. . .] Bless me for I have sinned terribly, but how I have been punished! May my soul at least be saved from the everlasting flames since my body and my heart are burning here on earth.[52]

Less dramatically, he wrote in the same month to Simone Girard, 'I think those terrible women, before losing their heads, determined that I should sacrifice one to them. That's not impossible.'[53] But central to his mental distress was the breakdown of his love life. A November tour of Germany lay ahead and Bernac, with Poulenc's Amsterdam mood in mind, was understandably worried and felt it was time to speak his mind:

> You have, sadly, through your lack of moral courage, worn out the affection of this boy who was loyal, even if not particularly interesting. I regret this for you, if indeed you loved him as much as you think, which I don't believe. You loved the character he needed to play in your presence. When you truly love someone, you love him for himself, not for yourself. And that was not the case. The only proof I put forward is that, before this break-up, you would not have hesitated to enter into another relationship, but that you were jealous of him because he could have done so. [. . .] You are not the first nor the last to have love problems. It's too easy, really, to blame everything on illness. This is not the first time you've followed the pattern of letting youself go. There is after all a human dignity that needs to be preserved. I suffer greatly to see you losing it entirely in the eyes of the world, and not only among your friends. Francis Poulenc, even on the human level, should be different from that. You may be certain that this weakness will end up manifesting itself in your art. Life is not made up of easy solutions.

Apologizing for his bluntness, Bernac went on to explain that he could not stand Poulenc moaning endlessly about Lucien, and finished by saying 'There are some things I'm afraid I can no longer tolerate; I feel tired, I've worked hard, and I am less in control of my nerves. I tell you frankly, Francis, I am *afraid* of this tour under these conditions. Forgive me.'[54] His fears were realized, and after only two concerts Poulenc collapsed and was taken into a clinic in the suburbs of Paris for three weeks. But a month later he lamented that he still felt exhausted: 'sleep still eludes me and dark thoughts are still floating round my brain. When shall I be myself again? And all because of one human being. At least I'm regaining a little willpower, there is that. I'm leaving for Cannes for the celebrations and can at least be certain he won't be there.'[55]

The year 1955 began with better hopes. On 15 January he and Bernac recorded a recital for the BBC, transmitted the next day, on the 16th Poulenc played his Two-Piano Concerto with Britten at the Festival Hall with the Liverpool Philharmonic under John Pritchard, and on the 18th and 20th he was again joined by Bernac in a recital of French songs in Carlisle and Newcastle upon Tyne. On 2 February the pair gave a 20th anniversary concert at the Salle Gaveau, although owing to Poulenc's illness *Le Travail du peintre*, which he had intended for this occasion, was not completed. But at least he was playing in public again.

The value that Poulenc attached to *Carmélites* is confirmed by Henry Barraud, Head of French Radio and Television: 'The more difficulties over it beset him, the more this work took on importance in his eyes. [. . .] He explained to me somewhat naively that, if he died, his standing with posterity would be irremediably affected if it were not enriched by this major work, in the absence of which all the rest would be insignificant. This risk threatened to become reality since he was in a deep depression and haunted by thoughts of suicide.' Barraud adds a happier envoi, in that his young daughter told him she was praying for three things: the success of Barraud's own opera, Désormière's return to health, and the completion and performance of *Carmélites*. A few days later Barraud met a Poulenc transformed: by a miracle, as he said, the copyright problems had been resolved, and ever after he would refer to Barraud's daughter as his 'guardian angel'.[56] Some financial costs may well have been incurred, but the only visible legacy is a prescribed acknowledgement, probably the most cumbersome in operatic history, that still today appears at the head of programmes for the opera: 'from the drama by Georges Bernanos, adapted with the authorization of Emmet Lavery from a story by Gertrud von le Fort and a scenario by Rev. Bruckberger and Philippe Agostini'.

This resolution happened in March, during which Poulenc returned to the opera, composing the first interlude of Act II. A signed agreement was made on 30 March. But in the meantime Lucien had been diagnosed in February with a serious attack of pleurisy. Poulenc saw to his hospitalization in Cannes and the illness brought them together again. This fact partly explains why the next four scenes of the opera were composed in Cannes, though Poulenc was no stranger to its Hôtel Majestic, and he stayed on when Lucien went home to Toulon. His temporary abandonment of the opera in March 1954 had coincided with the end of what he envisaged as Act I. But at some point in the ensuing twelve months the director chosen by La Scala for the opera, Margarita Wallmann, met him in his rue Médicis flat and, after he had played it through, assumed from its length (seven scenes and an interlude) that he had in fact written two acts. Poulenc retorted, ' "I've only written the first! You aren't going to try to convince me that I am capable of writing an opera in three acts?" "Precisely." "But where will the first act end in that case?" "With the death of the first Prioress, obviously." Francis looked at me with astonishment: "That's tremendous! That's marvellous!" and he took me in his arms, whirling me all round the room . . .'[57] This disposition not only produced three acts of practicable length (of circa 55, 40 and 40 minutes) but, as Gianfranco Vinay points out, meant that each one 'corresponded with a crucial moment in the evolution of the main dramatic theme'.[58]

In April the Renaud-Barrault company revived Giraudoux's *Intermezzo* with Poulenc's music. He reported to Milhaud, 'Apart from Boulez's concerts, nothing interesting in Paris this winter. At the Théâtre Marigny the revival of *Intermezzo* is excellent and Boulez conducts the music (and my God what frippery it is) with marvellous *honesty*.'[59] For this we also have the testimony of Jean-Louis Barrault himself, that 'we produced plays with incidental music by Auric, Poulenc, Honegger, Milhaud, Sauguet and Offenbach, all of which – although Boulez did not like them – he conducted with extreme vigour and authority'.[60] No letters from Poulenc to Boulez survive, but one from Boulez, probably in answer to thanks from Poulenc, ends with a reference to Boulez's first incidental music for the company, for Aeschylus's *Oresteia*. Barrault reported that Boulez 'thought he could marry the antique theatre with the musical language of serialism'; Boulez's own review of a provincial performance was that 'the reception in Bordeaux was very warm, despite the shock effect of this spectacle which is not entirely comforting'.[61] Boulez's friendly sign-off to Poulenc ('Veuillez croire à mes sentiments très dévoués') shows that the two composers were not allowing their views on composition to alienate them, whatever the supporting phalanx of twelve-toners might say or do.

On 5 May, writing from the Hôtel Majestic, Poulenc thanked Benjamin Britten for his 'songs which I like more and more!' These were presumably the songs in the cycle *Winter Words*, published in 1954. Poulenc's response was both predictable from his own point of view as well as accurate from that of the music: 'What I find remarkable, beyond the musical quality, is that your accompaniments are so rich with such simple means. One is astonished, when one looks at the score, that the music isn't "blacker". It's what I, for my part, have always tried to do.'[62] Shades of Matisse! Poulenc remained in Cannes through May and June, when he made his first mention of the three-act version of the opera.[63] After taking the cure at Évian, and with just two of the twelve scenes still to write, he received from Albert Béguin, Bernanos's executor, an extract from the judgement of the Revolutionary tribunal of 17 July 1794, parts of which Poulenc added to Bernanos's text. At Le Tremblay in July he began the third scene of Act III, finishing his autograph of the whole opera in August while staying with Richard Chanlaire in Tourrettes-sur-Loup, between Nice and Cannes.

By now his health, bar some residuary insomnia when off his drugs, had returned so that he could claim, 'I'm now so much back to being the person I was several years ago that I'm judging everything from a different angle.' More than that, he could now accept that 'Sometimes there are trials that are necessary. Without doubt my *Carmélites* were demanding all that.'[64] But further trials were in store, not least the death of three of his close friends. On 19 June Adrienne Monnier put an end to her suffering from Ménière's Disease with an overdose of sleeping pills. To the memorial number published in *Le Mercure de France* Poulenc contributed a short memoir, recalling the days some thirty years earlier when he had frequented her bookshop and met luminaries such as Fargue, Valéry, Gide, Claudel, Breton, Aragon and, most importantly, Éluard. He concluded his tribute, 'Dear Adrienne, you wanted to leave us without fuss. Our thanks for that. The surroundings of the mortuary were not the place for a final meeting. I prefer to imagine you, with your pretty, rosy smile, flying off, with your famous grey skirt inflated like a hot-air balloon, up to the heaven of poets where you were awaited, with joyful hearts, by so many of the departed.'[65]

Then on 27 November Honegger died, after a long and only partial recovery from the triple infarctus he had suffered in 1947. That Poulenc had never had as close a relationship with him as with Milhaud and Auric did not signal so much a lack of affection as the difficulty, even after Honegger's attack, of prising him away from his work – a difficulty also felt to some extent by his wife and daughter, who would never dare to beard him in his study, in a different street from their home, and the door of which was emblazoned with the command 'Do Not Disturb' in fifty languages.[66] But he was the first of Les Six to die, and with him (and Adrienne Monnier) another part of Poulenc's youth.

Between these two deaths came the one that was much the nearest to his heart. In mid-August Lucien's health took a sharp turn for the worse, but already his lungs had been declared cancerous and the end was not in doubt. 'I've entrusted his future to the blessed Carmelites,' Poulenc wrote to Bernac:

. . . so that they may protect his going, since it will have been so closely linked with their history. I actually began the work beside him, in happy days, in Lyon in the August of 53. After the great crisis you know of, I have just finished it sitting by him in the last days of his earthly life. As I've already mentioned to you, I'm haunted by Bernanos's words, 'Each of us does not die for ourselves ... but some in the place of others.' If Raymond remains the secret of *Les Mamelles* and *Figure humaine*, Lucien is certainly that of the *Stabat* and the *Carmélites*. Yes, I've finished my opera. All that's left are a few small touches.[67]

Those haunting words of Bernanos, sung by Sister Constance at the end of the first interlude of Act II, were felt by Poulenc to lie at the centre of the opera, and their link with his own life was only one of those that made the opera into his profoundly necessary work, as recounted by Barraud. Lucien died on 21 October as Poulenc was putting those finishing touches to his score; he then returned to Noizay to be tended by Raymond and his wife.[68]

In her memoirs Gertrude von le Fort explained that 'The point of departure of my own version was not initially the destiny of the sixteen Carmelites of Compiègne, but the figure of the little Blanche. Historically she never existed, but the breath of her tremulous nature came exclusively from within me and she can absolutely not be dissociated from her true origin.' Von le Fort was a child of the tumultuous Germany of the 1920s and:

> ... this girl, constantly anxious and known in the family as 'the little hare', this young woman who, through fear of the world, takes refuge in a convent and there seeks, through a mystic impulse, to infuse her religious life with the Agony of Christ, was already present in sketches of my literary composition before her destiny was included in that of the sixteen Carmelites of Compiègne. I came across this story by accident. A little footnote, at the bottom of a book about Catholic orders, on the Carmelites singing as they went to the scaffold, decided me to move the theatrical appearance of my little Blanche from the present to the French Revolution.[69]

A French opera foregrounding a brutal invasion of privacy and multiple executions cannot have failed to resonate with a composer and an audience who barely a decade earlier had been undergoing the terrors of the Occupation. Steven Huebner sensibly cautions against any facile identification of the sisters with the forces of the Resistance, not renowned for turning the other cheek,[70] but it's not hard to see how a story of conservatives being overthrown by revolutionaries might have spoken to Poulenc the composer, with his many references to 'dodécaca' (the joke to allay his anxiety?). Clearly it made sense to treat the nuns as normal and the revolutionaries as abnormal, so that the musical language for the former could be that espoused by Poulenc in many of his songs: basically tonal or modal, with chromatic decorations and fairly free movement between keys.

The work is dedicated 'to the memory of my Mother, who revealed music to me, of Claude Debussy, who gave me the desire to write it, of Claudio Monteverdi, Giuseppe Verdi and Modest Musorgsky who have served me here as models'. Although he does not designate Debussy as one of his models, Debussy's influence is the easiest of the four to recognize, in the refusal to write anything that can unambiguously be called an aria and instead to explore the possibilities of recitative and arioso, a style made possible by the fact that both *Pelléas et Mélisande* and *Dialogues des Carmélites* are settings of prose, and for the most part casually conversational prose at that. Monteverdi's influence may also in part relate to this, given that Vincent d'Indy in his 1902 review of *Pelléas* wrote:

> There is indeed, although the composer has probably not thought of it, a close relationship between his style of word setting and the 'stile rappresentativo' of Caccini, Gagliano and Monteverdi; I will even say – and it is, in my opinion, no faint praise – that it is with the marvellous cantor of *Orfeo*, *Ariana* and *L'Incoronazione di Poppea* that the composer of *Pelléas* has the nearest connection.[71]

Poulenc of course had, thanks to Nadia Boulanger, heard a lot more Monteverdi than Debussy ever did. Poulenc's correspondence with Bernac shows us what care he lavished both on the word setting, the ranges of particular voices, and not least on their necessary sonorities, always with an imperative that the words be heard. It needs to be said that, by staying within his familiar melodic and harmonic styles, Poulenc was not necessarily making life easier for himself. Certainly the generally regular rhythmic pulse of the first half or more of the opera makes the subsequent irruption of the revolutionary world all the more shocking. But he would undoubtedly have been aware of the danger of monotony, especially with a cast of almost entirely female voices (and here the similarly monochrome *Billy Budd* might have served as an awful warning: had the total absence of women's voices been a factor in his truanting?). One of the glories of the opera is that Poulenc managed to invest so much interest through the tiniest nuances, in the vocal line but also in the underlying harmonies and orchestral colours.

The only obvious structural elements are a number of repeated motifs. If these conjure up the figure of Richard Wagner and his leitmotifs, it's relevant to note Poulenc's views on the subject. Where Debussy was sarcastic about Wagner's 'unending catapults'[72] which, presumably, in his view were launched too directly at a precise meaning (not that *Pelléas* is free of them . . .), Poulenc used a caustic comment on Boulez's mathematical tendencies as pretext for a riff on the subject: 'I'm told he's a "polytechnicien". Not that I have anything against that noble institution [the École polytechnique] but it brings to mind two polytechnicians who were dancing partners of my sister and who liked nothing but Wagner, because they knew all the leitmotifs and could dig each other in the ribs and say "that's the magic potion, that's the spear" etc. How sad to react in this way.'[73] Poulenc's motifs are therefore rather less demonstrative than Wagner's, lacking what Liszt called the 'persistance systématique' of the latter,[74] and certainly they never provide the substance of any extended orchestral development. As Steven Huebner suggests, the opera 'invites an approach to leitmotifs and recurring melodies that underscores a cumulative web of meanings around concepts rather than around people or objects'.[75] Richard Langham Smith, referring to the motif that accompanies the memory of the death of Blanche's mother at her birth, says 'It's a motif we follow, more in the spirit of Debussy than of Wagner, asking us what it means rather than telling us.'[76]

Poulenc would surely have also agreed with Debussy that 'music has a rhythm that directs the development; the movements of the soul have another, by instinct more generalized. From the juxtaposition of these two rhythms springs a perpetual conflict. It doesn't happen simultaneously: either the music gets out of breath running after a character, or the character sits on a note waiting for the character to catch up.'[77] In Poulenc's opera the text and its singers rule the roost, and in a manner quite different from Debussy's, since in Poulenc's opera 'the category of the unsayable and the unsaid is absolutely not present among the work's features'.[78] There is no Mélisande mysteriously scattering mayhem. People mean what they say, even if brief silences ensue for digesting their message. The orchestra meanwhile is used to introduce, add colour (but 'almost no percussion, no special instruments', commented Poulenc),[79] contribute interludes and make brief final comments. Of the interludes, Pierre-Emmanuel Lephay justly writes:

It's also curious to note that these interludes, in which Musorgsky's influence is so striking, had to be composed rapidly as being needed for extending the intervals with curtain down between scenes [. . .], that's to say a similar situation to that of Debussy who had to compose interludes in a hurry (and for exactly the same practical reason) for the premiere of *Pelléas et Mélisande* – interludes in which the shadow of Wagner is so patent – as though, under time pressure, influences manifest themselves in a particularly obvious way . . .[80]

As for the text, Poulenc made many cuts and a few additions and transpositions, but basically followed that of Bernanos.[81]

The first scene opens on the library in the house of Blanche's father, the Marquis de la Force. His son, the Chevalier, bursts in and asks, 'Where's Blanche?' The Marquis complains of his bad manners, and already the atmosphere of tension is palpable in disjunct syntax and sudden silences in the orchestra. The reference of the opening motif, of two rising tones repeated an octave higher, is initially unclear: it may hark back to the 'Agnus Dei' of the Mass in G, or to the first movement of the Piano Concerto, or it may not. It's as well to accept that the frequent borrowings in the opera from Poulenc's previous works may simply be matters of convenience and should not be expected necessarily to carry over specific meanings. The tension is increased by the Chevalier's news that the carriage in which Blanche was coming home has been stopped by the mob. This of course reminds the Marquis of the occasion when this happened to his wife, pregnant with Blanche, and of her subsequent death in childbirth, his fearful memories reflected in the pulsing minor thirds in the bass that will recur throughout the opera. Blanche returns and makes light of her journey, and the first appearance of what may be termed her motif, borrowed from the opening and closing *Nocturnes*, occurs relevantly as she gives her opinion on the nature of fear, the emotion that drives the whole opera: 'danger,' she says 'is perhaps like cold water, which first of all knocks the breath out of you, and in which you feel comfortable when in it up to your neck.' She leaves the room, but soon we hear a scream. She has been frightened merely by the shadow of the servant lighting the lamps . . . Now, in a brief speech over repeated Gs in the bass that spell 'importance', she tells her father she has decided to enter Carmel. The Marquis initially questions her decision but, over the repeated quavers that feature in so many of Poulenc's songs, she holds firm.

After an interlude added following the Paris premiere in June 1957 and further bars of the original score, the curtain rises on the Prioress, Mme de Croissy and

Blanche in the parlour of the convent, on the lines that in 1953 had given Poulenc the confidence he could write the opera. As he explained, the scene moves from calm to the Prioress's severe recitation of the Order's rules: Blanche is attracted by 'a heroic life'? She shouldn't imagine that such a thing can just be taken down from the shelf. Convents are not 'museums of virtue, but houses of prayer' – at which point the orchestra falls silent, leaving the voice, as so often at crucial points, alone. But even if the Prioress 'does point out that there is nothing automatic about the heroic life, she does not deny the reality of Blanche's aspiration [. . .] The nun Blanche has become is, by profession, a soldier in Christ's army.'[82] After her definitive pronouncement, marked 'rude' and punctuated with a single dissonant chord, that 'Our Rule is not a refuge. It is not the Rule that keeps us, my child, it is we who keep the Rule', finally her affectionate nature wins through as she asks Blanche what name she wishes to take. 'Sister Blanche of the Agony of Christ,' she replies. The score indicates that 'The Prioress gives an imperceptible start then, peacefully and firmly' says 'Go in peace, my child.'

The Prioress's surprise stems from the fact that she too had taken this name and that her Superior had replied, 'Be very sure that you are strong. Whosoever enters Gethsemane can never again leave it.' 'Both women, the novice and the old Prioress, have felt mysteriously called to dedicate their lives within the mystery of Christ's agony in the garden, when he was utterly alone, knowing no consolation. Yet, in faith, we know that within that aloneness, he carried each one of us in our uttermost fragility' (Bishop Varden).

A second interlude and some stern, dissonant, Stravinskyan chords introduce Blanche and the young Sister Constance collecting various provisions and tools, accompanied by a 'giocoso' A major (a standard nineteenth-century key for light-heartedness). Constance's jolly gossip and memories of her recent dancing at a wedding shock Blanche: how can she speak like this when the Prioress . . . which is the first intimation that the latter is now ill. Constance, borrowing Blanche's motif for the moment, replies that she thinks death must be 'amusante' and, further, that she has prayed that she and Blanche might die young and on the same day. Blanche, horrified, rounds on her. Constance apologizes and all seems set for a gentle, accommodating final cadence in F major – suddenly, with a premonition of the future, twisted into A minor.

In the final scene of Act I the Prioress is in the infirmary on her deathbed, tended by Mother Marie of the Incarnation. The menacing introduction is made more so by a clanging bell and by timpani strokes on the rising minor thirds in the bass (possibly inspired by those in *Oedipus Rex* or in Debussy's *Le Martyre de Saint Sébastien*, an earlier work of Christian heroism under attack).[83] As the Prioress asks for a stronger painkiller, octave Es holding out against twelve different chords through twenty-six bars seem only to emphasize her immobility and inevitable fate. Mother Marie honestly repeats the doctor's opinion that the Prioress's death will be difficult. The Prioress commits Blanche to the care of Mother Marie, who leaves as Blanche enters the room. The Prioress tells Blanche that, as the last postulant to arrive, she is the dearest to her heart and blesses her. Blanche leaves, Mother Marie returns, and the rest of the scene, one of the most harrowing in the whole of opera, sees the Prioress experiencing a vision of the Carmel ransacked, and dying in agony. 'Think only of God,' urges Mother Marie: 'What am I, miserable wretch, that I should think of Him! Let Him first think of me!'

This has sometimes been interpreted as blasphemy. The truth is quite other. 'The Prioress has freely chosen, in union with Christ, to remain in Gethsemane "until the end" in order to bear her share of the Lord's cross and so to enable his grace to continue flowing into the world' (Bishop Varden). In the Agony in the Garden, Christ pleads with his Father to 'let this cup pass from me'. In her own outburst, the Prioress is therefore being entirely true to her union with Christ. Finally she calls for Blanche to return. She dies and Blanche, sobbing, buries her face in the bedclothes.

The first scene of Act II is set in the chapel, in the middle of which the open coffin is set. It is night-time, the only light coming from six candles round the coffin. Blanche and Constance are keeping vigil, the ceremonious nature of which is underlined by chords from Stravinsky's *Symphonies of Wind Instruments*. Bernanos having indicated here 'Récitation des psaumes' without specifying which, Poulenc properly inserts a Responsory from the Office for the Dead sung by the two nuns. A bell rings to signify a change of personnel for the vigil. Constance goes out to find replacements but Blanche, left alone with the coffin, is frightened and makes as if to leave (perhaps alone among mid-twentieth-century composers, Poulenc is content with diminished sevenths to depict her terror). Mother Marie enters, intercepts her, questions her, pardons her, gently leads her to the door.

In the interlude that follows, Blanche and Constance are in the garden making a cross of flowers for the Prioress's grave. Constance wonders whether what we call 'luck' is in fact God's logic and wonders whether the Prioress's painful death (low minor thirds again) was really someone else's, 'as in a cloakroom when someone gives you one coat instead of another'. Whose that 'another' might be in the present instance is made clear twice by Blanche's motif. This time, Blanche has nothing to say to Constance's musings.

In scene 2 the nuns are assembled in the chapter house to be addressed by the new Prioress, Madame Lidoine. Whereas the First Prioress came from the aristocracy, Mme Lidoine's father traded in cattle, but Poulenc seems at pains to disguise any class distinctions: the music introducing her is dignified, rather in the Baroque manner, and her lengthy discourse full of rhetorical contrasts. 'There is more than a hint in Bernanos's play that the election of Madame Lidoine was a matter of temporizing on the nuns' part: might this bourgeoise save them from the revolutionaries' fury? That the new Prioress is sensitive to this possibility is implicit when she invites Mother Marie to conclude her own inaugural address, as if admitting that she occupies a place that should have been Mother Marie's by right. And yet: Madame Lidoine shows herself, for all her commonness and talk of cabbage, able to rise to mystic levels, assuming the other sisters' vow in extremis, thus displaying a purity of faith that, in Mother Marie, is contaminated by self-will' (Bishop Varden).

The nub of her address, as often sung over a static bass line, is 'Beware of everything that could distract us from prayer.' The only possible sign of her upbringing comes in the warning that follows:

Prayer is a duty, martyrdom a reward. When a great king, in front of his whole court, beckons a servant girl to sit with him on the throne as if she were his beloved wife, it is better that she should not at first believe her eyes or ears, but should continue to polish the furniture.

This homely metaphor (which raised a laugh at the Milan premiere, though not at the Covent Garden one) would probably not have passed the lips of Madame de Croissy. The scene ends with Poulenc's interpolation of an Ave Maria, solos by Mother Marie and the Prioress being interspersed with a three-part choir of nuns that provides a satisfactorily conclusive texture.

At this point Poulenc made his longest cut, of four scenes, in Bernanos's text. Mother Marie doubts whether the timid Blanche is ready to receive the veil, but is overruled by the Prioress who, in any case, is under the Superior's order to conduct the ceremony. Poulenc, ever aware of the importance of vocal colour, may have realized that, in a vocal score of 242 pages, we are now on page 125 and have not heard a male voice since the Marquis on page twenty-nine. In the last of the four scenes cut, a conversation between the sisters shows there is some feeling against

Blanche as being an aristocrat; it ends with the Prioress assuring them that 'we risk being thrown out into the street, nothing worse than that'.

Back in the opera, a bell rings loudly and the orchestra responds 'molto agitato' in B flat minor, rending the convent's tranquillity. It is Blanche's brother, wanting to see her before he, very understandably, leaves France. The Prioress allows the visit as long as Mother Marie is present. Four times we now hear the indeterminate four-note motif that opened the whole opera: now it is becoming clearer that it could be a motif of Blanche's family – with resonances at the very end of the work. This interlude, surprisingly, ends with the loud B flat minor of its opening, as if to say 'The Chevalier's visit is not going to be helpful here.'

The introduction to their conversation indicates time passing, validating the Chevalier's opening words, 'Why have you been behaving like this for 20 minutes now, your eyes on the floor, hardly making any reply?' The fact that she then echoes his music tells us of the deep bond between them, whatever differences her new status may have made. Dotted rhythms in the orchestra accentuate the tension, the Chevalier telling Blanche she needs to come home to look after her father. In response to her claim that she is only slowly becoming used to happiness and freedom, he counters that she is inescapably bound to obey her own nature (in eight bars that, ironically, obey Poulenc's own nature in echoing Puccini, a composer he continued to love and admire against all 1950s orthodoxy). Her final answer is that 'I am no longer the little hare, I am a daughter of Carmel who is going to suffer for you', as the orchestra returns, discreetly, to Puccini. The Chevalier leaves and Mother Marie gently leads Blanche away, telling her to have courage.

Blanche's conversation with her brother and the mention of 'the little hare' 'raises a tantalizing possibility: that Blanche's extreme fragility may be, at least in part, the projection of others who purport to understand her and her "nature". In this projection she herself has sought refuge; but her entry into the *super*natural, oblative life of Carmel [. . .] enables her to touch a deeper truth, the experience of being strong in the strength of Another that will ultimately enable her to approach the scaffold singing, not just any pious song, but a doxology, a hymn of praise' (Bishop Varden).

Poulenc made more large cuts here, and the final scene of Act II takes place in the sacristy where all the nuns, having said mass, are assembled to say farewell to their priest, whose opening speech is underpinned yet again by the menace of the pulsing, low minor thirds. After they have all sung the 'Ave verum', the priest comforts Blanche, supported by Poulenc's most beguiling chords, but there is discord between Mother Marie, who insists that for priests to survive in France the Carmelites need to give their lives, and the Prioress who counters that it is not for them to choose martyrdom. Now the crowd is heard outside, shouting for the doors to be opened, and the discreet, regular accompaniment is broken up into jagged rhythms, with diminished sevenths abounding.

Two commissioners are admitted and their sentence of expulsion, read from a script, eerily and ironically echoes the rhythmic and harmonic regularity typical of Carmel itself. Mother Marie pointing out that they need to find other clothes since their habits are forbidden, one of the commissioners wonders, sarcastically, why she is so keen to look like everyone else, for which Poulenc allots him four bars that could have come straight from *Les Mamelles*. But the composer refuses to set the two styles off mechanically against each other. More subtly, we hear the commissioner being influenced at times by Mother Marie's sober responses. Intriguingly, it is the comic style he adopts for admitting that once he was a sacristan, and the sober one for explaining that in present circumstances he has no alternative but to 'howl with the wolves' – a discord between forced action and true feeling that would have been all too familiar to French audiences of the 1950s. It is not therefore all that surprising to read Poulenc's admitting, 'The weird thing is that it's not the religious dialogues that are giving me the most trouble, but on the contrary a narrative scene like the one with the People's Commissioner, which on the surface looks easier.'[84]

To conclude the act, Poulenc made his most radical intervention in Bernanos's original, inserting an earlier scene in which, on Christmas night, the statue of the Christ Child is taken round each cell to be venerated. Blanche, terrified by revolutionary chanting outside, drops the statue and it smashes. Replaced here, it allows Blanche's final words, 'The Little King is dead. We are left only with the Lamb of God', to portend the sacrifice of herself, 'the little hare'. The act ends with a final burst of revolutionary 'Ça ira', followed by a powerful consolidation of B flat minor complete with tremolando strings.

The Prioress has had to leave the convent for business in Paris so, as Mother Marie's motif tells us, it is she, with her desire for martyrdom, who now takes control. Marked 'Tempo de Sarabande', the opening of Act III takes its mood, dotted rhythms and key of A minor from the sarabande of 'Fac ut portem', the tenth movement of the *Stabat Mater*, and is the most obvious testimony to Poulenc's claim that 'my opera *Dialogues des Carmélites* is obviously the logical successor to my *Stabat Mater*'.[85] Richard Langham Smith also wonders whether Poulenc had 'the final chorus of the St Matthew Passion in mind when he began the final act with a Sarabande?' Certainly through its decisive, *ancien régime* character it portrays vividly both Mother Marie's determination and her aristocratic lineage.

The nuns are again assembled in the devastated chapel and Mother Marie explains that they will now vote secretly on the vow of martyrdom and that a single refusal will suffice to abandon it. Although initially Constance votes against, on learning that there is only one contrary vote she changes her mind (in taking this decision it is almost certain that the nuns would be remembering that 'in the early years of the 18th century, one of their number had prophesied that a collective martyrdom awaited them').[86] Constance and Blanche kneel before a book of the Gospels and make their devotions but, as the other sisters arrange themselves in order of age, Blanche escapes from the chapel.

To the opening music of the first interlude, taken from the Andante of the Sonata for two clarinets, three municipal officers appear in front of the curtain and are joined by the nuns. The chief officer pronounces the edict: no living in communities, no contact with enemies of the Republic or obstinate priests – instead certificates of freedom under the supervision of the laws. They leave and the Prioress, now returned from Paris, and Mother Marie have a short conversation full of unspoken tension. The Prioress feels it would be dangerous to have the priest now say mass for them, as was intended. Mother Marie declares obedience to her superior: but was the vow of martyrdom an error? Well, 'what's done is done. But how to reconcile our vow with such caution?' . . . all this over a pedal F, on which she leaves. Moving to a pedal B flat, which sounds like a conclusive tonic after Mother Marie's challenging dominant, the Prioress refuses to engage with her junior colleague. Instead she changes the terms of the debate: 'each of you,' she tells her flock, 'will answer for her vow before God, but it is I who will answer for you all, and I am old enough to know how to keep my accounts in order.' But again, Poulenc undermines the obvious, the brief orchestral epilogue ending the scene, for the first time in the opera, on an unresolved diminished seventh made more unsettling still by a timpani roll, as the Carmelites leave the convent for private homes in the town and the hostile outside world. Bernanos claims they do so wearing civilian clothes ('en civil'),[87] but in this he seems to have forfeited a crucial dramatic point. The truth is that they were removed from the convent on their washing day, so had only their religious habits left to wear; and, as already noted, they wore them throughout their trial. As far as is known, Poulenc did not specify in so many words which alternative he had in mind. But his remark to Maurice Jacquemont about the Milan production, that 'making the Carmelites into individuals was a mistake. Until Constance's arrival, they should be a flock with a single reaction: confidence', suggests that he wanted them to be wearing their habits.[88]

The introduction to the second scene begins with a slow passage inserted after the vocal score was published in which we hear the family motif, rather surprisingly omitted from the following faster, dotted section that originally introduced the scene. Blanche is back in the kitchen of the family home, her father guillotined, the house completely devastated. Mother Marie has come to fetch her but, in the face of her refusal, gives her an address where she will be safe, physically if not spiritually. The ensuing interlude, now purely orchestral, was originally spoken by citizens of the Bastille area, accompanied by tiny figures on percussion. Yes, life in Paris is no joke. And yesterday they arrested the nuns at Compiègne. Blanche joins them. Has she any relatives out in Compiègne? No, says Blanche, echoing Saint Peter's denial of Christ, I know not the place.

The penultimate scene of the opera, set in the Conciergerie prison on the Ile de la Cité where the nuns are confined, comes back to their habitual calm, but now coloured by the minor mode. In one of Poulenc's most inspired lyrical passages, the Prioress again takes upon herself the decision of martyrdom, but leaving each nun the merit of it, 'since I did not decide it myself'. She concludes with words Poulenc took from two other nuns much earlier in the play and which provide the ultimate consolation: 'In the Garden of Olives Christ was no longer master of anything. He knew the fear of death.' Constance asks, 'Where is Blanche?' But she is sure Blanche will return. Why? Her answer, 'Because of a dream I had', provokes general laughter.

But their hilarity is short-lived. The gaoler enters and reads out the Revolutionary tribunal's decree, naming each nun in a gruesome replica of a café-concert patter song ('as fast as possible but very articulated'). Finally he slows up for the crux of the message and the orchestra dies down suddenly to pianissimo for the word 'mort'. The Prioress responds, again 'très doux et calme', with her maternal benediction as the orchestra plays with the ubiquitous figure of a brief, quick descending scale that seems to play a purely functional role without attribution to any referent, personal or abstract.

The final interlude is played out in front of the curtain. Mother Marie meets the priest and tells him of the tribunal's decision; also (although this is not made as clear as could be by Poulenc) that, having been away looking for Blanche, she was not arrested with the others and that her sisters before the scaffold will look for her in vain. However, Bernanos does make clear that the sixteen nuns condemned to death included Mother Marie of the Incarnation, 'condamnée par contumace', that is in her absence.[89] As for Mother Marie's position in all this, Jean de Solliers puts it very clearly:

> It's been said that she was the most unhappy of all because she was deprived of the supreme reward of martyrdom. But nothing would have prevented her from joining her companions if she really wanted to. And we consider with a certain uneasiness that it was she who effectively challenged the Prioress, in the first interlude of Act III, over the strict fidelity to the vow which she had morally imposed on the community, and which now she does not have the courage to follow. Be that as it may, the irony of fate saw to it that the story of the Carmelites of Compiègne was preserved only in the memoirs of Mother Marie, the sole one to escape the convent.[90]

Wherever the truth lies here, the priest ends by telling Mother Marie she should not be concerned with the gaze of her sisters, but with responding to that of God.

The final scene of the opera is set in the Place du Trône (now Place de la Nation). While it may have been partly to give the time needed to arrange this new set that prompted Poulenc to insert before it, with the curtain down, music derived from the *Marche 1937*, written for that year's exhibition, this 'anticipation musicale' also had a dramatic function. As he wrote to Valcarenghi, 'this allows the people's agitation to be described before the entry of the Carmelites. The calmness of this entry makes a great impact by brusquely putting an end to the ferocity of the crowd. The absence of revolutionary words in Bernanos's text has always caused me a problem, which I think I have finally solved in this way.'[91] The pounding, menacing minor thirds in the bass, which have signalled 'dramatic tension' throughout the opera, are certainly revolutionary in their own right. But the March has the added value of presenting A major chords with C sharps above A minor with C naturals in the bass, the resultant grind of sharp against natural producing one of the most dissonant passages in the whole opera.[92] The nuns' relatively consonant procession to the scaffold, 'très calme et paisible', justifies Poulenc's remark that the scene 'is not strictly speaking a funeral march, rather a psalmody',[93] on the lines of 'Liberté' in *Figure humaine*. Melodically it echoes the Sarabande that opens Act III, also in A minor, but with the abrupt, dotted rhythm now smoothed over.

As the nuns intone the *Salve Regina*, the bass quavers pulse regularly through most of the scene, moving through a large number of keys but solidifying into crotchets as the end approaches. The only interruption in the flow comes with the first stroke of the guillotine that despatches the Prioress. As the crowd exclaims in horror (or approval?), the response of the nuns is to intone the *Salve Regina* a third higher and to increase the volume to fortissimo. From here, Poulenc indicates with each descent of the guillotine how many voices are left, and finally their identity. Here his dramatic antennae alerted him to a problem: 'it's horribly difficult to calculate a plausible timing for the decapitations of the poor nuns, which mustn't fall exactly on the beginnings or ends of phrases. I'll find a solution but it's a puzzle. I had wondered momentarily whether to take the line of a regular number of bars, but that sounded automatic. I'm trusting to instinct.'[94] His problem is manifest in the different placing of some of the decapitations in the Milan recording from those in the printed score. Here a few do indeed coincide with beginnings or ends of phrases, but the majority interrupt the pseudo-plainsong at apparently arbitrary points, even in the middle of words – an audible manifestation of the regime's increasing hostility to religion, as well as to the wealth of enclosed communities which hardly seemed to conform with Christ's own teaching: as Voltaire wrote of monks and nuns, 'they eat, they pray, they digest'.[95]

Sister Constance is finally the only one left singing. At this moment Blanche forces her way through the crowd, 'her countenance free of all fear' (in Bernanos's text she is pushed towards the scaffold by a group of women, but Poulenc's reading obviously makes a better fit with 'the transference of grace' through the old Prioress's sacrifice). 'Both opera and play display the working out of this life-giving sacrifice when Blanche, at the end, reaps the fruit of the old nun's free and loving gift of both her life and her death, finding herself astonishingly able to embrace her own death without terror, even with a kind of joy – the sting of death being no more [. . .] The Prioress, let's not forget, had taken upon herself to answer before God for Blanche's commitment, to see it through to the end' (Bishop Varden). Constance 'smiles gently at Blanche' and goes to her death. Blanche, intoning the *Veni Creator*, follows her, and the guillotine falls in a bar without music, a bar of stunned silence. The opera ends with what may be construed as her family motif: not only has she fulfilled her vow of martyrdom but, in doing so, has upheld the honour of her aristocratic family ('honour' being something much prized by Bernanos).[96]

For the composer, of course, his beginning is thus his end. What we find between the two is, in the words of Marcel Schneider, 'Poulenc's anxious religious belief that dies with the First Prioress, is reborn with the Second and sings the final *Salve Regina*. I imagine him, like those who commissioned paintings in the Middle Ages, in a corner of his opera, on his knees, piously reciting his text and his music.'[97] This piety led Poulenc to state that 'God invites us to heroism only in order to lead us to joy. Too many people make the mistake of thinking only of the sacrifice. It is a means, it is not an end . . .'[98]

This is not the place to consider all the other religious questions the opera throws up, which would need a book to themselves. For Poulenc the essence of the opera was, as already mentioned, the transference of grace from the First Prioress to Blanche and indeed to Constance, and he admitted being haunted by Constance's phrase at the end of the first interlude in Act II, 'Each of us does not die for ourselves, but for one another', taking this to refer to Lucien's impending death which, he felt, had saved himself from a suspected cancer.[99] Transference of grace in another aspect can be found in Poulenc's remark on completing the fair copy of the vocal score, justified by the event: 'Monsieur Lucien will die now, because I've finished.'[100] This implies that it was not only his depression that provided 'necessary experience' for writing the opera,[101] but also Lucien's illness. This link between suffering and creativity would prompt two, and possibly three, further vocal works in the years that followed.

By September, despite the anxious days spent by Lucien's deathbed, Poulenc's health seems to have fully returned, to judge by his workload: recitals of Schumann songs for the centenary of his death, recording Chabrier's *Valses romantiques* with Marcelle Meyer, planning a disc of *Babar* (eventually made in 1957), writing articles on Bartók and the Ballets Russes, and getting the vocal score of *Carmélites* ready for the printer. On the emotional front, things were perhaps not going as we might expect. Lucien's illness had brought him and Poulenc together again, and it's not unusual for a lover who has done everything humanly possible for the invalid to be able to weather their death with a certain equanimity. Even so we may be surprised to find that in mid-November, less than a month after Lucien died, Poulenc had already found a new lover about whom 'he talked at length over a lunch with Audel and Chanlaire'.[102] Benjamin Ivry identifies him as 'Claude, a 28-year-old junior executive at Citroën'.[103]

Poulenc was in Paris over Christmas and planned to spend the New Year with Raymond at Noizay. During the first months of 1956 he was travelling: to Greece, Italy and Britain (London and Liverpool). From Liverpool railway station, at 8 a.m. on 28 March, he wrote to his niece Brigitte one of his most delightful and informative letters: he and Jean Françaix had given a good performance of the Two-Piano Concerto; Victor de Sabata reckoned that *Carmélites* would need thirty orchestral rehearsals ('I must be dreaming!'); he had met Herbert von Karajan and Elisabeth Schwarzkopf and, having been warned of their combination of hysterics, skulduggery and musical professionalism, was determined not to get involved; his reception as an honourable member of the Accademia Santa Cecilia in Rome went very well; and on 21 March at the Domaine musical in Paris Boulez's *Le Marteau sans maître* 'is remarkable. If it weren't for the sawtooth nature of the prosody which makes the text unintelligible, it would really be first class'; the Webern too was very fine; but, as already quoted, 'I shall continue to write *do mi sol do* and do not approve of Stravinsky putting on hats that are too young for his age'.[104]

In the same letter Poulenc is pleased to report that the remastered version of his record of Satie piano music is excellent; also that Marcelle Meyer is pleased with their recording of Chabrier's *Valses romantiques* for two pianos. Technical excellence aside, both of these recordings are also historically important. He had of course heard Satie play, and Poulenc's embrace of strict tempi, with minimal rubato, undoubtedly stems from this experience, eschewing the rhythmic waywardness that disfigures so many modern Satie performances. As for the Chabrier pieces, Poulenc's authority is documented in his book on the composer:

> Having often had the honour and pleasure of playing them with Messager, who gave the first performance with the composer at the Société nationale on 15 December 1883, I take the liberty of suggesting the metronome marks, absent from the edition, which seem to me exact. The first waltz (dotted minim=88) must be played straight. The second (crotchet=112–120) very rubato. For the third, I realize that the right tempo is very hard to establish. It mustn't drag or hurry (dotted minim=84 seems to me to be the correct tempo).[105]

At the same time one has to admit that the speed of the third waltz in Poulenc's recording varies in fact between dotted minim = 60 and 72! But there is no reason to doubt his instruction to 'take care over the sonority and use lots of pedal. One should produce a sensuality in the notes that is reminiscent of Renoir's *Fillettes au piano* [Christine and Yvonne Lerolle]', an instruction tallying blatantly with his own inclination, so often repeated both orally and in writing.

After all this, his main task was completing the orchestration of *Carmélites* – La Scala wanted it by 1 June, but in the event Poulenc posted it on the 18th. On the 10th he had sent his niece Brigitte a card, noting a curious resemblance: 'Bichette, What a strange feeling it is to have finished the *Carmélites*. My finale is basically a bolero, because I've kept changing the orchestration of my unchanging rhythm.'[106]

His letters now contained thoughts about which singers for which parts. He soon came to accept that for the Milan premiere his wishes would go for rather little about both singers and decor, and wisely let things take their course. But for the following Paris production, which for him was the important one, not least because 'if Bernanos's fans will be irrelevant in Milan, they will certainly have to be considered in Paris',[107] he was lavish with advice, much of it taken, including Xavier Depraz and Régine Crespin as the Marquis and Mme Lidoine, and of course Denise Duval as Blanche, while Rita Gorr would be Mother Marie rather than his suggested Mme de Croissy.[108]

In the middle of orchestrating, Poulenc found time to write a short piece, 'Bucolique', for a set of eight *Variations sur le nom de Marguerite Long* – a slow, thoughtful little orchestral work, curiously at odds with Long's reputation as a somewhat brittle pianist. Then, with *Carmélites* finally out of his hands after three years, there was more travelling, to Aldeburgh, where he gave a ninety-minute talk ('I made them laugh a lot, which is the crucial thing'),[109] to Évian (with Claude), Milan, Fontainebleau, and in August to his sister in Normandy where he completed the Éluard song cycle *Le Travail du peintre*.

A few days earlier he had written about the cycle to Simone Girard, 'I'm really concentrating on it [. . .] the voice part's extremely contained – it doesn't go up beyond a high F$\sharp$ and, despite its inevitably Éluardian manner, the working-out of it is new. I hope to finish it over the next 10 days. It's true I'd been ruminating this masterpiece . . . for two years!!!'[110] In fact it had been longer than that, as he had talked about the project with Éluard some time before the poet's death in November 1952. His original intention was to have it ready for the twentieth anniversary in 1955 of his partnership with Bernac, but his illness and *Carmélites* between them had prevented this. The other disappointment was over the final song:

The seven poems that make up this collection are taken from the volume *Voir*, written to celebrate painters. I thought I might refresh my song writing by *painting in music*: Picasso, Chagall, Braque, Gris, Klee, Miró, Villon. When I'd talked to Éluard about my project, I'd asked him for a poem on Matisse, whom I adore. Paul sort of promised. I say 'sort of' because he didn't share my passion for this artist. In my imagination, 'Matisse' was to conclude the cycle in joy and sunshine. Now 'Villon' completes it lyrically and sombrely.[111]

A month after finishing the songs, Poulenc could write that they were 'beautiful and serious' and were 'as important as *Tel jour*'.[112] 'Villon' too has been praised by other voices, Graham Johnson finding it 'the most beautiful song' of the set,[113] while Benjamin Ivry, admitting that 'its subject is perhaps the weakest artist of the group', regards it as 'an artistic success; the composer adopted an air of farewell, producing a stern setting as he had done in Racine's *Hymne*. Éluard's text explained that "life is to be cherished in spite of plagues", a sentiment with which Poulenc, having weathered many inner crises, agreed. He believed that this would be his last melody, and the strong sign-off matches the impressive opening of the cycle.'[114]

The opening is impressive indeed, taking Mother Marie's forceful motif and transposing it from minor into major: this is the Picasso who, ploughing his own furrow, almost absent-mindedly dictates the course of contemporary painting, and Poulenc's observation that C major no longer spells 'peaceful happiness' is at one with what he calls the 'lofty tone' of the song. The problem was, what should come after this? He was not particularly fond of Chagall's work, and felt his setting of 'Braque' was too tasteful. He was happier with 'Gris', liking the rhythmic imitation between lines, and the melancholy that, again, derives from Mother Marie's rising A-B-C. 'Klee' was purely functional ('I needed a presto') and 'Miró' entailed problems in moving suddenly from stridency to gentle lyricism. Finally, ' "Villon" is, with "Gris", the song I like best. Everyone knows how much I like the litanic side of Éluard's poetry. The prosody of "l'aube, l'horizon, l'eau, l'oiseau, l'homme, l'amour" gives human relaxation to this poem that is so tight and violent.'[115] But we do not find Matisse's 'joy and sunshine', which surely would have been the ideal response and balance to the 'lofty tone' ('le ton altier') of 'Picasso' – a relationship summed up by one of that painter's biographers in her sentence, 'While Matisse was dazzling the art world with his wild outbursts of color and joy, Picasso was painting the portrait of Gertrude Stein in a brownish-gray monotone.'[116] As important as *Tel jour*? Not really. In any case such a miracle was unlikely to happen twice.

But Poulenc remained in melodic vein and in September wrote two more songs for favourite singers. On 12 December Marya Freund would be celebrating her eightieth birthday and her son Doda Conrad arranged for eighty compositions, dedications and letters to be presented to her on the day. Poulenc chose to set another poem, 'La souris', from Apollinaire's *Le Bestiaire* – or was it, with or without alterations, one of the songs he had removed at Auric's behest from his cycle of nearly forty years earlier? The mouse is time, which nibbles away at the poet's life: he'll soon be twenty-eight, years 'mal vécus, à mon envie'. Critics have agreed on them being 'badly lived', but 'à mon envie' continues to confuse translators a full century after it was written: 'despite my efforts'? 'just as I wanted'? or even as a casual homophone for 'à mon avis', 'in my opinion'. Poulenc is no help at all, giving the phrase exactly the same music as 'Et mal vécus'.

For Rose Dercourt-Plaut, another favourite singer, he set 'Nuage' by a contemporary poet Laurence de Beylié, relying on the regular quavers, harmonic sequences and 'doucement mélancolique' atmosphere that had always served him well. But no sooner had he finished it than he wondered to Henri Hell, 'What is this songful summer? My swansong in this domain?'[117] Not quite. But with retrospect we can see that it was almost that: in the slightly more than six years left to him he wrote just one light-hearted cycle of seven songs and three single ones. These apart, his vocal output now embraced an orchestra, as though *Carmélites* had given him a taste for the colours offered by this combination.

We might suppose from all this physical and creative activity that, spiritually, Poulenc was now in a good place. That it was otherwise is attested by an unpublished letter to John Howard Griffin of 17 August, which he begins by telling of the affair with Lucien, during which:

> I in some sense lost my faith – before this I had always relied on religion to help me to make a good death, and when I had that cancer scare praying did nothing for me – I hope that one day the source of grace will return. For the moment I am bored at Mass. I look forward to the 'Ite missa est' as I used to do, all those years ago, to the drum beat that signalled the end of lessons at the lycée. Pray God that he will allow me one day to find a good country priest to help me – intelligent priests depress me – Dominicans would turn me into a lifelong atheist.[118]

After an October in which he evades the attention of a biographer, he and Bernac were in England during November, giving recitals in Birmingham and Oxford and recording a programme for the BBC in London. On the 18th Poulenc left France for Milan in order to attend orchestral read-throughs of the opera on the 19th and 20th. 'There isn't a single bar,' he wrote, 'that I haven't scrutinized. Thanks to this, in January my orchestration will be exactly what I want it to be.'[119] He then spent over three weeks in his beloved Hôtel Majestic in Cannes, thinking about the opera and tidying up a few loose ends – as he said at the end of his life, 'working in a hotel is like being in a monastery; and when you get fed up with your own company, you can always go down to the bar.'[120] He also began his Flute Sonata and composed the song *Dernier Poème* on a text by Robert Desnos, written in his prisoner-of-war camp in Terezin, in which major/minor clashes characteristically tell of anxiety and loss.

To Maurice Jacquemont who was to produce the opera in Paris he wrote:

The Milan preparations are *fantastic* from all points of view (229 costumes, *astonishing singers* and everything to match). I don't want to play into the hands of those who, in advance, are saying that it's in Milan one needs to see and hear the *Carmélites*. Clearly, over there it's a sensational occasion. All the papers are talking about it, the senior clergy are asking for tickets etc. . . . I'm not asking for the same feverishness in Paris, but simply that work gets done.[121]

He sent a 'sweet' [sic] note to Lavery with Christmas greetings, and then there was the question of which critics to invite: Vuillermoz was to be shunned, likewise 'my greatest enemy' Robert Mooser, who had condemned the Piano Concerto. Poulenc had been terrified in Basle to see that *all* the musical journals contained articles by Antoine Goléa, a modern music specialist of whom, according to Alexander Goehr, even Messiaen was afraid.[122] 'I don't give a damn what he'll think of my music,' wrote Poulenc, 'but it's imperative to have him.'[123] There was to be no skulking in the traditionalist ghetto.

IX
JOY, SUFFERING AND FAREWELL
✦ 1957–1963 ✦

Poulenc reached Milan on 7 January 1957. Disappointment that he had not been consulted over the decor or production details was exacerbated by finding on his arrival his producer Margarita Wallmann 'deathly pale [. . .] like a refugee who's just got through the Hungarian border. To all my questions, merely a groan'. But then, the following evening, her face was transformed: 'It's astonishing how your score works by itself. I hadn't heard the singers before, but today I was able to rehearse the first scene. It's superb etc. . . .'[1] But he still had to hear them for himself, mindful no doubt of the fact that a failure in such a prestigious house as La Scala would probably condemn the opera to oblivion. Bernac, as often, was the first back home to hear his reaction: 'Pierre, old man, my cast is sen-sa-tio-nal!!! If *Carmélites* is a flop, I'll be the only one to blame.'[2]

His first impression of the decor was less than enthusiastic, but for the singers he ran through a whole list of admiring adjectives – 'magnifique', 'inouïe', 'formidable', etc. As the opera was sung in Italian, he had agreed that Denise Duval could not take the part of Blanche and had asked Virginia Zeani to sing the role after hearing her as Violetta in *La Traviata* in Paris the previous summer. Initially he found her 'not raucous and constricted enough', which is rather strange since elsewhere he explained that the voice-type he was after was the sensuous one of Thaïs in Massenet's opera.[3] Overall, though, he was greatly struck by her acting and singing, and she remembers that for Blanche 'the voice that he wanted had several colours from calm decision to great desperation'. Zeani felt that singing Violetta prepared her to some degree for Blanche in that both heroines suffer, Violetta physically, Blanche mentally. Of the production she recalled that 'the finale especially changed a lot. Margarita Wallmann dominated the dream and the desires of Poulenc and she changed a lot of things.'[4] This last point may explain why, at the end of the run, Poulenc felt that the production of the final scene had never quite worked. Throughout the rehearsal period Poulenc sent off a running commentary to Brigitte, of which the following is a fair sample:

> I've made some good changes to the melodic curve in the [Second] Prioress's great aria. It's in the 'great voice' manner, which goes better. I start my rehearsals at 10 a.m. and we finish at midnight. Every day there are one or two rehearsals with orchestra and voices. I think I must be dreaming! Ninety-four critics are coming from the four corners of the world. I await them *calmly*.[5]

The opening night on 26 January was sold out, with both Maria Callas and Gian Francesco Malipiero among many distinguished names in the audience, and over the previous three weeks Poulenc had exercised his charm to great effect: Fiorenza Cossotto, who sang Sister Mathilde, will never forget him as 'un grande musicista ed une meravigliosa persona' who used to call her 'La mia piccola Suor Matilde',[6] while Zeani says that 'a sweeter, more human, more intelligent person does not exist'.[7] Poulenc, for his part, was thrilled to have had some forty rehearsals, of which thirty had been unstaged with the orchestra (à l'italienne), and was delighted to have as conductor the experienced Nino Sanzogno, who had led the premiere of Prokofiev's *The Fiery Angel* in Venice in 1955. If Massimo Mila, Italy's major music critic, was cool about *Carmélites*, finding that 'Here we have a diligent, analytic representation of events and the environment (more than of the characters); but fear, the true subject of this story of militant nuns, is not in the music',[8] this was a minority view of the opera, even if Vincent Giroud is also right in affirming that 'it took a generation for its true greatness to be understood'.[9] The general response nevertheless was that Poulenc had surpassed all expectations, Claude Rostand in *Le Monde* claiming the work as 'A great international event. A great French victory.'[10] This victory, though, did not please everybody. Some hours before the curtain rose on the first night, a robust personage with enormous hands presented himself to Poulenc with much bowing and scraping. He was the leader of the *claque*, and had come for his instructions. Poulenc told him to let the work take its chance. At the reception after the performance the same gentleman begged for an audience. Why? 'He's furious,' explained the composer. 'He claims that this evening he had nothing to do!'[11]

Poulenc was back in Paris on 7 February and spent some weeks putting final corrections to the score of *Carmélites* before it went off to the printer. From late in the month he experienced one of his happiest periods for a long time. Comfortably settled in his regular room at the Hôtel Majestic in Cannes (between the lift and the reception counter, where other residents would not be disturbed by his piano),[12] and free from his opera after four years of worry and labour, an 'adorable meeting (a twenty-nine-year-old sergeant in the colonial infantry) made me forget everything including *Carmélites*. It's a long time since I enjoyed such *poetical* moments – that's the word.'[13] The twenty-eight-year-old Claude had clearly not stayed the course.

Poulenc also settled down to continuing his Flute Sonata, a project that had been in his mind since 1952, further encouraged by a commission in 1956 from the Elizabeth Sprague Coolidge Foundation. Like Raymond and Lucien before him, Sergeant Louis Gautier became identified in Poulenc's mind with a particular piece of his music, and he wrote to Simone Girard that 'The Flute Sonata is proof of the good effect of the French army on the mood of the old maestro.'[14] Louis, who would remain close to Poulenc until the latter's death, followed the pattern of metamorphosing from lover to friend, not without the usual storms and suspicions along the way.

Such things were, however, notably absent from the Flute Sonata, dubbed by Poulenc as being 'sans complexes', which we may take as denoting a lack of both complications as well as of complexes in the psychological sense. A letter to Bernac of 8 March, by which time the first two movements were completed, sums up the work with particular cogency:

> In working on this Flute Sonata I have the feeling of going back a long way, but with a more settled technique. It's a sonata of Debussyan dimensions. It's the French sense of balance [la mesure française]. [. . .] Finding the form for your language is the most difficult thing. It's what Webern has in the highest degree (as did Mallarmé) and what Boulez has not yet found.[15]

The nearest Poulenc comes to sonata tradition is in the 'cyclic' repeats of first movement material in the finale, but this influence from the Franck/d'Indy school is balanced by a phrase borrowed from the 'Interlude' of Debussy's Sonata for flute, viola and harp.[16] The only slight puzzle is the first movement's title Allegro malincolico, melancholy being no more than hinted at through minor triads. If there is melancholy, it is very much of the Poulenc variety, on the edge between clearly classifiable emotions, with cheerful ideas faintly inflected towards introspection. The flautist Michel Dubost remembers Poulenc's overall insistence on exactitude in the rhythms, 'still, with the inconsistency of great artists [he] wanted the first flourish soft and graceful, but not slow [. . .] He would compare the first four notes of the piece to a falling leaf. Thereafter the same pattern would be played in time.'[17] Melancholy is more patent in the Cantilena, borrowing from that in the song 'C' and couched in the key of B flat minor that figures so prominently in the more angst-ridden passages of *Carmélites*. The final Presto giocoso returns to the *voyou* persona of the 1920s with, as he says, a surer technique, but no loss of jaunty vim.

He played in two first performances in Paris over the next couple of months – of *Le Travail du peintre* with Alice Esty on 1 April and of the Flute Sonata with Jean-Pierre Rampal on 18 June – but his thoughts and energies were chiefly directed towards the Paris premiere of *Carmélites*, now fixed for 21 June. As early as 15 June 1956 he had told Georges Hirsch, the director of the Opéra, that 'Paris will be the original version, the premiere, the one that matters because it includes Bernanos's text. [. . .] With Wallmann and Wake [the designer Georges Wakhévitch] at Milan we shall have an ostentatious kind of poverty. I want the Paris sets to be purely French and according to my strict indications, knowing the *Carmélites* atmosphere profoundly as I do.'[18] Several weeks after the Milan premiere he wrote to Dugardin: 'With dear Marguerite [Wallmann] it wasn't worth interfering, since she, being a Viennese Jew, could see things only from the outside. [. . .] I really want people to see my work as it is. There's no Massenet or Puccini in it. It's much less simple than that. I prefer to have less success in Paris but that it should be tough [dur] and moving.'[19] How near the reality was coming to his wishes is expressed in a third letter of 9 June: 'Here I am in the final preparations for my great premiere, because for me it really is "my" premiere. In Milan everybody worked on my behalf. In Paris these are the *Carmélites* I dreamt of. I'm thrilled by everything: decors, production, casting. Denise is sublime! What an actress! I finally see in the flesh the character I have for so long borne within me.'[20]

The Paris press was a symphony of admiration. René Dumesnil wrote that the success of Poulenc's word setting 'cannot surprise those who have followed his music since his first songs on poems by Apollinaire: the prosody of *Dialogues des Carmélites* is their logical outcome.' On his choice of subject, 'it is certain that his religious feelings would have prompted it, but what aesthetic reasons supported a plan that was apparently so dangerous? Those that led Debussy to choose *Pelléas*, different though Maeterlinck's fluidity may be from Bernanos's robust prose.' Marcel Schneider reckoned that 'if he has not invented a new musical language, Poulenc has instead invented a new kind of opera. [. . .] As an intimate, psychological drama, Francis Poulenc's opera has no reference but itself; that is the highest praise one can confer upon it.' But perhaps the most welcome review for the composer was that of his ancient antagonist Émile Vuillermoz: '[Poulenc] had chosen a splendid text by Bernanos which not only did not call for music but rejected it. He accepted a highly disputable arrangement of this. He exposed himself to the grave danger of monotony. [. . .] He resigned himself to the lack of pace in certain scenes, counting on the terrible denouement of his plot to achieve ultimate victory. And in the event he was justified, being finally crowned with laurels.'[21]

Buoyed by the outright success of this work on which he felt his reputation would always rest, Poulenc now allowed himself some six months' relative respite. In early July he went to Rocamadour to give thanks to the Black Virgin, then to Cologne for the first German performance of the opera. He began the *Laudes de Saint Antoine de Padoue*, but did not finish them until March 1959, wrote an *Ave Maria*, now lost, began a Bassoon Sonata, never written, or lost, and the only work that was at all urgent was on the 'anticipations' for *Carmélites* – extensions of the interludes that had to marry seamlessly with existing material.[22] These additions, probably helpful for purely practical reasons of staging, were needed for the performances that were now being called for: before the end of the decade the opera was to be heard in Barcelona, Buenos Aires, Catania, Cologne, Geneva, Genoa, Ghent, Lisbon, London (Covent Garden), Naples, Palermo, Rome, San Francisco, Trieste and Vienna. In that period it was given at the Paris Opéra twenty-seven times.

In September Poulenc went with Bernac to the Edinburgh Festival, giving first performances of the *Deux Mélodies* ('La souris' and 'Nuage') and a second performance of *Le Travail du peintre*, though later he often referred to this also as a premiere. On the 16th he was present at Nadia Boulanger's seventieth birthday, for which he wrote a tribute all of five bars long. On the 25th, in a letter to Valcarenghi, he made his first known mention of what was to be his final opera: 'I definitely think I'll do *La Voix humaine*!!!! [Hans Werner] Henze has refused it. I regard this as a sign from Providence. Obviously it's a *tour de force*, but the *Mamelles* and *Dialogues* weren't a cinch for me. [. . .] Given her talents as an actress and her experience with my music, it is of course Duval who'll be the "voice", if

I take it on.'[23] The idea of setting Cocteau's text had come to Poulenc in Milan the previous January after a Verdi opera at La Scala with Maria Callas and Mario del Monaco: 'as the last notes faded beneath thunderous applause [. . .] Callas violently pushed the splendid Mario into the corner of the wings and advanced by herself into the middle of the stage. [. . .] At which point one of my dear friends, my publisher [Hervé Dugardin], who was sitting next to me, said; "You should write an opera just for her . . . that way, she wouldn't be such a b . . . nuisance.'[24]

The last quarter of the year was largely empty of engagements and devoted mostly to re-orchestrating his two numbers from *Les Mariés de la Tour Eiffel*, the full score of which had gone missing,[25] and to composing the *Élégie* for horn and piano in memory of Dennis Brain, whose death in a car accident on his way back from Edinburgh had cast a dark shadow over the Festival. Completed that December, the work is generally recognized as being enigmatic, not least because of its sharp contrasts and high levels of dissonance. There also seems to be no compelling reason for Poulenc to have written it since Brain was not a friend – a fact underlined by the misspelling of his first name in the published score. For analysts, it has marginal interest in beginning with a twelve-note row on solo horn, a similar though barely related one appearing soon afterwards on piano and a third one on horn ending the piece. But none of these three rows is incorporated into the body of the work, which sets angular repeated notes against the pulsing pairs of quavers, and suave tonality against brutal dissonance. Wilfrid Mellers is alone in finding justification beyond the music itself, claiming that 'it makes sense if the tone row "stands for" the immutable will of God which, since the work is not serially constructed, has a merely arbitrary connection with human destiny. The horn-song is Poulenc's quasi-vocal response to God's all-too-mysterious way, in which we as mourners may join vicariously.'[26] Whether Poulenc himself would have agreed over the will of God having 'a merely arbitrary connection with human destiny' is, of course, another matter.

In January 1958 Poulenc was mainly concerned with the British premiere of *Carmélites* at Covent Garden on the 16th in Wallmann's production and Wakhévitch's sets, though he also squeezed in some broadcasts and performances, including the Two-Piano Concerto with Jacques Février on the 5th. As always, Poulence was assiduous in attending rehearsals. Sir Humphrey Burton remembers a post-rehearsal conversation between the composer and Joan Sutherland, who was taking the role of Second Prioress. Poulenc launched at once on a cascade of admiring comments – 'vunderfool tone, superbe bress contrôle' – to which the diva replied, 'Oh, d'you think so? I've got the most frightful cold.' It was, as Burton remarks, a clash of two cultures – and an entirely honest one on both sides.[27] Poulenc was probably unaware that his opera had arrived in the midst of some disarray in the house. Although morale should have been high following the sensational performances, uncut, of Berlioz's *Les Troyens* the previous summer, Sir Thomas Beecham's grumbles about the preference for foreign conductors found some support and Rafael Kubelík, the house's music director who was conducting *Carmélites*, took these diatribes very much to heart. Within the house, though, Kubelík was popular: 'We learned so much from Kubelík,' said stage manager Elizabeth Latham. 'He was one of the few gentlemen that ever entered the theatre [. . .] I don't think he was right for Covent Garden – he was too nice.' On the musical front Elsie Morison who was singing Blanche, and who would marry Kubelík after the death of his first wife, remembered that 'he understood singers, he breathed with you',[28] while Sir John Tooley, then assistant director of the house, wrote later that 'It was Kubelík who really taught the orchestra to play with love and humanity.'[29] It is hardly surprising that such a man would appeal to Poulenc, especially as conductor of this particular opera: 'Composer Poulenc exclaimed between acts: "Kubelík is very, very wonderful. He is the finest living exponent of my work." '[30]

Critical reaction was mixed. Complaints were of tedium, stunted motivic development, false spirituality, unrelieved gloom, lack of characterization, through some of which a Protestant tone is discernible. We don't know how much of this Poulenc read, but he would have been more concerned about complaints that much of Joseph Machlis's English translation was inaudible, since he always insisted that the work be performed in the language of the host country. The most understanding review, and the most long-sighted in the context of the opera's future career, came from Peter Heyworth, whose article ended, 'In the final resort it is Poulenc's very restraint and scrupulousness that carry the day. There is no shadow of false rhetoric, dramatic attitudinising or exploitation of religious sentiment. Everything about the score rings true and that is perhaps why in the end the opera as a whole carries a conviction that far exceeds that of its parts. It is an honest work through and through.'[31]

It might have been expected that, as he had followed the Milan premiere with the Flute Sonata, he might now similarly turn to something cheerful – Sir John

Tooley recalls that theatre staff had to go round after a performance cheering everybody up.[32] Instead, as already noted, Poulenc followed up on the idea of a work for solo soprano and orchestra, and for his text chose Jean Cocteau's monologue *La Voix humaine*, first staged by the actress Berthe Bovy at the Comédie-Française in 1930. The story, quite simply that of a woman on the telephone to her ex-lover the day before he marries someone else, and suffering the nuances of anguish one might expect, could have suited the Callas of *Medea* or *Tosca* had the text been overtly dramatic. But Callas's name is never mentioned again, Poulenc immediately recognizing that the clipped, conversational style of Cocteau's writing would not suit her in the slightest. In any case, after *Carmélites* he knew what Duval could do in the way of subtle emotions, added to which she was on hand in Paris to advise during the compositional process, together with her singing teacher Janine Reiss: 'Each day Poulenc would bring one or two new pages of his score, with the ink barely dry, and immediately Janine and I would launch ourselves upon them. We worked on detail after detail, Poulenc staying to listen to us. Sometimes I would ask him to change a note or a phrase to make it fit my voice more perfectly.'[33] This cannot have happened exactly in the way she says, since the last page of the score bears the legend 'Février–Juin 1958, Cannes, Saint Raphaël, Noizay', but Reiss's 2013 memoir gives a lively account of their sessions: at one point Poulenc says one phrase sounds 'un peu dur à mon avis' [a bit harsh in my opinion], to which Duval replies, 'il est un peu dur parce qu'il est trop aigu' [it's a bit harsh because it's too high], and Poulenc duly transposes it down a third.[34]

Influences throughout operatic history have been cited on the work's musical style, from (again) the *seconda prattica* of Monteverdi, the word setting of Lully (likewise based on that of an actress), Gluck's reforms ('I thought I would restrict the music to its true function of serving the poetry in the expressions and situations of the story, without interrupting the action or chilling it with superfluous ornaments'),[35] and not least Debussy's *Pelléas et Mélisande*. The essential simplicity of Poulenc's drama can also be measured through its distance on every level except its subject from Schoenberg's monodrama *Erwartung*. This simplicity is most especially audible in the vocal lines and in the overall texture and syntax. Mostly the vocal line consists of repeated notes and small intervals, no more than a dozen of these altogether exceeding a perfect fifth. On the textural front, of the work's 780 bars no fewer than 186 are for solo voice entirely unaccompanied,[36] often containing tiny phrases with pauses between. Here Poulenc was possibly responding to the complaints in the British press mentioned above that much of the English text of *Carmélites* was inaudible. But over his syntax, of bars instantly repeated not merely one but twice or three times, he faced out complaints from the same source, citing *Pelléas* as a model (a model likewise contested in its time by critics): 'The orchestration, which is still more subtle than in *Carmélites*, permits this style through its varied colouring.'[37]

The size of Poulenc's orchestra lies between that of *Carmélites* and a chamber ensemble, with two horns instead of four and one trombone instead of three, as well as a much reduced percussion section of timpani, cymbals, tambourine, and xylophone for the telephone. He handles it too with extreme restraint, full orchestra being used only for short climaxes or at pianissimo level. This restraint mirrors that of the singer, known simply as 'Elle'. An affecting example is found at fig. 104 where the full orchestra pianissimo accompanies Elle, singing on a monotone *sans nuances*, as she pleads with her old lover not to take his new wife 'to the hotel where we used to go'. Here briefly the orchestra expresses the passion she dare not, their tune on octave strings 'très tendre', the whole passage 'extraordinairement doux et sensuel', while the pulsing off-beat chords on woodwind take us back to Massenet, and indeed to Debussy's *Faune*.[38] Having a rich orchestral sound to call on when he needed it, Poulenc was able to cut and abbreviate phases of Cocteau's text and allow the orchestra to take some of the emotional weight, though never at length. As Denis Waleckx points out, 'In general, Poulenc has tried to lighten the touch, cutting passages where the heroine's grief, verging on the paroxysmal, causes her to behave implausibly neurotically.'[39]

By the end of March 1958 Poulenc, in his favourite room at the Hôtel Majestic in Cannes, had completed not only the whole sketch of *La Voix humaine* but two more *Improvisations* (nos. 13 and 14) and a tiny song, *Une Chanson de porcelaine*, his last setting of Éluard and a present for Jane Bathori on her eightieth birthday. Marked 'Andante semplice', it begins with an almost complete cycle of fifths in the bass – a signal of harmonic control wickedly undermined by the unexpected, mysterious piano G on which the song ends. But despite the fine London performances of *Carmélites*, his promising work on *La Voix humaine* and the offices of his Chinese acupuncturist, Poulenc was still 'terribly nervous'.[40]

For Easter in early April he moved to St Raphaël, some twenty-five kilometres west of Cannes, close to where Louis was building himself a house at Bagnols-en-Forêt. From here he wrote to Bernac. He has turned down an invitation from

Britten to accompany a performance of *Mamelles* at Aldeburgh on 13 June, citing his fear of the sea, and claiming he was far happier in the mountains. His Chinese acupuncturist has had an excellent effect on him and he accepts that there's nothing physically wrong with him, that all his troubles are in the mind. He is also being treated by Dr Louis Chevalier who 'knows perfectly well that this began with doubts about my career. What people have often praised as my charming modesty is basically no more than an inferiority complex that has now taken a pathological turn.' Most alarming of all is 'the *total* absence of my faith at Mass this morning'.[41] A number of unpublished letters to Dr Chevalier over the next three years catalogue Poulenc's continuing nervous problems, notably including doubts whether his creative gifts were waning. One could possibly read these doubts into the apparently illogical last seven bars of the fourteenth *Improvisation*, where three bars of Stravinskyan tonal dissonance are followed by three more in octaves of almost twelve-note writing (in fact eleven, with only E flat missing), ending with one of his favourite dismissive sign-offs. But he kept these worries from all but a select few, and certainly the staff and audiences at Covent Garden would have had no idea that in January he had been 'dragging his ghost' round London. Chevalier thought travel would help his neuroses, but Poulenc was in fact dealing with the world through a fog of barbiturates and tranquillizers.[42]

In April he was in Lisbon for the Portuguese premiere of *Carmélites*, which went well like most of the premieres he visited, then he returned to Noizay. Apart from the first song recital by him and Duval on 15 May in Bordeaux ('the team lost its virginity', as he put it),[43] he spent May on *La Voix humaine*, completing the first draft on 2 June.[44] On the 13th, the day of the Aldeburgh performance of *Mamelles* with Peter Pears as the Husband, he wrote to Britten again apologizing for his defection but, according to Sir Charles Mackerras who conducted, it came off very well. In Poulenc's absence, Britten and Viola Tunnard played from annotated orchestral scores. (Mackerras later wrote that 'in all probability there is no two-piano version by Poulenc. [. . .] I remember that Britten was rather chary about adding pianistic flourishes to the basic orchestral score, which probably Poulenc himself would have done with that typical charm which is so evident in his music.')[45]

Whatever fears Poulenc may have felt over sea journeys, he did brave the Channel a few days later in order to reach Oxford where he was made a Doctor of Music on 25 June. Recounting the occasion later to Stéphane Audel, he had them both in stitches looking over the photos of him 'draped in the sacramental robe with broad moire facings and topped with a kind of royal cake' (see Plate 28). But

Audel had not seen him for years in such good form[46] and the impression he made on Oxford was of extreme good nature. Others being honoured at the Encaenia in the Sheldonian Theatre included the Prime Minister, Harold Macmillan, Lord Beveridge, Hugh Gaitskell and, also as a Doctor of Music, Shostakovich, closely shadowed by a couple of minders. The address by the Public Orator, T. F. Higham, spoke of Poulenc's dignity and majesty, as evinced 'in the cantata on France under German Occupation; or in his church music in which, as we expect of a Frenchman, he is able to mix fun and seriousness. [. . .] And he always appears, as is often the case with men of genius, to be younger than his years.'[47]

Poulenc was staying with Professor Hugh Trevor-Roper and his wife and on the evening before the ceremony a concert was arranged of songs and cello music by the two composers. A letter from Isaiah Berlin gives a graphic account of the occasion. After Shostakovich had 'immediately made for the nearest corner and sat there, contracted like a hedgehog', his Cello Sonata was played by the nineteen-year-old Rohan de Saram. The composer praised his playing, but pointed out that he had played two passages incorrectly; it turned out that the score had been 'edited' by Gregor Piatigorsky – cue the first sign of the emotional Shostakovich! 'Songs by Poulenc were then sung by Miss Margaret Ritchie, absurdly, in the ludicrous Victorian English fashion. Shostakovich writhed slightly, but Poulenc, very polite, very *mondain*, congratulated her and made grimaces to others behind her back. After this a movement [the slow movement] of Poulenc's Cello Sonata was played, to placate him.' Shostakovich, asked to play the piano, chose one of his recent Preludes and Fugues and played 'with such magnificence, such depth and passion, the work itself was so marvellous, so serious and so original and unforgettable, that everything by Poulenc flew through the window and could not be recaptured. [. . .] Poulenc, although looked after nicely, felt somewhat relegated, rather like Cocteau when Picasso is about.'[48] In fairness to Poulenc, and perhaps to French music in general, it may be noted that it was Berlin who, as a member of the Covent Garden board, had urged that 'a revival of an opera by Vivaldi would rivet international attention in a way in which *The Trojans* would not'.[49]

Rehearsal with de Saram, who had never seen the sonata before, went like clockwork. 'The one thing I do remember very, very clearly when playing with Poulenc was the extraordinary transparency and yet fullness of tone, not a pinched tone at all. One felt he was continually listening to what he was doing, and his tone was so transparent you felt you could do anything – it was wonderful. [. . .] And the style of the music, it communicated immediately, so there was hardly anything we worked at, as such.' Poulenc inscribed de Saram's score 'En souvenir de notre sonate'.[50]

❧

After all the travelling to premieres of *Carmélites* and the swift but taxing composition of *La Voix humaine*, Poulenc completed no new works until March 1959. The piano score of *La Voix* was finished on 7 August (1958) and he then took from 25 August to 19 September to orchestrate it. From 22 September to 21 October he was in the Villa d'Este on Lake Como as part of a jury arranged by the publishers Ricordi to find a new opera for La Scala, but after slogging through well over one hundred scores, 'mostly of a revolting amateurism', no prize was awarded. More to his taste was the first performance of Stravinsky's *Threni* in Venice the day after his arrival in Italy, which he found 'austere but real Stravinsky. Alas, he conducted very badly'. Although he thought the result 'very moving despite everything', this was not the general view, and certainly not of 'the horrible Goléa', who shouted 'it's not a concert, it's a cemetery'.[51] The same letter to Bernac rejoices in a forthcoming visit to Barcelona on 8 November for a performance of the *Stabat Mater* ('air fare and Ritz paid for!!!') and enthuses over Callas's new recording of Cherubini's *Medea*. Otherwise the last months of the year were quiet, overcast only by two deaths: of Duval's husband, and of Marcelle Meyer, Poulenc's partner in the wonderful 1955 recording of Chabrier's *Valses romantiques*.

Much of the first four months of 1959 was spent at performances of *Carmélites* throughout Europe (see list above, p. 253). The procession started badly at the end of January with a 'shabby performance' and 'wretched orchestra' in Barcelona,[52] Poulenc's mood not improved by weathering the arrival on the 7th of his sixtieth birthday. In any case his attention was focused on the premiere of *La Voix humaine* at the Opéra-Comique on 6 February, conducted by Georges Prêtre. Cocteau was not in good health, so Poulenc and Duval had gone down to Nice in early January to work on the production, and made another journey at the end of the month to put every detail in place. Poulenc, astonished at Cocteau's musical perception, surmised that 'I needed the experience of the metaphysical and spiritual anguish of *Dialogues des Carmélites* not to betray the terribly human anguish of Jean Cocteau's superb text'.[53] At the premiere Poulenc's opera was preceded by Messager's *Isoline*, condemned by one critic as a 'monstrous concoction of ugliness and stupidity',[54] but *La Voix* was a triumph: Milhaud congratulated Poulenc on 'winning 100% a wager that seemed impossible',[55] and even the 'horrible Goléa' was moved to write 'it could well be that this was Poulenc's masterpiece, and the most moving opera given in Paris these last years'.[56] 'But nothing could have given me more pleasure,' the composer admitted, 'than what [Cocteau] said: "My dear Francis, you have fixed, once and for all, the way in which my text should be spoken." '[57]

In April, a mere two months after the premiere, *La Voix* was recorded. The conductor Georges Prêtre recalled that during one of the rehearsals Poulenc's high, nasal voice was heard to insist 'je veux mes silences', and gently Prêtre had to explain to him that on record these could not afford to be so protracted. Felicity Lott, who has sung the role many times, remembers, 'it was so important for me that the pauses were the right length for me to sustain the emotion. If they were too long, everything kind of sank, and if they were too short, then it was impossible to make the emotional change in time.'[58] When Prêtre had also changed an orchestral nuance, he was relieved to see Poulenc coming down towards the orchestra with the brim of his hat turned up. Turned down meant gloom all round . . . After that, Poulenc only came to Prêtre's recordings for the champagne when they were all over.[59]

The downside to success was the old fear that he would never write anything so good again – something all composers have to deal with, though happily not with Poulenc's intensity. This made life hard for his close friends, Duval even 'fearing true insanity and suggesting some appropriate treatment such as electric shocks'.[60] Certainly his moods make for hard reading. But in the event his fears were, arguably, unrealized and at Cannes in March he wrote two more motets for male chorus, following two composed in July 1957 and June 1958, to form the four *Laudes de Saint Antoine de Padoue*. Curiously little is known about the genesis of these pieces: not the source of the texts, nor who they were written for (if they were), nor where or when they were first performed nor who by. Poulenc himself said and wrote nothing about them and their success has been widely doubted. Keith Daniel notes charitably that their writing, 'though still humble and introspective, is considerably more complicated [than that of the *Quatre petites prières* of 1948], with more dramatic melodic lines, more solo phrases, and a more unstable, complex harmonic style'.[61] Lacombe goes further, lamenting that 'the charm of his music is reduced without the new roughness achieving true grandeur or a persuasive directness of expression. The believer and the composer seem to be on the edge of a void.'[62]

The previous August Poulenc had written to Marie-Ange that he now wanted to write a cheerful opera to make her laugh.[63] While the texts of the *Laudes* are entirely upbeat ('Praise the Lord with a full heart', 'O most excellent Anthony', 'Dangers cease, want is no more'), the constraint of a male chorus here seems to prevent that expansion of the heart which blesses moments even in the *Stabat Mater*. In short, did Poulenc simply need an orchestra that he could treat cheerfully after its serious purposes in *Carmelites* and *La Voix*? Briefly he thought of setting Cocteau's *La Machine infernale*, a version of the Oedipus legend, telling Milhaud, 'I like its sarcasm and its picture of the old Jocasta',[64] but a month later admitted to Dugardin his fear that it was 'too literary'.[65] In any case, despite the comic elements in the first half of the play (Jocasta calls Tiresias 'Zizi' and blames him for everything that goes wrong, even for the palace staircases which, she's sure, are conspiring to trip her up), Tiresias is the blind old seer of Sophocles's *Oedipus Rex*, not the gender-bending personage of *Les Mamelles*, and the play ends as usual: Jocasta strangles herself with her scarf, Oedipus scratches out his eyes with the pin of her brooch. Not many jokes there.

Like Puccini before him, Poulenc remained, for the last four years of his life, on a quest for librettos – sadly, without success. But whatever the shortcomings of the *Laudes*, they had at least brought him once more into contact with Latin, and this was to be the language of his two last major choral works. The genesis of the *Gloria*, according to him, went back some four years to when he was finishing *Carmélites*, although precise dating is hard to establish. On 18 April he wrote from Bagnols-en-Forêt to Bernard Gavoty, 'I'm back at work, I've just begun a *Gloria* for chorus, soloist and orchestra in the Vivaldi style (words repeated *ad lib*). The use of Latin allows this macaronic arrangement.'[66] By this he presumably implied that he would not have been prepared to treat French in the same way, as Stravinsky had done in *Perséphone* to the horror of his librettist André Gide. Before this, the Koussevitzky Foundation had asked Poulenc for a symphony ('not my sort of thing'), then an organ concerto ('already done') and finally, on 7 July 1959, a composition of his own choosing for which the Advisory Board had approved a commission in the sum of $2,000.[67] Poulenc replied on 3 August that he had already begun the *Gloria*. It was therefore in only a rather loose sense a Koussevitzky commission.

The utterly joyful atmosphere of the *Gloria*, and its instant and lasting success, might suggest that now Poulenc had conquered his demons. Once more, not so. A letter to Dr Chevalier of 28 April admitted, 'what worries me profoundly is my work, which I have such need of *from all points of view*'. If this need is nothing unusual in the creative artist, more serious was 'a kind of laziness which soon drives me away from my piano [. . .] What I fail to understand is this fear of Paris, where I was born, where I have lived happily. Nothing there interests me any more (except the theatre). The society I used to enjoy bores me to tears and I never feel so lonely as in the rue de Médicis, in spite of the wonderful view. Luckily I can fall back on Noizay, *as the least worst*.'[68] Some weeks later he was realistic enough to write 'Enough misery and suffering. One has to say that, from the *Stabat* to *La Voix*, there haven't been any laughs.'[69] The *Gloria* then was to some extent a deliberate choice to cheer himself up, aided in this by an *Élégie* for two pianos, 'très Chabrier', written for Gold and Fizdale and dedicated to the memory of Marie-Blanche[70] – though the mention of Chabrier may also have been stirred by the death of Marcelle Meyer.

Poulenc's detailed comments on the progress of the *Gloria* show, as plainly as in any other of his works, the care he took over balance and structure. Possibly in no other piece of his has hard graft so obviously been the cause of easy listening, a phrase that in no way entails the superficial, despite Benjamin Ivry's claim that 'One can see why *Gloria* became instantly popular in Eisenhower's America: its sunny air was like the aftermath of a perfect tranquilliser' and his reference to 'The sedative quality to this pretty music'.[71] Nearer the mark is Richard Burton's observation that 'More than any other piece [by Poulenc] the *Gloria* fuses, rather than oscillates between, the *moine* and the *voyou*' and that 'no other modern Catholic music so uninhibitedly "[dances] before the Lord with all [its] might" – II Samuel: 6,14'.[72] Vivaldi's influence may not seem to have amounted to much: the rhythm of the phrase 'Laudamus te', female solos for the two 'Domine Deus' movements, Vivaldi's 'molto energico e ritmico' for 'Domine fili' (in Poulenc 'très vite et joyeux') and a reference towards the end of each work to its opening bars – in Poulenc's case loud, dramatic chords going back, through his piano 'Hymne' of 1928, to Stravinsky's *Serenade in A*. But it was obviously enough to get Poulenc started. Deep analysis of such an openly joyous work is barely justifiable. Perhaps the most important point to make is that it clings more nearly to tonality than either *Carmélites*, *La Voix humaine* or his final choral piece, *Sept Répons des ténèbres*: the second movement of the six, 'Laudamus te', beginning with twenty-one bars in C major and the fourth, 'Domine fili', with twenty in G major, all without accidentals. It hardly needs stressing how few composers can, like Poulenc, write singable, memorable, utterly characteristic music under such constraints. What he called the 'macaronic arrangement' does not in fact stretch syntax unduly, the boldest move being the 'Lauda . . . Lauda . . . Laudamus te' with which the second movement ends. Undoubtedly he borrowed this from Chabrier's 'Donnez-vous la . . . donnez-vous la . . . donnez-vous la peine de vous asseoir' in *L'Étoile*, itself borrowed, as Poulenc admits in his Chabrier biography, from Agamemnon's 'Le roi barbu qui s'avance, -bu qui s'avance, -bu qui s'avance' in Offenbach's *La belle Hélène*.[73]

Otherwise singularity is found only in some of the accentuation, such as the stressing of final syllables in 'Glori*a* in excels*is* De*o*', reflecting French practice, and especially in 'B*e*nedicim*u*s te', which must have put some Latinists seriously out of temper. But this latter treatment fits perfectly the 'très vif et joyeux' tone of the second movement, inspired according to the composer by the sight of footballing monks and Benozzo Gozzoli's frescos of carolling angels supposedly 'sticking their tongues out'[74] – in fact they don't, but in the circumstances we may allow Poulenc some artistic licence. But he *had* seen monks playing football.

There are, as usual with Poulenc, any number of self-quotations: the haunting phrase 'Pater omnipotens' that occurs four times in the third movement, 'Domine Deus', is taken from the middle movement of the wind trio of 1926. But the most curious borrowing, at least at first hearing, is the orchestral one at the end of the fifth movement, 'Domine Deus', from Verdi's *Otello* at the point where Iago finishes his narration of Cassio's dream. But in fact it's not so surprising. The moments of ecstasy, and notably the magical closing bars, are largely the domain of the soprano soloist – for whom Poulenc wanted one like Desdemona with 'a warm top to the voice but pianissimo'.[75]

Meanwhile other concerns were occupying him. On 27 May he and Bernac, with others, enjoyed a late celebration in the Salle Gaveau of Poulenc's sixtieth birthday. It was also the last time singer and accompanist worked together. Three days later Poulenc left for Vienna and the Austrian premiere of *Carmélites*, 'impeccable' with ten further performances in this run and fourteen more in view for the next.[76] In June he was in Brive composing a delightful third *Novellette*, based on a theme from Falla's *El Amor brujo* whose conjunct intervals chimed with his own preference, even if he regularized Falla's 7/8 metre into 3/8 (surprisingly, for Poulenc, maintained throughout). He also came back to his Bassoon Sonata, never completed. Then at Rocamadour in July he finished what he called the 'lamento' of a Clarinet Sonata, presumably the middle movement finally entitled 'Romanza', in which he borrowed a couple of fast upward scales from the 'Domine Deus' of the *Gloria*. As usual at this time of year he spent a fortnight with his sister at Le Tremblay before heading south to Bagnols and Louis, where he stayed until 1 September.

No important works were on the stocks for the remainder of the year, and the three short pieces he did compose all, like the *Novellette*, took their cheerful, relaxed tone to some extent from the *Gloria*. The song *Fancy*, a setting of 'Tell me where is fancy bred' from *The Merchant of Venice*, was commissioned by Marion Harewood for the volume *Classical Songs for Children*, edited by her and Ronald Duncan in 1962. In his letter to Bernac of 4 August [1959], Poulenc included an early version of the first four lines of the poem, immeasurably improved in the final one, and also asked Bernac's advice on accentuation. It's a pretty song, but it's a shame he didn't consult one of his many English-speaking friends, as the printed version does contain three doubtful stresses – all the more if we recall him rounding on Ned Rorem when the latter 'proudly showed him a setting of Ronsard, "Stick to American and leave French to us." '[77] He was on safer ground with the fifteenth and final *Improvisation*, dedicated to Edith Piaf, in which the strains of the *café concert* are decorated with elegant, chromatic harmonies, the underlying heartache in so many of Piaf's songs expressed through a struggle between major and minor. Minor wins . . . just. The last of the three works, the *Élégie* for two pianos, 'très Chabrier' as already mentioned, is a homage to the *Valses romantiques*, and little more needs to be said of it other than the instructions in the printed copy: 'This Elegy should be played as if you were improvising it, a cigar in your mouth and a glass of cognac on the piano. The syncopated notes (a kind of echo of the preceding chord) should barely be touched in. Overall you can never use too much pedal.' Although it is dedicated to the memory of Marie-Blanche, who had died in February 1958, the more recent death of Wanda Landowska on 16 August 1959 may also have contributed to the piece's intimate, elegiac tone.

The period of six months between finishing this piece by 28 September and writing the *Sarabande* for guitar the following March was one of Poulenc's longest fallow periods as a composer, even if he did work on orchestrating the *Gloria*, a task not completed until July 1960. Instead of composing, in November he started to write what would be his only book, a biography of Chabrier. What provoked this we do not know, other than his lifelong enthusiasm for Chabrier's music and the extraordinary fact that, over sixty years after the composer's death, although there were articles about him galore, there was still only one biography of him in any language (by René Martineau as long ago as 1910). He finished it at speed, telling Bernac at some point in December that 'the Chabrier book has been copied out. I think it's very lively, as if I'd known him.'[78]

Early in December he was in Milan to hear Renata Tebaldi, Mario del Monaco, Giuseppe di Stefano and Tito Gobbi in *Otello* and *Tosca*,[79] and returned to be greeted by a commission from Leonard Bernstein, musical director of the New York Philharmonic, to write a work for the inaugural season of the Philharmonic Hall at Lincoln Center in 1961–2. Poulenc had by now agreed to make a fourth American tour in February, this time with Duval and Prêtre, when this offer could be discussed. It would be his last choral work, the *Sept Répons des ténèbres*.

On the emotional front the decade was closing better than might have been expected. On 16 October he wrote to Rose Dercourt-Plaut, 'If I was really sensible, although my boy of the Midi is very handsome and very sweet, I would send all that packing, but now my 60 years can find pleasure in the 30 that have been difficult [. . .] Since I was 25, love has always made me suffer because I ask too much of people. As it is, 75% of boys would be thrilled by my situation. In my gloomy moments the thought of Raymond is the only thing that comforts me because he, truly, cares for me.'[80] A few weeks later though, his 'boy of the Midi' comes in for warmer approval in a letter from Bagnols: 'All's well here, where we live quite calmly with a bit of love . . . *conjugal* which is better.' Louis's completed house was a success, with room for Poulenc and an atmosphere in which he could work, even if it seems the neighbours may have complained about the noise of his piano.[81]

His sixtieth year was crowned with particular happiness in the form of a book: Sylvia Beach's *Shakespeare and Company*, dedicated to Adrienne Monnier. It contains a chapter on Raymonde.

The 1960s started less well, with flu and liver trouble, but right from his arrival in New York via Air France on 18 February everything fell into place, with warm greetings from friends and triumphant concerts. Over the four weeks between then and his return to France on 20 March the focus was on *La Voix humaine*, in which of course Duval's mastery was lauded from New York to Philadelphia, Chicago, Detroit and Washington. Poulenc, whose friendship with Virgil Thomson was tinged with respect for his critical acumen, was especially delighted by his claim that it was the greatest French musical success for years.[82] The award of the New York University Medal confirmed this. In the midst of all the concertizing and socializing, he just found time to write a tiny *Sarabande* for guitar, and we must assume there were also talks about Bernstein's commission, the *Sept Répons*, though only briefly mentioned at the time in Poulenc's known correspondence. He also took the opportunity to set American audiences straight on a number of points:

'Don't make me out to be a neo-classicist,' he said. 'I write as I want, as it comes to me. Some composers *innovent*, but some great composers do not *innovent*. Schubert did not *innove*. Wagner, Monteverdi, they *innovent*. Debussy *innove*; Ravel does not *innove*. It is not necessary that one *innove*. I am not against, you understand. Today there is the electronic music. Some I like, what I have heard. The *musique concrète* I do not like; it is *sale*. Music made with 'Teen pote'. 'Teen pote!' He went into a recess of the apartment and emerged with a small saucepan on which he hammered redoubtably with a spoon. 'Teen pote,' he said.[83]

On his return to France he wrote short articles for Ricordi's *Enciclopedia della musica* on Chabrier, Ravel, Satie and Massenet. While his views on the first three have been mentioned above, Massenet is not a name that figures importantly in Poulenc's writings or talks. His article expresses reservations – on the feebleness of Massenet's early operas and the flabbiness of his late ones – with praise for *Manon*, *Thaïs* and *Werther*. But his highest encomium is for Massenet's 'innate sense of prosody which makes everything that's sung perfectly intelligible',[84] a lesson, as we have seen, well taken by Poulenc himself. Apart from a brief visit to Rome for a concert on 5 May, he was mostly engaged in orchestrating the *Gloria* which, it is as well to report, was not completed until July, so certainly not dashed off. On 21 June he made his last recording with Bernac, of *Banalités*, *Tel jour telle nuit*, *Calligrammes* and *Le Travail du peintre*,[85] and in July was over the moon about the first performance at the Aix Festival of *La Voix* (Duval and Prêtre in Cocteau's production). This prompted him to think of a possible revival and recording of *Les Animaux modèles*, reminding Prêtre of the score he had given him eighteen months earlier, inscribed 'For Georges Prêtre, these animals all ready to form up under his baton'.[86]

That July he also began two works of antithetical character: the delightful 'chansons pour enfants', *La Courte Paille*, and what at this stage he referred to as the *Office des ténèbres* ('not without terror [. . .] May the Holy Virgin ensure that I succeed with this ambitious task!!!').[87] The Belgian writer Maurice Carême was a schoolteacher for many years and his poems for children testify to his happy familiarity with the infant mind. As he had done with Éluard, Poulenc asked the poet for a title to the cycle of seven songs, for which he balanced three patter songs and a complaining one against three in his most seductive, melancholy vein. Despite the above description 'chansons pour enfants', in fact he wrote them for Denise Duval to sing to her six-year-old son Richard, explaining that 'these sketches, alternately melancholic and witty, are without pretention. They need to be sung tenderly. It's the surest way to children's hearts.'[88] Carême's title, literally 'The Short Straw', doesn't indicate bad luck: merely a drawing of lots, or in this case a relaxed attitude in both performers and listeners.

'La Reine de coeur' (the Queen of Hearts) is Poulenc's own title for the third song, while 'Ba, be, bi, bo, bu' is, or was, the standard way of teaching young French children their pure vowels. What else can angels sing on Thursdays but Mozart? Unpretentious this music may be, but Poulenc the professional, wanting his legato in the left hand, insists on a particular fingering with fingers changing on notes organist-fashion. The final 'Lune d'Avril', 'très lent et irréel', looks back to the epilogue of *Babar* in its apparently effortless, seductive beauty: thirty-eight bars of which thirty-three are over a pedal C.[89] Simple too is the vocal line. As in *La Voix*, it moves conjunctly or in small intervals, with just one marvellous climax on a top G as the sunny landscape bedecked in primulas suddenly comes into view. The songs are dedicated to Duval and Richard and she owned the manuscript bearing the inscription 'To the sun of my heart/and of my music/to Denise/tenderly/Poupoule/60.' But, sadly for Poulenc, she never sang these songs. As she told Renaud Machart, she 'liked them but they didn't suit her from the point of view of vocal expressiveness'.[90] In any case it was surprising that Poulenc should have written them at all, given what he had said to an American interviewer a short time before about his songwriting:

'I'm too old,' he said, 'besides, Apollinaire, Éluard, Jacob are all dead – I was an intimate friend of all three – and somehow I understood their poetry extremely well. I was able to read between the lines of their poems; I was able to express in musical terms all that was left unsaid. Today poets do not write in a manner that inspires me to song. I once told the young French composer Boulez that I was too old for René Char and he was too young for Éluard. But aside from all that, I have written well over 100 songs and to write more would be to force myself in a direction in which I really have nothing further to say.'[91]

Hervé Lacombe informs us that the first performance of *La Courte Paille* was not given until 1 July 1962, by Colette Herzog and Claude Helffer.[92]

Another period mostly away from composing now followed, until he began *La Dame de Monte-Carlo* in April 1961. On 7 September he listened on the radio to the direct transmission of the French premiere of Dutilleux's Second Symphony, and next day sent him a telegram: 'Bravo de tout coeur. Raffinement orchestral exquis. Affections.'[93] At the end of the month he was again to serve on the Ricordi jury by Lake Como, and again the twelve one-act operas sent to him for study 'are not masterpieces'.[94] He was still working on his Chabrier biography, buying sixty-five unpublished letters and other mementos from a member of Chabrier's family, having stretched the deadline,[95] but his only composition, dated 9 November and dedicated to the memory of Raoul Dufy, was *La Puce*, a song on one of Apollinaire's poems from *Le Bestiaire*. Was this, like *Le Serpent*, a new song, or a revision of the original setting he had removed from his cycle on Auric's advice? There is no way of knowing for certain, and we are all at liberty to listen and judge, though the dissonance on which the piano epilogue ends may favour a revision.

In the run-up to Christmas he was in Rome, giving concerts and serving on the Santa Cecilia jury, but he was also planning his fifth and final American tour at the beginning of 1961. The main item would be the premiere of the *Gloria*, to which, after much negotiating, was added a performance of the Two-Piano Concerto. As Carl Schmidt records, 'In late November he learned that Evelyne Crochet, winner of the 1958 Tchaikovsky Competition, would play the second piano part so the Concerto "situation" was settled'[96] – the situation being Février's unavailability through illness, or possibly a clashing date. Accounts vary.

Poulenc flew into New York on 13 January and then travelled to Boston on the 15th to rehearse for the two identical concerts – originally scheduled for the following Friday and Saturday, but the Friday one had to be cancelled because of snow. The premiere of the *Gloria* with soprano Adèle Addison therefore took place on Saturday 21st. Poulenc's first experience of Charles Münch's conducting of the work had provoked him on the 17th to write, 'Arriving late at the first choir rehearsal, I heard something that was so far from being me that my legs gave way under me on the stairs. The choir is excellent but [Alfred Nash] Patterson [the choirmaster] is not Shaw-the-intuitive and these fine Protestants were making a shrill sound (especially the women) as they do in London, with an "Oh! my good Lord" tinge to it. [. . .] I didn't say anything till the interval, then I explained it all. Mr Patterson, hearing me sing, said, "Ah! it has to be sung like Maurice Chevalier." Exactly!'[97] Rehearsals continued with growing enthusiasm and the day after the Sunday performance Poulenc could write to Bernac:

> The Saturday performance went ahead. Very good, very fine, a success, but Münch less inspired than at the final rehearsal. Yesterday on the other hand (the critics were there) a *sublime* performance. Charlie [Münch] carried away but controlled, the choir incredible, Addison beyond belief, with ovation after ovation. I'm told today the press is excellent. [. . .] I'm *thrilled* because the public here are terrible, they *give out marks.*[98]

Replacing Février in the concerto was a red-letter day for the twenty-six-year-old Evelyne Crochet, as she remembers:

> I had less than three weeks to learn the concerto but when you're in your twenties, this is no problem. I knew it from memory when Poulenc arrived the week before the concerts. He was surprised and his famous wit showed immediately when he declared he had to practise to level with my playing. He was not secure with his memory and asked that we play the work from the score. Our rehearsals were full of good cheer, and he said he was reassured that it was so easy, because he actually told me he had not expected a young woman to be his partner. At the first concert, he was very excited to learn that Marlene Dietrich was in the audience and wanted me to spot her with 'my young eyes' through the backstage door. [. . .] He was a 'conteur'. He brought up our smiles and laughs and delighted all of us with many stories. [. . .] In his melodic music, he is also a 'conteur'.[99]

The mention of Crochet's 'young eyes' probably reflects trouble Poulenc had been having with his own, to add to those with his liver, his ears (after a flight) and of course his neuroses.

He then spent a week in New York, attending Leontyne Price's first performance in the city, with Franco Corelli in *Il Trovatore*, Laurence Olivier in Anouilh's

Becket, and recitals by Horowitz and Rubinstein.[100] After his return to Paris, his next important event was the French premiere of the *Gloria* on 14 February, with soprano Rosanna Carteri and a choir prepared by Yvonne Gouverné under the baton of Georges Prêtre. It is clear from Poulenc's 1962 talk at Les Trois Centres that he was undecided as to who was the ideal soprano for this work: Carteri, who had sung Blanche at the Naples and Catania premieres, had a tone he qualified as 'théâtral', which suited a work of brilliance; Adèle Addison, the soprano of the world premiere, one of 'extraordinary purity'; whereas Leontyne Price, whose *Trovatore* date at the Met prevented her from being considered, would later give a *Gloria* that was 'plus extérieur' than Addison's. Together they epitomized Poulenc's opinion, vouchsafed in the same talk, that the interpretation of any work had to move ('il faut que l'interprétation bouge'): one started, of course, with a scrupulous reading of the text, but then talent and personality began their work and a composer had to accept this, and indeed welcome it.

Prêtre's rendition of the *Gloria* was a success, but there were enough dissentient voices, especially over the unrestrained jollity of the 'Laudamus te', to worry the composer, and by early March his mood had sunk once more, necessitating treatment from Chevalier and the Chinese acupuncturist, and the reason was the same: not love any more – those problems at least were now in the past, even though there were regrets: for instance, that 'I have never slept with a Swiss. I regret it because it must be "clean" "very clean".'[101] Rather it was his reputation. Even Darius came in for a glancing blow:

> Not writing as much as Darius or others, it's vital for each one of my works to succeed, because I put all my energies into them. That's why, after the outright success of Boston (I'll show you the press clippings), Paris caused me maximum anxiety. Thank God people attached *importance* to this *Gloria*. I know perfectly well that I'm not fashionable, but I need to be 'recognized'. This has happened. Anyway I think that, in the future, I'll be played more than Barraqué or Pousseur [. . .] After all, my music is not that bad, even though sometimes I wonder why I go on, and for whom? [. . .] Do understand that I'm not jealous (there's room for everybody), but when I read that Messiaen and Jolivet are the two *important* composers, I question myself.[102]

It was just as well therefore that he never got to read a BBC memo about the *Gloria*, saying that those who had looked at the score were very chary of putting the BBC's resources at the disposal of a work which they truly believed could not do anything to enhance its composer's reputation. To them it seemed a curiously empty and unworthy way of treating words 'which are of great dignity, significance and familiarity'.[103] Those footballing Benedictines had a lot to answer for. In any case 'familiarity' was exactly what Poulenc was out to destroy, forcing us instead to hear the words with fresh ears.

But February brought two experiences of unalloyed happiness. Both he and Pathé-Marconi were delighted with Maurice Duruflé's recording of the Organ Concerto under Prêtre and no less with its companion, the *Gloria*, featuring the performers of the French premiere. Both recordings have rightly become iconic documents. Equally comforting was the reception given to his biography of Chabrier, published by La Palatine that February. The love inspired all those years ago by the recording of that composer's 'Idylle' had never left him. In 1947 the pianist Robert Casadesus, meeting Chabrier's daughter-in-law Mme Bretton-Chabrier, had been shown by her a number of unfinished manuscripts which he photographed; knowing Poulenc's affection for Chabrier, he showed these to him, but sadly both decided they were too fragmentary to be completed.[104] As to the value of the biography, a letter from the eighty-three-year-old Geneviève Sienkiewicz says it all, in words that must surely have banished any gloom:

> My dear Francis, I have just reread for the umpteenth time our *Chabrier* and there once again I find you, you, so alive, so characteristic, irreplaceable. It's exactly as though you were here, chatting, telling a story, remembering, loving and admiring without asking or borrowing anything from anyone. It's this 'striking' personality that will fix your place in French Music; keep it, guard it well. Three notes of Poulenc, three notes of Schubert, three notes of Mozart, three notes of Stravinsky, they're unmistakable. Not all are of the same value . . . of course there are semibreves, crotchets and semiquavers in all of them, as you know as well as I. Perfection is not human . . . and very tiresome that would be! But *originality*, that's what counts and what can't be had for the asking.[105]

Poulenc begins the book by explaining that its 'ton familier' suits the subject, whose music was 'at the same time so accessible and so lofty' and 'whose casualness is only skin-deep'. Noting Alfred Cortot's claim that Chabrier's late approach to musical technique left him fallible, Poulenc takes the line mentioned above concerning his own: 'If this pupil had been put in the hands of someone like Théodore Dubois, he would undoubtedly have acquired a feeling for ready-made formulas, but his inventiveness, his audacity would perhaps have been less marked.'[106]

In April Poulenc ended his six-month holiday from composition with a vengeance. *La Dame de Monte-Carlo*, a monologue for soprano and orchestra, 'is the story of an old female gambler at Monte-Carlo who throws herself into the sea after losing everything', so it's rather curious to read Poulenc saying, 'I needed this crazy piece to restore my taste for music.' However, the piece suggests a taste not so much for music as for death. Why he found it necessary to write it is unclear. The reason may simply have been one of desperation, since the same letter contains the admission, 'I'm in a period when I find *all* my music *dreadful* and I *must* work.'[107] He first read the monologue in a *Théâtre de poche* edition of Cocteau's collected plays in Cannes in late March, and not the least of the piece's appeal was its setting in Monte-Carlo which, as in *Les Mamelles*, held magic resonance for him. He never had much to say about the work, nor have subsequent commentators, perhaps because after *La Voix humaine* it seems somewhat supernumerary. Poulenc, though, justified it as reviving for him 'the years 1923–1925 when I lived in Monte-Carlo, with Auric, under the dominating shadow of Diaghilev'.[108] Richard Burton, always a voice of sanity and intelligence, suggests that 'once again, Poulenc has found the ideal female voice, sardonic, self-pitying and defiant, through which to express his own faintly absurd excess of melancholy'.[109] And once again Poulenc recognized that monotony was a major problem, which he aimed to solve by 'giving a different colour to each strophe of the text: melancholy, pride, lyricism, violence and sarcasm; finally unhappy love, anguish and a drop into the sea!' The orchestration too follows that of *La Voix*, plus 'a vibraphone, employed mechanically as in the music hall, a touch of castanets, and sound of the tam-tam at the end'.[110] In fact, according to a sheet inserted in the vocal score, after the Paris premiere on 5 December under Prêtre, Poulenc made corrections which included cutting the penultimate bar of the score, where the unaccompanied tam-tam stroke was to signify the woman's death – perhaps performance caused him to think this orchestral 'splash' too obvious. He also raised a number of low notes in the vocal line in passages where, as a recording of that premiere testifies,[111] Duval's words were slightly obscured by the orchestra.

In August Poulenc wrote to Bernac about his hopes over his reputation in America and a possible collaboration over a book on his songs: 'We shall perhaps manage to create, in America, a true Poulenc tradition. No question, it's there that I have my most receptive public, but it only needs a Teyte or a Frisch to screw everything up. I'm going to do the impossible and arrange for my book, our book, to be published over there with an introduction by Virgil [Thomson] instead of the letters, which will serve as preface in the [French] edition by Plon.'[112] In the event this book would be the *Journal de mes mélodies* written by Poulenc alone and published posthumously in French in 1964.

The Bernstein commission, which would become the *Sept Répons des ténèbres*, had been on the back burner for some time now, and a year later, Poulenc was to say to Bernac, 'I don't regret taking my time over it because it's composed with great care.'[113] This care also took the form of any number of false dawns, such as the admission in August, again to Bernac, that 'Yes, I had to start again from scratch and destroy pages that were *too pretty*. Basically I'm coming back to the austerity and violence I was looking for at the beginning.'[114] He spent most of May 1961 in Noizay with Richard Chanlaire and, after his restart in July, stayed at his desk most of the summer. By 2 October five of the seven movements were copied out and on 1 November Poulenc claimed the remaining two were done, with just the orchestration remaining. But the published score tells us that the work was not in fact complete until October 1962, and still in January 1963, the month of his death, he was correcting proofs.[115] One novelty of the work was that he wanted a boy soprano as soloist, with other boys joining the male chorus. 'It's very simple (because of the children),' he told Bernstein, 'but I think very moving, not at all decorative like the *Gloria* and entirely inward. It's penitence, but "poverty is not a vice" as we learn from Markévitch's *Rebus*.'[116]

Despite what some commentators have claimed, Poulenc added nothing whatever to the liturgical texts he chose from the *triduum* of Maundy Thursday, Good Friday and Holy Saturday. He set two from the Thursday, 'Una hora' and 'Judas mercator pessimus' (Responsories 8 and 5), three from the Friday, 'Jesum tradidit', 'Caligaverunt oculi mei' and 'Tenebrae factae sunt' (Responsories 8, 9 and 5), and two from the Saturday, 'Sepulto Domino' and 'Ecce quomodo' (Responsories 9 and 6). As can be seen from the numbering, he did allow himself to change the order of the texts from the liturgical one; he also repeated and intercalated phrases within the texts themselves according to his usual habit.

In July 1960 Poulenc had told Henri Hell of the definitive title of the work and explained what it would *not* be: that is, confined to Good Friday like Stravinsky's *Threni*.[117] Two months later he was admitting to Bernac that he found the project 'absorbing but terrifying' and that 'I have the impression of entering a tunnel'.[118] As often, he was greatly concerned with the 'colour' of the work, which began to change under his hand. In that same month he wrote again to Bernac that, with the first Response written, it was now 'more Mantegna than Zurbarán. It's not what I would have wanted, but too bad. It's either *superb* or too theatrical. Anyway it's "something".'[119] Biographers in general have, perhaps wisely, just accepted without comment this differentiation and Poulenc's further gloss that the two artists 'correspond in fact very precisely with my religious ideal: one with his mystic realism, the other with his ascetic purity which, even so, is not afraid sometimes to dress his saints like great ladies.'[120] From the dates of Mantegna (1431–1506) and Zurbarán (1598–1664) we may also conclude that the 'colour' had moved back in time from the Baroque to the Renaissance – whatever that may mean. On the other hand the two painters did agree on one aspect: where Mantegna demonstrated an absolute 'delight in the antique', Zurbarán 'made creative use of ruins'.[121] If nothing in Poulenc's work would qualify as a ruin, it does come over as one in which the composer looks back, and with affection, to earlier pieces of his own.

The most obvious quotation, right at the start, is from the *Litanies à la Vierge noire*, where Poulenc remembers a texture of high, consecutive sevenths rather than actual notes. The first three notes, A-B-C in A minor, come straight from the 'Fac ut portem' of the *Stabat Mater* via Mother Marie's theme in *Carmélites* and the two-piano Sonata, and would reappear in the Oboe Sonata: they then return, a tone higher, at the start of the final 'Ecce quomodo'. Such details aside, the colouring comes as much as anything from the instrumentation which, like that of *Carmélites*, includes 'almost no percussion, no special instruments'.[122] As Stéphan Etcharry notes, Poulenc's concern is to 'preserve the fragile, diaphanous timbre of the [soloist's] white voice and to make it audible: instrumental desks reduced by half for mezzo-sopranos and basses, for tenors reduced to three soloists, all instruments playing *pp*, low strings pizzicato, desks divided for violins and violas, woodwind mainly for touching in and often solo etc.'[123] Harry Christophers too writes that 'The orchestra is a large one but he uses it sparingly [. . .] his use of the harp is incredible, as are the high notes in the wind section.'[124]

The 'white voice' is that of the boy soloist Poulenc always had in mind. 'I'm no misogynist,' he told Bernac, 'but the idea of a woman's voice (replacing the child) doesn't satisfy me [. . .] Do you think that, instead of a child, one might not have a "white" tenor like [Hugues] Cuenod?'[125] Elsewhere it becomes clear that by 'enfant' Poulenc meant 'boy', and in a notice with the piano score he insisted that while women may be used for the chorus, girls must not. As for what kind of boy soprano, as late as September 1962 he was still on the hunt, having found unacceptable a boy whose voice and style were 'too "Plaine Monceau", which suits perfectly the music of Fauré's wealthy departed. I should like the son of a coal merchant or plumber from La Villette (with a lower range).'[126] Here again he was looking back, this time to his remarks, already noted, about his Mass of 1937 and its 'rough, direct style', recalling the fact that 'in the early Church those who had not been baptized were allowed to sing [the Kyrie] with the priests. This explains the almost savage side of my *Mass*.'[127] While the *Sept Répons* are rarely savage, Poulenc obviously wanted the work to express, among other things, his peasant side, and in particular that uncomplicated 'peasant faith' which he so much longed to be his own.

The seven movements cover much the same melodic and harmonic ground as the conclusion of the fourteenth *Improvisation* (see p. 258) Stravinskyan tonal dissonances, two twelve-note phrases and sign-offs, though these are now expressive rather than dismissive. To begin the second movement, 'Judas, mercator pessimus', Poulenc eschews complex, 'evil' dissonance for twenty-seven bars of C major – and somehow manages to imbue them with menace. Then the third movement, 'Jesum tradidit', begins with a twelve-note row orchestrated with Webernian *Klangfarbenmelodie* – that is with various instruments contributing to a single melodic line. But whatever this portends, it is surely not the ensuing fifteen bars of G minor . . . A second, quite different row is given to the basses in the next movement, 'Caligaverunt oculi mei', on the words 'O vos omnes qui transitis per viam': the whole text gives the meaning 'O all ye that pass by, behold and see if there be a sorrow like unto my sorrow.' Opinions have differed as to whether or not this note row might indicate the path of pain that Stravinsky embraced and Poulenc evaded.[128]

The boy soloist, who opened the third movement, does the same for 'Tenebrae factae sunt' and helps introduce Christ's despairing cry 'My God, why hast Thou forsaken me?', but has almost to himself the phrase 'inclinato capite', as Christ breathes His last, the sudden reduction in the texture wonderfully conveying the Saviour's final exhaustion. In 'Sepulto Domino' Poulenc makes further obeisance to figuration, with heavy consecutive fifths as the stone is rolled into the mouth of the cave and trumpet tuckets as the soldiers are set to guard it. For the final meditation on the death of this just man (and for the seventh and last time, with the indication 'calme'), Poulenc characteristically blends a steady quaver pulse, lasting through the whole movement (the sudden *ff* at fig. 56 is marked 'surtout sans presser'), with ever-changing phrase lengths, beginning with four phrases of ten, seven, fourteen and ten crotchets. A feeling of consummation is also induced in the exact repetition of the orchestral introduction by the choir. But what of the boy soloist? Poulenc the arch-dramatist knew, as he had in the *Stabat Mater*, that we would be waiting for his farewell entry. And again keeps us waiting. And when the boy does enter, it is again with the opening five bars of the movement, giving a feeling of arrival, albeit to one of pain and sacrifice. Finally, Christ's silence 'like the lamb before his shearer' is shadowed by the chorus's gradual withdrawal both from volume and from syntax, as they mutter 'os' (mouth), the basses having the last word, 'suum' (His). A melancholy ending in B minor seems inevitable. But instead, Poulenc crowns the work with his favourite, sensuous chord of a major thirteenth – here B major plus G♯ and A – spread widely between contrabassoon and piccolo. As one critic said after the Paris premiere, 'the composer wanted to offer the presence in these *Tenebrae* of a faint but persistent ray of hope, of faith in the promise given by Him who will return'.[129]

On 8 October Poulenc and Duval performed *La Voix humaine* in the theatre of Amboise to raise money for the church in Noizay, and at the end of the month he and Février played the D minor Concerto in Lausanne and recorded the 'valse-musette' *L'Embarquement pour Cythère*. Otherwise the final months of the year were quiet ones, with just one concert in London on 13 November. Work on *Sept Répons* was paramount.

'The last full year of Poulenc's life', as succinctly summarized by Schmidt, 'followed the now familiar pattern of a winter concert tour, composition at Brive, Noizay and Bagnols-en-Forêt, quick trips to Italy, Menton, Aix-en-Provence, Milan and Venice to attend or give concerts, as well as treks to summer spots such as Rocamadour and Le Tremblay.'[130] The Italian tour, from 3 to 16 February, saw Poulenc and Duval giving recitals in Trieste, Turin, Florence, Perugia and Naples. The programme was to consist of *La Voix*, together with four Debussy songs, three Ravel ones and, surprisingly, in view of her reservations, *La Courte Paille*. But in the end her reservations prevailed and she would never sing the cycle in public.[131] Poulenc meanwhile had suffered throughout the tour with neuritis in his right arm, telling Audel on his return that his hand was still tight when it came to writing.[132]

In December he had been asked by the publisher Hansen to orchestrate *Babar*, but for some reason refused. Instead he offered the job to Jean Françaix, who set to work in March. Poulenc allowed him to have a harp instead of a piano, as well as a trombone or a tuba which, as envisaged by Françaix, duly contribute 'some farts in the right places'.[133] Poulenc called the result a *chef d'oeuvre*.[134]

He was less happy about Louis's decision to leave Bagnols, where building and plumbing work had pretty well dried up, and open a bar in Cannes, but was grateful for 'a change [that] has come about in me, as some years ago with Raymond, so that I consider [Louis] as a child whom I *adore*. That makes everything easier.'[135] He would no doubt also have been content, had he known, that he had been included at some point in 1962 by Jolivet in his list of 'composers to be considered for state commissions in 1962', even if nothing in fact came his way.[136] The so-called 'complete' *Sept Répons* had been orchestrated by 2 April and Poulenc was 'going over it with a magnifying glass', a task which may even have been finished by 10 May when he again wrote, to Yvonne de Casa Fuerte, 'The *Répons* are finished.'[137]

If that was indeed true, it would to some extent explain a paragraph in the same letter: 'Listening to my songs the other day, I was saying to myself that of course they were good, but where to go now? Don't tell that to anybody, but it's good for me to open my heart to you. Perhaps at the moment too much lucidity is paralysing me?' This was to be a refrain throughout the remaining eight months of his life but, given his constantly shifting morale, it's hard to know how seriously to take it. Between April and June he composed incidental music for Cocteau's play *Renaud et Armide*, due to be performed in Baalbek in August, but whereas on 3 July he could write 'The recording of my *Renaud* music is splendid and I think these few notes will sound extremely well,' on 9 August he told Sauguet, 'I'm bored by *Renaud et Armide* and my music is totally uninteresting'.[138] In any case he had already answered the question 'where to go now?' by his intention 'to finish two sonatas (clarinet – bassoon) this summer which were sketched out two years ago', followed by the news that he has 'set stewing in the same pot a Sonata for oboe and the one for clarinet';[139] and a day later he tells Bernac more details of the Oboe Sonata with the rider 'I think the orientation towards woodwind is the solution for me at present'.[140] The Clarinet and Oboe sonatas were dedicated to the memories of Honegger and Prokofiev respectively.

These thoughts for the future were balanced by a dose of nostalgia, prompted by Stravinsky's eightieth birthday on 18 June. In a letter of good wishes, belated because he lacked Stravinsky's address, Poulenc says he has 'spent the spring listening every evening in the country to all your records. It's always exactly the same astonishment for me as when I was 20, and more so, if that's possible! [. . .] Alas! I no longer see you, which makes me really sad [. . .] If I no longer send you my music, that's quite simply because I think it wouldn't interest you.'[141] To which Stravinsky replied, with his typical, devastating honesty, 'when you tell me that your music no longer interests me, I have to reply that it's not a question of your music but of practically all contemporary music with which I'm in the process of losing touch'.[142] The truth of this is underlined by Robert Craft's diary for 2 August 1960: '[Stravinsky] is rather sharp about "Les Six", calling them "Six Characters in Search of an Author", and referring to an opera by one of them as "Les Mamelles de ma tante".'[143] Stravinsky's letter was the last contact between the two composers.

On 10 August Poulenc came close to disaster. A letter to Bernac tells the tale:

No Baalbek! So much the better in a sense, as I was dreading the heat and only agreed on the journey to please Louis. Three hours before taking the plane at Milan, 39.5 degrees and a *terrible* angina, in a Milan that was baking and empty. Luckily, thanks to my dear porter at the [Hôtel] Continental I had a very helpful doctor; I flew back to Paris, *stuffed* with penicillin and on the Friday [24 August], in a deserted Paris, saw a good doctor in Necker [15th arrondissement] [. . .] I leave tomorrow for Le Tremblay, dying for wind, humidity and flowers.[144]

This warning shot across his bows cannot have been totally unexpected. Back in February 1954 he had already been suffering from high blood pressure and was observing a strict diet.[145] Pictures of him in middle age reveal a body that might, to be polite, be described as 'full', and nowhere in the literature is there a mention of him going for walks as exercise: at best he would stroll (flâner) around his favourite Paris haunts. To these habits must be added the strain induced by his mental travails, whether caused externally, as by the legal problems with *Carmélites*, or internally by his chronic 'inquiétude'.

Having returned the first proofs of *Sept Répons* at the end September,[146] he now turned to copying out the Clarinet Sonata which he had finished by the beginning of that month, and continued work on the one for oboe. The paucity of correspondence during this autumn argues for the usual concentration that woodwind instruments inspired. He refused the cellist Pierre Fournier's request for a *Rapsodie*,[147] but took time to send Britten a letter for his fiftieth birthday, 'At 50, here you are, as glorious as a young Verdi', and remembered how at Aix-en-Provence, after Britten had accompanied Pears in Schubert songs, 'I declared to Pierre Bernac [. . .] "After Ben I give up playing Schubert." '[148] Perhaps surprisingly, Bernac would not have been totally distraught at such a decision. 'Naturally [Poulenc] loved and admired Schubert's Lieder, but he never managed to play them as well as I would have wished, and as he would have wished, because he was well aware of this fact. A certain rigour, a certain rhythmic firmness, which this music needs, was always hard for him. Even the technical side of his playing didn't suit Schubert, whereas on the contrary he was naturally in tune with the lyricism and suppleness of Schumann. In the French repertoire it was the music of Debussy, whom he adored, that he interpreted best – better even than Ravel and certainly than Fauré, whose music he didn't much like.'[149]

Raymonde Linossier's elder sister Suzanne Latarjet died during the autumn and Poulenc went to her funeral. He then continued work on the Oboe Sonata for a month in Cannes no doubt at the Hôtel Majestic, since Louis had now sold his house and was installed in his bar in the town. The piece was finished by 17 November.[150] Meanwhile Poulenc's 'sordid Paris apartment' was being repainted, and he warned Simone Girard that when she came on 1 January she would find 'an apartment that's clean and bold. I think our dear Pierre was slightly surprised by the colour combinations. It's quite Matisse.'[151] He ended the year with three days in Venice between sitting on a jury in Trieste and a visit to Milan where *Les Mamelles* was to be given from 2 March. But much of his attention was also directed towards his future in the United States. He acknowledged to Bernac, who had been replaced by Donald Gramm for the upcoming tour in April, that 'I set great store by these concerts to consolidate my position in America'[152] and told Fournier he was particularly keen for the New York performance of *Répons* scheduled for 11 April to be a success[153] – which indeed it would be, though without him.

Poulenc had first thought of writing sonatas for clarinet and oboe in 1957, when they were coupled in his mind with a bassoon sonata, and in 1959 he told his publisher R. Douglas Gibson of Chesters that he'd written the Andante of a Clarinet Sonata.[154] Around the same time he also told Simone Girard, 'I've finished the lamento of a Sonata for clarinet and piano dedicated to the memory of Arthur [Honegger]. I think it's very touching.'[155] The relationship between this and the final 'Romanza' is unknown, but in any case his attention then turned to the *Gloria*.

The structure of the sonata is of two parallel patterns:

I	II	III
fast - slow - fast	slow	fast
sad	sad	cheerful

This gives plenty of variety while ensuring that the unique fast+cheerful content of the third movement acts as a satisfying finale. Variety also obtains in the musical material, most notably at the start where challenging, dissonant chromaticism leads, with surreal abruptness, to the 'tune over pulsing quavers' familiar from the songs. This opening sets the scene for the sonata as a whole, where interruptions and changes of mood are the pattern: Wilfrid Mellers notes that the heading ' "Allegro tristamente" complements the "Allegretto malincolico" of the Flute Sonata's first movement', while finding the whole sonata 'life-asserting, yet a shade desperate'.[156] The slow section of the first movement, 'très calme, très doux', moves from *Babar*-like contentment to double-dotted adventure, borrowed from the 'Domine Deus' of the *Gloria*, though again there is a cross-current in the marking 'doucement monotone' that warns against any overt display. Finally, after the challenging chromaticism of the opening returns, it is placated to some extent by the final triad, but one that is minor rather than major.

The central 'Romanza' ('Lamento'?) begins by searching for some kind of certainty. This duly arrives after nine bars, in the form of the clarinet's rising minor third (here G-A-B flat), now familiar from *Carmélites* and *Sept Répons* and, in case there was any doubt, Poulenc labels the theme 'très doux et mélancolique', while the pianist is favoured with the familiar injunctions 'effleurer' ('stroke lightly') and 'beaucoup de pédale'. The clarinet plays the theme three more times, in G minor, B flat minor, then in G minor again, the key of the whole movement. This balance, together with the radiant harmonies and the apparently effortless flow of ideas, make this movement one of Poulenc's most beautiful creations, to which his 'très touchant' does scant justice.

The 'Allegro con fuoco' takes us back, in its energy and brassy confidence, to the wind sonatas of Poulenc's youth – in one important detail too: Pierre-Albert Castanet has discovered that the first seven notes of the phrase at rehearsal number 3 are taken from the 1917 song 'Titine, je cherche après Titine', made popular by Maurice Chevalier.[157] It seems only fitting that Poulenc should offer not just a lament for his friend, but remember too the young Honegger who, in those happy days of the early 1920s, had been so full of life and laughter.

The Oboe Sonata also displays Poulenc's interest in exploring new structures, ostensibly changing the traditional fast-slow-fast sequence to slow-fast-slow (Elégie – Scherzo – Déploration). But once more this simple structure is complicated by a slow section in the centre of the 'Scherzo' that introduces a new sensuousness, accompanied even by the very rare indication 'très légèrement rubato'. As in the

Clarinet Sonata, the body of the first movement is approached obliquely, but the eight bars there are now reduced to just four notes, which moreover never recur. Perhaps they are intended merely as a question mark in the minor? If so, they are answered convincingly by the opening theme in the major. Here, as in the memory of Chevalier mentioned above, we return to Poulenc's youth and the emphasis on conjunct intervals first found in the opening *Mouvement perpétuel*. The feeling of the oboe tune is distinctly neo-classical, but beneath it the piano left hand intones those hypnotic minor thirds which, borrowed from *Oedipus Rex* and the *Symphony of Psalms*, had signalled danger and disruption in *Carmélites*. The result is again that kind of mixed emotion in which Poulenc specialized, just as an 'Elégie' can be either consoling or lamenting – or both. Never one to waste a good idea, he repeats at fig. 6, and then somewhat altered in the finale, the double-dotted six bars from fig. 8 of the first movement of the Clarinet Sonata.

With the 'Scherzo' Poulenc seems to be recalling the diamantine sparkle of Prokofiev's own piano playing. Although the basic metre is 6/8, he throws in one or two 9/8s to keep everyone on their toes. That said, an unusual number of bars are immediately repeated, giving the whole movement a populist feel – unusual, because Poulenc's one quibble with his adored Debussy was his tendency to write what Poulenc called 'la musique bègue' or 'stuttering music'. In the sensuous central section which maybe remembers that among Prokofiev's many talents, when he chose to exercise it, was one for writing tunes, more frequent changes of metre give this section a more recherché and expressive air.

Wilfrid Mellers reminds us usefully that the finale 'pays deference to the "déplorations" that early French composers like Josquin and Ockeghem were wont to write for their revered masters'.[158] The composer described it as 'a sort of liturgical chant'.[159] Beginning with a reminiscence of the *Litanies à la Vierge noire* and with the familiar, angst-laden rising third (here A flat – B flat – C flat), the movement sets off monotone grief against rages 'at the dying of the light'. Dissonance too plays its part, especially in the final bars where C and C flat grind against each other, C flat and a minor key winning the struggle – something it has a claim to be even if Poulenc's mastery and affection are everywhere apparent.

It is tempting to regard this 'Déploration' as in some sense the final word from a composer aware of his impending death. While it is true that Poulenc had been haunted by death for years, worrying particularly about how his reputation would stand beyond the grave, the most one can truly say is that the attack of angina at Milan airport had undoubtedly fed into his long-standing hypochondria. But we need to beware of taking this a step further into some clear prescience of extinction. The hypochondria allied to his depressive tendencies made him say things that he would disown when the mood lifted – we should not, for example, necessarily take his word for his claim to Stéphane Audel, when the latter came to Noizay in early January 1963 to work on their conversations for Radio-Lausanne, that *Sept Répons*, the proofs of which he was correcting, would be his last religious work.[160] Altogether it is hard to gain a clear picture of Poulenc's mental and physical health during these last years. On the one hand, in October 1961 Audel had found a Poulenc who was 'aged, slightly shrunken, seriously pot-bellied. [. . .] He gives every impression of early-onset senility.'[161] Yet this was the Poulenc who, also according to Audel, could strike a hard bargain over payment for their conversations,[162] and who in February 1962 could give five successful concerts in Italy with Denise Duval, not to mention bringing *Sept Répons* to completion that April and composing these two wonderful wind sonatas during the summer and autumn.

The last weeks of Poulenc's life were marked by similar discordances. On 14 January he left Noizay with a heavy cold for Paris. On the 18th he went with Audel to a performance of Racine's *Andromaque* and on the 22nd again with him to Roger Vitrac's *Victor*, when he was struck by a serious coughing attack, leading to stomach pains so fierce he was afraid he was going to vomit. In spite of this, on the 24th he caught the train to Holland for concerts with Duval. On the 26th, after a concert in Maastricht, he sent Duval flowers to her hotel room with a card: 'Ma Denise, Je te dois ma dernière joie. Ton pauvre Fr.'[163] Is 'dernière' to be taken as 'most recent'? Or as 'final'? 'Pauvre' can be explained by the fact that on Monday the 28th he returned to Paris, exhausted and suffering from bronchitis, with a temperature of 39 degrees (102F). On the Tuesday he got his housekeeper Jeanne to phone Audel and postpone their recording session set for the Wednesday evening. At 9 o'clock on Wednesday morning Audel has a call from Jeanne saying 'Monsieur est très mal'. When, after trying to find a doctor and doing various other tasks, he reaches Poulenc's bedside, he finds the composer's sister Jeanne, her husband André and nephew Denis. Poulenc has died. His recent stomach pains and fear of vomiting, together with the high blood pressure diagnosed in 1954, all point to the cause being a heart attack. Recent research has also indicated that 'people who have heightened activity in a part of the brain linked to stress – the amygdala – are more likely to develop cardiovascular problems'.[164]

The date, 30 January, was that on which Raymonde Linossier had died thirty-three years earlier. Probably this would not have surprised Poulenc, since he somehow reconciled his Roman Catholic faith with a belief in astrology and was convinced that nothing good ever happened to him in January.[165] His death at barely sixty-four came as a terrible shock to all his family and friends: what the French call *une mort brutale* may be taken as signifying the suffering not only of the victims but also of their loved ones. It had become the custom to write off his depressions and complaints of ill-health merely as examples of his hypochondria, so that for some their sadness no doubt embraced a modicum of guilt. But for Poulenc himself it was exactly the end he had always wished for – anything rather than the protracted death-in-life of poor Déso.

His funeral took place at Saint-Sulpice on Saturday 2 February and, as he had instructed Brigitte to ensure, the Requiem Mass began and ended with cheerful organ music by Couperin and Nicolas de Grigny and peals of bells 'to swing my soul along'.[166] But there was to be no music by Poulenc and no *Dies irae*. 'Certainly I was disappointed,' wrote François Mauriac, 'not to hear the *Litanies à la Vierge noire*. And then I understood: it will always be possible to find Francis Poulenc again in his music [. . .] But that morning I was overcome by the composer's silence, a silence which was one with that of his dead body, and by his self-effacement before the ancient liturgy.'[167] He was buried in the cemetery of Père-Lachaise.

In his will, dated 2 June 1954, Poulenc insisted that Brigitte alone (*je dis bien seule*) was to 'have the right to look after the posthumous fate of my work, *in all its forms*'. She was to be the guardian 'of my work as well as all my books, music, papers, correspondence, manuscripts and photographs' – indeed everything except the ⅚ths of his copyright he gave to his daughter Marie-Ange and the ⅙th to Raymond Destouches. The furniture in his Paris flat went to his other niece Rosine. Brigitte, Marie-Ange and Raymond split his shares in Rhône-Poulenc. Throughout the will, Marie-Ange is referred to as 'my god-daughter' (see Appendix).

The three of his works he never heard performed were all given during 1963: the Clarinet Sonata on 10 April in Carnegie Hall by Benny Goodman and Leonard Bernstein, *Sept Répons* the following day in New York by the New York Philharmonic conducted by Thomas Schippers with boy soprano Jeffrey Meyer, and the Oboe Sonata on 8 June at the Strasbourg International Festival by Pierre Pierlot and Jacques Février. The two sonatas immediately became regulars in their respective repertoires, but *Sept Répons* for years was barely heard. For this, sadly, their first recording by Georges Prêtre must bear some responsibility, in which he was saddled with a dismal choir who were proof against even his musicianship and enthusiasm. But more recent recordings have confirmed Keith Daniel's claim that 'there is as much beauty, as much characteristic Poulenc writing, and perhaps more profundity and revelation of Poulenc's religious fervour and views of life and death in *Sept Répons* than in the vastly more popular *Stabat* and *Gloria*.'[168]

Overall, though, Poulenc's fears that his music would die with him have proved wholly unfounded. While he left no sketches or unfinished works to tempt the arts of scholars (nothing, for reasons already suggested, of Cocteau's *La Machine infernale* nor of a darkly dramatic opera he considered on the lines of Puccini's *Il Tabarro*, which he much admired),[169] what he did write never experienced that instant post-mortem slump which seems to afflict the music of most composers, and for years the *Gloria* was (has been?) the second best-selling French classical work after *Boléro*. If not all professional pianists play his piano music, this, as we have seen, is merely to echo his own distaste for most of it. Singers though, both solo and choral, will probably see to it forever that his vocal contributions are performed and loved as few others of their time. Those early quibbles about the populist features of his sacred music have long been dismissed and we may now glory guilt-free in his statement that 'pour moi, le véritable art sacré est sensuel.'[170]

It sometimes seems that everyone who came into contact with Poulenc had strong views about him; also that these covered a wide range of emotions, a fact embodied in Stéphane Audel's address to the composer, on the tenth anniversary of his death, as 'mon irrésistible, insupportable et cher Poulenc'. The following extracts come from some of those who knew him best:

Nadia Boulanger: I can't remember without laughing one dinner with friends where he told us an absolutely uninteresting story. He arrived at the Vienna railway station to board his sleeper; the sleeper was already occupied by somebody he had to turn out. A banal story. He told it to us so that we laughed until we cried, his description of the stunned expression of the rather dim carriage attendant, and of the man who had to be removed, was so droll. This was not at all amusing in itself and yet it was irresistible; so was his way of playing his own work at the piano.

(Bruno Monsaingeon, *Mademoiselle, Conversations with Nadia Boulanger*, Manchester, Carcanet Press, 1985, 103)

Pierre Bernac: To a young American student who was writing a doctoral thesis on his songs, and who was interviewing him, Poulenc, in my presence, replied: 'I beg you, don't analyse my songs or classify them, love them!' (Interviewed by Gérard Michel for *France Culture*, 11 December 1970)

Poulenc was extraordinarily visual, and if he had a very bad musical memory, his visual memory was wonderful. During our tours together we had the opportunity of visiting many museums and he would sometimes make remarks which illustrated how remarkable his visual memory was; for instance at the Phillips Gallery in Washington he once said: 'You see the green in the dress in this portrait; it is exactly the same as the green of the costume of the soldier in the Mantegna of San Zeno in Verona.' And you could be sure he was right. He used to say that he loved painting more than music. His favourite modern painters were Matisse, first of all, then Picasso and Bonnard; and he compared Dufy's paintings to his own music. (A talk given by Bernac on Poulenc on 20 January 1971 at the British Institute of Recorded Sound)

Sir Kenneth Clark: 'Eminent men are not always willing to make an effort, even in France [. . .] My favourite was Francis Poulenc; one felt, under his joyous participation in all that was amusing, the deep seriousness that is expressed in his religious music. He was a passionate lover of painting, and I have never known a man with whom I had rather visit a picture gallery. He had in the highest degree the gift of self-identification with each artist, without which no critic should open his mouth.' (*The Other Half*, London, John Murray, 1977, 120–1)

Marcel Schneider: 'You like painters as much as poets?' 'Yes, Matisse painted the pictures I dream of, which I shall never create; Éluard wrote the poems I would have loved to write. They are the ones who gave me most ideas about my art. Musicians can't teach me anything new.'

His suits were made to measure and from the best tailors. His elegance and social image damaged his reputation. He was seen as a socialite and we know, as Proust said, that people never attribute genius to a man they saw the previous evening at the opera. The traditional idea of the doomed poet is long-lasting; it satisfies some obscure delight in revenge among the well-heeled bourgeoisie.

In 1919 he was still in uniform, working in Paris for the Ministry of Aviation. One evening he was coming back along the Champs-Élysées when a woman came up to him: 'Handsome soldier, how about coming with me?' She didn't tempt Francis, neither by her figure, which wasn't of the slenderest, nor by her voice, which wasn't of the sweetest, but he agreed when she added: 'Come on, I'll make love to you in music!' They found a bench in a shady corner and there the woman fixed a bracelet on to her wrist covered with little bells. As Poulenc said, rocking with laughter, 'I remember it was in D major.'

He possessed the secret of knowing how to talk to everybody as an individual and to speak to their heart. That explains how this man who passed as communing only with high society was so at ease with the working class, and how his music, judged by some to be frivolous, carries more weight and gravity than many more austere compositions. Beyond social differences, he dealt in universal emotions and, beyond aesthetic principles and the disputes of cliques, he listened to the little song that sang within him: and he had the wisdom to prefer it to all others.

As Debussy was proud to admire Wagner and to have made the pilgrimage to Bayreuth, but to have warded off his influence, so Poulenc knew, from the age of eighteen, how to shake off the spiritual and artistic yoke of Stravinsky. It was his legitimate defence and also his salvation. Venerating Satie and Stravinsky, but keeping them at a distance, allowed Poulenc to see more clearly and to be more impartial than people of his generation. He admired Massenet's infallible prosody and melodic gifts and the Western genius of Tchaikovsky at a time when these composers were despised. Puccini's sense of theatre and dramatic structure as well as the professionalism of his orchestral writing seemed to him unsurpassable; how many times have I heard him say he would love to have written the 'glass of whisky' passage in the first act of *Madam Butterfly*! (*L'Éternité fragile, vol. 3, Le Palais des mirages*, Bernard Grasset, 1992, 215, 216, 217, 218, 222)

Michel Glotz (director of the French office of Pathé-Marconi, who in 1962 had been encouraging Poulenc for weeks to practise): Finally the day arrived for the recording of the famous Concerto for two pianos. What I feared duly happened:

Poulenc played very badly. At a certain point there was a conglomeration of wrong notes in passages that were so exposed it wasn't possible to ignore them, despite all the goodwill of Georges Prêtre, Jacques Février and myself. I said to him over the phone: 'Francis, it's not possible.' He came into the room in a rage and replied, in totally bad faith: 'It's not me, it's Jacques Février', curtly denouncing his lifelong colleague and friend. Unfortunately for him, we were recording in stereo and each piano had its own microphone. I asked Poulenc to come into the recording studio, told the technician to mute the loudspeaker connected to Février's piano, and got him to play the passage with the wrong notes. He was caught like a rat in a trap. Furious, he then said: 'Merde! At the end of the day, I'm the composer and I can do what I like!' Tricky situation . . . until I had the idea of saying to him, in the calmest tone imaginable: 'If you want that to be on the disc, that's fine, we can say in the liner notes that this "new version" of the concerto has been ratified by the composer himself . . .' From that moment he buckled to and we were able to finish the recording session in fairly good order. (*La Note bleue; une vie pour la musique*, JC Lattès, 2002, 100)

Madeleine Milhaud: He had his anxious side. And one has to admit, he was rather – how do you say? – 'close' with money. I remember at a party Darius and I gave, he found a one franc piece on the carpet and was going round the room asking 'C'est à vous? C'est à vous?' Eventually I said to him, 'For Heaven's sake, Francis, put it in your pocket.' (Madeleine Milhaud in conversation with the author)

When Poulenc died, I had really the feeling that Darius had lost a brother – a younger brother. It seemed that Francis was always the youngest. He was loveable and he loved. Of course, he went through certain little events which were sad: we had the impression that he was the only person who could be sad! (Barrie Gavin, Poulenc documentary, Hessischer Rundfunk, HR/RM Arts, 1988)

You feel a great sensitivity in the heart of Francis. You had the impression you could hear it beat, you know. So I will say [he had] more than two sides – Janus with three or four sides! (Ibid.)

Henri Sauguet: I owe him a lot. He taught me so many of the minute details of Parisian life, which I didn't know, coming from Bordeaux, from the provinces. He told me where I could buy good hats, nice ties, delicate scents. He was a connoisseur of Paris. (Ibid.)

Henri Hell: We had dinner and after dinner we listened to records – but never records of his own music, never. It was always music by other people, including Boulez. And we'd listen to a lot of Verdi. And I remember very well a recording of Wagner's *Götterdämmerung* – he said to me, 'It's very beautiful, but now please put on a record of Mozart to clean out my ears!' (Ibid.)

Gabriel Tacchino (after he had played Tchaikovsky's First Piano Concerto with Poulenc in the audience): My octaves were not extraordinary, and he said to me, 'There's a whole generation of Russian pianists arriving, you can't afford any weaknesses – work on your octaves!' I do what I can . . . And one day when I came to Noizay, I played his *Presto*, and very sweetly, because he had this sense of humour, he said, 'I always like to give you something as a souvenir', and he wrote on my score 'For my dear Tacchino, this *Presto* . . . without octaves'. It was a delicate way of reminding me of his advice. (Gabriel Tacchino in interview: https:www.youtube.com/watch?v=BUned9kjobI)

Stéphane Audel (on Le Grand Coteau): Francis, buried in a capacious armchair, followed the scores of operas by Verdi and Puccini, Mahler and Hindemith symphonies, Bartók concertos, music by Debussy, Chabrier (his beloved Chabrier), Musorgsky, Stravinsky, Prokofiev, and works by the Viennese serialists, whose rich vocal and orchestral scores sounded out from the gramophone. Being the man of order that he was, books, scores, collections of photos, autographs and letters he cherished were filed with the same precision as the times he devoted to work.

He got up very early and, after a breakfast of buttered rusks, jam and tea, would shut himself up in his studio. Turning his back to the windows through which came a blaze of sunlight, he worked at his table or at his piano. I used to hear him from my bedroom trying out chords, repeating a musical phrase, altering it, testing over and over until a sudden silence announced that he'd gone back to his table and was either writing out notes on his manuscript paper or else scratching out those that didn't satisfy him, with a scraper so worn down by use that it was now half its original size. This concentrated work continued until lunchtime. Francis would then go up to his bedroom, tidy himself briskly and, from that moment on, would devote himself to the calls of friendship. (JE 844, MMA 10–11; MFM 14–15)

Ned Rorem: Who will forget that voice, spoken or sung? The harmless venom, the malignant charity? His indiscriminate choice of friends, yet so discriminately faithful to a type; *la royauté des sergents de ville*! A few days later as a bread-and-butter gift I left a rare and fragrant package of Hindu joss-sticks (purchased the previous month near Tangier's Xoco Chico) with the concierge of Poulenc's Paris apartment. On returning to New York the following week, I found a letter from Francis thanking me for the incense, which he hoped would light the way toward one of *les beaux flics* that roamed his neighbourhood. The smoke, he said, weaved through his yellow plush armchairs, across the squeaking piano strings, and on out through the casements into the refracting sunlight of the Luxembourg Gardens, from whence it might float on the mist of his own song over the Atlantic to America where we would someday meet again. But we never did. ('Afterthoughts on Francis', *Settling the Score: Essays on Music*, New York, Doubleday, 1989, 133 – memoir written in 1967)

Since Jean Cocteau came back into Poulenc's life so productively at its very end, it seems fitting to let him offer the final souvenir:

Never again would we hear born and reborn that miracle of a mysterious equilibrium between the new and the classical, between the lessons learnt from the masters and the robust, almost peasant inspiration in his songs, in which technique and a childlike freshness were combined. (Quoted in Georges Hacquard, *Germaine Tailleferre. La Dame des Six*, Éditions de l'Harmattan, 1998, 195)

Yes, he could be 'insupportable', as when blaming Février for his own mistakes – a less appealing side of his childlike nature. But Audel spoke for many when he also called Poulenc 'irresistible' and 'dear'. Clearly the man's loveability matched that of his music. This has not been a quality much prized in classical music over the last century or so, and it has been far more the case that, as with Massenet, Poulenc's unstinting appeal to the heart has been written off as superficiality, and hence deeply suspect. One hears the voice of the analyst (for historical reasons, usually imitated with a cod German or at least mid-European accent) complaining that, 'Yes, this music works in practice. But does it work in theory?' Poulenc, as we have seen, had his harmonic and melodic preferences, so some kind of analysis was instinctively at work in that highly individual brain. But, to take just one aspect of his music, it's hard to envisage any textbook that could codify his blend of the popular with the recherché.

On this point, Poulenc's article 'In praise of banality' deserves close reading. As we have seen, in the 1920s he did make a couple of bids for stern modernity, but soon saw the error of his ways. It was Schoenberg, no less, who stated that there was still a lot of good music waiting to be written in C major. The difficulty, precisely, is to make it different, let alone good. That Poulenc was so often able to make his tonal music both different and good is not a gift to be sneered at.

Finally, we may remember Mme de Saint-Marceaux's 1927 diary in which she had written, 'Poulenc sang his *Chansons gaillardes* and played his *Napoli*. He plays the piano well. His compositions don't lack talent but he's not a genius, and I'm afraid he thinks he is.' Nearly 100 years later, we are better able to see that his 'inquiétude' never allowed him to think he was; but that in his finest works he comes very close, at the least, to joining that small and illustrious band.

APPENDIX

Just as first proofs of this book became available, news arrived of the publication of the vital document printed below.

This letter was published for the first time by Pierre Miscevic, in his book *Francis Poulenc, Lettres inédites à Brigitte Manceaux*, Éd. Orizons, Paris, 2019. It is reproduced by kind permission of Éditions Orizons.

The author is deeply grateful for their authorisation to Pierre Miscevic, to his publisher Daniel Cohen, and to Marie-Ange Lebedeff whom this letter touches so nearly.

2 June 1954

My dear little Brigitte,

Simply from reading my will you'll have learnt the truth about my god-daughter Marie-Ange. You must admit, it's as unfortunate as unexpected.

How ironic that Fate should have played this trick on me. The sweet little girl was born from a simple New Year's game between childhood friends.[1] There lies the real drama, because of course I've *never loved* Freddy. The only woman for whom I've ever felt love, as you know, was Raymonde. But there's no point going on about what's happened and I've never been able to blame Fred, who has *paid dearly* for her folly.

That's the truth of it: I have a daughter who is, I repeat, exquisite because she is the image of your Poulenc grandmother.[2] She has her gestures, her posture, her taste – for better or worse; she is 100% me. I ask you to *look after her always*, because I adore her. See to it that the poor little girl, who instinctively idolizes me, doesn't have to suffer for all that. You promise?

Next I must urge you never to abandon Raymond who is, with Raymonde, the person who has played the greatest role in my life. Be sure to tell him that and *try to keep an eye on him*. Tell Lucien the truth – it's thanks to him I wrote the *Stabat*. I'd been blocked from 1948 to 1950 by the M. Ange business – that he has been *the love* of my life: these feelings are so nuanced that they can run in parallel; you're capable of understanding that.

Do what you like with Noizay³ and everything I leave you. Sadly, I'm afraid that doesn't amount to much but . . . think if I'd got married! And anyway, you don't care about all that, do you? But I do leave you the *best of me*, that's to say my spiritual legacy, and that I give you from the bottom of my heart. I entrust my music to your hands. When it comes to republishing it, never go back to the manuscripts but to the last editions corrected by me. Never, on any account, allow publication of sketches for incidental music, songs etc., because I was lucky enough in my lifetime to publish everything I wanted.

One more word. I inherited from my mother a large diamond, which your mother will hand on to you. Give it to Marie-Ange for her 18th birthday. I think that's only fair. If things get tight for you both, sell it and share the proceeds with my little darling.

Think of me without bitterness – I have *loved* you *so much* (you've been a second Raymonde for me). Pray constantly for me. Talking of which, I want a funeral that's dignified and simple, with no flowers (I've loved them too much). Plainsong with *cheerful*⁴ organ prelude [?] and recessional by Couperin, Grigny and Bach. If possible, Dominicans and Benedictines because I should so much have liked, if I had had their faith, to have been one of them. And then lots of bells since they speed the soul onwards, I'm sure. Try and see to it that no one holds any grudges against me. *I have loved all of you so much*. And above all try and keep Marie-Ange's secret.

With which I embrace you most tenderly and count on you for everything.

Your old teacher

Francis

P.S. Sariac,⁵ who has always been the truest of friends, will advise you over everything.

---

1. At the time of their liaison Poulenc had known Frédérique Lebedeff for about twenty years.
2. Poulenc's mother.
3. Poulenc left Le Grand Coteau to Brigitte, who had in mind to sell it. But she died only a few months after Poulenc, and the house stayed in the family until 2016.
4. The adjective '*gaie*' is underlined three times.
5. Bernard de Sariac was the lawyer for the Poulenc-Manceaux family.

ENVOI

Those who have handled sciences have been either men of experiment or men of dogmas. The men of experiment are like the ant, they only collect and use; the reasoners resemble spiders, who make cobwebs out of their own substance. But the bee takes a middle course: it gathers its material from the flowers of the garden and of the field, but transforms and digests it by a power of its own. Not unlike this is the business of philosophy; for it neither relies solely or chiefly on the powers of the mind, nor does it take the matter which it gathers from natural history and mechanical experiments and lay it up in the memory whole, as it finds it, but lays it up in the understanding altered and digested. Therefore from a closer and purer league between these two faculties, the experimental and the rational (such as has never yet been made), much may be hoped. (Francis Bacon, *The New Organon*, Book One, 1620)

ENDNOTES

ABBREVIATIONS

ABR	*À bâtons rompus*, ed. Lucie Kayas, Arles, Actes Sud, 1999
Bernac	Pierre Bernac, *Francis Poulenc et ses mélodies*, Buchet-Chastel, 1978/2014 (see FPMS below; page references are to the second edition)
Cat.	Carl B. Schmidt, *The Music of Francis Poulenc: A Catalogue*, Oxford, Clarendon Press, 1995
CFP	*Cahiers de Francis Poulenc*: I ed. Simon Basinger, Éditions Eastern, 2008; II, III ed. Michel de Maule, 2009, 2011
CIREM	'In Memoriam Francis Poulenc', *Les Cahiers du Centre International de Recherches en Esthétique Musicale*, ed. Michelle Biget-Mainfroy, University of Tours, 2004
Collaer	Paul Collaer, *Correspondance avec des amis musiciens*, Sprimont, Mardaga, 1996
Corr.	Myriam Chimènes, ed., *Francis Poulenc: Correspondance 1910–1963*, Paris, Fayard, 1994
Daniel	Keith W. Daniel, *Francis Poulenc: His Artistic Development and Musical Style*, Ann Arbor, UMI Research Press, 1982
Diary	*Diary of my Songs*, partially trans. Winifred Radford, London, Gollancz, 1985 (see JMM below)
EM	Carl B. Schmidt, *Enchanting Muse: A Documented Biography of Francis Poulenc*, Hillsdale, Pendragon Press, 2001
ES	Sidney Buckland, ed. and trans, *Francis Poulenc, 'Echo and Source', Selected Correspondence 1915–1963*, London, Victor Gollancz, 1991
Fortune	*Fortune de Francis Poulenc: diffusion, interprétation, réception*, ed. Hervé Lacombe and Nicolas Southon, Presses universitaires de Rennes, 2016
FPF	interview with Bernard Gavoty in the Salle Gaveau in 1959, with English subtitles and performances of his music by him, Jean-Pierre Rampal and Denise Duval, in *Francis Poulenc & Friends*, DVD, EMI Classics, 1962/2005
FPMS	Pierre Bernac, *Francis Poulenc: The Man and his Songs*, trans. Winifred Radford, London, Gollancz, 1977; paperback reprint, London, Kahn & Averill, 2001 (see Bernac above)
FPV	*Francis Poulenc et la voix*, ed. Alban Ramaut, Symétrie/Université de Saint-Étienne, 2002
GAFP	*Centenaire Georges Auric–Francis Poulenc*, ed. Josiane Mas, Montpellier, 2001
HH	Henri Hell, *Francis Poulenc*, Paris, Fayard, 1978
HL	Hervé Lacombe, *Francis Poulenc*, Paris, Fayard, 2013
Ivry	Benjamin Ivry, *Francis Poulenc*, London, Phaidon, 1996
JE	Nicolas Southon, ed., *Francis Poulenc: J'écris ce qui me chante*, Fayard, 2011; partial English translation by Roger Nichols, NFH, *Francis Poulenc: Articles and Interviews, Notes from the Heart*, Farnham, Ashgate, 2014
JMM	*Journal de mes mélodies*, ed. Renaud Machart, Paris, Cicero, 1993 (see Diary above)

Langage	*Du langage au style: singularités de Francis Poulenc*, ed. Lucie Kayas and Hervé Lacombe, Paris, Société française de musicologie, 2016
Les Trois Centres	*Francis Poulenc par lui-même*, two audio cassettes of a talk given on 19 January 1962 at the Club des Trois Centres, Voxigrave, n.d.
MAL	Sidney Buckland and Myriam Chimènes, eds, *Francis Poulenc: Music, Art and Literature*, Aldershot, Ashgate, 1999
Mellers	Wilfrid Mellers, *Francis Poulenc*, Oxford, Oxford University Press, 1993
MFM	*My Friends and Myself*, trans. James Harding, London, Dennis Dobson, 1978, of *Moi et mes amis*, ed. Stéphane Audel, Paris-Genève, La Palatine, 1963; French text reprinted in JE 843–929
MMA	*Moi et mes amis*
MMM	Médiathèque musicale Mahler, Paris
NFH	*Francis Poulenc: Articles and Interviews, Notes from the Heart*, ed. Nicolas Southon, trans. Roger Nichols, Farnham, Ashgate, 2014
ReM	*Revue musicale*
Texas	Harry Ransom Humanities Research Center, University of Texas at Austin
Wendel	*Francis Poulenc: Correspondance 1915–1963*, ed. Hélène de Wendel, Paris, Éditions du Seuil, 1967
Yale	Beinecke Rare Book and Manuscript Library, New Haven, Yale University Press

PREFACE

1. Colin Jones, *Paris: The Biography of a City*, New York, Viking, 2005, 360
2. Alistair Horne, *Seven Ages of Paris*, London, Pan, 2003, 341
3. Unpublished letter of 11 [Oct 1954], Texas

I. OVERTURE AND BEGINNERS: 1899–1918

1. Corr. 19–18
2. Interview 12, JE 800; NFH 245
3. 'Notes sur Massenet', *Enciclopedia della musica*, 3, Milan, Ricordi, 1964, 124: JE 368
4. Boulez in conversation with the author
5. *Le Coq et l'Arlequin*, Paris, Stock, 1979, 79
6. Letter to Humbert Ferrand, 5 Nov 1863, *Selected Letters of Berlioz*, ed. Hugh Macdonald, trans. Roger Nichols, London, Faber, 421
7. Interview with Paul Guth, *Le Figaro littéraire*, 17 May 1952; JE 601–2; NFH 149–50
8. Stéphane Audel in Haine, CIREM 160
9. 'How I composed *Les Dialogues des Carmélites*', *L'Opéra de Paris*, 14, 1957, 15–17; JE 196; NFH 55
10. Mary Garden and Louis Biancolli, *Mary Garden's Story*, London, Michael Joseph, 1952, 64
11. HL 15
12. See n.7
13. Jacques Soulé, 'Francis Poulenc dans ses jeunes années', privately printed for 'Les Amis de Francis Poulenc', n.d., 17
14. Corr. 10–1, n.6
15. Rosine Seringe in conversation with the author
16. JE 189
17. JE 756; NFH 191
18. JE 754–5; NFH 190
19. JE 750; NFH 184
20. The first twenty-six bars of the piece are published in HL 27. The autograph is in BnF Mus. MS 23589.
21. HL 30
22. Corr. 10–1
23. *Mes amis musiciens*, Paris, Les éditeurs français réunis, 1955, 130

24. ABR 25
25. JE 751; NFH 185
26. HL 46
27. Soulé, 14, 15
28. JE 856; MFM 33
29. JE 774; NFH 212
30. JE 857; MFM 35
31. HL 73
32. HL 73–4
33. ABR 197
34. Letter to Milhaud of 29 Sept 1922, Corr. 22–31
35. BnF Mus. MS 23581
36. BnF Mus. MS 23584
37. JE 755; NFH 190. As Lacombe notes, the question of whether Poulenc had seen the stage version of *Le Sacre* the year before remains open, given his myth-making tendencies (HL 75 and n.259)
38. JE 605; NFH 151
39. JE 858; MFM 37
40. Mildred Clary, *Ricardo Viñes, un pèlerin de l'absolu*, Arles, Actes Sud, 2011, 194
41. JE 757; NFH 192
42. Edith Wharton, *Fighting France: From Dunquerque to Belfort*, New York, Charles Scribner's Sons, 1915, 25
43. JE 752; NFH 187. The reference is to Stravinsky's edited version of *The Sleeping Beauty* made for Diaghilev in 1921 and to his use of extracts from Tchaikovsky in his own ballet *Le Baiser de la fée* in 1928.
44. Originals of responses in BnF Mus. LA 41; those of Debussy, Saint-Saëns, Satie and Roussel in Corr. 15–2, 3, 4, 6
45. Maurice Barrès, *Les Traits éternels de la France*, translated as *The Undying Spirit of France*, New Haven, Yale University Press, 1917, 2–3
46. FPF
47. HL 96
48. JE 859–60; MFM 38
49. *Art and the Everyday: Popular Entertainment and the Circle of Erik Satie*, Oxford, Clarendon Press, 1991, 112
50. Francis Steegmuller, *Cocteau: A Biography*, London, Constable, 1986, 160
51. *Hommage à Maurice Ravel*, in *Revue musicale*, no. spécial, December 1938, 205
52. Letter of 2 June 1917, Texas. Poulenc identifies himself as 'Compositeur Futuriste', a description he disowned shortly afterwards.
53. JE 807; NFH 253
54. Corr. 17–1; ES 2
55. Corr. 17–4; ES 4
56. JE 916–17; MFM 126
57. 'The public worship Ennui. For them, Ennui is mysterious and profound', *A Mammal's Notebook*, ed. Ornella Volta, trans. Antony Melville, London, Atlas Press, 1996, 149
58. This octatonic chord probably came from a study of Ravel's music.
59. *The Chesterian*, 1/2, Oct 1919, 55–6
60. Preface to M. Storez, *L'Architecture et l'art décoratif en France après la guerre (comment préparer leur renassissance)*, Paris, 1918, n.p.
61. Derain to Vlaminck in Cabanne, *Le Siècle de Picasso*, I, Paris, Denoël, 1975, 284–5
62. Paris, Dorbon Aîné, 1910, 10
63. Frederick Brown, *An Impersonation of Angels*, London, Longmans, 1969, 156–7
64. *Notes sans musique*, Paris, Julliard, 1949, 96
65. HL 119–20
66. *The Very Rich Hours of Adrienne Monnier*, trans. Richard McDougall, New York, Charles Scribner's Sons, 1976, 38

67. Sophie Robert, 'Raymonde Linossier: "Lovely soul who was my flame"', trans. Sidney Buckland, MAL 109
68. Corr. 17–3
69. BnF Mus. MS 17676
70. Stravinsky, *Chroniques de ma Vie*, Denoël/Gonthier, 1962, 13
71. EM 47
72. JE 861; MFM 41
73. Letters to Viñes of 28 and 18 Feb 1918, Corr. 18–3 and 18–2
74. BnF Mus. NLA 39 (27)
75. Undated letter from between 23 Aug and Sept 1918, Texas
76. Undated letter from between Jan and July 1918, Texas
77. Letter to Viñes of 3 Sept 1918, Corr. 18–7; ES 27–8
78. 26 Sept 1939, Corr. 39–14
79. HL 130–1
80. Rosenthal in conversation with the author
81. *An Impersonation of Angels*, 190
82. Letter of early Oct 1918 to Édouard Souberbielle, Corr. 18–11
83. Letter of 18 Oct 1918, Corr. 18–14
84. JE 796; NFH 240
85. Daniel,108
86. JE 246
87. JE 878; MFM 69
88. JE 322–3; ABR 213 (these two accounts differ)
89. Letters to Valentine Gross of 1 Oct 1918, 18–10, and to Souberbielle of 31 December 1918, Corr. 18–22
90. Roger Nichols, *Conversations with Madeleine Milhaud*, London, Faber, 1996, 23
91. Georges Auric, *Quand j'étais là*, Paris, Grasset, 1979, 26; trans. in Robert Orledge, *Satie Remembered*, London, Faber, 1995, 115
92. Letter of 2 Sept 1918 to Édouard Souberbielle, Corr. 18–6
93. Programme printed in EM 59
94. JE 903; MFM 197
95. See n.74
96. JE 803–4; NFH 248–9
97. Letter to Poulenc of 15 Oct 1918, Corr. 18–12
98. Nancy Perloff, *Art and the Everyday: Popular Entertainment and the Circle of Erik Satie*, Oxford, Clarendon Press, 1991, 154
99. Letter of 14 March 1919, Texas; quoted Cat. 26
100. Letter to Souberbielle, Corr. 18–18
101. Letter to Valentine Gross of 14 [March 1919], Corr. 19–6
102. *Mes amis musiciens*, 74
103. 'Mes maîtres et mes amis', JE 468–9; NFH 99
104. Letter to Pierre Bertin of Nov 1918, Erik Satie, *Correspondance presque complète*, ed. Ornella Volta, Paris, Fayard, 2000, 346; Michael Bullock, *Satie Seen through his Letters*, London, Marion Boyars, 1989, 97
105. Letter to Comte Étienne de Beaumont of end Dec 1918, Corr. 18–19
106. Corr. 18–20

II. 'NOW WE ARE SIX': 1919–1924

1. *Lettres et écrits*, ed. Nicole Labelle, Paris, Flammarion, 1987, 61
2. Paris, Stock, 1979, 61
3. *La Musique française de piano*, Paris, Quadrige/Presses universitaires de France, 1981, 499–500
4. HL 165
5. Letter of 7 Feb 1921, Corr. 21–1

6. Mary Garden and Louis Biancolli, *Mary Garden's Story*, London, Michael Joseph, 1952, 64
7. This similarity was pointed out by David Drew in *European Music in the Twentieth Century*, ed. Howard Hartog, London, Pelican, 1961, 280
8. *Le Nocturne. Fauré, Chopin et la nuit, Satie et le matin*, Paris, Albin Michel, 1957, 158
9. JE 547; NFH 125
10. JE 759; NFH 194
11. JE 756; NFH 192
12. 'Maurice Ravel', *ReM* 2/6, April 1921, 17; quoted in Barbara L. Kelly, *Music and Ultra-Modernism in France*, Woodbridge, The Boydell Press, 2013, 60
13. JE 758; NFH 193
14. Doda Conrad, *Dodascalies*, Arles, Actes Sud, 1997, 30
15. Ivry 30
16. Corr. 21–20; ES 32
17. 'Apollinaire et la musique', *ReM*, Jan 1952, 148
18. Alain Corbillari, 'Les sept péchés capitaux de Francis Poulenc', *Revue musicale de Suisse Romande*, 56/1 (March 2003), 44
19. JE 772; NFH 211
20. Letter of January/February 1919, Texas
21. Bernac 191; FPMS 183
22. Poulenc to Stravinsky, Letter of 26 Sept 1919, Corr. 19–19 and n.
23. JMM, 15
24. Louise Varèse, *A Looking-Glass Diary*, London, Eulenburg, 1975, 161–2
25. Darius Milhaud, *Ma Vie heureuse*, Paris, Belfond, 1973, 32
26. Letter of 'Lundi' (April–July 1919), Texas
27. Albert Roussel, *Lettres et écrits*, ed. Nicole Labelle, Paris, Flammarion, 1987, 81; the article 'Young French Composers' appeared in *The Chesterian*, I/2, October 1919, 33–7.
28. Ibid.
29. Letter to Poulenc of 27 Sept 1919, Corr. 19–20
30. MFM 138
31. Corr. 19–8; ES 17
32. Letter of 30 Aug 1919, Corr. 19–17; ES 36
33. 'Satie & Les Six', *French Music since Berlioz*, ed. Richard Langham Smith and Caroline Potter, Aldershot, Ashgate, 2006, 223–48
34. Ibid. 234
35. Corr. 19–22
36. *Ma Vie heureuse*, 83
37. Letter postmarked 8 Nov 1919, Cat. 54
38. JE 764; NFH 201
39. JE 759; NFH 194
40. Daniel 175
41. Cat. 56, Jean Chantavoine, *L'Excelsior*, 12 April 1920
42. See n.20 above
43. Robert Orledge, *Satie the Composer*, Cambridge University Press, 1990, 320
44. Ibid. 143
45. Bengt Häger, *Ballets suédois*, trans. Ruth Sharman, London, Thames & Hudson, 1990, 68. An illustration of Börlin in the role appears on p. 69.
46. JE 918–19; MFM 128–9 and Roger Nichols, *Ravel Remembered*, London, Faber, 1987, 118
47. Bronislava Nijinska, 'Reflections about the Production of *Les Biches* and *Hamlet* in Markova-Dolin Ballets', trans. Lydia Lopokova, in *Dancing Times*, February 1937, 617–18; Lynn Garafola, *Diaghilev's Ballets Russes*, New York, Oxford University Press, 1989, 127; Roger Nichols, *The Harlequin Years*, London, Thames & Hudson, 2002, 138
48. *L'Information musicale*, 7, Jan 1941, 195; JE 85
49. Letter of 22 June 1920, Yale f.978
50. L. Dunton Green, 'The Chamber Music Festival at Salzburg, *The Chesterian*, 4/25 (Sept 1922), 10

51. JE 61–3; NFH 17–19
52. Letter to Milhaud of 8 July 1920, Corr. 20–5; letters to Cocteau and Radiguet, dated respectively 'Mercredi' and 'Lundi', Texas
53. *Excelsior*, 6 March 1922, quoted in Albert Roussel, *Lettres et écrits*, 304
54. EM 34–5
55. 6/44, Jan/Feb 1925, 133
56. Paul Collaer, 'I "Sei"; Studio dell' evoluzione della musica francese dal 1917 al 1924', *L'Approdo musicale* 19–20, 1965, 53–4
57. Letter to Poulenc, 1921, Wendel 38
58. Henry Bidou, *L'Opinion*, 22 Jan 1921, quoted in HL 240
59. Corr. 21–2
60. Letter to Ansermet of Oct 1923, Corr. 23–34
61. Cat. 74
62. HH 55
63. Madeleine Milhaud in conversation with the author
64. Letter of 28 July 1921, Corr. 21–16
65. Review of 4 April 1921 in Arthur Bliss, *As I Remember*, London, Faber, 1970, 61
66. Letter of 22 Dec 1921 to Guy de Lioncourt, Vincent d'Indy, *Ma Vie*, ed. Marie d'Indy, Paris, Seguier, 2001, 790
67. Letter to Cocteau, summer 1921, Texas
68. Letter to Poulenc of 16 Dec 1921, Corr. 21–27
69. Letter [of Sept 1921], Corr. 21–19
70. *Ma Vie heureuse*, 32
71. The authoritative source for details of these lessons is Robert Orledge, 'Poulenc and Koechlin: 58 Lessons and a Friendship', MAL 9–47
72. JE 859; MFM 35
73. Orledge, op. cit. Exx 1.2 and 1.3a
74. Corr. 21–23
75. Corr. 21–27
76. Freund's son, Doda Conrad, in conversation with the author
77. Jean Wiéner, *Allegro appassionato*, Belfond, 1978, 51
78. Letter of 17 Oct 1921, Yale, f.978. 17–19
79. Eric Walter White, *Stravinsky: The Composer and his Works*, London, Faber, 1966, 291; from Alfredo Casella, *Strawinski*, Brescia, La Scuola, 1947
80. *Fanfare*, I/4, 15 Nov 1921
81. *The Music of Stravinsky*, Oxford, Clarendon Press, 1993, 102
82. See n.80
83. *Fanfare*, I/6, 15 Dec 1921
84. Virgil Thomson, *Virgil Thomson*, London, Weidenfeld and Nicolson, 1967, 55
85. *Ma Vie heureuse*, 117–18
86. 'Le musicien et le sorcier', *Les Lettres françaises*, 5 May 1945, JE 114; NFH 35
87. Ibid. 140, 142
88. Henri Sauguet, *La musique, ma vie*, Séguier, 1990, 88
89. Letter to his wife on 10 April 1922; Ravel, *L'Intégrale: Correspondance (1895–1937), écrits et entretiens*, ed. Manuel Cornejo, Paris, Le Passeur, 2018, letter 1424 n.1
90. Letter to Milhaud of 13 April 1922, Corr. 22–3
91. Letter to Jean-Aubry, Yale f.978, 24
92. Stephen Walsh, *Igor Stravinsky: A Creative Spring*, London, Jonathan Cape, 2000, 350, 349
93. *Ma Vie heureuse*, 110–11
94. Letter to Milhaud of June 1922, Corr. 22–9
95. Article in *Feuilles libres*, 27, June–July 1922; JE 68–9; NFH 22
96. Letter to Stravinsky of 9 July 1922, Corr. 22–15
97. Letter to Milhaud of 16 Aug 1922, Corr. 22–22

98. BnF Mus. MS 19340 (1, 2)
99. J. & W.C. 2122 (1–3)
100. Letter of 7 July 1922, Corr. 22–14
101. *Études*, Paris, Claude Aveline, 1927, 19
102. HL 179–80; Jean-Claire Vançon, 'Langage, matériau et forme dans les sonates de jeunesse pour instruments à vent de Francis Poulenc', *Langage*, 102
103. See n.72
104. Stock, 1979, 51
105. Spoken by Picasso in Rome in 1917; quoted in Kenneth E. Silver, *Esprit de Corps: The Art of the Parisian Avant-Garde and the First World War, 1914–1925*, London, Thames & Hudson, 1989, 211
106. Letter to Milhaud of 22 June 1922, Corr. 22–11
107. Letter to Koechlin of early Sept 1922, Corr. 22–26
108. Letter of 17 Nov 1922, in Auric, *Quand j'étais là*, Paris, Grasset, 1979, 57
109. Letter to Milhaud of 29 Sept 1922, Corr. 22–31
110. Facsimile in HL 254
111. Letter to Milhaud of Jan 1923, Corr. 23–3
112. *Revue musicale*, 1 March 1923, A. Getteman, 'Musique à Bruxelles', 176
113. Letter to Stravinsky of 17 Jan 1923, Corr. 23–4
114. See n.81
115. Victor Hugo's '*Préface de Cromwell*, published on 5 Dec 1827, was the codification of the precepts, the hoisting of the Romantic flag, the hors-d'oeuvre of an unperformable play which turned into the main course.' Graham Robb, *Victor Hugo*, London, Picador, 1997, 134
116. 'Les concerts Straram', ReM 1 June 1923, 133
117. Letter to Milhaud of 30 Jan 1923, Corr. 23–7
118. Letter to Koechlin, Corr. 23–26; ES 60–1
119. Letter of 8 Oct 1923, Erik Satie, *Correspondance presque complète*, ed. Ornella Volta, Paris, Fayard, 2000, CMXCV
120. Letter to Comte Étienne de Beaumont of 14 April 1923, Corr. 23–10
121. JE 924; MFM 137–8
122. Letter to Paul Collaer of 12 June, from Vichy, Corr. 23–15
123. See n.1
124. HL 259
125. Wendel 49–50
126. 'Apollinaire et Poulenc', *Apollinaire et la musique, actes du colloque Stavelot*, 27–29 Aug 1965, ed. Michel Décaudin, 1967, 54
127. Cat. 537
128. Cat. 371
129. Letter from Ravel to Georges Jean-Aubry of 13 Dec 1923, in *A Ravel Reader*, ed. and trans. Arbie Orenstein, New York, Columbia University Press, 1990, 247
130. Letters of 11 Sept, 19 Sept, 6 Oct 1923, Corr. 23–29, 23–33 (ES 63), 23–36 (ES 64)
131. Letter to Koechlin of 27 Oct 1923, Corr. 23–38
132. Letter of Nov 1923, Corr. 23–39. The reference is to the ballet by Delibes.
133. JE 767; NFH 205
134. Paul Levy reviewing Richard Bradford, *The Man who Wasn't There: A Life of Ernest Hemingway*, in *The Spectator*, 26 Jan 2019, 35. See Christopher Moore, 'Camp in Francis Poulenc's Early Ballets', *MQ*, 95, Sept 2012, 299–342; and '*Camp* et ambiguïté formelle dans le *Concert champêtre*', *Langage*, 319–30
135. Letter marked 'Vendredi soir', Corr. 23–47
136. *Diaghilev's Ballets Russes*, New York, Oxford University Press, 1989, 129–32
137. Ibid. 130
138. 'Francis Poulenc on His Ballets', *Ballet*, 4/2, Sept 1946, 57–8: JE 125–9; NFH 39–41
139. *Francis Poulenc par lui-même*, talk of 10 Jan 1962 at the Club des Trois Centres, Voxigrave, n.d.
140. *The Harlequin Years*, 138

141. *Comoedia*, 11 Jan 1924
142. HH 74–5
143. Quoted in André Coeuroy, *Panorama de la musique contemporaine*, Éditions Kra, 1928, 118
144. Letter to Paul Collaer, Collaer 164
145. *Passport to Paris*, Boston, Little, Brown, 1955, 119
146. Quoted by Rainer Peters in notes for *Les Fâcheux* and *La Pastorale*, Hänssler Classic, Les Ballets Russes, vol. 7, CD 93.265
147. Letter to Louis Durey of May 1924, Corr. 24–10
148. Letter to Armand Lunel of 10 May 1924, Corr. 24–11
149. Corr. 24–17; ES 72

III. DREAMING OF MATURITY: 1924–1928

1. Letter to Collaer of 8 April 1924, Corr. 24–9
2. Letter to Collaer [of 13 April 1924], Collaer 181
3. See n.1
4. Ibid.
5. Letters to Collaer of 21 Feb and 8 April 1924, to Durey of May 1924, and to Nora Auric of 23 Jan 1933, Corr. 24–8, 24–9, 24–10, 33–1
6. ReM 1 July 1924; HL 284–5
7. Paul Collaer, *Darius Milhaud*, trans. Jane Hohfeld Galante, San Francisco, San Francisco Press, 1988, 75
8. 'Erik Satie', *Paris Journal*, 27 June 1924, 1: Robert Orledge, *Satie Remembered*, trans. Roger Nichols, London, Faber, 1995, 194
9. René Gimpel, *Diary of an Art Dealer*, trans. John Rosenberg, London, Hamish Hamilton, 1986, 264. I am grateful to Sidney Buckland for sending me this text.
10. Letter to Collaer of 12 Dec 1924, Corr. 24–32
11. Collaer, *Darius Milhaud*, 76
12. Ibid. 78
13. Letter to Sauguet of Oct 1924, Corr. 24–25
14. Stravinsky, *Selected Correspondence*, ed. and trans. Robert Craft, vol. 3, London, Faber, 1985, 210
15. Daniel, 60
16. JE 796; NFH 240–1
17. Daniel, 111–13
18. JE 796; NFH 240
19. Médiathèque Mahler, Fonds Schaeffner, 196
20. Cat. 114–15. The orchestral version is available on the EMI box 7243 5 66849, disc 1, sung by François Le Roux with the Orchestre Philharmonique de Monte-Carlo conducted by John Nelson.
21. JE 641–2; NFH 158
22. JE 772–3; NFH 211–12
23. André George, *Les nouvelles littéraires*, 21 Mar 1925, Cat. 118
24. Letter to Auric of 15 March 1925, Corr. 25–5
25. ReM 1 Feb 1924, 164
26. Pierre Hermant, 'Musique de chambre et de piano', L. Rohozinski, *Cinquante ans de musique française de 1874 à 1925*, Paris, Les Éditions musicales de la Librairie de France, 1925, II, 135
27. 'Côte d'azur 47. Rêverie monégasque', *Opera*, 89, 22 Jan 1947, 1 and 6: JE 136–9
28. Hélène Jourdan-Morhange, 'Entretien avec F. Poulenc', unidentified newspaper cutting, around May/June 1957: JE 621–3
29. John Drummond, *Speaking of Diaghilev*, London, Faber, 1998, 262
30. Madeleine Milhaud in conversation with the author
31. Corr. 25–5. I have adopted the different but clearly correct order of events set out in EM 144–5.
32. Cyril W. Beaumont, *The Diaghilev Ballet in London*, London, Putnam, 1945, 246
33. Milhaud, *Ma Vie heureuse*, Paris, Belfond, 1973, 145

34. Sophie Robert's article, 'Raymonde Linossier: "Lovely soul who was my flame"', trans. Sidney Buckland, MAL 87–139, is an indispensable source of information on Linossier.
35. Letter of 6 July 1925, Corr. 255–7; ES 76–8
36. Yale f.978. 13–14
37. Letter to Collaer, Corr. 26–1
38. Letter to Jean Wiéner, Corr. 22–24
39. Letter of 22 Nov 1926, Corr. 26–9
40. JMM 16; Diary 25
41. An identical texture appears in 'Le mendiant', *Chansons villageoises*, which Poulenc noted was influenced by Musorgsky (*Journal de mes mélodies*, 40). Pierre-Emmanuel Lephay makes the link to the opening of 'Bydlo', *Pictures at an Exhibition* (*Langage*, 149–51).
42. JE 781–2; NFH 221–2
43. *The Chesterian*, 8, 57, Sept–Oct 1926, 25 in EM 149–50
44. *Les nouvelles littéraires*, 22 May 1926, 7
45. ReM, 1 Feb 1927, 169
46. Letter to Valentine Hugo of July 1926, Corr. 26–6
47. Richard Buckle, *Diaghilev*, London, Hamish Hamilton, 1984, 453
48. Corr. 26–7
49. Letter to Collaer, Corr. 26–8
50. Manuel Rosenthal, *Satie, Ravel, Poulenc*, Madras and New York, Hanuman Books, 1987, 55–6: Roger Nichols, *Ravel*, London, Yale University Press, 2011, 350
51. Corr. 27–1; ES 82–3
52. Roger Nichols, *Conversations with Madeleine Milhaud*, London, Faber, 1996, 81
53. Marguerite de Saint-Marceaux, *Journal, 1894–1927*, ed. Myriam Chimènes, Paris, Fayard, 2007, 1254
54. Letter of 22 June 1927, Ravel, *L'Intégrale: Correspondance (1895–1937), écrits et entretiens*, Letter 2054
55. EM 162
56. JMM 16; Diary 25
57. 'La Musique et les Ballets Russes de Serge Diaghilev', JE 358
58. Richard Buckle, *Diaghilev*, London, Hamish Hamilton, 1984, 489
59. Corr. 27–4
60. Igor Stravinsky and Robert Craft, *Dialogues and a Diary*, London, Faber, 1968, 25
61. Ibid. 26
62. Stephen Walsh, *The Music of Stravinsky*, Oxford, Clarendon Press, 1993, 135
63. See n.61
64. Letter of 9 Aug 1927, Corr. 27–6
65. Corr. 27–8
66. Corr. 27–10
67. JE 362
68. JE 823; NFH 273
69. *Dial*, July 1929, 608, reprinted in Lynn Garafola, *Diaghilev's Ballets Russes*, New York, Oxford University Press, 1989, 140 (the translation is by Ezra Pound)
70. JE 757; NFH 192
71. Interview with Lucien Chevaillier, 26 April 1929, JE 538; NFH 120
72. JE 777; NFH 217
73. HL 329–30
74. Daniel, 138
75. Letter to Émile Vuillermoz of 20 Aug [1928], Texas
76. Letter to Charles de Noailles of 16 July [1928], Corr. 28–2
77. Corr. 28–4
78. JE 548; NFH 126
79. Letter to Henri Sauguet of 9 Aug [1945], Corr. 45–19; ES 162–3
80. JE 546; NFH 125
81. Letter [of 24 January 1929], Corr. 29–1
82. Letter [of 3 December 1928], Corr. 28–13

IV. DEPRESSION AND RECOVERY: 1929–1934

1. Corr. 29–2
2. Letter of Tuesday [March 1929], Corr. 29–3, ES 103
3. Letter [of March 1929], Corr. 29–4
4. HL 333
5. Ibid. 326
6. Letter of 19 April 1929, Corr. 29–6
7. Letter of 10 May 1929, Corr. 29–8
8. For a summary of this text see Robert Graves, 'Artemis's Nature and Deeds', *The Greek Myths*, I, section 22, London, Penguin Books, 1955, 83–4
9. Letter to André Schaeffner of 11 Nov [1929], Corr. 29–20
10. JE 129; NFH 40
11. Letter to Claire Croiza [of Aug 1929], Corr. 29–15
12. See n.9
13. Letter of 13 Dec 1929, Collaer 29–13
14. Letter of 11 March 1932, ibid. 32–11
15. See n.9
16. JE 779; NFH 218
17. Corr. 29–14; ES 86
18. Myriam Chimènes, *Mécènes et Musiciens*, Fayard, 2004, 614 n.2
19. Corr. 29–17
20. Cat. FP 53
21. Letter [of 31 January 1930], Corr. 30–1
22. JMM 55; partly in Diary 96–7
23. Corr. 30–3
24. Letters to Marie-Laure de Noailles [of 11 April and 1 May 1930], Corr. 30–5 and 30–7
25. Postcard from Poulenc, Adolfo Salazar and Oscar Esplá to Ravel [of c.9 April 1930], Ravel, *L'Intégrale: Correspondence (1895–1937)*, *écrits et entretiens*, Letter 2296
26. Letter [of Aug 1929], Corr. 10–1, n.6
27. Letter [of summer 1930], Corr. 30–9
28. *Journal de musicologie* 16–17
29. Letter to Marie-Laure de Noailles [of 10 Oct 1930], Corr. 30–15
30. Letter to his publishers Salabert of 27 March 1931, Cat. 181
31. JE 844, MMA 10; MFM 14
32. Roger Shattuck, *The Banquet Years*, New York, Vintage Books, 1968, 270–1
33. Letter of Marie Laurencin to Poulenc [of 1931], Corr. 31–6; ES 90–1
34. Bernac 72; FPMS 56
35. JMM 17; Diary 27
36. Ibid.
37. Bernac 73; FPMS 57
38. JMM 17; Diary 27
39. JE 75; NFH 25
40. Corr. 31–9; ES 93–4
41. Letter of 6 April 1931, Corr. 31–10; ES 94
42. Letter to Poulenc of 24 Aug 1931, Corr. 31–14
43. Letter to the Comtesse Charles de Polignac [of 13 Aug 1931], Corr. 31–13
44. Letter to the Comtesse Charles de Polignac [of Oct 1931], Corr. 31–19
45. Quoted by Richard Langham Smith, 'Poulenc et Edward Lockspeiser: une amitié professionnelle', Fortune, 213; translation by Edward Lockspeiser
46. Bernac 166; FPMS 153
47. JMM 18; Diary 27
48. Henri Sauguet, *La musique, ma vie*, Séguier, 1990, 290
49. Michel Duchesneau, *L'Avant-garde musicale à Paris de 1871 à 1939*, Sprimont, Mardaga, 1997, 124

50. Darius Milhaud, *Ma Vie heureuse*, Paris, Belfond, 1973, 190
51. Corr. 31–28
52. René Bizet, 'Naissance d'une oeuvre. Les confidences de Maurice Ravel à la veille de l'exécution de son Concerto', Ravel, *L'Intégrale*, Document 2664, p.1559 n.1
53. Letter of 12 Jan [1932], Corr. 32–2
54. Letter of 14 Feb [1932], Corr. 32–3
55. Letters of 17 Feb 1932 and [1 March 1932], Corr. 32–5 (ES 96–7) and 32–6
56. Letter to André Latarjet [of summer 1932], Corr. 32–13
57. JE 805–6; NFH 252
58. JMM 34–5; Diary 61
59. Ibid.; Diary 63
60. HL 378
61. See n.43
62. JMM 33; Diary 59
63. Corr. 32–16
64. JE 915; MFM 123–4
65. Letter to Marguerite Long of 16 July [1932], MMM, Fonds Marguerite Long
66. JE 779; NFH 219
67. Rosenthal in conversation with the author
68. Letter [of Sep 1932], Corr. 32–17
69. JE 779; NFH 218708. JE 554 and 296; NFH 130 and 78
70. JE 554 and 296; NFH 130 and 78
71. Renaud Machart, *Poulenc*, Éditions du Seuil, 1995, 83
72. MMM, unpublished letter of 1932, Fonds Schaeffner 204
73. Machart 84
74. Letter of 1 Oct [1932], Corr. 32–19
75. Letter [of 10 Aug 1932], Corr. 32–14
76. Edmund Rubbra in conversation with the author
77. Jean Roy, *Francis Poulenc*, Paris, Éditions Seghers, 1964, 42–3
78. JE 758–9; NFH 193–4
79. Corr. 32–20; ES 98–9
80. Cat. 208–9
81. *Le Ménestrel*, 10 Mar 1933, in Cat. 207
82. Ibid. 208
83. Daniel 185
84. 'Les "Six" et le piano', in *La Musique française de piano*, Paris, Quadrige Presses universitaires de France, 1981, 528–9
85. EM 205
86. JE 783; NFH 223
87. HL 400
88. Eugen Weber, *The Hollow Years: France in the 1930s*, London, Sinclair-Stevenson, 1995, 134
89. Corr. 34–1
90. Stephen Walsh, *Igor Stravinsky: A Creative Spring*, London, Jonathan Cape, 2000, 530
91. Ibid. 534
92. Corr. 34–2
93. JE 81; NFH 28
94. Pierre Boulez in conversation with the author
95. *La Musique française de piano*, 524
96. Recorded by Berkeley's friend and biographer Tony Scotland in Peter Dickinson, *The Music of Lennox Berkeley*, Woodbridge, The Boydell Press, 2/2003, 16
97. Corr. 34–3
98. JE 280–3; NFH 65–7
99. JE 284–7; NFH 69–71
100. JE 290; NFH 74

101. Corr. 34–5; ES 123
102. JE 783–4; NFH 223

V. SURREALISM AND FAITH: 1934–1939

1. Corr. 34–6
2. JE 480; NFH 107
3. Letter to Marie-Blanche de Polignac, Corr. 31–11
4. JE 784–5; NFH 224
5. JE 480; NFH 108
6. JMM 19; Diary 31
7. HL 408
8. EM 215
9. Letter to Jeanne Manceaux [of 10 May 1935], Corr. 35–5
10. *Alexeieff, le cinéma épinglé*, www.cinedoc.org
11. Cat. 234–5
12. JE 461–73; NFH 95–103
13. JE 77–83; NFH 27–29
14. JE 78
15. JMM 30
16. Letter from Éluard of 4 April 1926, Corr. 36–5
17. Alban Ramaut, 'Francis Poulenc et les Latarjet', FPV 184 and 186
18. Corr. 36–2
19. JE 786–7; NFH 228
20. Letter of 15 Mar 1936, Corr. 36–3, and n.1, quoting from Koechlin's articles of 10 and 17 April
21. Letters to Nadia Boulanger of Sept 1936, Corr. 36–20 and BnF Mus. NLA 95, 88–9 and 90
22. Letter to Auric [of 25 Aug 1936], Corr. 36–18
23. JE 787; NFH 229
24. HL 417
25. A dominant 13th on A (A-G-C$\sharp$-F$\sharp$-B-E)
26. *Mes amis musiciens*, Paris, Les éditeurs français réunis, 1955, 132
27. HL 419
28. Corr. 36–9; ES 106
29. Letter to Auric [of 25 Aug 1936], Corr. 36–18
30. Corr. 36–17
31. See n.22
32. Graham Johnson and Richard Stokes, *A French Song Companion*, Oxford University Press, 2000, 353
33. *Francis Poulenc*, Paris, Zodiaque, 1974, 21
34. Yvonne Gouverné in conversation with the author
35. Corr. 36–20
36. Renaud Machart, *Poulenc*, Paris, Éditions du Seuil, 1995, 104
37. Letter to Marc Pincherle [of 30 Jan 1954], *Les Autographes* sale catalogue, Sept 2011, item 133
38. See n.22
39. JE 791; NFH 233
40. Letter to Nora Auric [of 11 Sept 1936], Corr. 36–22
41. JE 471; NFH 100
42. JE 759, 834; NFH 194, 286
43. Interview of 2013: https://www.youtube.com/watch?v=BUned9kjobI
44. Bernac 113; FPMS 98
45. JMM 21; this line is no longer in use.
46. Daniel 39
47. Letter [of spring 1945], Corr. 45–9; ES 155–6
48. 'Éluard, Poulenc and *Tel jour telle nuit*', MAL 161, 171

49. Ibid. 146
50. Letter to Poulenc of 2 Jan 1937, Corr. 37–1; ES 109
51. JMM 46
52. JMM 22
53. JE 771; NFH 210
54. JE 921; MFM 133
55. Cat. 267
56. *La Musique française après Debussy*, Paris, Gallimard, 1943, 161–2
57. Letter to Lunel [of April 1937], Corr. 37–3
58. 'In Search of a Libretto', MAL 255
59. Letter to Nora Auric [of 17 Aug 1937], Corr. 37–9
60. Letter of 19 Aug [1937], Corr. 37–10
61. Letter to Madame Albert Roussel [of 27 Aug 1937], Corr. 37–13
62. JE 812; NFH 260
63. JE 790; NFH 231
64. ABR 85
65. Vincent Cronin, *Paris, City of Light 1919–1939*, London, HarperCollins, 1994, 280
66. Ibid. 279
67. Ned Rorem, *Settling the Score*, New York, Doubleday, 1989, 175
68. HH 129
69. Daniel 225
70. Mellers 79
71. Letter to Collaer [of 12 Oct 1937], Corr. 37–18
72. JE 769; NFH 207
73. HH 163
74. JMM 44; Diary 39
75. 'Le coeur de Maurice Ravel', *La nouvelle Revue française*, 323, 1 Jan 1941; JE 293, NFH 79
76. JMM 26; Diary 45
77. JE 788; NFH 229
78. Alban Ramaut, 'Francis Poulenc et les Latarjet', FPV 181
79. Letter to Yvonne Gouverné of Monday [May 1938], Corr. 38–4, ES 114
80. Alastair Sooke, 'The Crucifixion of Pablo Picasso', *Daily Telegraph*, 3 Mar 2018
81. Harry Halbreich, *Arthur Honegger*, trans. Roger Nichols, Portland, Amadeus Press, 1999, 417
82. Ibid. 128
83. René Kerdyk, 'Portrait, Francis Poulenc', *Gringoire*, 11 Feb 1938, BnF Mus., Fonds Montpensier
84. Letters [of 30 April 1936] and 15 Aug to Marie-Blanche de Polignac, Corr. 36–9; ES 129 and Corr. 36–15; ES 130
85. Letter [of May 1938], Corr. 38–6
86. Ibid. n.1, letter [of 27 May 1938]
87. *L'Orgue*, no. 154, April–June 1975, trans. *Music*, The AGO-RCCO Magazine, vol. 8, issue 7, July 1974
88. Mellers 90
89. Letter [of July 1939], Corr. 39–4,
90. JMM 24–5; Diary 43
91. JMM 25; Diary 43
92. JMM 26; Diary 45
93. HL 471
94. Bernac 124; FPMS 111
95. JMM 28; Diary 49
96. Corr. 39–3, n.2
97. Guy de Maupassant, *A Parisian Affair and Other Stories*, trans. Sian Miles, London, Penguin, 2004, 78–9
98. See n.89
99. JE 759; NFH 194

100. *Les Trois Centres*
101. Letter to Marie-Blanche [of 17 April 1939], Corr. 39–3; ES 118–19
102. Corr. 39–14
103. *Les Trois Centres*
104. Hell 161
105. Ivry 117
106. See n.104
107. Letter to Collaer [of 27 Nov 1939], Corr. 39–22
108. Nicolas Nabokov, *Old Friends and New Music*, London, Hamish Hamilton, 1951, 149
109. See n.104

VI. THE YEARS OF DARKNESS: 1939–1944

1. Nabokov, op. cit. 149
2. Bernac 150; FPMS 137
3. JMM 62; Diary 111. Poulenc's opinion is dated Sept 1960.
4. JMM 32; Diary 57
5. Letter [of Oct 1939], Corr. 39–19 n.2; ES 122
6. *A French Song Companion*, Oxford University Press, 2000, 354
7. JMM 33; Diary 57
8. Letter to Agathe Rouart-Valéry [of Oct 1939], Corr. 39–19; ES 150
9. Letter to Simone Girard [of Oct 1939], Corr. 39–20
10. Letter to Édouard Bourdet [of Dec 1939], Corr. 39–23
11. Myriam Chimènes, 'Alfred Cortot et la politique musicale du gouvernement de Vichy', *La Vie musicale sous Vichy*, ed. Myriam Chimènes, Paris, Éditions Complexe, 2001, 36
12. EM 265
13. JMM 13; Diary 19
14. HL 486
15. Letter of 19 April 1940, BnF Mus. NLA-37 (253)
16. Letter of 13 May 1940, BnF Mus. NLA-37 (191)
17. *L'Éternité fragile, vol. 3, Le Palais des mirages*, Bernard Grasset, 1992, 218
18. Letter [of 10 July 1940], Corr. 40–5
19. Letter of 10 July [1940], Corr. 40–6, ES 152
20. Jean Dutourd, *Les Taxis de la Marne*, Paris, Gallimard, 1956/1992, 120, trans. Richard D. E. Burton; *Olivier Messiaen, Texts, Contexts, & Intertexts (1937–1948)*, ed. Roger Nichols, New York, Oxford University Press, 2016, 37
21. Vercors (Jean Bruller), *Le silence de la mer*, Paris, Albin Michel, 1942/1951
22. Letter [of 20 Aug 1940], Corr. 40–10
23. Mellers 46–7
24. Corr. 45–13, n.1; ES 160–1
25. Letter of 9 Sept 1940, Corr. 40–12; ES 154
26. HL 505
27. Letter to Nora Auric of 1 Jan [1941], partially in Cat. 307, complete in Yale GEN MSS MUSIC MISC f. 326
28. JMM 36; Diary 65
29. JE 274; NFH 77
30. JE 82; NFH 28
31. Bernac 88; FPMS 72
32. Ibid. 87
33. HH 168
34. Yale GEN MSS 601, box 48, f.982, 2–3
35. MMA 61; MFM 49
36. Letter of Tuesday [Jan 1941], Corr. 41–1; ES 157
37. Details in EM 488–9, App 2

38. Letter to Gret of Wednesday [15 Jan 1941], Corr. 41–2
39. Cat. 324
40. Letter of 28 July [1941], Corr. 41–6
41. Letter of Friday [1 Aug 1941], Corr. 41–7
42. Corr. 41–11
43. HL 507
44. Pascale Honegger in conversation with the author
45. Alexandra Laederich, 'Les associations symphoniques parisiennes', *La Vie musicale sous Vichy*, ed. Myriam Chimènes, Paris, Éditions Complexe, 2001, 217, 225, 223
46. Letter of 3 Jan to Koechlin, Robert Orledge, 'Poulenc and Koechlin', MAL 37
47. Corr. 42–4
48. Letter [of 12 Oct 1937], Corr. 37–18
49. Mellers 96
50. See n.37
51. Corr. 42–6
52. Letter [of Aug 1942], Corr. 42–7; ES 159
53. JE 823; NFH 273
54. 'Entretien avec A.P.: Francis Poulenc nous parle de son nouveau ballet *Les animaux modèles*', *Le Figaro*, 14 Aug 1942, JE 568; NFH 134
55. Letter to Colette of 22 Aug [1942], Corr. 42–8, n.1
56. Ibid.
57. See n.45
58. Alfred Cobban, *A History of Modern France*, vol. 3, London, Penguin, 1975, 187
59. See the memoirs of the schoolmaster Jean Guéhenno, *Journal des années noires*, Paris, Gallimard, 1947: for example, his entry for 21 Aug 1941, 'In the "communist" quarter in which I live [. . .] the common people, resigned for so long, are falling into despair. [. . .] There is nothing we can do and there will be nothing for a long time yet.' (p.178)
60. 'Un ballet de Francis Poulenc à l'Opéra', *Comoedia*, 15 Aug 1942, reprinted (as 'Les animaux modèles') in *Incantation aux fossiles*, Lausanne, Aux Éditions d'Ouchy, 1948, 111
61. Henri Dutilleux in conversation with the author
62. Letter to Schaeffner [of Oct 1942], Corr. 42–20, ES 160
63. Letter [of 10 July 1940], Corr. 40–5
64. *A Ned Rorem Reader*, New Haven and London, Yale University Press, 2001, 221
65. JMM 39; Diary 71
66. Bernac 182
67. Daniel 271
68. JMM 39; Diary 71
69. Letters of Saturday [20 Aug 1938], Tuesday [29 Aug 1939] and [Aug 1942], Corr. 38–11, 39–10 (ES 120) and 42–7 (ES 128–9)
70. Corr. 42–18
71. Letter of 3 Dec [1942] from Brive-la-Gaillarde, Corr. 42–21
72. Ian Ousby, *Occupation: The Ordeal of France, 1940–1944*, London, Pimlico, 1999, 268
73. JE 834 and 759; NFH 287 and 194
74. 'Sur deux premières auditions', *Comoedia*, 103, 19 June 1943, JE 106. In Spanish, 'La guitarra hace llorar a los sueños'; in French, 'La guitare fait pleurer les songes'
75. Rostand 11, JE 796; NFH 240
76. Letter [of July 1943], Corr. 43–2
77. Letter [of July 1943], Corr. 43–3
78. Letter of 25 Sept 1946, Paul Collaer, *Correspondance avec des amis musiciens*, Sprimont, Mardaga, 46–12. From Beaulieu Poulenc was thrilled to see, on the hills, a *maquis* campfire.
79. Letter to Bernac of 17 Aug [1943], Corr. 43–4; ES 131–2
80. Letter to Victor Hely-Hutchinson [of 1 Dec 1944], Corr. 44–18
81. Letter to Roland-Manuel of 1 Mar [1950], Corr. 50–14
82. Hervé Lacombe, 'Puissance expressive et "plastique chorale" dans *Figure humaine*', FPV 217

83. 'Entretien avec Jeannie Chauveau: "Secrètement élaborée sous l'Occupation, l'oeuvre de deux grands artistes français va être révélée au monde par la chorale d'Anvers" ', *Ce soir*, 994, 25 Nov 1944, JE 572; NFH 137–8

84. JE 789; NFH 230

85. FPV 220

86. Pierre Michaut, *Libération soir*, 18 Nov 1944, BnF Mus., Fonds Montpensier

87. 'Mes mélodies et leurs poètes', *Conferencia*, 36, 15 Dec 1947, JE 482; NFH 109

88. Ibid.

89. See Geoffrey Treasure, *The Huguenots*, New Haven and London, Yale University Press, 2013, 254

90. Brigitte Massin, *Les Joachim, une famille de musiciens*, Paris, Fayard, 1999, 286–7

91. Letter of 20 Aug 1943, Corr. 43–6

92. Letter [of Oct 1943], Corr. 43–9. Another reason for Poulenc's distaste might have been that Delforge was close to the Nazis.

93. Letter to Roland-Manuel [of 8 Nov 1943], Corr. 43–13

94. Frederic Spotts, *The Shameful Peace*, New Haven and London, Yale University Press, 2008, 3, 249

95. Cat. 342–4; HL 541–2. *Souvenirs*, in an edition by Hervé Lacombe, was published by Salabert in 2016.

96. Haine, CIREM 210

97. Corr. 44–1

98. Letter of 10 April 1944, Corr. 44–2

99. Corr. 44–4; ES 164

100. Letter to Bernac [of 9 June 1944], Corr. 44–3

101. See n.81

102. 'Poulenc's Les Mamelles de Thirésias', *MQ*, xxv, April 1949, 318

103. Letter to Bernac of 29 June [1944], Corr. 44–4; ES 164

104. Letter [of 5 July 1944], Corr. 44–7, n.6; ES 137

105. Letter [of 22 July 1944], Corr. 44–8; ES 138–9

106. Letter to Sauguet of 28 July [1944], Corr. 44–12; ES 143–4. Sauguet's long reply of 4 Aug 1944, Corr. 44–14; ES 144–6

107. 'The archives of the Ville de Paris record 2,873 Parisians, including inhabitants of the inner suburbs, killed during the month of August.' Anthony Beevor and Artemis Cooper, *Paris after the Liberation*, London, Hamish Hamilton, 1994, 58n

108. Letter [of 27 Aug 1944], Corr. 44–16

VII. 'LIBERTY, I WRITE YOUR NAME': 1944–1952

1. The following paragraphs owe much to Langham Smith's excellent article 'Poulenc et Edward Lockspeiser: une amitié professionnelle', Fortune, 197–219

2. Letter to René Lara of 8 Oct [1898], Gabriel Fauré, *Correspondance*, ed. Jean-Michel Nectoux, Paris, Flammarion, 1980, 233,

3. 'De l'avenir au présent', *La Bataille*, 5 April 1945, BnF Mus., Fonds Montpensier

4. Letter of 6 Nov 1944, Corr. 44–17

5. Letter [of 1 Dec 1944], Corr. 44–18

6. Renaud Machart, *Poulenc*, Paris, Éditions du Seuil, 1995, 149; Jean Roy, *Francis Poulenc*, Paris, Éditions Seghers, 1964, 54

7. 'Le figuralisme dans la musique profane a cappella de Francis Poulenc', FPV 198–9

8. *Untwisting the Serpent*, Chicago and London, University of Chicago Press, 2000, 296–7; though I don't concur with Albright that Ravel's usage is in any way comical or burlesque.

9. Graham Johnson and Richard Stokes, *A French Song Companion*, Oxford University Press, 2000, 357

10. JMM 43; Diary 77

11. Philip Reed, 'Poulenc, Britten, Aldeburgh: A Chronicle', MAL, 349–50

12. JE 789; NFH 230–1

13. Gillian Opstad, *Debussy's Mélisande*, Woodbridge, The Boydell Press, 2009, 290
14. 'Poulenc et Edward Lockspeiser', n.1, 202. Later, Poulenc complained, 'With *Figure humaine* in English, I was suffering at every word.' Pierre Miscevic, *Lettres inédites à Brigitte Manceaux*, 226
15. Ibid. 205
16. Letter of 27 March 1945, Corr. 45–4; ES 175
17. 'Vive Strawinsky!', *Le Figaro*, 199, 7 April 1945, JE 108–12; NFH 31–3
18. Manuel Rosenthal in conversation with the author
19. Letter to Bernac [of May 1945], Corr. 45–11; ES 157–8
20. Letter of 9 Aug [1945], Corr. 45–19; ES 162–3
21. Machart 154
22. HL 574
23. Letter of Sunday [Aug 1945], Corr. 45–13, n.1; ES 160–1
24. Letter of 10 [Sept 1945], Corr. 45–21; ES 185
25. Letter to Paul Rouart of 2 Oct [1945], Corr. 45–26
26. Letter to Bernac [of Sept 1945], Corr. 45–25
27. Letter of 28 Dec [1945], Corr. 45–31
28. Pierre Boulez in conversation with the author
29. 'Le musicien et le sorcier', *Les lettres françaises*, 54, 5 May 1945, JE 115; NFH 36
30. Joan Peyser, *Boulez: Composer, Conductor, Enigma*, London, Cassell, 1977, 75
31. See n.26
32. Letter of 30 Dec [1945], Corr. 45–34
33. Anthony Beevor and Artemis Cooper, *Paris after the Liberation*, London, Hamish Hamilton, 1994, 90, 94
34. Letter of 15 March [1946], Corr. 46–2
35. Letter to Bernac [of summer 1946], BnF, MS, NAF 27139
36. Letter of 5 May [1946], ed. Peter Dickinson, *Lennox Berkeley and Friends*, Woodbridge, The Boydell Press, 2012, 74–5
37. Manuel Rosenthal, *Satie, Ravel, Poulenc*, Madras and New York, Hanuman Books, 1987, 74
38. JMM 48–9; Diary 83
39. JMM 53; Diary 91
40. Letter of 4 Dec 1946, Corr. 46–15
41. Letter of 28 Dec 1946, Corr. 46–16. Then as now, the Paris gutters were flushed out daily, so there could be no second thoughts.
42. JE 798; NFH 242
43. Letter of Désormière to Collaer of 16 Nov 1944, Collaer 44–5
44. JE 809; NFH 255
45. Letter [of 13 Jan 1947], Corr. 47–1; ES 169. In the circumstances, this date must be regarded as questionable.
46. *Folies de Paris*, London, Chappell, 1979, 173
47. Dominique Sordet, *Douze chefs d'orchestre*, Paris, Librairie Fischbacher, 1924, 50, 51
48. HL 586, 588
49. Letter of 11 June 1947, Corr. 47–5; ES 169–70
50. Roger Shattuck, 'Surrealism at the Opéra-Comique', *Theatre Arts*, xxxii, Jan 1948, 51
51. Ivry 138
52. HL 588
53. Letter to Bernac of 24 June [1944], Corr. 44–4; ES 134–6
54. HH 194
55. Letter of 12 Oct [1937], Corr. 37–17
56. 'In Search of a Libretto', MAL 255
57. Francis Steegmuller, *Apollinaire: Poet among the Painters*, Harmondsworth, Penguin, 1973, 262
58. Ibid.
59. Cat. 351
60. JMM 44; partially in Diary 79
61. *Untwisting the Serpent*, 304

62. JongEun Yim, 'Therapeutic Benefits of Laughter in Mental Health: A Theoretical Review', *Tohoku Journal of Experimental Medicine*, July 2016, vol. 239/3, 243–9

63. JE 474–83; NFH 105–9

64. Memorandum to Mr Lowe of 24 Feb 1947, BBC, Caversham

65. Letter to Rose Lambiotte, Corr. 47–9

66. Letters to Bernac [of Aug or Sept 1947] and to Schaeffner of 23 Aug [1947], Cat. 377

67. JMM 53, 57; Diary 90–1

68. *A French Song Companion*, 358

69. Cat. 380

70. Corr. 47–8

71. HL 607

72. Unpublished letter to Bernac of 23 Sept [1947], Yale GEN MSS 601, Box 48 f.969, 29

73. Published under their original title *À bâtons rompus*, ed. Lucie Kayas, Arles, Actes Sud, 1999

74. Arthur Gold and Robert Fizdale, *Misia*, London, Macmillan, 1980, 306

75. Letter of 15 Sept [1948], Corr. 48–6

76. JMM 54; Diary 92–3

77. Letter to Bernac of 18 July [1948], Corr. 48–2; ES 170–2

78. Ibid.

79. Letter to Bernac of 31 July [1948], Cat. 386

80. BnF Mus. MS 20244

81. See n.77

82. Letter of 8 Sept 1948, Cat. 386

83. JMM 55; partially in Diary 96–7

84. Carl Schmidt, 'La méthode de composition de Francis Poulenc', *Langage*, 365–81

85. Letter to Marie-Blanche [of May 1949], Corr. 49–6

86. 'Hommage à Jean Witkowski', JE 402–3

87. Letter to Bernac of 8 March [1957], Corr. 57–11

88. Daniel 123

89. Corr. 48–3 n.1

90. JE 870

91. Letter of 18 Aug [1947], Corr. 47–11

92. Ibid., n.1

93. Cat. 389

94. 'Poulenc's choral works with orchestra', MAL, 51, 55

95. Daniel 61

96. Mellers 159

97. Jacques Lonchampt, 'À la radio. La Tribune libre de la musique vivante', *Le Monde*, 18 Jan 1962, 13, in JE 177–8

98. Letters to Alice Ardoin [of 21 July 1928], Corr. 28–4, to André Jolivet of [Oct 1943], Corr. 43–9, and two letters to Bernac of 10 [Sept 1945] and [Sept 1945], Corr. 45–21 (ES 163–4) and 45–25

99. *Dodascalies*, 329–30

100. Corr. 48–6

101. HL 617

102. Letter to Brigitte Manceaux of 3 Nov 1948, Corr. 48–8; ES 194

103. *Dodascalies*, Arles, Actes Sud, 1997, 330

104. JMM 53–4; Diary 92–3

105. Bernac 232–3

106. Letter to Denise Bourdet of 5 Dec [1948], Corr. 48–11

107. Letter to Elvira Viñes Soto of 10 Mar 1949, Corr. 49–3; ES 174–5. Viñes's recorded legacy, lasting just a fraction over one hour, has been reissued with the biography by Mildred Clary, *Ricardo Viñes, un pèlerin de l'absolu*, Arles, Actes Sud, 2011.

108. Letter to Marie-Blanche [of May 1949], Corr. 49–6

109. Letter [of October 1943], Corr. 43–9

110. Letters to Bernac of 10 [Sept 1945], Corr. 45–21, and [Sept 1945], Corr. 45–25; ES 163–4

111. Corr. 49–9 n.3
112. JMM 55; Diary 96–7
113. Letter to Irène Aïtoff [end of 1949], Corr. 49–16
114. Corr. 49–13
115. Yale f.974, 24–6, partially in Corr. 49–14 n.1
116. Corr. 49–14; ES 178
117. *Music and People*, New York, George Braziller, 1968, 28
118. 'Petits conseils à un grand chanteur', *Candide*, 11 Feb 1957, BnF Mus., Fonds Montpensier
119. Pierre Gervasoni, *Henri Dutilleux*, Arles, Actes Sud / Philharmonie de Paris, 2016, 1637 (n.27)
120. Letter of 18 Sept [1949], Corr. 49–13
121. 'Feuilles américaines', JE 161; NFH 46
122. Dominique Jameux, *Pierre Boulez*, trans. Susan Bradshaw, Cambridge, MA, Harvard University Press, 1991, 14
123. 'Debussy's "Jeux"', *Die Reihe*, 5, Bryn Mawr, Theodore Presser Company, 1959, 3–20
124. JE 161–2
125. Letter to Jolivet of 28 Feb [1950], Corr. 50–13
126. Roy, *Francis Poulenc*, 106
127. Daniel 154
128. Letter of 16 Feb [1950], Corr. 50–8
129. This last admission from Henri Hell in conversation with the author. His biography was published in 1958 and revised in 1978.
130. See n.128
131. Letter to Roland-Manuel of 1 March [1950], Corr. 50–14
132. Letter to Yvonne de Casa Fuerte of 10 March [1950], Corr. 50–17; ES 183–4
133. Letter to Bernac [of 19 Aug 1955], Corr. 55–11
134. *A French Song Companion*, 358
135. JMM 56
136. Letter of 6 Sept [1950], Corr. 50–28
137. 'Encore BOLIVAR!', Poulenc and Gavoty, *Le Figaro*, 6 June 1950, 6
138. Letter to Hélène Jourdan-Morhange of 22 Aug [1950], Corr. 50–25
139. Henry Barraud, *Un Compositeur aux commandes de la Radio*, Paris, Fayard, 2010, 474–5
140. Letter of 6 Sept [1950], Corr. 50–28
141. Letter of 1 Aug [1950], Corr. 50–22
142. JE 814–15; NFH 262–3
143. *Les Trois Centres*
144. JE 792; NFH 234
145. E. Abry, C. Audic and P. Crouzet, 'Bossuet (1627–1704)', *Histoire illustrée de la Littérature Française*, Paris, Henri Didier, 1922, 257
146. Ivry 158
147. Markus Schneider, 'La Mère des douleurs dansante: une analyse du *Stabat Mater* de Francis Poulenc', *Langage*, 245–6
148. 'Poulenc's choral works with orchestra', MAL 55
149. Letter of 6 Jan 1951, Corr. 50–24 n.2
150. Ibid. in the body of the letter
151. Letter of 22 Aug [1950], Corr. 50–25
152. Mellers 141
153. I am grateful to Andrew McCrae for bringing this to my notice.
154. Letter to Sauguet of 5 Oct [1950], Corr. 50–30
155. W. R. Anderson, 'Round about Radio', *Musical Times*, Dec 1950, 477; C. M., 'New Music in London', ibid. 482
156. Letter to Poulenc [of 22 Nov 1950], Corr. 50–33
157. JE 857; MFM 35
158. Corr. 51–3; ES 215
159. Letter from Turin to Dr Claudine Escoffier-Lambiotte of 3 Feb [1951], Corr. 51–2

160. Letter of 15 Aug [1951], Corr. 51–11; ES 191
161. Letter [of 24 Jan 1951], Corr. 51–3 n.8; ES 381–2
162. Manuel Rosenthal in conversation with the author
163. Letter to Pierre Souvtchinsky of 31 Aug [1951], Corr. 51–14
164. 'La musique de piano de Prokofieff', *Musique russe*, vol. 2, ed. Pierre Soutvtchinsky, Paris, Presses universitaires de France, 1953, 269–76; JE 322–38
165. Letter to Simone Girard [of 10 Dec 1951], Corr. 51–16; ES 221
166. Ibid.
167. Bernac recorded Schumann's *Dichterliebe* with Robert Casadesus for Columbia.
168. Letter to Simone Girard [of 28 Jan 1952], Corr. 52–3; ES 222
169. Letter of 13 Feb [1952], Corr. 52–6
170. Letter to Landowska of 8 July [1952], Corr. 52–18
171. Brigitte Massin, *Les Joachim*, Paris, Fayard, 1999, 338
172. Pierre Boulez, *Points de repère*, Paris, Éditions du Seuil, 1981, 394; trans. Martin Cooper, *Orientations*, London, Faber, 1986, 505
173. Letter of 21 April [1952], Corr. 52–12; ES 227
174. Cat. 420
175. HL 636
176. JE 812–13; NFH 261
177. Daniel 231
178. See n.173
179. François Porcile, *Les conflits de la musique française, 1940–1965*, Paris, Fayard, 2001, 141–2
180. Letter to Yvonne de Casa Fuerte of 27 May [1952], Corr. 52–14
181. Issue of 28 May 1952
182. Paul Kildea, *Benjamin Britten: A Life in the Twentieth Century*, London, Allen Lane, 2013, 361
183. See n.180
184. MAL 348–62
185. Letter to Marc Pincherle of 16 April [1952], Corr. 52–10 n.2
186. Letter to Pincherle of 18 April [1952], Corr. 52–11
187. Letter to Milhaud of 10 July 1952, Corr. 52–17 n.8

VIII. MAD ABOUT NUNS: 1952–1956

1. Cat. 439
2. Letter to Nora Auric of 12 Jan [1932], Corr. 32–2
3. Letter to Simone Girard of 24 Dec 1951, Corr. 51–16, n.4; ES 384
4. Letter to Bernac of 20 Aug [1952], 52–21
5. Ibid.
6. Letter to Sidney Buckland of 2 July 1988, sent by her to the author
7. Letter to Gold and Fizdale of 17 Sept 1955, Corr. 55–14; ES 235–6
8. Letter to Simone Girard [of Nov 1953], BnF Mus. NLA-37, 241
9. *Mes amis musiciens*, Paris, Les éditeurs français réunis, 1995, 137
10. HL 638
11. Letter to Simone Girard of 10 July 1952, Corr. 52–21, n.2
12. Letter to Yvonne de Casa Fuerte of 3 Oct [1952], Corr. 52–26
13. Letter to Bernac of 20 Aug [1952], Corr. 52.21
14. Letter to Bernac of 2 Sept [1952], Corr. 52–22
15. See n.12
16. Letter to Bernac [of 6 Jan 1953], Corr. 53–1; ES 200–1
17. Letter of 8 Jan 1953, Corr. 53–3
18. Letter to Igor Markévitch, Corr. 53–5
19. Letter to Simone Girard [of March 1953], Corr. 53–6; ES 201–2
20. 'Comment j'ai composé *Les Dialogues des Carmélites*', *L'Opéra de Paris*, 14, 1957 in JE 197–8; NFH 56–7

21. Margarita Wallmann, *Les Balcons du ciel*, Paris, Éditions Robert Laffont, 1976, 150
22. Colin Jones, 'The Carmelites of Compiègne', programme of the Royal Opera House, Covent Garden, May/June 2014, 25
23. Pierre Enckell, 'Les vraies Carmélites de Compiègne', 'Dialogues des Carmélites', *L'Avant-Scène Opéra*, 257, 2010, 46–7
24. All of this paragraph is indebted to Claude Gendre's fine article '*Dialogues des Carmélites*: The historical background, literary destiny and genesis of the opera', MAL 274–319
25. Letter to Bernac of 22 [Aug 1953], Corr. 53–16; ES 206
26. Letter to Audel of 31 Aug [1953], Corr. 53–18; ES 206
27. Letter to Bernac of 1 Sept [1953], Corr. 53–19; ES 207–8
28. Letter to Simone Girard of 4 Dec [1953], Corr. 53–30
29. See n.27
30. Corr. 53–26
31. *The Musical Times*, Dec 1953, 577
32. Letter to Doda Conrad of 6 Dec [1953], Cat. 443
33. Letter to Pierre Souvtchinsky of 27 Jan [1954], Corr. 54–4
34. Report in *Le Figaro*, 9 May 1952
35. Boulez in conversation with the author
36. Letter to his father of 1 June 1953, Pierre Gervasoni, *Henri Dutilleux*, Arles, Actes Sud/Philharmonie de Paris, 2016, 486
37. Dutilleux in conversation with the author
38. Letter to Brigitte Manceaux of 28 March 1956, Corr. 56–4; ES 237–9
39. Letter of 10 May 1954, Corr. 54–16; ES 218
40. Letter [of ?28 Jan or 4 Feb 1954], Corr. 54–5; ES 215
41. JMM 37–8; Diary 99
42. Bernac 173; FPMS 161
43. See n.25
44. Letter of 22 Aug [1953], Corr. 53–17
45. Corr. 53–31, n.1
46. Letter of 27 Jan 1954, Yale GEN MSS 601, Box 48, f.971,8; partially in Corr. 54–8, n.1
47. '*Les Dialogues des Carmélites*: Métamorphoses de la victime sacralisée', CIREM, 109
48. Letter to Brigitte Manceaux [of 21 July 1954], Corr. 54–19
49. Collaer, *Correspondance*, letter from Sauguet to Collaer of 22 Nov 1954, 428
50. Cat. 395
51. Letter [of July 1954], Corr. 54–20
52. Unpublished letter of 11 [Oct 1954], Texas
53. Letter [of Oct 1954], Corr. 54–32; ES 223–4
54. Letter of 4 Nov [1954], Corr. 54–34; ES 225–6
55. Letter to Rose Dercourt-Plaut of 20 Dec [1954], Corr. 54–37
56. Henry Barraud, *Un Compositeur aux commandes de la Radio*, Paris, Fayard, 2010, 826
57. Claude Gendre, '*Dialogues des Carmélites*: The historical background, literary destiny and genesis of the opera', trans. Sidney Buckland, MAL 305
58. '*Les Dialogues des Carmélites*: Métamorphoses de la victime sacralisée', CIREM, 115
59. Letter of 5 April [1955], Corr. 55–2
60. Joan Peyser, *Boulez: Composer, Conductor, Enigma*, London, Cassell, 1977, 52
61. Letter [of April 1955], Corr. 55–3
62. Letter of 5 May 1955, Corr. 55–4; ES 228–9
63. Letter to Honegger of 1 July [1955], Denis Waleckx, 'Chronologie de la composition', *Dialogues des Carmélites*, *L'Avant-Scène Opéra*, 257, 2010, 83
64. Letter to Rose Dercourt-Plaut of 2 July [1955], Corr. 55–7; ES 230–1
65. 'Lorsque je suis mélancolique', *Le Mercure de France*, 1109, Jan–April 1956, 72–3, in JE 409–12
66. Honegger's daughter Pascale in conversation with the author
67. Letter [of 19 Aug 1955], Corr. 55–11; ES 231–3
68. Letter to Simone Girard of 31 Oct [1955], Corr. 55–16; ES 236

69. *Aufzeichnungen und Erinnerungen*, Cologne, Benziger, 1951, 93, accessed from the French translation in Gianfranco Vinay, '*Les Dialogues des Carmélites:* Métamorphoses de la victime sacralisée', CIREM, 111

70. Steven Huebner, 'Francis Poulenc's "Dialogues des Carmélites": Faith, Ideology and Love', *Music & Letters*, 97/2, 2016, 278

71. 'À propos de *Pelléas et Mélisande*. Essai de psychologie du critique d'art', *L'Occident*, I/7 (June 1902), reprinted in *Pelléas et Mélisande cent ans après: études et documents*, ed. Jean-Christophe Branger, Sylvie Douche and Denis Herlin, Lyon, Symétrie, 2012, 499

72. Letter to Ernest Guiraud of early Aug 1889, *Correspondance*, ed. François Lesure and Denis Herlin, Paris, Gallimard, 2005, 78

73. Letter to Henry Barraud of 1 June [1953], Corr. 53–10

74. Quoted by Baudelaire in 'Richard Wagner et Tannhauser à Paris', *L'Art romantique*, Paris, Calmann-Lévy, 1924, 243

75. See n.70, 288, n.53

76. 'Poulenc's Musical Procession', programme book of Covent Garden Opera, *Dialogues des Carmélites*, 2014, 32

77. Review of Alfred Bruneau's *L'Ouragan*, *La Revue blanche*, 15 May 1901, reprinted in *Monsieur Croche et autres écrits*, ed. François Lesure, Paris, Gallimard, 1987, 41

78. Violaine Anger, 'Du silence au chant: l'imaginaire de la parole dans les *Dialogues des Carmélites*', *Langage*, 228

79. 'Comment j'ai composé Les Dialogues des Carmélites', JE 199; NFH 57

80. 'Moussorgski, modèle de Poulenc?', *Langage*, 157

81. Georges Bernanos, *Dialogues des Carmélites*, Neuchâtel, La Baconnière, Collection Les Cahiers du Rhône/Paris, Éditions du Seuil, 1949

82. In this and succeeding paragraphs I am deeply indebted to the insights of Bishop Erik Varden of Trondheim. Quotations marked (Bishop Varden) are taken verbatim from his texts of 19 Jan and 28 April 2019.

83. The second possibility is mentioned by Steven Huebner, see n.70, 306–7

84. JE 819; NFH 268–9

85. JE 802; NFH 248

86. Colin Jones, 'The Carmelites of Compiègne', programme book of Covent Garden Opera, *Dialogues des Carmélites*, 2014, 22–3

87. Bernanos, *Dialogue des Carmélites*, 187

88. Letter of 28 Feb 1957, Corr. 57–9

89. Bernanos, *Dialogue des Carmélites*, 225

90. Jean de Solliers, 'Introduction et Guide d'écoute, Dialogues des Carmélites', Paris, *L'Avant-Scène Opéra*, 257, 2010, 42

91. Letter to Valcarenghi of 18 Aug [1957], Cat. 447

92. On the question of the major-over-minor chord, it is worth quoting Ernest Ansermet's reminiscence: 'One evening when Ravel, Stravinsky and I were discussing Schönberg's idea of using a major/minor chord – it was one of his earlier innovations – Ravel said "But it's possible so long as the minor third is above and the major third is below." "If this arrangement is possible," replied Stravinsky, "I don't see why the inverse shouldn't be; and *if I will it, I can do it.*"' Ansermet, *Les fondements de la musique dans la conscience humaine*, Neuchâtel, À la Baconnière, 1961, 267. Eric Walter White notes this disposition in bars 3 ff. of Stravinsky's *Symphonies of Wind Instruments*, which could be the site of Poulenc's borrowing. White, *Stravinsky, The Composer and his Works*, London, Faber, 2/1979, 557

93. Letter to Bernac [of 19 Aug 1955], Corr. 55–11; ES 232

94. Letter to Bernac [of 9 Sept 1955], Corr. 55–13; ES 234

95. See n.86

96. See n.70, 283 and 295–8

97. *La Symphonie imaginaire*, Paris, Le Seuil, 1981, 256, quoted in Fortune, 192 n.49

98. Interview with Bernard Gavoty, *Le Figaro littéraire*, 2 Feb 1957, JE 627

99. See n.70

100. See n.68
101. See n.64
102. Malou Haine, 'Mon irrésistible, insupportable et cher Poulenc . . .', CIREM, 2004, 179
103. Ivry 186
104. Corr. 56–4; ES 271. Robert Craft's response was that 'as Poulenc now goes about belittling I.S. as too old for the new hats he tries on in *Canticum sacrum*, the French composer shouldn't mind being told that those new hats are part of the reason why I.S. is I.S. and Poulenc is only Poulenc.' Stravinsky and Craft, 'Diaries, 1956', *Retrospectives and Conclusions*, New York, Knopf, 1969, 193–4
105. *Emmanuel Chabrier*, Paris / Geneva, La Palatine, 1961, 76
106. Pierre Miscevic, *Poulenc et l'Italie*, Ambassade de France en Italie, 2006, 31
107. Letter to Georges Hirsch of 12 Sept [1956], Corr. 56–19
108. Letter to Georges Hirsch of 15 June [1956], Corr. 56–6
109. Letter to Jacques Leguerney of 3 July [1956], Corr. 56–9
110. Letter of 8 Aug, Corr. 56–15, n.1
111. JMM 58; Diary 100–1
112. Letters to Simone Girard [of 26 Sept 1956] and to Nadia Boulanger [of 17 Sept 1956], quoted in Corr. 56–20 n.2
113. Graham Johnson and Richard Stokes, *A French Song Companion*, Oxford University Press, 2000, 359
114. Ivry 199
115. JMM 59; Diary 102–3
116. Arianna Stassinopoulos Huffington, *Picasso, Creator and Destroyer*, London, Pan, 1988, 85
117. Letter [of 16 Sept 1956], Corr. 56–20
118. Texas
119. Letter to Hervé Dugardin of 17 Nov [1956], Corr. 56–22, n.1
120. FPF
121. Letter [of 7 Dec 1956], Corr. 56–24
122. Alexander Goehr in conversation with the author
123. Letter to Hervé Dugardin [of 12 Dec 1956], Corr. 56–25

IX. JOY, SUFFERING AND FAREWELL: 1957–1963

1. Letter to Hervé Dugardin [of 8 Jan 1957], Corr. 57–2
2. Corr. 57–3
3. Denise Bourdet, 'Comment Blanche de la Force . . .', *Le Figaro littéraire*, 22 June 1957, in HL 653
4. E-mail to the author of 28 July and phone conversation with him of 3 Aug 2016
5. Pierre Miscevic, *Poulenc et l'Italie*, Ambassade de France en Italie, 2006, 43
6. Letter to the author of 19 July 2017
7. Roger Pines, 'Reunion: Virginia Zeani', *Opera News*, Jan 2003
8. Massimo Mila, *Cronache musicali*, 1955–1959, Turin, Giulio Einaudi, 1959, 343–6, in Piero Weiss, *Opera: A History in Documents*, New York and Oxford, Oxford University Press, 2002, 322
9. *French Opera: A Short History*, New Haven and London, Yale University Press, 2010, 291
10. See n.8, 319
11. Bernard Gavoty, 'Près de Francis Poulenc, j'ai vu créer à la Scala *Dialogues des Carmélites*', *Le Figaro littéraire*, 363, 2 Feb 1957, 31, in JE 624–31
12. Entretien avec Pierre Descargues: 'Carmélites et tango', *La Tribune de Lausanne*, 24 March 1957; JE 632
13. Letter to Dugardin [of 3 March 1957], Corr. 57–10, n.2
14. Ibid., letter [of 13 July 1957]
15. Corr. 57–11
16. David Owen Norris, 'Francis Poulenc, Sonata for flute and piano', *BBC Music Magazine*, April 2018, 120–1
17. Unidentifiable source
18. Corr. 56–6
19. Letter of 8 March 1957, Corr. 57–9. n.5.

20. Letter to Rose Dercourt-Plaut, Corr. 57–20; ES 246
21. *Le Monde*, 23/24 June, *Combat*, 24 June, *L'Intransigeant*, June 1957, 'Les échos de la presse française', *L'Avant-Scène Opéra*, 52, May 1983, 122–3
22. Cat. 447. A long letter of Sept 1957 to Maurice Jacquemont, the producer of the Paris performances, shows the extreme details of staging with which Poulenc engaged, Corr. 57–28
23. Cat. 477
24. 'Citoyen de Noizay [. . .] Il donnera *La Voix humaine* demain soir à Amboise avec Denise Duval', *La Nouvelle République*, 7 Sept 1961, JE 663–5; NFH 171–2. In fact, Poulenc myth-making!
25. The original autograph is now in the Dansmuseet, Stockholm.
26. Mellers, 162
27. Sir Humphrey Burton in conversation with the author
28. Norman Lebrecht, *Covent Garden: The Untold Story*, London, Simon & Schuster, 2001, 184
29. John Tooley, *In House: Covent Garden 50 Years of Opera and Ballet*, London, Faber, 1999, 22
30. Anonymous journalist, *The Daily Mail*, 17 Jan 1958, in Nigel Simeone, 'Les *Dialogues des Carmélites* dans la presse anglaise', FPV, 28. This article contains nine notices of the opening run.
31. *The Observer*, 19 Jan 1958, see n.22, 30
32. Sir John Tooley in conversation with the author
33. 'Une oeuvre que j'ai vu naître', *L'Avant-Scène Opéra*, 52, May 1983, 134
34. Broadcast on *France Culture*, 16 Mar 2013
35. Preface to the 1769 edition of *Alceste*, Piero Weiss, ed., *Opera: A History in Documents*, New York and Oxford, Oxford University Press, 2002, 119
36. Daniel 307
37. Letter of 30 March 1958 to Hervé Dugardin, Corr. 58–7
38. See example 12.3 in Waleckx, 'Poulenc, Cocteau and *La Voix humaine*', MAL 334–5
39. Ibid. 330
40. Letter to Bernac [of March 1958], Corr. 58–4; ES 250–1
41. Letter to Bernac of Easter [6 April] 1958, Corr. 58–8; ES 251–2
42. Letter to Rose Dercourt-Plaut of 20 April 1958, Corr. 58–9
43. Letter to Simone Girard [of May 1958], Corr. 58–10; ES 253
44. Letter to Hervé Dugardin, Corr. 58–11
45. Letter from Sir Charles Mackerras to Sidney Buckland of 19 Dec 2000
46. Haine, CIREM 181
47. Programme of the proceedings, BnF Mus. Rés. Vma 469
48. Letter from Berlin to Rowland Burdon-Muller, 28 June 1958, printed in *The New York Review of Books*, 16 July–12 Aug 2009, LVI, 12
49. *Covent Garden: The Untold Story*, 186
50. Rohan de Saram in conversation with the author
51. Letter to Bernac [of 4 Oct 1958], Corr. 58–19
52. Letter to Rose Dercourt-Plaut of 30 Jan [1959], Corr. 59–1; ES 257
53. Letter to Louis Aragon of 1 Feb [1959], Corr. 59–2; ES 258
54. Édouard Dermit, cited in HL 728
55. Letter [of Feb 1959], Corr. 59–5 n.1
56. HL 729
57. 'La musique de *La Voix humaine*', JE 644; NFH 160
58. Dame Felicity Lott in an e-mail to the author of 23 Feb 2019
59. Roger Nichols, 'Le gourmand fastidieux', *International Opera Collector*, 6, Winter 1997, 33
60. Haine, CIREM 193
61. Daniel 233
62. HL 751
63. Corr. 58–18
64. Letter of 10 Mar [1959], Corr. 59–5
65. Letter of 13 April [1959], ibid. n.5
66. Corr. 59–6
67. Cat. 490–1

68. Yale f.975, 10–12; HL 751–2
69. Letter to Simone Girard [of 13 June 1959], Corr. 59–13; ES 261–2
70. Letter to Bernac of 24 July 1959, Corr. 59–21 n.7
71. Ivry 204
72. Richard D. E. Burton, *Francis Poulenc*, Bath, Absolute Press, 2002, 113
73. *Emmanuel Chabrier*, Paris/Geneva, La Palatine, 1961, 43; *Emmanuel Chabrier*, trans. Cynthia Jolly, London, Dennis Dobson, 1981, JE 693
74. ES 403, Letter 298 n.1
75. Letter to Leonard Burkat of 28 July 1960, Corr. 60–13
76. Letter to Paul Rouart of 4 June [1959], Corr. 59–11
77. Ned Rorem, *Settling the Score*, New York, Doubleday, 1989, 175
78. Unpublished letter [of Dec 1959], Yale f.972, 16–17
79. EM 437
80. HL 722
81. Letter to Stéphane Audel of 5 Dec 1959, *Catalogue de la Librairie de l'Abbaye*, April 2016, 359, item 67
82. Letter to Bernac of 26 Feb [1960], Corr. 60–3
83. John M. Conly, 'Memoir of Francis Poulenc', *The Atlantic Monthly*, Boston, June 1960
84. JE 368–9
85. Véga C 30 A 293
86. Letter to Prêtre [of July 1960], Corr. 60–12
87. Letter from Rocamadour to Bernac [of July 1960], Corr. 60–10; ES 273
88. Journal 62; Diary 108–11
89. Bernac's claim (p. 180) that 'In the fourth bar of the last page, the low C in the bass is clearly a sharp' is a curious aberration in such a useful book.
90. Journal 132, n.258
91. John Gruen, 'Poulenc', *Musical America*, April 1960, 7, 24
92. HL 757
93. Gervasoni, op. cit., 613
94. Letter to Audel [of 19 Aug 1960], Corr. 60–20
95. Letter to Sauguet of 12 December 1960, Corr. 60–32
96. EM 444
97. Letter to Bernac, Corr. 61–3
98. Letter [of 23 Jan 1961], Corr. 61–6; ES 281–2
99. Evelyne Crochet in an e-mail to the author of 6 Nov 2017
100. See n.98
101. Letter to Audel of 19 July 1960, *Catalogue de la Librairie de l'Abbaye*, no. 358, 2016, item 91
102. Letter to Henri Hell of 2 Mar 1961, Corr. 61–9; ES 282–3
103. Memo of 1 May 1961, BBC Caversham Archives
104. Gaby Casadesus, *Mes Noces musicales*, Buchet-Chastel, 1989, 152
105. Letter of 9 Mar 1961, Corr. 61–10
106. *Emmanuel Chabrier*, 7, 8, 55, 30; tr. Jolly, 9, 36
107. Letter to Rose Dercourt-Plaut of 6 April 1961, Corr. 61–17, n.2; partially in ES 413
108. Journal 63; Diary 110–11
109. Burton, *Francis Poulenc*, 114
110. Journal 63; Diary 112–13
111. 'Francis Poulenc: Créations mondiales et inédites', INA, Mémoire vive, 2013, I, tr 5
112. Partially unpublished letter, Yale, f.974, 29–31. The 'Frisch' Poulenc mentions would be the Danish soprano Povla Frijsh (1881–1960) who specialized in the songs of modern composers, including Poulenc, and recorded 'Avant le cinéma' (I am grateful to Jon Tolansky for this information). Exactly what were the crimes of her and Maggie Teyte is unknown. On the credit side, Adèle Addison was one of Frijsh's pupils.
113. Letter of 26 Mar 1962, Corr. 62–4; ES 288
114. Letter of Aug 1961, Corr. 61–17 n.1: see also ES 410, letter 320 n.1

115. See letter 61–22 n.1; ES 413, letter 333 n.1
116. Letter of 1 Nov 1961, Corr. 61–26. Markévitch's ballet for orchestra *Rebus* was composed in 1931. The reference is to two of the movements of the work entitled 'Danse du pauvreté' and 'Fugue des vices' (I am grateful to Nigel Simeone for this information). Even so, Poulenc's remark remains somewhat mysterious.
117. Letter of 21 July 1960, Corr. 60–21 n.2
118. Letter of 5 Sept 1960, Corr. 60–23; ES 275
119. Corr. 60–25; ES 275–6
120. JE 871
121. J. H. Plumb, *The Horizon Book of the Renaissance*, London, Collins, 1961, 96; Kenneth Clark, ibid. 109. To Brigitte Poulenc wrote, 'If possible, Mantegna since I thought it preferable to have a more colourful palette.' Ibid. 322
122. Poulenc, 'Comment j'ai composé *Les Dialogues des Carmélites*', JE 199
123. 'L'écriture choro-orchestrale dans les *Sept Répons des ténèbres*', *Langage*, 286
124. *Poulenc our Contemporary*, Paris, Universal Music, 2013, 20
125. See n.93c
126. Letter to Michel Garcin of 29 Sept 1962, Corr. 62–21
127. JE 812; NFH 260
128. Renaud Machart, Poulenc, Paris, Éditions du Seuil, 1995, 232
129. René Dumesnil, 'La musique. *Répons des ténèbres* de Poulenc', *Le Monde*, 17 Dec 1963, reprinted in HL 777
130. EM 455
131. Letter to Duval [of early Jan 1962], Corr. 62–1; ES 286–7
132. Letter of 20 Feb 1962, *Catalogue de la Librairie de l'Abbaye*, 355, 2015, item 40
133. Letter to Poulenc of 24 Mar 1962, Corr. 62–3
134. EM 457
135. Letter to Bernac of 26 Mar 1962, Corr. 62–4; ES 288–9
136. Lucie Kayas, *André Jolivet*, Paris, Fayard, 2005, 444
137. Corr. 62–9
138. Cat. 507
139. Letters of 23 June 1962 to Rose Dercourt-Plaut and of 13 July 1962 to R. Douglas Gibson, Corr. 62–13 n.4
140. Letter to Bernac of 14 July 1962, ibid. text of letter itself; ES 290
141. Letter of 5 Aug 1962, Corr. 62–16; ES 293
142. Letter [of 12 Aug 1962], Corr. 62–20; ES 296
143. Igor Stravinsky and Robert Craft, *Dialogues and a Diary*, London, Faber, 1968, 206
144. Unpublished [?] letter of 20 Aug 1962, Yale f.973, 12–14. One has to be careful translating 'angine', as in this simple form it can mean 'quinsy' or 'suppurating tonsilitis'. But since that has a slow onset, it is clear from the suddenness of this attack that Poulenc did suffer an 'angine de poitrine' (angina pectoris).
145. Haine, CIREM 168
146. Cat. 505
147. Letter of 1 Nov 1962, Corr. 62–24
148. Letter of Oct 1962, Corr. 62–23; ES 296
149. Pierre Bernac, interview with Gérard Michel, *France Culture*, 4 Dec 1970
150. Letter of 17 Nov to Doda Conrad, Cat. 509
151. Letter of 9 Dec 1962, Corr. 62–25 n.3
152. Unpublished letter of 10 Nov 1962, Yale f.973, 20–21
153. See n.142
154. Letter of 10 Aug 1959, Cat. 509
155. Letter [of 3 July 1959], Corr. 59–18
156. Mellers 165
157. 'La clarinette dans les sonates de Francis Poulenc', CIREM 134
158. Mellers 170–1

159. Letter of 14 July 1962 to Bernac, Corr. 62–13; ES 290–1
160. Haine, CIREM 201
161. Ibid. 199
162. Ibid. 162
163. Corr. 63–1
164. Sarah Knapton, 'Scientists pinpoint how stress causes heart attacks', *Daily Telegraph*, 12 Jan 2017, referencing Dr Ahmed Tawakol et al., 'Relation between resting amygdalar activity and cardiovascular events: a longitudinal and cohort study', *The Lancet*, 389, issue 10071, 25 Feb 2017, 834–45. More specifically, the doctor who examined Poulenc after his death diagnosed a ruptured aorta. Pierre Miscevic, Francis Poulenc, *Lettres inédites à Brigitte Manceaux*, Paris, Éditions Orizons, 2019, 18, n.12.
165. Pierre Meylan, 'Francis Poulenc à Lausanne', *Feuilles musicales*, numéro spécial Poulenc, Lausanne, 1961/4–5, 80
166. Marcel Schneider, op. cit., 221
167. *Bloc-notes*, vol. 3 (1961–64), 9 Feb, ed. J. Touzot, Seuil, 1993, 300–3
168. MAL 84
169. *Les Trois Centres*
170. FPF

CHRONOLOGY

1855   5 July: Émile Poulenc born, Paris

1862   31 March: Marcel Royer (Papoum) born, Paris

1864   20 June: Jenny Royer born, Paris

1885   16 March: Émile and Jenny married, Paris

1886   24 May: Jeanne Poulenc born, Nogent

1888   8 July: Louis Poulenc born, Nogent

1891   17 May: Louis dies

1892   23 June: child stillborn

1899   7 January: Francis Poulenc born, Paris

1904   First piano lessons with his mother

1907   Lessons with Mlle Melon; he hears gramophone for first time, Vichy; revelation of Debussy's music, *Danses*

1910   January: Seine overflows; 10 May, he celebrates first communion; discovers *Winterreise*, music of Stravinsky; *En Barque*

1911   15 August: begins holiday diary, Luchon

1912   April: continued in Biarritz; September, enters Lycée Condorcet

1913   14 March: *Mélopée d'automne*; 2 June: *Viens! une flûte invisible*

1914   March: leaves lycée; April: at concert performance of Stravinsky, *Le Sacre*; introduced to Ricardo Viñes; 1 August: French troops mobilized; *Processional pour la crémation d'un mandarin* (destroyed)

1915   7 June: mother dies; he meets Milhaud

1916   21 February: battle of Verdun begins

1 July–September: battle of the Somme

3 October: returns to Lycée Condorcet; through Viñes meets Satie, Auric; *Préludes* (destroyed)

1917   1 February: Milhaud reaches Brazil

Spring: composes *Rapsodie nègre*

5 May: at premiere of Debussy's Violin Sonata

18 May: attends premiere of Satie's *Parade*

24 June: attends premiere of Apollinaire's *Les Mamelles de Tirésias*

15 July: father dies; Poulenc moves in with sister, her husband and daughter

August: *Zèbre* (destroyed)

Autumn: *Trois Pastorales*

11 December: premiere of *Rapsodie nègre*; comes to notice of Stravinsky, Diaghilev

With Linossier, at Monnier bookshop; hears Apollinaire; meets Aragon, Breton, Éluard

Meets Cocteau, Radiguet, Max Jacob, Bathori, Honegger, Durey, Tailleferre

1918   17 January: mobilized for military service

Meets Falla chez Viñes

? 5 February: first 'Nouveaux Jeunes' concert ?

19 March: premiere of *Poèmes sénégalais*

25 March: death of Debussy

3 April: private premiere of Satie, *Socrate*

Spring: Sonata for two clarinets

June: Sonata for piano duet; two meetings with Aragon

Late summer: Cocteau's 'Séance Music-Hall'

Autumn: *Toréador*

October: *Prélude* for percussion, *Le Jongleur* (destroyed), Sonata for violin and piano (destroyed), Sonata for piano trio (lost or destroyed)

5 November: Viñes gives premiere of *Pastorales*, Hôtel Ritz, Madrid

9 November: death of Apollinaire

11 November: armistice

December: *Trois Mouvements perpétuels, Trois Pastorales*

21 December: premieres of Piano Duet Sonata, Violin Sonata

Milhaud returns from Brazil

1919   9 February: premiere of *Trois Mouvements perpétuels*

5 April: premiere of Sonata for two clarinets

April–June: *Cocardes*

May: *Le Bestiaire* (premiere during the year); *Deux Mélodies inédites du Bestiaire*

19 June: plays percussion in 'Exhortation' from *Choéphores*

28 June: signature of Treaty of Versailles

July: 'Valse' for *Album des Six*; becomes secretary at war office in Paris

November: *Quadrille* for piano duet (lost or destroyed)

1920   16, 23 January: Collet's articles in *Comoedia*

2 February: premiere of Stravinsky, *Le Chant du rossignol*, Ballets Russes

23 February: premiere of *Cocardes* at Spectacle-Concert (Sch EM 78)

8 March: premiere of Satie's *musique d'ameublement*

March: Suite in C for piano

10 April: premiere of Suite

? May: at Ravel's playthrough of *La Valse* for Diaghilev chez Misia

15 May: at premiere of Stravinsky, *Pulcinella*

May–November: three articles in nos. 1, 2 and 4 of *Le Coq*

July: visits Roussel

September–March 1921: *Impromptus*

October–November: *Le Gendarme incompris*

12 December: concert premiere of Ravel, *La Valse*

First setting of *Paul et Virginie*

1921   9 January: working on *Impromptus, Gendarme, Quatre Poèmes de Max Jacob* (EM 92)

17 January: demobilized

5 March: to Rome – first time outside France! Concerts with Milhaud; meets Casella, Malipiero, Rieti. First mention of *Biches* (EM 93)

6 March: 'La baigneuse de Trouville' for *Les Mariés de la Tour Eiffel*; first mention of what will be *Les Biches*

22 April: Schoenberg *Five Orchestral Pieces*, conducted by Caplet at Concerts Pasdeloup

24 May: premieres of *Le Gendarme incompris*, Satie, *Le Piège de Méduse*, Milhaud, *Caramel mou*, Auric, *Les Pélicans*; Diaghilev attends, commissions Poulenc ballet (EM 123 – but see letter 21–6 for dating)

?18 or 19 June: premiere of *Les Mariés*

21 June: premiere of *Le Jongleur*

July: *Trois Études de pianola*, *Première Suite d'orchestre*, String Quartet, Trio for piano, clarinet and cello (all abandoned, destroyed, lost, or possibly never begun)

Summer: *Promenades*; *Esquisses d'une fanfare*

September: *Quatre Poèmes de Max Jacob* completed; writes to Koechlin regarding lessons; first sketches for *Les Biches*

8 November: begins lessons

November–December: Two articles for *Fanfare*; *Études pour pianola* (abandoned)

Meets Sauguet

16 December: death of Saint-Saëns

1922   7 January: premiere of *Quatre Poèmes* (then burnt, but Milhaud had a copy . . .)

12 January: Paris premiere of Schoenberg, *Pierrot lunaire*

end January: to Vienna with Milhaud and Marya Freund

February: chez Schoenberg, meets Berg, Webern

13 February: operation on throat abscess

30 March: Second Paris performance of Schoenberg, *Pierrot lunaire*

April: meets Bartók on visit to Paris (EM 112–3)

18 May: Opéra premiere of Stravinsky, *Renard*

29 May: private premiere of Stravinsky, *Mavra*

3 June: Opéra premiere of *Mavra*

Summer: *Marches militaires* (lost or destroyed)

7 and 10 August: Salzburg Festival

16 August: to Houlgate, then Nazelles till at least 22 September

August–October: Sonata for horn, trumpet and trombone

Early September: *Chanson à boire*; Sonata for clarinet and bassoon; *Caprice espagnol* (lost or destroyed)

Autumn: begins work on *Les Biches*

–1925: *Napoli*

14 December: French premiere of Webern, *Five movements for string quartet* (see inscribed copy HL 254)

First edition of *Impromptus*

1923   4 January: premiere of Sonata for clarinet and bassoon, Sonata for horn, trumpet and trombone

9/10–19 January: visits Brussels; back in Paris on 29 January

26 March: death of Sarah Bernhardt

Late March, early April: contracts jaundice, goes to Vichy, Nazelles (at least 14 April–24 May)

1 June: premiere of Roussel, *Padmâvatî*

12 June: at Vichy again

13 June: premiere of Stravinsky, *Les noces*; FP too ill to play, but attends

25 June: premiere of Falla, *El Retablo de maese Pedro* (meets Landowska during rehearsals)

September: Clarinet Quintet (lost or destroyed)

18 October: premiere of Stravinsky Octet

25 October: premiere of Milhaud, *La Création du monde*, Ballets Suédois

Autumn: recitatives for Gounod, *La Colombe*; completes *Les Biches*

12 December: death of Raymond Radiguet

1924   6 January: premiere of *La Colombe*, premiere of *Les Biches*, Monte-Carlo

14 March: third version of Honegger, *Le Roi David*

24 April: Paris premiere of Stravinsky, *L'Histoire du soldat*

Early May: at Nazelles

8 May: premiere of Honegger, *Pacific 231*

17 May: premiere of Milhaud *Salade*, Beaumont

26 May: Paris premiere of *Les Biches*

May–April 1926: Trio for oboe, bassoon and piano

2 June: Cocteau *Roméo et Juliette* + Poulenc *Fanfare*

4 June: Paris premiere of Auric, *Les Fâcheux*

15 June: Paris premiere of Satie, *Mercure*

20 June: Paris premiere of Milhaud, *Le Train bleu*

5 July: Olympic Games open

4 November: death of Fauré

December: premiere of Satie, *Relâche*; Sonata 2 for violin and piano (destroyed); *Poèmes de Ronsard*; Second edition of (5) *Impromptus*

1925   January: in Amboise

10 March: premiere of *Poèmes de Ronsard*

27 March: final lesson with Koechlin

22 April: death of Caplet

30 April: Exposition des Arts Décoratifs opens

April–July: in Cannes, Monte-Carlo, Vichy

4 May: at Milhaud's wedding in Aix

25 May: London premiere of *Les Biches*

1 July: death of Satie

August: transcription for piano of Mozart's *Ein musikalischer Spass*

–1926: *Chansons gaillardes*

September: in Nazelles, completes *Napoli*

14 November: first Surrealist exhibition opens

November: accident to thumb

CHRONOLOGY

1926   1 February: Paris premiere of Ravel, *L'Enfant et les sortilèges*

Further work on Trio up to . . .

2 May: premieres of *Napoli*, *Chansons gaillardes* and Trio (Auric/Poulenc concert)

2 June: leaves for London with Sauguet

13 June: premiere of Ravel, *Chansons madécasses*

14 June: plays in *Les Noces*, London; stays to hear *Les Biches* on 29 June

7 July: returns to France

Summer in Nazelles

26 November: Chabrier, *Gwendoline* revived at Opéra

1927   February: *Vocalise*; premiere 7 May (possibly)

April: 'Pastourelle' for *L'Éventail de Jeanne*; premiere 16 June

–August 1928: *Concert champêtre*

May–May 1928: *Airs chantés*

14 May: Falla in first Paris performance of his Harpsichord Concerto

27 May: premiere of Sauguet, *La Chatte*

30 May: premiere of Stravinsky, *Oedipus Rex*

7 June: premiere of Prokofiev, *Le Pas d'acier*

16 June: *L'Éventail de Jeanne* chez Dubost; popularity of 'Pastourelle' (EM 162; Cat 137)

5 July: to London with Sauguet and Auric (EM 163)

?28 July: buys Le Grand Coteau; living for some months at the Lion d'Or and with Tante Liénard

18 October: Salle Pleyel opened

October–1928: *Deux Novellettes* written in Nazelles, Amboise

8 December: Schoenberg conducts his works at Concerts Colonne

16 December: premiere of Milhaud, *Le pauvre Matelot*

1928   3 March: premiere of incomplete *Airs chantés* (nos. 1 and 4)

12 March: Falla, *El Retablo*, *La Vida breve*, *El Amor brujo* at Opéra-Comique

29 March: French premiere of Puccini, *Turandot* at Opéra

10 June: premiere of *Deux Novellettes*, *Trois pièces pour piano*, complete *Airs chantés* (Auric/Poulenc concert) – first appearance of FP as solo pianist in Paris?

12 June: European premiere of Stravinsky, *Apollon musagète*

Summer: *Aubade* commissioned; invited to Kerbastic; begins reviewing for *Arts phoniques*

August: completes *Concert champêtre*

19 October: premiere of Honegger, *Rugby*

22 November: premiere of Ravel, *Boléro*

27 November: premiere of Stravinsky, *Le Baiser de la fée*

1929   4 March: *L'Éventail de Jeanne* at Opéra

March: 'Pièce brève sur le nom d'Albert Roussel' for *Hommage à Albert Roussel*

18 April: premiere of *Hommage*; private premiere of *Concert champêtre*

3 May: public premiere of *Concert champêtre*

23 May: Ravel, *La Valse* at Opéra

10 May, 18 June: letters of 'love' to Chanlaire

May–June: *Aubade*; premiere 19 June at Noailles' Materials Ball

19 August: death of Diaghilev

2 September: *Fanfare*

24 October: Wall Street crash

3 November: *Valse* (for Raymonde Linossier; fragment only, Sch EM 160)

November: Sonata 3 for violin and piano (unfinished, lost)

11, 18 December: 10th anniversary concerts for Les Six

–1938: begins *Nocturnes* (1–8)

1930   30 January: death of Raymonde Linossier

April: visits Falla in Spain (Sch EM 177)

July: *Épitaphe*

Summer: based in Noizay; preliminary sketches for *Les Soirées de Nazelles*

13 December: Ansermet conducts world premiere of Stravinsky's *Symphony of Psalms* in Brussels

1931   February: Poulenc reviews *Symphony of Psalms*; *Trois Poèmes de Louise Lalanne*; premiere 1 June

—March: *Quatre Poèmes de Guillaume Apollinaire*; premiere 1 June

9 March: Festival Francis Poulenc in Strasbourg

24 March: at French premiere of *Symphony of Psalms* conducted by Stravinsky

Spring: low mood, bank failure

19 June: premiere of first version of Sextet

July: first mention of Éluard songs

—December: *Cinq Poèmes de Max Jacob*

Mid-August: informal and (24th) formal commission of new concerto

24 September: death of his nanny Marie Françoise Lauxière

Autumn: commission from Noailles

18 November: decides on *Le Bal masqué*

1 December: first concert of La Sérénade; FP an artistic advisor (others EM 190)

2 December: death of d'Indy

1932   14 January: at premiere of Ravel G major Concerto

February–10 April: *Le Bal masqué*; premiere 20 April

13 June: repeated at fourth Sérénade concert

July, August: hard work on Concerto for two pianos and orchestra; premiere 5 September, Venice; last meeting with Falla

8 October: 'Valse-improvisation sur le nom de Bach' for *Hommage à J. S. Bach*

December–May 1934: *Improvisations* 1–10; premiere of seven of them 4 February 1933

Mid-December–1 Jan: Auric joins him in Noizay

1933   17 January: at Ravel LH concerto, Wittgenstein

20–21 January: buys inscribed copies of *Gwendoline* + *Le Roi* from d'Indy sale

23 January: presents Two-Piano Concerto MS to Winnie + private performance

February: *Villageoises*; incidental music to *Intermezzo*

1 February: Two-Piano Concerto with Février, Beecham, Queen's Hall (Sch C 195 review)

25 February: *Concert champêtre*

1 March: premiere of Giraudoux's *Intermezzo*

19 May: *Pierrot*

Autumn: song for play *Pétrus*; chorus for *M. Le Trouhadec saisi par la débauche* (both lost)

Feuillets d'album, *Improvisation 7*

24 December: 'Bal de jeunes filles' (Nocturne 2)

1934   January–April: *Huit Chansons polonaises*

6 February: attempted *coup d'état* by leagues

30 March: at Stravinsky, *Perséphone* premiere, Opéra

May–August: *Deux intermezzi*

July: *Presto in B flat*

9–18 July: Vichy

4–11 August: Kerbastic

13 August: Salzburg Festival; beginning of FP/PB duo

Summer: ? *Quatre Chansons pour enfants*

September–October: orchestrates *Poèmes de Ronsard*

October: first ideas for Organ Concerto

December: *Badinage*

Humoresque; *Improvisations 8–10*; 'Villanelle' for *Pipeaux*

1935   February: concert tour of North Africa with Modrakowska [see Sch EM App 2]

March: *Cinq Poèmes de Paul Éluard*; premiere 3 April [FP 3000fr; PE 350fr !]

3 April: debut concert with PB, École normale de musique

April–May: tour of provincial towns with Modrakowska; victory of Front populaire

11 May: death of Tante Liénard

? July: *La Belle au bois dormant*, Alexeieff film

August: *Margot* at Kerbastic

September: *À sa guitare*

October: *Suite française*; premiere of small orchestra version 11 December

25/28 October: *Le Bal masqué* in Lausanne/Geneva, prepared by 'Éloge de la banalité'

26 November: premiere of *Margot*

1936 March–April: *Sept Chansons* (first version); incomplete premiere 15 November

April: acquires unfurnished room at 5 rue de Médicis

10–13 April: Edward James at Noizay, also the Latarjets, Rieti, Sauguet and Rostand

30 April: Organ Concerto reaching end

15 August: to Uzerche with PB and Gouverné

17 August: death of Pierre-Octave Ferroud

22–29 August: *Litanies à la Vierge noire*; premiere 17 November

September: *Petites voix; Plain-chant*

1 October: *Les Soirées de Nazelles* completed; premiere 1 December, BBC

17 November: premiere of *Litanies*, Boulanger/BBC

December: Songs on Cocteau's *Plain-chant* (destroyed)

–January 1937: *Tel jour telle nuit*

1937 3 February: premiere of *Tel jour telle nuit*

April–October: search for libretto with Lunel [see Waleckx, MAL]

7 May: 'Bourrée, au Pavillon d'Auvergne' for *À l'Exposition*; premiere 24 June

June: *Deux Marches et un intermède*; premiere 24 June

August: Mass in G major

23 August: death of Roussel

September–December: *Sécheresses*

October: first thoughts of ballet for Rouché

December: *Trois Poèmes de Louise de Vilmorin*

28 December: death of Ravel

30 December: Poulenc at his funeral in Levallois

1938 March: 'Le Portrait'; concerts with PB in London including all Debussy songs for BBC, then Italy

April: Organ Concerto

3 April: premiere of Mass in G major

May: 'Allons plus vite'

2 May: premiere of *Sécheresses*, Colonne, Paray

May–August: *Deux Poèmes de Guillaume Apollinaire*

July: at Kerbastic, then Le Tremblay

–January 1939: *Quatre Motets pour un temps de pénitence*

31 July–28 August: in Anost with PB; Organ Concerto completed; 'Dans le jardin d'Anna', 'Tu vois le feu du soir'

–January 1939: *Miroirs brûlants*

5–8 September: at Venice Biennale with PB

29 September: *Priez pour paix* [one of few he allowed to be transposed]

October: *La Grenouillère*; concerts with PB in Holland

–November: then in eastern France

28 November: premiere of *Trois Poèmes de Louise de Vilmorin*

December: Nocturne 8

16 December: private premiere of Organ Concerto chez la Princesse de Polignac

1939 7 January: premiere of 'Je nommerai ton front'

January–February: Two tours of England and Ireland with PB

16 February: premieres of 'Le Portrait', 'Tu vois le feu du soir'

April: *Ce doux petit visage*

7 April (Good Friday): premiere of *Quatre Motets pour un temps de pénitence*

17 April: ideas regarding *The Tempest* or *Pericles*

May–January 1940: re-orchestrates *Les Biches*

21 June: public premiere of Organ Concerto, Salle Gaveau

August: definitive version of *Sextuor*

6–16 August: at Kerbastic

Summer: early sketches for *Les Mamelles de Tirésias*

3 September: France and Great Britain declare war on Germany; Le Grand Coteau full of refugees

September–October: *Fiançailles pour rire*

October: *Bleuet*

1 October: Le Grand Coteau free of refugees

3 November: starts *Journal de mes mélodies*

Française d'après Claude Gervaise

Deux Préludes posthumes et une gnossienne (orchestrations of Satie)

1940   January: completes re-orchestration of *Les Biches*

January–March: tour with PB of Portugal (2nd–10th Jan), Italy, Holland and Switzerland – musical propaganda

June–August: *Mélancolie*

2 June–18 July: military service

14 June: Germans occupy Paris

1 July: Pétain government installed in Vichy

19 July–9 September: in Brive: *L'Histoire de Babar* and beginning of Cello Sonata sketched out

August–June 1942: *Les Animaux modèles*

9 September: returns to Paris

October: *Léocadia*; premiere 3 November

–November: *Banalités*; premiere 14 December

3 November: premiere of *Léocadia*

December: *Colloque*; sketch of *Animaux modèles* completed; writing article on Stravinsky

9 December: premiere of final version of Sextet

1941   3 January: Stravinsky article appears in *L'Information musicale*

25 January–25 March: Nine Paris concerts [EM App 2]

4 February: premieres of *Colloque, Ce doux petit visage*

23 May: premiere of *Mélancolie*

May: *Exultate Deo*; *Salve Regina*

June–November: *Improvisations 11, 12*

September: String Trio (unfinished, lost); *Montparnasse* begun

October: begins orchestrating *Les Animaux modèles*

? November: *La Fille du jardinier* (lost)

Piece for solo flute

La Duchesse de Langeais (film)

1942 27 March: premiere screening of *La Duchesse de Langeais*

21 May: premiere of *Fiançailles pour rire*

Summer–Easter 1943: Sonata 4 for violin and piano

June: completes orchestration of *Les Animaux modèles*

July: founding of Comité national des musiciens

8 August: premiere of *Les Animaux modèles*, Opéra

October–December: *Chansons villageoises*

8 November: Operation Torch, allied invasion of North Africa

11 November: all France occupied

1943 March: Intermezzo in A flat

20 March: article on Fauré's orchestration in *Comoedia*

29 April: death of Viñes

21 June: premiere of Violin Sonata 4/5

28 June: premiere of *Chansons villageoises*

Summer: *Figure humaine;* Mussolini falls

August–October: *Métamorphoses*

September: Allied landing in Sicily

September–October: *Deux Poèmes de Louis Aragon*; premiere 8 December

Métamorphoses; premiere 8 December

Le Voyageur sans bagages

1944   4 March: death of Max Jacob

1 April: premiere of *Le Voyageur sans bagage*

May–October: *Les Mamelles de Tirésias*

6 June: D-Day

24–26 December: *Un Soir de neige*

La Nuit de la Saint-Jean (lost)

1945   January: *Deux Mélodies de Guillaume Apollinaire*; premiere 27 April

2–15 January: in London

6 January: plays Two-Piano Concerto with Britten

February: completes *Montparnasse*, *Hyde Park*

March: back in London

25 March: premiere of *Figure humaine*

27 March: at work on String Quartet 2

7 April: article 'Vive Strawinsky' in *Le Figaro*

21 April: premiere of *Un Soir de neige*, together with Milhaud's *Quatrains valaisans* and Messiaen's *Trois petites Liturgies de la Présence divine*, La Pléiade

May: at Noizay

8 June: death of Desnos

9 July–26 August: at Larche; *L'Histoire de Babar* completed

August–April 1946: *Chansons françaises*

9 August: completes orchestration of *Mamelles*

September: *Le Soldat et la sorcière* (lost); premiere 5 December

26 September: death of Bartók

24 November: death of Oncle Papoum; Jeanne moves into his flat; Poulenc from maid's quarters to new flat on 7th floor

1946   January–30 March: concerts with PB in France, Belgium, Switzerland, Holland

18 January: appointed chevalier de la Légion d'honneur

April: completes *Chansons françaises*

14 June: premiere of *Babar* on French Radio

17 June: Légion ceremony

18 June–?9 July: with Bernac in England

July: *Deux Mélodies sur des poèmes de Guillaume Apollinaire*; premiere 9 November

–summer 1947: *Le Disparu*

Late July–mid-August: working with Bernac at Le Tremblay

August: second version of *Paul et Virginie*

–summer 1947: *Main dominée par le coeur*

13 September: birth of Marie-Ange

14 November: death of Falla

28 November: death of Nusch Éluard

2 December: *Figure humaine*, Brussels, Belgian radio (Collaer)

1947   January: String Quartet 2 destroyed by this date

February, March, May, June, October, December: London, mainly playing for BBC

20 March: talk 'Mes mélodies et leurs poètes' at l'Université des Annales

22 May: Paris premiere of *Figure humaine* (Pléiade)

3 June: premiere of *Les Mamelles de Tirésias*

End July: Paris

Summer–September: *Trois Chansons de F. Garcia Lorca*; premiere 12 November

1 August–September 1948: *Sinfonietta*, Noizay

? September: *Amphitryon*; premiere 5 December; begins recording 'À bâtons rompus'

1 September: orchestrates *Litanies*, Noizay

October: . . . *mais mourir*

? November: *L'Invitation au château*; premiere 5 November

15 December: 'Mes mélodies et leurs poètes' published in *Conferencia*

1948   19 January: to Holland with Bernac, fifteen concerts

April–October: Cello Sonata

May–August: *Calligrammes*; premiere 20 November

Spring: meets 'les boys' in Paris

August: *Quatre petites Prières de Saint François d'Assise*

16 October: private premiere of *Calligrammes*, chez Marie-Blanche

22 October–23 December: first US tour [EM App 2]; friendship with Bernstein

24 October: premiere of *Sinfonietta*, Philharmonia, Déso, 3rd prog

2–8 November: *Hymne*; premiere 28 December

24 November: public premiere of *Calligrammes*, New York Town Hall

1949   January: resumes 'À bâtons rompus'

8–20 February: concerts with Bernac in England [EM App 2]

12 February: death of Christian Bérard

April: 2 weeks with Bernac in Spain

18 May: premiere of Cello Sonata

May–October: Piano Concerto

June: short trip to England

July: 'Mazurka' for *Mouvements de cœur*; premiere 6 November

6 July: Ned Rorem chez Poulenc

–end July; usual three weeks chez Jeanne at Le Tremblay

13 August: first two movements of Piano Concerto written

28 December–29 March 1950: second US tour [fourteen concerts, two recordings: EM App 2]

1950   6 January: premiere of Piano Concerto

29 March: flies back from New York

Spring: meets Lucien Roubert

April–July: *La Fraîcheur et le feu*; premiere 1 November

24 July: European premiere of Piano Concerto, Aix, Münch; 25 July, *Turangalîla*

July–22 April 1951: *Stabat Mater*

August, September: Noizay

15 October: back to Paris

28 October: start of concert season, Paris, London, Paris

1 November: premiere of *La Fraîcheur et le feu* in Birmingham

31 December: death of Koechlin

1951   February: concerts in Italy, North Africa

February–September: *Thème varié*

13 June: premiere of *Stabat Mater*, Strasbourg

July: *Le Voyage en Amérique*, *L'Embarquement pour Cythère*; Brive, Hyères

August: Noizay

1–7 September: concerts in Edinburgh, London, Bournemouth, London

November–May 1952: *Quatre Motets pour le temps de Noël*

1952   4 January–5 March: third US tour + Caracas with PB [EM App 2]

–12 March: Paris; –19 March: Midi

March: Désormière suffers paralytic stroke

21 March–?: Munich

April–23 May: Noizay

27 April: Robert Shaw conducts US premiere of *Stabat Mater* in New York

30 April: Paris premiere of *Stabat*

–11 June: Festival du XXe siècle

Late June: tour in England (27th at Aldeburgh)

June: 'Matelote provençale' for *La Guirlande de Campra*; premiere 31 July; first thoughts of *Carmélites*

Early July: Le Tremblay

August: Noizay, *Ave verum corpus*; premiere 25 November; persistent eye problem

September: *Capriccio d'après Le Bal masqué*

Autumn–July 1953: Sonata for two pianos

October: Lyon, Avignon

20 November–20 December: Marseille hotel, composing

18 November: death of Éluard; 22nd: funeral, Poulenc present

15 December: premiere of *Thème varié*

1953   4–28 January: Ouchy-Lausanne, preparing Rostand and Audel interviews; decides on *Le Travail du peintre*

–18 February: Paris; then to London, back by 27th

5 March: death of Prokofiev

18–?30 March: Italy with Fournier; meets Valcarenghi in Milan; first thoughts of *Carmélites*

10 April: Poulenc festival in Monte-Carlo

23 July: Le Tremblay, completes Sonata for two pianos

15 August: begins *Carmélites*; 18 September: I/1 written; 3 October: I/2, 3

1 September: officier de la Légion d'honneur

31 October: awarded by Colette

2 November: premiere of Sonata for two pianos, 'Les boys', Wigmore

December: *Carmélites* I/4; 4–19th, Lausanne

6 December: problems over opera rights

1954   January: Bernac passed over for Conservatoire post

?16 January–15 February: Cannes, *Carmélites* II/1, 2

21 February: Britten invites him again to Aldeburgh, refused

?9–?24 March: Egypt with PB; *Carmélites* II/3

27, 28 March: Greece

April: Noizay, *Parisiana*; premiere 12 October; *Carmélites* II, interlude 2

May: still at Noizay, 'Rosemonde'; premiere 12 October

June: health worries – cancer?

July: in Pyrenees

7 August:: Rocamadour

16 August: starts orchestrating *Carmélites*

September, October: Noizay

November: Poulenc pulls out of German tour; in clinic for three weeks

20 December: flies to Cannes

1955   13–23 January: England with Bernac

16 January: Two-Piano Concerto with Britten, Liverpool PO/Pritchard, RFH

2 February: 20th anniversary concert with Bernac, Salle Gaveau [*Le Travail* not ready]

Mid-February: Lucien develops pleurisy

1 March: Cannes, *Carmélites* II/interlude 1, II/4, III/1

30 March: final permission granted regarding *Carmélites* libretto

April: Cannes, *Carmélites* III/1, III/interlude 1, III/2

May: Cannes, *Carmélites* III/2

17 June–3 July: Évian

19 June: death of Adrienne Monnier

July–August: Le Tremblay–Tourrettes-sur-Loup, *Carmélites* III/3

August: Tourrettes-sur-Loup, *Carmélites* III/4

21 October: death of Lucien Roubert

27 November: death of Honegger

1956   March: Greece, Italy

21 March: At premiere of Boulez, *Le Marteau sans maître*

27 March: Two-Piano Concerto with Françaix, Liverpool

April: Cannes, finishes orchestration of *Carmélites* Act II

5 May: 'Bucolique' for *Variations sur le nom de Marguerite Long*; premiere 4 June

1 June: La Scala deadline for orchestral score [not met!]

18 June: Brive, finishes orchestration of Act III = whole score

24 June: gives talk at Aldeburgh

26 June–12 July: Évian; 12–20 July: Milan; 20–23 July: Aix; 24–28 July: Fontainebleau;

28 July–19 August: Le Tremblay; 19 August: Noizay: completes *Le Travail du peintre*

September: *Deux Mélodies*

6–12 November: Birmingham, Oxford, London

18–25 November: Milan for first orchestral read-through of *Carmélites*

–1 December: Berlin

1–25 December: Cannes

December: *Dernier Poème*

December–March 1957: Sonata for flute and piano

1957   7 January: Milan

26 January: Milan, premiere of *Dialogues des Carmélites*

7 February: back to Paris; end of February: changes to *Carmélites*

28 February–17 March: Cannes

March: completes Flute Sonata, movements 1 and 2

9 March: 'rencontre divine avec un sergent de 29 ans . . .' [Louis Gautier]

1 April: premiere of *Le Travail du peintre*, Alice Esty with Poulenc

12–15 April: Milan: 12th, Callas in *Anna Bolena*

May: completes Flute Sonata

18 June: premiere of Sonata for flute and piano with Jean-Pierre Rampal

21 June: Paris premiere of *Dialogues des Carmélites*

Early July: Rocamadour

14 July: at Cologne premiere of *Dialogues des Carmélites*

July–March 1959: *Laudes de Saint Antoine de Padoue*

August: *Ave Maria* (lost); Sonata for bassoon and piano (never written or lost)

August–September: adding 'anticipations' in *Carmélites*

1 September: death of Dennis Brain

4 September–?: Edinburgh

5 September: premiere of *Deux Mélodies* and first performance with Bernac of *Le Travail du peintre*

16 September: *Vive Nadia*; premiere that same day for her 70th birthday

20 September: San Francisco premiere of *Dialogues des Carmélites*

25 September: first mention of *Voix humaine* (letter to Valcarenghi)

September: begins *Élégie* for horn and piano

11–15 November: Cannes: re-orchestrates two numbers from *Les Mariés de la Tour Eiffel*

15 November: Paris

December: completes *Élégie* for horn and piano

1958   New Year: Milan

5 January: London; Poulenc and Février play Two-Piano Concerto, LSO/Gibson

16 January: Covent Garden premiere of *Dialogues des Carmélites*; BBC recording of Flute Sonata

January: *Élégie*, *Sextuor*

February–June: *La Voix humaine*

17 February: premiere of *Élégie*

March: Cannes, *Une Chanson de porcelaine*; *Improvisations* 13, 14

18–21 April: Lisbon for premiere of *Dialogues des Carmélites*

21 April: Noizay

15 May: first FP/Duval recital, Bordeaux

2 June: *La Voix humaine* completed

13 June: Aldeburgh, *Mamelles* [without Poulenc]; festival day of St Anthony of Padua

25 June: Oxford D Mus

Early July: Évian; 21–25 July: Aix; –21 August: Tourrettes; –19 September: Noizay

7 August: completes piano score of *La Voix humaine*

25 August–19 September: orchestrates *La Voix humaine*

22 September–21 October: Venice, Lake Como (jury Ricordi), Florence

23 September: premiere of Stravinsky, *Threni*, conducted by composer

8 November: Barcelona, *Stabat Mater*

18 November: death of Marcelle Meyer

1959   January–June: nine venues for *Carmélites*

6 February: premiere of *La Voix humaine*

Mid-February: Naples, *Dialogues des Carmélites*

March: completes *Laudes de Saint Antoine de Padoue*

April: pondering *Gloria* for Koussevitzky commission

May–December: working on it

27 May: last recital with Bernac [also here with others], celebration of 60th birthday, Salle Gaveau

30 May: leaves for Vienna and *Dialogues des Carmélites*

May–June 1960: *Gloria*

June: Brive, *Novellette 3*, 'Lamento' for Clarinet Sonata

26 June: still at work on Bassoon Sonata

Early July: fortnight at Le Tremblay

21 July–30 August: Bagnols-en-Forêt (Louis Gautier)

August: *Fancy*, *Improvisation 15*

16 August: death of Wanda Landowska

Summer–September: *Élégie pour deux pianos*, completed by 28th

1 September: Noizay

5–19 October: 'monastery' in the Midi

Early November: orchestrates *Gloria*; starts Chabrier book

20 November: cabled commission from New York Philharmonic Orchestra = *Sept Répons*

Late November–28 December: Bagnols

8–12 December: Milan, *Otello* and *Tosca*

1960   2 January: Noizay; liver problems, flu

18 February: Air France to New York [fourth US tour with Duval, Prêtre], Chicago, Detroit, New York

March: *Sarabande* for guitar, in New York

April: Noizay, orchestrates *Gloria*

–24 August: Bagnols

25 April: *Gloria*, five of six movements done

30 April–7 May: Rome

21 June: last recording with Bernac (Véga C30 A293)

July: completes orchestration of *Gloria*; begins to plan fifth and last US tour

July–August: *La Courte Paille*; texts chosen for *Sept Répons*

24 August: leaves Bagnols for Noizay

Mid-October: Milan

November: Noizay, *La Puce*; finishes *Chabrier*

16–22 December: Rome (Santa Cecilia jury, concerts)

1961   13–29 January: fifth and last US tour (New York, Boston, New York)

21 January: premiere of *Gloria*, Concerto for two pianos with Evelyne Crochet

February: *Chabrier* published

14 February: Paris premiere of *Gloria* (Carteri)

March: anxiety . . .

April: *La Dame de Monte-Carlo*; premiere November; begins work on *Sept Répons des ténèbres*

May: Noizay with Chanlaire

27 July: starts *Sept Répons* over again

October–March 1962: *Sept Répons*

1962   3–16 February: Italian tour with Duval

26 March: finishes *Sept Répons*

April: Venice festival

April–June: *Renaud et Armide* (lost); premiere 18 August

May: revises orchestration of *Mamelles*

12 June: Jean Françaix finishes orchestration of *Babar*; Poulenc reduces orchestration of *Mamelles* for La Scala in 1963

22 June: Bagnols; 26 June: Paris

1 July: premiere of *La Courte Paille*

Summer: Brive (Bosredon) Sonata for clarinet and piano; Sonata for oboe and piano

10 August: attack of angina at Milan airport – back to Paris

Autumn: work continues on two wind sonatas

Late October–22 November: Cannes

3–12 December: Italy

Christmas: Bagnols

1963   Early January: Noizay with Chanlaire

14 January: to Paris

22 January: at theatre, crisis of coughing and stomach pains

24–28 January: concerts in Holland with Duval

26 January: last note to Duval ('ma dernière joie')

28 January: returns to Paris

30 January: Poulenc dies in his flat, 5 rue de Médicis

2 February: funeral mass, St Sulpice

10 April: premiere of Sonata for clarinet and piano, Carnegie Hall (Goodman, Bernstein)

11 April: premiere of *Sept Répons des ténèbres*, Philharmonic Hall, New York

8 June: premiere of Sonata for oboe and piano, Strasbourg (Pierlot, Février)

CATALOGUE OF WORKS

In each case the three dates are those of composition/first public performance/publication(s).

BALLETS AND OPERAS

La Colombe, recitatives by Poulenc	1923/1924/–
Les Biches	1923/1924/1924, 1943
L'Éventail de Jeanne, 'Pastourelle'	1927/1929/1929
Aubade	1929/1930/1931
Les Animaux modèles	1940–2/1942/1944
Les Mamelles de Tirésias	1944/1947/rev. 1962
Dialogues des Carmélites	1953–5/1957/1957
La Voix humaine	1958/1959/1959

ORCHESTRAL WORKS AND CONCERTOS

Les Biches, orchestral suite	1924/1924/1924, 1943
L'Éventail de Jeanne, 'Pastourelle'	1927/1929/1929
Concert champêtre	1927–8/1929/?1929
Aubade	1929/1930/1931
Concerto for two pianos and orchestra	1932/1932/1934
Suite française	1935/1935/1935
Deux Marches et un intermède	1937/1937/1938
Concerto for organ and orchestra	1938/1939/1939
Les Animaux modèles, orchestral suite	1940–2/1943/1949
Amphitryon	1947/1947/–
Sinfonietta	1947–8/1948/1948
Concerto for piano and orchestra	1949/1950/1950
La Guirlande de Campra, 'Matelote provençale'	1952/1952/1954
Variations sur le nom de Marguerite Long, 'Bucolique'	1956/1956/1956

PIANO MUSIC – SOLO PIANO

En Barque	1910/?/–
Mélopée d'automne	1913/?/–
Processional pour la crémation d'un mandarin	1914/?/–
Préludes	1916/?/–
Trois Pastorales	1917/?/no. 1 rev. 1928
Trois Mouvements perpétuels	1918/1919/1919
L'Album des Six, 'Valse'	1919/1919/1920

CATALOGUE OF WORKS

Suite pour piano	1920/1920/1920
Le Gendarme incompris, piano score	1920/?/–
Impromptus	1920–1/1922/1922, 1924, 1939
Promenades	1921/1923/1923, 1952
Esquisse d'une fanfare	1921/?/1921
Sonata for two clarinets, piano score	1918/?/1925
Sonata for clarinet and bassoon, piano score	1922/?/1925
Sonata for horn, trumpet and trombone, piano score	1922/?/1925
Les Biches, piano score	1924/?/1924, 1947
Napoli	1922–5/1926/1926
L'Éventail de Jeanne, 'Pastourelle'	1927/?/1929
Deux Novellettes	1927–8/1939/1930, 1939
Trois pièces pour piano	1918–28/1953/1928/1931, 1953
Hommage à Albert Roussel, 'Pièce brève sur le nom d'Albert Roussel'	1929/1929/1929
Nocturnes 1–8	1929–38/?/1932–9
Intermède, no. 2 of *Le Bal masqué*	1932/?/1932
Caprice, no. 6 of *Le Bal masqué*	1932/?/1932
Hommage à J. S. Bach, 'Valse-improvisation sur le nom de Bach'	1932/?/1932
Improvisations 1–10	1932–4/1933 (7 only)/1933–4
Villageoises	1933/?/1933
Feuillets d'album	1933/?/1933
Presto in B flat	1934/?/1934
Deux intermezzi	1934/?/1934
Humoresque	1934/?/1935
Badinage	1934/?/1935
Suite française	1935/?/1935
Les Soirées de Nazelles	1930–6/1936/1937
À l'Exposition, 'Bourrée, au Pavillon d'Auvergne'	1937/1937/1937
Française d'après Claude Gervaise	1939/?/1940
Mélancolie	1940/1941/1941
Les Animaux modèles, piano score	1940–2/?/1942
Improvisations 11, 12	1941/?/1945
Intermezzo in A flat major	1943/?/1947
Thème varié	1951/1952/1952
Improvisations 13, 14	1958/?/1958
Novellette in E minor 'sur un thème de Manuel de Falla'	1959/?/1960
Improvisation 15 (Hommage à Édith Piaf)	1959/?/1960

PIANO MUSIC – PIANO DUET

Sonata for piano duet	1918, 1939/1918/1919, 1939

PIANO MUSIC – TWO PIANOS

Zèbre, scherzo for two pianos	1917/?destroyed
Jongleur, arr. two pianos	?1918/?destroyed
Concert champêtre, arr. two pianos	1927–8/?/1929
Aubade, arr. two pianos	1929/?/1930
Concerto for two pianos, arr. two pianos	?/?/1933
Concerto for piano and orchestra, arr. two pianos	1949/?/1950
L'Embarquement pour Cythère	1951/?/1952

Capriccio d'après Le Bal masqué	1952/?/1953
Sonata for two pianos	1952–3/1953/1954
Élégie (in alternating chords) for two pianos	1959/?/1960

PIANO AND RECITER

L'Histoire de Babar le petit éléphant (Brunhoff)	1940–5/1946/1949
orchestrated by Jean Françaix	1962/?/1963

CHAMBER MUSIC

(a) Wind instruments

Sonata for two clarinets	1918, 1945/1919/1919, 1945
Sonata for clarinet and bassoon	1922, 1945/1923/1924, 1945
Sonata for horn, trumpet and trombone	1922, 1945/1923/1924, 1945
Trio for oboe, bassoon and piano	1926/1926/1926
Pipeaux, 'Villanelle' for pipe	1934/?/1934
Un Joueur de flûte berce les ruines for flute	1941/?/–
Sonata for flute and piano	1956–7/1957/1958
Élégie for horn and piano	1957/1958/1958
Sonata for clarinet and piano	1962/1963/1963
Sonata for oboe and piano	1962/1963/1963

(b) Strings

Ire Bagatelle for violin and piano (from *Le Bal masqué*)	1932/?/1932
Sérénade for cello and piano (from *Chansons gaillardes*)	1948/?/1950
Suite française for cello and piano	1953/?1953/–
Sonata for violin and piano	1942–3, 1949/1943/1944, 1949
Souvenirs for cello and piano	1944/2013/2016
Sonata for cello and piano	1948, 1953/1949/1949, 1953

(c) Guitar

Sarabande	1960/?/1961

(d) Ensembles

Trois Mouvements perpétuels	1919/1927/1948
Suite française	?/1935/1948
Sextuor	1931–9/1933, 1940/1939

INCIDENTAL MUSIC

Le Gendarme incompris (Cocteau/Radiguet)	1920/1921/1988
Les Mariés de la Tour Eiffel (Cocteau)	1921, 1957/1921/n.d.
Roméo et Juliette (Shakespeare/Cocteau)	1921/?1924/1921
Orphée (Cocteau)	1926/?1926/–
Intermezzo (Giraudoux)	1933/1933/–
Monsieur Le Trouhadec saisi par la débauche (Romains)	1933/?/lost
Pétrus (Achard)	1933/1933/–
Margot (Bourdet) see *À sa guitare* below	1935/?/1935
Léocadia (Anouilh) see *Les Chemins de l'amour* below	1940/1940/1961

La Fille du jardinier (Exbrayat)	1941/1941/lost
Le Voyageur sans bagage (Anouilh)	1943/1944/–
La Nuit de la Saint-Jean (Barrie)	1944/1944/–
Le Soldat et la sorcière (Salacrou)	1945/1945/lost
L'Invitation au château (Anouilh)	1947/1947/1948
Amphitryon (Molière)	1947/1947/–
Renaud et Armide (Cocteau)	1962/1962/lost

FILM MUSIC

La Belle au bois dormant (Alexeieff)	1935/1935/–
La Duchesse de Langeais (Baroncelli)	1941–2/1942/1942
Le Voyageur sans bagage (Anouilh)	1943/1944/–
Le Voyage en Amérique (Lavorel)	1951/1951/–

SONGS

(a) for voice unaccompanied

Petite complainte	1918/?/Corr. p. 79

(b) for voice and piano

Viens! une flûte invisible (Hugo)	1913/?/–
Le Toréador (Cocteau)	1919/?/1933
Le Bestiaire (Apollinaire)	1919/1919/1920
Cocardes (Cocteau)	1919, 1939/1920/1920
Quatre Poèmes de Max Jacob	1921/1922/1993
Poèmes de Ronsard	1924–5/1925/1925
Chansons gaillardes (anon.)	1925–6/1926/1926
Vocalise	1927/1927/1929
Airs chantés (Moréas)	1927–8/1928/1928
Épitaphe (Malherbe)	1930/?/1930
Trois Poèmes de Louise Lalanne (Laurencin/Apollinaire)	1931/1931/1931
Quatre Poèmes de Guillaume Apollinaire	1931/1931/1931
Cinq Poèmes de Max Jacob	1931/?/1931
Pierrot (Banville)	1933/?/–
Huit Chansons polonaises (anon.)	1934/?/1934
Cinq Poèmes de Paul Éluard	1935/1935/1935
À sa guitare (Ronsard)	1935/?/1935
Tel jour telle nuit (Éluard)	1936–7/1937/1937
Trois Poèmes de Louise de Vilmorin	1937/1938/1938
Le Portrait (Colette)	1938/1939/1939
Deux Poèmes de Guillaume Apollinaire	1938/1939/1938
Priez pour paix (Orléans)	1938/?/1939
La Grenouillère (Apollinaire)	1938/?/1939
Miroirs brûlants (Éluard)	1938–9/1939/1939
Ce doux petit visage (Éluard)	1939/1941/1941
Fiançailles pour rire (Vilmorin)	1939/1942/1940
Bleuet (Apollinaire)	1939/?/1940
Les Chemins de l'amour (Anouilh)	1940/1940/1945
Banalités (Apollinaire)	1940/1940/1941
Colloque (Valéry) duet	1940/1941/1978
Chansons villageoises (Fombeure)	1942/?/1943

Métamorphoses (Vilmorin)	1943/1943/1944
Deux Poèmes de Louis Aragon	1943/1943/1944
Deux Mélodies de Guillaume Apollinaire	1945/1945/1945
Le Pont (Apollinaire)	1946/1946/1947
Un Poème (Apollinaire)	1946/1946/1947
Paul et Virginie (Radiguet)	1946/?/1947
Le Disparu (Desnos)	1946–7/?/1947
Main dominée par le coeur (Éluard)	1946–7/?/1947
Trois Chansons de F. Garcia Lorca	1947/1947/1947
. . . mais mourir (Éluard)	1947/?/1948
Calligrammes (Apollinaire)	1948/1948/1948
Hymne (Racine)	1948/1948/1949
Mazurka (Vilmorin)	1949/1949/1949
La Fraîcheur et le feu (Éluard)	1950/1950/1951
Parisiana (Jacob)	1954/1954/1954
Rosemonde (Apollinaire)	1954/1954/1955
Le Travail du peintre (Éluard)	1956/1957/1957
Deux Mélodies (Apollinaire/Beylié)	1956/1957/1957
Dernier Poème (Desnos)	1956/?/1957
Une Chanson de porcelaine (Éluard)	1958/?/1959
Fancy (Shakespeare)	1959/?/1962
La Courte Paille (Carême)	1960/1962/1960
La Dame de Monte-Carlo (Cocteau)	1961/?/1961

(c) for voice and ensemble

Rapsodie nègre (Prouille/Moulié)	1917, 1933/1917/1919, 1933
Poèmes sénégalais (?), ? destroyed	1918/1918/–
Le Toréador (Cocteau)	1919/?/–
Le Bestiaire (Apollinaire)	1919/?/1920
Cocardes (Cocteau)	1919/1920/1920
Quatre Poèmes de Max Jacob	1921/1922/1993
Poèmes de Ronsard	1934/1934/–
Le Bal masqué (Jacob)	1932/1932/1932
À sa guitare (Ronsard)	1935/?/–
Chansons villageoises (Fombeure)	1942/1943/1943
La Dame de Monte-Carlo (Cocteau)	1961/1961/1961

CHORAL MUSIC (UNACCOMPANIED MIXED CHOIR, UNLESS OTHERWISE INDICATED)

Chanson à boire (anon.) men's voices	1922/?/1923
Quatre Chansons pour enfants	1934/?/1935, 1937
Sept Chansons (Apollinaire/Éluard)	1936, 1937, 1943/ 1936, 1937, 1943/ 1937, 1943
Litanies à la Vierge noire (anon.) women's voices with organ	1936/1936/1937
with orchestra	1947/?/1947
Petites voix (Ley) children's voices	1936/?/1936
Mass in G major	1937/1938/1937
Sécheresses (James) with orchestra	1937/1938/1952
Quatre Motets pour un temps de pénitence	1938–9/1939/1938
Hymne à la Touraine men's voices	1939/1939/–
Exultate Deo	1941/?/1941

Salve Regina	1941/?/1941
Figure humaine (Éluard)	1943, 1959/1945/1945, 1959
Un Soir de neige (Éluard)	1944/1945/1945
Chansons françaises (anon.)	1945–6/?/1948
Quatre petites prières de Saint François d'Assise men's voices	1948/?1949/1949
Stabat Mater with soprano solo and orchestra	1950–1/1951/1951
Quatre Motets pour le temps de Noël	1951–2/?/1952
Ave verum (Pope Innocent VI) women's voices	1952/1952/1952
Vive Nadia (Poulenc)	1957/1957/Corr. p. 875
Laudes de Saint Antoine de Padoue men's voices	1957–9/?/1959
Gloria with soprano solo and orchestra	1959–60/1961/1960
Sept Répons des ténèbres with solo (boy) soprano and orchestra	1961–2/1963/1962

TRANSCRIPTIONS OF WORKS BY OTHERS

Mozart, *Ein musikalischer Spass*, arranged for piano	1925/?/1927
Satie, *Deux Préludes posthumes et une Gnossienne*, arranged for orchestra	1939/?/1949

SELECT BIBLIOGRAPHY

The site of publication is Paris unless otherwise indicated.

Albright, Daniel, *Untwisting the Serpent*, Chicago and London, University of Chicago Press, 2000

Aldeburgh Britten Festival 20–23 Oct 1994, quoting from 1964 Festival programme book

Alexeieff, Alexandre, analysis of film of *La Belle au bois dormant*

Amis, John, *Amiscellany*, London, Faber, 1985, 85–6

Anger, Violaine, 'Du silence au chant: l'imaginaire de la parole dans les *Dialogues des Carmélites*', *Langage*, 225–34

Anon., ed., *Francis Poulenc*, Yonne, Cahiers Zodiaque, 1974

Auric, Georges, 'Apollinaire et la musique,' *ReM*, Jan 1952, 147–9

— *Quand j'étais là*, Grasset, 1979

L'Avant-Scène Opéra, *Dialogues des Carmélites*, nos 52 (May 1983) and 257 (July/August 2010)

Barraud, Henry, *Un Compositeur aux commandes de la Radio*, Fayard, 2010

Barrès, Maurice, *The Undying Spirit of France*, New Haven, Yale University Press, 1917

Basinger, Simon, 'Ma rencontre avec Henri Dutilleux', CFP III, 2012, 103–7; about Francis Poulenc

Beaumont, Cyril W., *The Diaghilev Ballet in London*, London, Putnam, 1945

Beevor, Anthony and Artemis Cooper, *Paris after the Liberation*, London, Hamish Hamilton, 1994

Bellas, Jacqueline, 'Apollinaire et Poulenc,' *Apollinaire et la musique, actes du colloque Stavelot*, 27–29 August 1965, ed. Michel Décaudin, 1967

Berenguer, Bruno, 'Une amitié intime', CFP I, 73–103

Berlin, Isaiah, 'Shostakovich at Oxford', *New York Review of Books*, 16 July–12 Aug 2009, LVI/12, 22–3

Bernac, P., 'Poulenc', British Institute of Recorded Sound, talk given 20 Jan 1971, Lennox Berkeley in the chair

— *Entretiens avec Gérard Michel*, 20 Nov 1970–15 Jan 1971

— *Francis Poulenc et ses mélodies*, Buchet-Chastel, 1978/2014; *Francis Poulenc: The Man and his Songs*, trans. Winifred Radford, London, Gollancz, 1977; paperback reprint, London, Kahn & Averill, 2001

Bernanos, Georges, *Dialogues des Carmélites*, Neuchâtel, La Baconnière, Collection Les Cahiers du Rhône/Éditions du Seuil, 1949

Bertin, Pierre, 'Erik Satie et le Groupe des Six', *Annales Conferencia*, LVIII, Feb 1951, 49–60

Biget-Mainfroy, Michelle, ed., *In memoriam Francis Poulenc*, Rouen, CIREM, 2004

Bliss, Arthur, *As I Remember*, London, Faber, 1970

Boulez, Pierre, *Points de repère*, ed. Christian Bougois, Éditions du Seuil, 1981; trans. Martin Cooper in *Orientations*, London, Faber, 1986

Bourdet, Denise, 'Images de Paris', *La Revue de Paris*, March 1957

Britten, Benjamin and Peter Pears, brief tribute to Francis Poulenc, Aldeburgh Festival Programme 1964

Brown, Frederick, *An Impersonation of Angels*, London, Longmans, 1969

Buckle, Richard, *Diaghilev*, London, Hamish Hamilton, 1984

Bullock, Michael, *Satie Seen through his Letters*, London, Marion Boyars, 1989

SELECT BIBLIOGRAPHY

Burton, Richard D. E., *Francis Poulenc*, Bath, Absolute Press, 2002

Cabanne, Pierre, *Le Siècle de Picasso*, I, Denoël, 1975

Caré, Claude, 'Francis Poulenc et Paul Eluard: une seule musique sous les deux espèces', n.d.

— 'Francis Poulenc et le mécénat privé', Nov 2007

Casella, Alfredo, *Strawinski*, Brescia, La Scuola, 1947

Castanet, Pierre-Albert, 'La clarinette dans les sonates de Francis Poulenc', CIREM, 119–36

Chimènes, Myriam, 'Geneviève Sienkiewicz et Francis Poulenc: correspondance inédite', GAFP, 239–85

— *Mécènes et musiciens*, Fayard, 2004

— *La Musique à Paris sous l'Occupation*, Fayard, 2013

— ed., *La Vie musicale sous Vichy*, Éditions Complexe, 2001

Clary, Mildred, *Ricardo Viñes, un pèlerin de l'absolu*, Arles, Actes Sud, 2011

Cobban, Alfred, *A History of Modern France*, London, Penguin, 1975

Cocteau, Jean, *Le Coq et l'Arlequin*, Stock, 1979

— *Cahiers Jean Cocteau*, nouvelle série no. 4, 'Cocteau et la musique', ed. David Gullentops, 2006

Coeuroy, André, *Panorama de la musique contemporaine*, Éditions Kra, 1928

Collaer, Paul, 'I "Sei"; Studio dell' evoluzione della musica francese dal 1917 al 1924', *L'Approdo musicale* 19–20, 1965, 53–4

— *Darius Milhaud*, trans. Jane Hohfeld Galante, San Francisco, San Francisco Press, 1988

— *Correspondance avec des amis musiciens*, ed. Robert Wangermée, Sprimont, Mardaga, 1996

Conly, John M., 'Memoir of Francis Poulenc', *The Atlantic Monthly*, Boston, June 1960

Conrad, Doda, *Dodascalies*, Arles, Actes Sud, 1997

Corbillari, Alain, 'Les sept péchés capitaux de Francis Poulenc,' *Revue musicale de Suisse Romande*, 56/1, March 2003

Cortot, Alfred, *La Musique française de piano*, Quadrige/Presses universitaires de France, 1981

Coste, Claude, *Les Malheurs d'Orphée*, L'Improviste, 2003

Covent Garden, Royal Opera House programme for *Dialogues des Carmélites*, May/June 2014

Cronin, Vincent, *Paris, City of Light 1919–1939*, London, HarperCollins, 1994

Cuénod, Hugues, Interview with François Hudry, 11 July 1997, on Dante LYSD254

Daniel, Keith W., *Francis Poulenc: His Artistic Development and Musical Style*, Ann Arbor, UMI Research Press, 1982

Debost, Michel, Memoir of Francis Poulenc, in English

Décaudin, Michel, ed., *Apollinaire et la musique*, Stavelot, Les Amis de Guillaume Apollinaire, 1967

Denis, Maurice, preface to *L'architecture et l'art décoratif en France après la guerre (comment préparer leur renaissance)*, Verneuil sur Avre, A. Aubert, 1915

Dickinson, Peter, *Lennox Berkeley and Friends*, Woodbridge, The Boydell Press, 2012

D'Indy, Vincent, *Ma Vie*, ed., Marie d'Indy, Seguier, 2001

Drew, David, *European Music in the Twentieth Century*, ed. Howard Hartog, London, Pelican, 1961

Drummond, John, *Speaking of Diaghilev*, London, Faber, 1998

Duchesneau, Michel, *L'Avant-garde musicale à Paris de 1871 à 1939*, Sprimont, Mardaga, 1997

Dumesnil, René, *La Musique en France entre les deux guerres, 1919–1939*, Édition Milieu du Monde, 1946

— '*Répons des ténèbres* de Poulenc', HL 777

Dutourd, Jean, *Les Taxis de la Marne*, Gallimard, 1956/1992

Duval, Denise, 'J'ai détesté chanter', *Libération*, 6/7 Nov 2004

— 'Des Folies-Bergère aux DIALOGUES', 'Dialogues des Carmélites', *L'Avant-Scène Opéra*, 257, 2010, 98–9

Eberle, Kevin Ryland, 'How Queer! Camp Aesthetics and Francis Poulenc's Trio for Oboe, Bassoon and Piano,' University of Nevada, Las Vegas, 2016

Enckell, Pierre, 'Les vraies Carmélites de Compiègne', *L'Avant-Scène Opéra*, 257, 2010

Fauré, Gabriel, *Correspondance*, ed. Jean-Michel Nectoux, Flammarion, 1980

Faure, Michel, *Du Néoclassicisme musical dans la France du premier xxe siècle*, Klincksieck, 1997

Ferraty, Franck, *La Musique pour piano de Francis Poulenc ou le temps de l'ambivalence*, L'Harmattan, 2009

— *Francis Poulenc à son piano: un clavier bien fantasmé*, L'Harmattan, 2011

354

Franceschini, Stefania, *Francis Poulenc, una biographia*, Varese Zecchini, 2014

Frazier, James E., *Maurice Duruflé, the Man and his Music*, University of Rochester Press, 2007

Garafola, Lynn, *Diaghilev's Ballets Russes*, New York, Oxford University Press, 1989

Garden, Mary and Louis Biancolli, *Mary Garden's Story*, London, Michael Joseph, 1952

Gavin, Barrie, quotes from TV film 1988 (Mady, Sauguet, Hell, Prêtre, Poulenc)

Gavoty, Bernard, 'Poulenc contre Rossini', *Le Figaro*, 15 June 1951

Gendre, Claude, '*Dialogues des Carmélites*: The historical background, literary destiny and genesis of the opera', MAL 274–319

Gervasoni, Pierre, *Henri Dutilleux*, Arles, Actes Sud/Philharmonie de Paris, 2016

Glotz, Michel, *La Note bleue*, Lattès, 2002, 89–104

Gold, Arthur and Robert Fizdale, *Misia*, London, Macmillan, 1980

Gonnard, Henri, 'La voix et le surréalisme, une rencontre problématique', in P. Lécroart and F. Toudoire-Surlapierre, eds, *Éclats de voix: l'expression de la voix en littérature et musique*, Éditions de l'improviste, 2005

Gouverné, Yvonne, 'Hommage à Francis Poulenc', in *Poulenc et Rocamadour*, 1974

Gruen, John, 'Poulenc', *Musical America*, April 1960

Guth, Paul, 'Des "Mamelles de Tirésias" au "Stabat Mater": Francis Poulenc a deux côtés', *Le Figaro littéraire*, 17 May 1952

Hacquard, Georges, *Germaine Tailleferre. La Dame des Six*, Harmattan, 1998, 194–5

Häger, Bengt, *Ballets suédois*, trans. Ruth Sharman, London, Thames & Hudson, 1990

Haine, Malou, ' "Mon irrésistible, insupportable et cher Poulenc . . .": Poulenc à travers le *Journal intime* de son ami Stéphane Audel', CIREM, 157–227

Halbreich, Harry, *Arthur Honegger*, trans. Roger Nichols, Portland, Amadeus Press, 1999

Harding, James, *Folies de Paris*, London, Chappell, 1979

Hell, Henri, 'Les dernières oeuvres de Francis Poulenc', *Fontaine*, Sept 1957

'Hommage à Maurice Ravel', *Revue musicale*, December 1938

Honegger, Arthur, 'Un ballet de Francis Poulenc à l'Opéra', *Comoedia*, 15 Aug 1942

— 'Les animaux modèles', *Incantation aux fossiles*, Lausanne, Aux Éditions d'Ouchy, 1948, 111

Huebner, Steven, 'Francis Poulenc's "Dialogues des Carmélites": Faith, Ideology and Love,' *Music & Letters*, 97/2, 2016

Hurard-Viltard, Éveline, *Le Groupe des Six, ou le matin d'un jour de fête*, Méridiens Klincksieck, 1987

Ivry, Benjamin, *Francis Poulenc*, London, Phaidon, 1996

Jameux, Dominique, *Pierre Boulez*, trans. Susan Bradshaw, Cambridge, MA, Harvard University Press, 1991

Jankélévitch, Vladimir, *Le Nocturne. Fauré, Chopin et la nuit, Satie et le matin*, Albin Michel, 1957

Johnson, Graham and Richard Stokes, *A French Song Companion*, Oxford University Press, 2000

Jones, Colin, 'The Carmelites of Compiègne', programme of the royal Opera House, Covent Garden, May/June 2014, 22–3

Jost, Peter, 'Les mélodies de Georges Auric et de Francis Poulenc d'après Paul Éluard', GAFP, 115–41

Jourdan-Morhange, Hélène, *Mes amis musiciens*, Les éditeurs français réunis, 1955

Kayas, Lucie ed., *À bâtons rompus*, Arles, Actes Sud, 1999

— *André Jolivet*, Fayard, 2005

— and Hervé Lacombe, eds, *Du langage au style*, Société française de musicologie, 2016

Kelly, Barbara L., ed., *French Music, Culture and National Identity, 1870–1939*, University of Rochester Press, 2008

— *Music and Ultra-Modernism in France*, Woodbridge, The Boydell Press, 2013

Kildea, Paul, *Benjamin Britten: A Life in the Twentieth Century*, London, Allen Lane, 2013

Lacombe, Hervé, 'Puissance expressive et "plastique chorale" dans *Figure humaine*', FPV, 213–27

— *Poulenc Our Contemporary*, London, Universal Music, 2013

— and Nicolas Southon (eds), *Fortune de Francis Poulenc: diffusion, interprétation, réception*, Presses universitaires de Rennes, 2016

Landormy, Paul, *La Musique française après Debussy*, Gallimard, 1943

SELECT BIBLIOGRAPHY

Langham Smith, Richard, 'Poulenc et Edward Lockspeiser: une amitié professionnelle', *Fortune*, 197–219

Lebrecht, Norman, *Covent Garden: The Untold Story*, London, Simon & Schuster, 2001

Lécroart, Pascal, '*La Voix humaine* de Poulenc et sa prosodie', in *Éclats de voix* (see Gonnard above)

Lephay, Pierre-Emmanuel, 'Moussorgski, modèle de Poulenc?', *Langage*, 149–58

Machart, Renaud, *Poulenc*, Éditions du Seuil, 1995

Malherbe, Henry, 'Au Théâtre des Champs-Élysées: Ballets russes', *Le Temps*, 11 June 1924

Markévitch, Igor, *Etre et avoir été*, Gallimard, 1980

Mas, J., ed., *Centenaire Georges Auric-Francis Poulenc*, Montpellier (Centre d'étude du xxe siècle), 2001

Massin, Brigitte, *Les Joachim, une famille de musiciens*, Fayard, 1999

Maupassant, Guy de, *A Parisian Affair and Other Stories*, trans. Sian Miles, London, Penguin, 2004

Mellers, Wilfrid, *Francis Poulenc*, Oxford University Press, 1993

Menasce, Jacques de, 'Poulenc's Les Mamelles de Thirésias', *MQ*, xxv (April 1949), 315–22

Meylan, Pierre, 'Francis Poulenc à Lausanne', *Feuilles musicales*, 1961/4–5, 78–81

Milhaud, Darius, *Études*, Claude Aveline, 1927

— *Notes sans musique*, Julliard, 1949

— *Ma Vie heureuse*, Belfond, 1973

— *Notes sur la musique. Essais et chroniques*, ed. Jeremy Drake, Flammarion, 1982

Miscevic, Pierre, *Poulenc et l'Italie*, Ambassade de France en Italie, 2006

— *Francis Poulenc et la mélodie*, Musée des Beaux-Arts, Tours, 2016

— and Francis Poulenc, *Lettres inédites à Brigitte Manceaux*, Orizons, 2019

Monnier, Adrienne, *The Very Rich Hours of Adrienne Monnier*, trans. Richard McDougall, New York, Charles Scribner's Sons, 1976

Moore, Christopher, 'Camp in Francis Poulenc's Early Ballets,' *MQ*, xiv/2–3 (2012), 299–342

— 'Camp et ambiguité formelle dans le Concert champêtre', *Langage*, 319–30

Nabokov, Nicolas, *Old Friends and New Music*, London, Hamish Hamilton, 1951

Nichols, Roger, *Ravel Remembered*, London, Faber, 1987

— *Conversations with Madeleine Milhaud*, London, Faber, 1996

— 'Le gourmand fastidieux', *International Opera Collector*, 6, Winter, 1997, 30–4

— *The Harlequin Years*, London, Thames & Hudson, 2002

— *Ravel*, London, Yale University Press, 2011

Opstad, Gillian, *Debussy's Mélisande*, Woodbridge, The Boydell Press, 2009

Orledge, Robert, *Satie the Composer*, Cambridge University Press, 1990

— *Satie Remembered*, London, Faber, 1995

— 'Satie & Les Six', *French Music since Berlioz*, ed. Richard Langham Smith and Caroline Potter, Aldershot, Ashgate, 2006

— 'Poulenc and Koechlin: 58 Lessons and a Friendship', MAL 9–47

Ousby, Ian, *Occupation, the Ordeal of France, 1940–1944*, London, Pimlico, 1999

Peignot, Suzanne, Unpublished article on Poulenc intended for the magazine *Adam* (kindly supplied by Sidney Buckland)

Perloff, Nancy, *Art and the Everyday: Popular Entertainment and the Circle of Erik Satie*, Oxford, Clarendon Press, 1991

Peyser, Joan, *Boulez: Composer, Conductor, Enigma*, London, Cassell, 1977

Pistone, Danièle, *Poulenc et ses amis*, in *Revue internationale de musique française*, Honoré Champion, 1994

— ed., *Musique et musiciens à Paris dans les années 30*, Champion, 2000

Porcile, François, *Les conflits de la musique française, 1940–1965*, Fayard, 2001

Pouille, Marcel and Charles Moulié, *Les poèmes de Makoko Kangarou*, Dorbon Aîné, 1910

Poulenc, Francis, 'Three SQs' 1921 b,c, *Fanfare*, 15 Nov 1921, etc.

— 'Le coeur de Maurice Ravel', *La nouvelle Revue française*, 1 Jan 1941: JE 293; NH 79

— 'Francis Poulenc on His Ballets,' *Ballet*, 4/2, Sept 1946: JE 57–8; NH 39–41

— 'On cooking', *Harper's Bazaar* (CS 1946e)

— 'Ma bibliothèque idéale', *Pour une bibliothèque idéale*, Gallimard, 1950

— 'Souvenirs', *Cahiers Renaud/Barrault*, I/2, Juilliard, 1953

— 'La musique de piano de Prokofieff', *Musique russe*, vol. 2, ed. Pierre Souvtchinsky, Presses universitaires de France, 1953, 269–76: JE 322–38

— 'Lorsque je suis mélancolique', *Le Mercure de France*, Jan–April 1956: JE 409–12

— *Emmanuel Chabrier*, Paris/Geneva, La Palatine, 1961

— 'Hommage à Ben B', October 1962, *Tribute to BB*, Faber

— *Moi et mes amis*, confidences recueillies par Stéphane Audel, La Palatine, 1963; *My Friends and Myself*, trans. James Harding, London, Dennis Dobson, 1978

— Poulenc Concert 'IN MEMORIAM', Arts Council, 7 May 1963, with address by Lennox Berkeley

— 'Francis Poulenc à l'heure de la revanche', *Le Figaro*, 25 January 1993 (DTLX and his reserves, Florentz)

— *Journal de mes mélodies*, ed. Renaud Machart, Cicero, 1993; this contains additions not found in *Diary of my Songs*, trans. Winfred Radford, London, Victor Gollancz, 1985

— *À bâtons rompus, écrits radiophoniques*, ed. Lucie Kayas, Arles, Actes Sud, 1999

— *J'écris ce qui me chante*, ed. Nicolas Southon, Fayard, 2011

Ramaut, Alban, ed., *Francis Poulenc et la voix*, Publications de l'Université de Saint-Étienne, 2002

Ravel, Maurice, *A Ravel Reader*, ed. and trans. Arbie Orenstein, New York, Columbia University Press, 1990

— *L'Intégrale: Correspondance (1895–1937), écrits et entretiens*, ed. Manuel Cornejo, Le Passeur, 2018

Reibel, Emmanuel, *Les Concertos de Poulenc*, Bourg-la-Reine, Zurfluj, 1999

Revue musicale, La, 'Hommage à Maurice Ravel', numéro spécial, Dec 1938

Robert, Sophie, 'Raymonde Linossier: "Lovely soul who was my flame"', trans. Sidney Buckland, MAL 109

Rohozinski, Ladislas, *Cinquante ans de musique française de 1874 à 1925*, Les Éditions musicales de la Librairie de France, 1925

Rorem, Ned, *Music and People*, New York, George Braziller, 1968

— *Settling the Score*, New York, Doubleday, 1989

— *A Ned Rorem Reader*, New Haven and London, Yale University Press, 2001

Rosenthal, Manuel, *Satie, Ravel, Poulenc*, Madras and New York, Hanuman Books, 1987

Rostand, Claude, 'Le Concerto de Poulenc à Aix-en-Provence', *Carrefour*, 1 Aug 1950

Roussel, Albert, *Lettres et écrits*, ed. Nicole Labelle, Flammarion, 1987

Roy, Jean, *Francis Poulenc*, Éditions Seghers, 1964

— *Le Groupe des Six*, Seuil, 1994

Royal Opera House, Covent Garden, programme for *Dialogues des Carmélites*, May/June 2014

Saint-Marceaux, Marguerite de, *Journal, 1894–1927*, ed. Myriam Chimènes, Fayard, 2007

Satie, Erik, *A Mammal's Notebook*, ed. Ornella Volta, trans. Antony Melville, London, Atlas Press, 1996

— *Correspondance presque complète*, ed. Ornella Volta, Fayard, 2000

Sauguet, Henri, 'Figure humaine', *La Bataille*, 28 May 1947

— *La musique, ma vie*, Séguier, 1990

Schmidt, Carl, 'La méthode de composition de Francis Poulenc', *Langage*, 365–81

Schneider, Marcel, *L'Éternité fragile, vol. 3, Le Palais des mirages*, Bernard Grasset, 1992

— 'Francis Poulenc: l'entretien des muses', *Le Monde de la Musique*, Jan 1999, 42–5

Shattuck, Roger, 'Surrealism at the Opéra-Comique', *Theatre Arts*, xxxii (Jan 1948), 51–2

— *The Banquet Years*, New York, Vintage Books, 1968

Silver, Kenneth E., *Esprit de Corps: The Art of the Parisian Avant-Garde and the First World War, 1914–1925*, London, Thames & Hudson, 1989

Simeone, Nigel, *Poulenc in London and Dreamland*, Cambridge, Mirage Press, 2000

— 'Les *Dialogues des Carmélites* dans la presse anglaise', FPV 23–33

— 'Making Music in Occupied Paris,' *Musical Times*, Spring 2006, 23–50

Simon, Yannick, *Composer sous Vichy*, Lyon, Symétries, 2009

Smith, Cecil, 'Music: More Emissaries from France', *The New Republic*, cxix (13 Dec 1948)

Sordet, Dominique, *Douze chefs d'orchestre*, Librairie Fischbacher, 1924

Soulé, Jacques, 'Francis Poulenc dans ses jeunes années', booklet published by Les Amis de Francis Poulenc, n.d.

Spotts, Frederic, *The Shameful Peace*, New Haven and London, Yale University Press, 2008

Steegmuller, Francis, *Apollinaire: Poet among the Painters*, Harmondsworth, Penguin, 1973

— *Cocteau: A Biography*, London, Constable, 1986

Stravinsky, Igor, *Selected Correspondence*, vol. 3, ed. and trans. Robert Craft, London, Faber, 1985

— and Robert Craft, *Dialogues and a Diary*, London, Faber, 1968

— *Retrospectives and Conclusions*, New York, Knopf, 1969

Tacchino, Gabriel, 'Qui était Francis Poulenc?', CFP III, 2011, 29–34

Thomson, Virgil, *Virgil Thomson*, London, Weidenfeld and Nicolson, 1967

Vançon, Jean-Claire, 'Langage, matériau et forme dans les sonates de jeunesse pour instruments à vent de Francis Poulenc', *Langage*, 93–106

Varèse, Louise, *A Looking-Glass Diary*, London, Eulenburg, 1975

Vercors (Jean Bruller), *Le silence de la mer*, Albin Michel, 1942/1951

Waleckx, Denis, '*Les mamelles de Tirésias*, pierre angulaire de la production dramatique de Francis Poulenc', GAFP, 157–74

— 'Chronologie de la composition', *Dialogues des Carmélites*, in *L'Avant-Scène Opéra*, 257, 2010, 82–3

Wallmann, Margarita, *Les Balcons du ciel*, Éditions Robert Laffont, 1976

Walsh, Stephen, *The Music of Stravinsky*, Oxford, Clarendon Press, 1993

— *Igor Stravinsky: A Creative Spring*, London, Jonathan Cape, 2000

Weber, Eugen, *The Hollow Years: France in the 1930s*, London, Sinclair-Stevenson, 1995

Weiss, Piero, ed., *Opera: A History in Documents*, New York and Oxford, Oxford University Press, 2002

Welsh National Opera, programme for *Dialogues des Carmélites*, 1999

Werck, Isabelle, *Francis Poulenc*, Bleu nuit, 2018

Wharton, Edith, *Fighting France: From Dunquerque to Belfort*, New York, Charles Scribner's Sons, 1915

White, Eric Walter, *Stravinsky: The Composer and his Works*, London, Faber, 1966

Wiéner, Jean, *Allegro appassionato*, Belfond, 1978

Wolff, Stéphane, *Un demi-siècle d'Opéra-Comique (1900–1950)*, Éditions André Bonne, 1953

VISUAL SOURCES

Gavin, Barrie, *Poulenc*, a TV documentary, Hessischer Rundfunk, HR/RM Arts, 1988

Moriarty, Denis, *Poulenc*, a TV documentary devised and introduced by John Amis, BBC, 1973

Poulenc, Christophe, *Francis Poulenc: Impressions*, a TV documentary, Aquarius Visual and Sound Arts, 1999

INDEX

Achard, Marcel
  Pétrus, 105
Addison, Adèle, 269, 270, 271
Agostini, Philippe, 220, 227
Albert-Birot, Pierre, 15
Albright, Daniel, 173, 185
Alexeieff, Alexandre, 114
  Belle au bois dormant, La, 114
Anouilh, Jean
  Becket, 271
  L'Invitation au château, 188
  Léocadia, 147
  Voyageur sans bagage, Le, 169
Ansermet, Ernest, 56, 86, 89, 161, 330
Apaches, Les, 20
Apollinaire, Guillaume, 14, 19, 27, 33, 66, 92,
    94, 117, 118, 119, 130, 134, 136, 137, 138,
    143, 144, 148, 149, 151, 160, 173, 179,
    184, 186, 187, 189, 191, 247, 252, 268,
    269, 330, 333, 336, 337
  Alcools, 223
  Bestiaire, Le, 32
  Calligrammes, 189
  Mamelles de Tirésias, Les (play), 15, 128, 184,
    323
Aragon, Louis, 15, 19, 63, 166–7, 168, 170, 173,
    229, 323, 335
  Yeux d'Elsa, Les, 166
d'Aranyi, Jelly, 50, 62
Arbeau, Thoinot
  Orchésographie, 114
Ardoin, Alice, 83, 84, 89, 91
Auber, Daniel François Esprit
  Domino noir, Le, 52
Aubert, Louis, 34, 65
Aubin, Tony, 105, 163
Audel, Stéphane, 91, 114, 193, 217, 218, 243,
    258–9, 277, 283, 285, 289, 290, 340
Auric, Georges, 11, 13, 15, 21, 22, 25, 26, 31,
    32, 33, 35, 37, 39, 40, 41, 49, 51, 54, 55,

56, 57, 60, 61, 62, 63, 65, 67, 68, 71,
    72, 73, 79, 83, 96, 97, 100, 113, 114,
    120, 122, 127, 129, 134, 147, 178, 204,
    228, 229, 269, 273, 323, 325, 327, 328,
    329, 330
  Fâcheux, Les, 47, 61
  Matelots, Les, 61
  Pastorale, La, 61
Auric, Nora, 97, 101

Bach, Carl Philipp Emanuel, 23
Bach, Johann Sebastian, 46, 102, 104
  Fantasia in G minor, 136
  Mass in B minor, 172
  Musical Offering, 165
  St Matthew Passion, 239
Balanchine, Georges, 89, 213
Ballets Russes, 14, 28, 44, 51, 54, 63, 71, 75, 78,
    243, 322
  see also Diaghilev, Sergei
Ballets Suédois, 39, 63
Balzac, Honoré de, 128
Barber, Samuel, 211, 216
  Mélodies passagères, 211
Barbette (female impersonator), 59
Barraqué, Jean, 271
Barraud, Henri, 204, 227, 230
Barrie, James Matthew, 172
Barsacq, André, 107
Bartók, Béla, 24, 47, 50, 52, 73, 243, 289
  Allegro barbaro, 24
  String Quartet no. 2, 47
  Suite op. 14, 50
  Violin Sonata no. 1, 50
Bathori, Jane, 18, 21, 23, 24, 25, 26, 56, 73,
    257, 323
Baudelaire, Charles, 66, 137, 151
Beach, Sylvia, 20, 266
Beaumarchais, Pierre, 184
Beaumont, Cyril W., 68

Beaumont, Count Étienne de, 22, 56, 63, 68, 89, 327
Beckmans, José, 185
Beecham, Thomas, 105, 255, 331
Beethoven, Ludwig van, 3, 6, 15, 52
   An die ferne Geliebte, 31
   Fidelio, 110
   Symphony no. 9, 172
Béguin, Albert, 220, 228
Bérard, Christian, 98, 183, 188, 199, 205, 206, 217, 338
Berg, Alban, 50
   Chamber Concerto, 78
   Lyric Suite, 104
   Violin Concerto, 177
   Wozzeck, 213
Bergès, Arlette, 7
Berkeley, Lennox, 108, 174, 179
Berlin, Isaiah, 259
Berlioz, Hector, 2, 3, 97
   Grande symphonie funèbre et triomphale, 97
   Requiem, 97
   Symphonie fantastique, 148
   Troyens, Les, 255, 259
Bernac, Pierre, 3, 34, 35, 56, 57, 71, 92, 93, 95, 110, 111, 112, 120, 121, 122, 124, 128, 132, 133, 135, 136, 138, 139, 142, 144, 145, 146, 148, 149, 152, 159, 160, 166, 167, 170, 171, 174, 175, 176, 179, 185, 187, 189, 190, 192, 195, 196, 197, 198, 199, 200, 202, 206, 208, 209, 210–11, 213, 217, 218, 223, 224, 225, 226, 229, 231, 245, 248, 249, 251, 253, 257, 260, 264, 265, 266, 267, 270, 273, 274, 275, 278, 279, 280, 286, 337, 338, 340, 341, 343, 344, 345
Bernanos, Georges, 219, 220, 224, 227, 228, 230, 233, 235, 236, 238, 239, 241, 242, 245, 252, 253
Bernouard, François, 41
Bernstein, Leonard, 198, 266, 267, 274, 284, 338, 346
Bertin, Pierre, 19, 49
Beveridge, William, 259
Bizet, Georges, 2, 3, 24
   Carmen, 1, 2
Blanche, Jacques-Émile
Bliss, Arthur, 52
Böhm, Karl, 213
Bonham Carter, Violet, 175
Bonnard, Pierre, 286
Bonnet, Joseph, 136
Borel, Jeanne, 32
Börlin, Jean, 39

Bosredon, Marthe, 12, 346
Bossuet, Jacques-Bénigne, 144, 205, 213
Boulanger, Nadia, 12, 22, 106, 114, 117, 122, 127, 136, 140, 141, 179, 211, 231, 253, 285, 332
Boulez, Pierre, 1, 2, 23, 30, 108, 175, 177, 178, 200, 212, 221–2, 228
   conducting Poulenc's incidental music for *Intermezzo*, 232, 244, 251, 269, 289
   Marteau sans maître, Le, 177, 244, 341
   Piano Sonata no. 2, 206
   Soleil des eaux, Le, 222
Boult, Adrian, 175
Bourdet, Édouard
   Margot, 114–15
Bourdin, Roger, 98, 162
Boutet de Monvelle, Mlle, 5
Bovy, Berthe, 256
Brahms, Johannes, 1, 102, 115, 143, 208
Brailowsky, Alexander, 82
Brain, Dennis, 254, 342
Braque, Georges, 15, 19, 246
Breton, André, 15, 19, 63, 116, 229
British Institute of Recorded Sound, 286
Britten, Benjamin, 174, 175, 213, 217, 224, 226, 228, 258, 279, 336, 340, 341
   Billy Budd, 213, 231
   Peter Grimes, 174
   Turn of the Screw, The, 4
   Winter Words, 228
Brown, Frederick, 23
Bruckberger, Raymond, 220, 227
Bruckner, Anton, 1, 204
Brunhoff, Jean de, 146, 147
Buckland, Sidney, 125
Burton, Humphrey, 254, 255
Burton, Richard D. E., 263, 273
Buxtehude, Dietrich, 135

Caccini, Giulio, 231
Caffaret, Lucie, 87
Callas, Maria, 250, 254, 256, 260, 342
Calvet Quartet, 182
Cameron, Basil, 174, 208
Campagnola, Léon, 7
Campra, André
   Camille, 213
Caplet, André, 34, 49, 65, 120, 325, 327
Carême, Maurice, 268
Carpenter, John Alden, 40
Carteri, Rosanna, 271, 345
Casa Fuerte, Yvonne de, 96, 212, 278
Casella, Alfredo, 21, 48, 73, 79, 104
Casella, Hélène, 145

Cendrars, Blaise, 19, 41
Chabrier, Emmanuel, 2, 7, 17, 26, 64, 70, 113,
    150, 151, 158, 201, 244, 263, 264, 266,
    267, 269, 272, 289, 344, 345
    Éducation manquée, Une, 55
    L'Étoile, 150, 184, 264
    Gwendoline, 150, 328, 330
    Idylle, 7
    Valses romantiques, 243, 244, 260
Chagall, Marc, 246
Chalupt, René, 71
Chamberlain, Neville, 138
Chanlaire, Richard, 86, 87, 90, 151, 181, 229,
    243, 274, 329, 345, 346
Char, René, 269
Charpentier, Marc-Antoine, 206
Cherubini, Luigi
    Medea, 256, 260
Chester, J. & W., 1, 17, 35, 36, 37, 46, 161,
    174, 280
Chesterian, The, 17, 35, 41, 42, 43
Chevalier, Louis (doctor), 258, 263, 271
Chevalier, Maurice, 26, 149, 160, 171, 173, 270,
    281, 282
Chœurs de Lyon, 118, 128, 131
Chopin, Frédéric, 2, 70, 108, 115, 124, 197,
    216
    Étude in G flat, op. 25, no. 9, 75, 143
    Sonata in B flat minor, 92
Christiné, Henri, 7
Christophers, Harry, 275
'Clarendon', *see* Gavoty, Bernard
Clark, Kenneth, 175
Claudel, Paul, 22, 139, 229
Clément, Edmond, 2–3, 9
Clementi, Muzio, 31
Cluytens, André, 221
Cocteau, Jean, 1, 14, 15, 20, 22–3, 25, 26, 27, 29,
    33–4, 35, 36, 37, 38, 41, 43, 44, 47, 50,
    54, 56, 58, 59, 61, 64, 69, 115, 124–5,
    181, 259, 260, 290, 323, 332
    Coq et l'Arlequin, Le, 22, 23, 29, 37, 38, 41,
    54, 334
    Dame de Monte-Carlo, La, 273, 345
    Machine infernale, La, 262, 285
    Mariés de la Tour Eiffel, Les, 44–5, 47, 50, 325
    Orphée, 72
    Renaud et Armide, 278
    Roméo et Juliette, 63, 327
    Voix humaine, La, 253–4, 256, 257, 267, 343,
    344
Collaer, Paul, 30, 45, 53, 56, 62, 70, 84, 88, 98,
    102, 154, 163, 168, 177, 181, 182, 337
Collet, Henri, 37, 38, 41, 324

Colette, Sidonie-Gabrielle, 12, 133, 156,
    221, 340
Columbia (record company), 84, 104
Comoedia, 37, 38, 156, 158
Concerts de la Pléiade, 161–2, 164, 168, 213,
    336, 337
Conrad, Doda, 33, 127, 195, 196, 197, 211, 247
Coolidge, Elizabeth Sprague (Foundation), 251
Copeau, Jacques, 18, 19
Corelli, Franco, 270
Cortot, Alfred, 29–30, 106, 108, 144, 145, 178, 272
Cossotto, Fiorenza, 250
Couperin, François, 154, 213, 284
Craft, Robert, 279
Crespin, Régine, 245
Crochet, Evelyne, 269, 270
Croiza, Claire, 32, 58
Crusell, Bernhard, 23
Cuenod, Hugues, 127, 275

Daladier, Édouard, 138
Daniel, Keith, 38, 64, 65, 81, 105, 125, 194, 201,
    206, 212, 261, 285
Daniel-Lesur, Jean-Yves, 204
David, Félicien
    Désert, Le, 11
Debussy, Claude, 2, 3, 5, 11, 12, 13, 14, 16, 17,
    19, 24, 29, 31, 33, 43, 49, 52, 57, 64, 66,
    82, 92, 109, 110, 111, 113, 115, 116, 133,
    151, 162, 172, 200, 201, 208, 231, 232,
    233, 251, 267, 277, 280, 282, 287
    Ariettes oubliées, 66
    Trois Ballades de François Villon, 127
    Danses sacrée et profane, 5, 24, 54
    Études, 16
    L'Isle joyeuse, 82
    Jardins sous la pluie, 5
    Jeux, 16, 200
    Martyre de Saint Sébastien, Le, 235
    Mer, La, 200
    Pelléas et Mélisande, 3, 31, 82, 175, 180–1,
    217, 231, 232, 233, 253, 256, 257
    Prélude à l'après-midi d'un faune, 111, 257
    Promenoir des deux amants, Le, 19, 57
    Soirée dans Grenade, La, 5
    Sonata for flute, viola and harp, 251
    String Quartet, 82
    Syrinx, 150
Delage, Maurice, 51, 65
Delannoy, Marcel, 73
Delbos, Claire, 124
Delgrange, Félix, 19
Delibes, Léo, 3
    Sylvia, 57

Delmas-Marsalet, Paul, 224
Delvincourt, Claude, 147, 153, 223
Demets (publisher), 37
Denis, Maurice, 18
Dent, Edward, 175
Depraz, Xavier, 245
Derain, André, 15, 18
Dercourt-Plaut, Rose, 247, 266
Deslys, Gaby, 21
Desnos, Robert, 175, 248, 334
Désormière, Roger, 74, 88, 96, 98, 134, 136, 167,
    175, 182, 185, 211–12, 217, 227, 284,
    338, 339
Destouches, Raymond, 145, 151, 163, 169, 170,
    178, 197, 202, 215, 217, 221, 230, 244,
    251, 266, 278, 284
Dhérin, Gustave, 81
Diaghilev, Sergei, 14, 15, 21, 36, 39, 40, 47, 55,
    57, 58, 60, 61, 63, 75, 89, 90, 92, 98, 273,
    323, 324, 325, 329
Diderot, Denis, 13
Dietrich, Marlene, 270
Dior, Christian, 183, 195
Dolin, Anton, 71
Domaine musical (concerts), 221, 244
Doucet, Clément, 47
Doumer, Paul, 107
Dubost, Jeanne, 73, 74, 328
Dubost, Michel, 252
Dubout, Albert, 98
Duchamp, Marcel, 116
Dufy, Raoul, 15, 23, 32, 269, 286
    Fée electricité, La, 128
Dugardin, Hervé, 252, 254, 262
Dukas, Paul, 16, 29, 65, 171, 198, 204
Duke, Vernon (born Vladimir Dukelsky), 60
Dumesnil, René, 252
Duncan, Ronald, 265
Duparc, Henri, 151, 208
Dupré, Marcel, 136, 204
Durand (publisher), 134
Durey, Louis, 21, 22, 26, 31, 35, 36, 37, 323
Duruflé, Maurice, 135, 136, 272
Dutilleux, Henri, 158, 199, 222, 269
    Métaboles, 222
    Symphony no. 1, 222
Duval, Denise, 182–3, 185, 186, 206, 221, 245,
    249, 254, 256, 258, 260, 261, 266, 267,
    268, 273, 277, 283, 343, 344, 345
Dvořák, Antonín, 206

Éluard, Nusch, 126, 181, 188, 337
Éluard, Paul, 15, 56, 66, 94, 112, 113, 116, 117,
    118, 124, 125, 126, 127, 130, 131, 134,
    137, 138, 142, 156, 163, 164, 170, 173,
    175, 180, 181, 191, 202, 208, 217, 229,
    245, 246, 257, 268, 269, 286, 323, 330,
    331, 340
    Facile, 126
    'Liberté', 164
    Livre ouvert I, Le, 202
    Poésie et vérité, 164
    Répétitions, 117
    Vie immédiate, La, 117
    Yeux fertiles, Les, 125
Emmauel, Maurice, 114
Enesco, Georges
    Oedipe, 203
Erté [Romain de Tirtoff], 183
Esty, Alice, 252, 342
Etcharry, Stéphan, 275
Etcheverry, Henri, 185, 217
Evans, Edwin, 175
Exposition coloniale (1931), 94, 102
Exposition Internationale des Arts et des
    Techniques Appliqués à la Vie
    Moderne (1937), 127, 130

Falla, Manuel de, 47, 56, 57, 73, 78, 80–1, 90, 98,
    101, 121, 158, 181, 194, 323, 326, 328,
    329, 330, 337
    El amor brujo, 264–5
    Fanfare pour une fête, 47
    Harpsichord Concerto, 73, 80–1, 97
    El retablo de maese Pedro, 56, 73, 326
Fanfare (journal), 47, 325
Fargue, Léon-Paul, 19, 22, 229
Fauré, Gabriel, 2, 13, 65, 82, 92, 101, 115, 151,
    161, 172, 276, 280, 297, 327, 335
    Bonne chanson, La, 82
    Cinq Mélodies de Venise, 101
    Naissance de Vénus, La, 172
    Pénélope, 82
Ferroud, Pierre-Octave, 73, 100, 115, 120–1, 332
Feuillère, Edwige, 152
Février, Jacques, 74, 97, 98, 101, 105, 106, 124,
    192, 217, 254, 269, 270, 277, 284, 288,
    290, 331, 343, 346
Figaro, Le, 109, 110, 133, 138, 199, 213
Fizdale, Robert, 189, 209, 216, 217, 221, 263
Flament, Édouard, 61
Fleury, Louis, 49
Flonzaley Quartet, 47, 48
Fombeure, Maurice, 159
Fort, Gertrude von le, 220, 227, 230
Fort, Paul, 19
Fournier, Pierre, 192, 197, 218, 279, 280, 340
Françaix, Jean, 135, 158, 244, 277, 341, 345

Franck, César, 3, 6, 12, 13–14, 251
Franco, Francisco, 130
Fresnay, Pierre, 147
Freund, Marya, 33, 47, 49, 50, 107, 174, 196, 247
Frisch, Povla, 273

Gabrieli, Giovanni, 140
Gagliano, Marco da, 231
Gaitskell, Hugh, 259
Gallimard, Gaston, 117, 118, 161, 170
Garafola, Lynn, 59
Garban, Lucien, 97
Garvey, David, 197
Gaulle, Charles de, 178
Gautier, Louis, 151, 251, 257, 265, 266, 277, 278,
    279, 280, 342, 344
Gavoty, Bernard ('Clarendon'), 199, 203, 213,
    262
Gedalge, André, 35, 46
Gervaise, Claude
    Livre de danceries, 114
Gibson, R. Douglas, 280
Gide, André, 19, 229, 262
Girard, Simone, 210, 215, 218, 223, 225, 245,
    261, 280
Giraud, Yvonne, see Casa Fuerte, Yvonne de
Giraudoux, Jean, 105, 151
    Intermezzo, 105, 240
Giroud, Vincent, 250
Glotz, Michel, 287–8
Gluck, Christoph Willibald, 256
Godebska, Ida, 106
Goehr, Alexander, 248
Goethe, Johann Wolfgang von, 184
Gold, Arthur, 189, 209, 216, 217, 221, 263
Goldbeck, Fred, 81
Goléa, Antonie, 248, 260, 261
Goodman, Benny, 284, 346
Goossens, Eugene, 71
Gorr, Rita, 245
Gounod, Charles, 2, 3, 55, 326
    Colombe, La, 55, 326
    Faust, 41
    Médecin malgré lui, Le, 55
    Philémon et Baucis, 55
    Roméo et Juliette, 41
Gouverné, Yvonne, 120, 121–2, 126, 134, 221,
    271, 332
Gouy d'Arcy, François de, 68
Granados, Enrique
    Goyescas (opera), 203
Greeley, Russel, 68
Green, Julien
    Visionnaire, Le, 108

Grétry, André, 3
Grieg, Edvard
    Piano Concerto, 6
Griffin, John Howard, 224–5, 247
Grigny, Nicolas de, 284
Gris, Juan, 19, 246
Guillaume, Paul, 14
Guimard, Hector, 73

Hahn, Reynaldo, 132, 169
Hansen (publisher), 277
Harding, James, 183
Harewood, Marion, 265
Haydn, Joseph, 64, 65
Helffer, Claude, 269
Hell, Henri, 131, 141, 149, 184, 185, 201, 247,
    274, 289
Henze, Hans Werner, 253
Hepp, François, 74
l'Hermite, Tristan, 57
Herzog, Colette, 269
Heseltine, Philip, see Warlock, Peter
Hettich, Amédée-Louis
    Répertoire moderne de vocalise-études, 73
Higham, Thomas Farrant, 259
Hindemith, Paul, 52, 158, 194, 289
Hitler, Adolf, 109, 138, 175
Hoffmansthal, Hugo von, 109
Honegger, Arthur, 21, 22, 26, 37, 49, 52, 55, 58,
    65, 104, 113, 127, 128, 134, 151, 158, 168,
    178, 199, 204, 222, 228, 229, 278, 280,
    281, 323, 326, 327, 329, 341
    Cantique de Pâques, 55
    Cris du monde, 134
    Judith, 153
    Pacific 231, 337
    Roi David, Le, 45, 62
    Rugby, 84
Honegger, Pascale, 153
Horowitz, Vladimir, 9, 74, 79, 80, 104, 168, 195,
    211, 271
Howells, Herbert, 174
Hüe, Georges, 82
Huebner, Steven, 230, 232
Hugo, Jean, 34
Hugo, Valentine, 27, 34, 69, 87
Hugo, Victor, 10
Huyghens, Salle (in rue Huyghens), 14, 19,
    27, 31

Ibert, Jacques, 73, 74, 199
d'Indy, Vincent, 1, 6, 13, 48, 62, 96, 192, 231,
    251, 330
Ivry, Benjamin, 33, 141, 205, 243, 246, 263

Jaboune, *see* Legrand, Jean-Marie
Jacob, Max, 39, 41, 42, 43, 44, 45, 66, 92, 95, 96,
    98, 99, 115, 117, 169, 217, 223, 268, 323,
    325, 330, 336
Jacquemont, Maurice, 240, 248
James, Edward, 131, 134, 332
Jankélévitch, Vladimir, 31
Jean-Aubry, Georges, 35, 38, 40, 47, 69
Joachim, Irène, 167, 211
Jobin (singer), 49
Johnson, Graham, 121, 143, 173, 188, 202, 246
Jolivet, André, 94, 168, 197, 204, 271, 278
Jourdan-Morhange, Hélène, 6, 27, 119, 206,
    216
Jouvet, Louis, 105

Karajan, Herbert von, 111, 244
Ketèlbey, Albert
    In a Persian Market, 204
Kisling, Moïse, 14
Klee, Paul, 246
Klemperer, Otto, 209
Kling, Otto Marius, 1, 36
Kochno, Boris, 98
Kodály, Zoltán, 47
Koechlin, Charles, 26, 46, 48, 49, 50, 54, 55, 66,
    67, 85, 103, 117, 118, 119, 155, 160, 209,
    325, 327, 339
Koussevitzky, Serge, 73
Koussevitzky Foundation, 262, 344
Krauss, Clemens, 110, 209
Krenek, Ernst, 116
Kubelík, Rafael, 255

La Fontaine, Jean de, 131, 146, 154, 156–8
Lacombe, Hervé, 4, 6, 22, 30, 86, 87, 99, 113,
    118, 145, 153, 164, 176, 195, 216, 261,
    269
Lalande, Michel Richard de, 206
Lalanne, Louise, 92
Lalo, Édouard
    Roi d'Ys, Le, 2
Laloy, Louis, 51, 60
Lamorlette, Roger, 81
Landormy, Paul, 128, 160
Landowska, Wanda, 12, 56, 73, 80, 87, 94, 107,
    113, 195, 211, 265
Lapeyrette, Ketty, 224
Larbaud, Valéry, 19
Lassus, Orlando di, 140
Latarjet, André, 100, 117
Latarjet, Suzanne, 6, 117, 280
Latham, Elizabeth, 255
Laure, Jean, 7

Laurencin, Marie, 12, 33, 41, 57, 60, 63, 92,
    132, 191
Lauxière, Marie Françoise ('Nounou', Poulenc's
    nanny), 4, 330
Lavery, Emmet, 220, 224, 227, 248
Lavorelle, Henri, 209
Lebedeff, Marie-Ange (Poulenc's daughter),
    181, 262, 284, 337
Lecanu, Maurice, 84
Leclair, Jean-Marie, 72
Léger, Fernand, 15
Legrand, Jean-Marie ('Jaboune'), 9–10, 117–18
Lehmann, Lotte, 110
Leibowitz, René, 177, 178, 209
Lejeune, Émile, 19
Lephay, Pierre-Emmanuel, 232
Lerolle, Jacques, 106, 116
    see also Rouart Lerolle
'Les boys', *see* Fizdale, Robert; Gold, Arthur
Lévy, Lazare, 178
Ley, Madeleine, 123
Liénard, Virginie ('Tante Liénard'), 12, 67, 77,
    79, 113, 123, 328, 331
Lifar, Serge, 111, 154
Linossier, Alice, *see* Ardoin, Alice
Linossier, Dr Georges, 2
Linossier, Raymonde, 6, 7, 19, 20, 32, 33, 68, 69,
    83, 85, 86, 87, 89, 90, 91, 92, 93, 117,
    157, 162, 176, 191, 192, 266, 280, 284,
    323, 329
    Bibi-la-Bibiste, 20
Linossier, Suzanne, *see* Latarjet, Suzanne
Liszt, Franz, 127, 232
    Faust Symphony, A, 102
Lockspeiser, Edward, 172, 175, 178, 187, 188,
    191, 193, 194
Loeillet, Jean-Baptiste, 72
Long, Marguerite, 74, 101, 245, 341
Lorca, Federico García, 162, 188
Loriod, Yvonne, 153
Lubin, Germaine, 110
Lully, Jean-Baptiste, 206, 256
Lunel, Armand, 128, 129, 184, 332
Lurçat, Jean, 170
Lycée Condorcet, 9, 10, 14, 18, 41, 118, 322, 323
Lyre et Palette (concerts), 19, 31

Maar, Dora, 181
Mabille, Marie-Thérèse, 150
Machart, Renaud, 101–2, 136, 173, 176, 268
Machlis, Joseph, 255
Mackerras, Charles, 258
Macmillan, Harold, 259
Mahler, Alma, 49

Mahler, Gustav, 289
Malherbe, François de, 91
Malherbe, Henri, 182
Malipiero, Gian Francesco, 47, 48, 104, 250, 325
  Rispetti e strambotti, 47, 48
Mallarmé, Stéphane, 10, 30, 43, 150, 186, 251
Manceaux, André (Poulenc's brother-in-law), 10
Manceaux, Brigitte, (Poulenc's niece), 15, 100, 198, 224, 244, 245, 250, 284, 292
Manceaux, Denis (Poulenc's nephew), 15
Manceaux, Jeanne, *see* Poulenc, Jeanne Élise Marguerite
Manceaux, Rosine (Poulenc's niece; later Rosine Seringe), 4, 15, 146, 225, 284
Mantegna, Andrea, 275
Marchal, André, 136, 207
Margueritte, Victor
  Garçonne, La, 59
Maritain, Jacques, 220
Markévitch, Igor, 96, 100
  Rebus, 274
Martineau, René, 266
Massenet, Jules, 2, 3, 200, 249, 252, 257, 267, 287, 290
  Grisélidis, 203
  Manon, 2, 41, 267
  Thaïs, 249, 267
  Werther, 267
Massine, Léonide, 15, 39, 131
Materlinck, Maurice, 253
Matisse, Henri, 14, 15, 19, 113, 152, 202, 228, 246, 280, 286
Maupassant, Guy de
  Femme de Paul, La, 138
Mauriac, François, 179, 218, 284
Mayol, Félix, 41
Mellers, Wilfrid, 131, 136, 147, 154, 194, 207, 254, 281, 282
Melon, Mlle (piano teacher), 5
Mendelssohn, Felix, 16, 101, 153
Menotti, Gian Carlo
  Consul, The, 213
Messager, André, 3, 71, 74, 244
  Isoline, 260
Messiaen, Olivier, 65, 122, 124, 128, 158, 170, 171, 175, 177, 198, 200, 204–5, 206, 216, 222, 248, 271
  Corps glorieux, Les, 204
  Trois petites Liturgies de la Présence divine, 170, 171, 175, 177, 336
  Poèmes pour Mi, 124
  Cinq Rechants, 204
  Vingt Regards sur l'Enfant-Jésus, 176

  Technique de mon langage musical, 171
  Turangalíla Symphony, 171, 198, 204–5, 338
  Visions de l'Amen, 171, 204
Meyer, Jeffrey, 284
Meyer, Marcelle, 27, 39, 40, 49, 69, 71, 151, 243, 244, 260, 263, 344
Meyerbeer, Giacomo
  Robert le diable, 218
Mila, Massimo, 250
Milhaud, Darius, 19, 22, 26, 31, 35, 37, 39, 41, 43, 44, 45, 46, 47, 49, 50, 51, 52, 53, 54, 55, 57, 60, 62, 63, 67, 68, 71, 73, 77, 96, 98, 103, 127, 128, 132, 146, 147, 152, 175, 176, 177, 182, 183, 194, 198, 199, 203, 209, 215, 217, 228, 229, 260, 262, 322, 323, 324, 325, 326, 328, 336
  Bolivar, 203
  Boeuf sur le toit, Le, 39, 48, 50, 57
  Création du monde, La, 39, 57, 326
  Deux Cités, Les, 139
  Esther de Carpentras, 128
  Maximilien, 97, 215
  Organ Sonata, 98
  Pauvre Matelot, Le, 78, 328
  Salade, 63, 327
  Train bleu, Le, 47, 63, 64, 327
  Violin Sonata no. 1, 35
Milhaud, Madeleine, 25, 44, 45, 67, 68, 73, 288
Miró, Joan, 246
Mitchell, Donald, 221
Modigliani, Amadeo, 14, 15, 19
Modrakowska, Maria, 106, 107, 112, 115, 331
Monaco, Mario del, 254, 266
Monnier, Adrienne, 19, 20, 28, 32, 92, 112, 229, 266, 323, 341
Montesquieu, 14
Monteux, Pierre, 10
Monteverdi, Claudio, 117, 231, 256, 267
  Ariana, 231
  L'incoronazione di Poppea, 231
  motets (unspecified), 117
  Orfeo, 231
Mooser, Robert, 248
Morand, Paul, 74
Moréas, Jean, 74, 75
Moreau, Léon, 34
Morison, Elsie, 255
Moryn, Gilbert, 98, 99
Moulié, Charles, 18
Moulton, Mrs (patron), 111
Moyse, Marcel, 82
Mozart, Wolfgang Amadeus, 2, 47, 64, 65, 101, 102, 109, 115, 120, 148, 268, 272, 289
  Divertimento K439b, 88

musikalischer Spass, Ein, K522, arr. Poulenc
    for piano, 67, 69, 327
  Piano Concerto K467, 102
  Piano Concerto K537, 102
  Requiem K626, 129
Münch, Charles, 115, 148, 203, 209, 210, 268,
    269–70, 338
Münch, Fritz, 209–10, 213
Muratore, Lucien, 182
Mussolini, Benito, 138, 333
Musorgsky, Modest, 70, 160, 231, 233, 289
  Nursery Songs, 6
Myers, Rollo, 175

Nabokov, Nicolas, 96, 100, 213
Némirovsky, Irène
  Suite française, 145
Neveu, Ginette, 161, 162, 163, 175
Nicoloson, Harold, 128
Nijinska, Bronislava, 47, 57–9, 60, 88
Nijinsky, Vaslav, 47
Noailles, Charles de, 83, 85, 86, 87, 89, 91, 95,
    99, 329, 330
Noailles, Marie-Laure de, 83, 89, 90, 91, 96, 97,
    98, 99, 100, 103, 329
Nobel, Félix de, 212
Nohain, Jean, *see* Legrand, Jean-Marie
Nono, Luigi, 221
Nouveaux Jeunes (group), 19, 21, 22, 25, 27,
    36, 323

Offenbach, Jacques, 3, 13, 64, 228
  Belle Hélène, La, 264
  Grande-Duchesse de Géroldstein, La, 12
Olivier, Laurence, 270
Orledge, Robert, 36, 155

Palffy, Count Paul, 143, 166
Papoum, *see* Royer, Marcel
Paray, Paul, 133, 331
Pasquier Trio, 152
Pathé-Marconi (record company), 221, 272,
    287
Patterson, Alfred Nash, 270
Pears, Peter, 174, 175, 217, 258, 279
Peignot, Suzanne, 40, 66, 79, 98, 100, 110
Peinture et musique (concerts), 19
Penrose, Roland, 175
Pergolesi, Giovanni Battista, 206
Perloff, Nancy, 14
Pétain, Philippe, 145
Petits Chanteurs à la Croix de bois, 139
Pfitzner, Hans
  Palestrina, 158

Philipp, Isidore, 178
Piaf, Edith, 180, 265
Picasso, Pablo, 14, 15, 19, 27, 52, 63, 66, 115,
    126, 181, 246, 259, 286
  Guernica, 128, 130–1
Pierlot, Pierre, 284, 346
Pilcer, Harry, 21
Pincherle, Marc, 213
Planté, Francis, 82, 178
Platard, André, 180
Plautus, Titus Maccius, 184
Polignac, Jean de, 109, 114
Polignac, Marie-Blanche de, 4, 91, 104, 109, 114,
    119, 138, 139, 143, 145, 160, 163, 195,
    197, 263, 265, 338
Polignac, Winaretta [Princess Edmond] de, 12,
    24, 56, 76, 94, 97, 102, 105, 106, 112,
    117, 135, 333
Pons, Lily, 195
Potassons (group), 19, 20, 21, 28, 68
Poulenc, Camille (uncle), 3
Poulenc, Émile (father), 3, 4, 9, 10, 11, 13, 14,
    15, 18, 20, 129, 322, 323
POULENC, FRANCIS
  artists, favourite, 286
  as record critic, 81–2
  baccalauréat, 13–14
  Chabrier, biography of, 266, 269, 272
  Chabrier, borrowings from, 184, 264
  childhood, 4–14
  description as 'moine et voyou', 203–4
  destruction of works, 27, 42, 44, 45, 182
  earliest compositions, 6
  Exposition 1937, 127–8
  first public performance of his music, 14
  French 'temperament', 1, 2, 13
  homosexuality, 5, 58, 69, 125, 181
  ill health, 56, 224–5, 226, 279, 283–4
  meets Debussy, 5
  meets Viñes, 11
  military service, 20–21
  orchestration of three pieces by Satie, 145
  parents, 2–4
  recordings by, 32, 64, 81, 82, 84, 104, 175,
    243, 244, 267, 283, 287–8
  religion, 3–4, 121–2
  schooling, 9
  self-borrowing, 169, 233, 238, 239, 265, 265,
    281
  studies with Koechlin, 46
  views on other composers
    Berg, 177
    Boulez, 177–8, 221–2
    Debussy, 200

Fauré, 82
Honegger, 45
Massenet, 267
Messiaen, 198, 204–5
Mozart, 109
Prokofiev, 210,
Puccini, 203, 237, 285, 287
Ravel, 97–8, 132–3, 148, 155; attends Ravel's funeral, 132
Satie, 24, 287
Strauss, 109
Stravinsky, 51–2, 55, 76, 78, 84
Wagner, 115, 267, 289
Webern, 52, 165, 244, 251
WORKS
À sa guitare, 114, 115
Airs chantés, 72, 74–5, 79, 83, 328, 329
Amphitryon, 188, 189, 337
Animaux modèles, Les, 131, 146, 148, 149, 154–8, 159, 160, 162, 192, 267, 334, 335
Aubade, 78, 79, 83, 84, 85–6, 87, 88–9, 93, 98, 100, 103, 117, 135, 141, 329
Ave verum, 215, 339
Badinage, 106, 331
Bal masqué, Le, 95, 97, 98, 99–100, 102, 103, 105, 115, 140, 223, 330, 332
Banalités, 148–9, 267, 334
Belle au bois dormant, La, 114, 331
Bestiaire, Le, 32, 33, 34, 40, 50, 51, 52, 92, 113, 187, 247, 269, 324
Biches, Les, 40, 47, 52, 54, 57–60, 61, 62, 63, 65, 66, 67, 68, 69, 70, 71, 74, 77, 78, 81, 84, 87, 88, 89, 90, 132, 140, 145, 151, 155, 192, 325, 326, 327, 328, 334
Bleuet, 143, 144, 334
'Bourée, au Pavillon d'Auvergne', for *À l'Exposition*, 127, 332
'Bucolique' for *Variations sur le nom de Marguerite Long*, 245, 341
Calligrammes, 189–92, 193, 195, 197, 267, 338
Capriccio d'après Le Bal masqué, 216, 339
Ce doux petit visage, 151, 331, 335
Une Chanson de porcelaine, 257, 343
Chansons gaillardes, 67, 70, 71, 74, 77, 110, 138, 291, 327, 328
Chansons villageoises, 145, 159–60, 162, 335
Chemins de l'amour, Les (for *Léocadia*), 147
Cinq Poèmes de Max Jacob, 94, 95, 142, 330
Cinq Poèmes de Paul Éluard, 119, 124, 143, 331
Cinq Poèmes de Ronsard, 65–6, 71, 109, 325, 331
Cocardes, 34–5, 36, 38, 39, 43, 324
Colloque, 150, 151, 334, 335

Concert champêtre, 73, 74, 78, 79, 80–1, 83, 87, 88, 90, 103, 113, 211, 328, 329, 331
Concerto for organ, 112, 119, 122, 127, 128, 135–6, 139, 272, 331, 332, 333
Concerto for piano, 168, 197, 198, 200–1, 208, 209, 233, 248, 338
Concerto for two pianos, 11, 94–5, 97, 100–1, 102–3, 104, 105, 109, 112, 117, 119, 134, 135, 174, 192, 226, 244, 254, 269, 277, 287–8, 330, 331, 336, 341, 343, 345
Courte Paille, La, 268, 269, 277, 345, 346
Dame de Monte-Carlo, La, 269, 273, 345
Dernier Poème, 248, 342
Deux Marches et un intermède, 128, 332
Deux Mélodies (1956–7), 253, 342
Deux Novellettes, 78, 79, 328, 329
Deux Poèmes de Guillaume Apollinaire ('Dans le jardin d'Anna'; 'Allons plus vite'), 136–7, 333
Deux Poèmes de Louis Aragon, 166–8, 335
Dialogues des Carmélites, 2, 12, 24, 32, 100, 128, 130, 160, 215–48, 249, 250, 251, 252, 253, 254, 255, 256, 257, 258, 260, 262, 263, 264, 275, 279, 281, 282, 339, 340, 341, 342, 343, 344
Disparu, Le, 180, 337
Duchesse de Langeais, La, 151, 152, 154, 335
Élégie for horn and piano, 254, 343
Élégie for two pianos, 263, 265, 344
L'Embarquement pour Cythère, 209, 277, 339
En barque (first composition), 8, 322
Épitaphe, 75, 91, 113, 329
Esquisse d'une fanfare, 47, 325
L'Eventail de Jeanne, see 'Pastourelle' for *L'Éventail de Jeanne*
Exultate Deo, 150, 193, 335
Fancy, 265, 344
Feuillets d'album, 106
Fiançailles pour rire, 132, 141, 142, 154, 166, 181, 334, 335
Figure humaine, 130, 163, 165–6, 169, 171, 172, 173, 175, 178, 179, 181, 182, 183, 193, 201, 202, 205, 230, 241, 335, 336, 337
Fille du jardinier, La (lost), 152, 335
Fraîcheur et le feu, La, 202, 205, 208, 339
Française d'après Claude Gervaise, 145
Gendarme incompris, Le, 42, 43, 44, 46, 47, 324, 325
Gloria, 65, 80, 140, 262–4, 265, 267, 269, 271–2, 274, 280–1, 285, 344, 345
Grenouillère, La, 132, 138, 333
L'Histoire de Babar, le petit éléphant, 146, 147, 169, 176, 179, 186–7, 192, 243, 268, 277, 281, 334, 336, 337

orchestrated by Françaix, 277, 345

Huit Chansons polonaises, 106–7

Humoresque, 106, 331

Hyde Park, 173, 336

Hymne (Racine), 195–6, 246, 338

Hymne à la Touraine, 136

Improvisations, 104, 147 (no. 11), 195, 209, 257, 265 (no. 15), 328, 331, 335, 343

Intermezzi (for piano), 106, 109, 331

Intermezzo (incidental music), 105, 228, 331

L'Invitation au château (incidental music), 188, 189, 337

Jeunesse de Gargantua, La (project), 128, 184

Laudes de Saint Antoine de Padoue, 253, 261, 262, 342, 344

Léocadia (incidental music), 147, 334

Litanies à la Vierge noire, 121, 122, 123, 124, 127, 138, 156, 275, 282, 284, 332, 337

Main dominée par le coeur, 180, 188, 337

. . . mais mourir, 181, 188, 337

Mamelles de Tirésias, Les, 114, 128, 140, 160, 169, 170, 171, 172, 176, 178, 182–7, 188, 189, 191, 202, 221, 230, 238, 253, 258, 262, 273, 280, 334, 336, 337, 343, 345

Marches militaires (lost), 50, 62, 67, 70, 72, 91, 100, 326

Mariés de la Tour Eiffel, Les (two numbers), 44–5, 47, 254, 325, 343

Mass in G major, 128, 129–31, 133, 233, 276, 332, 333

'Matelote provençale' for *La Guirlande de Campra*, 213, 339

'Mazurka' for *Mouvements du coeur*, 197–8

Mélancolie, 146, 147, 151, 192, 209, 334, 335

Mélopée d'automne, 10, 322

Métamorphoses, 166, 167, 176, 335, 336

Miroirs brûlants ('Tu vois le feu du soir', 'Je nommerai ton front'), 136–8, 333

Monsieur le Trouhadec (lost), 105, 331

Montparnasse, 100, 152, 173, 335, 336

Napoli, 42, 52, 62, 67, 69–70, 71, 74, 124, 291, 326, 327, 328

Nocturnes, 91, 105, 108, 139, 209, 233, 329

Novellette in E minor on a theme by Falla [Novellette no. 3], 264–5, 344

Nuit de la Saint-Jean, La (lost), 172, 336

Parisiana, 223, 225, 340

'Pastourelle' for *L'Éventail de Jeanne*, 72, 73, 74, 86, 328, 329

Paul et Virginie, 57, 180, 324, 337

Petites voix, 123, 151, 332

Pétrus (lost), 105, 331

Piano Trio (lost), 45, 323

Piece for solo flute, 150, 335

Pièce brève (on the name Albert Roussel), 86–7

Pierrot, 105, 331

Poèmes sénégalais (lost), 21, 24, 323

Pont, Le, 179, 180

Portrait, Le, 133, 136, 137, 139, 333

Première Suite d'orchestre (lost), 45, 325

Priez pour paix, 131, 138, 333

Processional pour la crémation d'un mandarin, 11, 322

Promenades, 45, 46, 49, 57, 200, 325

Puce, La, 269, 345

Quadrille for piano duet (lost), 38, 324

Quatre Chansons pour enfants, 10, 109, 331

Quatre Motets pour le temps de Noel, 210, 212, 339

Quatre Motets pour un temps de Pénitence, 131, 139–40, 333

Quatre Petites Prières de Saint-François d'Assise, 193, 261, 338

Quatre Poèmes de Guillaume Apollinaire, 92, 98, 113, 330

Quatre Poèmes de Max Jacob, 42, 43, 45, 49, 95, 324, 325

Rapsodie nègre, 14, 15, 16, 17, 18, 19, 20, 21, 23, 24, 25, 32, 38, 39, 75, 323

Récitatif pour précéder Orphée, 72

Renaud et Armide (lost), 278, 345

Rosemonde, 223, 225, 340

Salve Regina (motet), 150, 193, 335

Sarabande, 265, 267, 344

Sécheresses, 103, 131, 133–5, 332, 333

Sept Chansons, 10, 117–19, 124, 332

Sept Répons des ténèbres, 263, 266, 267, 268, 274, 276–7, 278, 279, 280, 281, 283, 284, 285, 344, 345, 346

Sextet, 94, 100, 104, 105, 140, 141, 148, 330, 334, 343

Sinfonietta, 182, 187–8, 193, 194, 195, 337, 338

Soir de neige, Un, 173, 174, 175, 336

Soirées de Nazelles, Les, 90, 91, 122, 123, 329, 332

Soldat et la sorcière, Le (lost), 178, 336

Sonata for bassoon (unfinished), 253, 265, 278, 280, 342, 344

Sonata for cello and piano, 146, 192, 193, 197, 259–60, 334, 338

Sonata for clarinet and bassoon, 52–3, 54, 55, 326

Sonata for clarinet and piano, 265, 278, 279, 280–1, 282, 284, 344, 346

Sonata for flute and piano, 217, 248, 251–2, 255, 281, 342, 343

Sonata for horn, trumpet and trombone, 53, 326

Sonata for oboe and piano, 275, 276, 278, 279, 280, 281–2, 284, 346
Sonata for piano duet, 24–5, 27, 47, 323, 324
Sonata for piano trio (lost), 27
Sonata for two clarinets, 13, 23, 31, 33, 34, 36, 37, 47, 53, 239, 323, 324
Sonata for two pianos, 216–17, 219, 221, 339, 340
Sonata for violin and piano, 158, 161–2, 192, 335
Sonatas for violin and piano (lost), 27, 62, 72, 89, 100, 105, 116, 324, 327, 329
Stabat mater, 140, 194, 199, 202, 205–8, 209, 210, 211, 212, 218, 230, 238, 239, 260, 262, 263, 275, 277, 285, 339, 343
String Quartet (1945, destroyed after private performance; partly reworked as *Sinfonietta*), 179, 182, 192, 336, 337
String Quartets (lost), 45, 163, 176, 325
String Trio (lost), 151–2, 335
Suite in C for piano, 13, 34, 38, 39, 40, 42, 51, 324
Suite française d'après Claude Gervaise, 114, 115, 145, 219, 332
Tel jour telle nuit, 124, 126, 133, 148, 163, 174, 181, 191, 246, 247, 267, 332
Thème varié, 209, 217, 339, 340
Toréador, Le, 26–7, 124, 323
Travail du peintre, Le, 227, 245–7, 252, 253, 267, 340, 341, 342
Trio for oboe, bassoon and piano, 62, 64–5, 67, 71, 81, 90, 105, 110, 264, 327, 328
Trio for piano, clarinet and cello (lost), 45, 325
Trois Chansons de F. Garcia Lorca, 188, 337
Trois Études de Pianola (lost), 45, 325
Trois Mouvements perpétuels, 28, 29–30, 31, 32, 33, 36, 42, 50, 51, 82, 161, 168, 324
Trois Pastorales (revised as *Trois Pièces*), 11, 21, 79, 323, 324
Trois Pièces pour piano, 11, 21, 40, 79, 329
Trois Poèmes de Louise de Vilmorin, 131–2, 332, 333
Trois Poèmes de Louise Lalanne, 92, 98, 132, 330
'Valse' for *Album des Six*, 37, 324
Valse-improvisation sur le nom de Bach, 103–4, 330
Viens! une flûte invisible, 10, 322
Villageoises, 105, 331
Villanelle, 109, 331
Vocalise, 72, 73, 328
Voix humaine, La, 124, 253, 256, 257, 258, 260–1, 262, 263, 266, 267, 268, 273, 277, 343, 344

Voyage en Amérique, Le (later reworked as *L'Embarquement pour Cythère*), 209, 339
Zèbre (lost), 20, 323
Poulenc Frères, 3
see also Rhône-Poulenc
Poulenc, Jeanne Élise Marguerite (Poulenc's sister), 4, 10
Poulenc, Jenny Zoé (Poulenc's mother), 2, 3, 4, 5, 6, 9, 12, 322
Poulenc, Louis Étienne (Poulenc's brother), 4
Pousseur, Henri, 271
Prêtre, Georges, 135, 260, 261, 266, 267, 272, 273, 285, 288, 344
Price, Leontyne, 270, 271
Printemps, Yvonne, 92, 114, 147, 209
Pritchard, John, 226, 341
Prokofiev, Sergei, 70, 100, 158, 210, 278, 282, 328, 340
  Chout, 54
  Classical Symphony, 78, 187
  Fiery Angel, The, 250
  Pas d'acier, Le, 75
  Sarcasmes, 24
  'Suggestion diabolique', 24
Prouille, Marcel, 18
Proust, Marcel, 58, 123, 286
Prunières, Henry, 64, 65, 103
Puccini, Giacomo, 2, 17, 183, 185, 200, 237, 252, 287, 289
  Bohème, La, 2, 17
  Madam Butterfly, 185, 287
  Tabarro, Il, 285
  Tosca, 7, 182, 185, 215, 256, 266, 344
  Turandot, 78, 203, 329

Rabelais, François, 128, 129, 184
Rachmaninov, Sergei, 113, 201
Racine, Jean, 108, 196, 246
  Andromaque, 283
Radiguet, Raymond, 41, 43, 56, 57, 58, 61, 180, 323, 326
Rampal, Jean-Pierre, 252, 342
Ravel, Maurice, 2, 9, 11, 13, 15, 16, 17, 19, 20, 24, 27, 29, 38, 39, 40, 43, 49, 50, 51, 52, 57, 65, 66, 67, 72, 73, 75, 82, 90, 113, 115, 127, 132–3, 134–5, 140, 148, 155, 162, 171, 179, 184, 194, 208, 267, 277, 280, 324, 328, 329, 330, 332
  Boléro, 40, 84, 90, 285, 329
  Concerto for piano left hand, 101, 102, 330
  Concerto in G major, 97, 101, 102, 330
  L'Enfant et les sortilèges, 67, 71, 72, 132, 140, 173, 184, 328
  'Fanfare' for *L'Éventail de Jeanne*, 74

Gaspard de la nuit, 82
L'Heure espagnole, 168, 184
Histoires naturelles, 19, 127, 133
Miroirs, 108
Ronsard à son âme, 65
Trois Chansons, 26
Trois Poèmes de Stéphane Mallarmé, 23
Valse, La, 38, 39–40, 324, 329
Ray, Man, [Emmanuel Radnitzky], 126, 181
Reed, Philip, 174, 213
Reinhardt, Max, 109
Reiss, Janine, 256
Renaud-Barrault theatre company, 228
Renoir, Pierre-Auguste, 138, 245
Reverdy, Pierre, 19, 66
Revue musicale, La, 50, 51, 65, 86, 103
Rhône-Poulenc, 3, 155, 284
Ricordi (publisher), 214, 218, 260, 267, 269
Rieti, Vittorio, 96, 100, 325, 332
Rimsky-Korsakov, Nikolai, 21, 23
Antar, 48
Risler, Édouard, 7
Ritchie, Margaret, 259
Robert, Sophie, 20
Rocamadour, 121, 164, 188, 205, 224, 253, 265, 277
Roland-Manuel, Alexis, 19, 21, 22, 31, 65, 204, 217
Romains, Jules, 19, 105
Roosevelt, Franklin Delano, 112
Ropartz, Joseph Guy Marie, 12–13
Rorem, Ned, 131, 159, 198, 265, 290, 338
Rosenthal, Manuel, 22, 72, 101, 128, 175
Rossini, Gioacchino, 206
Rostand, Claude, 1, 65, 74, 78, 98, 101, 106, 112, 118, 129, 131, 155, 174, 201, 203, 204, 218, 221, 250, 332, 340
Rouart, Paul, 177, 204
Rouart Lerolle (publisher), 161
Roubert, Lucien, 151, 202, 211, 215, 216, 224, 226, 227, 229, 230, 243, 247, 251, 338, 341
Rouché, Jacques, 74, 131, 132, 147, 152, 154, 160, 182, 215, 332
Roussel, Albert, 29, 35, 36, 38, 41, 42, 46, 47, 56, 65, 73, 77, 86–7, 104, 129, 324, 329, 332
Padmâvatî, 56, 326
Pour une fête de printemps, 48
Symphony no. 2, 42
Roy, Claude, 170
Roy, Jean, 104, 173
Royer, Jenny Zoé, *see* Poulenc, Jenny Zoé
Royer, Marcel (Poulenc's uncle 'Papoum'), 2, 4, 11, 120, 136, 146, 170, 178, 322, 336

Rubinstein, Anton
Romance in F, 12
Rubinstein, Arthur, 45, 101, 271
Rubinstein, Ida, 107
Rubinstein, Nela (Mme Arthur Rubinstein), 107, 271

Sabata, Victor de, 200, 214, 244
Sainte Cécile Choral Society, Antwerp, 172
Saint-Marceaux, Marguerite de, 73, 291
Saint-Saëns, Camille, 2, 12, 27, 171, 208, 325
Le Déluge, 45
Piano Concerto no. 2, 65
Salabert (publisher), 43
Salles, Georges, 93, 98, 120, 150
Samazeuilh, Gustave, 163
Sanzogno, Nino, 250
de Saram, Rohan, 259–60
Satie, Erik, 2, 11, 13, 14–15, 16, 17, 19, 22, 23, 25, 26, 27, 29, 30, 31, 32, 33, 36, 37, 38, 40, 41, 47, 49, 50, 53, 54, 55, 56, 57, 60, 62, 63, 64, 68, 69, 71, 73, 103, 105, 145, 158, 201, 244, 267, 287, 323, 334
Avant-dernières pensées, 29
Gymnopédies, 29
Mercure, 63, 327
Musique d'ameublement, 39, 324
Nocturnes, 17
Parade, 14–15
Piège de Méduse, Le, 97, 98, 325
Relâche, 63, 327
Socrate, 24, 55, 323
Sonatine bureaucratique, 40
Sonnerie pour réveiller le bon gros Roi des Singes, 47
Trois Morceaux en forme de poire, 105
Trois petites pièces montées, 39
Sauer, Emil von, 178
Sauguet, Henri, 50, 71, 75, 84, 89, 96, 97, 100, 120, 151, 160, 171, 172, 176, 204, 209, 213, 217, 222, 224, 228, 278, 288
Chatte, La, 75, 328
Gageure imprévue, La, 171
Plumet du colonel, Le, 62
Sazonova, Julie, 107
Scarlatti, Domenico, 2, 53, 70
Schaeffner, André, 65, 158, 159, 188
Scherchen, Hermann, 221
Schippers, Thomas, 284
Schloezer, Boris de, 60, 68, 71, 78, 107
Schmidt, Carl, 21, 42, 74, 113, 212, 215, 224, 269, 275
Schmitt, Florent, 49, 51, 73, 79, 116, 199
Schneider, Marcel, 145, 243, 253, 286

Schoenberg, Arnold, 6, 11, 33, 49–50 78, 116, 177–8, 291, 325, 328
   Erwartung, 256
   Five Orchestral Pieces op. 16, 49, 325
   Herzgewächse, 47
   Pierrot lunaire, 17, 47, 49, 50, 325
   Six Little Piano Pieces op. 19, 6, 33, 49
   Three Pieces op. 11, 49
Schubert, Franz, 2, 6, 33, 115, 143, 145, 152, 187, 267, 272, 279, 280
   Die Nebensonnen, 187
   String Quintet, 104
   Winterreise, Die, 6, 121, 206, 322
Schumann, Robert, 16, 124, 127, 143, 243, 280
   Carnaval, 16
   Dichterliebe, 121, 127
   Frauenliebe und Leben, 127
Schwarzkopf, Elisabeth, 244
Scotto, Vincent, 7
Screpel, Henri, 164, 178
Sculpture nègre (ballet), 39
Sérénade, La (concert society), 96, 98, 99, 104, 105, 115, 118, 124, 168, 330
Seringe, Rosine, *see* Manceaux, Rosine
Sert, Misia, 106, 324
Shakespeare, William
   Coriolanus, 107
   Merchant of Venice, The, 265
   Pericles, 140
   Romeo and Juliet, 47
   Tempest, The, 140
Shakespeare & Co. (bookshop), 20, 266
Shattuck, Roger, 183
Shaw, Robert, 212
Shostakovich, Dmitri, 259
Sibelius, Jean, 201, 204
Sienkiewicz, Geneviève, 11
Singer, Winaretta, *see* Polignac, Winaretta
Six, Les (group), 4, 19, 22, 23, 29–61 *passim*, 63, 89, 222, 229, 279
Smith, Richard Langham, 172, 232, 239
Smyth, Ethel, 52
Société musicale indépendante (SMI), 13
Société nationale de musique (SNM), 13
Soëtens, Robert, 110
Soirées de Paris (ballet season), 63, 89
Souberbielle, Édouard, 7, 23
Soulé, Jacques, 4, 8, 14
Souzay, Gérard, 154
Spotts, Frederic, 169
Stein, Gertrude, 189, 246
Stendhal [Marie-Henri Beyle], 128
Stockhausen, Karlheinz, 221

Stokowski, Leopold, 211
Strauss, Johann II
   Fledermaus, Die, 109
Strauss, Richard, 109
   Ägyptische Helena, Die, 109
   Arabella, 213
   Elektra, 109
   Rosenkavalier, Der, 109
Stravinsky, Igor, 10, 11, 12, 16, 17, 20, 21, 23, 29, 34, 36, 39, 40, 44, 47, 51–2, 54, 55, 57, 60, 63, 64, 88, 94, 95, 115, 132, 136, 141, 142, 144, 146, 150, 158, 159, 168, 173, 174, 175, 177, 179, 186, 202–3, 206, 212, 221, 222, 224, 234, 244, 258, 260, 272, 276, 278–9, 287, 289, 322, 323, 326, 326, 334
   Apollon musagète, 78, 89, 88, 94, 329
   Baiser de la fée, Le, 78, 84, 329
   Capriccio, 93
   Chant du rossignol, Le, 38, 324
   Concertino, 47
   Danses concertantes, 175
   Firebird, The, 10, 76, 93
   Fireworks, 10
   Four Norwegian Moods, 175
   Histoire du soldat, 34, 55, 63, 326
   Jeu de cartes, 94
   Mavra, 40, 51–2, 53, 56, 69, 78, 94, 168, 221, 325
   Noces, Les, 44, 47, 55, 56, 58, 61, 71, 78, 86, 160, 326
   Octet, 97, 326
   Oedipus Rex, 76, 78, 136, 158, 185, 207, 213, 235, 282, 328
   Perséphone, 107–8, 262, 331
   Petrushka, 10, 23
   Piano Rag-Music, 34
   Pribaoutki, 159
   Pulcinella, 40, 41, 52, 53, 78, 115, 324
   Rag-Time, 34
   Renard, 47, 51, 221, 325
   Rite of Spring, see Sacre du printemps, Le
   Rossignol, Le, 11
   Sacre du printemps, Le, 6, 10–11, 23, 51, 116, 175, 322
   Serenade in A, 263
   Symphonies of Wind Instruments, 104, 235
   Symphony of Psalms, 93, 94, 207, 282, 330
   Three Japanese Lyrics, 23
   Three Shakespeare Songs, 222
   Threni, 260, 274, 343
Sutherland, Joan, 255
Sylphides, Les (ballet), 60
Szymanowski, Karol, 73

Tacchino, Gabriel, 124, 289
Taffanel, Paul, 82
Tailleferre, Germaine, 26, 45, 48, 127, 189, 290, 323
Tchaikovsky, Piotr Ilyich, 12, 60, 78, 194, 287
Tebaldi, Renata, 140, 266
Teyte, Maggie, 175, 273
Thomson, Virgil, 48, 189, 195, 267, 274
    Cello Concerto, 202
    Four Saints in Three Acts, 213
Tilliard, Simone, 7, 177
Tooley, John, 255–6
Toscanini, Arturo, 101, 200
Touraine, Geneviève, 154
Tournemire, Charles, 136
Trevor-Roper, Hugh, 259
Triton (concert society), 115
Tual, Denise, 213
Tunnnard, Viola, 258

Universal Edition, 17

Valcarenghi, Guido, 218, 219, 241, 253
Valéry, Paul, 19, 144, 150, 229
Varden, Bishop Erik, 234, 235, 236, 237, 242
Varèse, Edgard, 35
Vaurabourg, Andrée, 55, 58
Verdi, Giuseppe, 2, 64, 122, 160, 185, 206, 208, 231, 279, 289
    Falstaff, 1–2
    Otello, 128, 264, 266, 344
    Traviata, La, 249
    Trovatore Il, 270
Victoria, Tomás Luis de, 130, 139, 212
Vidal, Paul, 16, 17, 19, 22, 46
Vierne, Louis, 136
Villa-Lobos, Heitor
    Chôros no. 8, 101
Villon, Jacques, 246
Vilmorin, Louise de, 131, 132, 141, 142, 143, 166, 197
    Chevaliers de la Garde blanche, 131
Vincent, José, 10, 11
Viñes, Elvira, 11

Viñes, Ricardo, 11, 13, 14, 16, 20, 21, 26, 31, 33, 34, 38, 40, 56, 79, 101, 132, 162, 197, 210, 322, 323, 335
Vivaldi, Antonio, 72, 259, 262, 263
Vuillard, Édouard, 92
Vuillermoz, Émile, 42, 55, 63, 114, 199, 248, 253

Wagner, Erika, 49
Wagner, Richard, 1, 3, 10, 45, 115, 116, 232, 233, 267, 287, 289
    Götterdämmerung, 289
    Lohengrin, 3
    Meistersinger von Nürnberg, Die, 1
    Parsifal, 33
    Tannhäuser, 3
    Tristan und Isolde, 3
Wakhevitch, Georges, 252, 254
Waleckx, Denis, 128, 184, 257
Wallmann, Margarita, 219, 227, 249, 252, 254
Walsh, Stephen, 48, 76, 107
Warlock, Peter, 47
    Capriol Suite, 114
Watteau, Jean-Antoine, 59, 201
Weber, Carl Maria von, 81, 127
    Oberon, 110
Webern, Anton, 50, 52, 165, 244, 251, 276, 325
    Concerto op. 24, 221
    Five Movements for String Quartet op. 5, 54, 326
Weill, Kurt,
    Jasager, Der, 97
    Mahagonny, 97
Wellesz, Egon, 47, 50
Wendel, Hélène de, 150
Wharton, Edith, 12, 13
Wiéner, Jean, 47, 54, 101
Witkowski, Jean, 192
Wolff, Albert, 182, 183
Woodgate, Leslie, 175

Yvain, Maurice, 64

Zeani, Virginia, 249, 250
Zurbarán, Francisco de, 275